THE INVISIBLES

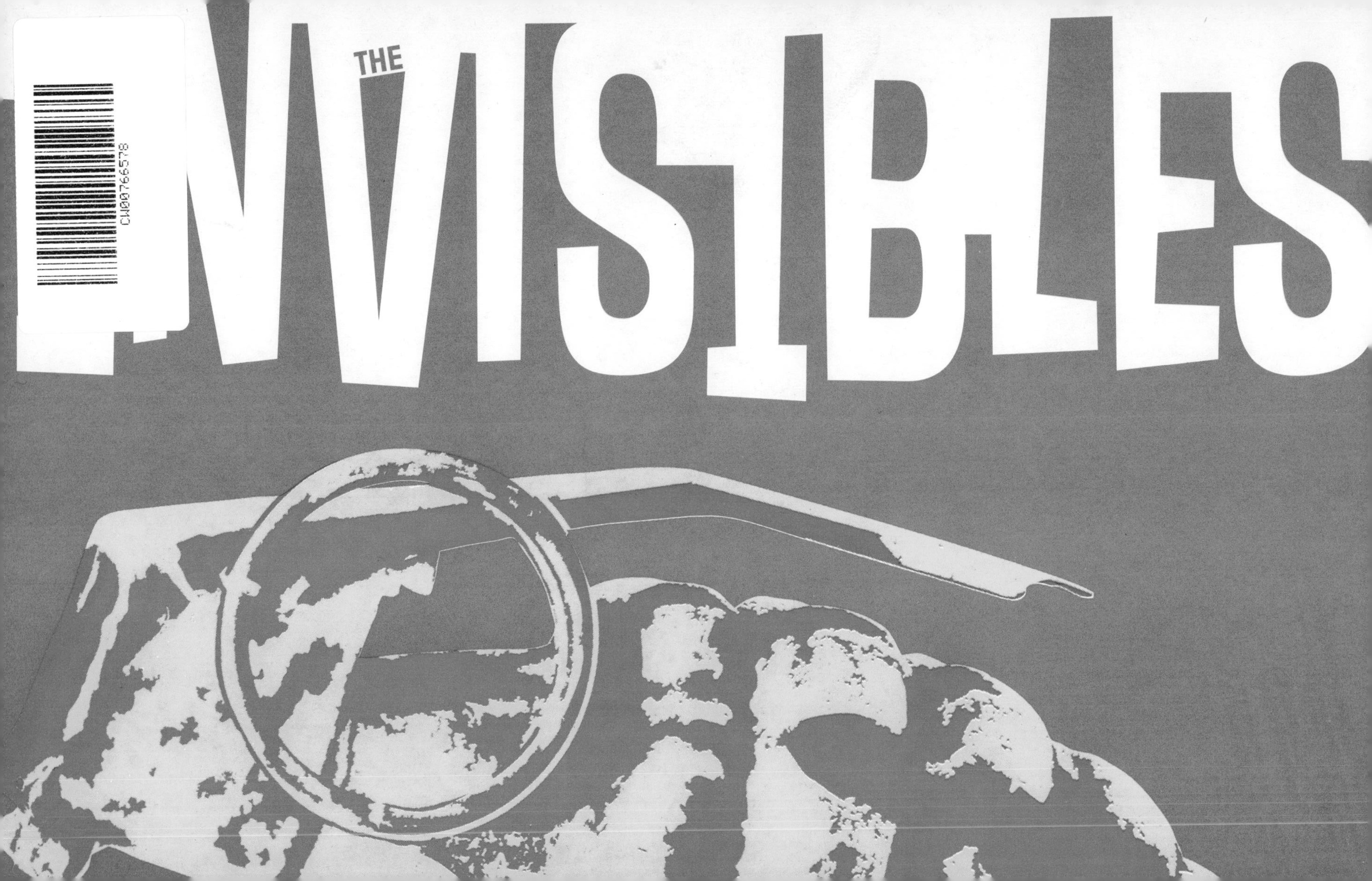

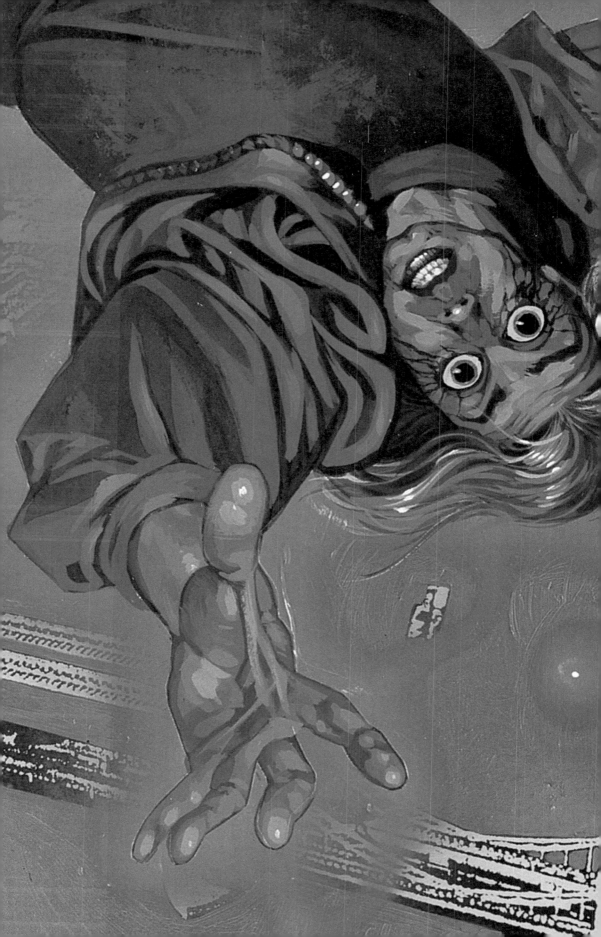

BOOK ONE

THE INVISIBLES

Grant Morrison Writer

Steve Yeowell
Jill Thompson
Dennis Cramer
Chris Weston
John Ridgway
Steve Parkhouse
Duncan Fegredo
Artists

Daniel Vozzo Colorist

Clem Robins
Annie Parkhouse
Letterers

Rian Hughes
Sean Phillips
Original Series Covers

Brian Bolland
Cover Artist

THE INVISIBLES created by Grant Morrison

Stuart Moore Editor – Original Series   Julie Rottenberg Associate Editor – Original Series   Jamie S. Rich Group Editor – Vertigo Comics
Jeb Woodard Group Editor – Collected Editions   Scott Nybakken Editor – Collected Edition   Steve Cook Design Director – Books   Louis Prandi Publication Design

Diane Nelson President   Dan DiDio Publisher   Jim Lee Publisher   Geoff Johns President & Chief Creative Officer
Amit Desai Executive VP – Business & Marketing Strategy, Direct to Consumer & Global Franchise Management   Sam Ades Senior VP – Direct to Consumer
Bobbie Chase VP – Talent Development   Mark Chiarello Senior VP – Art, Design & Collected Editions   John Cunningham Senior VP – Sales & Trade Marketing
Anne DePies Senior VP – Business Strategy, Finance & Administration   Don Falletti VP – Manufacturing Operations
Lawrence Ganem VP – Editorial Administration & Talent Relations   Alison Gill Senior VP – Manufacturing & Operations
Hank Kanalz Senior VP – Editorial Strategy & Administration   Jay Kogan VP – Legal Affairs   Thomas Loftus VP – Business Affairs
Jack Mahan VP – Business Affairs   Nick J. Napolitano VP – Manufacturing Administration   Eddie Scannell VP – Consumer Marketing
Courtney Simmons Senior VP – Publicity & Communications   Jim (Ski) Sokolowski VP – Comic Book Specialty Sales & Trade Marketing
Nancy Spears VP – Mass, Book, Digital Sales & Trade Marketing

DC Comics, 2900 West Alameda Avenue, Burbank, CA 91505. Printed in the USA. First Printing.
ISBN: 978-1-4012-6795-7

Library of Congress Cataloging-in-Publication Data

Names: Morrison, Grant, author. | Yeowell, Steve, illustrator. | Thompson, Jill, 1966- illustrator.
Title: Invisibles book one / Grant Morrison, writer ; Steve Yeowell, Jill Thompson, artists.
Description: Burbank, CA : DC Comics, [2016] | "Vertigo" —Cover.
Identifiers: LCCN 2015044890 | ISBN 9781401261405 (paperback)
Subjects: LCSH: Graphic novels. | BISAC: COMICS & GRAPHIC NOVELS / Superheroes. | GSAFD: Comic
books, strips, etc.
Classification: LCC PN6728.I58 M6643 2017 | DDC 741.5/973—dc23
LC record available at https://lccn.loc.gov/2015044890

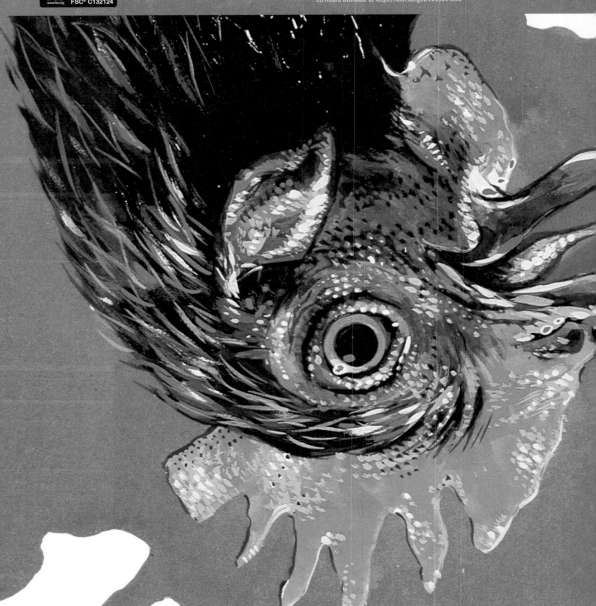

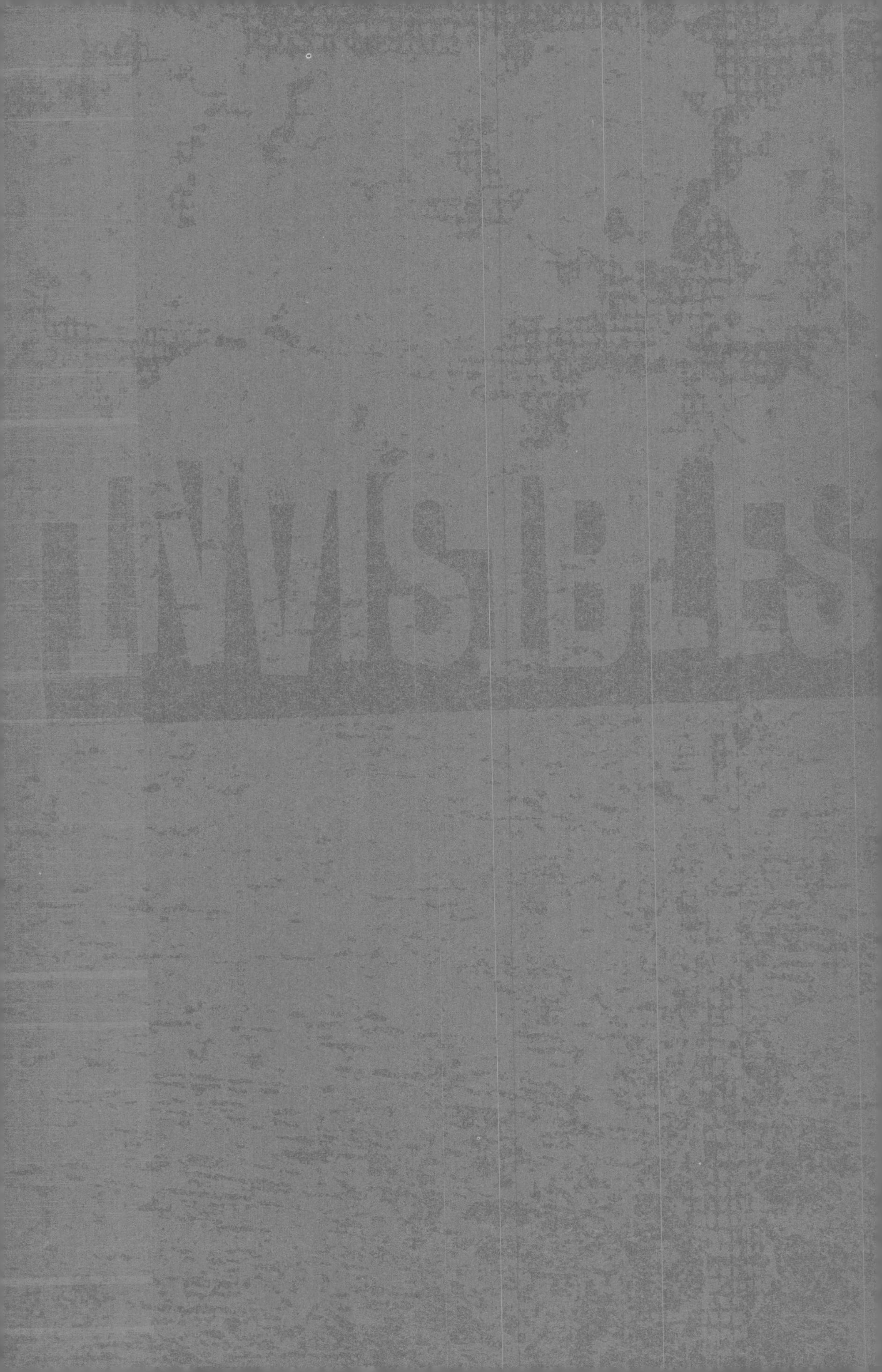

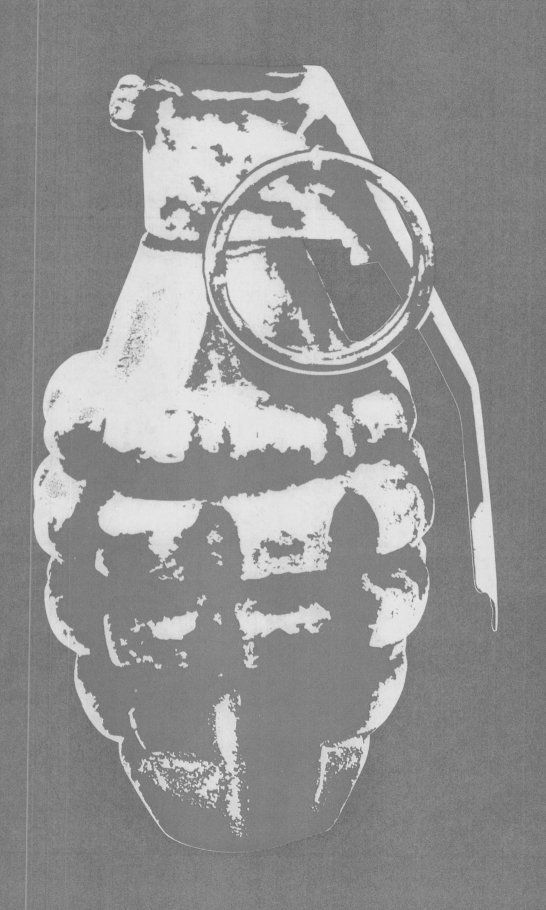

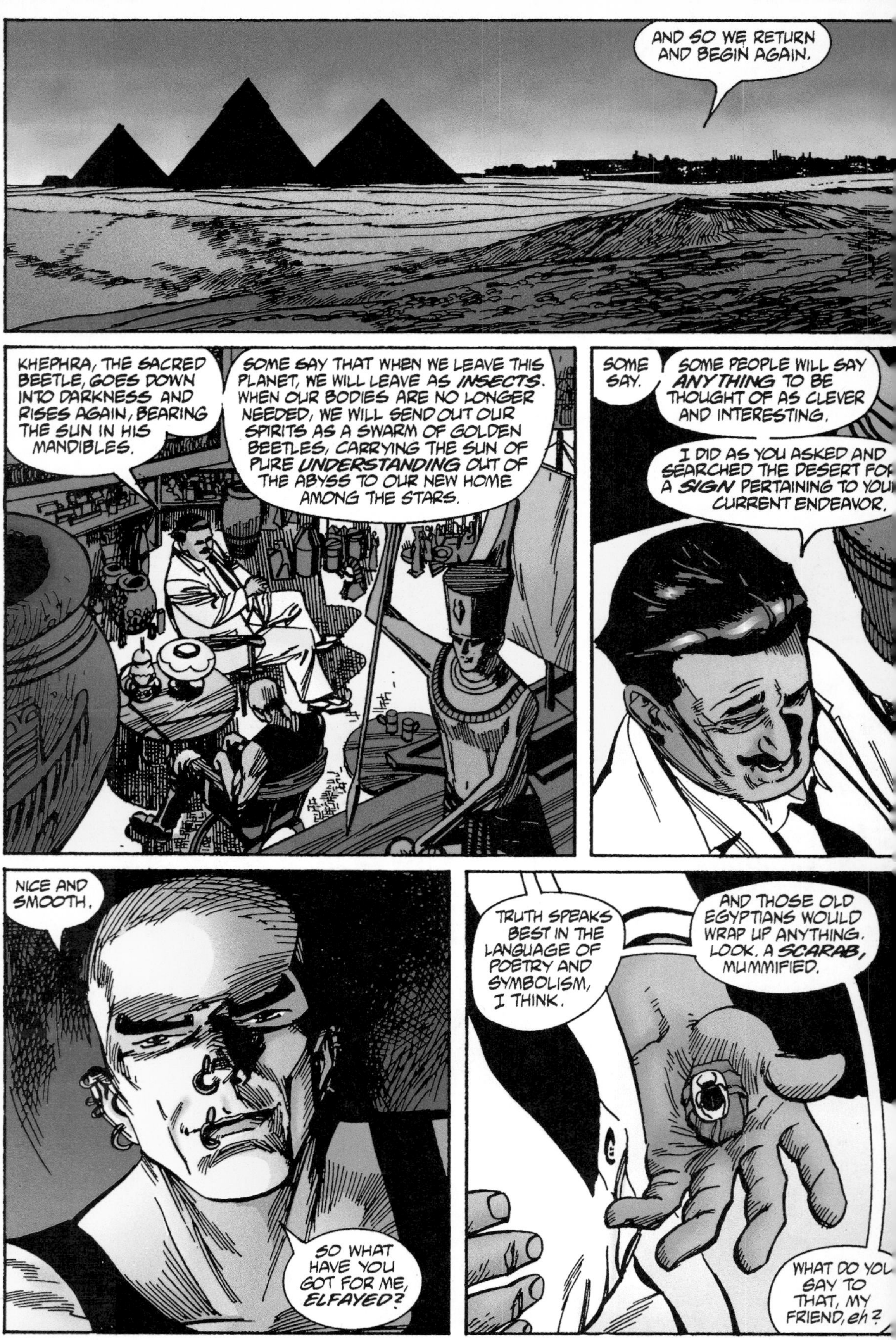
AND SO WE RETURN AND BEGIN AGAIN.
KHEPHRA, THE SACRED BEETLE, GOES DOWN INTO DARKNESS AND RISES AGAIN, BEARING THE SUN IN HIS MANDIBLES.
SOME SAY THAT WHEN WE LEAVE THIS PLANET, WE WILL LEAVE AS INSECTS. WHEN OUR BODIES ARE NO LONGER NEEDED, WE WILL SEND OUT OUR SPIRITS AS A SWARM OF GOLDEN BEETLES, CARRYING THE SUN OF PURE UNDERSTANDING OUT OF THE ABYSS TO OUR NEW HOME AMONG THE STARS.
SOME SAY.
SOME PEOPLE WILL SAY ANYTHING TO BE THOUGHT OF AS CLEVER AND INTERESTING.
I DID AS YOU ASKED AND SEARCHED THE DESERT FOR A SIGN PERTAINING TO YOUR CURRENT ENDEAVOR.
NICE AND SMOOTH.
SO WHAT HAVE YOU GOT FOR ME, ELFAYED?
TRUTH SPEAKS BEST IN THE LANGUAGE OF POETRY AND SYMBOLISM, I THINK.
AND THOSE OLD EGYPTIANS WOULD WRAP UP ANYTHING. LOOK. A SCARAB, MUMMIFIED.
WHAT DO YOU SAY TO THAT, MY FRIEND, eh?

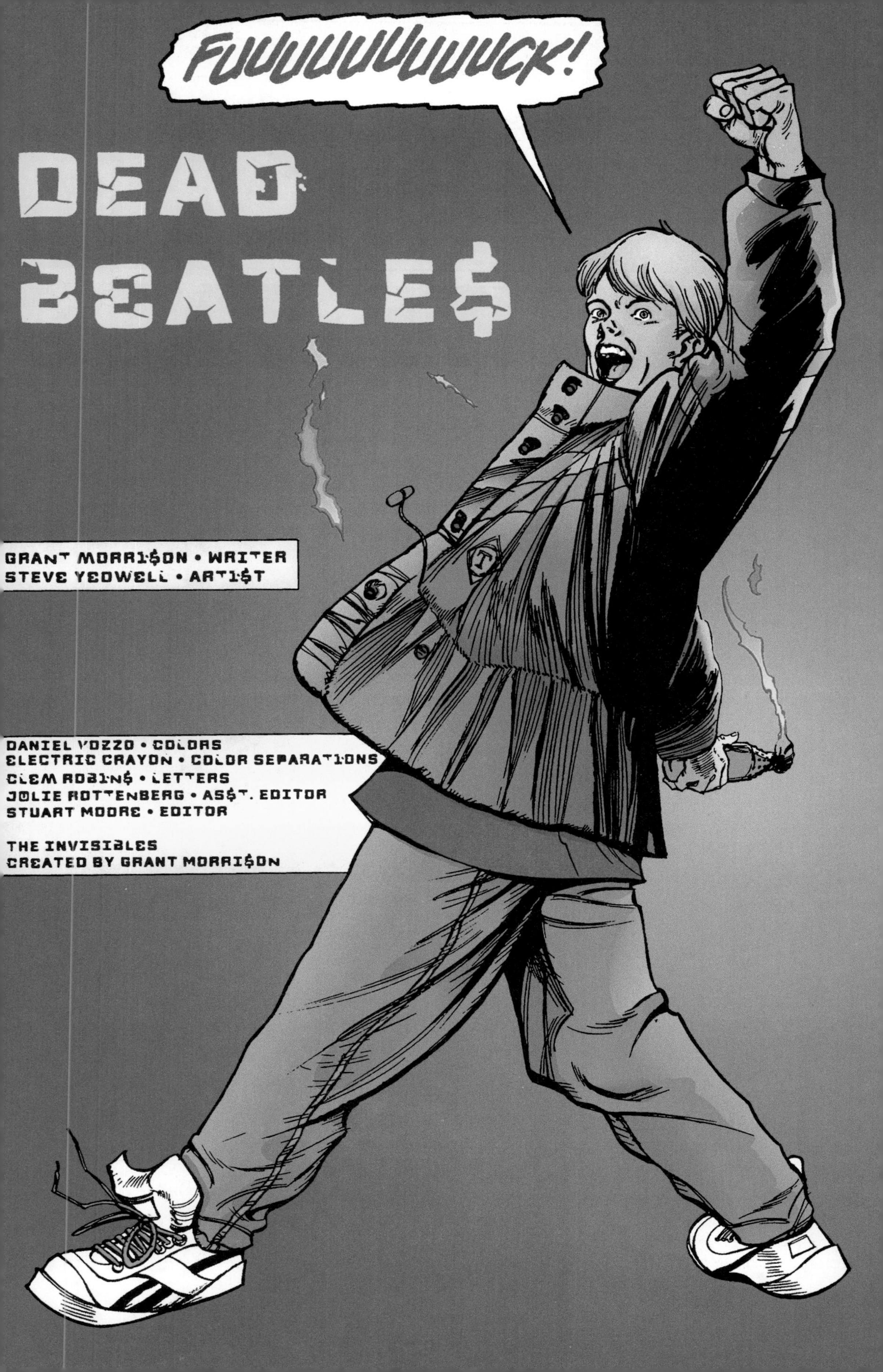
FUUUUUUUUUUCK!
DEAD BEATLE$
GRANT MORRI$ON • WRITER
STEVE YEOWELL • ARTI$T
DANIEL VOZZO • COLORS
ELECTRIC CRAYON • COLOR SEPARATIONS
CLEM ROBIN$ • LETTERS
JOLIE ROTTENBERG • AS$T. EDITOR
STUART MOORE • EDITOR
THE INVISIBLES
CREATED BY GRANT MORRI$ON

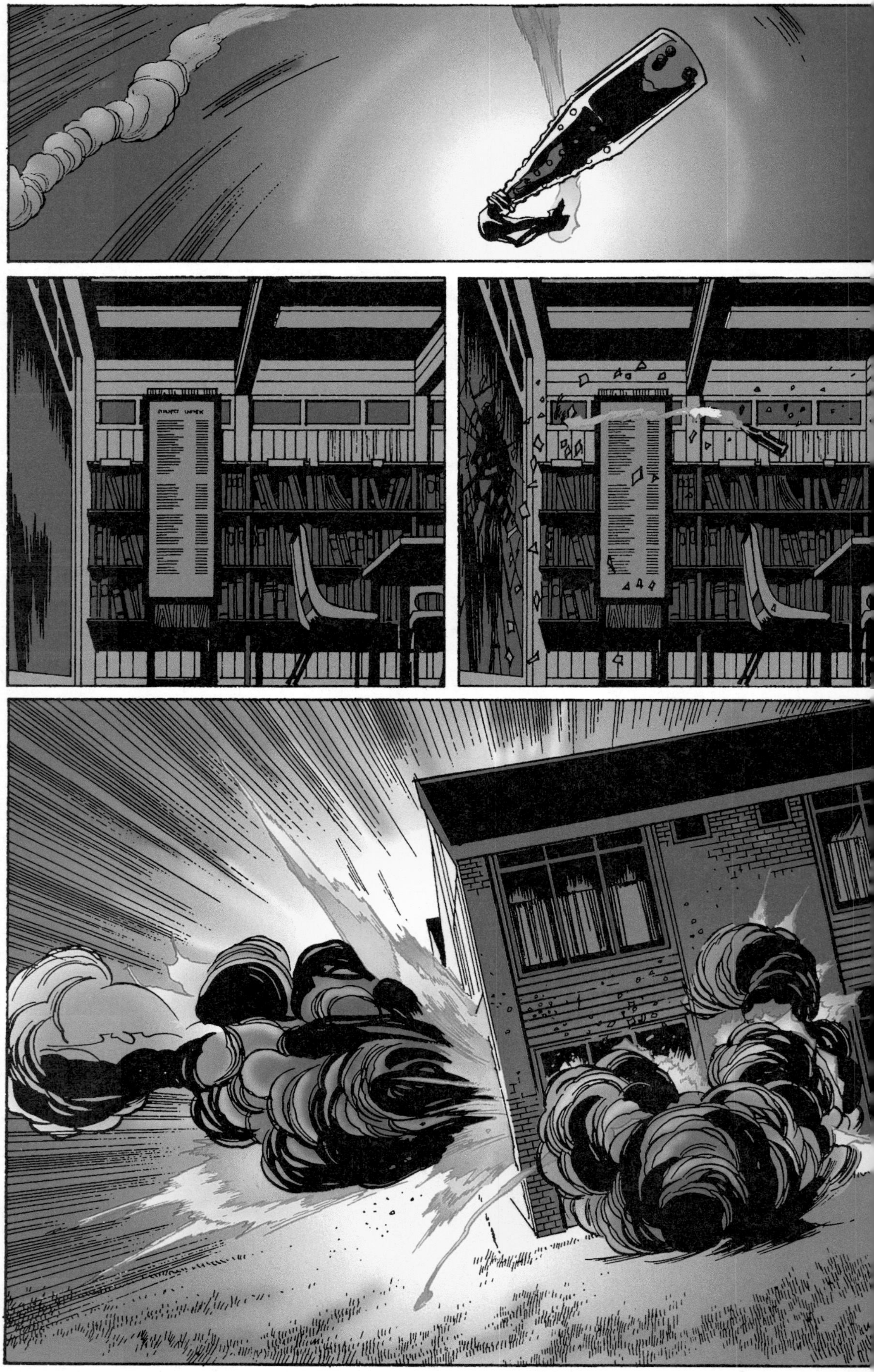

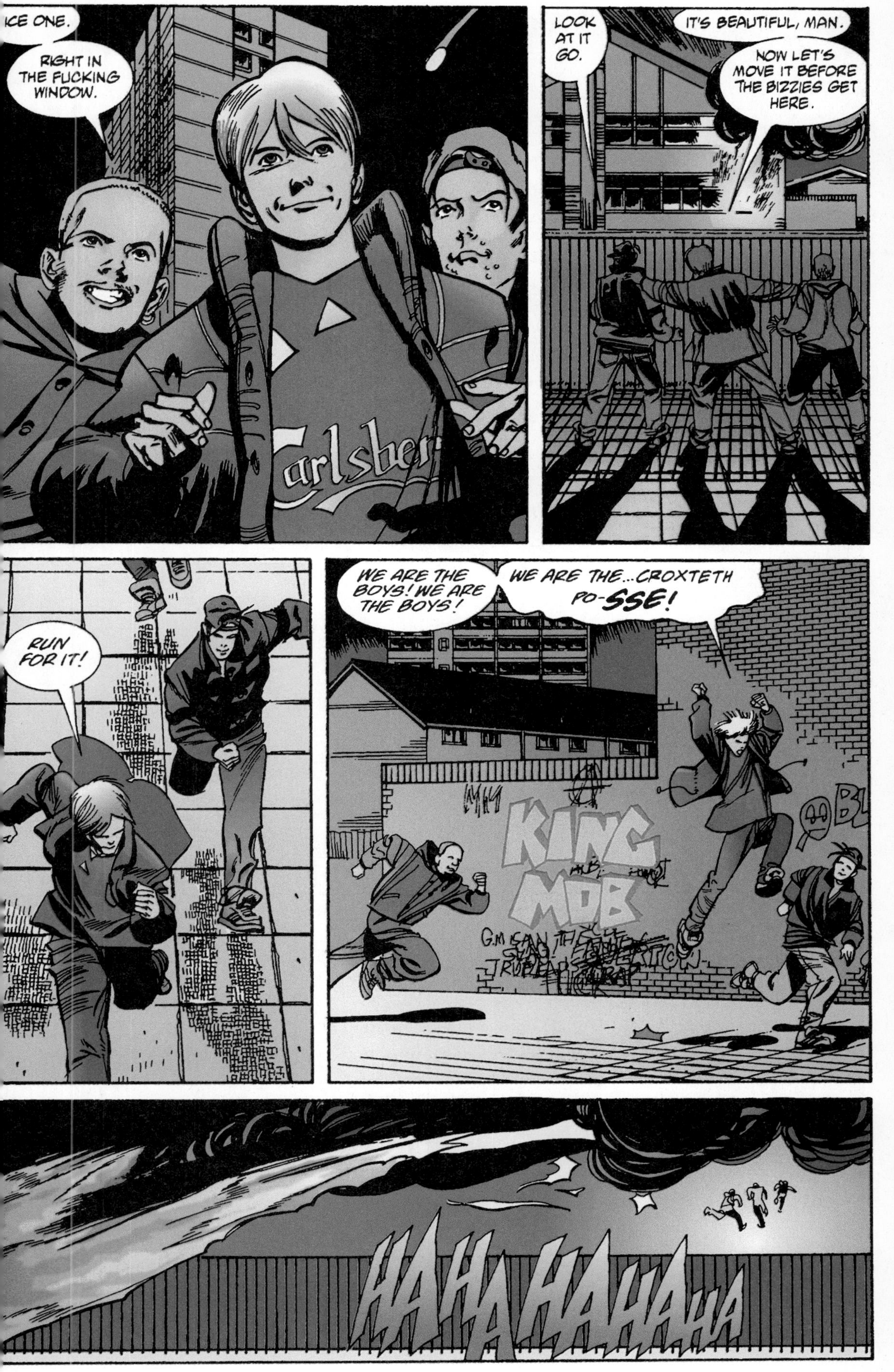

ICE ONE.
RIGHT IN THE FUCKING WINDOW.
LOOK AT IT GO.
IT'S BEAUTIFUL, MAN.
NOW LET'S MOVE IT BEFORE THE BIZZIES GET HERE.
RUN FOR IT!
WE ARE THE BOYS! WE ARE THE BOYS!
WE ARE THE...CROXTETH PO-SSE!
KING MOB
HAHAHAHAHAHA

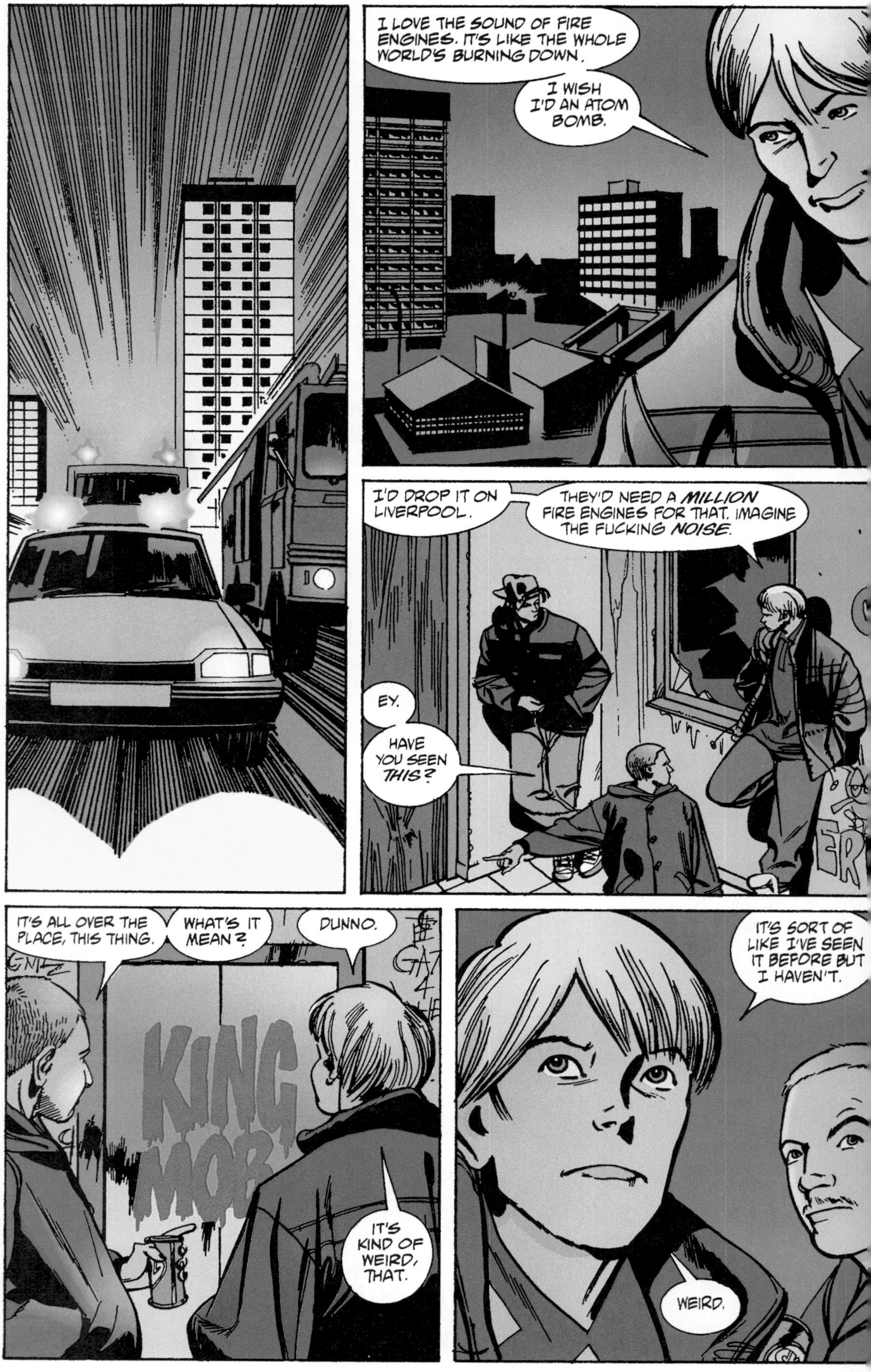
I LOVE THE SOUND OF FIRE ENGINES. IT'S LIKE THE WHOLE WORLD'S BURNING DOWN.
I WISH I'D AN ATOM BOMB.
I'D DROP IT ON LIVERPOOL.
THEY'D NEED A MILLION FIRE ENGINES FOR THAT. IMAGINE THE FUCKING NOISE.
EY.
HAVE YOU SEEN THIS?
IT'S ALL OVER THE PLACE, THIS THING.
WHAT'S IT MEAN?
DUNNO.
KING MOB
IT'S KIND OF WEIRD, THAT.
IT'S SORT OF LIKE I'VE SEEN IT BEFORE BUT I HAVEN'T.
WEIRD.

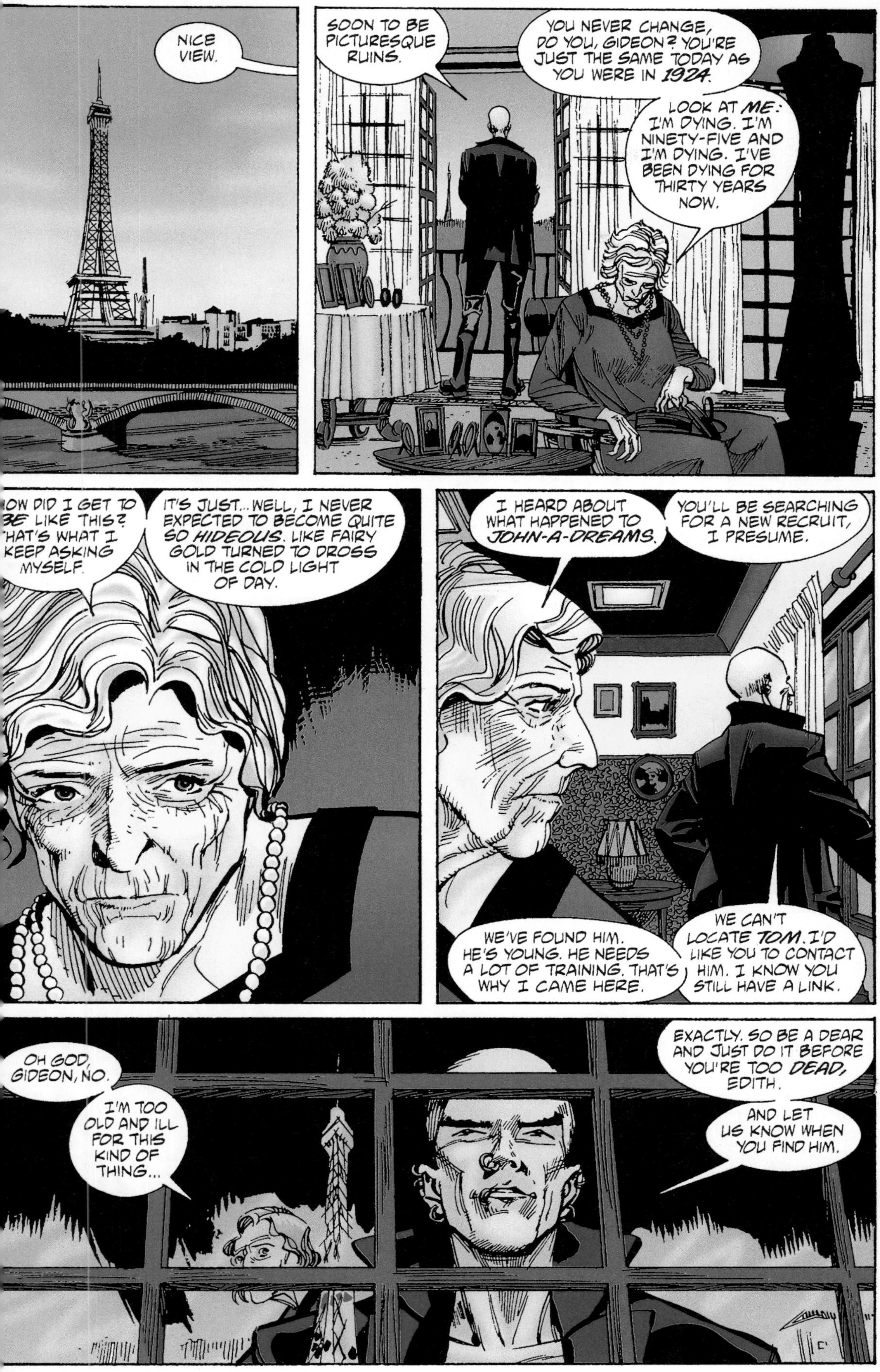
NICE VIEW.
SOON TO BE PICTURESQUE RUINS.
YOU NEVER CHANGE, DO YOU, GIDEON? YOU'RE JUST THE SAME TODAY AS YOU WERE IN 1924.
LOOK AT ME: I'M DYING. I'M NINETY-FIVE AND I'M DYING. I'VE BEEN DYING FOR THIRTY YEARS NOW.
HOW DID I GET TO BE LIKE THIS? THAT'S WHAT I KEEP ASKING MYSELF.
IT'S JUST... WELL, I NEVER EXPECTED TO BECOME QUITE SO HIDEOUS. LIKE FAIRY GOLD TURNED TO DROSS IN THE COLD LIGHT OF DAY.
I HEARD ABOUT WHAT HAPPENED TO JOHN-A-DREAMS.
YOU'LL BE SEARCHING FOR A NEW RECRUIT, I PRESUME.
WE'VE FOUND HIM. HE'S YOUNG. HE NEEDS A LOT OF TRAINING. THAT'S WHY I CAME HERE.
WE CAN'T LOCATE TOM. I'D LIKE YOU TO CONTACT HIM. I KNOW YOU STILL HAVE A LINK.
OH GOD, GIDEON, NO.
I'M TOO OLD AND ILL FOR THIS KIND OF THING...
EXACTLY. SO BE A DEAR AND JUST DO IT BEFORE YOU'RE TOO DEAD, EDITH.
AND LET US KNOW WHEN YOU FIND HIM.

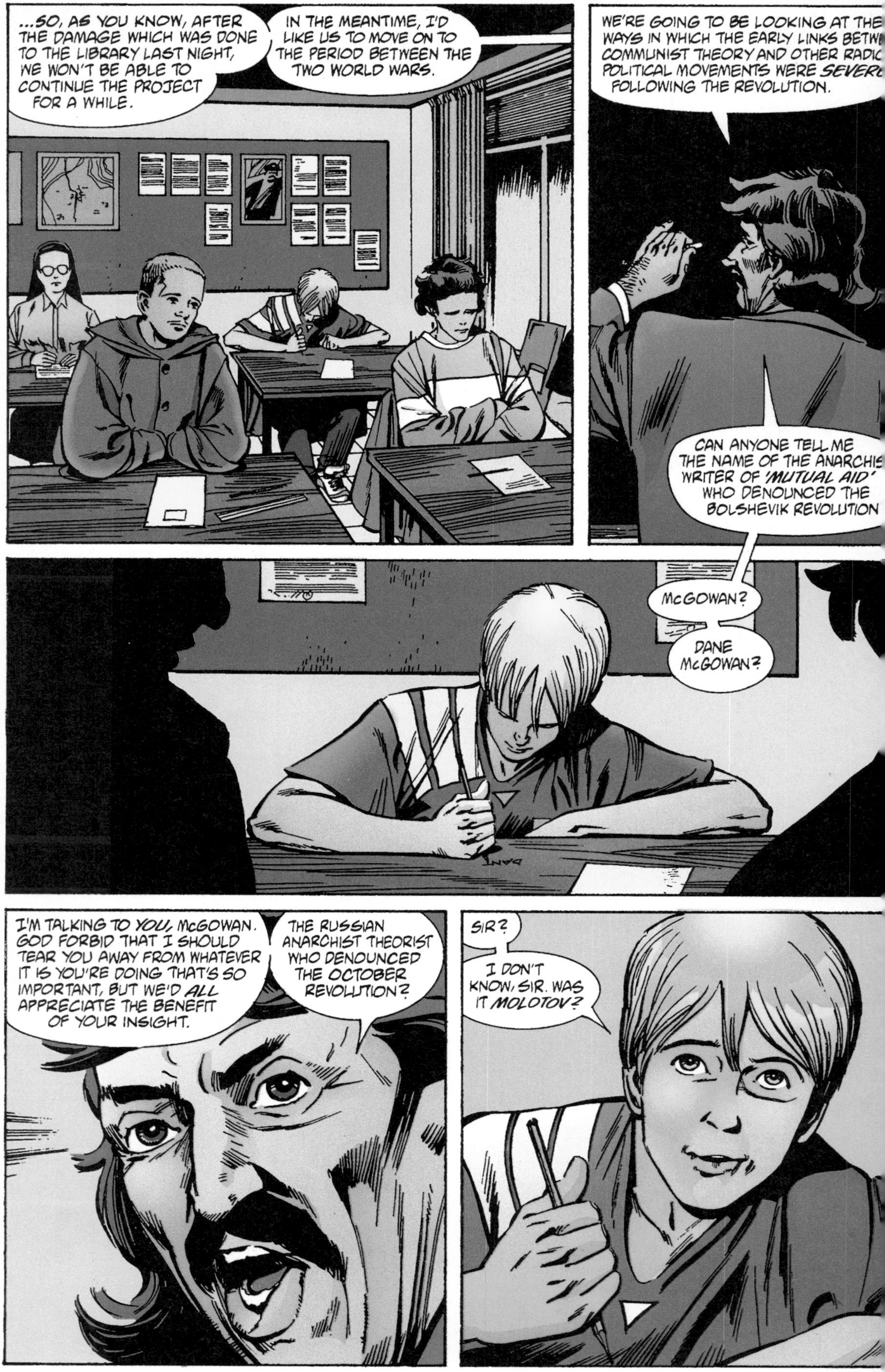
...SO, AS YOU KNOW, AFTER THE DAMAGE WHICH WAS DONE TO THE LIBRARY LAST NIGHT, WE WON'T BE ABLE TO CONTINUE THE PROJECT FOR A WHILE.
IN THE MEANTIME, I'D LIKE US TO MOVE ON TO THE PERIOD BETWEEN THE TWO WORLD WARS.
WE'RE GOING TO BE LOOKING AT THE WAYS IN WHICH THE EARLY LINKS BETW COMMUNIST THEORY AND OTHER RADIC POLITICAL MOVEMENTS WERE SEVER FOLLOWING THE REVOLUTION.
CAN ANYONE TELL ME THE NAME OF THE ANARCHIS WRITER OF 'MUTUAL AID' WHO DENOUNCED THE BOLSHEVIK REVOLUTION
McGOWAN?
DANE McGOWAN?
I'M TALKING TO YOU, McGOWAN. GOD FORBID THAT I SHOULD TEAR YOU AWAY FROM WHATEVER IT IS YOU'RE DOING THAT'S SO IMPORTANT, BUT WE'D ALL APPRECIATE THE BENEFIT OF YOUR INSIGHT.
THE RUSSIAN ANARCHIST THEORIST WHO DENOUNCED THE OCTOBER REVOLUTION?
SIR?
I DON'T KNOW, SIR. WAS IT MOLOTOV?

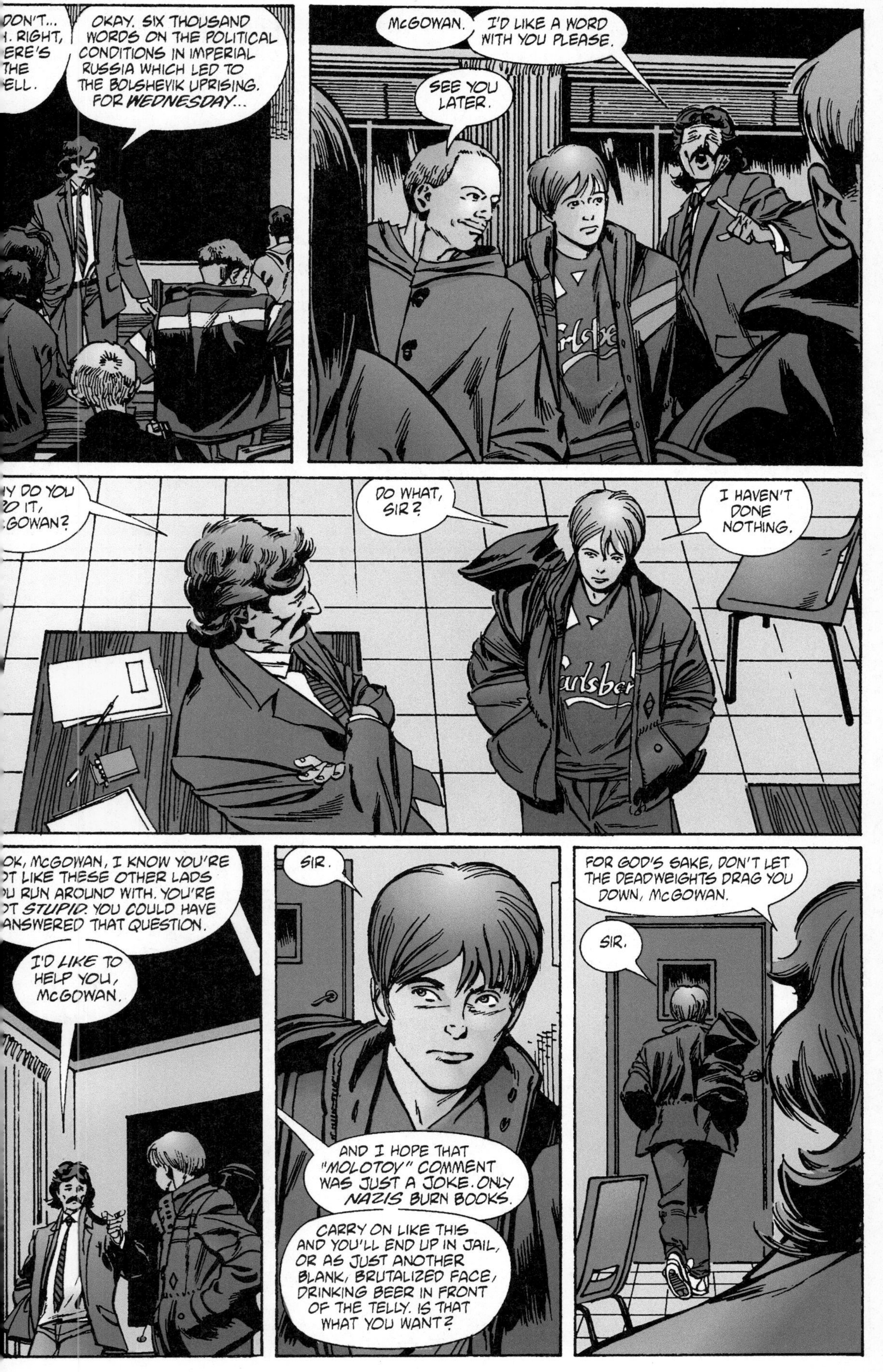
DON'T... H. RIGHT, ERE'S THE ELL.
OKAY. SIX THOUSAND WORDS ON THE POLITICAL CONDITIONS IN IMPERIAL RUSSIA WHICH LED TO THE BOLSHEVIK UPRISING. FOR WEDNESDAY...
McGOWAN.
I'D LIKE A WORD WITH YOU PLEASE.
SEE YOU LATER.
Y DO YOU O IT, GOWAN?
DO WHAT, SIR?
I HAVEN'T DONE NOTHING.
OK, McGOWAN, I KNOW YOU'RE T LIKE THESE OTHER LADS U RUN AROUND WITH. YOU'RE T STUPID. YOU COULD HAVE ANSWERED THAT QUESTION.
I'D LIKE TO HELP YOU, McGOWAN.
SIR.
AND I HOPE THAT "MOLOTOV" COMMENT WAS JUST A JOKE. ONLY NAZIS BURN BOOKS.
CARRY ON LIKE THIS AND YOU'LL END UP IN JAIL, OR AS JUST ANOTHER BLANK, BRUTALIZED FACE, DRINKING BEER IN FRONT OF THE TELLY. IS THAT WHAT YOU WANT?
FOR GOD'S SAKE, DON'T LET THE DEADWEIGHTS DRAG YOU DOWN, McGOWAN.
SIR.

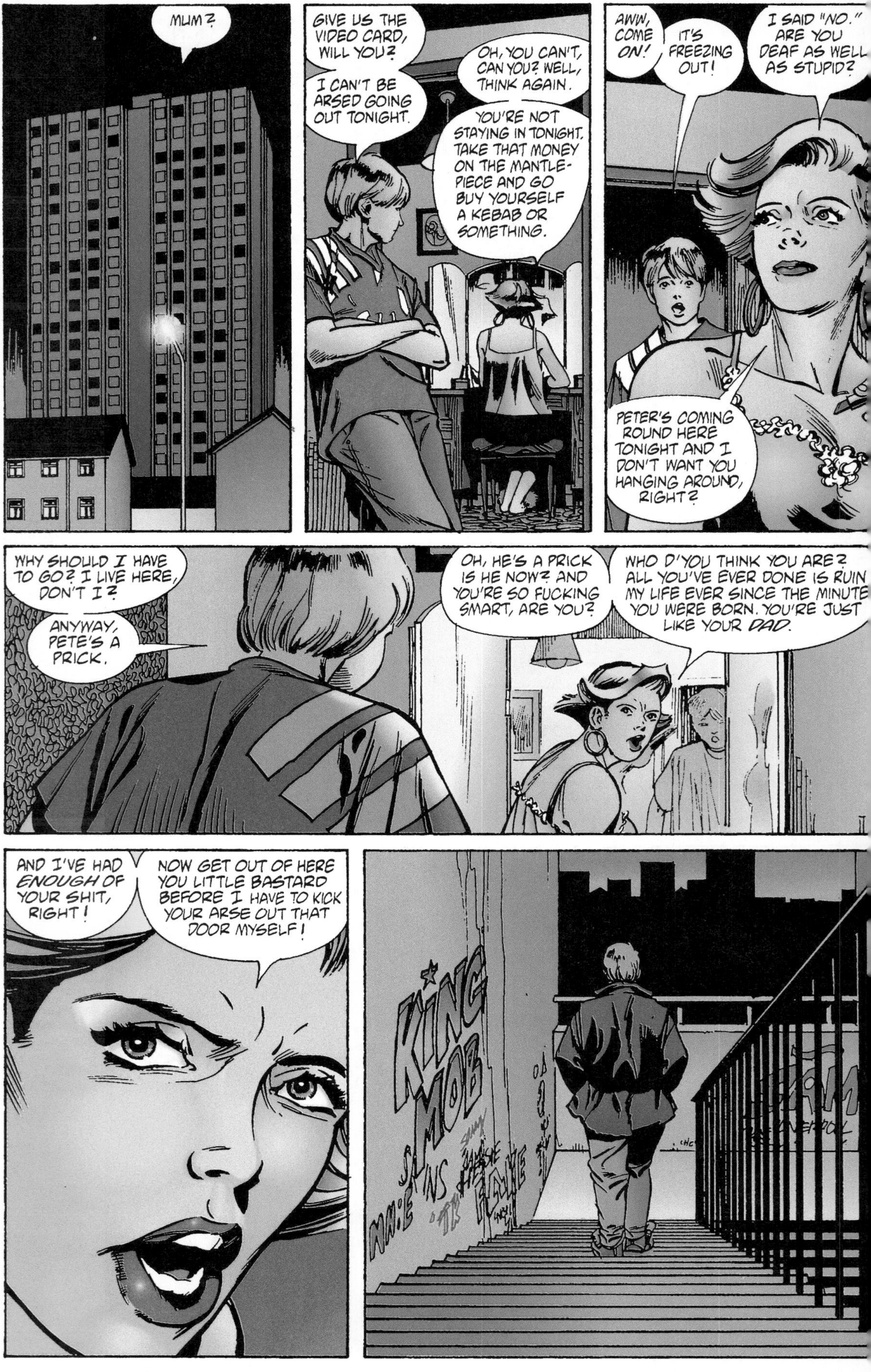
MUM?
GIVE US THE VIDEO CARD, WILL YOU?
I CAN'T BE ARSED GOING OUT TONIGHT.
OH, YOU CAN'T, CAN YOU? WELL, THINK AGAIN.
YOU'RE NOT STAYING IN TONIGHT. TAKE THAT MONEY ON THE MANTLE-PIECE AND GO BUY YOURSELF A KEBAB OR SOMETHING.
AWW, COME ON!
IT'S FREEZING OUT!
I SAID "NO." ARE YOU DEAF AS WELL AS STUPID?
PETER'S COMING ROUND HERE TONIGHT AND I DON'T WANT YOU HANGING AROUND, RIGHT?
WHY SHOULD I HAVE TO GO? I LIVE HERE, DON'T I?
ANYWAY, PETE'S A PRICK.
OH, HE'S A PRICK IS HE NOW? AND YOU'RE SO FUCKING SMART, ARE YOU?
WHO D'YOU THINK YOU ARE? ALL YOU'VE EVER DONE IS RUIN MY LIFE EVER SINCE THE MINUTE YOU WERE BORN. YOU'RE JUST LIKE YOUR DAD.
AND I'VE HAD ENOUGH OF YOUR SHIT, RIGHT!
NOW GET OUT OF HERE YOU LITTLE BASTARD BEFORE I HAVE TO KICK YOUR ARSE OUT THAT DOOR MYSELF!
KING MOB

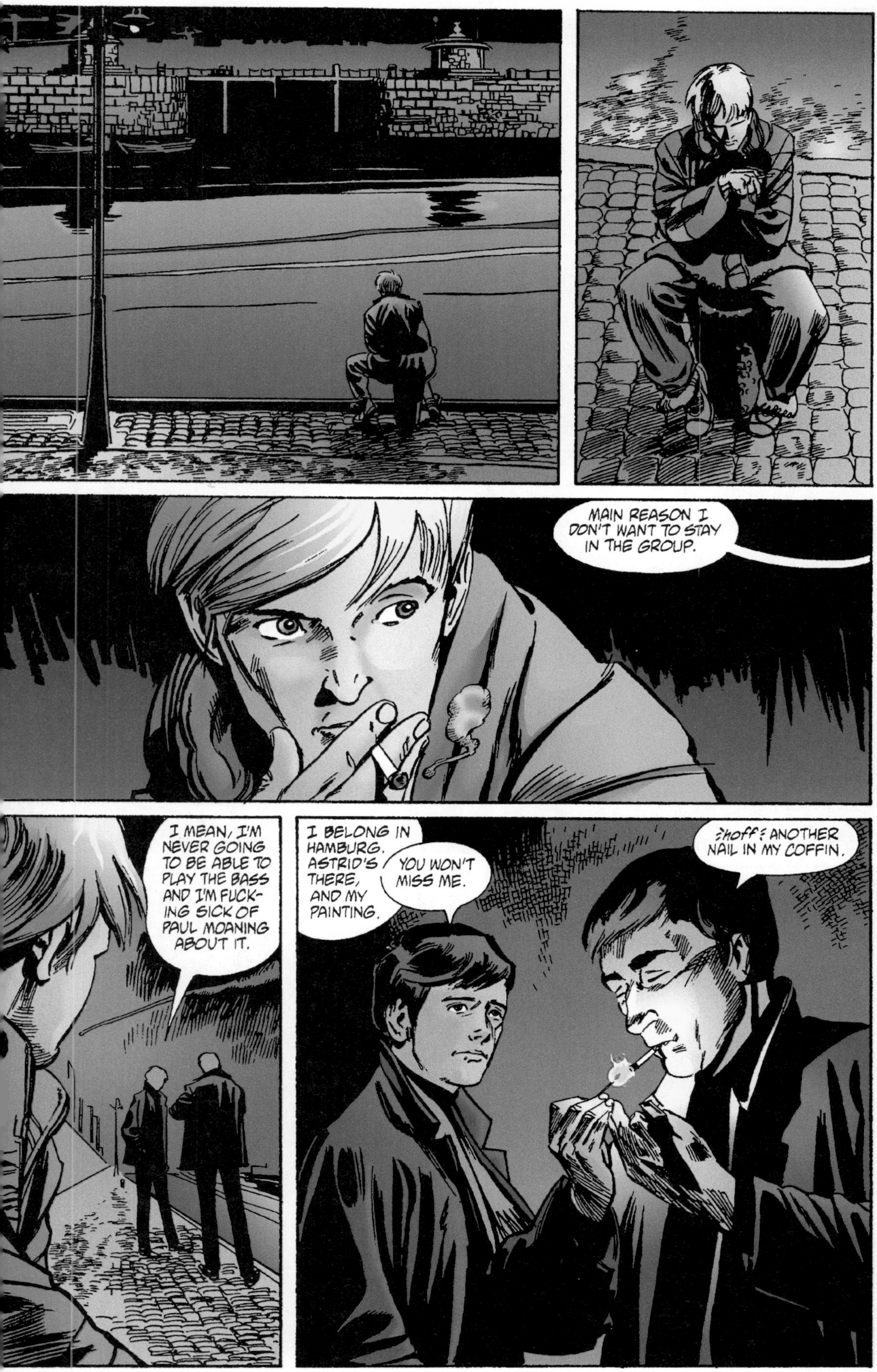
MAIN REASON I DON'T WANT TO STAY IN THE GROUP.
I MEAN, I'M NEVER GOING TO BE ABLE TO PLAY THE BASS AND I'M FUCKING SICK OF PAUL MOANING ABOUT IT.
I BELONG IN HAMBURG. ASTRID'S THERE, AND MY PAINTING.
YOU WON'T MISS ME.
hoff ANOTHER NAIL IN MY COFFIN.

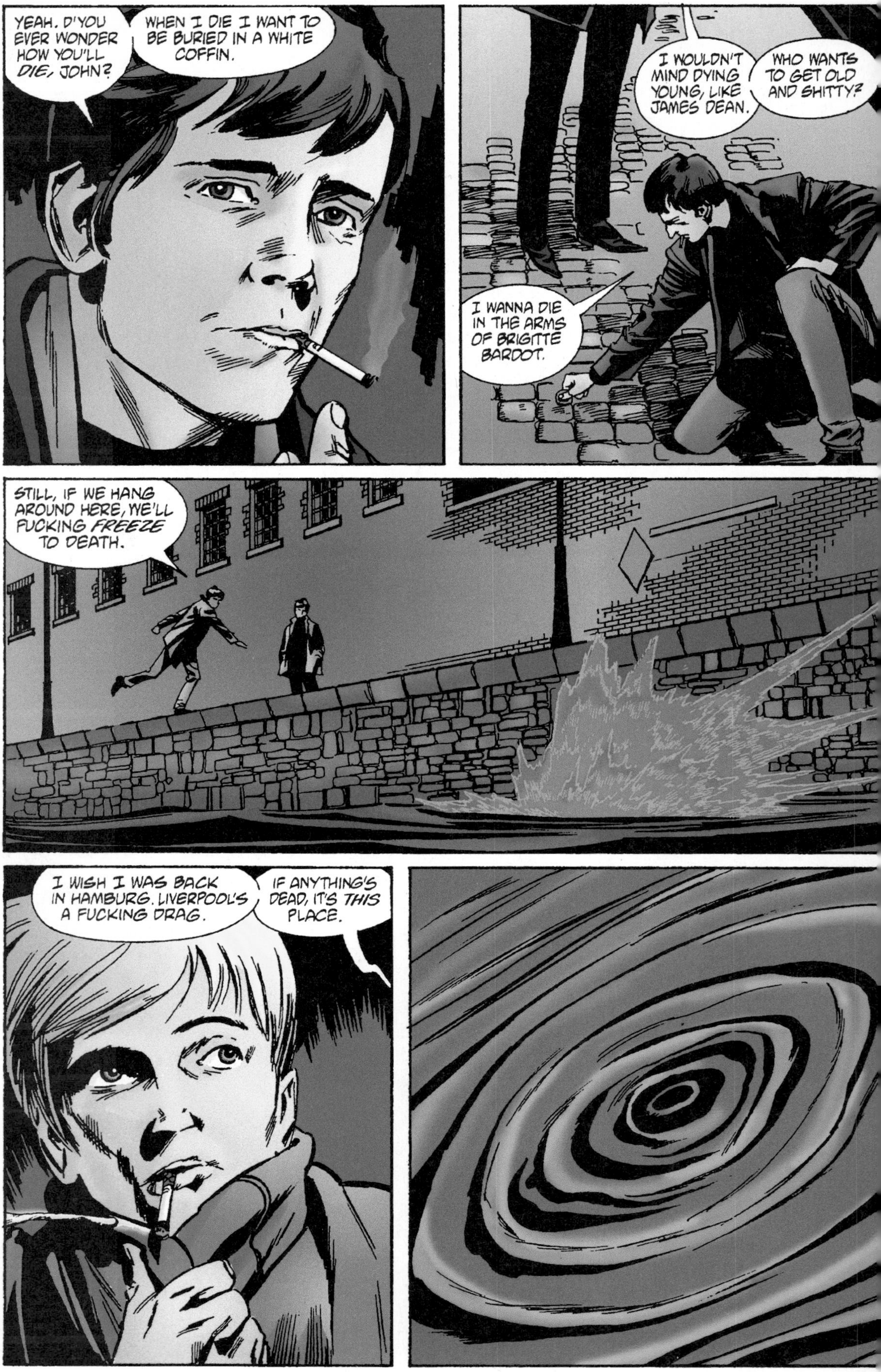
YEAH. D'YOU EVER WONDER HOW YOU'LL *DIE*, JOHN?
WHEN I DIE I WANT TO BE BURIED IN A WHITE COFFIN.
I WOULDN'T MIND DYING YOUNG, LIKE JAMES DEAN.
WHO WANTS TO GET OLD AND SHITTY?
I WANNA DIE IN THE ARMS OF BRIGITTE BARDOT.
STILL, IF WE HANG AROUND HERE, WE'LL FUCKING *FREEZE* TO DEATH.
I WISH I WAS BACK IN HAMBURG. LIVERPOOL'S A FUCKING DRAG.
IF ANYTHING'S DEAD, IT'S *THIS* PLACE.

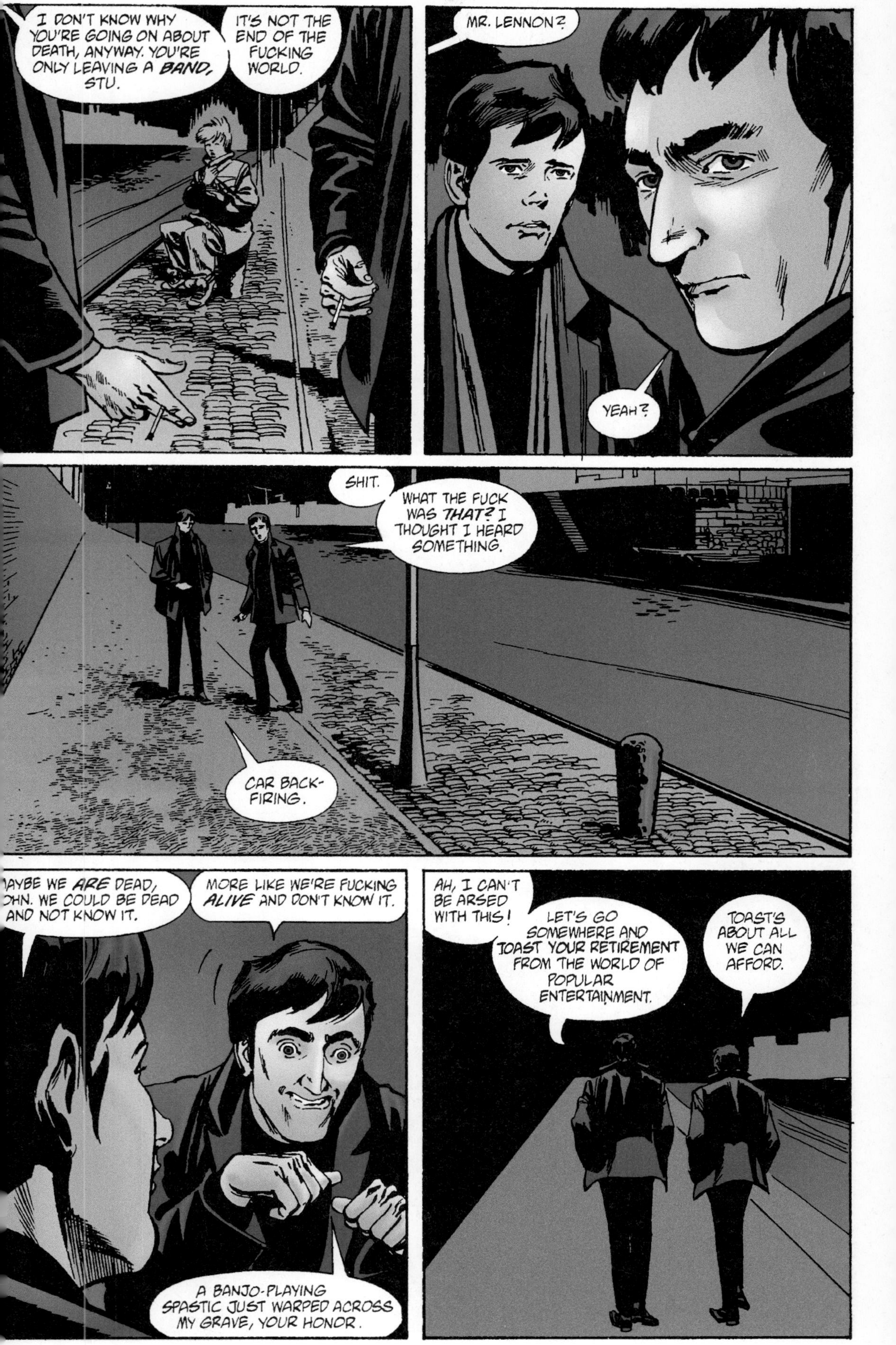
I DON'T KNOW WHY YOU'RE GOING ON ABOUT DEATH, ANYWAY. YOU'RE ONLY LEAVING A BAND, STU.
IT'S NOT THE END OF THE FUCKING WORLD.
MR. LENNON?
YEAH?
SHIT.
WHAT THE FUCK WAS THAT? I THOUGHT I HEARD SOMETHING.
CAR BACK-FIRING.
MAYBE WE ARE DEAD, JOHN. WE COULD BE DEAD AND NOT KNOW IT.
MORE LIKE WE'RE FUCKING ALIVE AND DON'T KNOW IT.
A BANJO-PLAYING SPASTIC JUST WARPED ACROSS MY GRAVE, YOUR HONOR.
AH, I CAN'T BE ARSED WITH THIS!
LET'S GO SOMEWHERE AND TOAST YOUR RETIREMENT FROM THE WORLD OF POPULAR ENTERTAINMENT.
TOAST'S ABOUT ALL WE CAN AFFORD.

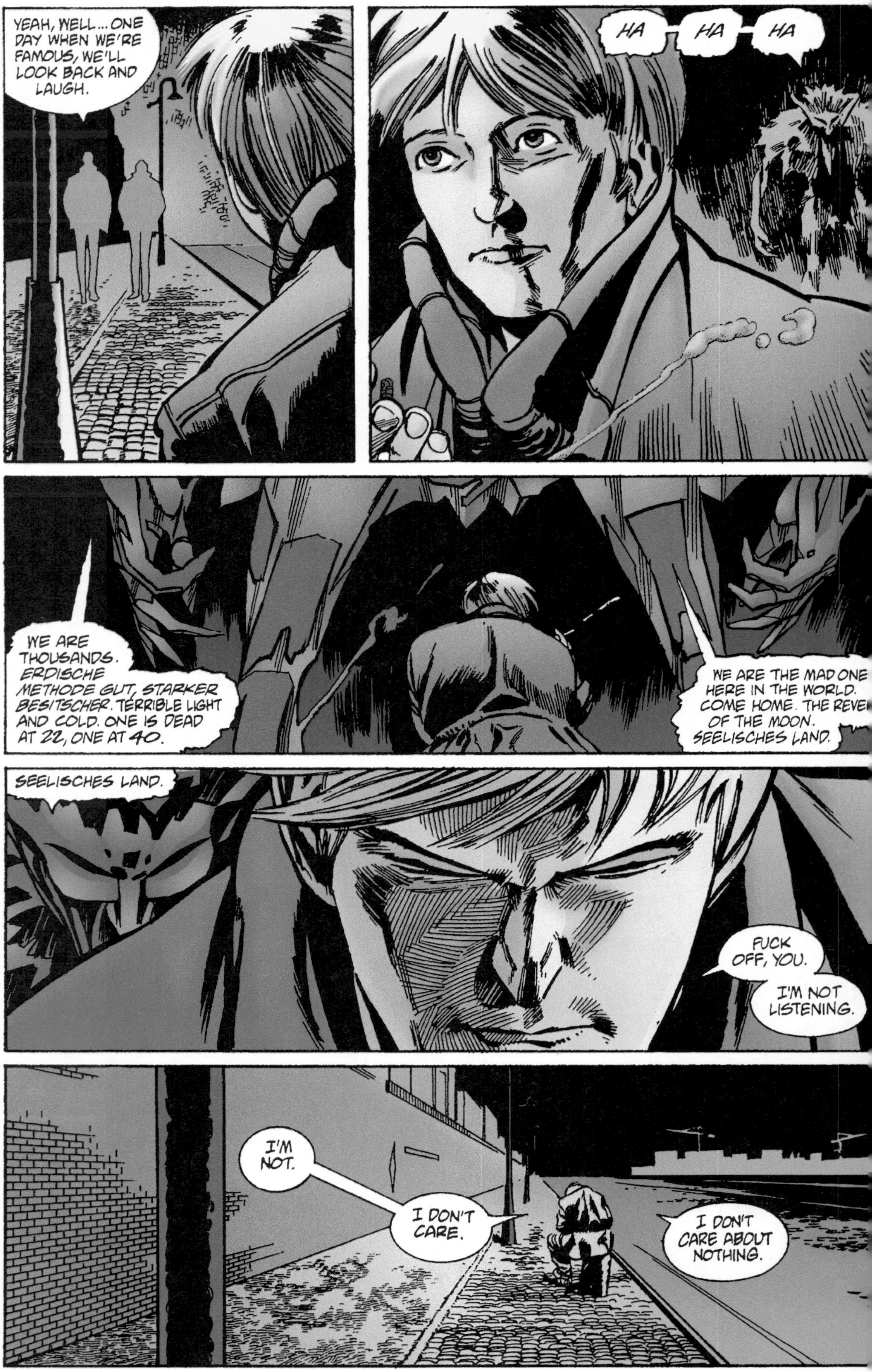
YEAH, WELL... ONE DAY WHEN WE'RE FAMOUS, WE'LL LOOK BACK AND LAUGH.
HA
HA
HA
WE ARE THOUSANDS. ERDISCHE METHODE GUT, STARKER BESITSCHER. TERRIBLE LIGHT AND COLD. ONE IS DEAD AT 22, ONE AT 40.
WE ARE THE MAD ONE HERE IN THE WORLD. COME HOME. THE REVE OF THE MOON. SEELISCHES LAND.
SEELISCHES LAND.
FUCK OFF, YOU.
I'M NOT LISTENING.
I'M NOT.
I DON'T CARE.
I DON'T CARE ABOUT NOTHING.

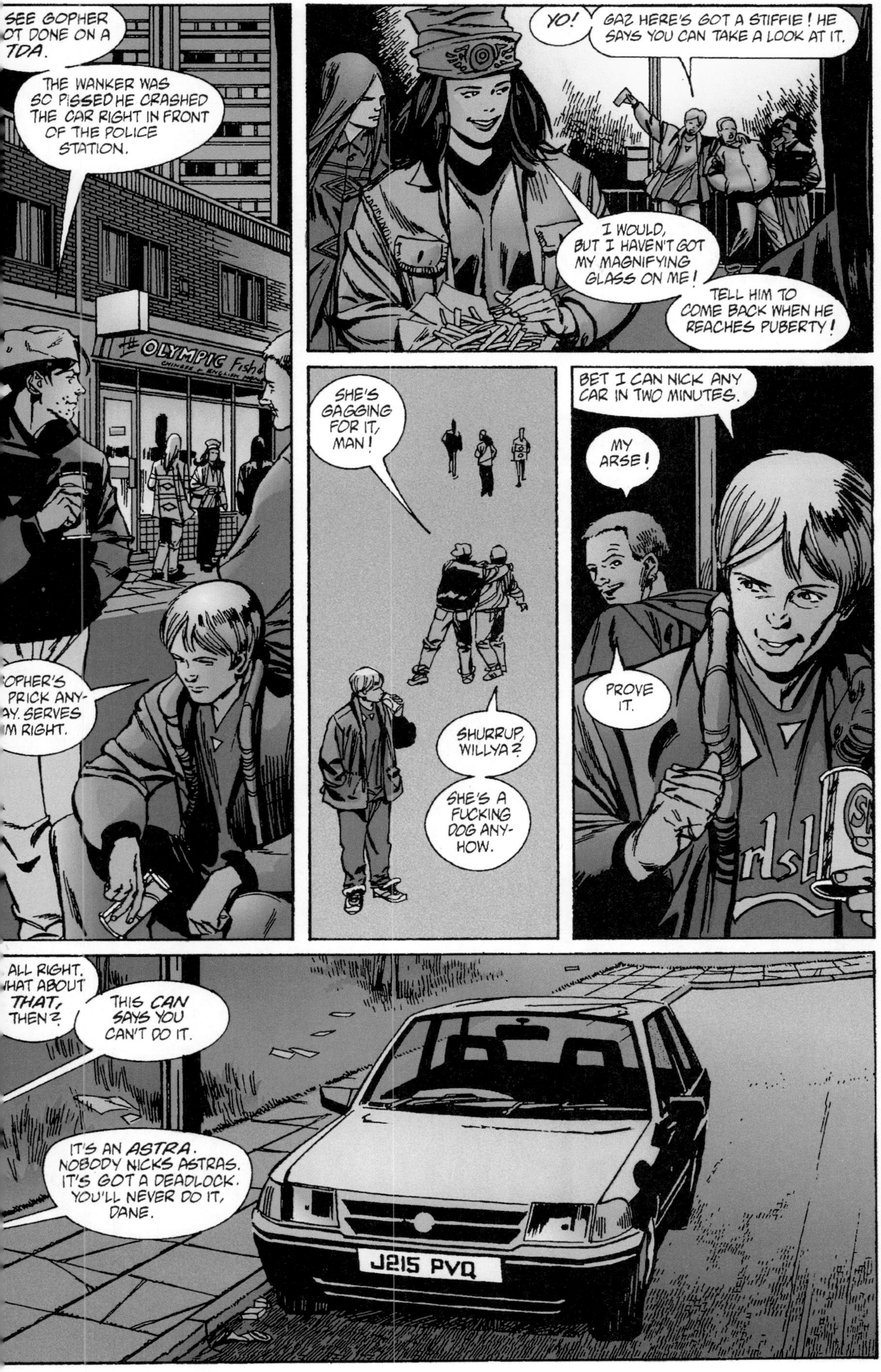

SEE GOPHER
OT DONE ON A
TDA.
THE WANKER WAS SO PISSED HE CRASHED THE CAR RIGHT IN FRONT OF THE POLICE STATION.
OLYMPIC Fish
OPHER'S PRICK ANY-
AY. SERVES
M RIGHT.
YO!
GAZ HERE'S GOT A STIFFIE! HE SAYS YOU CAN TAKE A LOOK AT IT.
I WOULD, BUT I HAVEN'T GOT MY MAGNIFYING GLASS ON ME!
TELL HIM TO COME BACK WHEN HE REACHES PUBERTY!
SHE'S GAGGING FOR IT, MAN!
SHURRUP, WILLYA?
SHE'S A FUCKING DOG ANY-HOW.
BET I CAN NICK ANY CAR IN TWO MINUTES.
MY ARSE!
PROVE IT.
ALL RIGHT.
HAT ABOUT
THAT,
THEN?
THIS CAN SAYS YOU CAN'T DO IT.
IT'S AN ASTRA. NOBODY NICKS ASTRAS. IT'S GOT A DEADLOCK. YOU'LL NEVER DO IT, DANE.
J215 PVQ

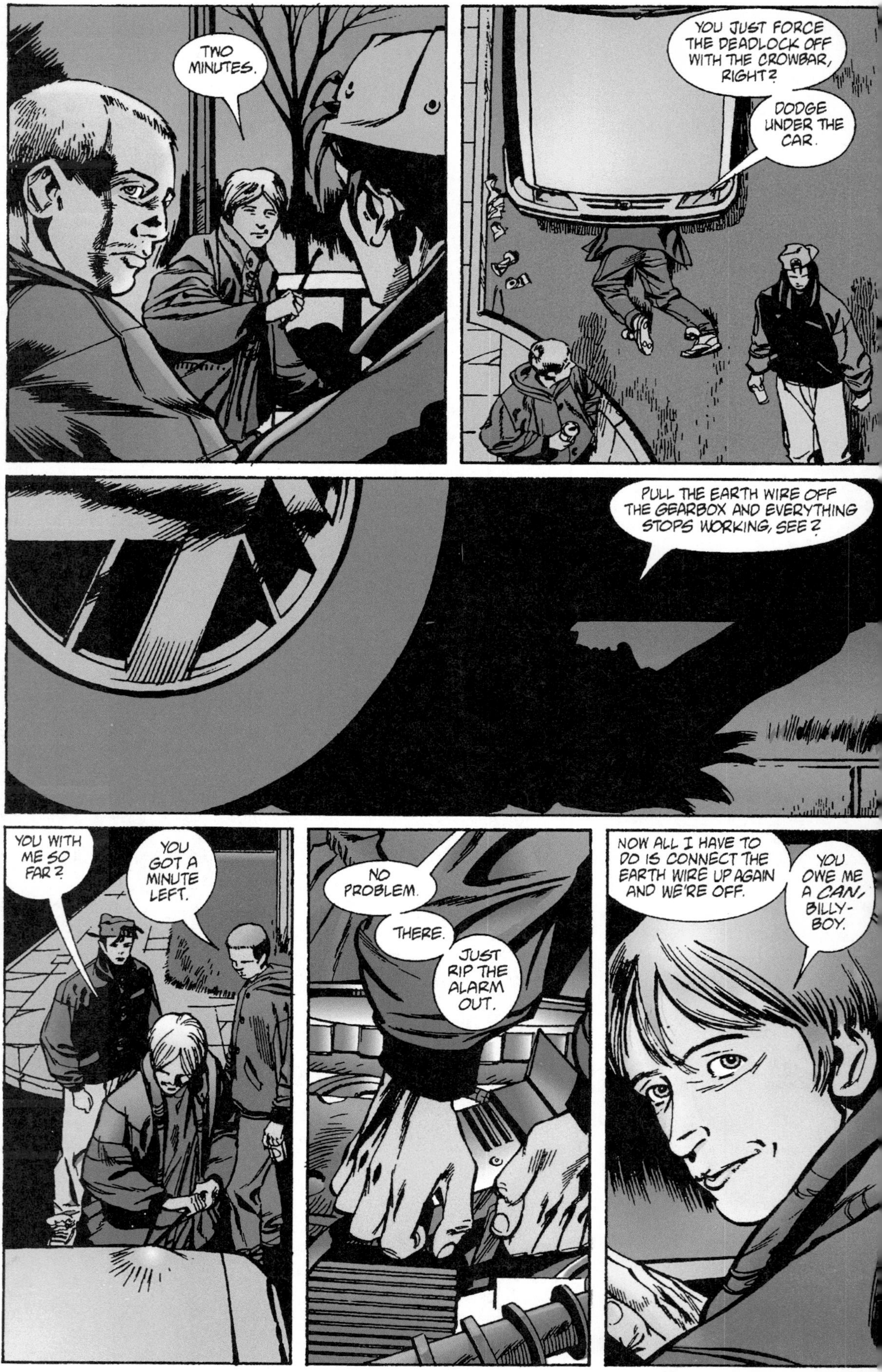
TWO MINUTES.
YOU JUST FORCE THE DEADLOCK OFF WITH THE CROWBAR, RIGHT?
DODGE UNDER THE CAR.
PULL THE EARTH WIRE OFF THE GEARBOX AND EVERYTHING STOPS WORKING, SEE?
YOU WITH ME SO FAR?
YOU GOT A MINUTE LEFT.
NO PROBLEM.
THERE.
JUST RIP THE ALARM OUT.
NOW ALL I HAVE TO DO IS CONNECT THE EARTH WIRE UP AGAIN AND WE'RE OFF.
YOU OWE ME A CAN, BILLY-BOY.

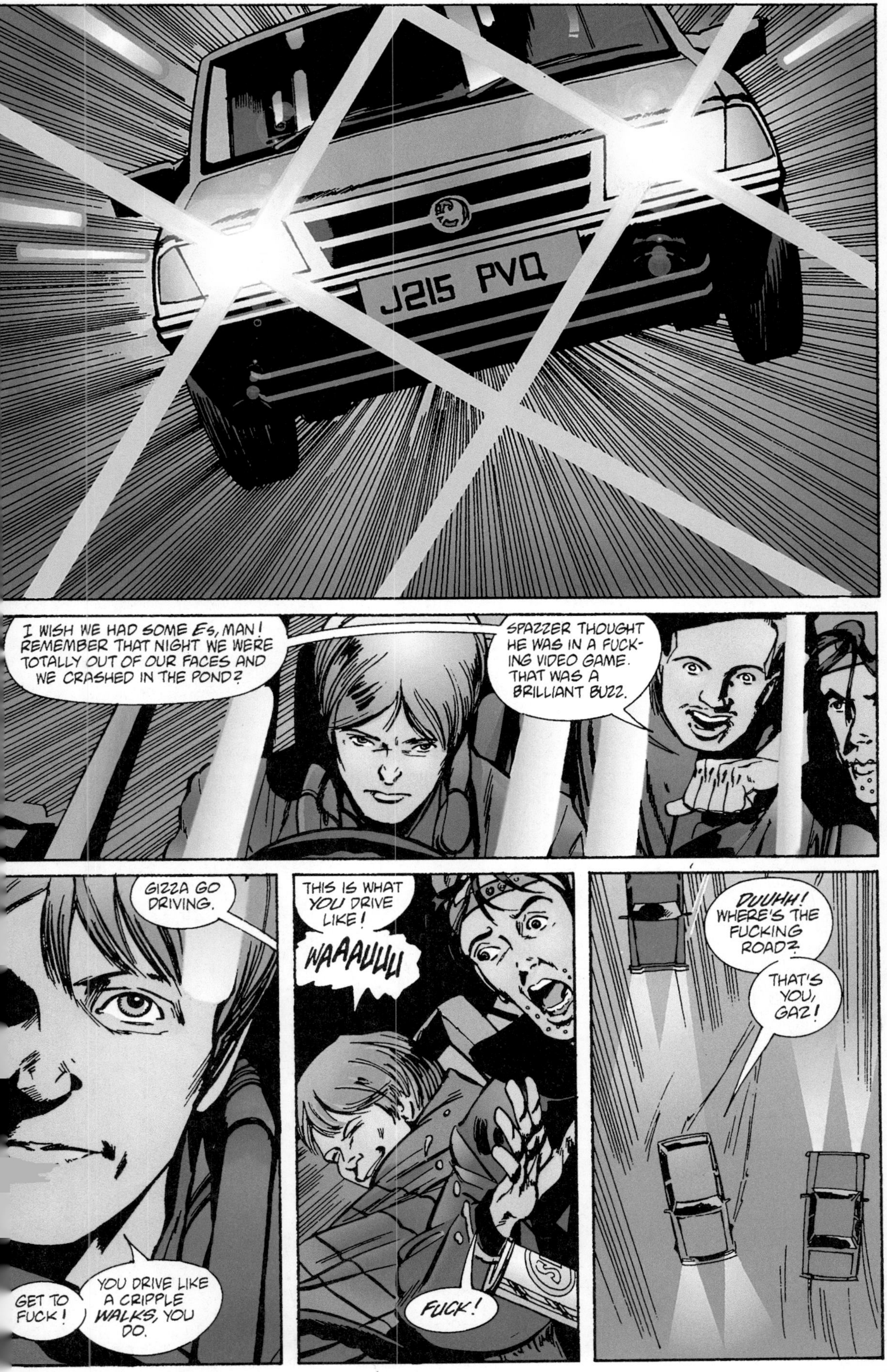
J215 PVQ
I WISH WE HAD SOME Es, MAN! REMEMBER THAT NIGHT WE WERE TOTALLY OUT OF OUR FACES AND WE CRASHED IN THE POND?
SPAZZER THOUGHT HE WAS IN A FUCKING VIDEO GAME. THAT WAS A BRILLIANT BUZZ.
GIZZA GO DRIVING.
GET TO FUCK!
YOU DRIVE LIKE A CRIPPLE WALKS, YOU DO.
THIS IS WHAT YOU DRIVE LIKE!
WAAAUUU
FUCK!
DUUHH! WHERE'S THE FUCKING ROAD?
THAT'S YOU, GAZ!

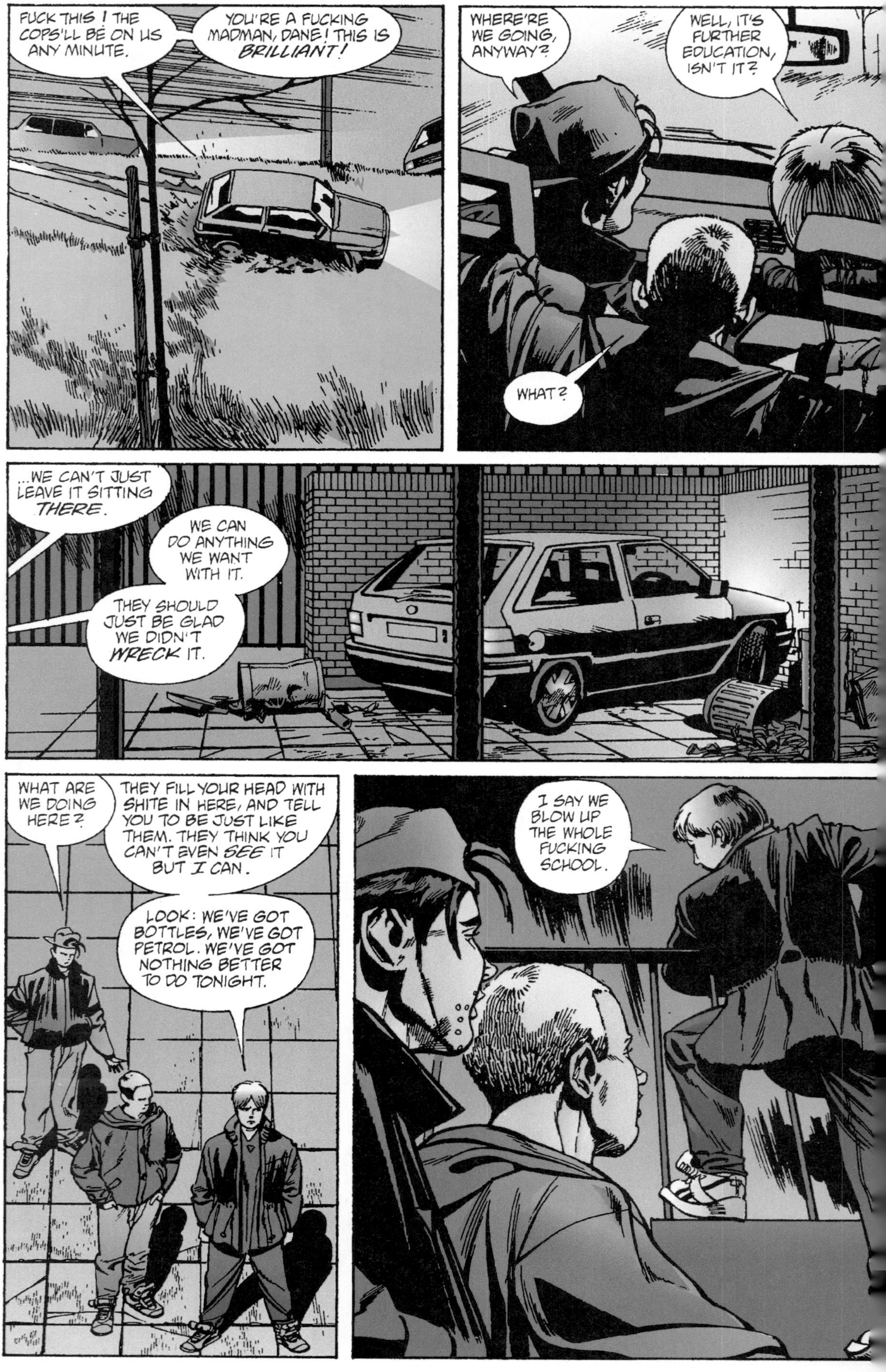
FUCK THIS ! THE COPS'LL BE ON US ANY MINUTE.
YOU'RE A FUCKING MADMAN, DANE! THIS IS BRILLIANT!
WHERE'RE WE GOING, ANYWAY?
WELL, IT'S FURTHER EDUCATION, ISN'T IT?
WHAT?
...WE CAN'T JUST LEAVE IT SITTING THERE.
WE CAN DO ANYTHING WE WANT WITH IT.
THEY SHOULD JUST BE GLAD WE DIDN'T WRECK IT.
WHAT ARE WE DOING HERE?
THEY FILL YOUR HEAD WITH SHITE IN HERE, AND TELL YOU TO BE JUST LIKE THEM. THEY THINK YOU CAN'T EVEN SEE IT BUT I CAN.
LOOK: WE'VE GOT BOTTLES, WE'VE GOT PETROL. WE'VE GOT NOTHING BETTER TO DO TONIGHT.
I SAY WE BLOW UP THE WHOLE FUCKING SCHOOL.

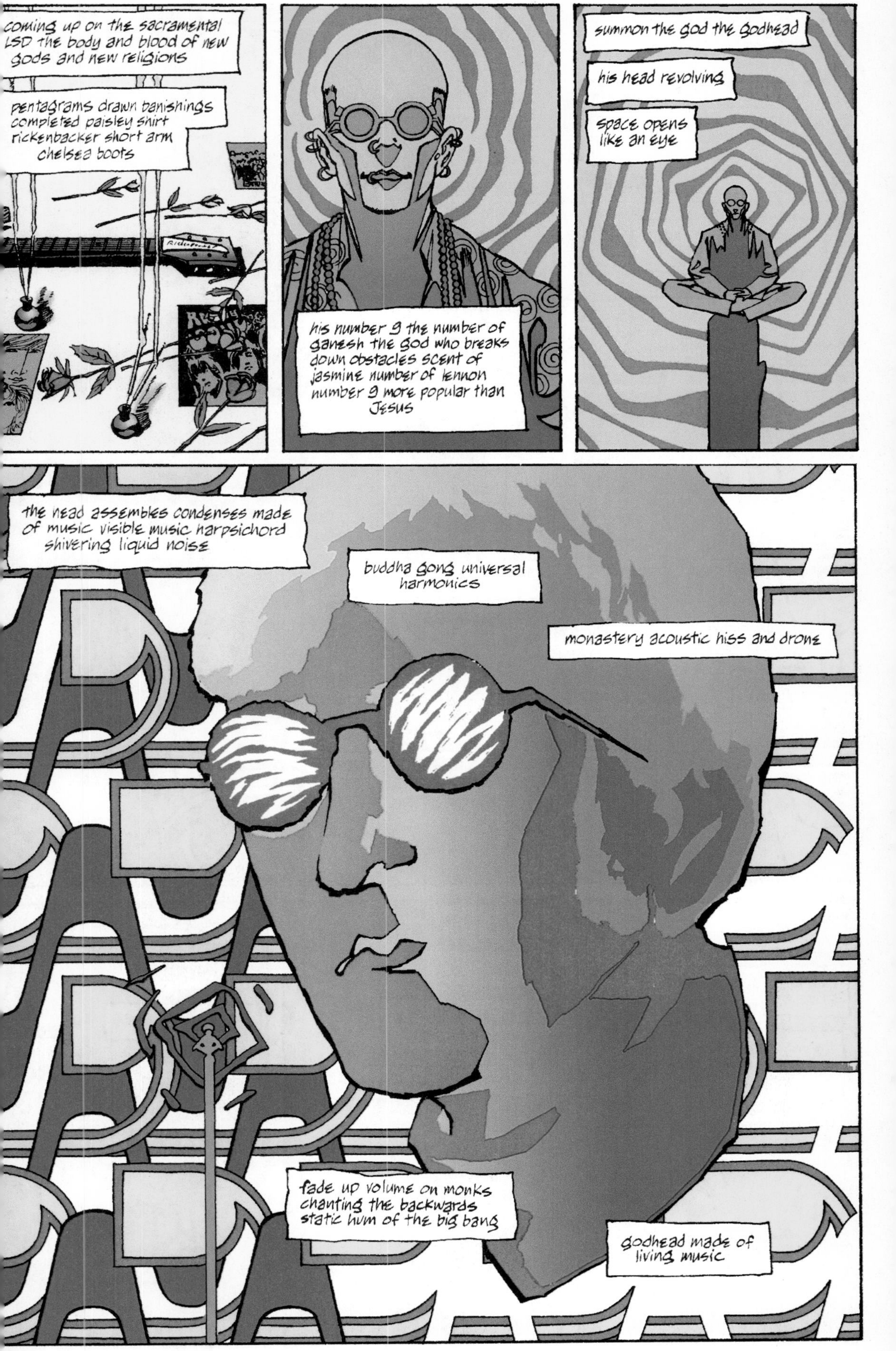

coming up on the sacramental LSD the body and blood of new gods and new religions
pentagrams drawn banishings completed paisley shirt rickenbacker short arm chelsea boots
his number 9 the number of ganesh the god who breaks down obstacles scent of jasmine number of lennon number 9 more popular than Jesus
summon the god the godhead
his head revolving
space opens like an eye
the head assembles condenses made of music visible music harpsichord shivering liquid noise
buddha gong universal harmonics
monastery acoustic hiss and drone
fade up volume on monks chanting the backwards static hum of the big bang
godhead made of living music

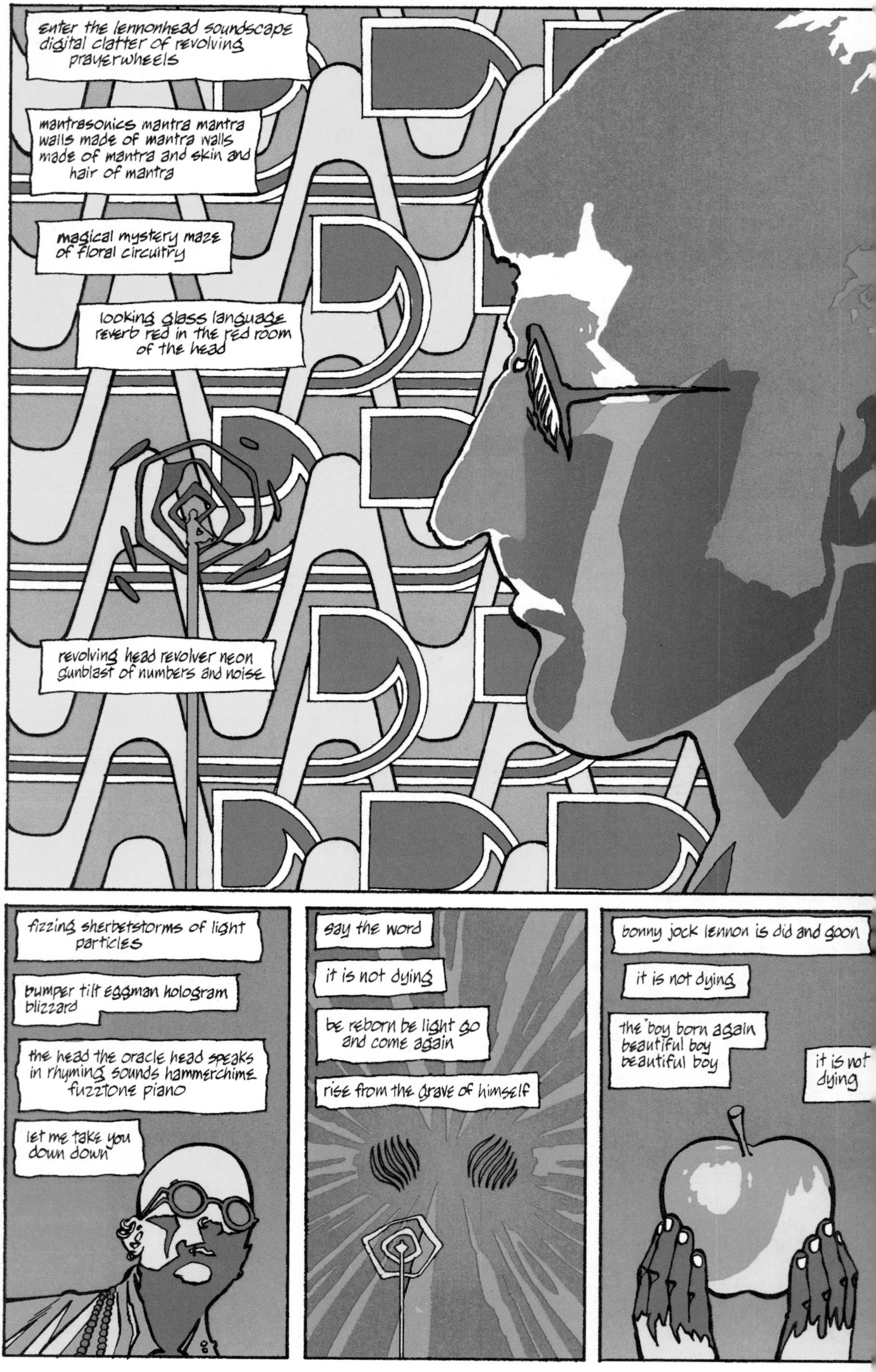
enter the lennonhead soundscape digital clatter of revolving prayerwheels
mantrasonics mantra mantra walls made of mantra walls made of mantra and skin and hair of mantra
magical mystery maze of floral circuitry
looking glass language reverb red in the red room of the head
revolving head revolver neon gunblast of numbers and noise
fizzing sherbetstorms of light particles
bumper tilt eggman hologram blizzard
the head the oracle head speaks in rhyming sounds hammerchime fuzztone piano
let me take you down down
say the word
it is not dying
be reborn be light go and come again
rise from the grave of himself
bonny jock lennon is did and goon
it is not dying
the boy born again beautiful boy beautiful boy
it is not dying

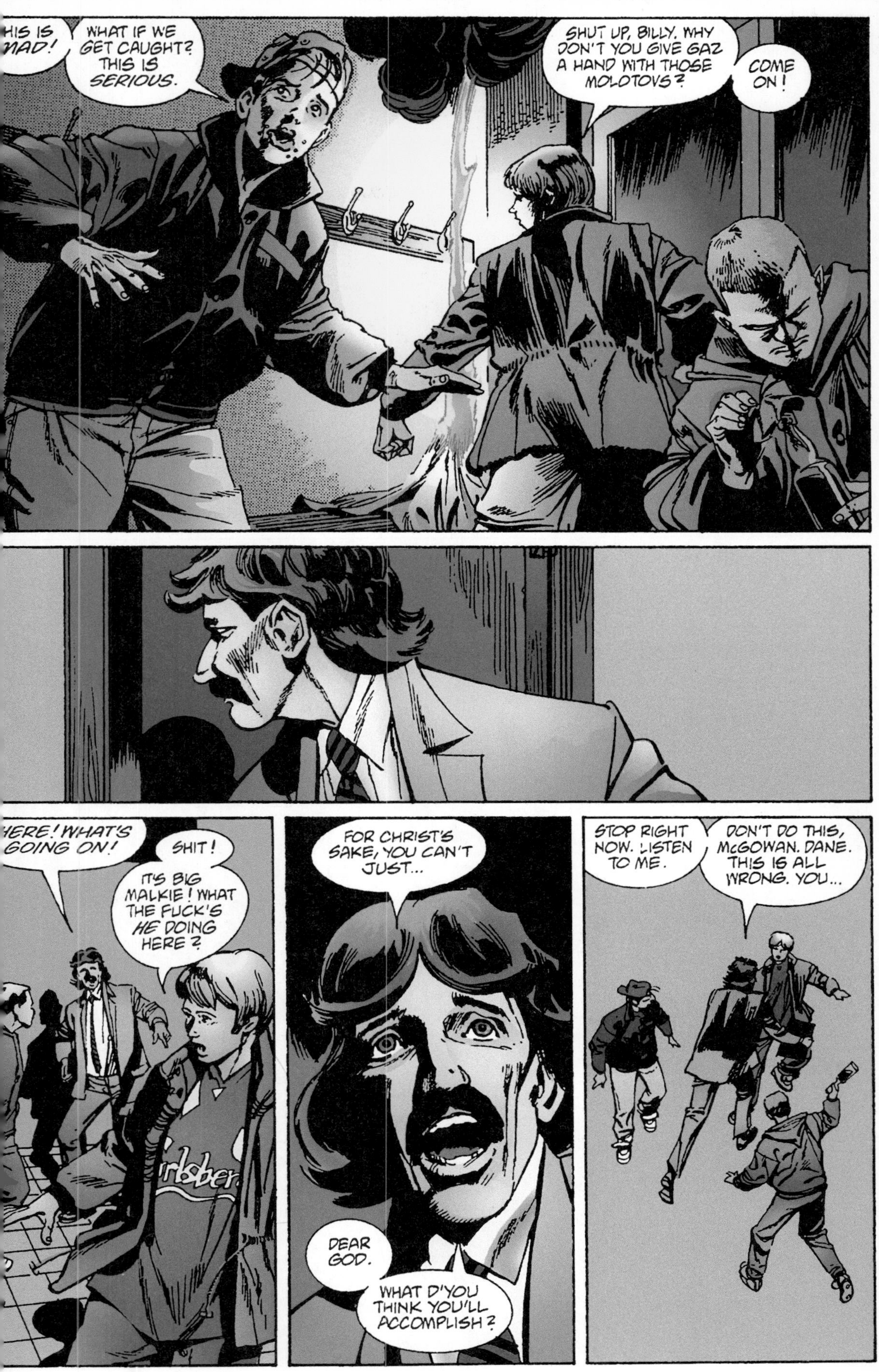
HIS IS MAD!
WHAT IF WE GET CAUGHT? THIS IS SERIOUS.
SHUT UP, BILLY. WHY DON'T YOU GIVE GAZ A HAND WITH THOSE MOLOTOVS?
COME ON!
HERE! WHAT'S GOING ON!
SHIT!
IT'S BIG MALKIE! WHAT THE FUCK'S HE DOING HERE?
FOR CHRIST'S SAKE, YOU CAN'T JUST...
DEAR GOD.
WHAT D'YOU THINK YOU'LL ACCOMPLISH?
STOP RIGHT NOW. LISTEN TO ME.
DON'T DO THIS, McGOWAN. DANE. THIS IS ALL WRONG. YOU...

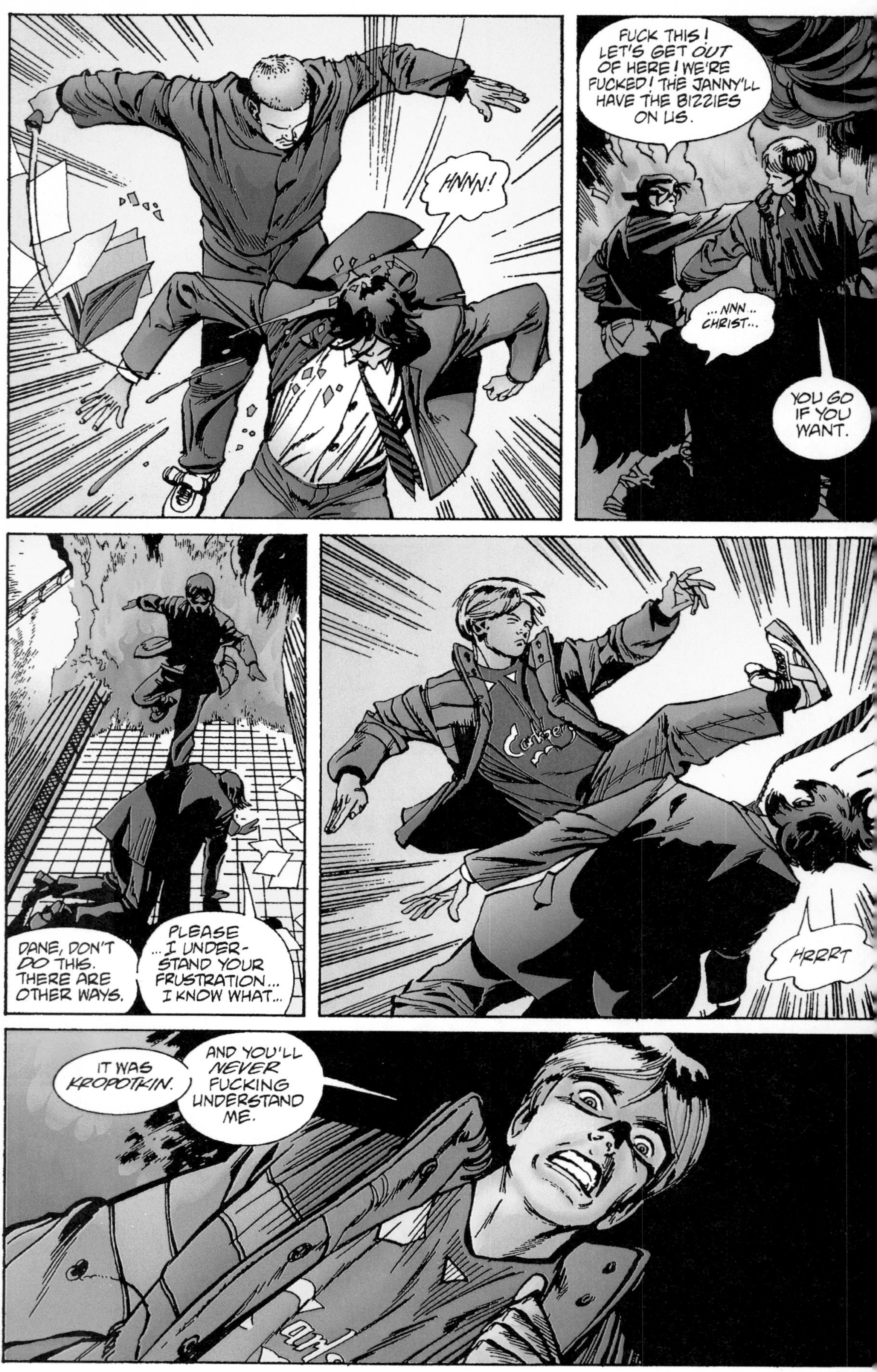
HNNN!
FUCK THIS! LET'S GET OUT OF HERE! WE'RE FUCKED! THE JANNY'LL HAVE THE BIZZIES ON US.
...NNN... CHRIST...
YOU GO IF YOU WANT.
DANE, DON'T DO THIS. THERE ARE OTHER WAYS.
PLEASE ...I UNDERSTAND YOUR FRUSTRATION... I KNOW WHAT...
HRRRT
IT WAS KROPOTKIN.
AND YOU'LL NEVER FUCKING UNDERSTAND ME.

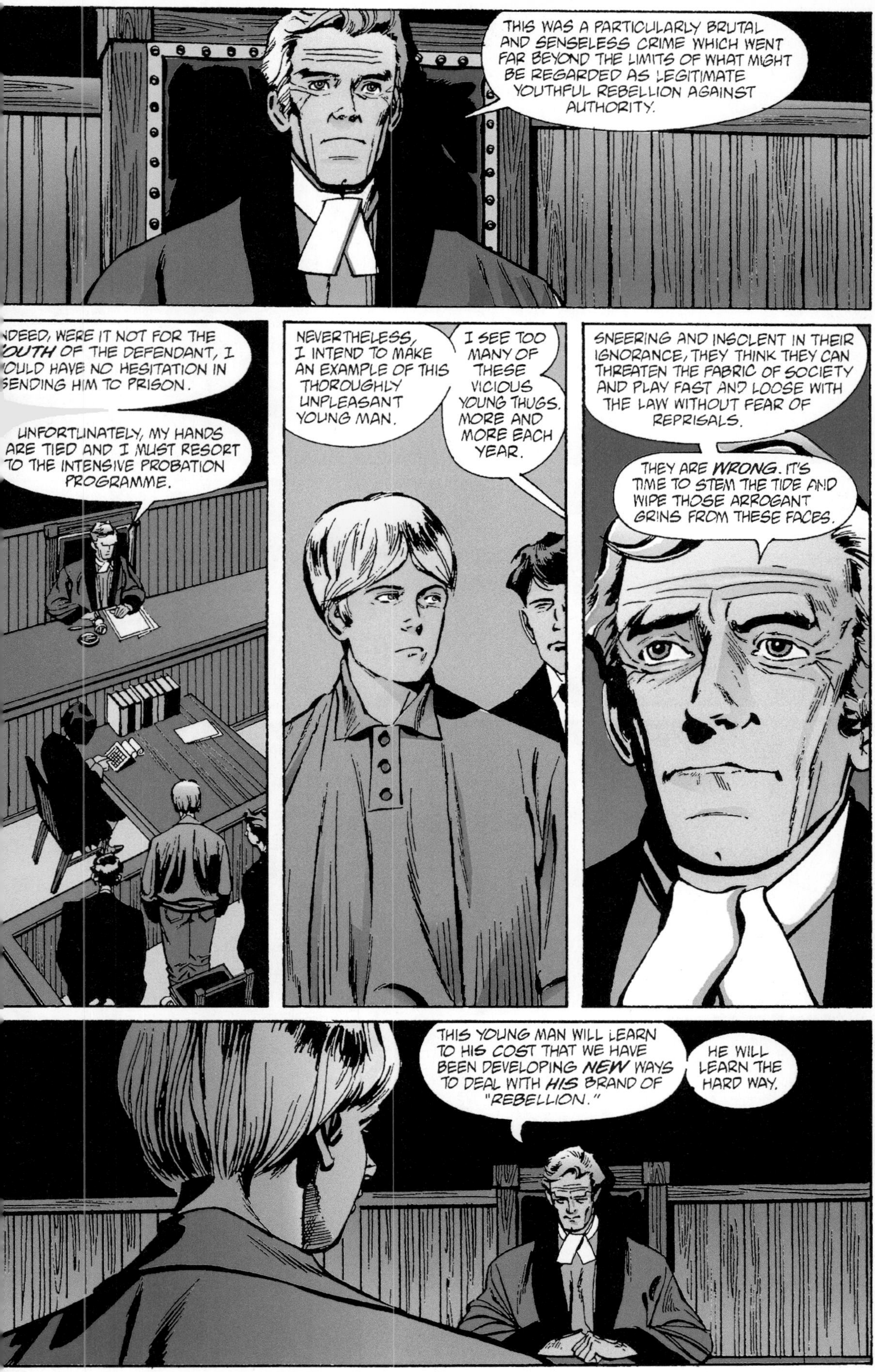
THIS WAS A PARTICULARLY BRUTAL AND SENSELESS CRIME WHICH WENT FAR BEYOND THE LIMITS OF WHAT MIGHT BE REGARDED AS LEGITIMATE YOUTHFUL REBELLION AGAINST AUTHORITY.
NDEED, WERE IT NOT FOR THE OUTH OF THE DEFENDANT, I OULD HAVE NO HESITATION IN SENDING HIM TO PRISON.
UNFORTUNATELY, MY HANDS ARE TIED AND I MUST RESORT TO THE INTENSIVE PROBATION PROGRAMME.
NEVERTHELESS, I INTEND TO MAKE AN EXAMPLE OF THIS THOROUGHLY UNPLEASANT YOUNG MAN.
I SEE TOO MANY OF THESE VICIOUS YOUNG THUGS. MORE AND MORE EACH YEAR.
SNEERING AND INSOLENT IN THEIR IGNORANCE, THEY THINK THEY CAN THREATEN THE FABRIC OF SOCIETY AND PLAY FAST AND LOOSE WITH THE LAW WITHOUT FEAR OF REPRISALS.
THEY ARE WRONG. IT'S TIME TO STEM THE TIDE AND WIPE THOSE ARROGANT GRINS FROM THESE FACES.
THIS YOUNG MAN WILL LEARN TO HIS COST THAT WE HAVE BEEN DEVELOPING NEW WAYS TO DEAL WITH HIS BRAND OF "REBELLION."
HE WILL LEARN THE HARD WAY.

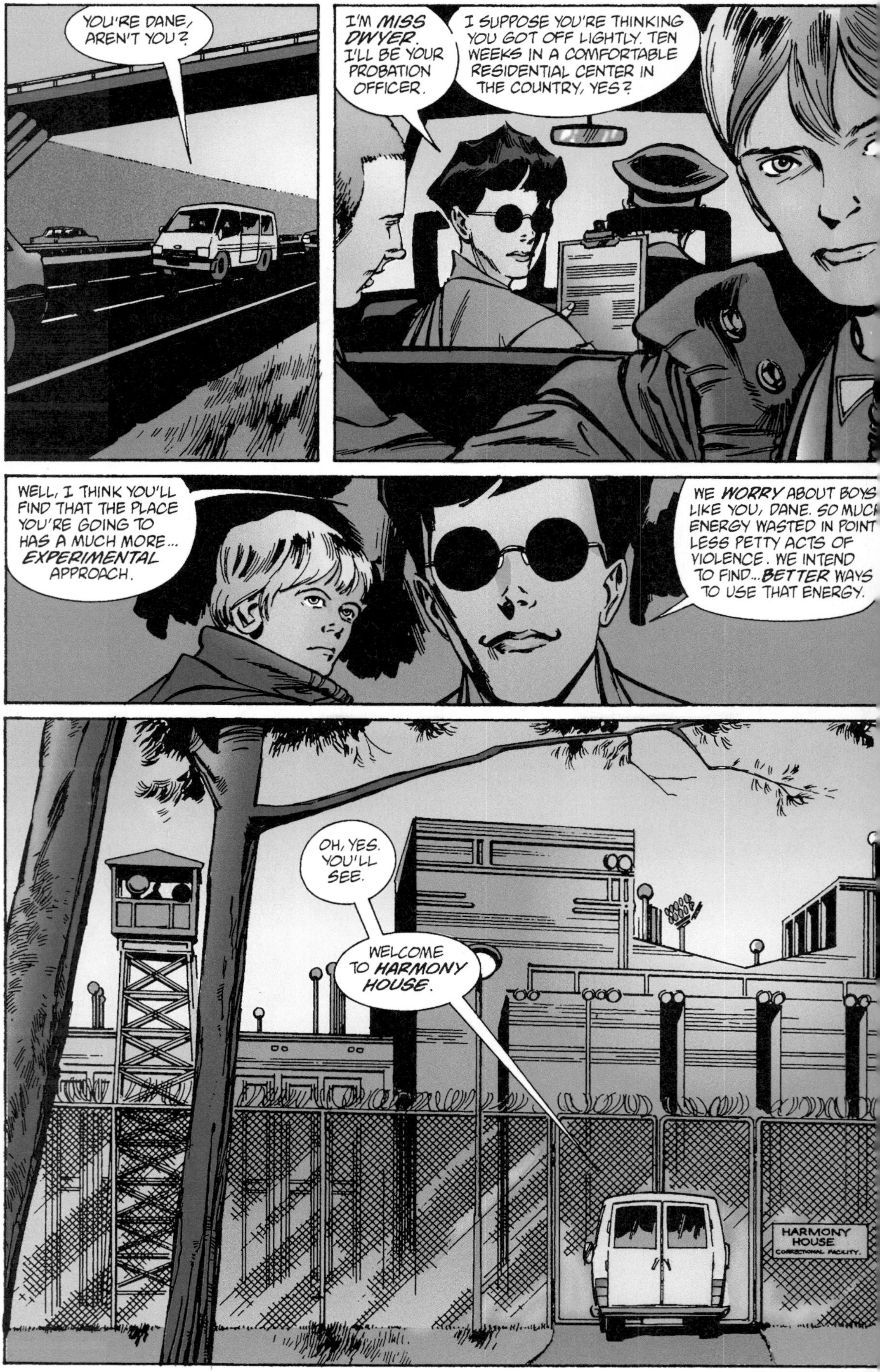
YOU'RE DANE, AREN'T YOU?
I'M MISS DWYER. I'LL BE YOUR PROBATION OFFICER.
I SUPPOSE YOU'RE THINKING YOU GOT OFF LIGHTLY. TEN WEEKS IN A COMFORTABLE RESIDENTIAL CENTER IN THE COUNTRY, YES?
WELL, I THINK YOU'LL FIND THAT THE PLACE YOU'RE GOING TO HAS A MUCH MORE... EXPERIMENTAL APPROACH.
WE WORRY ABOUT BOYS LIKE YOU, DANE. SO MUCH ENERGY WASTED IN POINTLESS PETTY ACTS OF VIOLENCE. WE INTEND TO FIND... BETTER WAYS TO USE THAT ENERGY.
OH, YES. YOU'LL SEE.
WELCOME TO HARMONY HOUSE.
HARMONY HOUSE
CORRECTIONAL FACILITY.

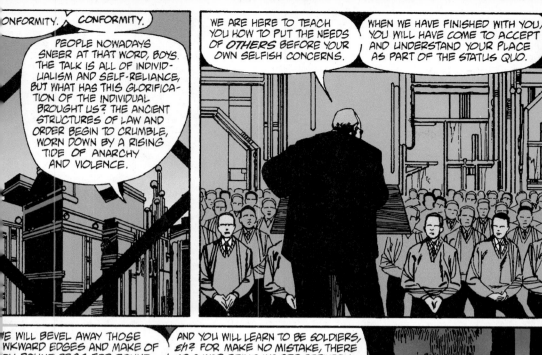

CONFORMITY. CONFORMITY.

PEOPLE NOWADAYS SNEER AT THAT WORD, BOYS. THE TALK IS ALL OF INDIVID-UALISM AND SELF-RELIANCE, BUT WHAT HAS THIS GLORIFICA-TION OF THE INDIVIDUAL BROUGHT US? THE ANCIENT STRUCTURES OF LAW AND ORDER BEGIN TO CRUMBLE, WORN DOWN BY A RISING TIDE OF ANARCHY AND VIOLENCE.

WE ARE HERE TO TEACH YOU HOW TO PUT THE NEEDS OF *OTHERS* BEFORE YOUR OWN SELFISH CONCERNS.

WHEN WE HAVE FINISHED WITH YOU, YOU WILL HAVE COME TO ACCEPT AND UNDERSTAND YOUR PLACE AS PART OF THE STATUS QUO.

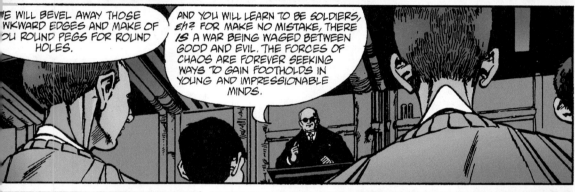

WE WILL BEVEL AWAY THOSE AWKWARD EDGES AND MAKE OF YOU ROUND PEGS FOR ROUND HOLES.

AND YOU WILL LEARN TO BE SOLDIERS, EH? FOR MAKE NO MISTAKE, THERE *IS* A WAR BEING WAGED BETWEEN GOOD AND EVIL. THE FORCES OF CHAOS ARE FOREVER SEEKING WAYS TO GAIN FOOTHOLDS IN YOUNG AND IMPRESSIONABLE MINDS.

BUT FEAR NOT: WE ARE HERE TO PULL YOU OUT OF THE SHADOWS, BOYS.

WE ARE HERE TO MAKE YOU MARCH IN STEP.

AND HERE AT HARMONY HOUSE YOU WILL LEARN TO HAVE *PRIDE* IN YOUR ROLE AS A COG IN THE GREAT MACHINE OF SOCIETY.

MAKE NO MISTAKE, BOYS: WE *WILL* MAKE YOU CONFORM.

AND, WHAT IS MORE, IN THE END YOU WILL *THANK* US FOR IT.

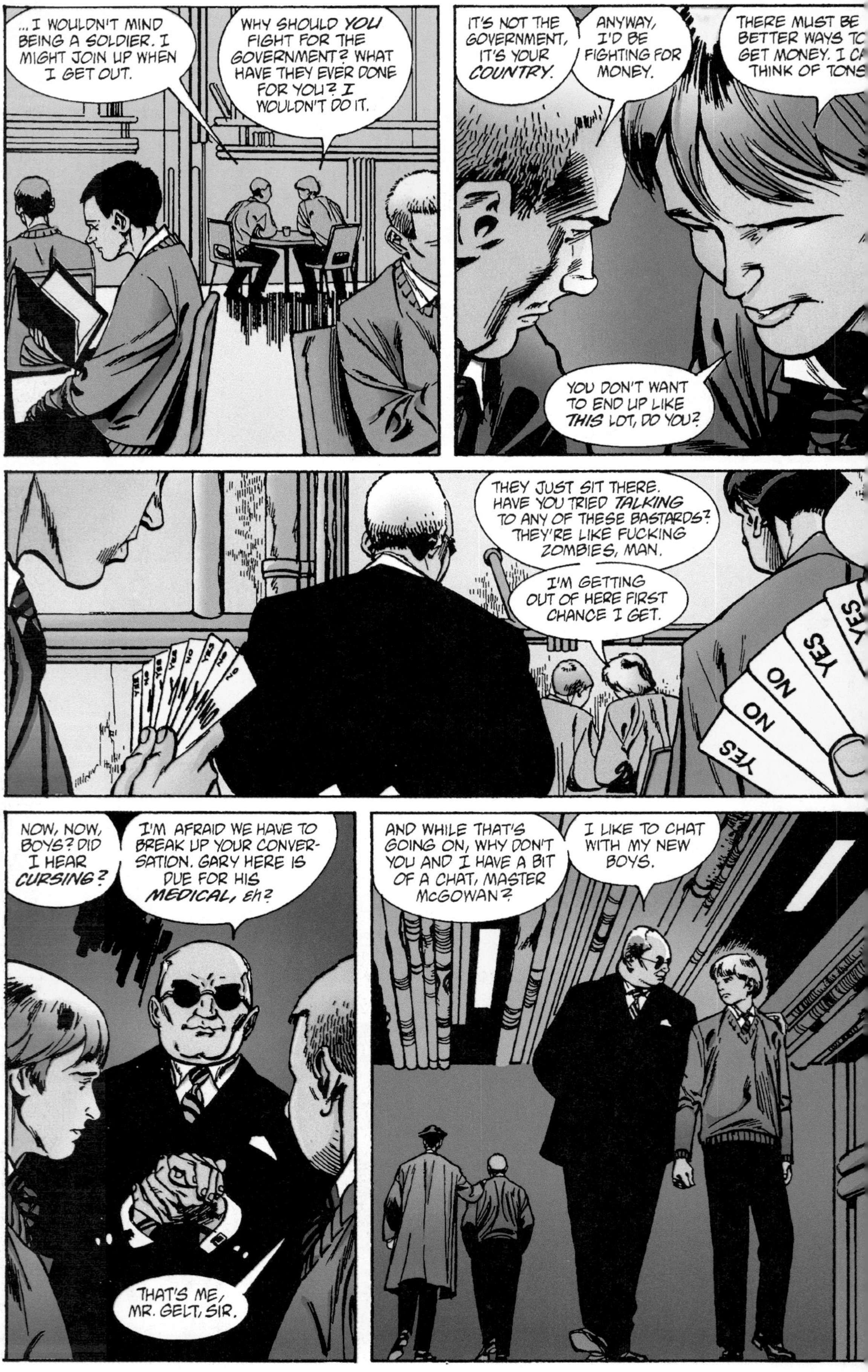
...I WOULDN'T MIND BEING A SOLDIER. I MIGHT JOIN UP WHEN I GET OUT.
WHY SHOULD YOU FIGHT FOR THE GOVERNMENT? WHAT HAVE THEY EVER DONE FOR YOU? I WOULDN'T DO IT.
IT'S NOT THE GOVERNMENT, IT'S YOUR COUNTRY.
ANYWAY, I'D BE FIGHTING FOR MONEY.
THERE MUST BE BETTER WAYS TO GET MONEY. I CA THINK OF TONS
YOU DON'T WANT TO END UP LIKE THIS LOT, DO YOU?
THEY JUST SIT THERE. HAVE YOU TRIED TALKING TO ANY OF THESE BASTARDS? THEY'RE LIKE FUCKING ZOMBIES, MAN.
I'M GETTING OUT OF HERE FIRST CHANCE I GET.
YES
NO
NO
YES
YES
NOW, NOW, BOYS? DID I HEAR CURSING?
I'M AFRAID WE HAVE TO BREAK UP YOUR CONVERSATION. GARY HERE IS DUE FOR HIS MEDICAL, EH?
THAT'S ME, MR. GELT, SIR.
AND WHILE THAT'S GOING ON, WHY DON'T YOU AND I HAVE A BIT OF A CHAT, MASTER McGOWAN?
I LIKE TO CHAT WITH MY NEW BOYS.

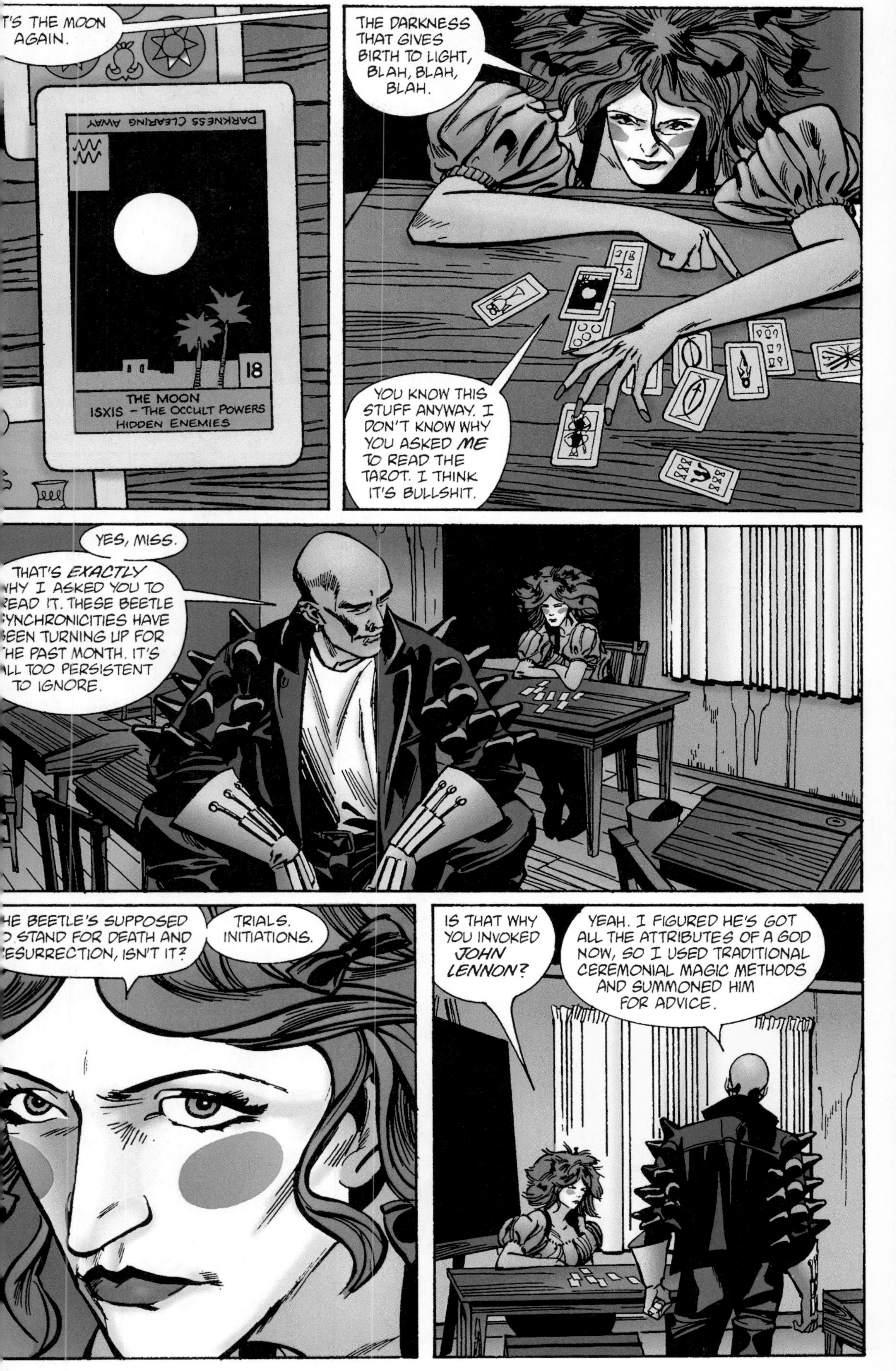
T'S THE MOON AGAIN.
DARKNESS CLEARING AWAY
18
THE MOON
ISXIS - THE OCCULT POWERS
HIDDEN ENEMIES
THE DARKNESS THAT GIVES BIRTH TO LIGHT, BLAH, BLAH, BLAH.
YOU KNOW THIS STUFF ANYWAY. I DON'T KNOW WHY YOU ASKED ME TO READ THE TAROT. I THINK IT'S BULLSHIT.
YES, MISS.
THAT'S EXACTLY HY I ASKED YOU TO EAD IT. THESE BEETLE YNCHRONICITIES HAVE EEN TURNING UP FOR HE PAST MONTH. IT'S LL TOO PERSISTENT TO IGNORE.
HE BEETLE'S SUPPOSED O STAND FOR DEATH AND ESURRECTION, ISN'T IT?
TRIALS. INITIATIONS.
IS THAT WHY YOU INVOKED JOHN LENNON?
YEAH. I FIGURED HE'S GOT ALL THE ATTRIBUTES OF A GOD NOW, SO I USED TRADITIONAL CEREMONIAL MAGIC METHODS AND SUMMONED HIM FOR ADVICE.

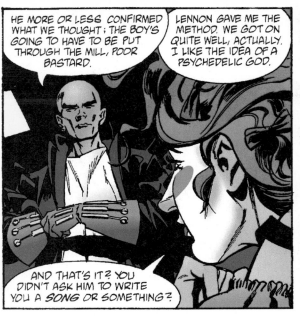

HE MORE OR LESS CONFIRMED WHAT WE THOUGHT; THE BOY'S GOING TO HAVE TO BE PUT THROUGH THE MILL, POOR BASTARD.

LENNON GAVE ME THE METHOD. WE GOT ON QUITE WELL, ACTUALLY. I LIKE THE IDEA OF A PSYCHEDELIC GOD.

AND THAT'S IT? YOU DIDN'T ASK HIM TO WRITE YOU A *SONG* OR SOMETHING?

HE JUST SUGGESTED I GIVE YOU *THIS*.

AN APPLE FOR THE TEACHER.

EVE MAY HAVE FALLEN FOR THAT ONE. *RAGGED ROBIN'S* NOT SO DUMB.

I GUESS YOU WANT ME TO CONTACT THE *OTHERS* NOW. BOY'S STILL IN NEW YORK. FANNY'S AT THE ACADEM—

I'M GOING TO NEED *ALL* OF YOU. WE HAVE TO SET THIS ONE UP REALLY CAREFULLY. WE CAN'T AFFORD TO LOSE THIS KID.

THAT'S IF WE HAVEN'T ALREADY LOST HIM.

I'VE BEEN LOOKING FORWARD TO VISITING HARMONY HOUSE.

YOU KNOW, WHEN *I* WAS A KID, I WANTED TO GROW UP AND FIND MYSELF LIVING IN A '60s *SPY* SERIES.

FUNNY HOW THINGS TURN OUT, ISN'T IT?

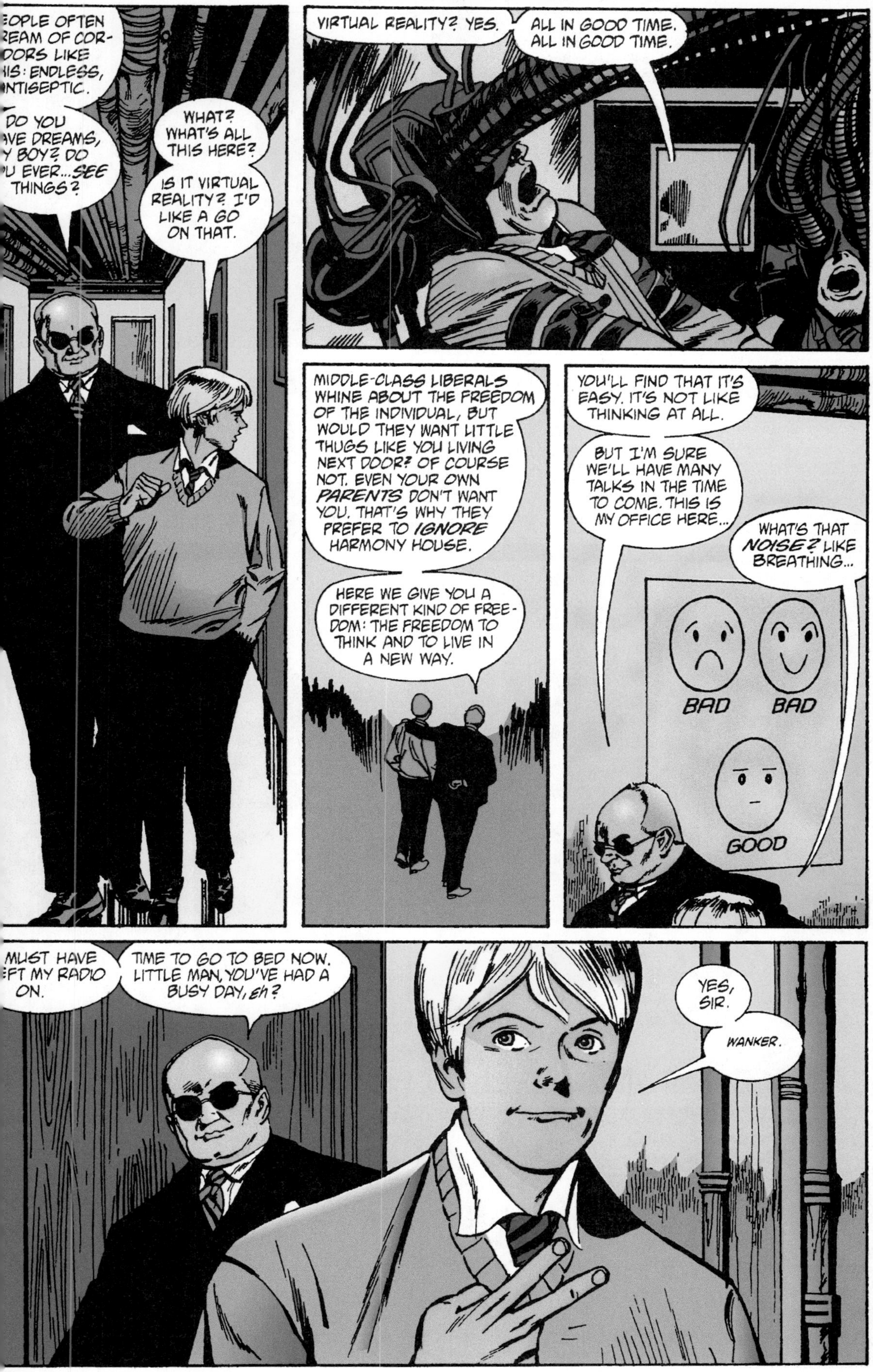
EOPLE OFTEN REAM OF COR- DORS LIKE HIS: ENDLESS, NTISEPTIC.
DO YOU AVE DREAMS, Y BOY? DO U EVER...SEE THINGS?
WHAT? WHAT'S ALL THIS HERE?
IS IT VIRTUAL REALITY? I'D LIKE A GO ON THAT.
VIRTUAL REALITY? YES.
ALL IN GOOD TIME. ALL IN GOOD TIME.
MIDDLE-CLASS LIBERALS WHINE ABOUT THE FREEDOM OF THE INDIVIDUAL, BUT WOULD THEY WANT LITTLE THUGS LIKE YOU LIVING NEXT DOOR? OF COURSE NOT. EVEN YOUR OWN PARENTS DON'T WANT YOU. THAT'S WHY THEY PREFER TO IGNORE HARMONY HOUSE.
HERE WE GIVE YOU A DIFFERENT KIND OF FREE- DOM: THE FREEDOM TO THINK AND TO LIVE IN A NEW WAY.
YOU'LL FIND THAT IT'S EASY. IT'S NOT LIKE THINKING AT ALL.
BUT I'M SURE WE'LL HAVE MANY TALKS IN THE TIME TO COME. THIS IS MY OFFICE HERE...
WHAT'S THAT NOISE? LIKE BREATHING...
BAD
BAD
GOOD
MUST HAVE EFT MY RADIO ON.
TIME TO GO TO BED NOW. LITTLE MAN, YOU'VE HAD A BUSY DAY, eh?
YES, SIR.
WANKER.

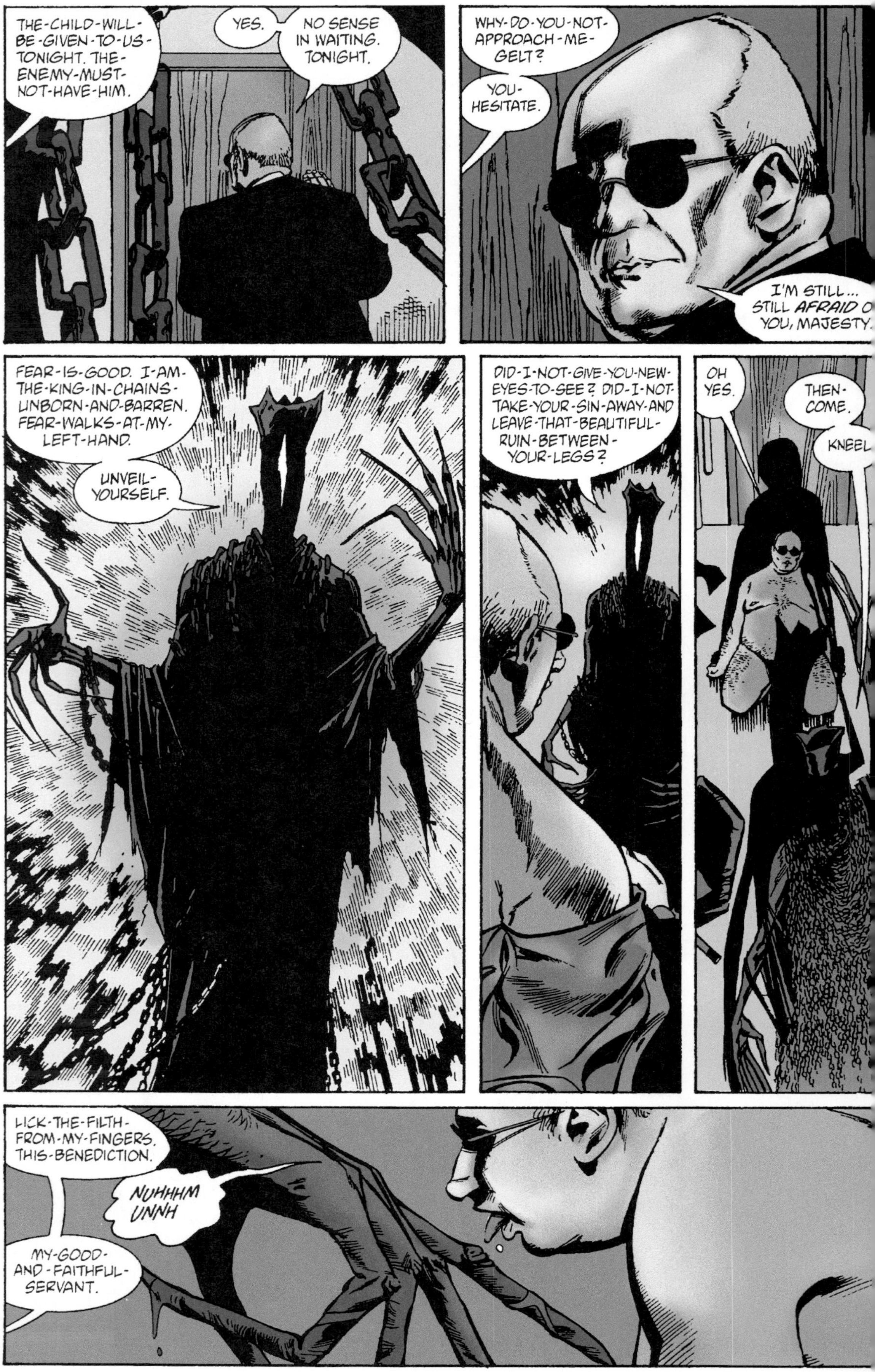
THE-CHILD-WILL-BE-GIVEN-TO-US-TONIGHT. THE-ENEMY-MUST-NOT-HAVE-HIM.
YES.
NO SENSE IN WAITING. TONIGHT.
WHY-DO-YOU-NOT-APPROACH-ME-GELT?
YOU-HESITATE.
I'M STILL... STILL AFRAID O YOU, MAJESTY.
FEAR-IS-GOOD. I-AM-THE-KING-IN-CHAINS-UNBORN-AND-BARREN. FEAR-WALKS-AT-MY-LEFT-HAND.
UNVEIL-YOURSELF.
DID-I-NOT-GIVE-YOU-NEW-EYES-TO-SEE? DID-I-NOT-TAKE-YOUR-SIN-AWAY-AND LEAVE-THAT-BEAUTIFUL-RUIN-BETWEEN-YOUR-LEGS?
OH YES.
THEN-COME.
KNEEL
LICK-THE-FILTH-FROM-MY-FINGERS. THIS-BENEDICTION.
NUHHHM UNNH
MY-GOOD-AND-FAITHFUL-SERVANT.

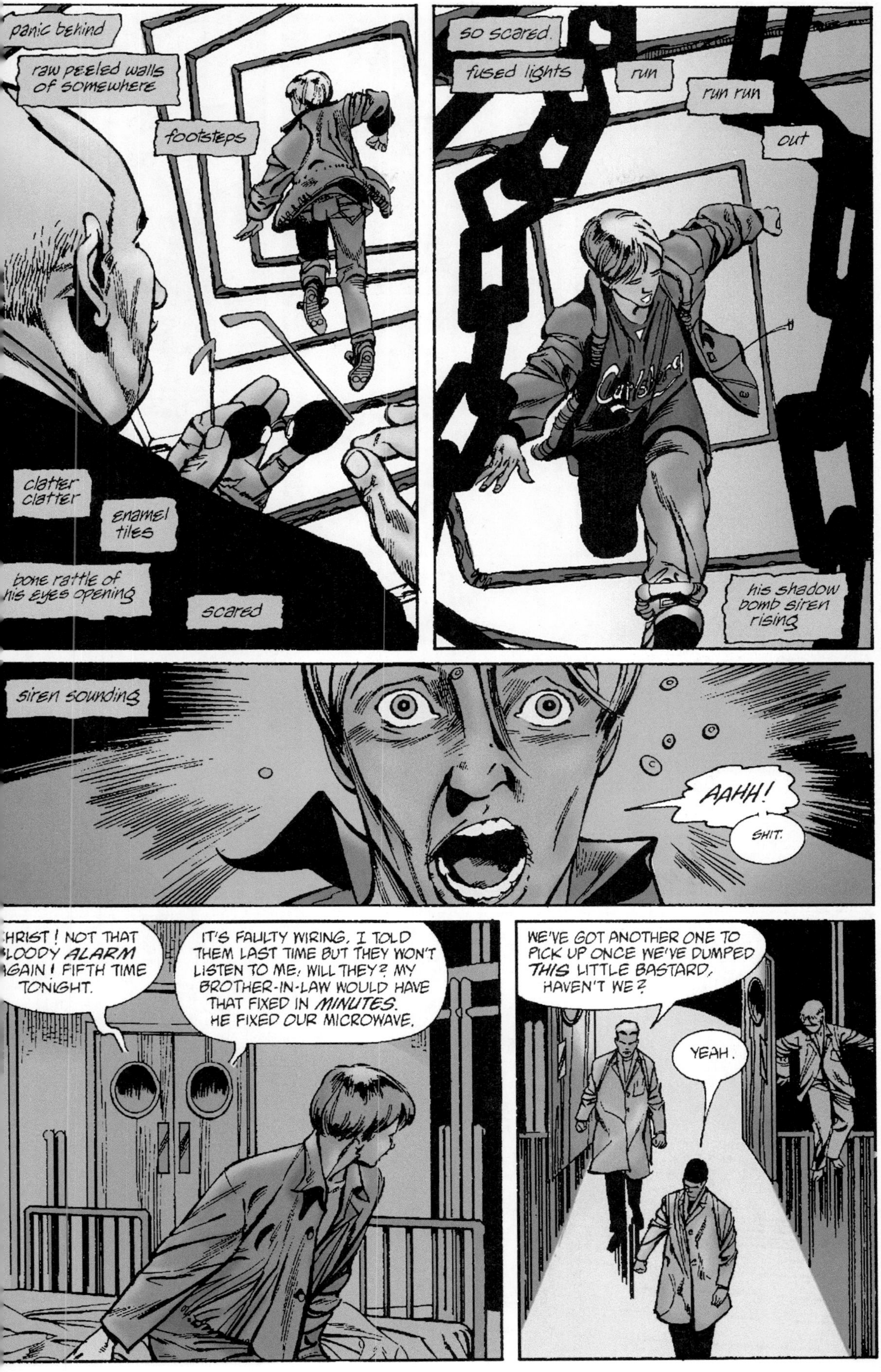
panic behind
raw peeled walls of somewhere
footsteps
clatter clatter
enamel tiles
bone rattle of his eyes opening
scared
so scared.
fused lights
run
run run
out
his shadow bomb siren rising
siren sounding
AAHH!
SHIT.
CHRIST! NOT THAT BLOODY ALARM AGAIN! FIFTH TIME TONIGHT.
IT'S FAULTY WIRING, I TOLD THEM LAST TIME BUT THEY WON'T LISTEN TO ME, WILL THEY? MY BROTHER-IN-LAW WOULD HAVE THAT FIXED IN MINUTES. HE FIXED OUR MICROWAVE.
WE'VE GOT ANOTHER ONE TO PICK UP ONCE WE'VE DUMPED THIS LITTLE BASTARD, HAVEN'T WE?
YEAH.

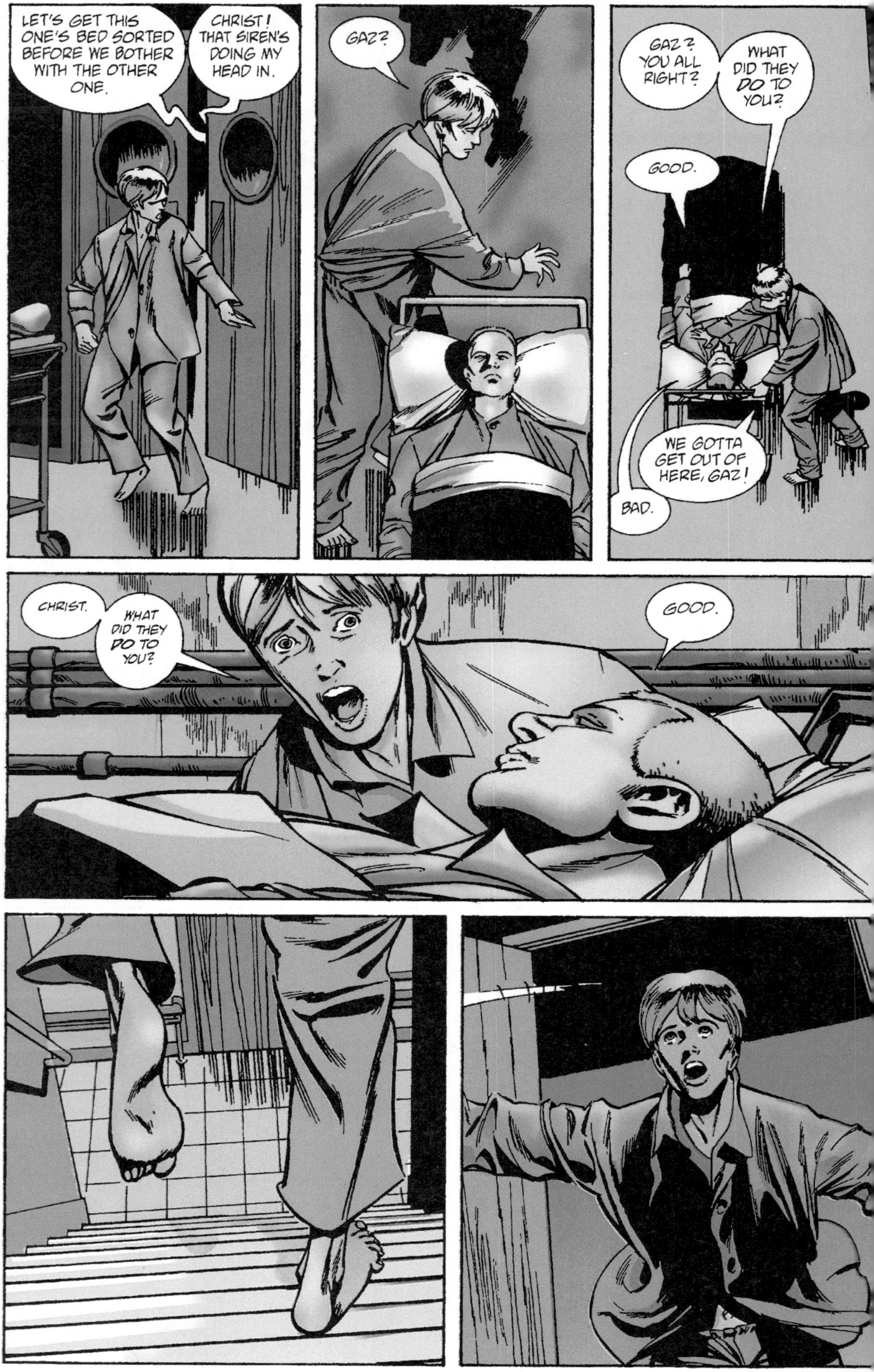
LET'S GET THIS ONE'S BED SORTED BEFORE WE BOTHER WITH THE OTHER ONE.
CHRIST! THAT SIREN'S DOING MY HEAD IN.
GAZ?
GAZ? YOU ALL RIGHT?
WHAT DID THEY DO TO YOU?
GOOD.
BAD.
WE GOTTA GET OUT OF HERE, GAZ!
CHRIST.
WHAT DID THEY DO TO YOU?
GOOD.

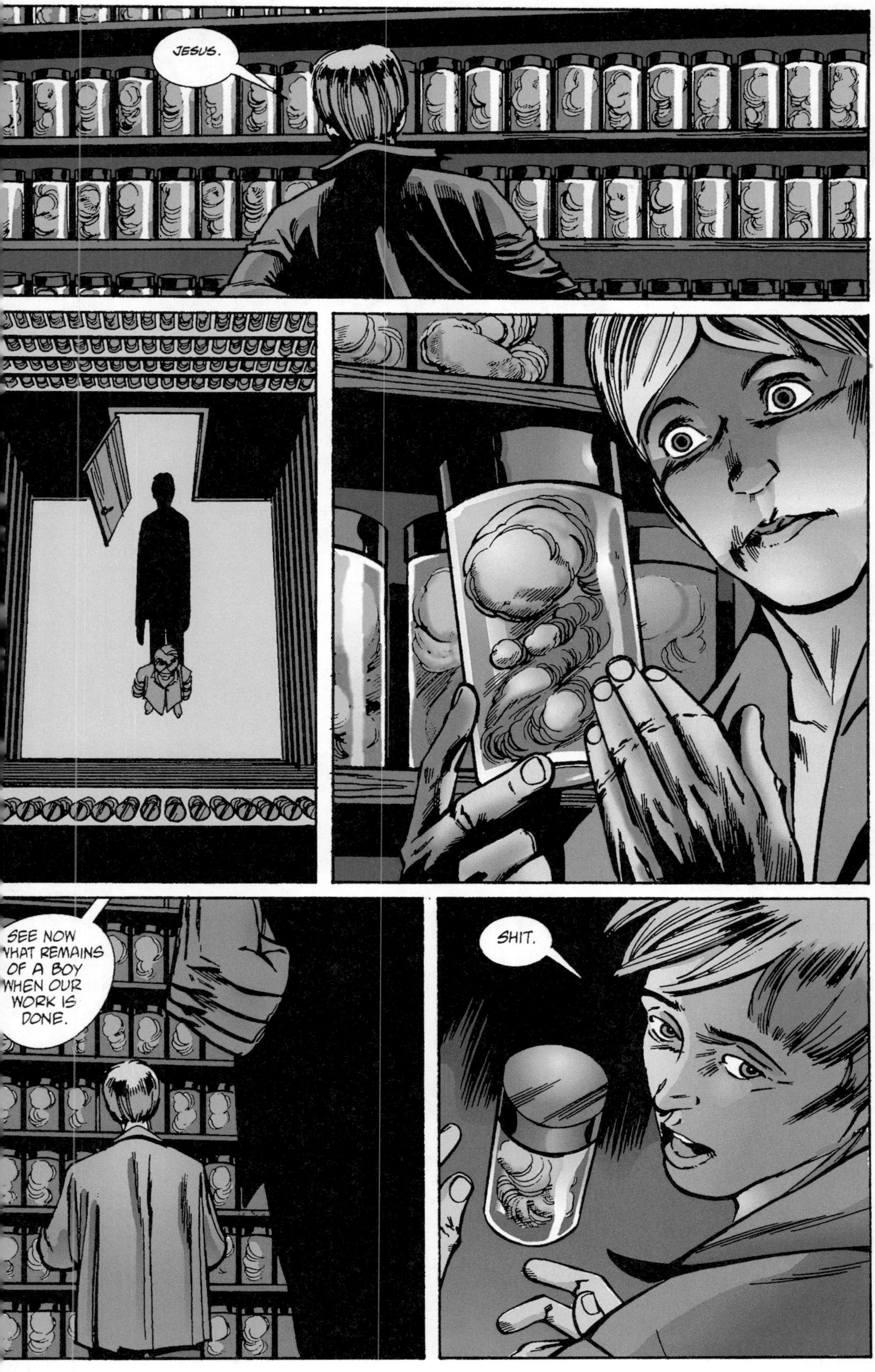
JESUS.
SEE NOW WHAT REMAINS OF A BOY WHEN OUR WORK IS DONE.
SHIT.

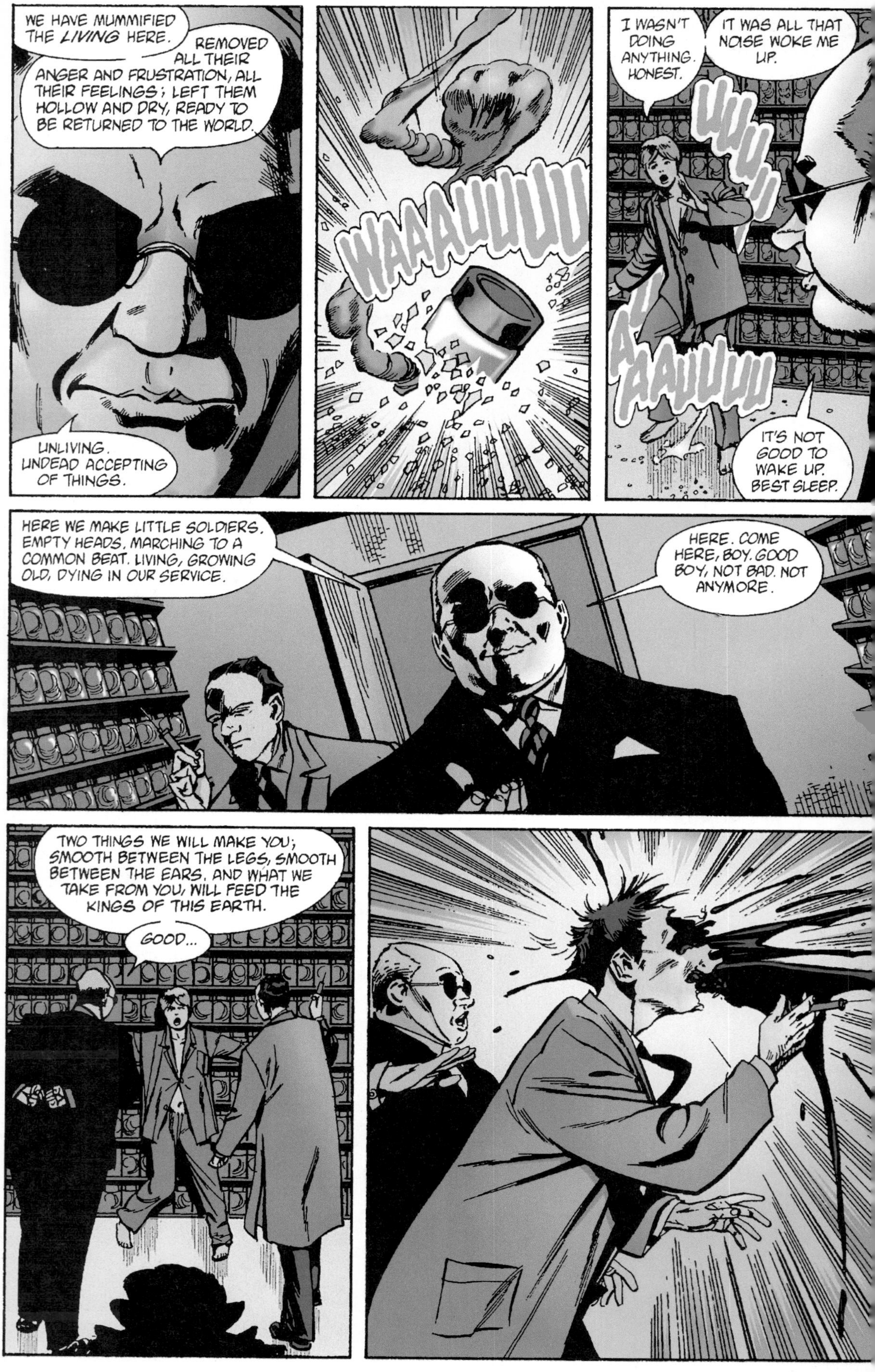
WE HAVE MUMMIFIED THE *LIVING* HERE.
REMOVED ALL THEIR ANGER AND FRUSTRATION, ALL THEIR FEELINGS; LEFT THEM HOLLOW AND DRY, READY TO BE RETURNED TO THE WORLD.
UNLIVING. UNDEAD ACCEPTING OF THINGS.
WAAAUUUUU
I WASN'T DOING ANYTHING. HONEST.
IT WAS ALL THAT NOISE WOKE ME UP.
UUUUU
AAAAUUUU
IT'S NOT GOOD TO WAKE UP. BEST SLEEP.
HERE WE MAKE LITTLE SOLDIERS. EMPTY HEADS, MARCHING TO A COMMON BEAT. LIVING, GROWING OLD, DYING IN OUR SERVICE.
HERE. COME HERE, BOY. GOOD BOY, NOT BAD. NOT ANYMORE.
TWO THINGS WE WILL MAKE YOU; SMOOTH BETWEEN THE LEGS, SMOOTH BETWEEN THE EARS. AND WHAT WE TAKE FROM YOU, WILL FEED THE KINGS OF THIS EARTH.
GOOD...

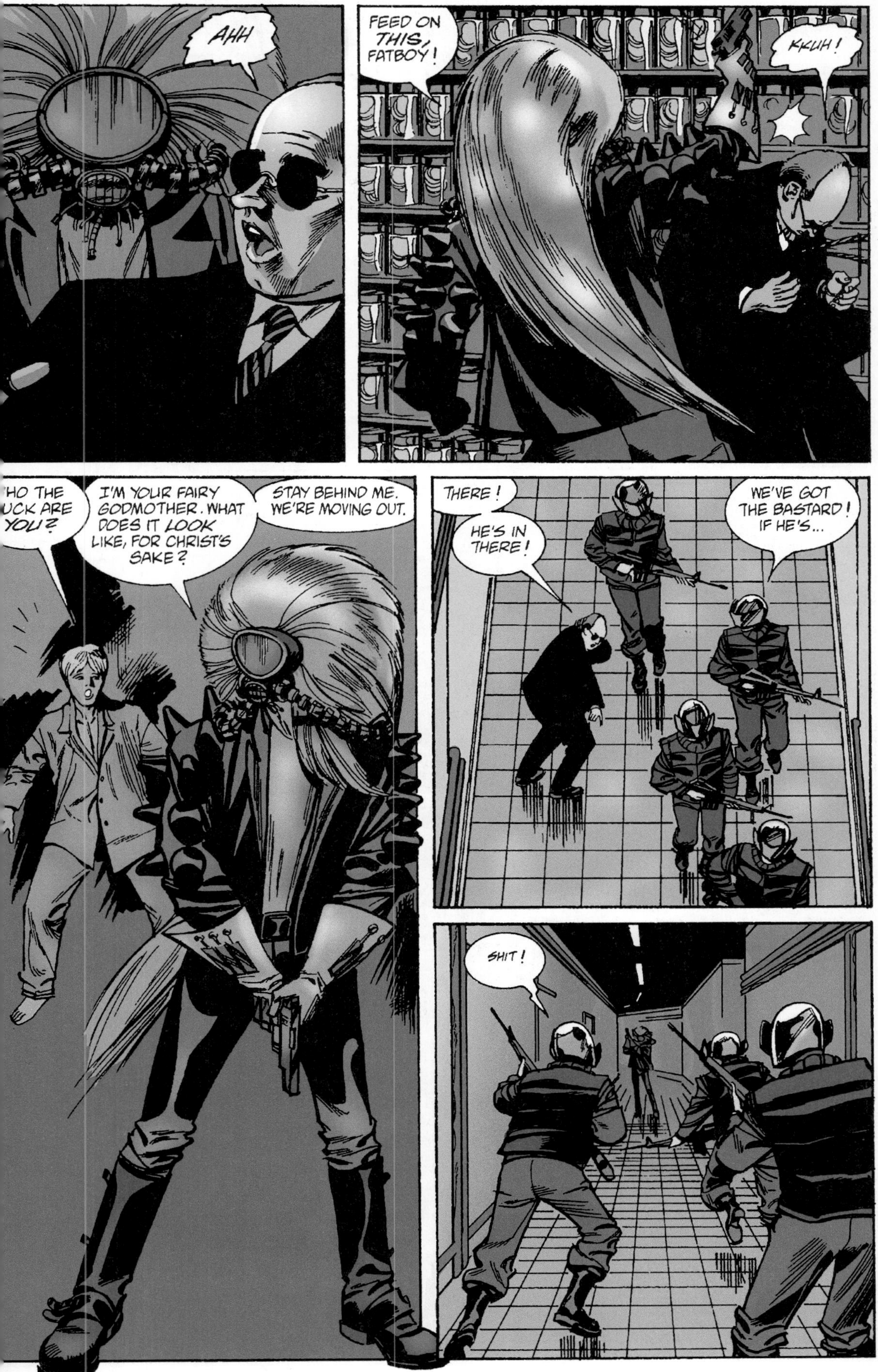
AHH
FEED ON THIS, FATBOY!
KKUH!
HO THE UCK ARE YOU?
I'M YOUR FAIRY GODMOTHER. WHAT DOES IT LOOK LIKE, FOR CHRIST'S SAKE?
STAY BEHIND ME. WE'RE MOVING OUT.
THERE!
HE'S IN THERE!
WE'VE GOT THE BASTARD! IF HE'S...
SHIT!

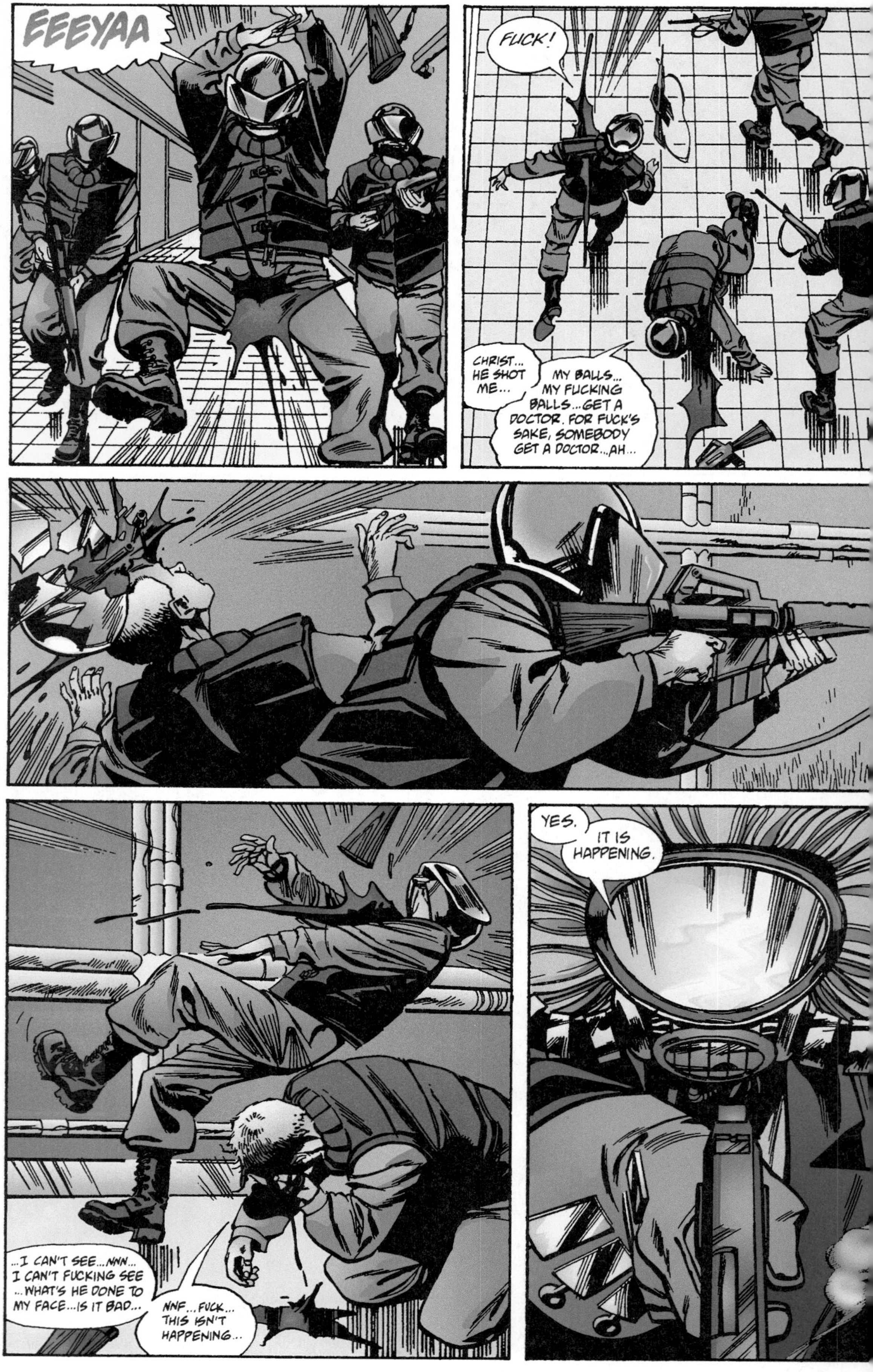
EEEYAA
FUCK!
CHRIST... HE SHOT ME...
MY BALLS... MY FUCKING BALLS...GET A DOCTOR. FOR FUCK'S SAKE, SOMEBODY GET A DOCTOR...AH...
YES.
IT IS HAPPENING.
...I CAN'T SEE...NNN... I CAN'T FUCKING SEE ...WHAT'S HE DONE TO MY FACE...IS IT BAD...
NNF...FUCK... THIS ISN'T HAPPENING...

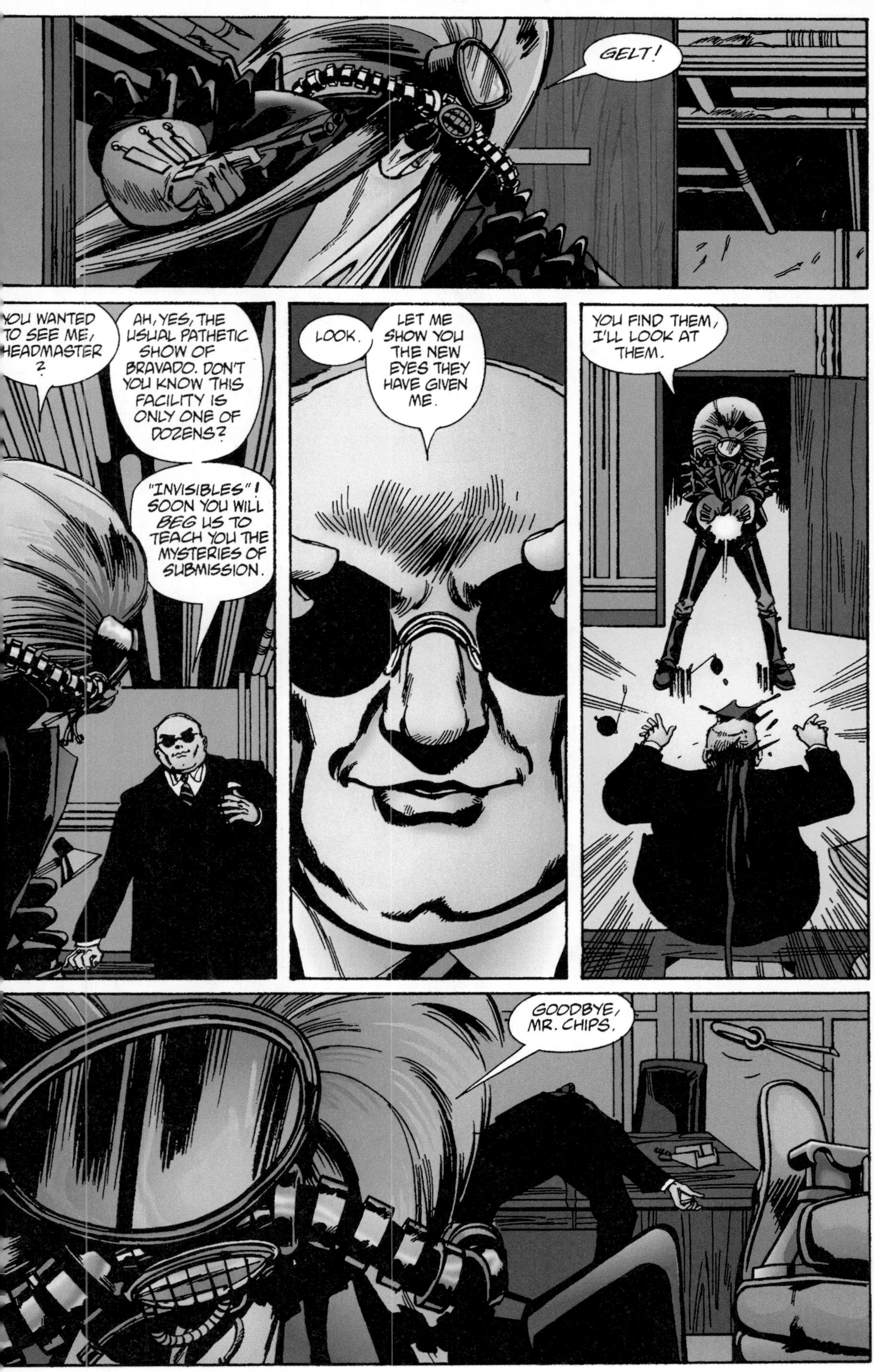
GELT!
YOU WANTED TO SEE ME, HEADMASTER?
AH, YES, THE USUAL PATHETIC SHOW OF BRAVADO. DON'T YOU KNOW THIS FACILITY IS ONLY ONE OF DOZENS?
"INVISIBLES"! SOON YOU WILL BEG US TO TEACH YOU THE MYSTERIES OF SUBMISSION.
LOOK.
LET ME SHOW YOU THE NEW EYES THEY HAVE GIVEN ME.
YOU FIND THEM, I'LL LOOK AT THEM.
GOODBYE, MR. CHIPS.

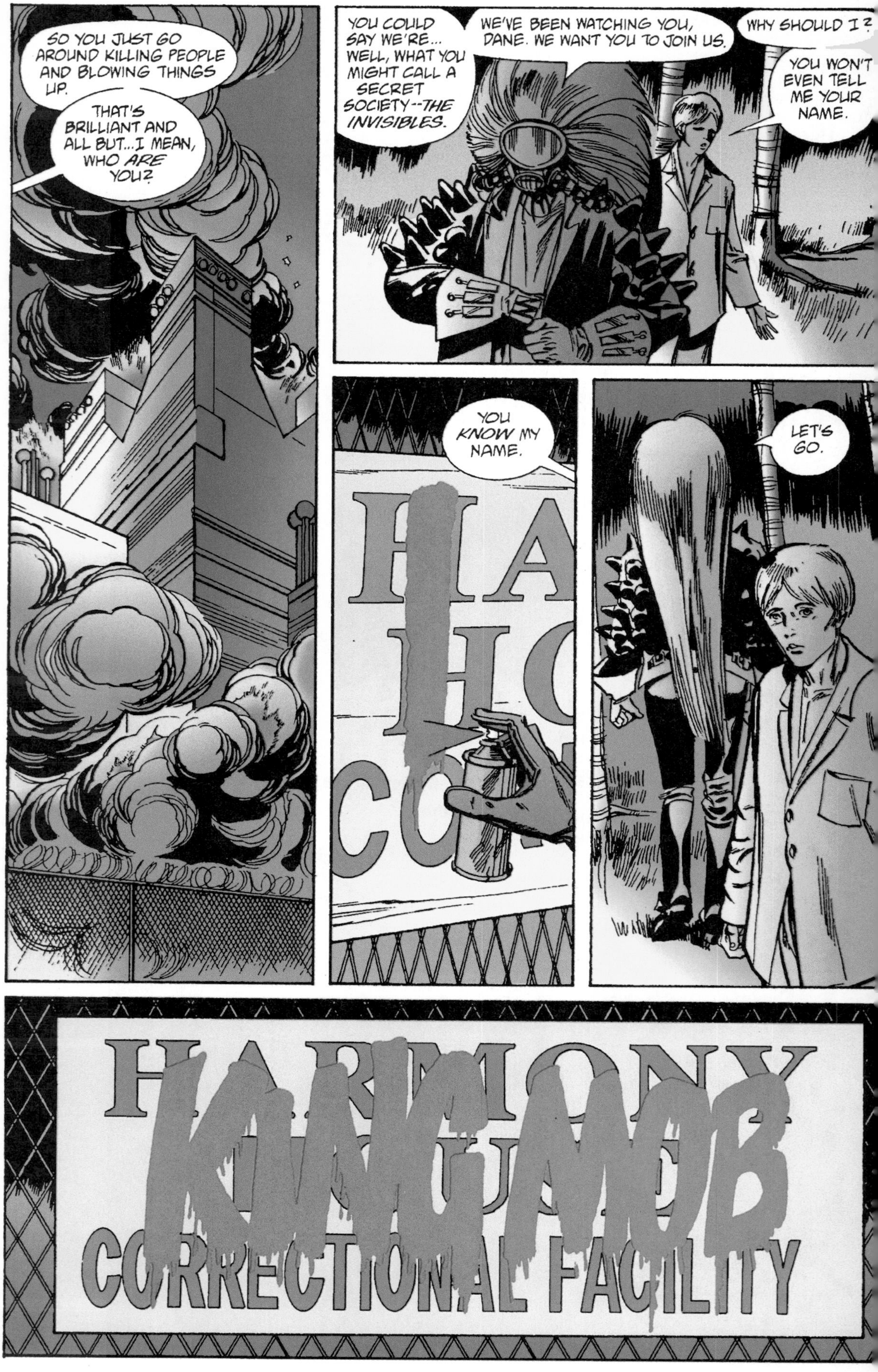
SO YOU JUST GO AROUND KILLING PEOPLE AND BLOWING THINGS UP.
THAT'S BRILLIANT AND ALL BUT...I MEAN, WHO *ARE* YOU?
YOU COULD SAY WE'RE... WELL, WHAT YOU MIGHT CALL A SECRET SOCIETY--*THE INVISIBLES.*
WE'VE BEEN WATCHING YOU, DANE. WE WANT YOU TO JOIN US.
WHY SHOULD I?
YOU WON'T EVEN TELL ME YOUR NAME.
YOU *KNOW* MY NAME.
LET'S GO.
HARMONY HOUSE CORRECTIONAL FACILITY
KING MOB

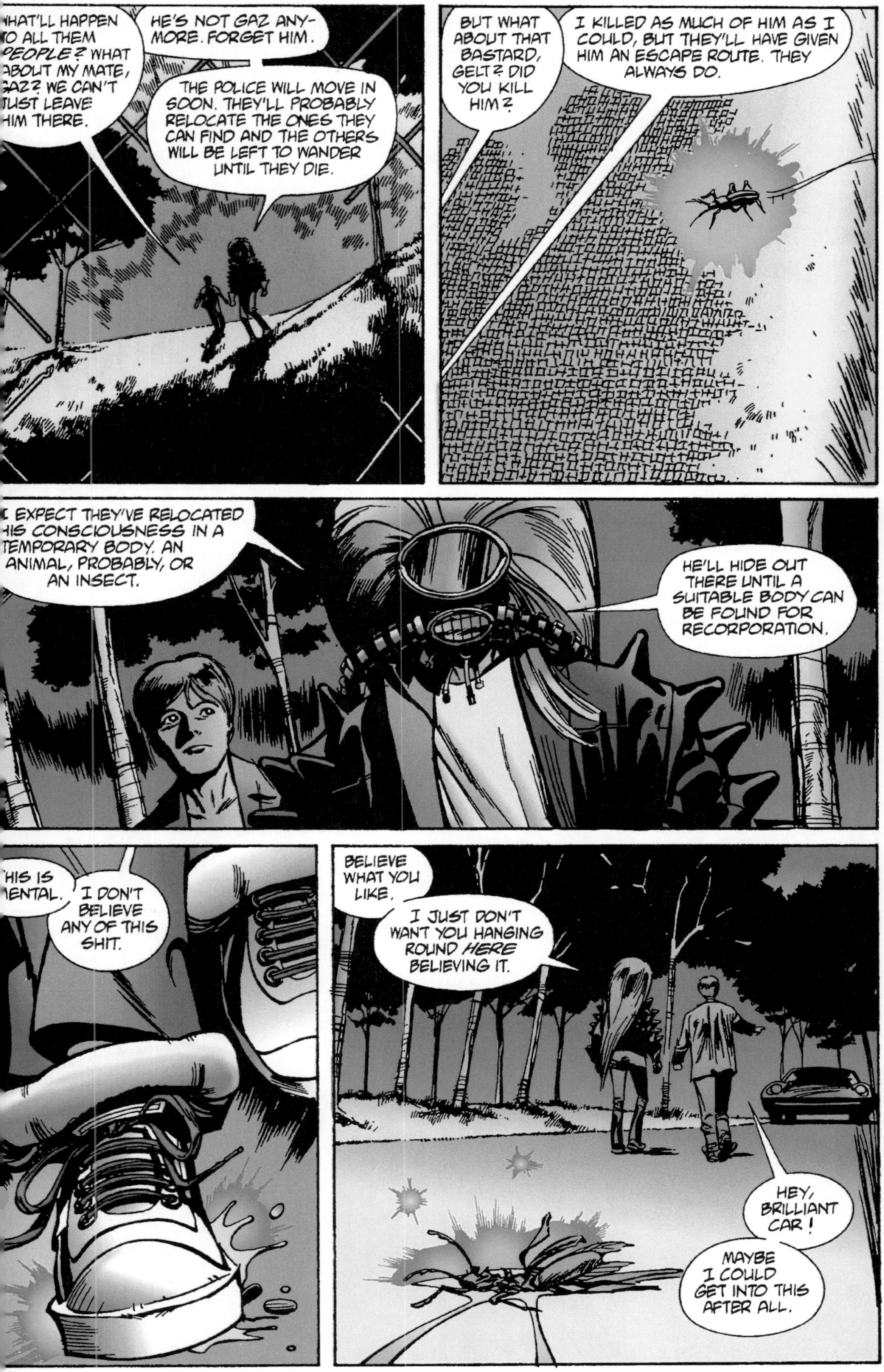
HAT'LL HAPPEN TO ALL THEM PEOPLE? WHAT ABOUT MY MATE, GAZ? WE CAN'T JUST LEAVE HIM THERE.
HE'S NOT GAZ ANY-MORE. FORGET HIM.
THE POLICE WILL MOVE IN SOON. THEY'LL PROBABLY RELOCATE THE ONES THEY CAN FIND AND THE OTHERS WILL BE LEFT TO WANDER UNTIL THEY DIE.
BUT WHAT ABOUT THAT BASTARD, GELT? DID YOU KILL HIM?
I KILLED AS MUCH OF HIM AS I COULD, BUT THEY'LL HAVE GIVEN HIM AN ESCAPE ROUTE. THEY ALWAYS DO.
EXPECT THEY'VE RELOCATED HIS CONSCIOUSNESS IN A TEMPORARY BODY. AN ANIMAL, PROBABLY, OR AN INSECT.
HE'LL HIDE OUT THERE UNTIL A SUITABLE BODY CAN BE FOUND FOR RECORPORATION.
THIS IS MENTAL.
I DON'T BELIEVE ANY OF THIS SHIT.
BELIEVE WHAT YOU LIKE.
I JUST DON'T WANT YOU HANGING ROUND HERE BELIEVING IT.
HEY, BRILLIANT CAR!
MAYBE I COULD GET INTO THIS AFTER ALL.

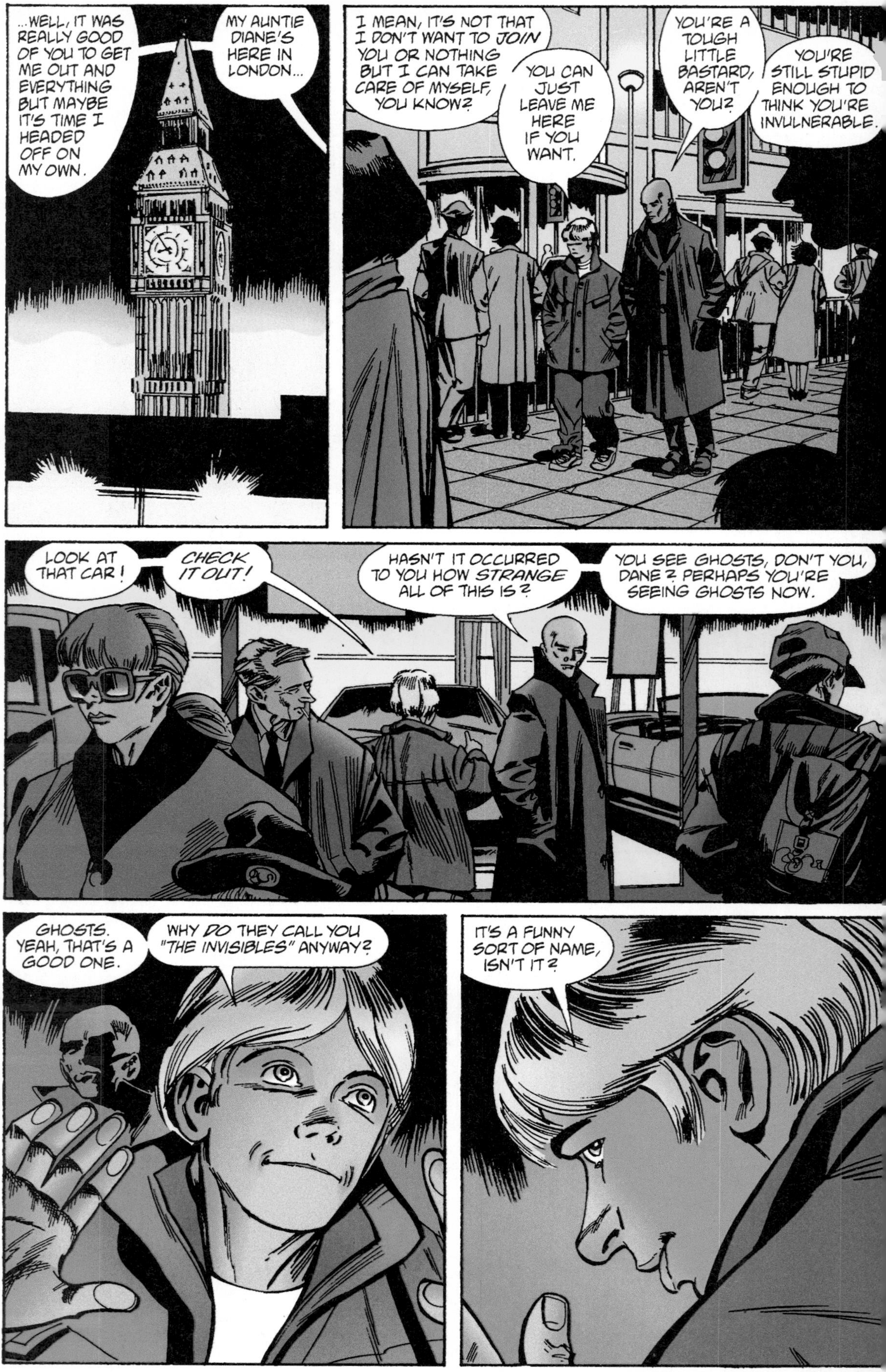
...WELL, IT WAS REALLY GOOD OF YOU TO GET ME OUT AND EVERYTHING BUT MAYBE IT'S TIME I HEADED OFF ON MY OWN.
MY AUNTIE DIANE'S HERE IN LONDON...
I MEAN, IT'S NOT THAT I DON'T WANT TO JOIN YOU OR NOTHING BUT I CAN TAKE CARE OF MYSELF, YOU KNOW?
YOU CAN JUST LEAVE ME HERE IF YOU WANT.
YOU'RE A TOUGH LITTLE BASTARD, AREN'T YOU?
YOU'RE STILL STUPID ENOUGH TO THINK YOU'RE INVULNERABLE.
LOOK AT THAT CAR!
CHECK IT OUT!
HASN'T IT OCCURRED TO YOU HOW STRANGE ALL OF THIS IS?
YOU SEE GHOSTS, DON'T YOU, DANE? PERHAPS YOU'RE SEEING GHOSTS NOW.
GHOSTS. YEAH, THAT'S A GOOD ONE.
WHY DO THEY CALL YOU "THE INVISIBLES" ANYWAY?
IT'S A FUNNY SORT OF NAME, ISN'T IT?

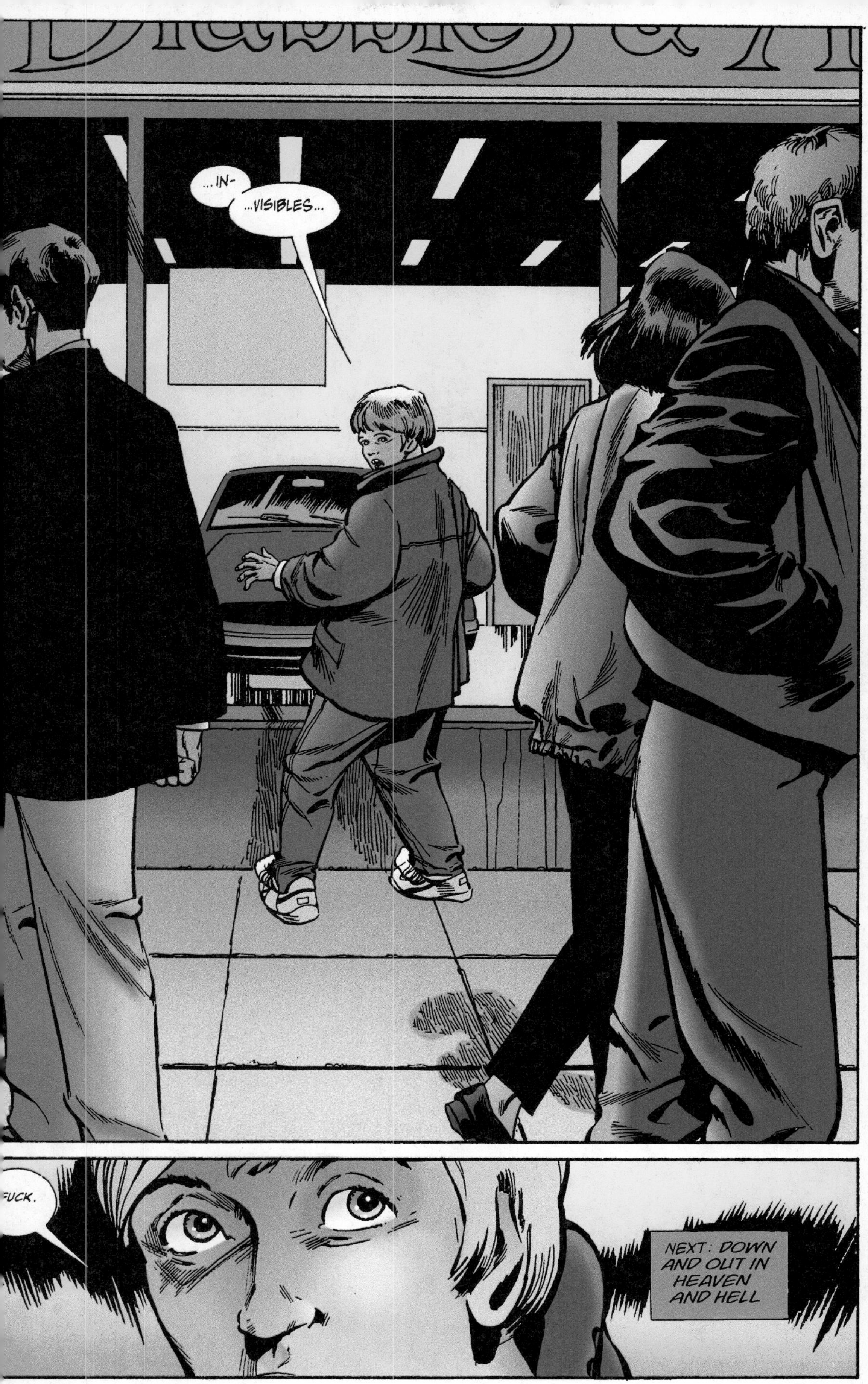
...IN-
...VISIBLES...
FUCK.
NEXT: DOWN AND OUT IN HEAVEN AND HELL

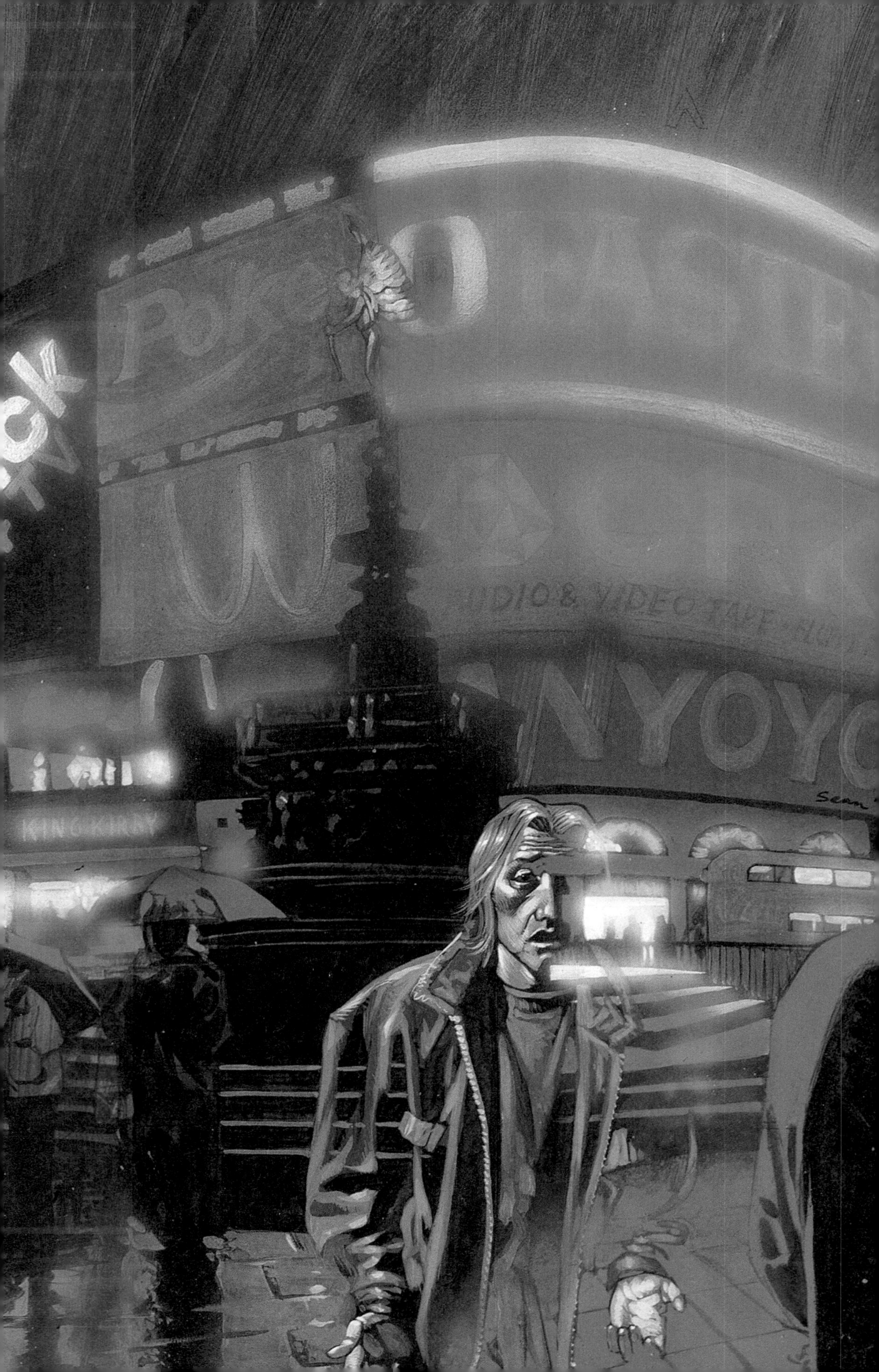

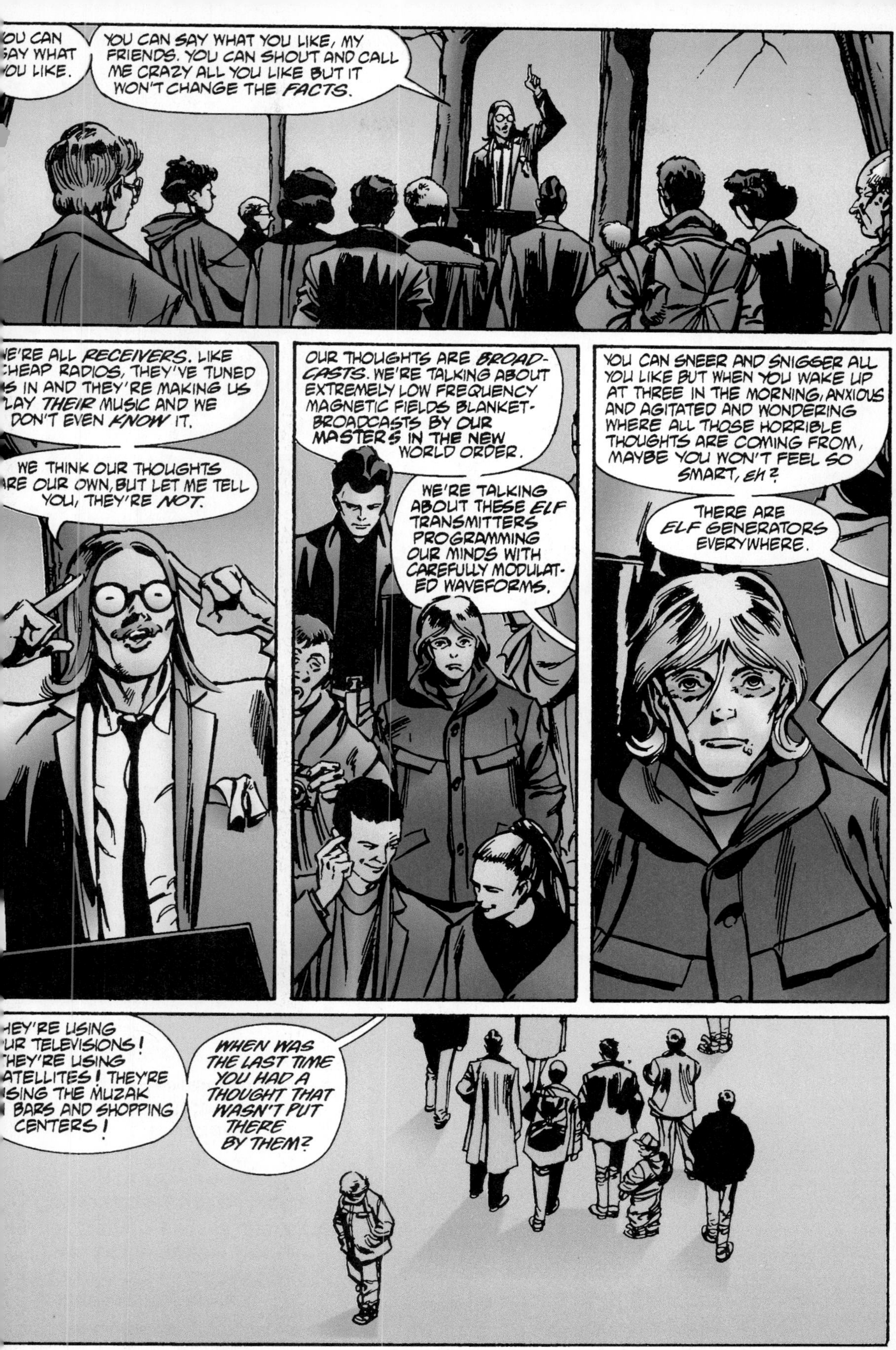
OU CAN
SAY WHAT
OU LIKE.
YOU CAN SAY WHAT YOU LIKE, MY FRIENDS. YOU CAN SHOUT AND CALL ME CRAZY ALL YOU LIKE BUT IT WON'T CHANGE THE FACTS.
E'RE ALL RECEIVERS. LIKE CHEAP RADIOS, THEY'VE TUNED S IN AND THEY'RE MAKING US LAY THEIR MUSIC AND WE DON'T EVEN KNOW IT.
WE THINK OUR THOUGHTS RE OUR OWN, BUT LET ME TELL YOU, THEY'RE NOT.
OUR THOUGHTS ARE BROADCASTS. WE'RE TALKING ABOUT EXTREMELY LOW FREQUENCY MAGNETIC FIELDS BLANKET-BROADCASTS BY OUR MASTERS IN THE NEW WORLD ORDER.
WE'RE TALKING ABOUT THESE ELF TRANSMITTERS PROGRAMMING OUR MINDS WITH CAREFULLY MODULATED WAVEFORMS.
YOU CAN SNEER AND SNIGGER ALL YOU LIKE BUT WHEN YOU WAKE UP AT THREE IN THE MORNING, ANXIOUS AND AGITATED AND WONDERING WHERE ALL THOSE HORRIBLE THOUGHTS ARE COMING FROM, MAYBE YOU WON'T FEEL SO SMART, EH?
THERE ARE ELF GENERATORS EVERYWHERE.
HEY'RE USING UR TELEVISIONS! THEY'RE USING ATELLITES! THEY'RE SING THE MUZAK BARS AND SHOPPING CENTERS!
WHEN WAS THE LAST TIME YOU HAD A THOUGHT THAT WASN'T PUT THERE BY THEM?

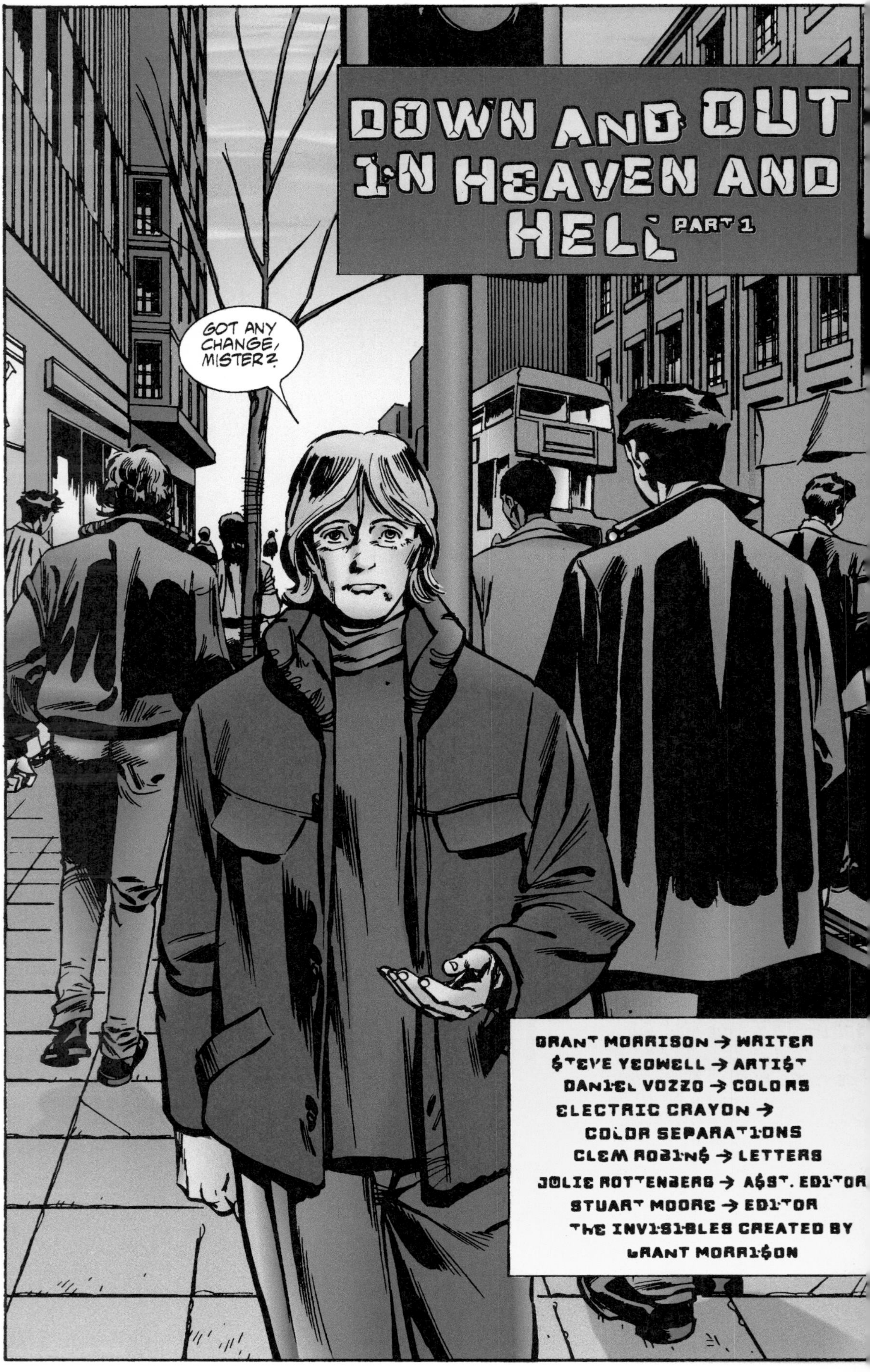
DOWN AND OUT IN HEAVEN AND HELL PART 1
GOT ANY CHANGE, MISTER?
GRANT MORRISON → WRITER
STEVE YEOWELL → ARTIST
DANIEL VOZZO → COLORS
ELECTRIC CRAYON → COLOR SEPARATIONS
CLEM ROBINS → LETTERS
JULIE ROTTENBERG → ASST. EDITOR
STUART MOORE → EDITOR
THE INVISIBLES CREATED BY GRANT MORRISON

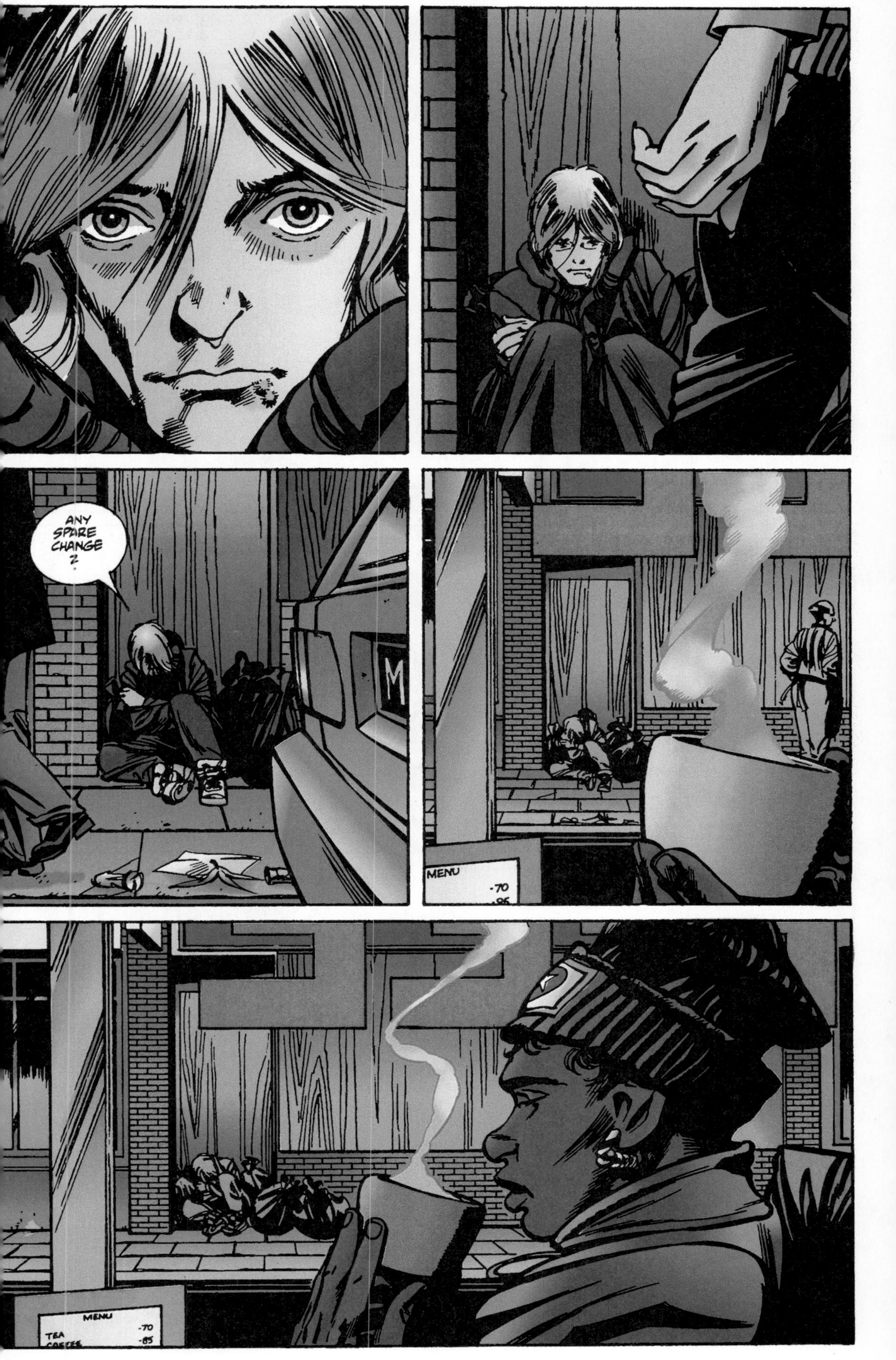
ANY SPARE CHANGE ?
MENU
-70
MENU
TEA -70
COFFEE -85

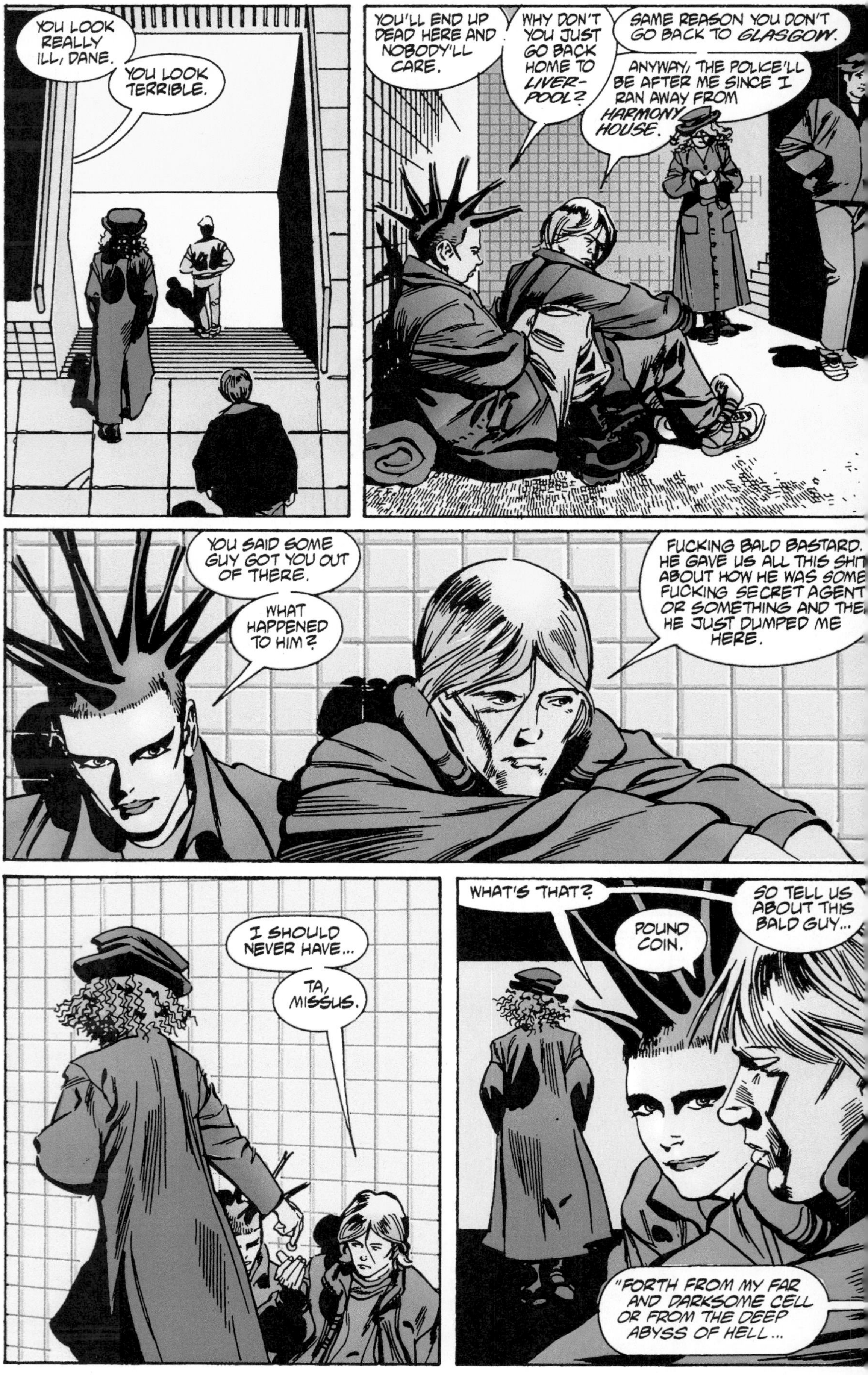
YOU LOOK REALLY ILL, DANE.
YOU LOOK TERRIBLE.
YOU'LL END UP DEAD HERE AND NOBODY'LL CARE.
WHY DON'T YOU JUST GO BACK HOME TO LIVERPOOL?
SAME REASON YOU DON'T GO BACK TO GLASGOW.
ANYWAY, THE POLICE'LL BE AFTER ME SINCE I RAN AWAY FROM HARMONY HOUSE.
YOU SAID SOME GUY GOT YOU OUT OF THERE.
WHAT HAPPENED TO HIM?
FUCKING BALD BASTARD. HE GAVE US ALL THIS SHIT ABOUT HOW HE WAS SOME FUCKING SECRET AGENT OR SOMETHING AND THEN HE JUST DUMPED ME HERE.
I SHOULD NEVER HAVE...
TA, MISSUS.
WHAT'S THAT?
POUND COIN.
SO TELL US ABOUT THIS BALD GUY...
"FORTH FROM MY FAR AND DARKSOME CELL OR FROM THE DEEP ABYSS OF HELL...

"MAD TOM IS COME TO VIEW THE WORLD AGAIN TO EASE HIS POOR DISTEMPERED BRAIN.

"PLUTO LAUGHS AND PROSERPINE IS GLAD TO SEE POOR NAKED TOM O'BEDLAM MAD..."

OH CHRIST, IT'S *MAD TOM*.

KID ON YOU'RE ASLEEP.

"THROUGH THE WORLD I'LL WANDER NIGHT AND DAY, TO FIND MY STRAGGLING SENSES..."

HELLO, YOUNG LOVERS! TOM'S A-COLD! O DO, DE, DO, DE, DO DE. BLESS THEE FROM WHIRLWINDS, STAR-BLASTING AND TAKING.

"POOR NAKED TOM IS VERY DRY A LITTLE DRINK FOR CHARITY..."

TAKE HEED O'TH' FOUL FIEND; OBEY THY PARENTS; KEEP THY WORDS' JUSTICE; SWEAR NOT; COMMIT NOT WITH MAN'S SWORN SPOUSE; SET NOT THY SWEET HEART ON PROUD ARRAY...

FUCK OFF, TOM.

WHO GIVES ANYTHING TO POOR TOM, WHOM THE FOUL FIEND HATH LED THROUGH FIRE AND THROUGH FLAME? YOU THING RIKE JELLYFISH PRETTY SOON NOW.

HA HA HA HA HA

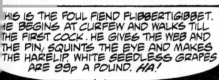

THIS IS THE FOUL FIEND FLIBBERTIGIBBET. HE BEGINS AT CURFEW AND WALKS TILL THE FIRST COCK. HE GIVES THE WEB AND THE PIN, SQUINTS THE EYE AND MAKES THE HARELIP. WHITE SEEDLESS GRAPES ARE 99p A POUND. HA!

"THE MAN IN THE MOON DRINKS CLARET, WITH POWDER-BEET, TURNIP AND CARROT...

"A CUP OF OLD MALLIGO SACK WILL FIRE THE BUSH AT HIS BACK."

WHAT'S THAT ALL ABOUT?

MAD TOM, HAVE YOU NEVER SEEN HIM?

HE'S A PAIN IN THE ARSE. BELIEVE ME, THAT'S ALL YOU NEED TO KNOW.

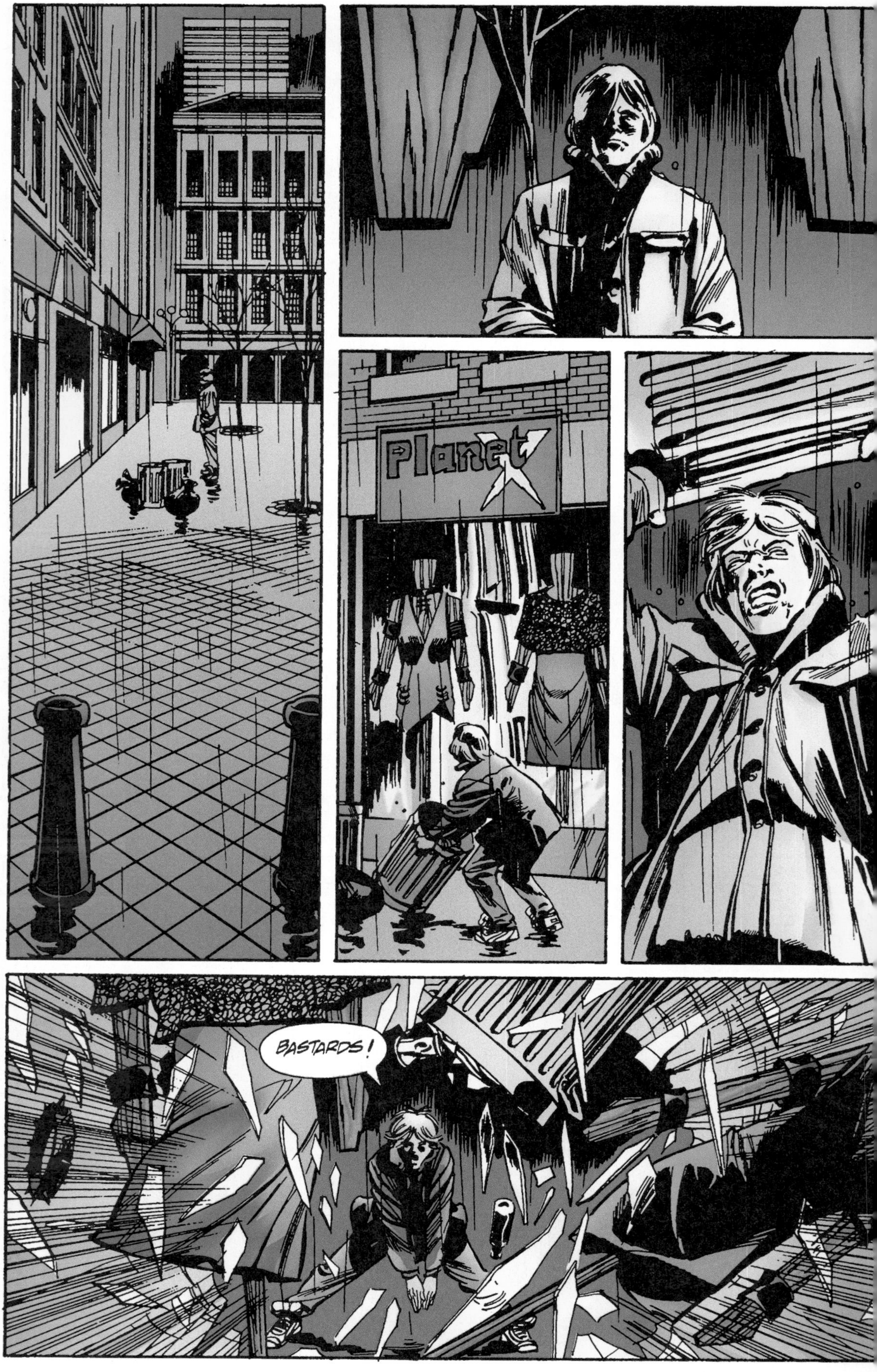
Planet X
BASTARDS!

OI! YOU!

SHIT.

ADULT BOOKS

KMAKER

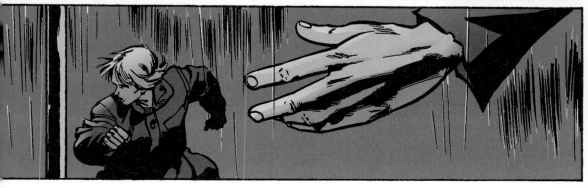

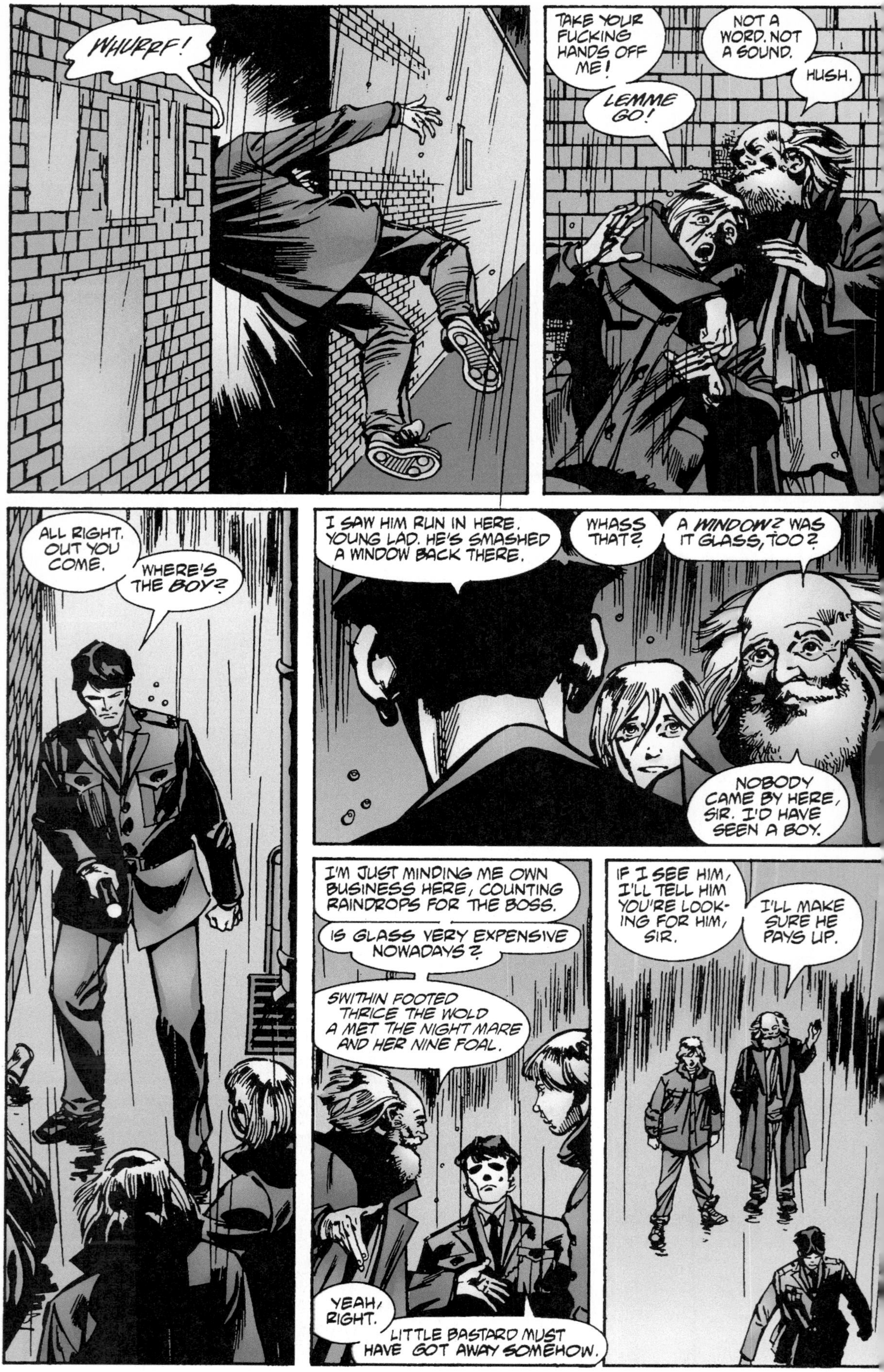
WHURRF!
TAKE YOUR FUCKING HANDS OFF ME!
LEMME GO!
NOT A WORD. NOT A SOUND.
HUSH.
ALL RIGHT. OUT YOU COME.
WHERE'S THE BOY?
I SAW HIM RUN IN HERE. YOUNG LAD. HE'S SMASHED A WINDOW BACK THERE.
WHASS THAT?
A WINDOW? WAS IT GLASS, TOO?
NOBODY CAME BY HERE, SIR. I'D HAVE SEEN A BOY.
I'M JUST MINDING ME OWN BUSINESS HERE, COUNTING RAINDROPS FOR THE BOSS.
IS GLASS VERY EXPENSIVE NOWADAYS?
SWITHIN FOOTED THRICE THE WOLD A MET THE NIGHT MARE AND HER NINE FOAL.
YEAH, RIGHT.
LITTLE BASTARD MUST HAVE GOT AWAY SOMEHOW.
IF I SEE HIM, I'LL TELL HIM YOU'RE LOOKING FOR HIM, SIR.
I'LL MAKE SURE HE PAYS UP.

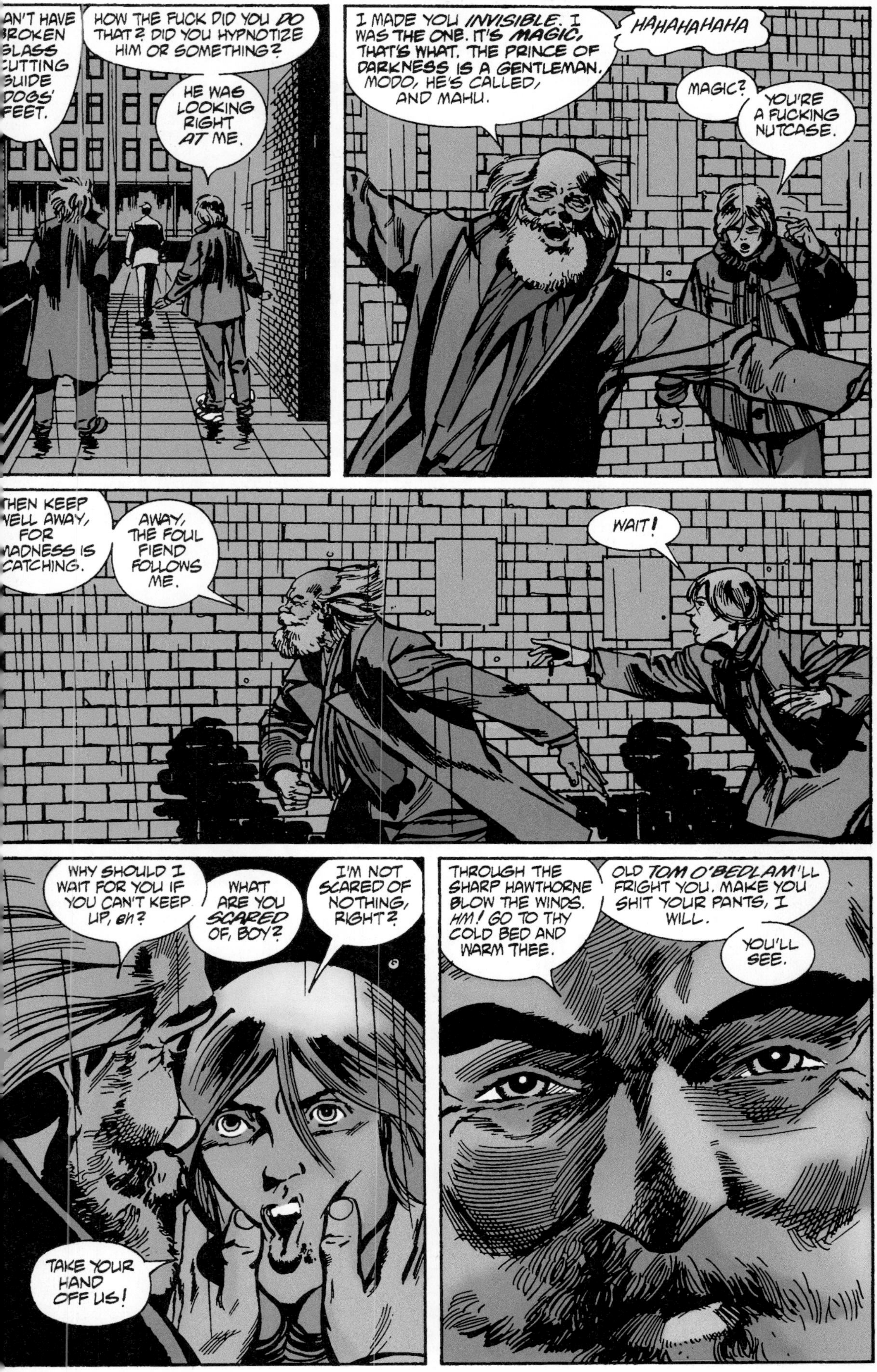

AN'T HAVE BROKEN GLASS CUTTING GUIDE DOGS' FEET.
HOW THE FUCK DID YOU DO THAT? DID YOU HYPNOTIZE HIM OR SOMETHING?
HE WAS LOOKING RIGHT AT ME.
I MADE YOU INVISIBLE. I WAS THE ONE. IT'S MAGIC, THAT'S WHAT. THE PRINCE OF DARKNESS IS A GENTLEMAN. MODO, HE'S CALLED, AND MAHU.
HAHAHAHAHA
MAGIC?
YOU'RE A FUCKING NUTCASE.
THEN KEEP WELL AWAY, FOR MADNESS IS CATCHING.
AWAY, THE FOUL FIEND FOLLOWS ME.
WAIT!
WHY SHOULD I WAIT FOR YOU IF YOU CAN'T KEEP UP, eh?
WHAT ARE YOU SCARED OF, BOY?
I'M NOT SCARED OF NOTHING, RIGHT?
TAKE YOUR HAND OFF US!
THROUGH THE SHARP HAWTHORNE BLOW THE WINDS. HM! GO TO THY COLD BED AND WARM THEE.
OLD TOM O'BEDLAM'LL FRIGHT YOU. MAKE YOU SHIT YOUR PANTS, I WILL.
YOU'LL SEE.

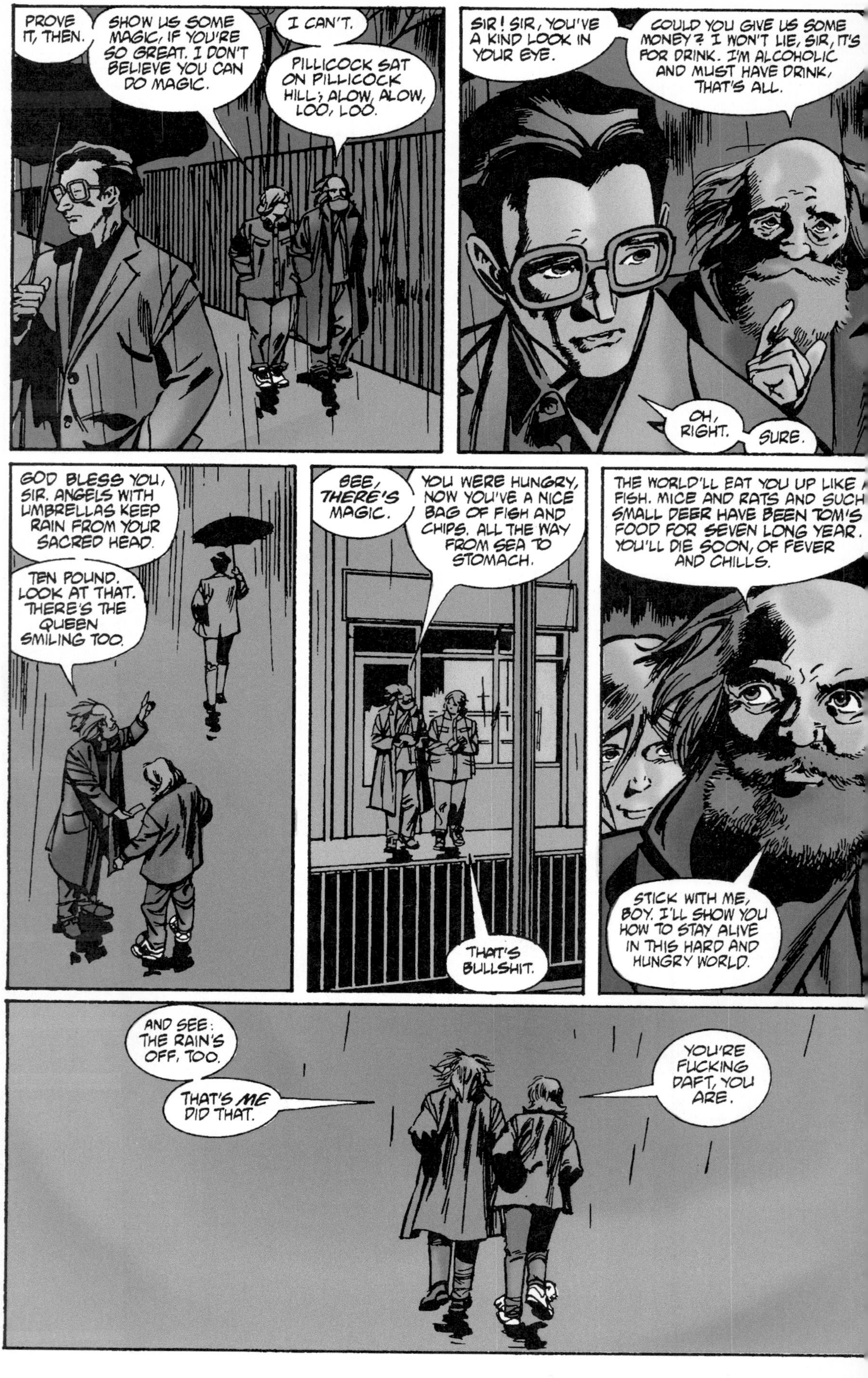
PROVE IT, THEN.
SHOW US SOME MAGIC, IF YOU'RE SO GREAT. I DON'T BELIEVE YOU CAN DO MAGIC.
I CAN'T.
PILLICOCK SAT ON PILLICOCK HILL; ALOW, ALOW, LOO, LOO.
SIR! SIR, YOU'VE A KIND LOOK IN YOUR EYE.
COULD YOU GIVE US SOME MONEY? I WON'T LIE, SIR, IT'S FOR DRINK. I'M ALCOHOLIC AND MUST HAVE DRINK, THAT'S ALL.
OH, RIGHT.
SURE.
GOD BLESS YOU, SIR. ANGELS WITH UMBRELLAS KEEP RAIN FROM YOUR SACRED HEAD.
TEN POUND. LOOK AT THAT. THERE'S THE QUEEN SMILING TOO.
SEE, THERE'S MAGIC.
YOU WERE HUNGRY, NOW YOU'VE A NICE BAG OF FISH AND CHIPS. ALL THE WAY FROM SEA TO STOMACH.
THAT'S BULLSHIT.
THE WORLD'LL EAT YOU UP LIKE A FISH. MICE AND RATS AND SUCH SMALL DEER HAVE BEEN TOM'S FOOD FOR SEVEN LONG YEAR. YOU'LL DIE SOON, OF FEVER AND CHILLS.
STICK WITH ME, BOY. I'LL SHOW YOU HOW TO STAY ALIVE IN THIS HARD AND HUNGRY WORLD.
AND SEE: THE RAIN'S OFF, TOO.
THAT'S ME DID THAT.
YOU'RE FUCKING DAFT, YOU ARE.

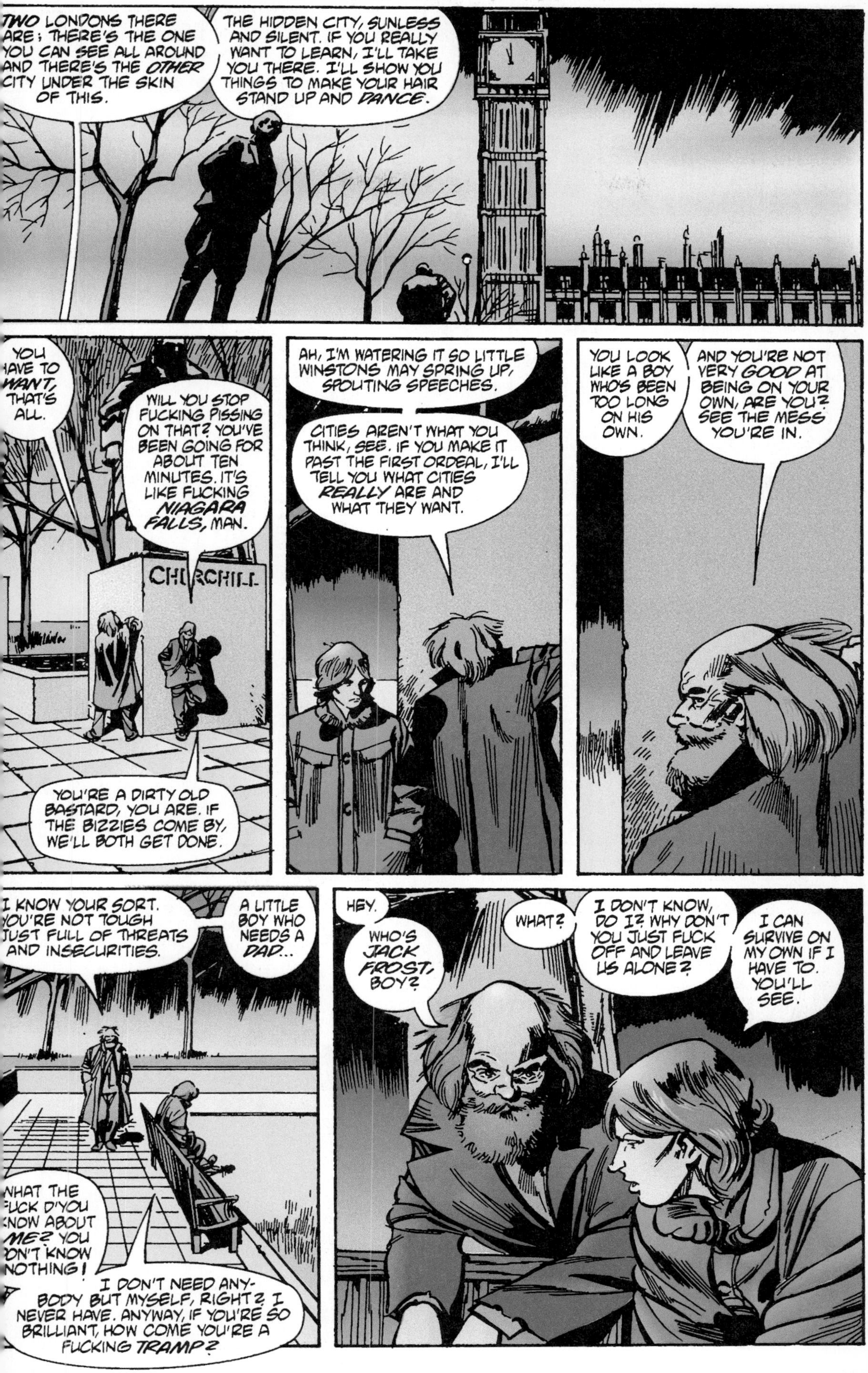
TWO LONDONS THERE ARE; THERE'S THE ONE YOU CAN SEE ALL AROUND AND THERE'S THE OTHER CITY UNDER THE SKIN OF THIS.
THE HIDDEN CITY, SUNLESS AND SILENT. IF YOU REALLY WANT TO LEARN, I'LL TAKE YOU THERE. I'LL SHOW YOU THINGS TO MAKE YOUR HAIR STAND UP AND DANCE.
YOU HAVE TO WANT, THAT'S ALL.
WILL YOU STOP FUCKING PISSING ON THAT? YOU'VE BEEN GOING FOR ABOUT TEN MINUTES. IT'S LIKE FUCKING NIAGARA FALLS, MAN.
CHURCHILL
YOU'RE A DIRTY OLD BASTARD, YOU ARE. IF THE BIZZIES COME BY, WE'LL BOTH GET DONE.
AH, I'M WATERING IT SO LITTLE WINSTONS MAY SPRING UP, SPOUTING SPEECHES.
CITIES AREN'T WHAT YOU THINK, SEE. IF YOU MAKE IT PAST THE FIRST ORDEAL, I'LL TELL YOU WHAT CITIES REALLY ARE AND WHAT THEY WANT.
YOU LOOK LIKE A BOY WHO'S BEEN TOO LONG ON HIS OWN.
AND YOU'RE NOT VERY GOOD AT BEING ON YOUR OWN, ARE YOU? SEE THE MESS YOU'RE IN.
I KNOW YOUR SORT. YOU'RE NOT TOUGH JUST FULL OF THREATS AND INSECURITIES.
A LITTLE BOY WHO NEEDS A DAD...
WHAT THE FUCK D'YOU KNOW ABOUT ME? YOU DON'T KNOW NOTHING!
I DON'T NEED ANYBODY BUT MYSELF, RIGHT? I NEVER HAVE. ANYWAY, IF YOU'RE SO BRILLIANT, HOW COME YOU'RE A FUCKING TRAMP?
HEY.
WHO'S JACK FROST, BOY?
WHAT?
I DON'T KNOW, DO I? WHY DON'T YOU JUST FUCK OFF AND LEAVE US ALONE?
I CAN SURVIVE ON MY OWN IF I HAVE TO. YOU'LL SEE.

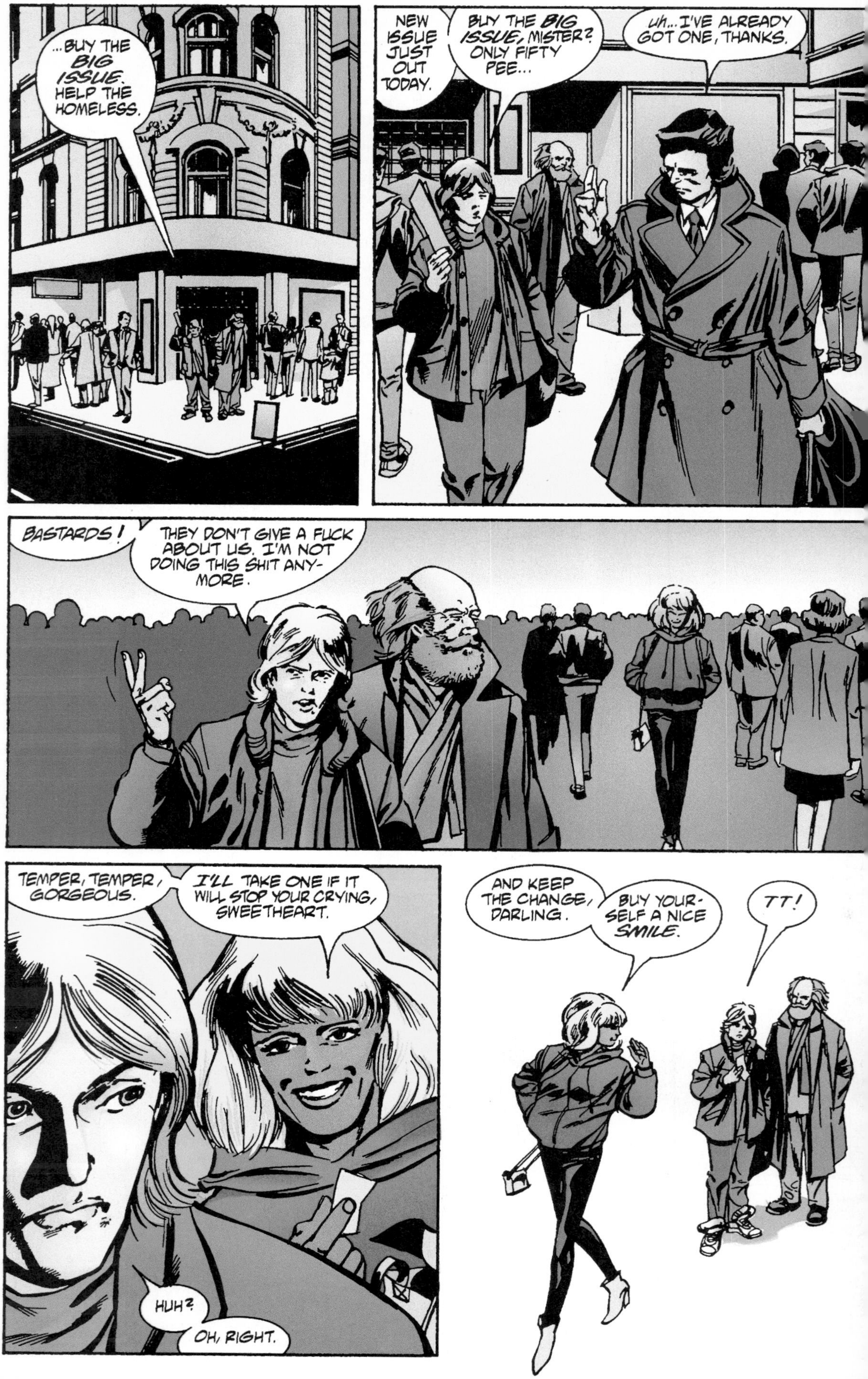
...BUY THE BIG ISSUE. HELP THE HOMELESS.
NEW ISSUE JUST OUT TODAY.
BUY THE BIG ISSUE, MISTER? ONLY FIFTY PEE...
UH... I'VE ALREADY GOT ONE, THANKS.
BASTARDS!
THEY DON'T GIVE A FUCK ABOUT US. I'M NOT DOING THIS SHIT ANY-MORE.
TEMPER, TEMPER, GORGEOUS.
I'LL TAKE ONE IF IT WILL STOP YOUR CRYING, SWEETHEART.
HUH?
OH, RIGHT.
AND KEEP THE CHANGE, DARLING.
BUY YOUR-SELF A NICE SMILE.
TT!

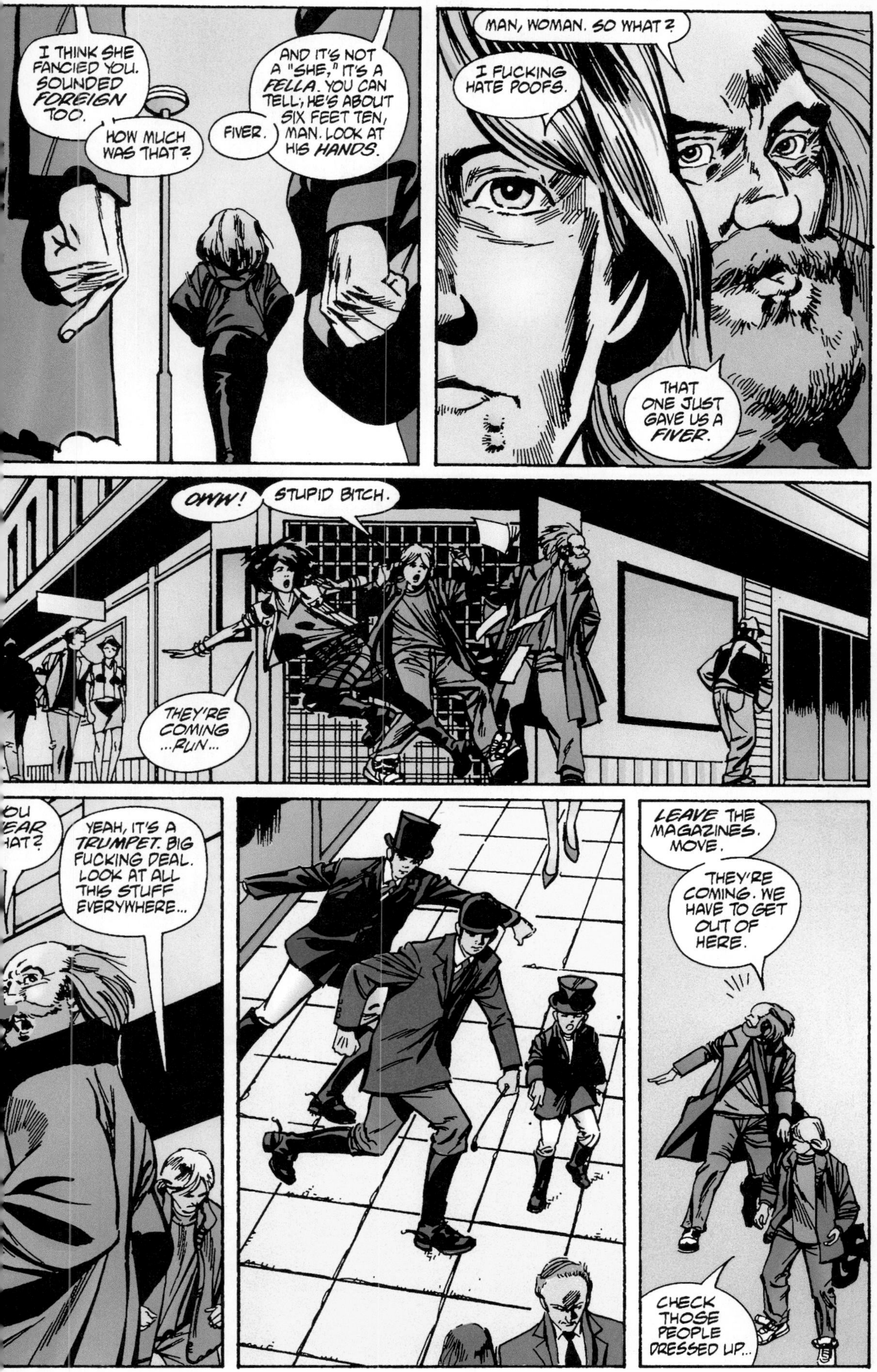

I THINK SHE FANCIED YOU. SOUNDED FOREIGN TOO.
HOW MUCH WAS THAT?
FIVER.
AND IT'S NOT A "SHE," IT'S A FELLA. YOU CAN TELL; HE'S ABOUT SIX FEET TEN, MAN. LOOK AT HIS HANDS.
MAN, WOMAN. SO WHAT?
I FUCKING HATE POOFS.
THAT ONE JUST GAVE US A FIVER.
OWW!
STUPID BITCH.
THEY'RE COMING ...RUN...
YEAH, IT'S A TRUMPET. BIG FUCKING DEAL. LOOK AT ALL THIS STUFF EVERYWHERE...
LEAVE THE MAGAZINES. MOVE.
THEY'RE COMING. WE HAVE TO GET OUT OF HERE.
CHECK THOSE PEOPLE DRESSED UP...

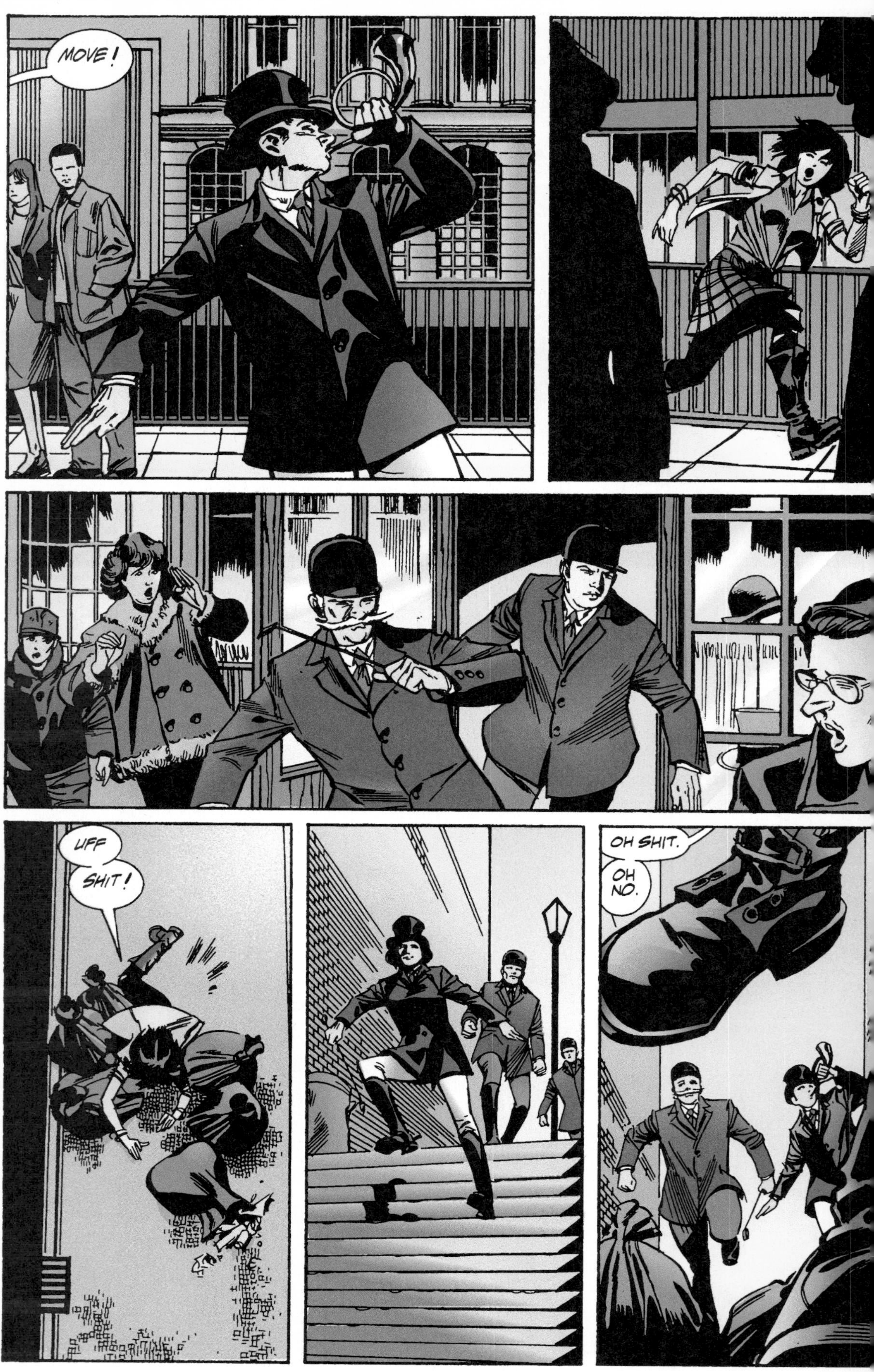
MOVE!
UFF
SHIT!
OH SHIT.
OH NO.

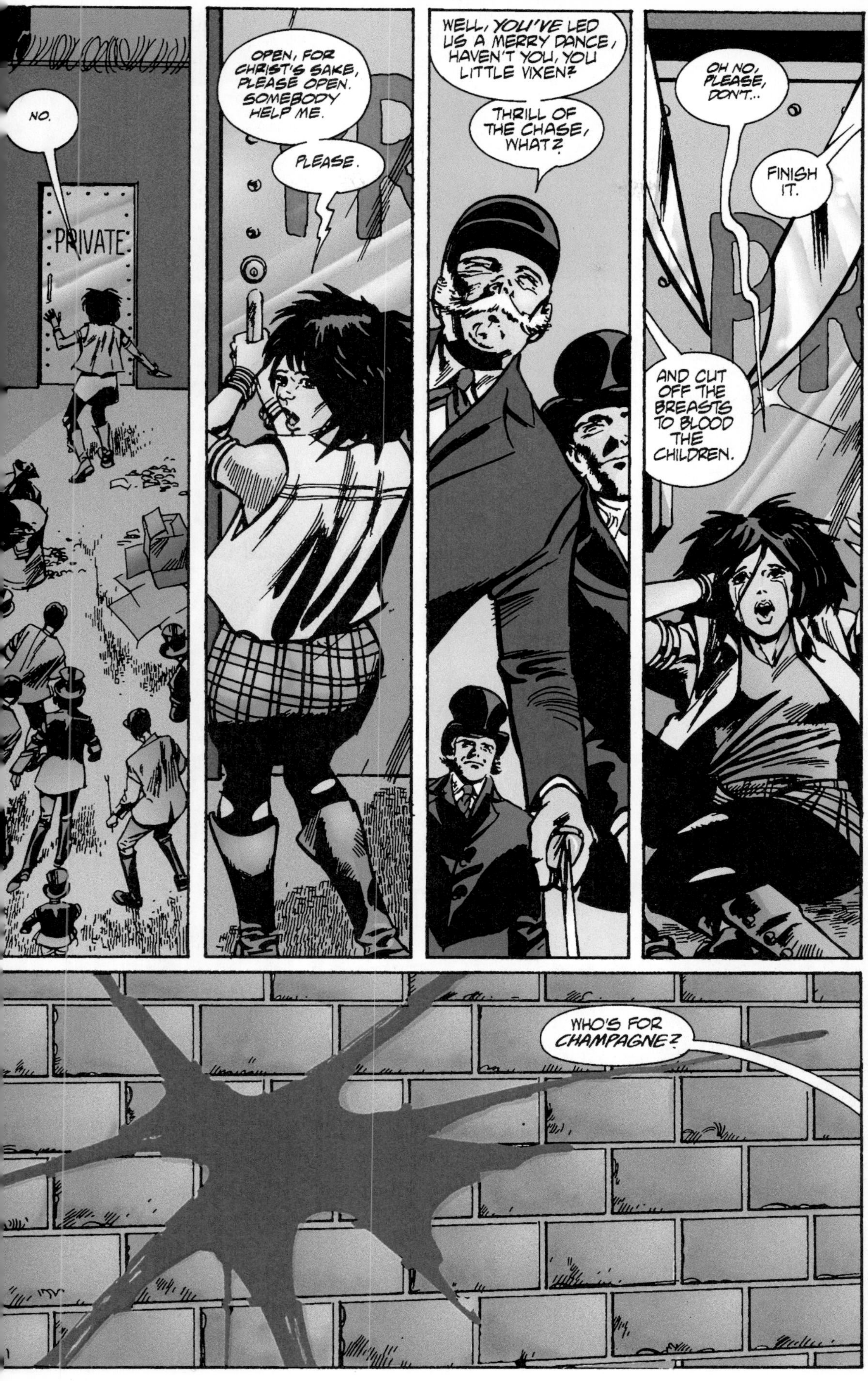
NO.
OPEN, FOR CHRIST'S SAKE, PLEASE OPEN. SOMEBODY HELP ME.
PLEASE.
WELL, YOU'VE LED US A MERRY DANCE, HAVEN'T YOU, YOU LITTLE VIXEN?
THRILL OF THE CHASE, WHAT?
PRIVATE
OH NO, PLEASE, DON'T...
FINISH IT.
AND CUT OFF THE BREASTS TO BLOOD THE CHILDREN.
WHO'S FOR CHAMPAGNE?

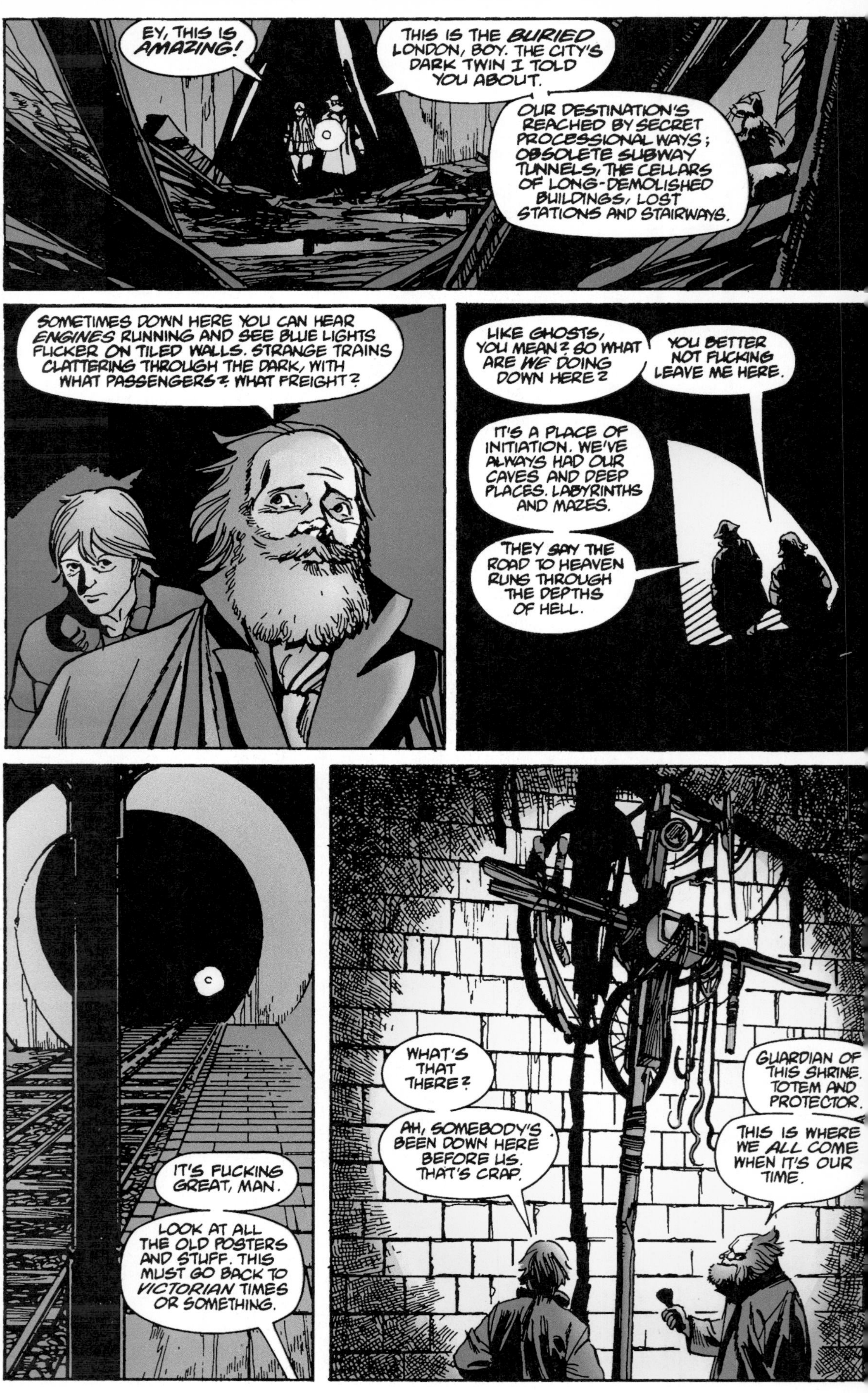
EY, THIS IS AMAZING!
THIS IS THE BURIED LONDON, BOY. THE CITY'S DARK TWIN I TOLD YOU ABOUT.
OUR DESTINATION'S REACHED BY SECRET PROCESSIONAL WAYS; OBSOLETE SUBWAY TUNNELS, THE CELLARS OF LONG-DEMOLISHED BUILDINGS, LOST STATIONS AND STAIRWAYS.
SOMETIMES DOWN HERE YOU CAN HEAR ENGINES RUNNING AND SEE BLUE LIGHTS FLICKER ON TILED WALLS. STRANGE TRAINS CLATTERING THROUGH THE DARK, WITH WHAT PASSENGERS? WHAT FREIGHT?
LIKE GHOSTS, YOU MEAN? SO WHAT ARE WE DOING DOWN HERE?
YOU BETTER NOT FUCKING LEAVE ME HERE.
IT'S A PLACE OF INITIATION. WE'VE ALWAYS HAD OUR CAVES AND DEEP PLACES. LABYRINTHS AND MAZES.
THEY SAY THE ROAD TO HEAVEN RUNS THROUGH THE DEPTHS OF HELL.
IT'S FUCKING GREAT, MAN.
LOOK AT ALL THE OLD POSTERS AND STUFF. THIS MUST GO BACK TO VICTORIAN TIMES OR SOMETHING.
WHAT'S THAT THERE?
AH, SOMEBODY'S BEEN DOWN HERE BEFORE US. THAT'S CRAP.
GUARDIAN OF THIS SHRINE. TOTEM AND PROTECTOR.
THIS IS WHERE WE ALL COME WHEN IT'S OUR TIME.

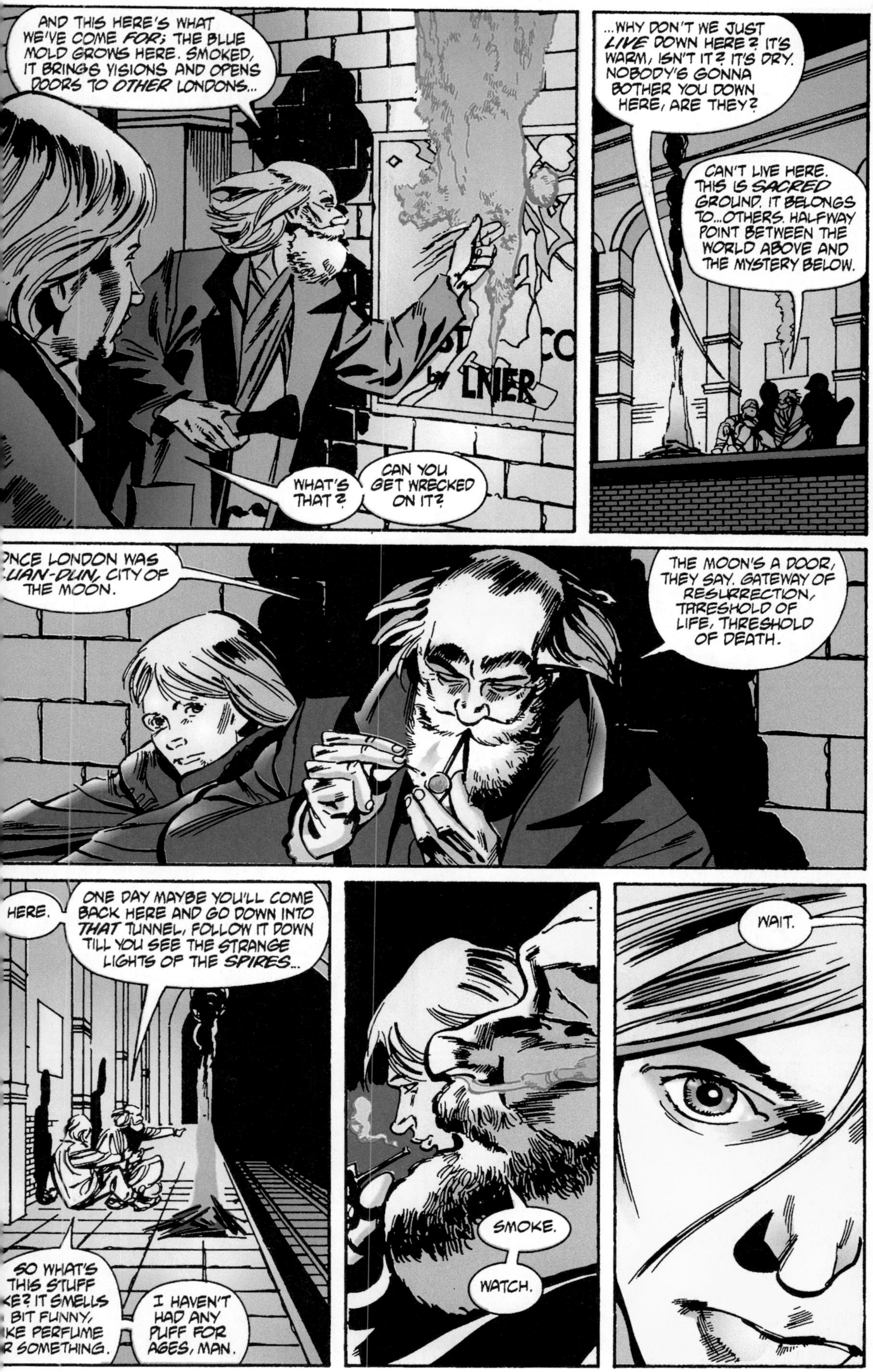
AND THIS HERE'S WHAT WE'VE COME *FOR*; THE BLUE MOLD GROWS HERE. SMOKED, IT BRINGS VISIONS AND OPENS DOORS TO *OTHER* LONDONS...
WHAT'S THAT?
CAN YOU GET WRECKED ON IT?
...WHY DON'T WE JUST *LIVE* DOWN HERE? IT'S WARM, ISN'T IT? IT'S DRY. NOBODY'S GONNA BOTHER YOU DOWN HERE, ARE THEY?
CAN'T LIVE HERE. THIS IS *SACRED* GROUND. IT BELONGS TO...OTHERS. HALFWAY POINT BETWEEN THE WORLD ABOVE AND THE MYSTERY BELOW.
ONCE LONDON WAS LUAN-DUN, CITY OF THE MOON.
THE MOON'S A DOOR, THEY SAY. GATEWAY OF RESURRECTION, THRESHOLD OF LIFE, THRESHOLD OF DEATH.
HERE.
ONE DAY MAYBE YOU'LL COME BACK HERE AND GO DOWN INTO *THAT* TUNNEL, FOLLOW IT DOWN TILL YOU SEE THE STRANGE LIGHTS OF THE *SPIRES*...
SO WHAT'S THIS STUFF LIKE? IT SMELLS BIT FUNNY, LIKE PERFUME OR SOMETHING.
I HAVEN'T HAD ANY PUFF FOR AGES, MAN.
SMOKE.
WATCH.
WAIT.

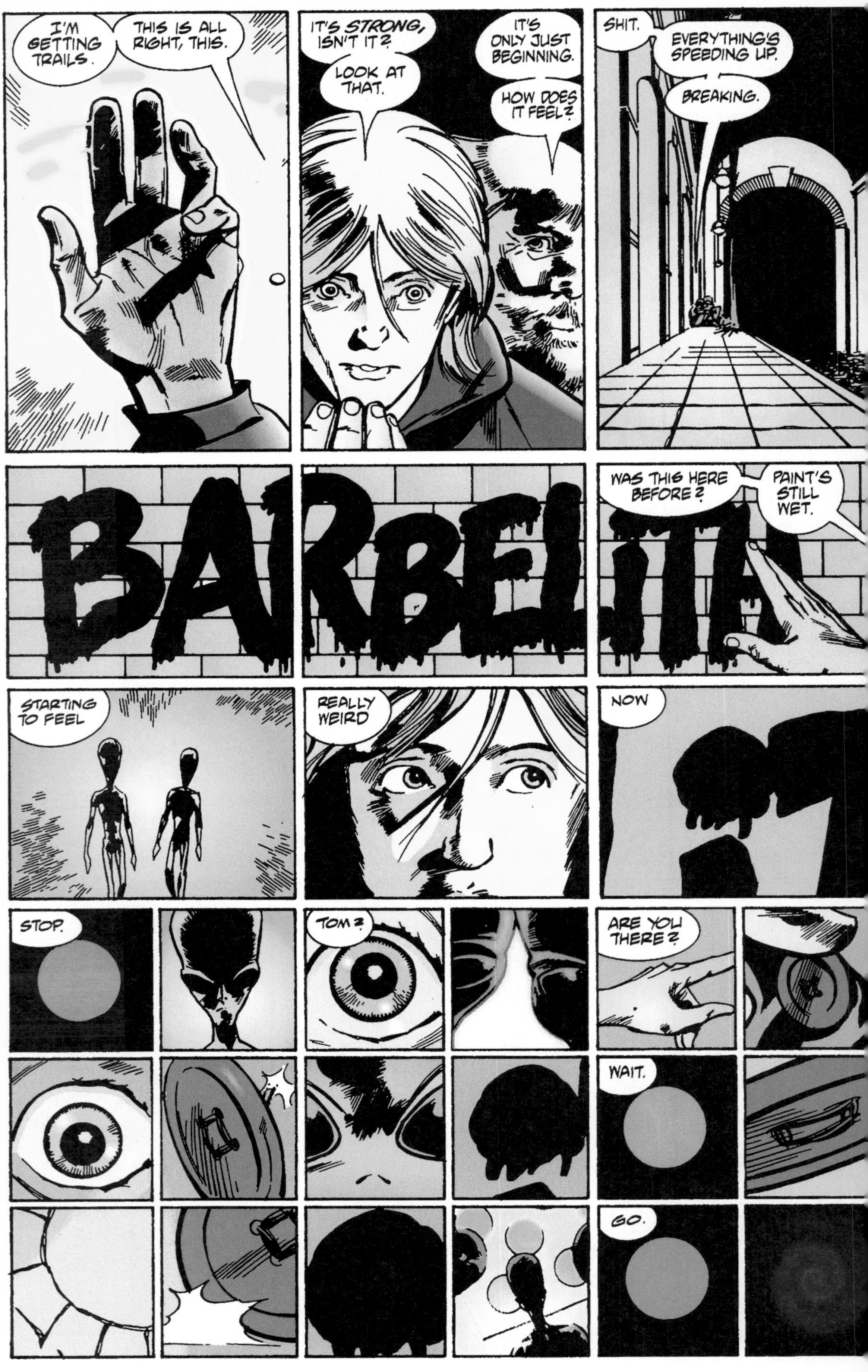
I'M GETTING TRAILS.
THIS IS ALL RIGHT, THIS.
IT'S *STRONG*, ISN'T IT?
LOOK AT THAT.
IT'S ONLY JUST BEGINNING.
HOW DOES IT FEEL?
SHIT.
EVERYTHING'S SPEEDING UP.
BREAKING.
BARBELITH
WAS THIS HERE BEFORE?
PAINT'S STILL WET.
STARTING TO FEEL
REALLY WEIRD
NOW
STOP.
TOM?
ARE YOU THERE?
WAIT.
GO.

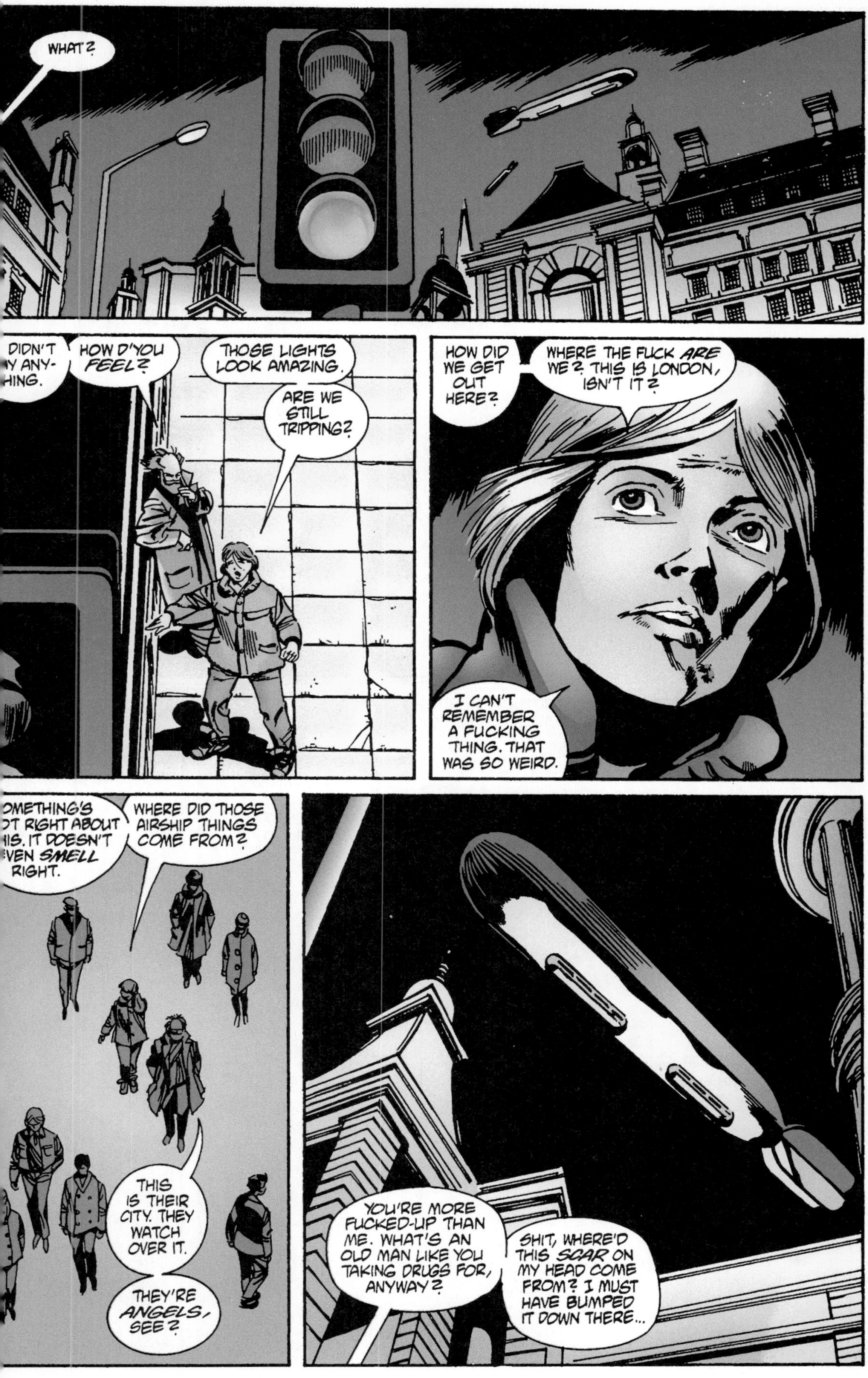
WHAT?
DIDN'T Y ANY- HING.
HOW D'YOU FEEL?
THOSE LIGHTS LOOK AMAZING.
ARE WE STILL TRIPPING?
HOW DID WE GET OUT HERE?
WHERE THE FUCK ARE WE? THIS IS LONDON, ISN'T IT?
I CAN'T REMEMBER A FUCKING THING. THAT WAS SO WEIRD.
OMETHING'S OT RIGHT ABOUT HIS. IT DOESN'T VEN SMELL RIGHT.
WHERE DID THOSE AIRSHIP THINGS COME FROM?
THIS IS THEIR CITY. THEY WATCH OVER IT.
THEY'RE ANGELS, SEE?
YOU'RE MORE FUCKED-UP THAN ME. WHAT'S AN OLD MAN LIKE YOU TAKING DRUGS FOR, ANYWAY?
SHIT, WHERE'D THIS SCAR ON MY HEAD COME FROM? I MUST HAVE BUMPED IT DOWN THERE...

NOW WHERE ARE WE GOING?

NOWHERE IN PARTICULAR. THE PARIS *SITUATIONISTS* USED TO CALL THIS SORT OF THING A *DÉRIVE*--DRIFTING AIMLESSLY THROUGH THE CITY, MAKING IT NEW AND STRANGE. THE STREET OF LITTLE GIRLS, SUN STREET, THE OCEAN BAR AND THE SQUARE OF THE APPALLING MOBILE.

PEOPLE LOOK AT US AND SEE THE POOR AND THE MAD, BUT THEY'RE LOOKING AT US THROUGH THE BARS OF THEIR *CAGES.*

THERE'S A PALACE IN YOUR HEAD, BOY. LEARN TO LIVE IN IT ALWAYS.

I'VE JUST REALIZED *BIG BEN'S* THE WRONG WAY ROUND.

WHAT THE FUCK'S GOING ON?

I WANT TO GET BACK TO NORMAL.

THERE'S NO GOING BACK. WE'VE UNPICKED THE THREAD OF THE WORLD.

LOOK THERE! "URIZEN, DEADLY BLACK, IN CHAINS BOUND."

BUT WHAT ABOUT THE *REAL* WORLD?

YOU DON'T THINK *THIS* WORLD IS ANY LESS REAL THAN THE ONE YOU LEFT, DO YOU?

EVERYTHING THAT EVER HAPPENED TO YOU IS REAL, EVEN YOUR *DREAMS.* THEM, MOST OF ALL.

THERE ARE MANY WORL MANY CITIES, AND ALL O THEM ARE JUST *SHOCK WAVES* SPREADING OU FROM ONE SINGLE MOMENT OF CLARITY AN UNDERSTANDING.

RIPPLES.

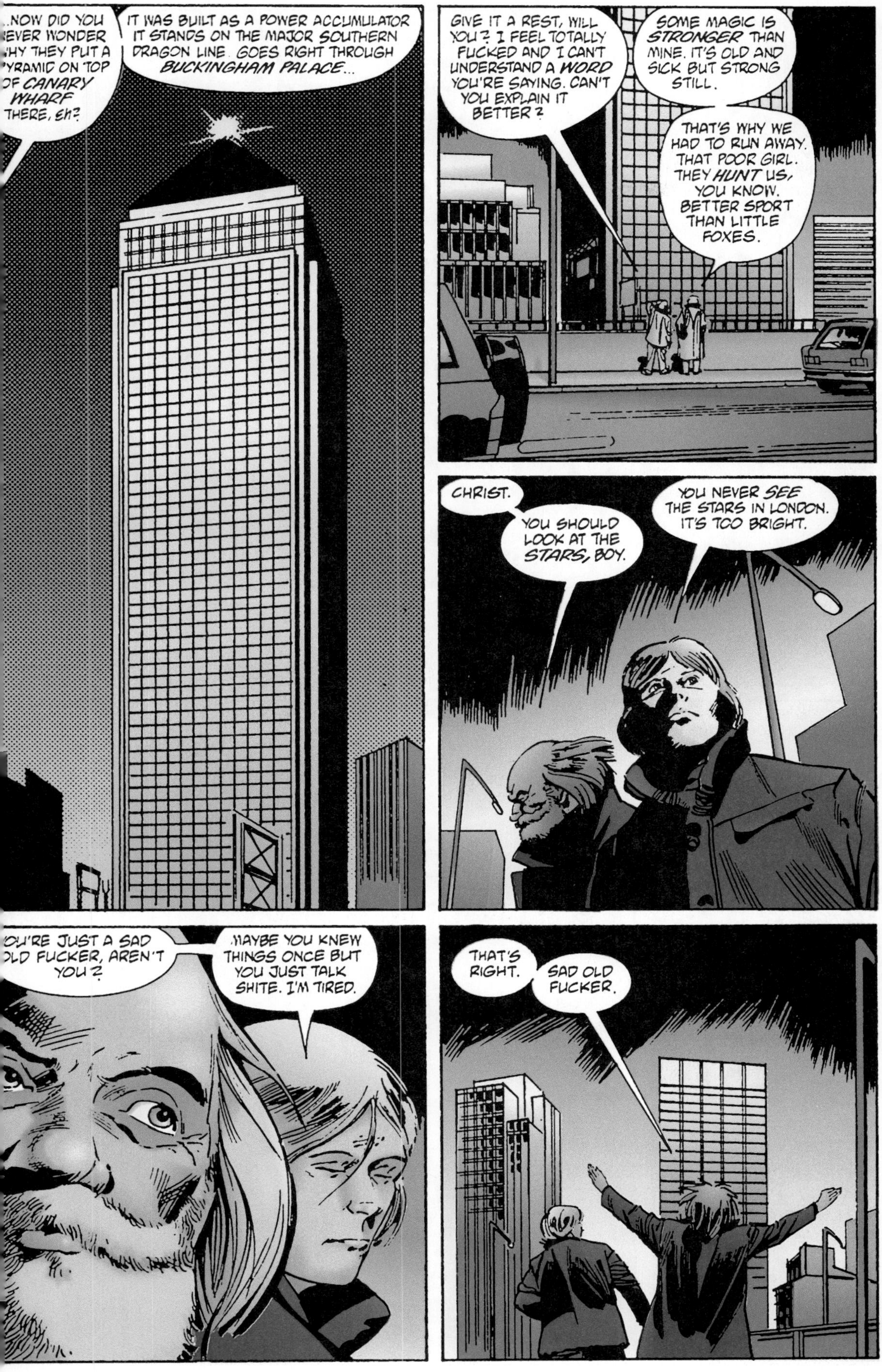
..NOW DID YOU NEVER WONDER WHY THEY PUT A PYRAMID ON TOP OF CANARY WHARF THERE, EH?
IT WAS BUILT AS A POWER ACCUMULATOR IT STANDS ON THE MAJOR SOUTHERN DRAGON LINE. GOES RIGHT THROUGH BUCKINGHAM PALACE...
GIVE IT A REST, WILL YOU? I FEEL TOTALLY FUCKED AND I CAN'T UNDERSTAND A WORD YOU'RE SAYING. CAN'T YOU EXPLAIN IT BETTER?
SOME MAGIC IS STRONGER THAN MINE. IT'S OLD AND SICK BUT STRONG STILL.
THAT'S WHY WE HAD TO RUN AWAY. THAT POOR GIRL. THEY HUNT US, YOU KNOW. BETTER SPORT THAN LITTLE FOXES.
CHRIST.
YOU SHOULD LOOK AT THE STARS, BOY.
YOU NEVER SEE THE STARS IN LONDON. IT'S TOO BRIGHT.
YOU'RE JUST A SAD OLD FUCKER, AREN'T YOU?
MAYBE YOU KNEW THINGS ONCE BUT YOU JUST TALK SHITE. I'M TIRED.
THAT'S RIGHT.
SAD OLD FUCKER.

LOOK AT THE STARS!

"LAST NIGHT I HEARD THE DOG STAR BARK MARS MET VENUS IN THE DARK..."

HA HA HA HA

FUCK.

NO WAY, MAN.

IT'S A POWER CUT. IT'S JUST A COINCIDENCE.

YOU'RE RIGHT.

AND THIS, TOO.

COINCIDENCE.

DID YOU REALLY DO THAT?

YOU GOTTA SHOW US HOW TO DO THAT.

SO YOU STILL WANT TO BE INVISIBLE THEN?

IS THAT WHAT YOU REALLY WANT?

ARE YOU READY TO SIGN ON THE DOTTED LINE?

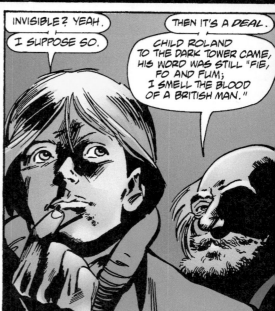

INVISIBLE? YEAH.

I SUPPOSE SO.

THEN IT'S A DEAL.

CHILD ROLAND TO THE DARK TOWER CAME, HIS WORD WAS STILL "FIE, FO AND FUM; I SMELL THE BLOOD OF A BRITISH MAN."

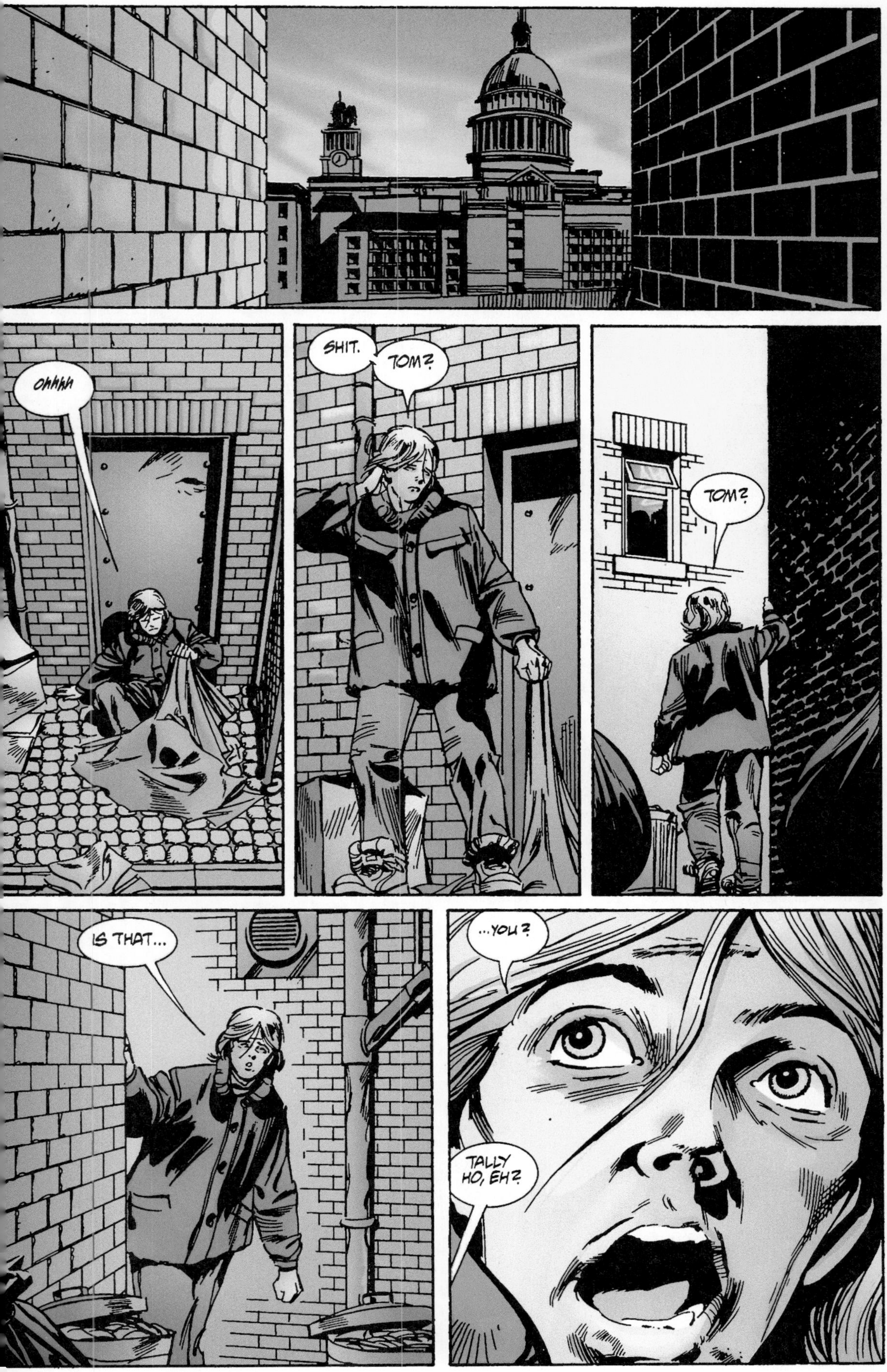
ohhhh
SHIT.
TOM?
TOM?
IS THAT...
...YOU?
TALLY HO, EH?

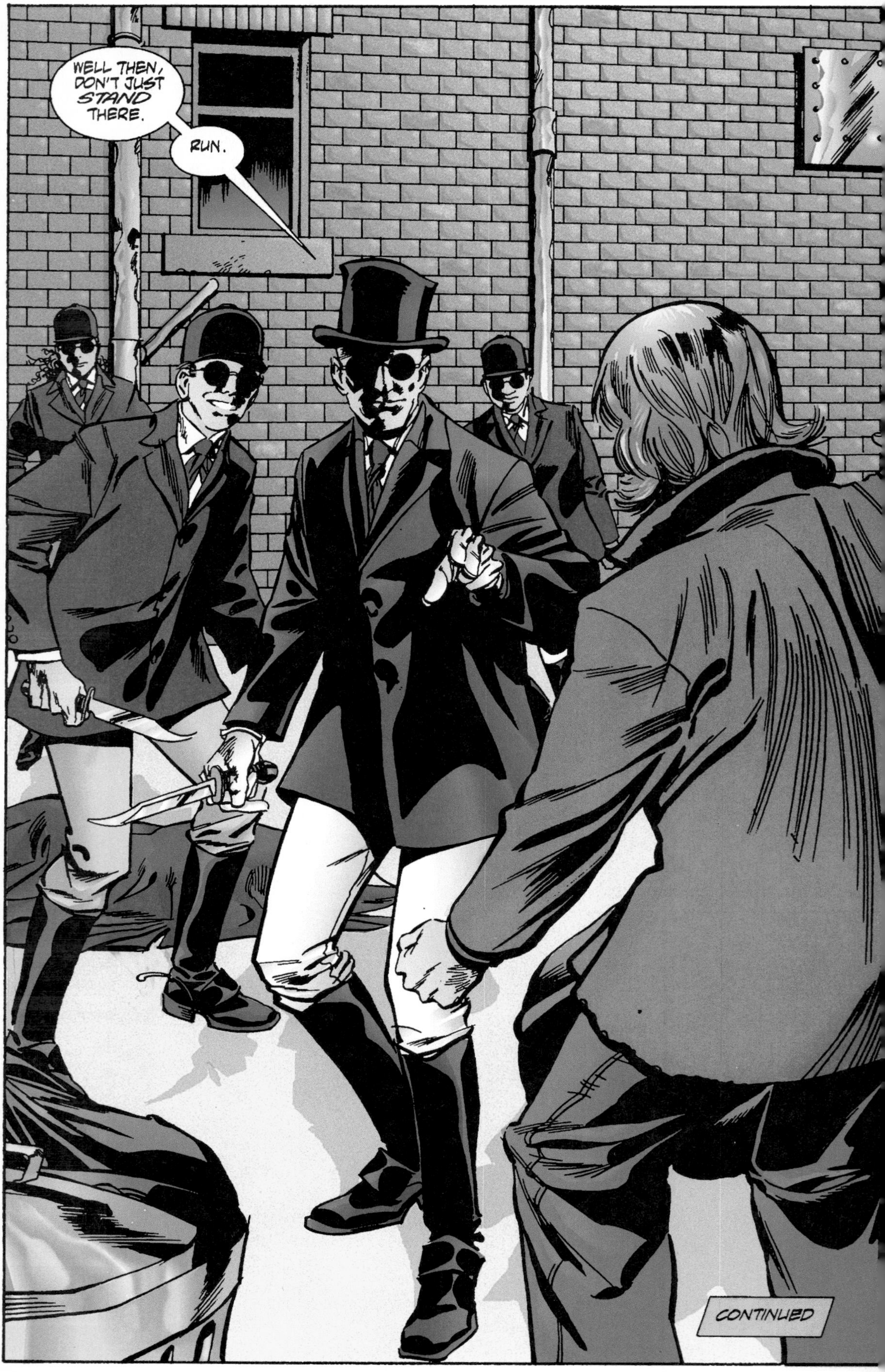
WELL THEN, DON'T JUST STAND THERE.
RUN.
CONTINUED

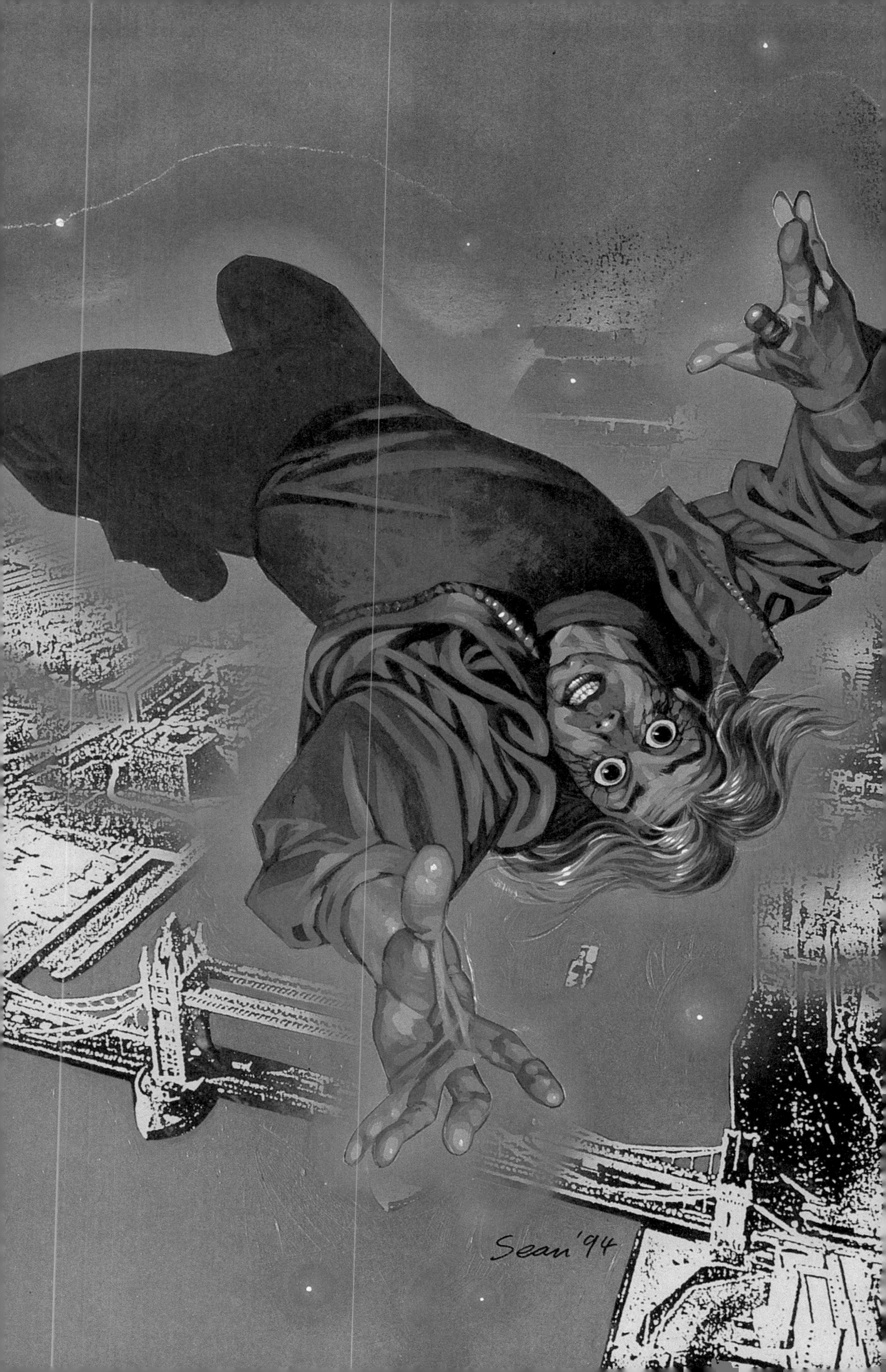
Sean '94

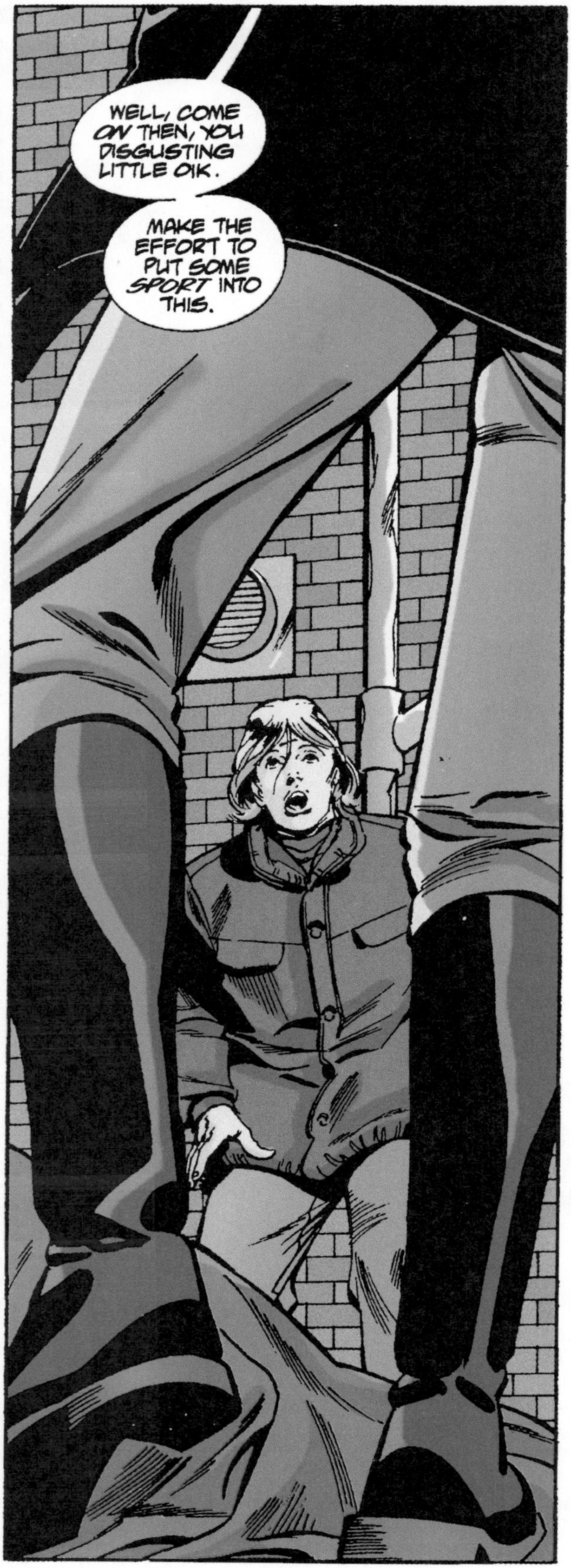
WELL, COME ON THEN, YOU DISGUSTING LITTLE OIK.
MAKE THE EFFORT TO PUT SOME SPORT INTO THIS.

DOWN AND OUT IN HEAVEN AND HELL

PART 2

GRANT MORRISON → WRITER

STEVE YEOWELL → ARTIST

DANIEL VOZZO → COLORS

ELECTRIC CRAYON → COLOR SEPARATION

CLEM ROBINS → LETTERS

JULIE ROTTENBERG → ASST. EDITOR

STUART MOORE → EDITOR

THE INVISIBLES CREATED BY GRANT MORRISON

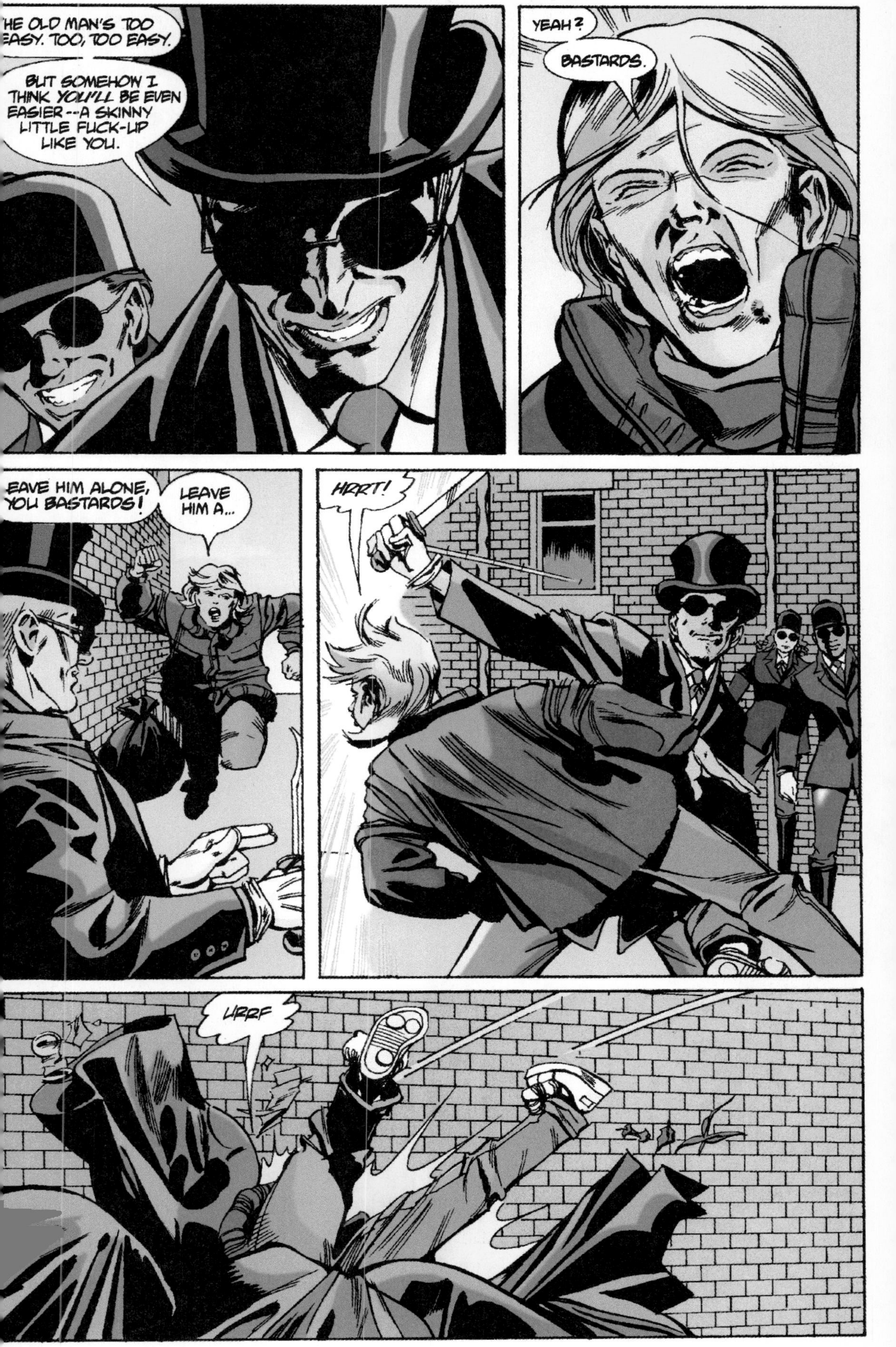
THE OLD MAN'S TOO EASY. TOO, TOO EASY.
BUT SOMEHOW I THINK YOU'LL BE EVEN EASIER--A SKINNY LITTLE FUCK-UP LIKE YOU.
YEAH?
BASTARDS.
LEAVE HIM ALONE, YOU BASTARDS!
LEAVE HIM A...
HRRT!
URRF

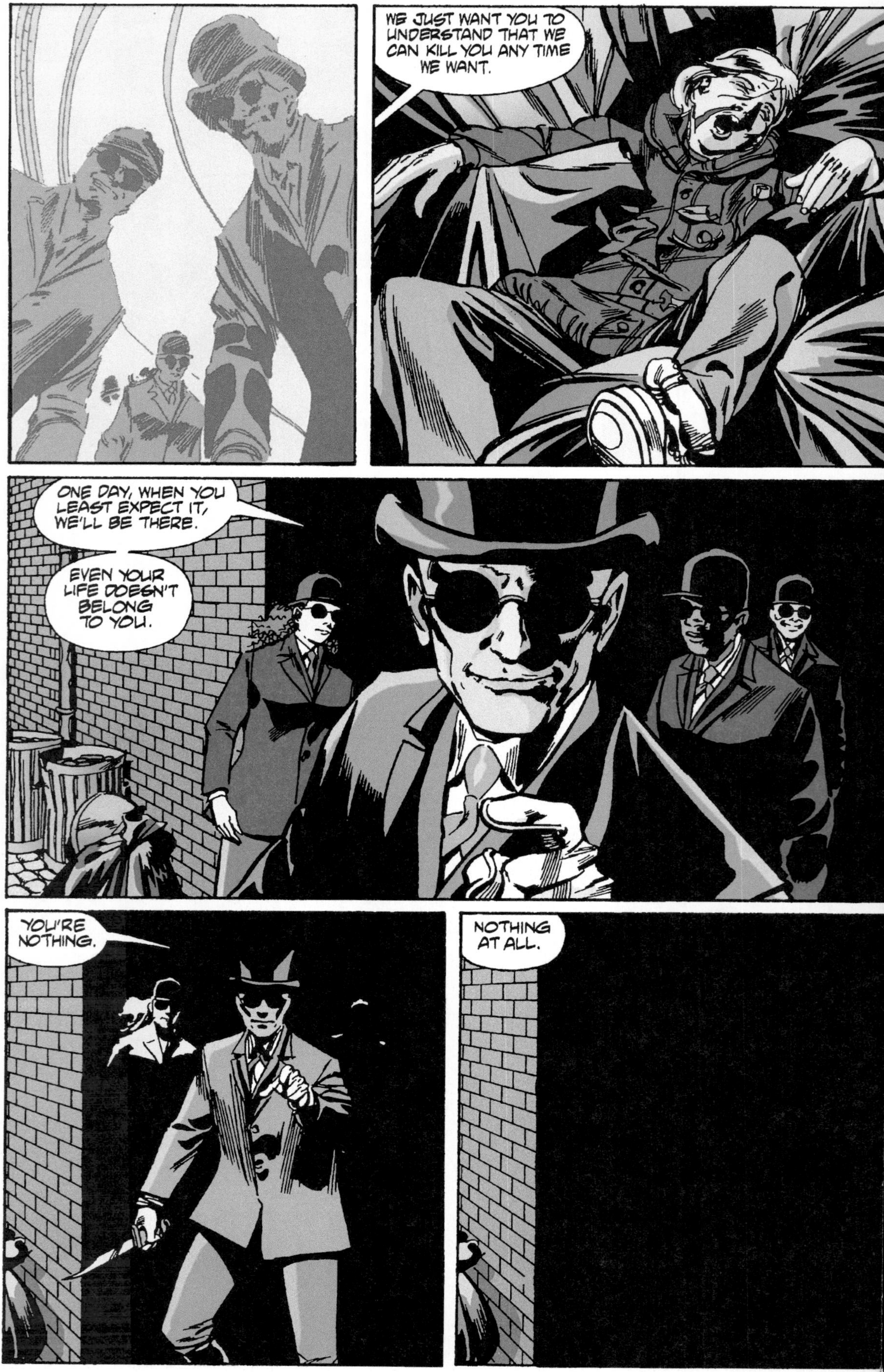
WE JUST WANT YOU TO UNDERSTAND THAT WE CAN KILL YOU ANY TIME WE WANT.
ONE DAY, WHEN YOU LEAST EXPECT IT, WE'LL BE THERE.
EVEN YOUR LIFE DOESN'T BELONG TO YOU.
YOU'RE NOTHING.
NOTHING AT ALL.

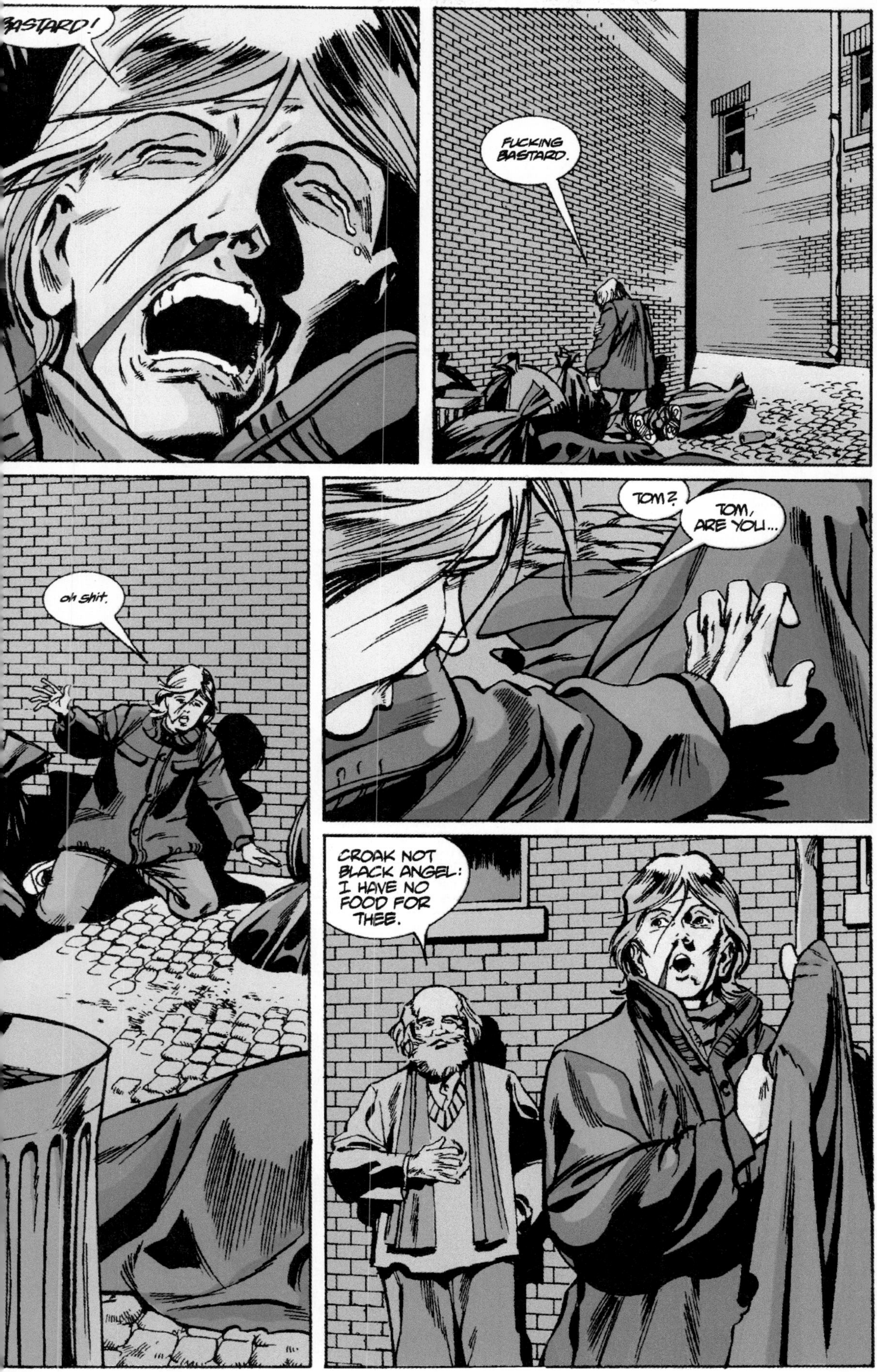
BASTARD!
FUCKING BASTARD.
oh shit.
TOM?
TOM, ARE YOU...
CROAK NOT BLACK ANGEL: I HAVE NO FOOD FOR THEE.

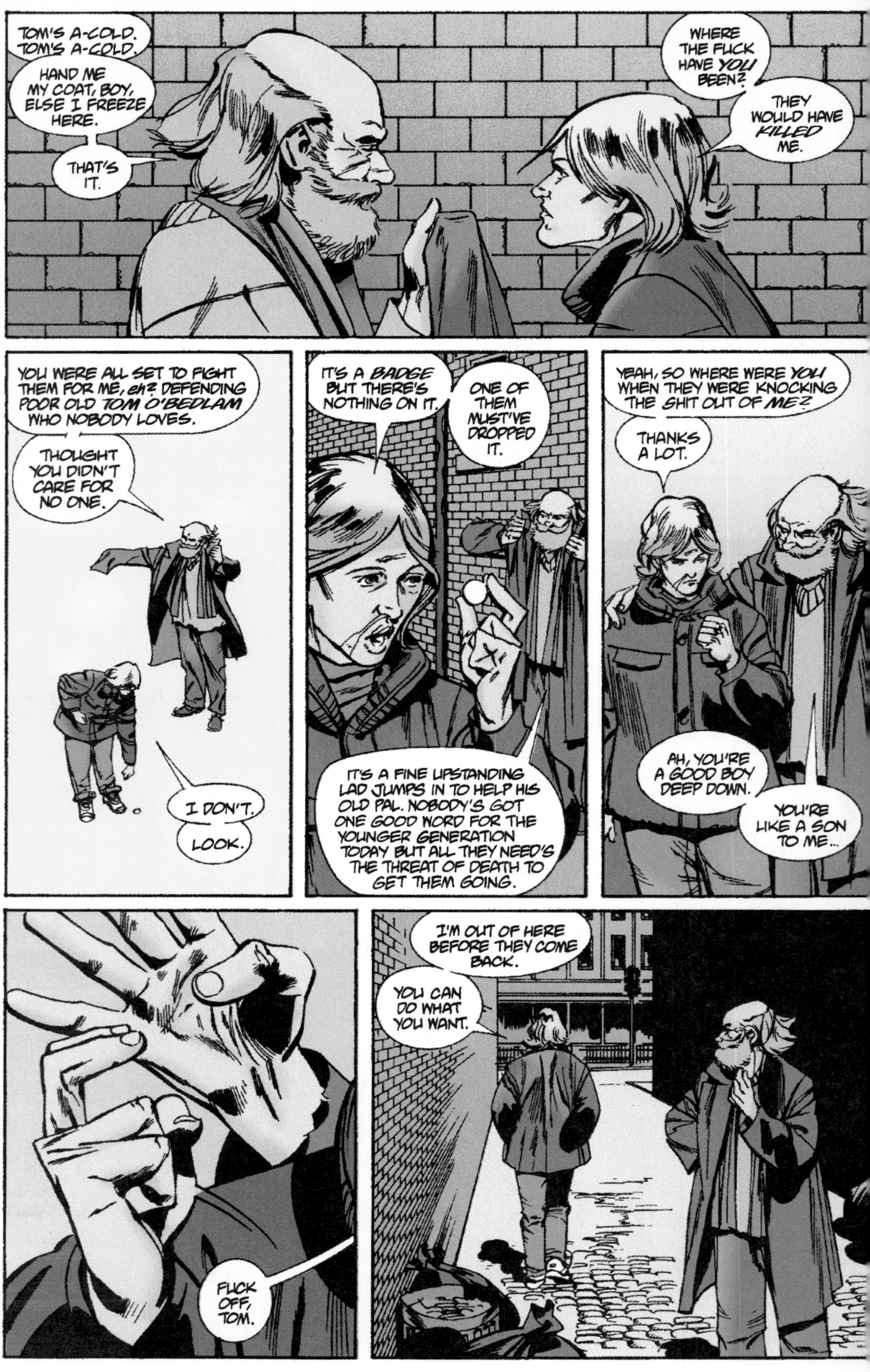
TOM'S A-COLD. TOM'S A-COLD.
HAND ME MY COAT, BOY, ELSE I FREEZE HERE.
THAT'S IT.
WHERE THE FUCK HAVE YOU BEEN?
THEY WOULD HAVE KILLED ME.
YOU WERE ALL SET TO FIGHT THEM FOR ME, eh? DEFENDING POOR OLD TOM O'BEDLAM WHO NOBODY LOVES.
THOUGHT YOU DIDN'T CARE FOR NO ONE.
I DON'T.
LOOK.
IT'S A BADGE BUT THERE'S NOTHING ON IT.
ONE OF THEM MUST'VE DROPPED IT.
IT'S A FINE UPSTANDING LAD JUMPS IN TO HELP HIS OLD PAL. NOBODY'S GOT ONE GOOD WORD FOR THE YOUNGER GENERATION TODAY BUT ALL THEY NEED'S THE THREAT OF DEATH TO GET THEM GOING.
YEAH, SO WHERE WERE YOU WHEN THEY WERE KNOCKING THE SHIT OUT OF ME?
THANKS A LOT.
AH, YOU'RE A GOOD BOY DEEP DOWN.
YOU'RE LIKE A SON TO ME...
FUCK OFF, TOM.
I'M OUT OF HERE BEFORE THEY COME BACK.
YOU CAN DO WHAT YOU WANT.

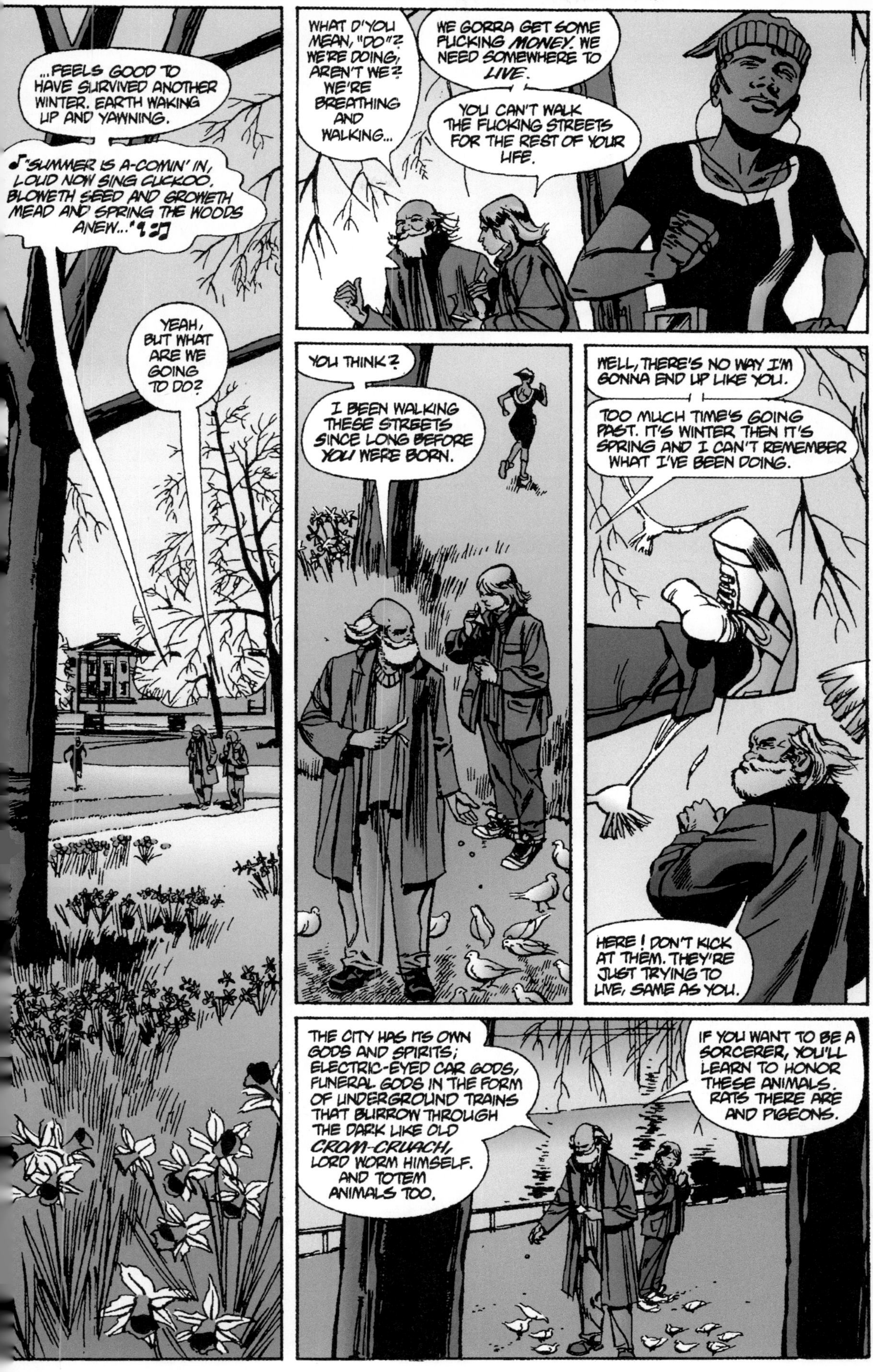
...FEELS GOOD TO HAVE SURVIVED ANOTHER WINTER. EARTH WAKING UP AND YAWNING.
"SUMMER IS A-COMIN' IN, LOUD NOW SING CUCKOO. BLOWETH SEED AND GROWETH MEAD AND SPRING THE WOODS ANEW..."
YEAH, BUT WHAT ARE WE GOING TO DO?
WHAT D'YOU MEAN, "DO"? WE'RE DOING, AREN'T WE? WE'RE BREATHING AND WALKING...
WE GORRA GET SOME FUCKING MONEY. WE NEED SOMEWHERE TO LIVE.
YOU CAN'T WALK THE FUCKING STREETS FOR THE REST OF YOUR LIFE.
YOU THINK?
I BEEN WALKING THESE STREETS SINCE LONG BEFORE YOU WERE BORN.
WELL, THERE'S NO WAY I'M GONNA END UP LIKE YOU.
TOO MUCH TIME'S GOING PAST. IT'S WINTER THEN IT'S SPRING AND I CAN'T REMEMBER WHAT I'VE BEEN DOING.
HERE! DON'T KICK AT THEM. THEY'RE JUST TRYING TO LIVE, SAME AS YOU.
THE CITY HAS ITS OWN GODS AND SPIRITS; ELECTRIC-EYED CAR GODS, FUNERAL GODS IN THE FORM OF UNDERGROUND TRAINS THAT BURROW THROUGH THE DARK LIKE OLD CROM-CRUACH, LORD WORM HIMSELF. AND TOTEM ANIMALS TOO.
IF YOU WANT TO BE A SORCERER, YOU'LL LEARN TO HONOR THESE ANIMALS. RATS THERE ARE AND PIGEONS.

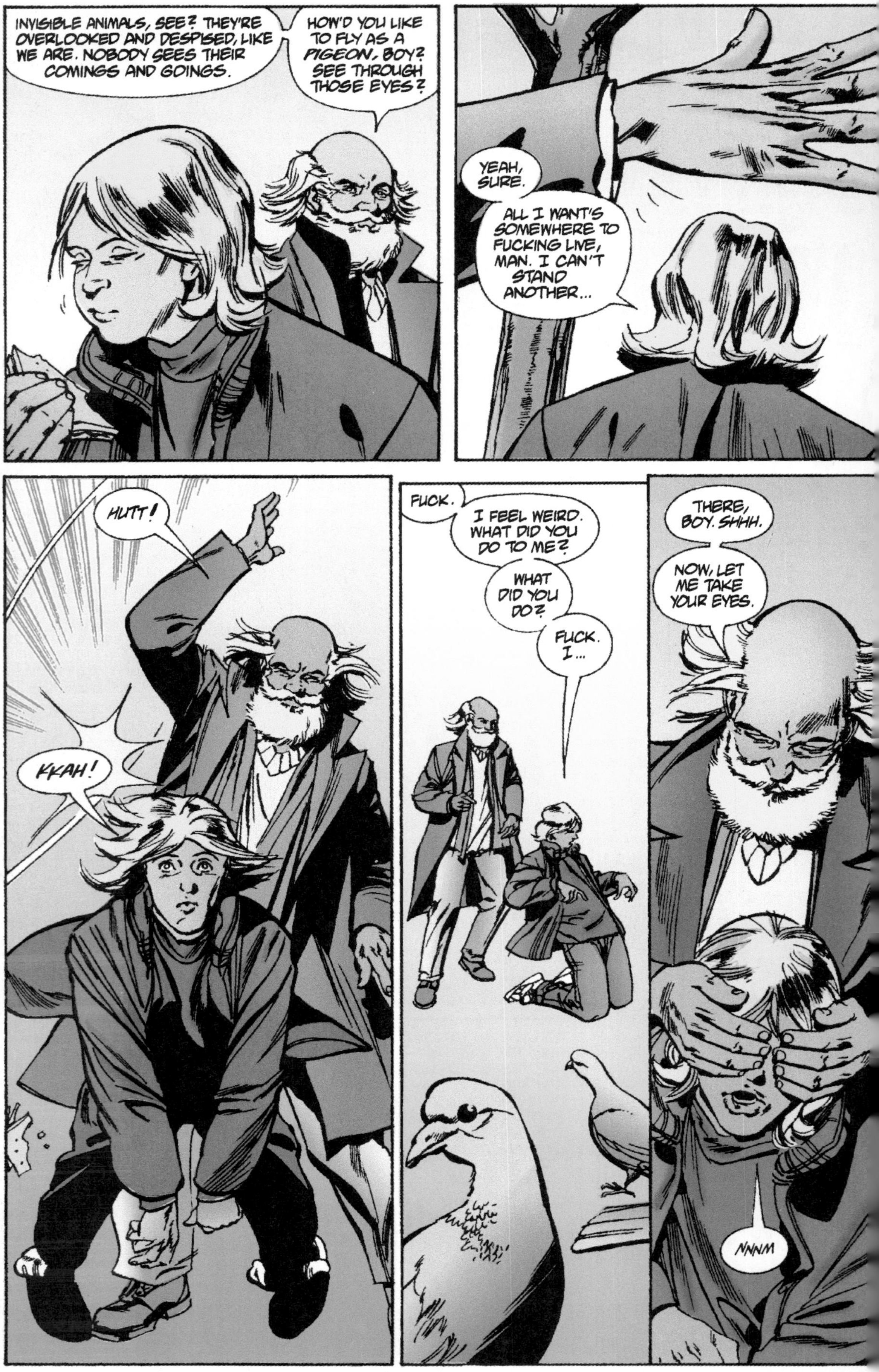
INVISIBLE ANIMALS, SEE? THEY'RE OVERLOOKED AND DESPISED, LIKE WE ARE. NOBODY SEES THEIR COMINGS AND GOINGS.
HOW'D YOU LIKE TO FLY AS A PIGEON, BOY? SEE THROUGH THOSE EYES?
YEAH, SURE.
ALL I WANT'S SOMEWHERE TO FUCKING LIVE, MAN. I CAN'T STAND ANOTHER...
HUTT!
KKAH!
FUCK.
I FEEL WEIRD. WHAT DID YOU DO TO ME?
WHAT DID YOU DO?
FUCK. I...
THERE, BOY. SHHH.
NOW, LET ME TAKE YOUR EYES.
NNNM

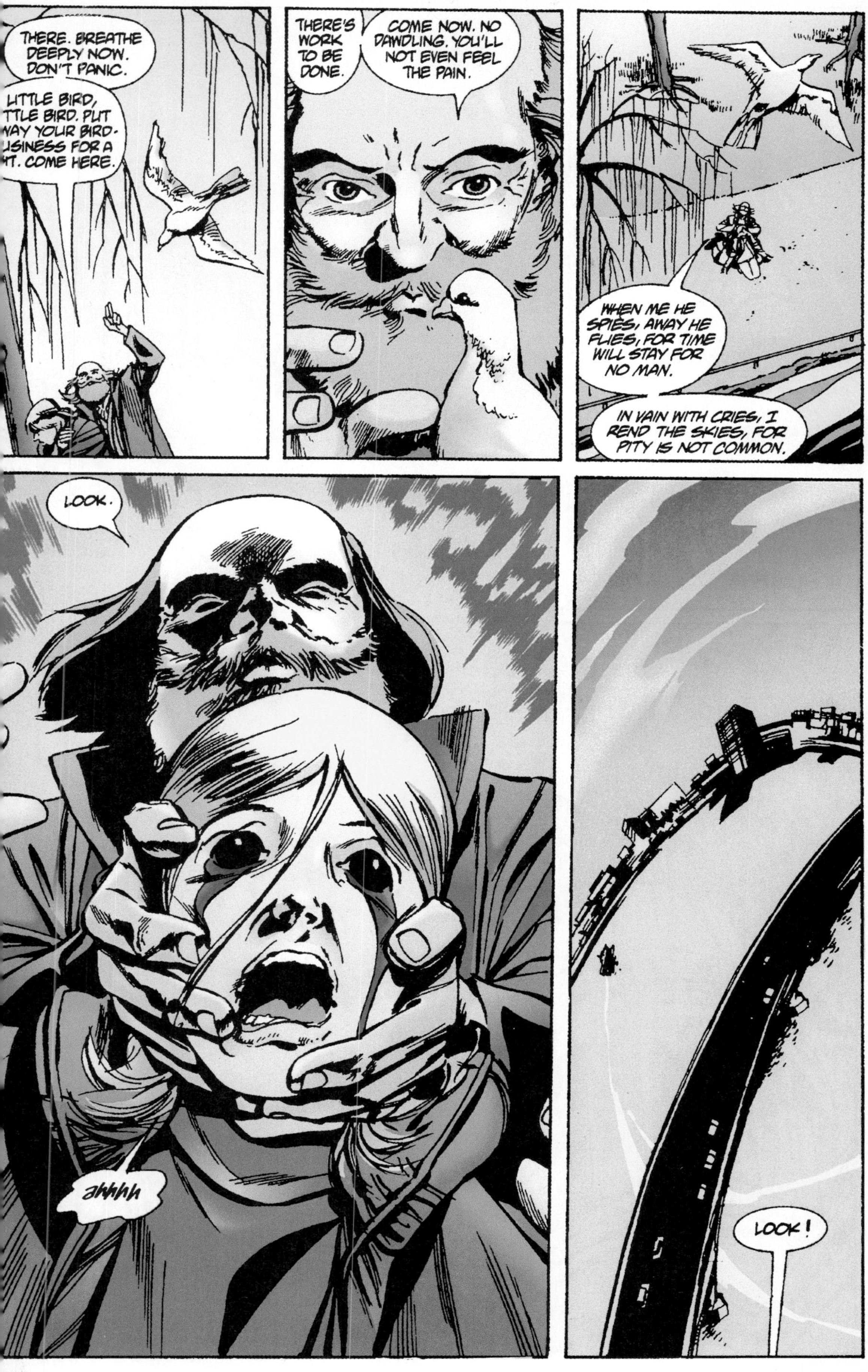
THERE. BREATHE DEEPLY NOW. DON'T PANIC.
LITTLE BIRD, TTLE BIRD. PUT WAY YOUR BIRD-USINESS FOR A HT. COME HERE.
THERE'S WORK TO BE DONE.
COME NOW. NO DAWDLING. YOU'LL NOT EVEN FEEL THE PAIN.
WHEN ME HE SPIES, AWAY HE FLIES, FOR TIME WILL STAY FOR NO MAN.
IN VAIN WITH CRIES, I REND THE SKIES, FOR PITY IS NOT COMMON.
LOOK.
ahhhh
LOOK!

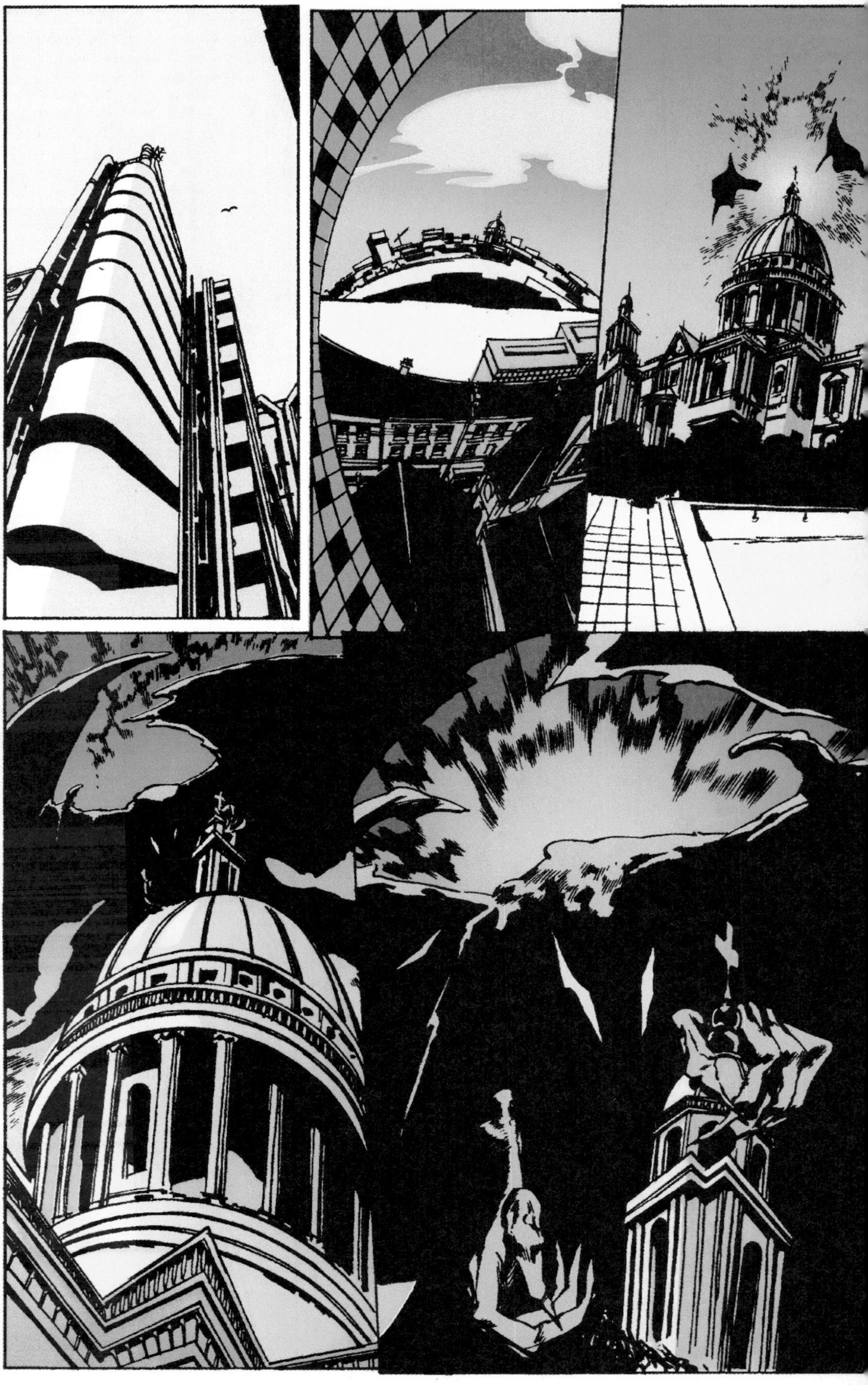

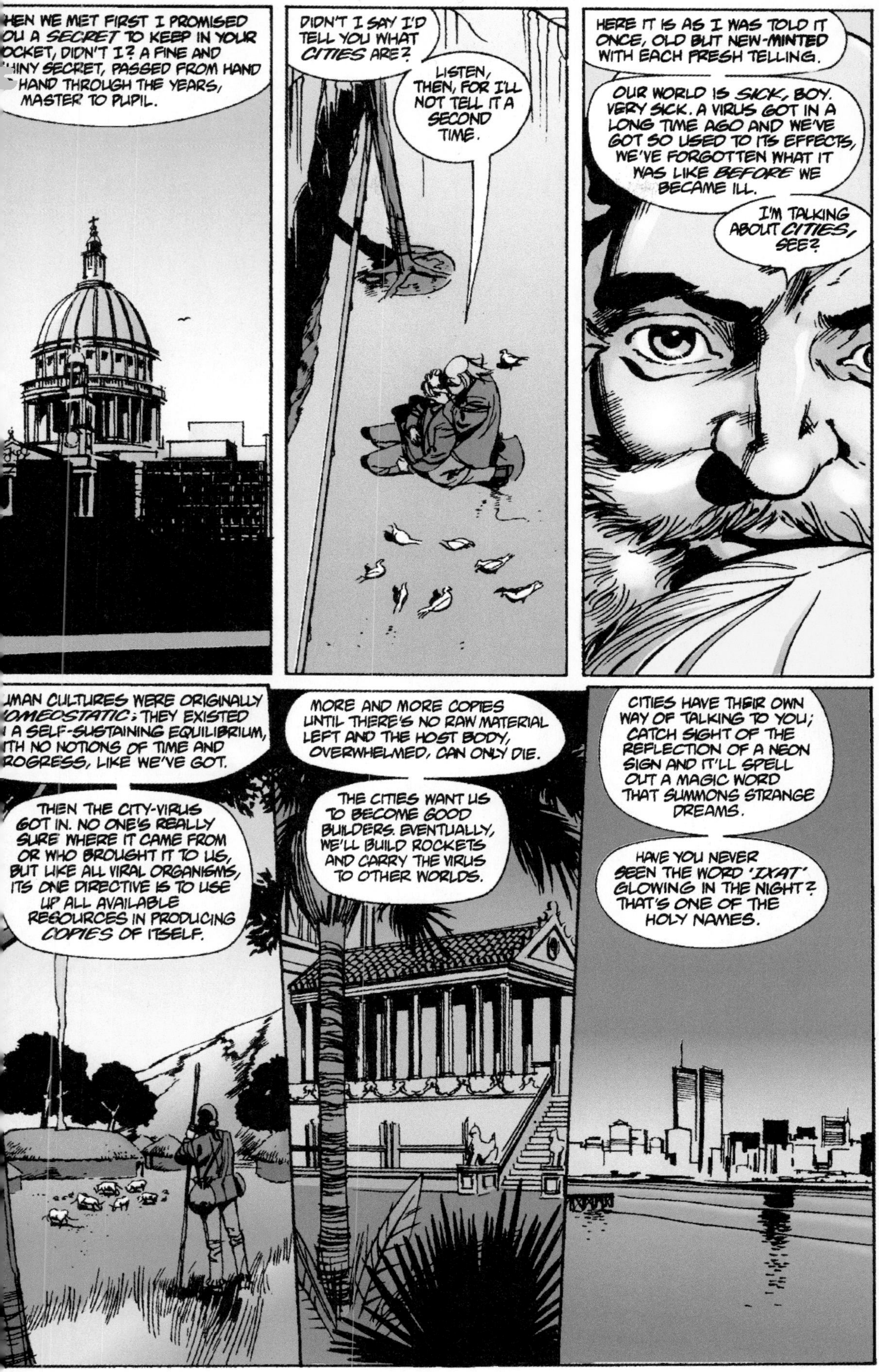
HEN WE MET FIRST I PROMISED OU A SECRET TO KEEP IN YOUR OCKET, DIDN'T I? A FINE AND HINY SECRET, PASSED FROM HAND HAND THROUGH THE YEARS, MASTER TO PUPIL.
DIDN'T I SAY I'D TELL YOU WHAT CITIES ARE?
LISTEN, THEN, FOR I'LL NOT TELL IT A SECOND TIME.
HERE IT IS AS I WAS TOLD IT ONCE, OLD BUT NEW-MINTED WITH EACH FRESH TELLING.
OUR WORLD IS SICK, BOY. VERY SICK. A VIRUS GOT IN A LONG TIME AGO AND WE'VE GOT SO USED TO ITS EFFECTS, WE'VE FORGOTTEN WHAT IT WAS LIKE BEFORE WE BECAME ILL.
I'M TALKING ABOUT CITIES, SEE?
UMAN CULTURES WERE ORIGINALLY OMEOSTATIC; THEY EXISTED A SELF-SUSTAINING EQUILIBRIUM, ITH NO NOTIONS OF TIME AND ROGRESS, LIKE WE'VE GOT.
THEN THE CITY-VIRUS GOT IN. NO ONE'S REALLY SURE WHERE IT CAME FROM OR WHO BROUGHT IT TO US, BUT LIKE ALL VIRAL ORGANISMS, ITS ONE DIRECTIVE IS TO USE UP ALL AVAILABLE RESOURCES IN PRODUCING COPIES OF ITSELF.
MORE AND MORE COPIES UNTIL THERE'S NO RAW MATERIAL LEFT AND THE HOST BODY, OVERWHELMED, CAN ONLY DIE.
THE CITIES WANT US TO BECOME GOOD BUILDERS. EVENTUALLY, WE'LL BUILD ROCKETS AND CARRY THE VIRUS TO OTHER WORLDS.
CITIES HAVE THEIR OWN WAY OF TALKING TO YOU; CATCH SIGHT OF THE REFLECTION OF A NEON SIGN AND IT'LL SPELL OUT A MAGIC WORD THAT SUMMONS STRANGE DREAMS.
HAVE YOU NEVER SEEN THE WORD 'IXAT' GLOWING IN THE NIGHT? THAT'S ONE OF THE HOLY NAMES.

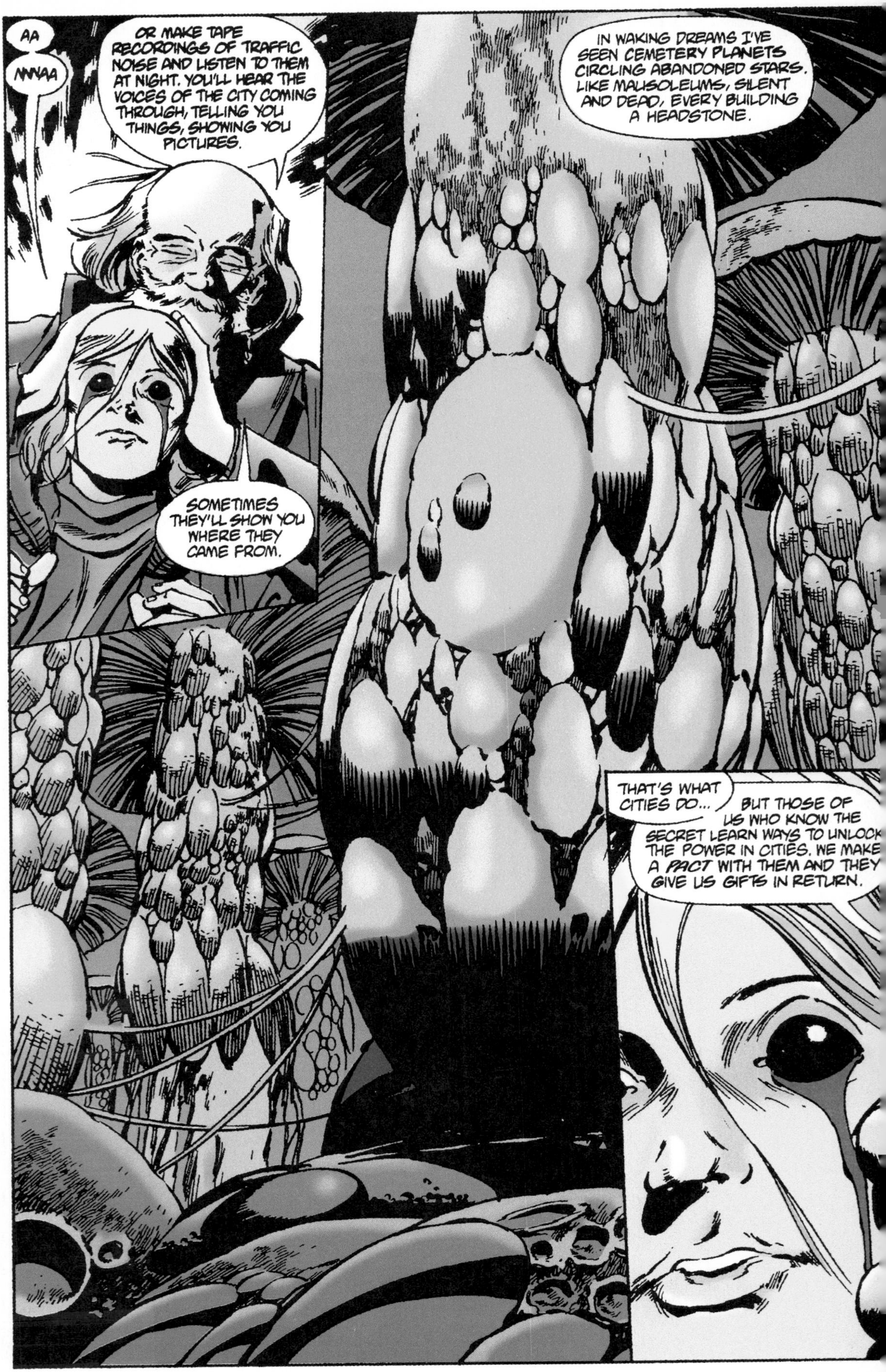
AA
NNNAA
OR MAKE TAPE RECORDINGS OF TRAFFIC NOISE AND LISTEN TO THEM AT NIGHT. YOU'LL HEAR THE VOICES OF THE CITY COMING THROUGH, TELLING YOU THINGS, SHOWING YOU PICTURES.
SOMETIMES THEY'LL SHOW YOU WHERE THEY CAME FROM.
IN WAKING DREAMS I'VE SEEN CEMETERY PLANETS CIRCLING ABANDONED STARS. LIKE MAUSOLEUMS, SILENT AND DEAD, EVERY BUILDING A HEADSTONE.
THAT'S WHAT CITIES DO...
BUT THOSE OF US WHO KNOW THE SECRET LEARN WAYS TO UNLOCK THE POWER IN CITIES. WE MAKE A PACT WITH THEM AND THEY GIVE US GIFTS IN RETURN.

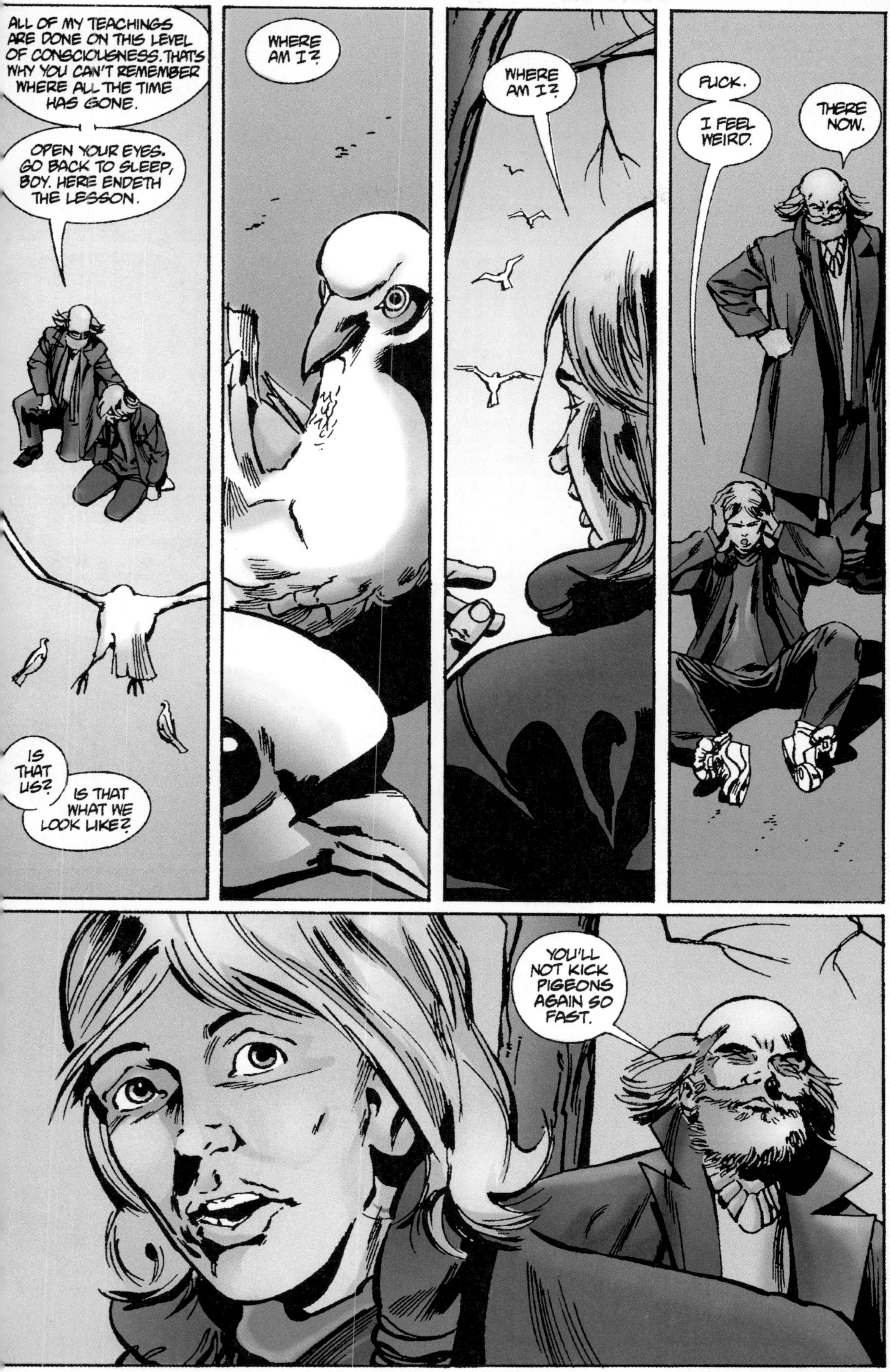

ALL OF MY TEACHINGS ARE DONE ON THIS LEVEL OF CONSCIOUSNESS. THAT'S WHY YOU CAN'T REMEMBER WHERE ALL THE TIME HAS GONE.
OPEN YOUR EYES. GO BACK TO SLEEP, BOY. HERE ENDETH THE LESSON.
IS THAT US?
IS THAT WHAT WE LOOK LIKE?
WHERE AM I?
WHERE AM I?
FUCK.
I FEEL WEIRD.
THERE NOW.
YOU'LL NOT KICK PIGEONS AGAIN SO FAST.

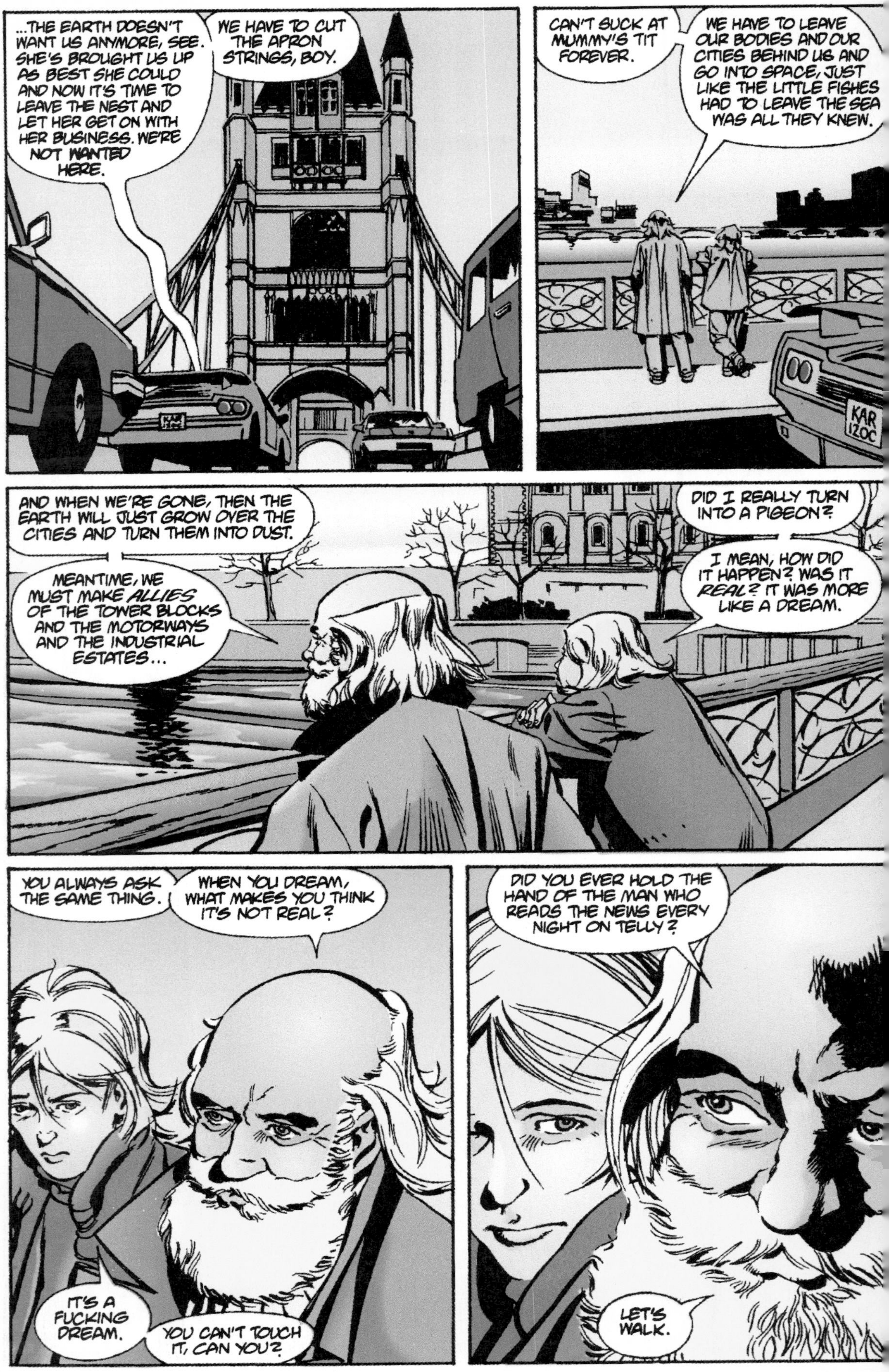
...THE EARTH DOESN'T WANT US ANYMORE, SEE. SHE'S BROUGHT US UP AS BEST SHE COULD AND NOW IT'S TIME TO LEAVE THE NEST AND LET HER GET ON WITH HER BUSINESS. WE'RE NOT WANTED HERE.
WE HAVE TO CUT THE APRON STRINGS, BOY.
KAR 120C
CAN'T SUCK AT MUMMY'S TIT FOREVER.
WE HAVE TO LEAVE OUR BODIES AND OUR CITIES BEHIND US AND GO INTO SPACE, JUST LIKE THE LITTLE FISHES HAD TO LEAVE THE SEA WAS ALL THEY KNEW.
KAR 120C
AND WHEN WE'RE GONE, THEN THE EARTH WILL JUST GROW OVER THE CITIES AND TURN THEM INTO DUST.
MEANTIME, WE MUST MAKE *ALLIES* OF THE TOWER BLOCKS AND THE MOTORWAYS AND THE INDUSTRIAL ESTATES...
DID I REALLY TURN INTO A PIGEON?
I MEAN, HOW DID IT HAPPEN? WAS IT *REAL*? IT WAS MORE LIKE A DREAM.
YOU ALWAYS ASK THE SAME THING.
WHEN YOU DREAM, WHAT MAKES YOU THINK IT'S NOT REAL?
IT'S A FUCKING DREAM.
YOU CAN'T TOUCH IT, CAN YOU?
DID YOU EVER HOLD THE HAND OF THE MAN WHO READS THE NEWS EVERY NIGHT ON TELLY?
LET'S WALK.

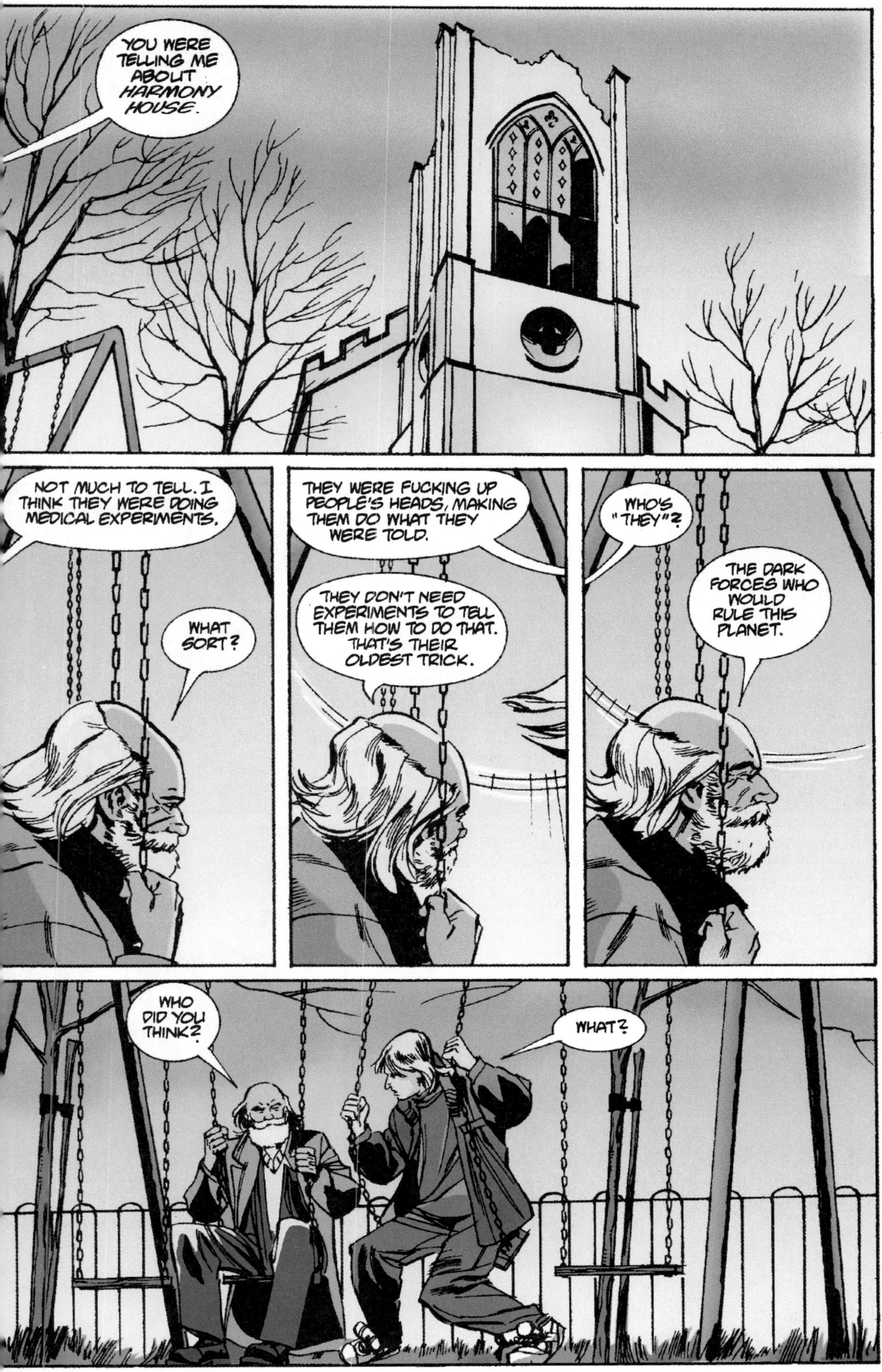
YOU WERE TELLING ME ABOUT HARMONY HOUSE.
NOT MUCH TO TELL. I THINK THEY WERE DOING MEDICAL EXPERIMENTS.
WHAT SORT?
THEY WERE FUCKING UP PEOPLE'S HEADS, MAKING THEM DO WHAT THEY WERE TOLD.
THEY DON'T NEED EXPERIMENTS TO TELL THEM HOW TO DO THAT. THAT'S THEIR OLDEST TRICK.
WHO'S "THEY"?
THE DARK FORCES WHO WOULD RULE THIS PLANET.
WHO DID YOU THINK?
WHAT?

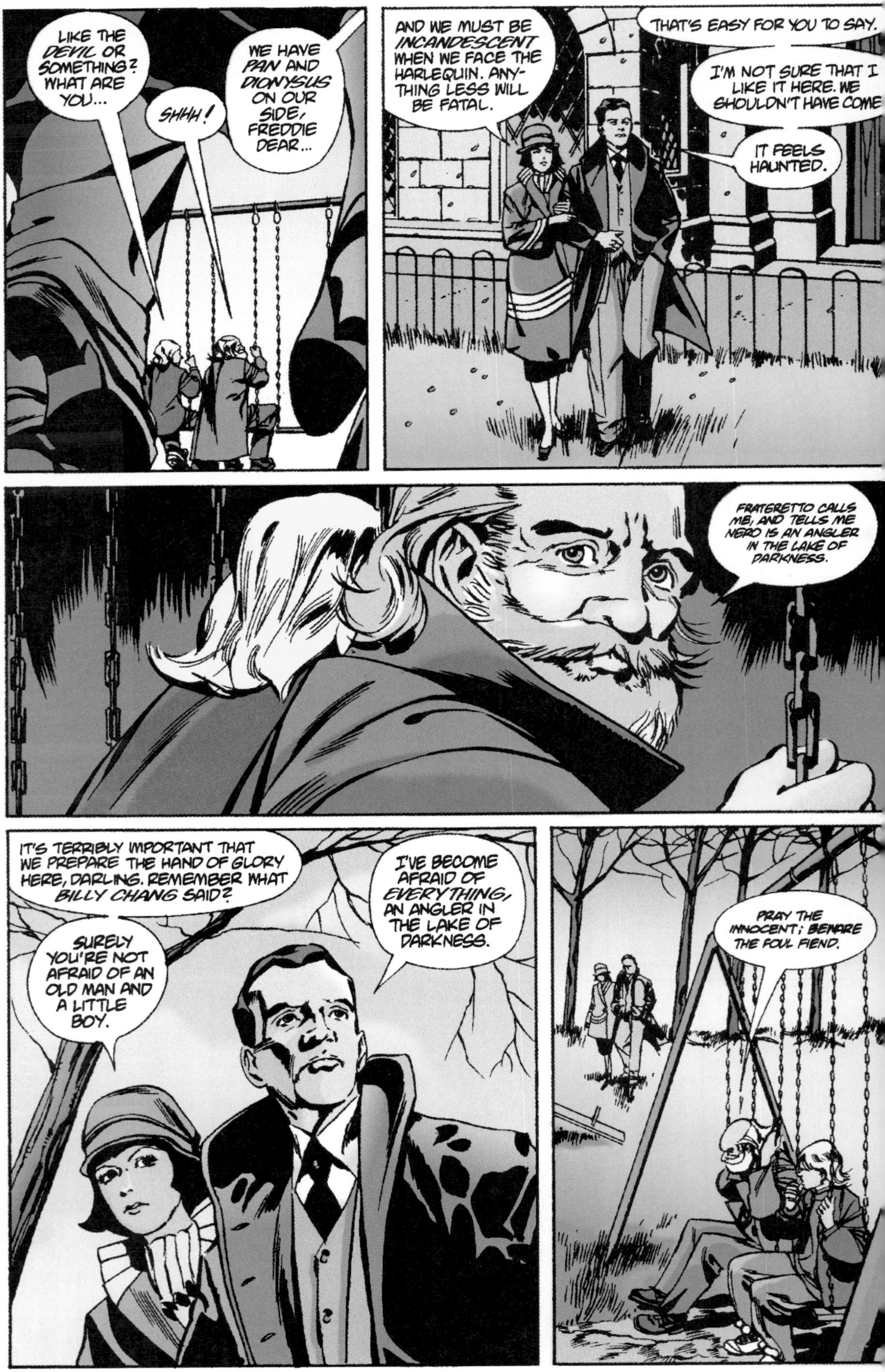
LIKE THE DEVIL OR SOMETHING? WHAT ARE YOU...
SHHH!
WE HAVE PAN AND DIONYSUS ON OUR SIDE, FREDDIE DEAR...
AND WE MUST BE INCANDESCENT WHEN WE FACE THE HARLEQUIN. ANYTHING LESS WILL BE FATAL.
THAT'S EASY FOR YOU TO SAY.
I'M NOT SURE THAT I LIKE IT HERE. WE SHOULDN'T HAVE COME
IT FEELS HAUNTED.
FRATERETTO CALLS ME, AND TELLS ME NERO IS AN ANGLER IN THE LAKE OF DARKNESS.
IT'S TERRIBLY IMPORTANT THAT WE PREPARE THE HAND OF GLORY HERE, DARLING. REMEMBER WHAT BILLY CHANG SAID?
SURELY YOU'RE NOT AFRAID OF AN OLD MAN AND A LITTLE BOY.
I'VE BECOME AFRAID OF EVERYTHING, AN ANGLER IN THE LAKE OF DARKNESS.
PRAY THE INNOCENT; BEWARE THE FOUL FIEND.

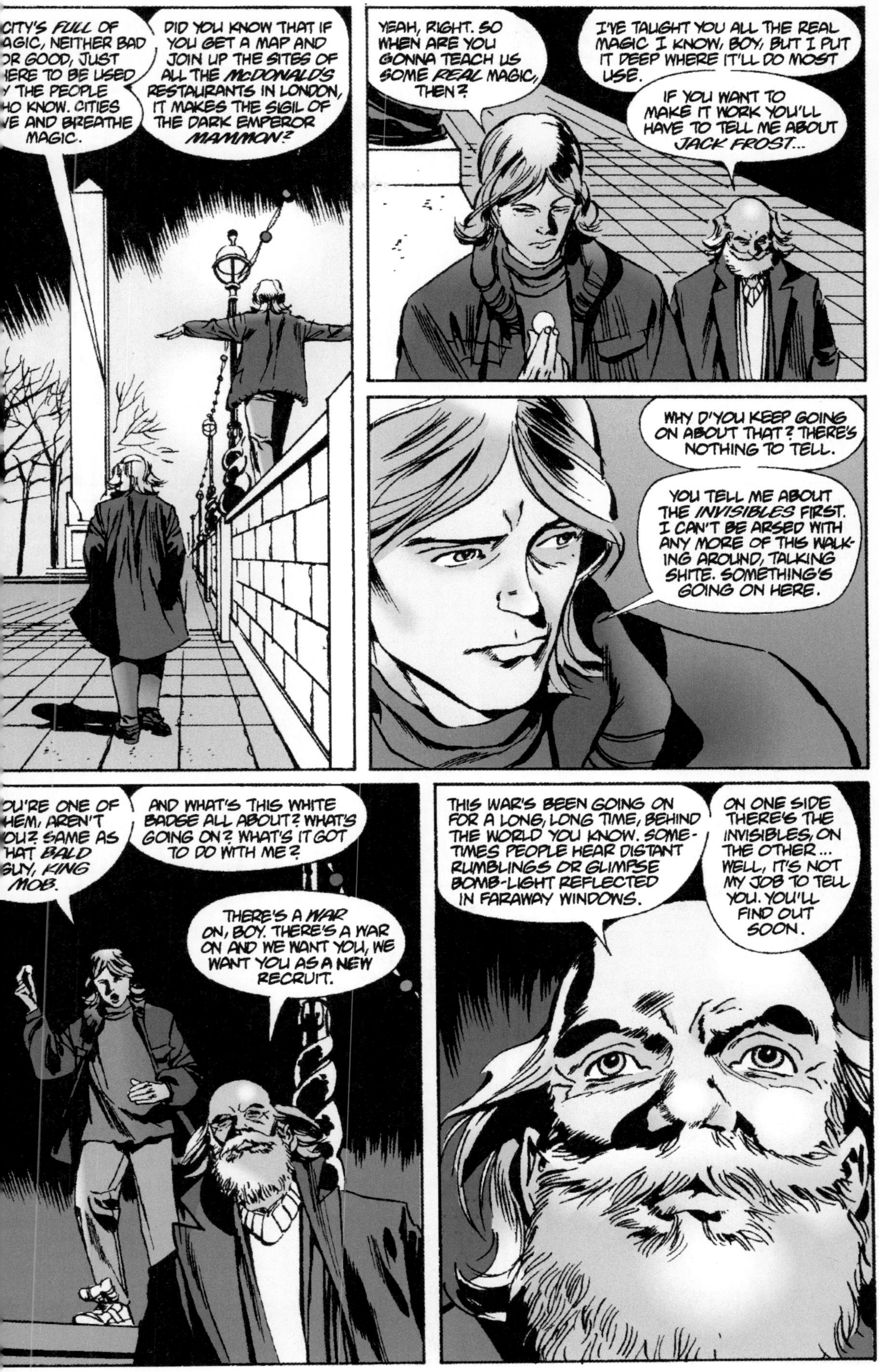

CITY'S FULL OF
AGIC, NEITHER BAD
OR GOOD, JUST
HERE TO BE USED
Y THE PEOPLE
HO KNOW. CITIES
VE AND BREATHE
MAGIC.
DID YOU KNOW THAT IF YOU GET A MAP AND JOIN UP THE SITES OF ALL THE McDONALD'S RESTAURANTS IN LONDON, IT MAKES THE SIGIL OF THE DARK EMPEROR MAMMON?
YEAH, RIGHT. SO WHEN ARE YOU GONNA TEACH US SOME REAL MAGIC, THEN?
I'VE TAUGHT YOU ALL THE REAL MAGIC I KNOW, BOY, BUT I PUT IT DEEP WHERE IT'LL DO MOST USE.
IF YOU WANT TO MAKE IT WORK YOU'LL HAVE TO TELL ME ABOUT JACK FROST...
WHY D'YOU KEEP GOING ON ABOUT THAT? THERE'S NOTHING TO TELL.
YOU TELL ME ABOUT THE INVISIBLES FIRST. I CAN'T BE ARSED WITH ANY MORE OF THIS WALKING AROUND, TALKING SHITE. SOMETHING'S GOING ON HERE.
OU'RE ONE OF
HEM, AREN'T
OU? SAME AS
HAT BALD
GUY, KING
MOB.
AND WHAT'S THIS WHITE BADGE ALL ABOUT? WHAT'S GOING ON? WHAT'S IT GOT TO DO WITH ME?
THERE'S A WAR ON, BOY. THERE'S A WAR ON AND WE WANT YOU, WE WANT YOU AS A NEW RECRUIT.
THIS WAR'S BEEN GOING ON FOR A LONG, LONG TIME, BEHIND THE WORLD YOU KNOW. SOMETIMES PEOPLE HEAR DISTANT RUMBLINGS OR GLIMPSE BOMB-LIGHT REFLECTED IN FARAWAY WINDOWS.
ON ONE SIDE THERE'S THE INVISIBLES, ON THE OTHER... WELL, IT'S NOT MY JOB TO TELL YOU. YOU'LL FIND OUT SOON.

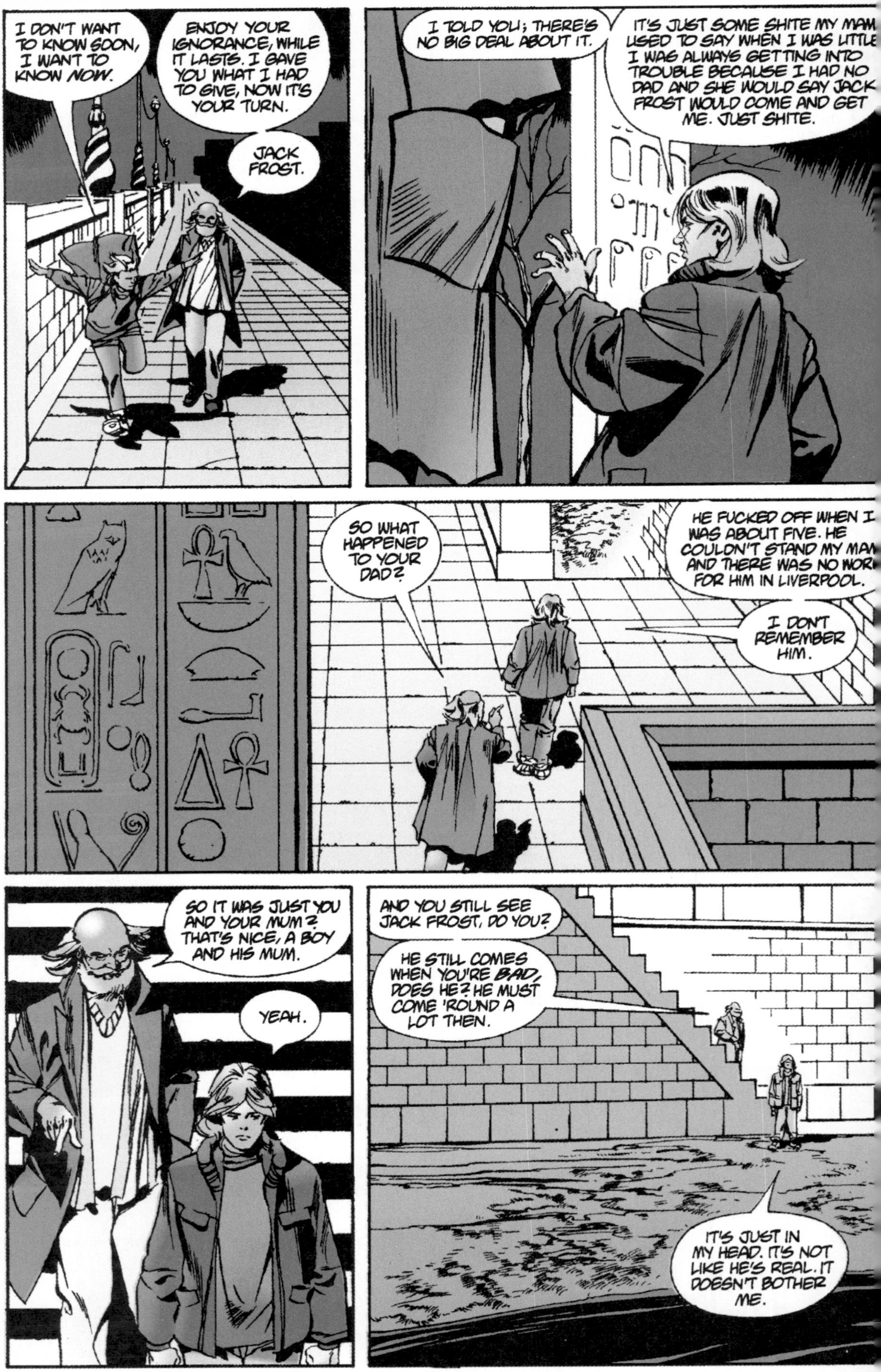
I DON'T WANT TO KNOW SOON, I WANT TO KNOW NOW.
ENJOY YOUR IGNORANCE, WHILE IT LASTS. I GAVE YOU WHAT I HAD TO GIVE, NOW IT'S YOUR TURN.
JACK FROST.
I TOLD YOU; THERE'S NO BIG DEAL ABOUT IT.
IT'S JUST SOME SHITE MY MAM USED TO SAY WHEN I WAS LITTLE. I WAS ALWAYS GETTING INTO TROUBLE BECAUSE I HAD NO DAD AND SHE WOULD SAY JACK FROST WOULD COME AND GET ME. JUST SHITE.
SO WHAT HAPPENED TO YOUR DAD?
HE FUCKED OFF WHEN I WAS ABOUT FIVE. HE COULDN'T STAND MY MAM AND THERE WAS NO WORK FOR HIM IN LIVERPOOL.
I DON'T REMEMBER HIM.
SO IT WAS JUST YOU AND YOUR MUM? THAT'S NICE, A BOY AND HIS MUM.
YEAH.
AND YOU STILL SEE JACK FROST, DO YOU?
HE STILL COMES WHEN YOU'RE BAD, DOES HE? HE MUST COME 'ROUND A LOT THEN.
IT'S JUST IN MY HEAD. IT'S NOT LIKE HE'S REAL. IT DOESN'T BOTHER ME.

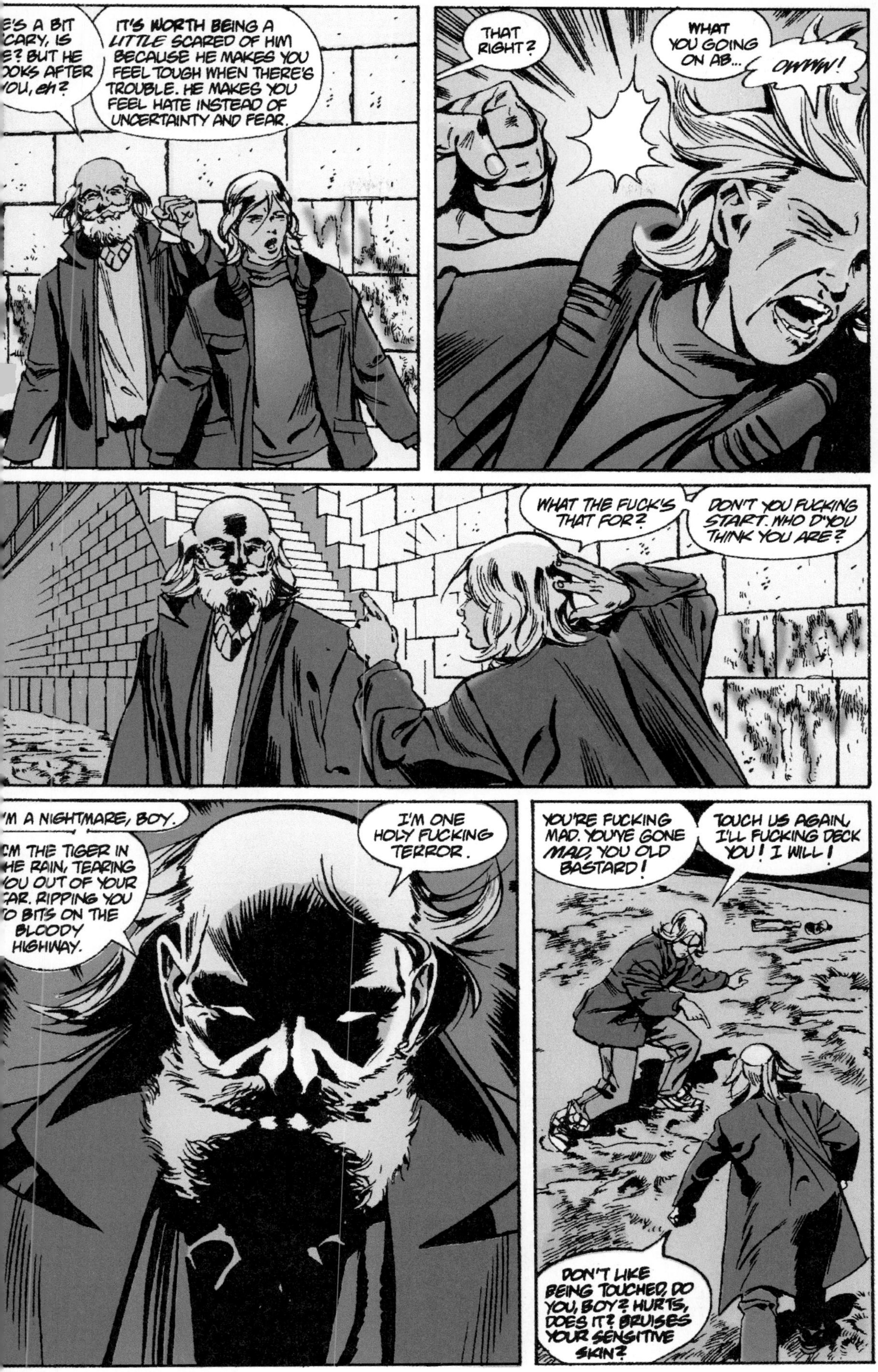
E'S A BIT
CARY, IS
E? BUT HE
OOKS AFTER
YOU, eh?
IT'S WORTH BEING A LITTLE SCARED OF HIM BECAUSE HE MAKES YOU FEEL TOUGH WHEN THERE'S TROUBLE. HE MAKES YOU FEEL HATE INSTEAD OF UNCERTAINTY AND FEAR.
THAT RIGHT?
WHAT YOU GOING ON AB...
OWWW!
WHAT THE FUCK'S THAT FOR?
DON'T YOU FUCKING START. WHO D'YOU THINK YOU ARE?
'M A NIGHTMARE, BOY.
'M THE TIGER IN HE RAIN, TEARING YOU OUT OF YOUR CAR. RIPPING YOU TO BITS ON THE BLOODY HIGHWAY.
I'M ONE HOLY FUCKING TERROR.
YOU'RE FUCKING MAD. YOU'VE GONE MAD, YOU OLD BASTARD!
TOUCH US AGAIN, I'LL FUCKING DECK YOU! I WILL!
DON'T LIKE BEING TOUCHED, DO YOU, BOY? HURTS, DOES IT? BRUISES YOUR SENSITIVE SKIN?

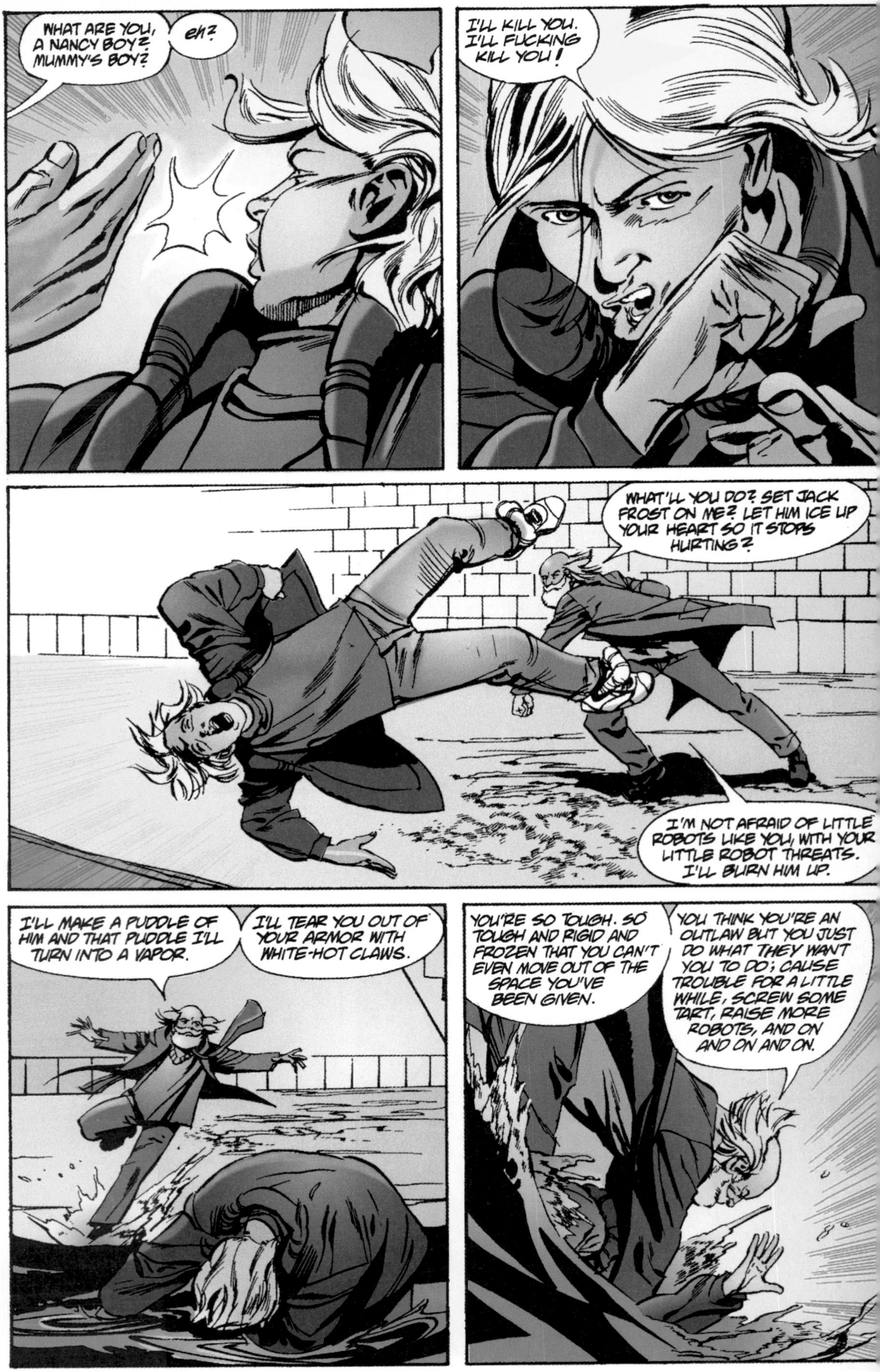
WHAT ARE YOU, A NANCY BOY? MUMMY'S BOY?
eh?
I'LL KILL YOU. I'LL FUCKING KILL YOU!
WHAT'LL YOU DO? SET JACK FROST ON ME? LET HIM ICE UP YOUR HEART SO IT STOPS HURTING?
I'M NOT AFRAID OF LITTLE ROBOTS LIKE YOU, WITH YOUR LITTLE ROBOT THREATS. I'LL BURN HIM UP.
I'LL MAKE A PUDDLE OF HIM AND THAT PUDDLE I'LL TURN INTO A VAPOR.
I'LL TEAR YOU OUT OF YOUR ARMOR WITH WHITE-HOT CLAWS.
YOU'RE SO TOUGH. SO TOUGH AND RIGID AND FROZEN THAT YOU CAN'T EVEN MOVE OUT OF THE SPACE YOU'VE BEEN GIVEN.
YOU THINK YOU'RE AN OUTLAW BUT YOU JUST DO WHAT THEY WANT YOU TO DO; CAUSE TROUBLE FOR A LITTLE WHILE, SCREW SOME TART, RAISE MORE ROBOTS, AND ON AND ON AND ON.

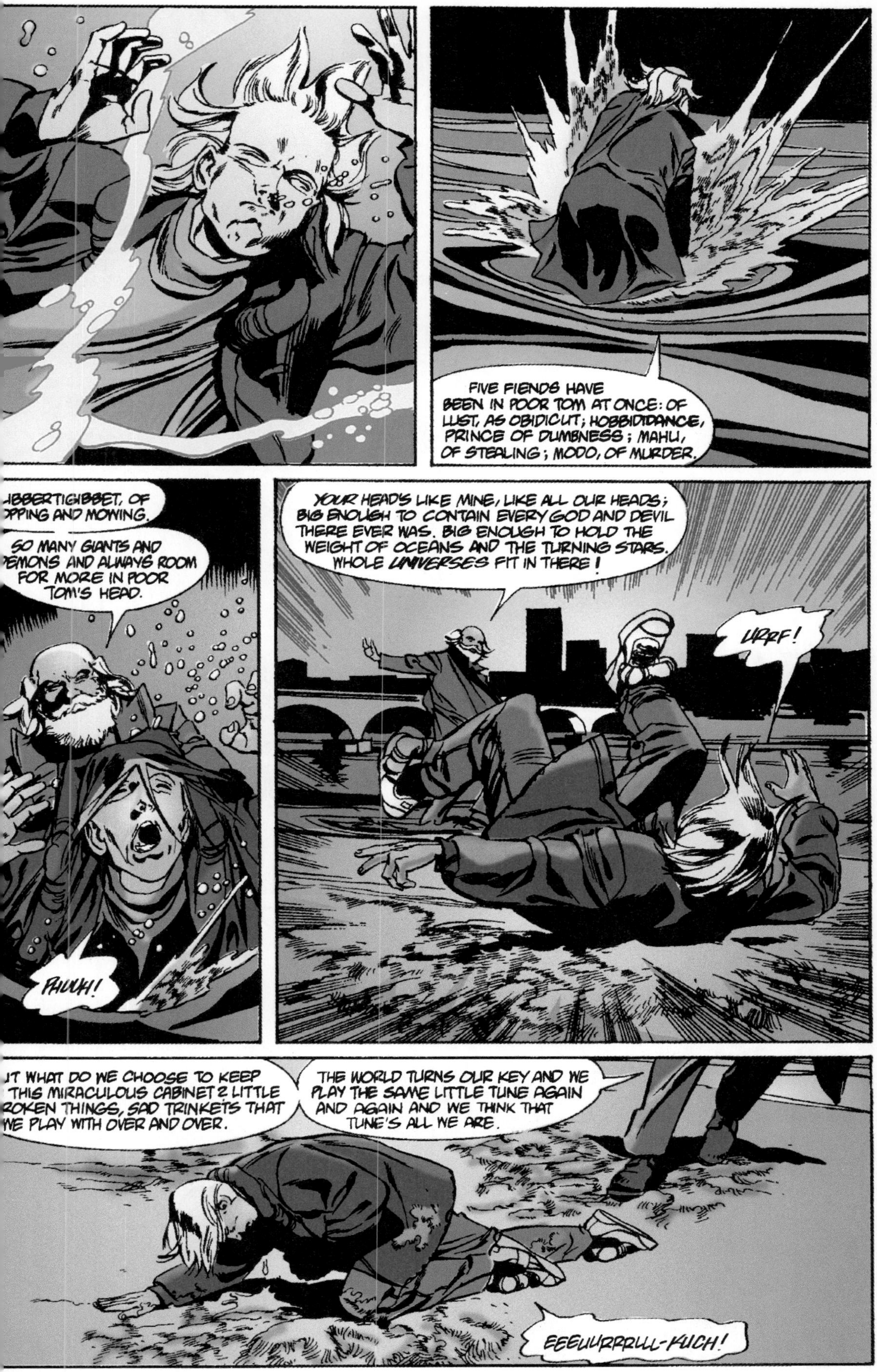

FIVE FIENDS HAVE BEEN IN POOR TOM AT ONCE: OF LUST, AS OBIDICUT; HOBBIDIDANCE, PRINCE OF DUMBNESS; MAHU, OF STEALING; MODO, OF MURDER.
LIBBERTIGIBBET, OF MOPPING AND MOWING.
SO MANY GIANTS AND DEMONS AND ALWAYS ROOM FOR MORE IN POOR TOM'S HEAD.
PHUUH!
YOUR HEAD'S LIKE MINE, LIKE ALL OUR HEADS; BIG ENOUGH TO CONTAIN EVERY GOD AND DEVIL THERE EVER WAS. BIG ENOUGH TO HOLD THE WEIGHT OF OCEANS AND THE TURNING STARS. WHOLE UNIVERSES FIT IN THERE!
URRF!
UT WHAT DO WE CHOOSE TO KEEP THIS MIRACULOUS CABINET? LITTLE ROKEN THINGS, SAD TRINKETS THAT WE PLAY WITH OVER AND OVER.
THE WORLD TURNS OUR KEY AND WE PLAY THE SAME LITTLE TUNE AGAIN AND AGAIN AND WE THINK THAT TUNE'S ALL WE ARE.
EEEUURRRLL-KUCH!

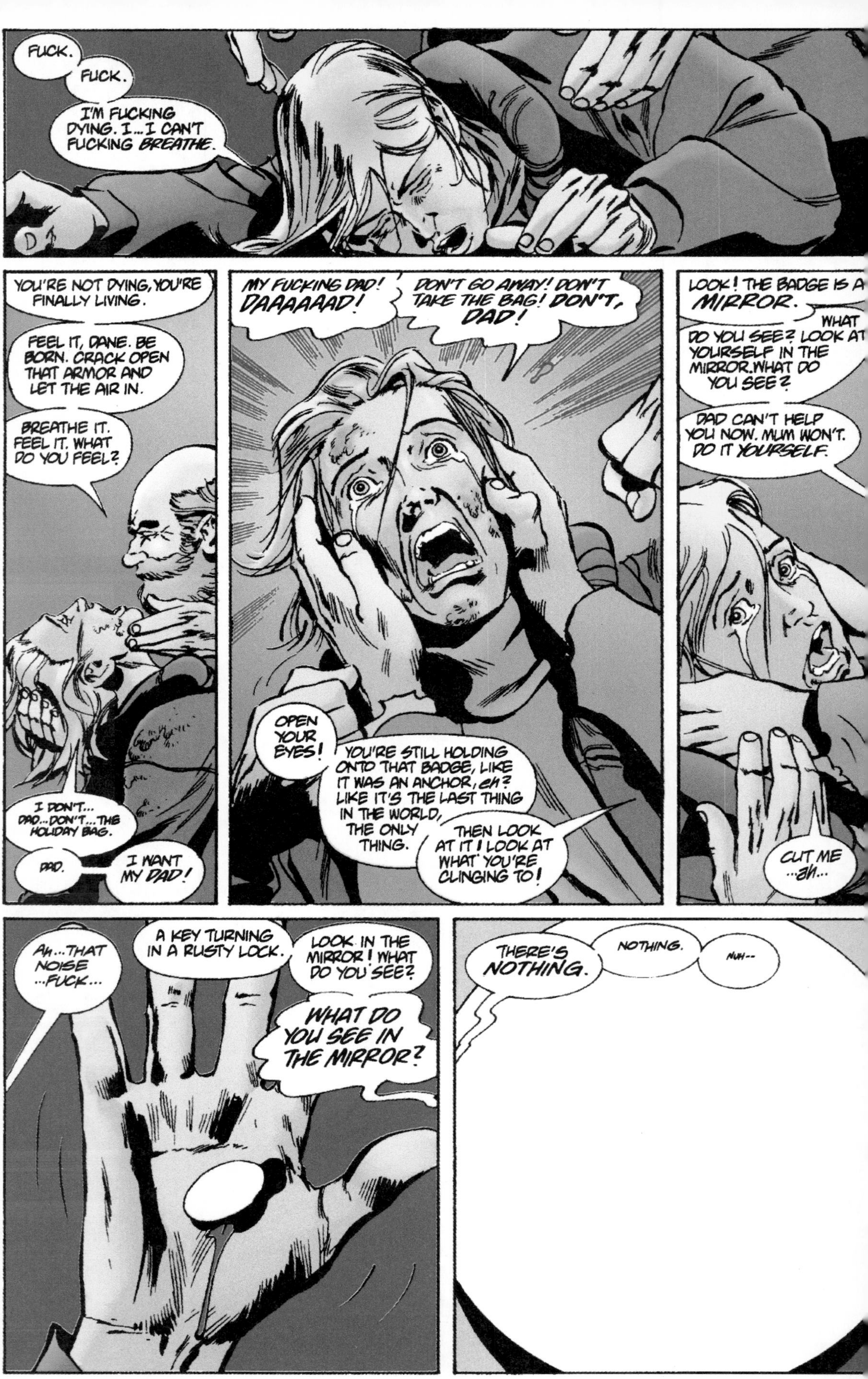
FUCK.
FUCK.
I'M FUCKING DYING. I...I CAN'T FUCKING BREATHE.
YOU'RE NOT DYING, YOU'RE FINALLY LIVING.
FEEL IT, DANE. BE BORN. CRACK OPEN THAT ARMOR AND LET THE AIR IN.
BREATHE IT. FEEL IT. WHAT DO YOU FEEL?
I DON'T... DAD...DON'T...THE HOLIDAY BAG.
DAD.
I WANT MY DAD!
MY FUCKING DAD! DAAAAAAD!
DON'T GO AWAY! DON'T TAKE THE BAG! DON'T, DAD!
OPEN YOUR EYES!
YOU'RE STILL HOLDING ONTO THAT BADGE, LIKE IT WAS AN ANCHOR, eh? LIKE IT'S THE LAST THING IN THE WORLD, THE ONLY THING.
THEN LOOK AT IT! LOOK AT WHAT YOU'RE CLINGING TO!
LOOK! THE BADGE IS A MIRROR.
WHAT DO YOU SEE? LOOK AT YOURSELF IN THE MIRROR. WHAT DO YOU SEE?
DAD CAN'T HELP YOU NOW. MUM WON'T. DO IT YOURSELF.
CUT ME ...ah...
Ah...THAT NOISE ...FUCK...
A KEY TURNING IN A RUSTY LOCK.
LOOK IN THE MIRROR! WHAT DO YOU SEE?
WHAT DO YOU SEE IN THE MIRROR?
THERE'S NOTHING.
NOTHING.
NUH--

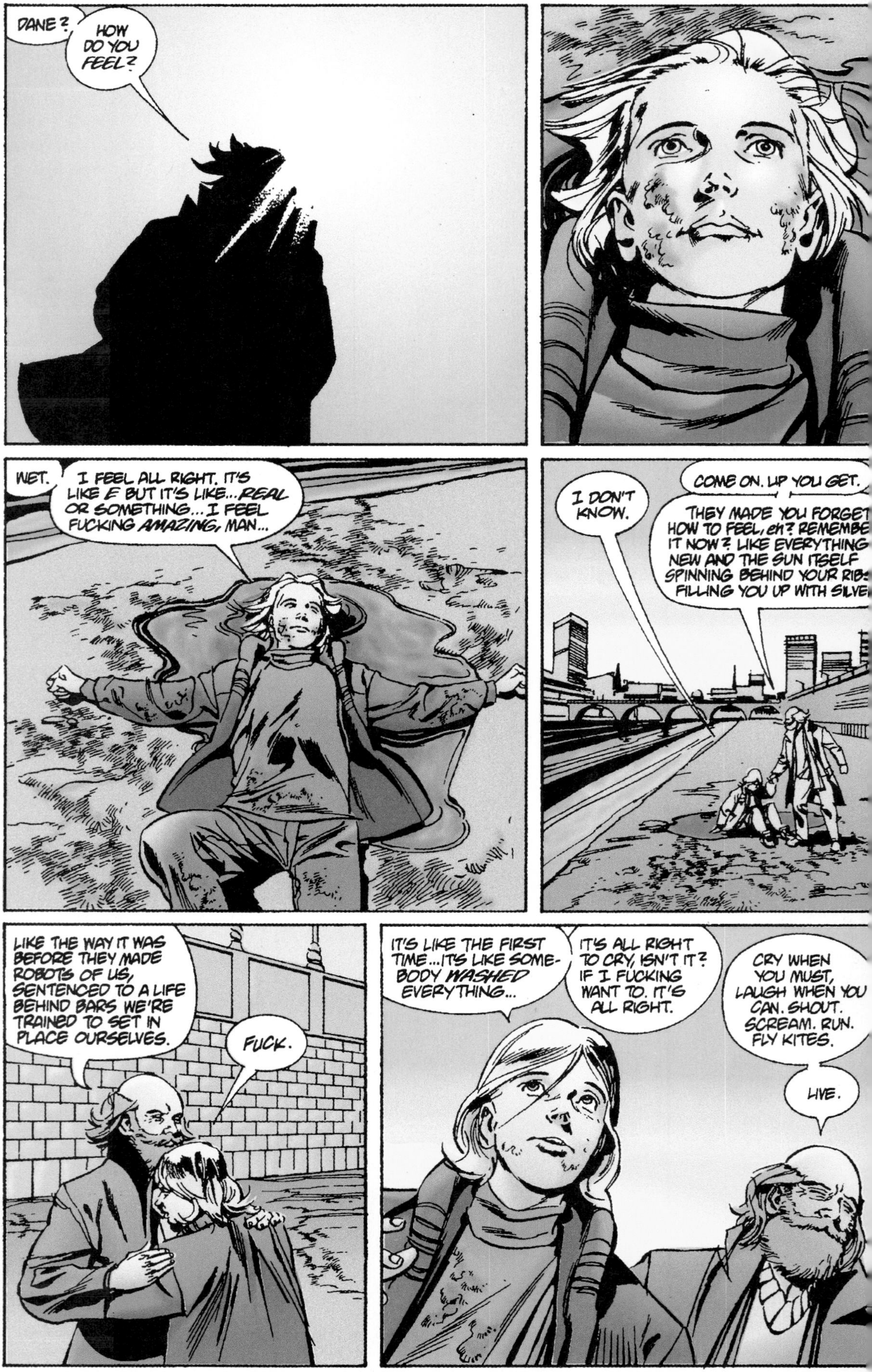
DANE?
HOW DO YOU FEEL?
WET.
I FEEL ALL RIGHT. IT'S LIKE E BUT IT'S LIKE... REAL OR SOMETHING... I FEEL FUCKING AMAZING, MAN...
I DON'T KNOW.
COME ON. UP YOU GET.
THEY MADE YOU FORGET HOW TO FEEL, eh? REMEMBE IT NOW? LIKE EVERYTHING NEW AND THE SUN ITSELF SPINNING BEHIND YOUR RIBS FILLING YOU UP WITH SILVE
LIKE THE WAY IT WAS BEFORE THEY MADE ROBOTS OF US, SENTENCED TO A LIFE BEHIND BARS WE'RE TRAINED TO SET IN PLACE OURSELVES.
FUCK.
IT'S LIKE THE FIRST TIME... IT'S LIKE SOMEBODY WASHED EVERYTHING...
IT'S ALL RIGHT TO CRY, ISN'T IT? IF I FUCKING WANT TO. IT'S ALL RIGHT.
CRY WHEN YOU MUST, LAUGH WHEN YOU CAN. SHOUT. SCREAM. RUN. FLY KITES.
LIVE.

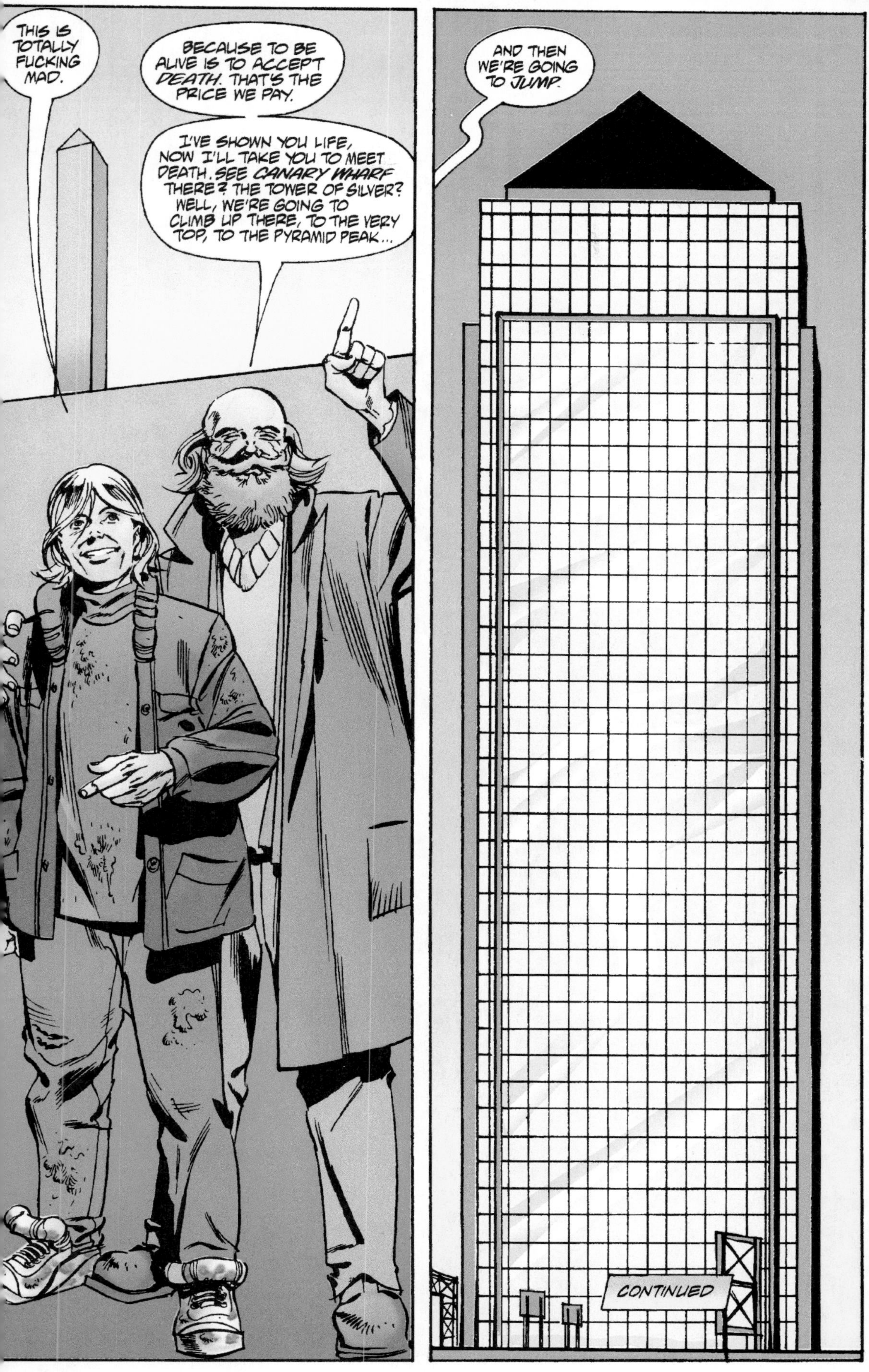
THIS IS TOTALLY FUCKING MAD.
BECAUSE TO BE ALIVE IS TO ACCEPT DEATH. THAT'S THE PRICE WE PAY.
I'VE SHOWN YOU LIFE, NOW I'LL TAKE YOU TO MEET DEATH. SEE CANARY WHARF THERE? THE TOWER OF SILVER? WELL, WE'RE GOING TO CLIMB UP THERE, TO THE VERY TOP, TO THE PYRAMID PEAK...
AND THEN WE'RE GOING TO JUMP.
CONTINUED

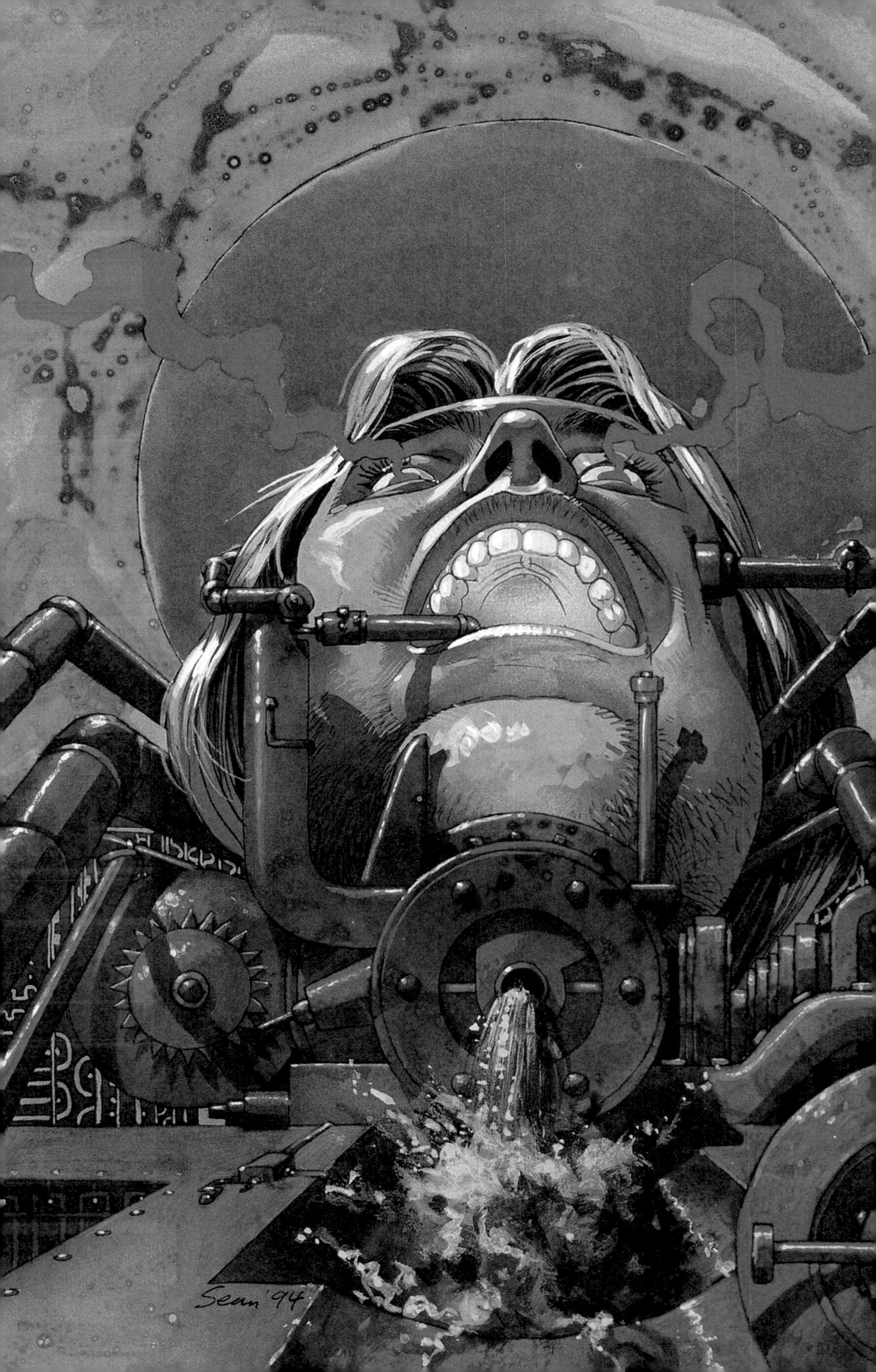
Sean '94

DOWN AND OUT IN HEAVEN AND HELL

PART 3

THE INVISIBLES CREATED BY
GRANT MORRISON

GRANT MORRISON → WRITER

STEVE YEOWELL → ARTIST

DANIEL VOZZO → COLORS

CLEM ROBINS → LETTERS

STUART MOORE → EDITOR

JULIE ROTTENBERG → ASST. EDITOR

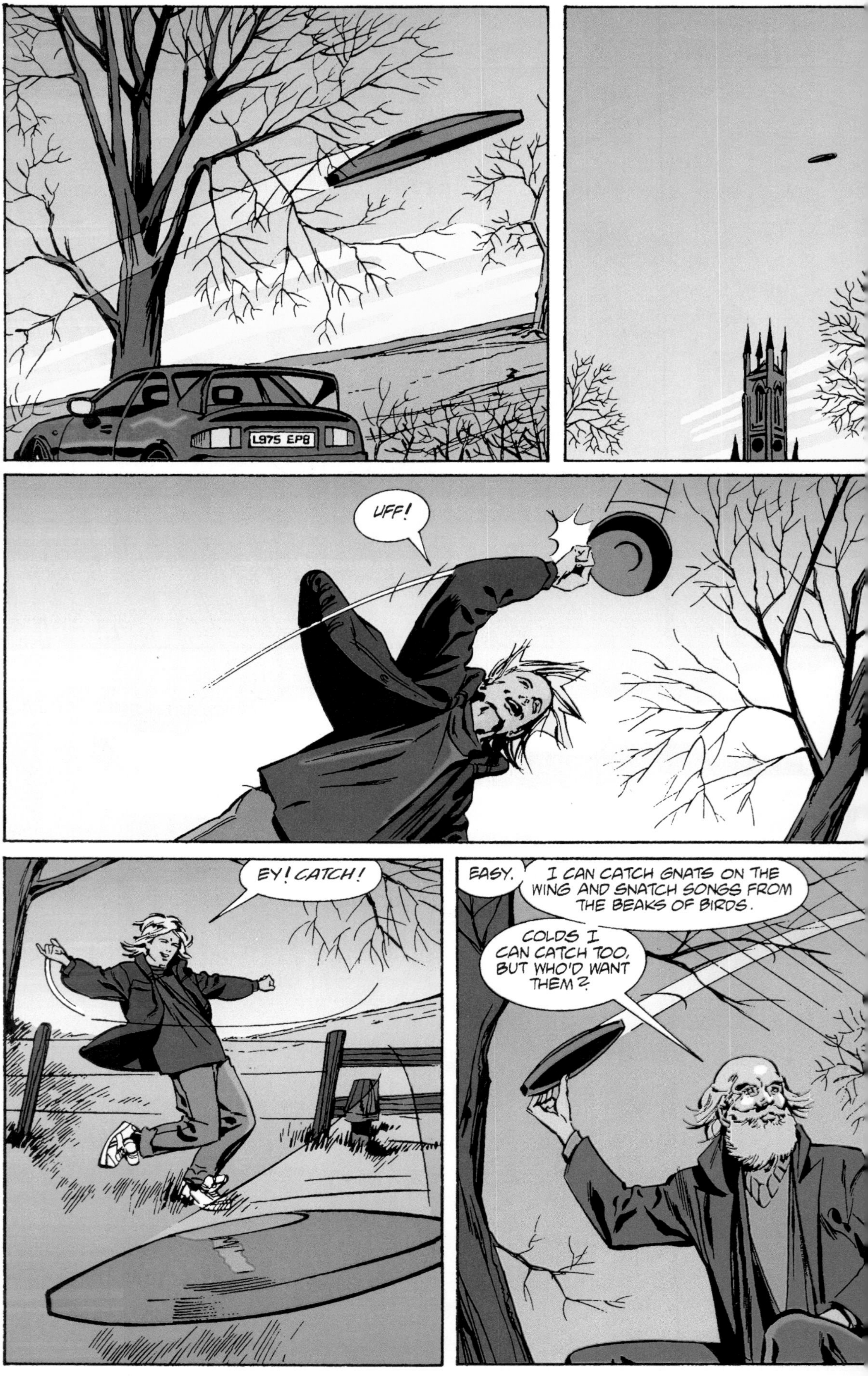
L975 EPB
UFF!
EY! CATCH!
EASY.
I CAN CATCH GNATS ON THE WING AND SNATCH SONGS FROM THE BEAKS OF BIRDS.
COLDS I CAN CATCH TOO, BUT WHO'D WANT THEM?

YOU CAN'T CATCH ME THOUGH, CAN YOU?

I'D LIKE TO SEE *YOU* TRYING TO RUN.

LOOK AT YOU! ALL FULL OF LIFE. SPARKS FLY FROM YOU WHERE MY FIRES ARE GONE TO EMBERS AND ASH NOW.

THERE'S SOMETHING I MUST TELL YOU, DANE. I EXPECTED TO BE GONE BY NOW BUT I STAYED FOR YOU BECAUSE I WAS ASKED. AN OLD FRIEND ASKED ME.

I STAYED FOR A WHILE AND NOW MY WORK'S ALL DONE.

LOUDLA, DOODLA! COME MARCH TO WAKES AND FAIRS AND MARKET TOWNS. POOR TOM, THY HORN IS DRY.

WHAT A LONG, STRANGE DREAM IT'S BEEN. POOR TOM'S A-COLD. I CANNOT DANCE IT FARTHER.

IT'S GETTING NEAR TIME FOR ME TO GO.

I SEE MY LIFE NOW AS ONE SHAPE. I CAN SEE ITS EDGES AND BOUNDARIES. SO SMALL IT SEEMS.

LOOK! LOOK AT THOSE BEAUTIFUL ELECTRICITY PYLONS!

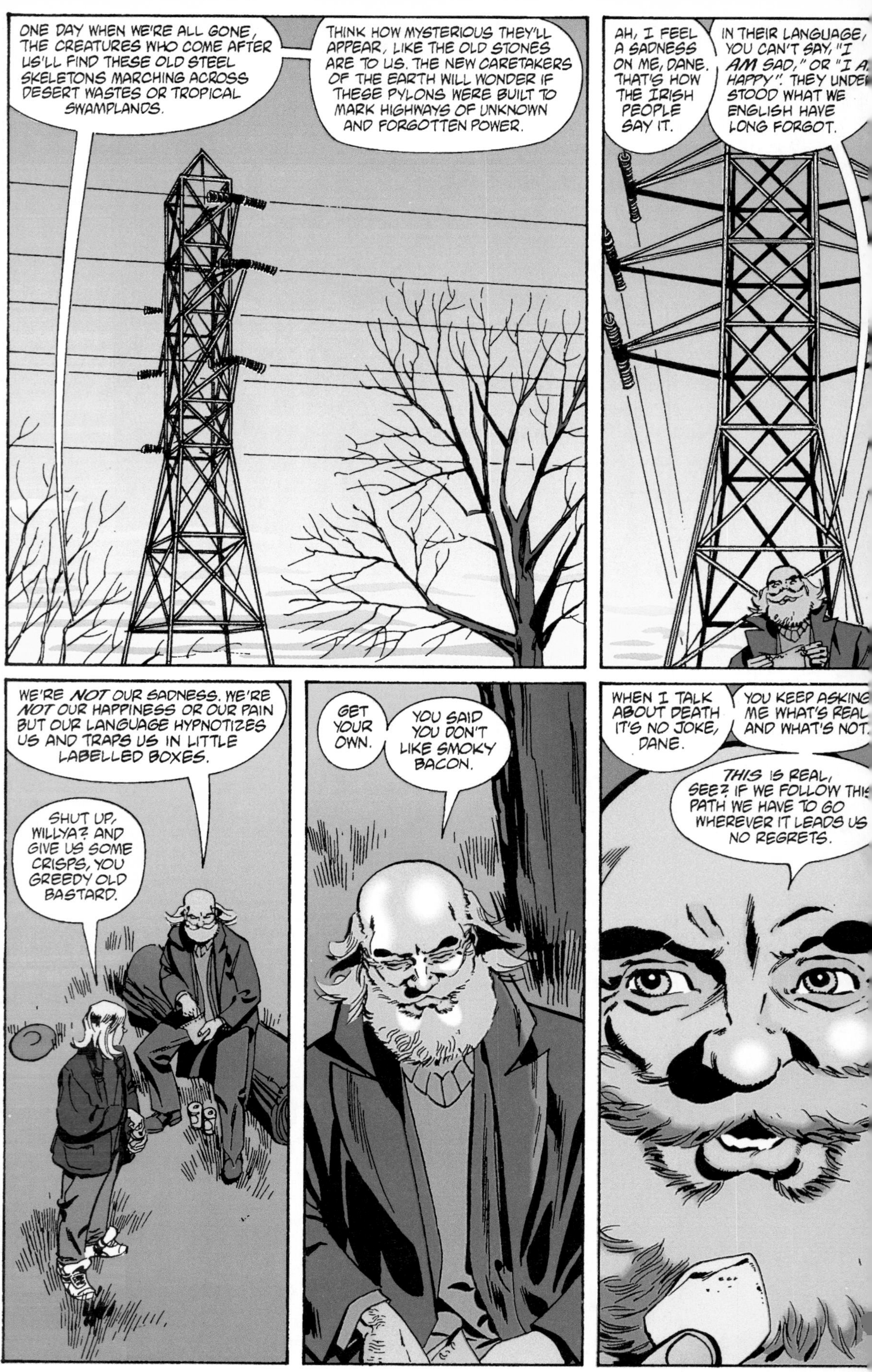
ONE DAY WHEN WE'RE ALL GONE, THE CREATURES WHO COME AFTER US'LL FIND THESE OLD STEEL SKELETONS MARCHING ACROSS DESERT WASTES OR TROPICAL SWAMPLANDS.
THINK HOW MYSTERIOUS THEY'LL APPEAR, LIKE THE OLD STONES ARE TO US. THE NEW CARETAKERS OF THE EARTH WILL WONDER IF THESE PYLONS WERE BUILT TO MARK HIGHWAYS OF UNKNOWN AND FORGOTTEN POWER.
AH, I FEEL A SADNESS ON ME, DANE. THAT'S HOW THE IRISH PEOPLE SAY IT.
IN THEIR LANGUAGE, YOU CAN'T SAY, "I AM SAD," OR "I A
HAPPY". THEY UNDE
STOOD WHAT WE ENGLISH HAVE LONG FORGOT.
WE'RE NOT OUR SADNESS. WE'RE NOT OUR HAPPINESS OR OUR PAIN BUT OUR LANGUAGE HYPNOTIZES US AND TRAPS US IN LITTLE LABELLED BOXES.
SHUT UP, WILLYA? AND GIVE US SOME CRISPS, YOU GREEDY OLD BASTARD.
GET YOUR OWN.
YOU SAID YOU DON'T LIKE SMOKY BACON.
WHEN I TALK ABOUT DEATH IT'S NO JOKE, DANE.
YOU KEEP ASKING ME WHAT'S REAL AND WHAT'S NOT.
THIS IS REAL, SEE? IF WE FOLLOW THIS PATH WE HAVE TO GO WHEREVER IT LEADS US NO REGRETS.

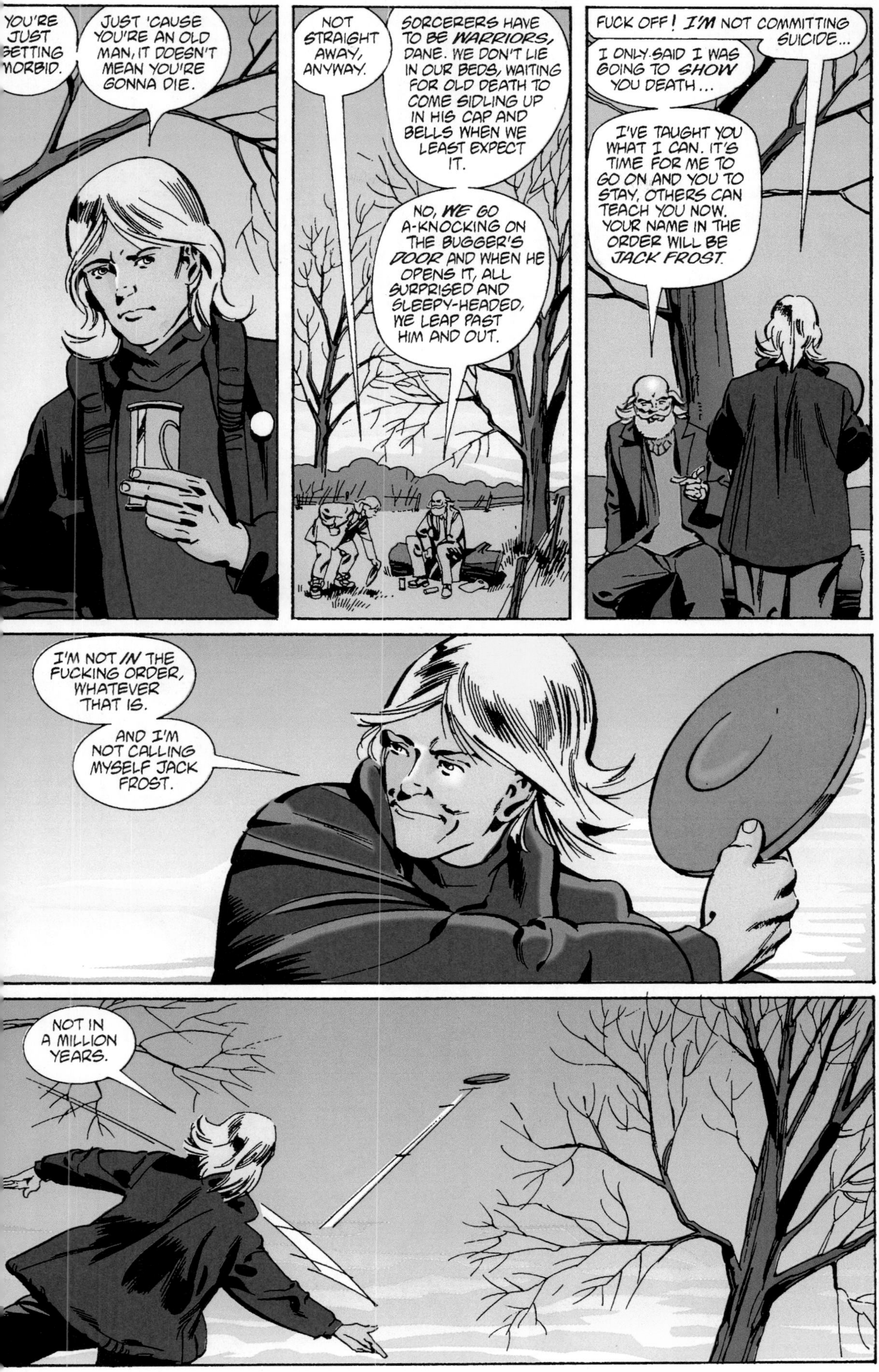
YOU'RE JUST GETTING MORBID.
JUST 'CAUSE YOU'RE AN OLD MAN, IT DOESN'T MEAN YOU'RE GONNA DIE.
NOT STRAIGHT AWAY, ANYWAY.
SORCERERS HAVE TO BE WARRIORS, DANE. WE DON'T LIE IN OUR BEDS, WAITING FOR OLD DEATH TO COME SIDLING UP IN HIS CAP AND BELLS WHEN WE LEAST EXPECT IT.
NO, WE GO A-KNOCKING ON THE BUGGER'S DOOR AND WHEN HE OPENS IT, ALL SURPRISED AND SLEEPY-HEADED, WE LEAP PAST HIM AND OUT.
FUCK OFF! I'M NOT COMMITTING SUICIDE...
I ONLY SAID I WAS GOING TO SHOW YOU DEATH...
I'VE TAUGHT YOU WHAT I CAN. IT'S TIME FOR ME TO GO ON AND YOU TO STAY. OTHERS CAN TEACH YOU NOW. YOUR NAME IN THE ORDER WILL BE JACK FROST.
I'M NOT IN THE FUCKING ORDER, WHATEVER THAT IS.
AND I'M NOT CALLING MYSELF JACK FROST.
NOT IN A MILLION YEARS.

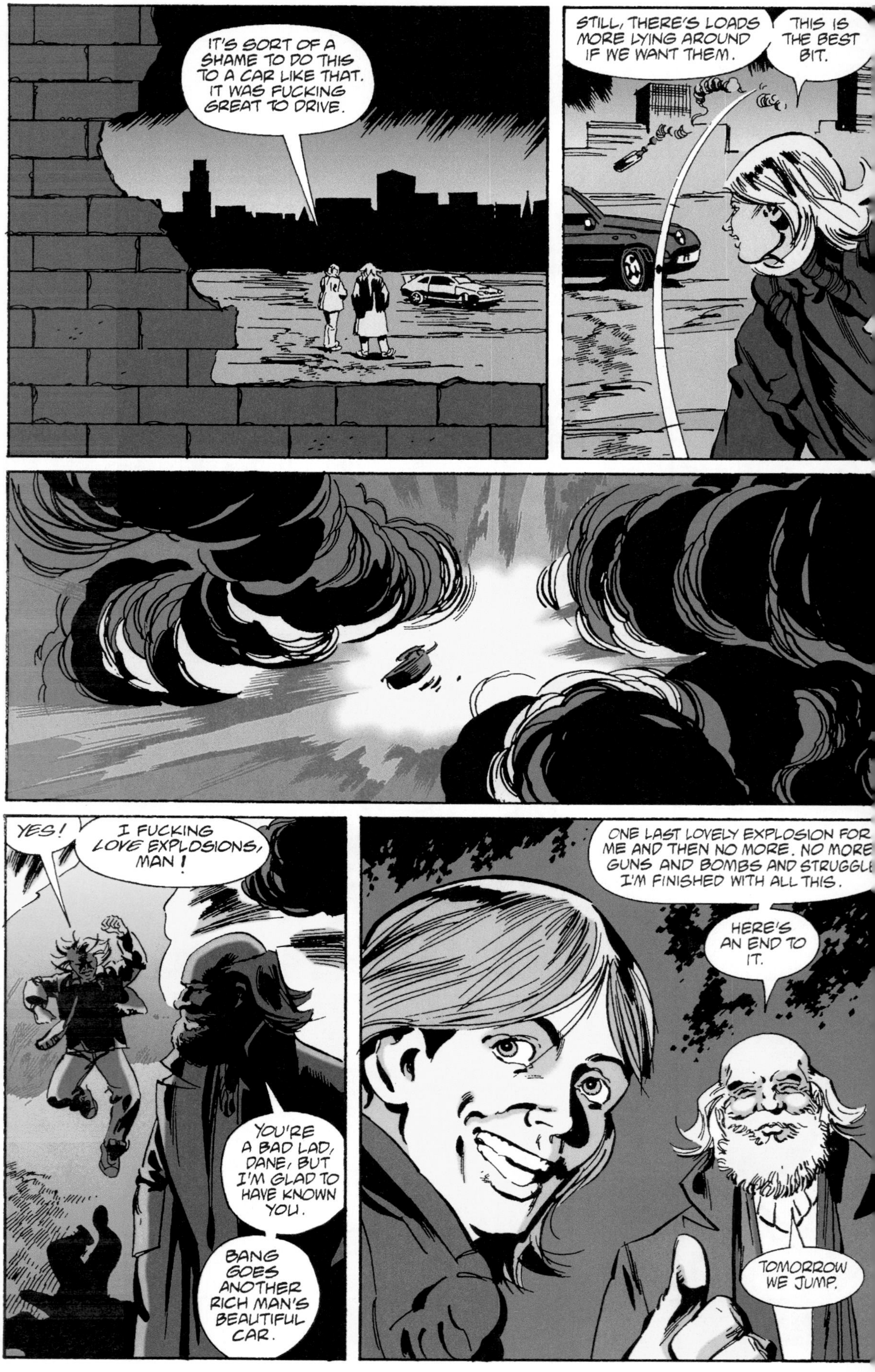
IT'S SORT OF A SHAME TO DO THIS TO A CAR LIKE THAT. IT WAS FUCKING GREAT TO DRIVE.
STILL, THERE'S LOADS MORE LYING AROUND IF WE WANT THEM.
THIS IS THE BEST BIT.
YES!
I FUCKING LOVE EXPLOSIONS, MAN!
YOU'RE A BAD LAD, DANE, BUT I'M GLAD TO HAVE KNOWN YOU.
BANG GOES ANOTHER RICH MAN'S BEAUTIFUL CAR.
ONE LAST LOVELY EXPLOSION FOR ME AND THEN NO MORE. NO MORE GUNS AND BOMBS AND STRUGGLE. I'M FINISHED WITH ALL THIS.
HERE'S AN END TO IT.
TOMORROW WE JUMP.

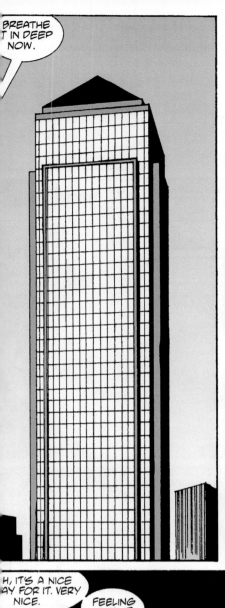

BREATHE
IT IN DEEP
NOW.

LET THE SMOKE SPILL
INTO YOUR BRAIN AND
OPEN ALL THOSE
STRANGE OLD DOORS
WITH FLAKING PAINT
IN THERE.

KKRRF!

WHAT
ABOUT
YOU?

I DON'T NEED
THE BLUE
MOLD NOW. I
GOT BETTER
WAYS TO GET
WHERE I'M
GOING.

THERE'S AN ADDRESS
ON THIS PIECE OF
PAPER HERE. I WANT
YOU TO KEEP IT IN
YOUR POCKET AND WHEN
WE'RE ALL DONE, THIS IS
WHERE YOU'LL FIND THEM
WAITING FOR YOU.

H, IT'S A NICE
AY FOR IT. VERY
NICE.

FEELING
OKAY?

I'M ALL RIGHT. I
DON'T FEEL THAT
OUT OF IT.

I DON'T
REALLY FEEL
OUT OF IT
AT ALL.

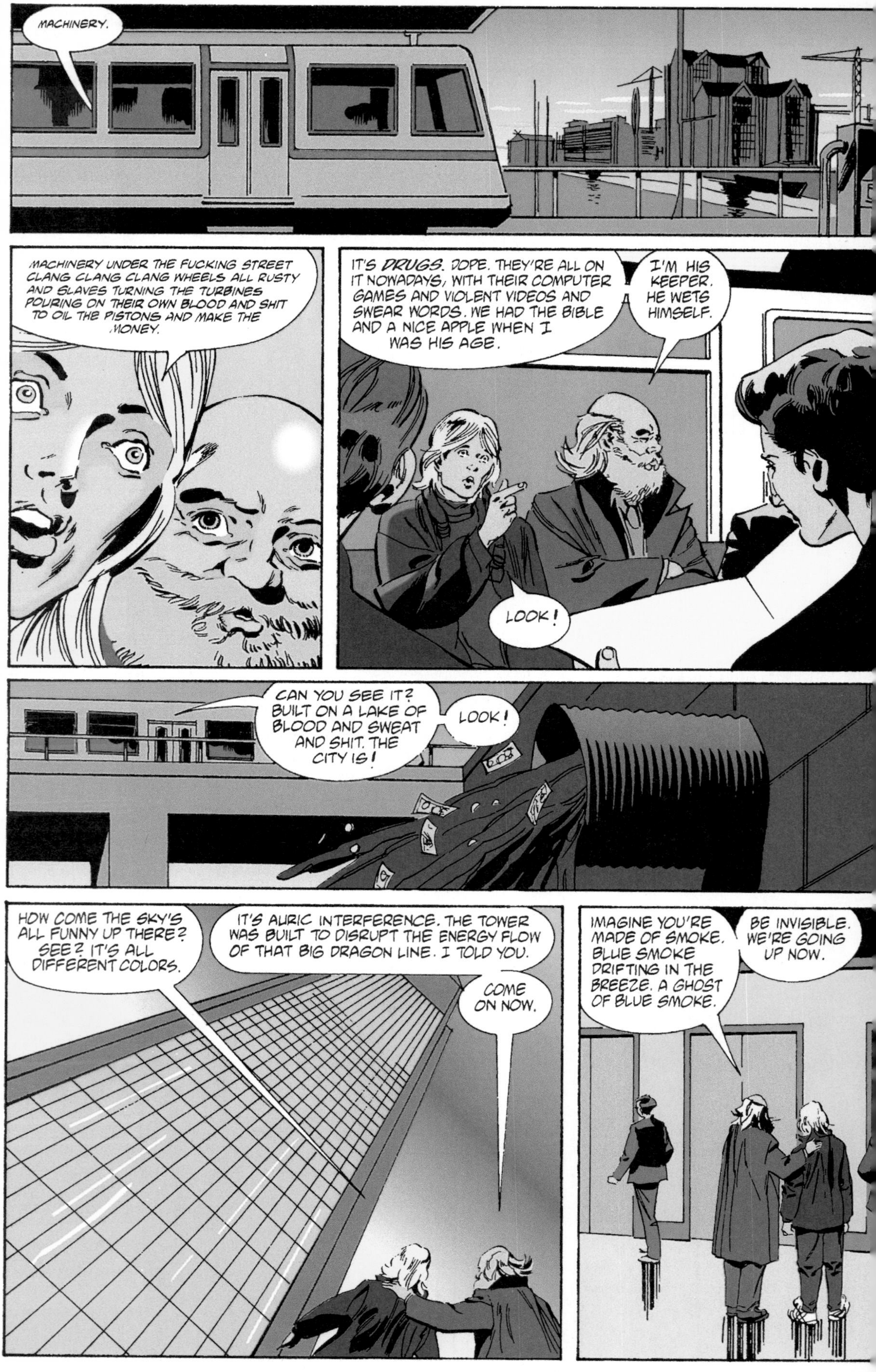
MACHINERY.
MACHINERY UNDER THE FUCKING STREET CLANG CLANG CLANG WHEELS ALL RUSTY AND SLAVES TURNING THE TURBINES POURING ON THEIR OWN BLOOD AND SHIT TO OIL THE PISTONS AND MAKE THE MONEY.
IT'S DRUGS. DOPE. THEY'RE ALL ON IT NOWADAYS, WITH THEIR COMPUTER GAMES AND VIOLENT VIDEOS AND SWEAR WORDS. WE HAD THE BIBLE AND A NICE APPLE WHEN I WAS HIS AGE.
I'M HIS KEEPER. HE WETS HIMSELF.
LOOK!
CAN YOU SEE IT? BUILT ON A LAKE OF BLOOD AND SWEAT AND SHIT. THE CITY IS!
LOOK!
HOW COME THE SKY'S ALL FUNNY UP THERE? SEE? IT'S ALL DIFFERENT COLORS.
IT'S AURIC INTERFERENCE. THE TOWER WAS BUILT TO DISRUPT THE ENERGY FLOW OF THAT BIG DRAGON LINE. I TOLD YOU.
COME ON NOW.
IMAGINE YOU'RE MADE OF SMOKE. BLUE SMOKE DRIFTING IN THE BREEZE. A GHOST OF BLUE SMOKE.
BE INVISIBLE. WE'RE GOING UP NOW.

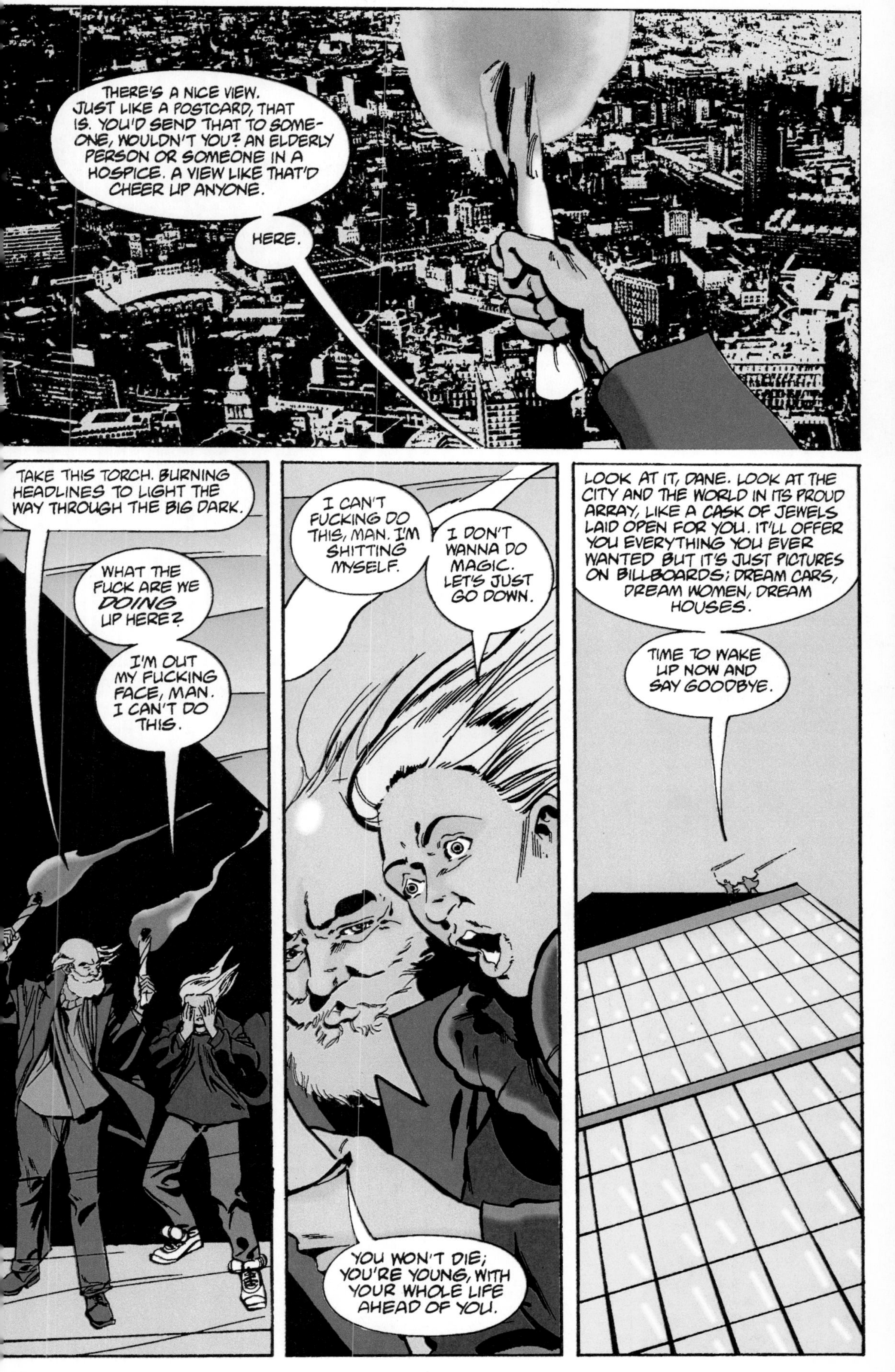
THERE'S A NICE VIEW. JUST LIKE A POSTCARD, THAT IS. YOU'D SEND THAT TO SOMEONE, WOULDN'T YOU? AN ELDERLY PERSON OR SOMEONE IN A HOSPICE. A VIEW LIKE THAT'D CHEER UP ANYONE.
HERE.
TAKE THIS TORCH. BURNING HEADLINES TO LIGHT THE WAY THROUGH THE BIG DARK.
WHAT THE FUCK ARE WE *DOING* UP HERE?
I'M OUT MY FUCKING FACE, MAN. I CAN'T DO THIS.
I CAN'T FUCKING DO THIS, MAN. I'M SHITTING MYSELF.
I DON'T WANNA DO MAGIC. LET'S JUST GO DOWN.
YOU WON'T DIE; YOU'RE YOUNG, WITH YOUR WHOLE LIFE AHEAD OF YOU.
LOOK AT IT, DANE. LOOK AT THE CITY AND THE WORLD IN ITS PROUD ARRAY, LIKE A CASK OF JEWELS LAID OPEN FOR YOU. IT'LL OFFER YOU EVERYTHING YOU EVER WANTED BUT IT'S JUST PICTURES ON BILLBOARDS; DREAM CARS, DREAM WOMEN, DREAM HOUSES.
TIME TO WAKE UP NOW AND SAY GOODBYE.

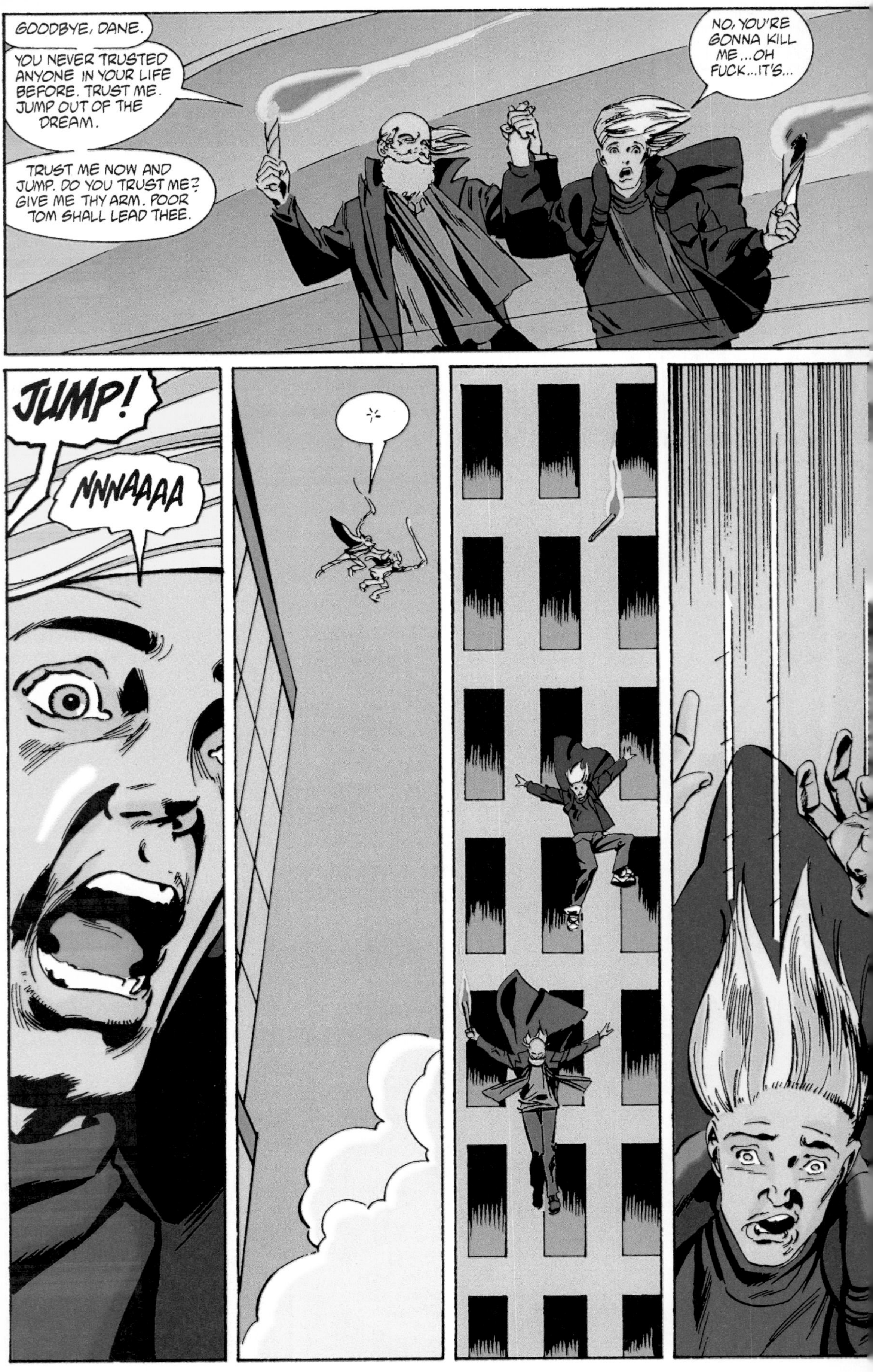
GOODBYE, DANE.
YOU NEVER TRUSTED ANYONE IN YOUR LIFE BEFORE. TRUST ME. JUMP OUT OF THE DREAM.
TRUST ME NOW AND JUMP. DO YOU TRUST ME? GIVE ME THY ARM. POOR TOM SHALL LEAD THEE.
NO, YOU'RE GONNA KILL ME...OH FUCK...IT'S...
JUMP!
NNNAAAA

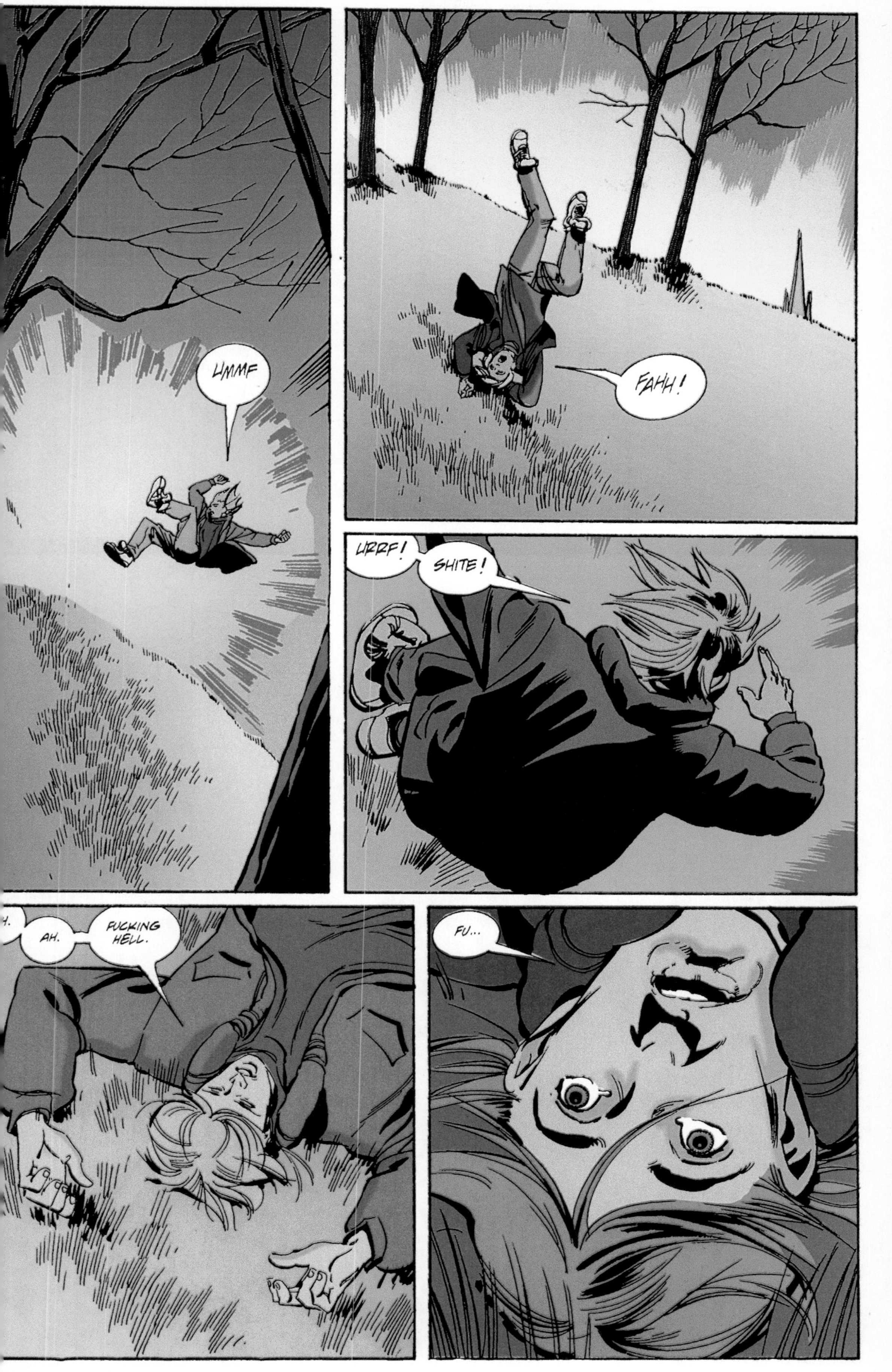
UMMF
FAHH!
URRF!
SHITE!
AH.
FUCKING HELL.
FU...

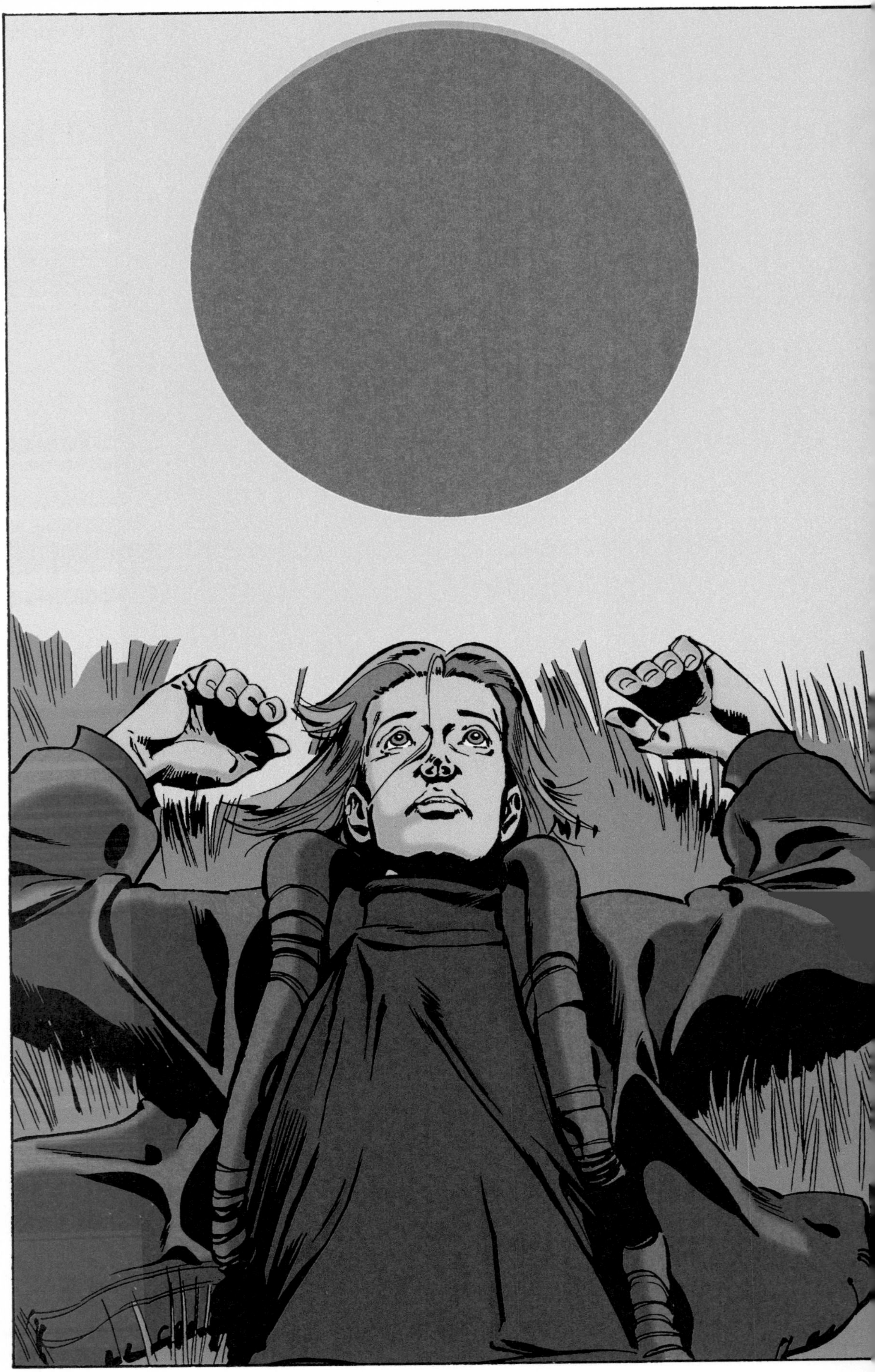

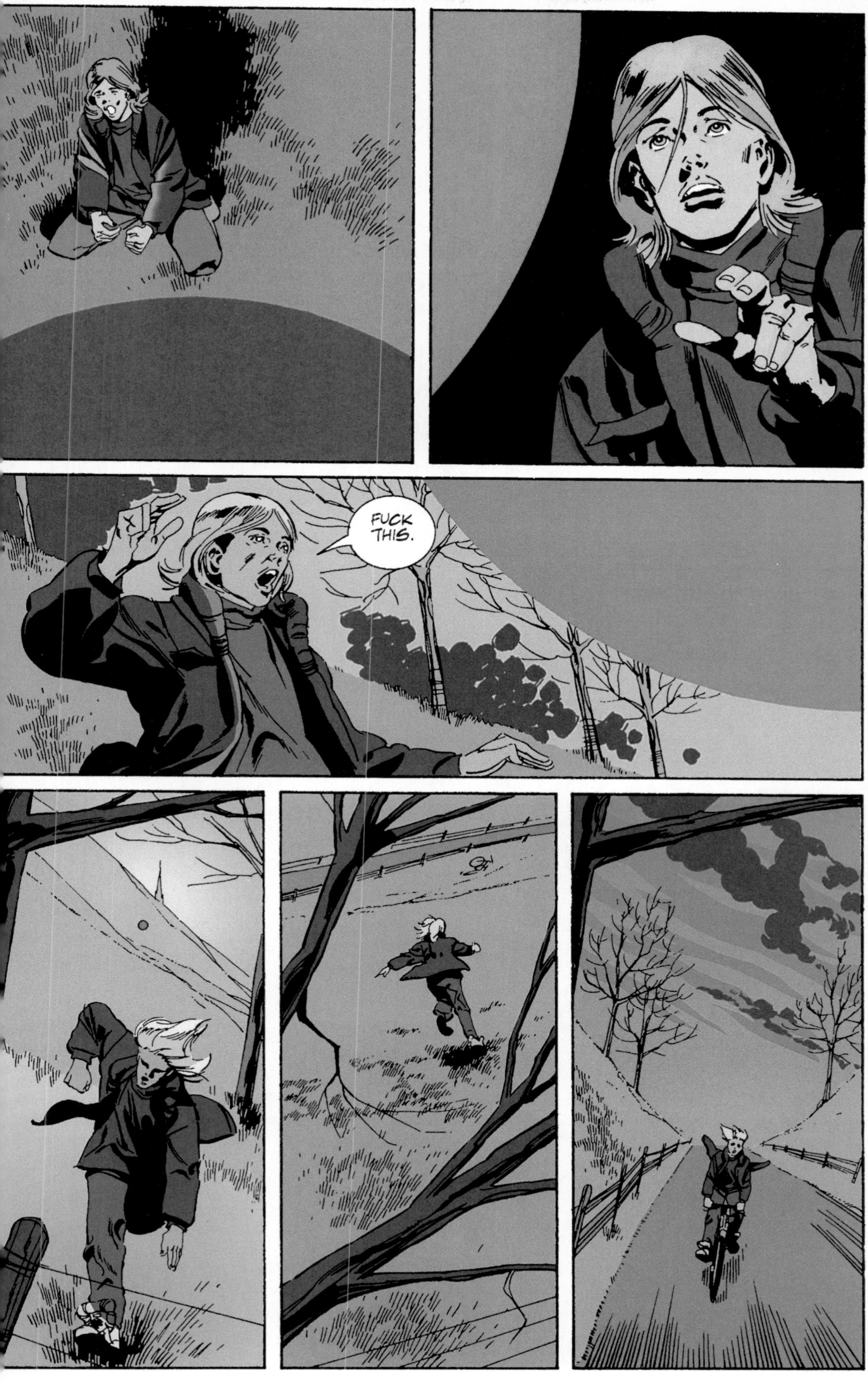
FUCK THIS.

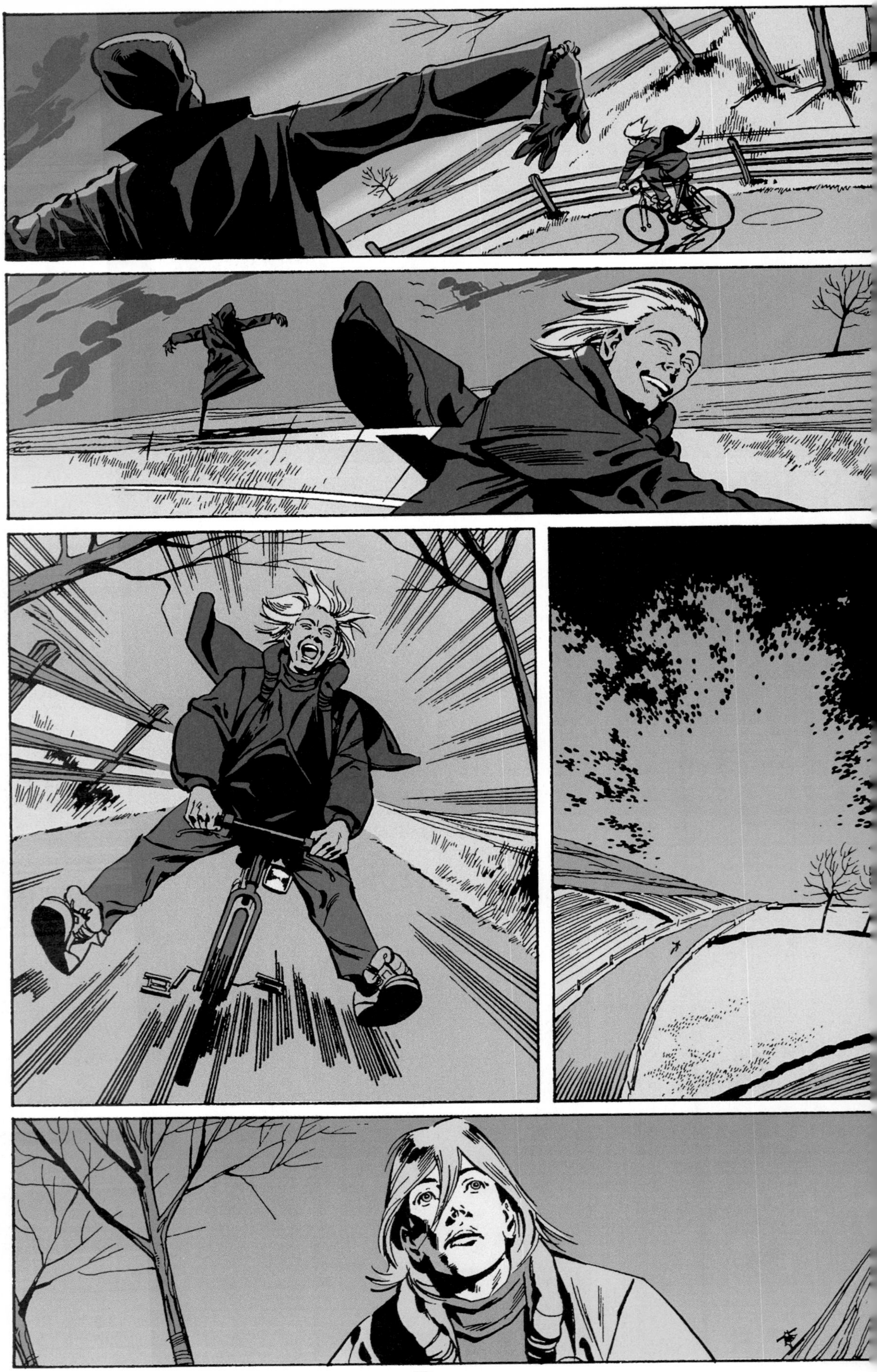

JESUS.

FUCKING HELL.

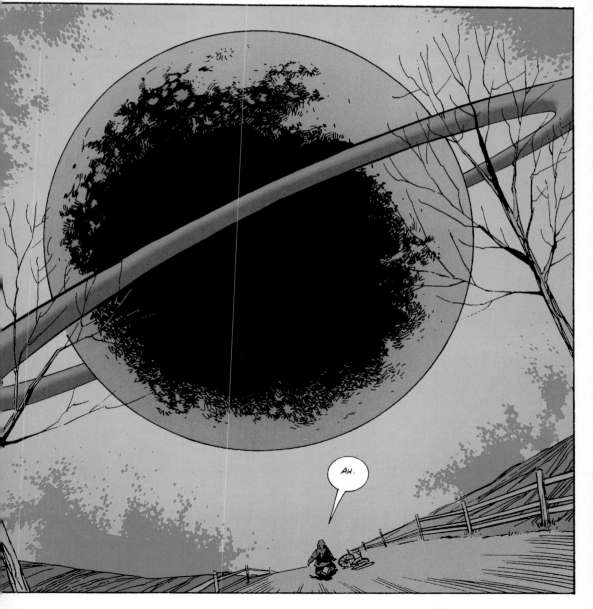

AH.

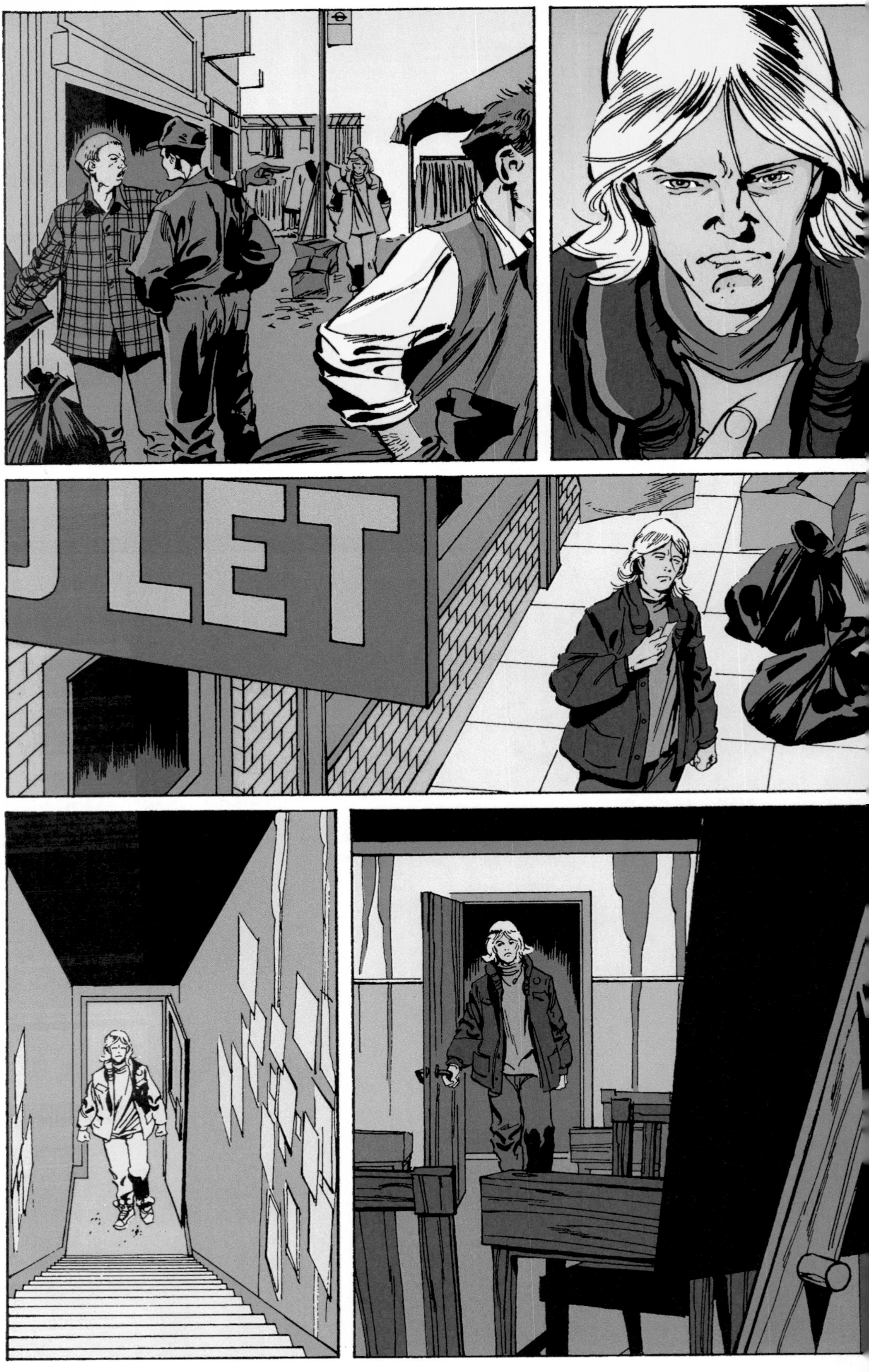

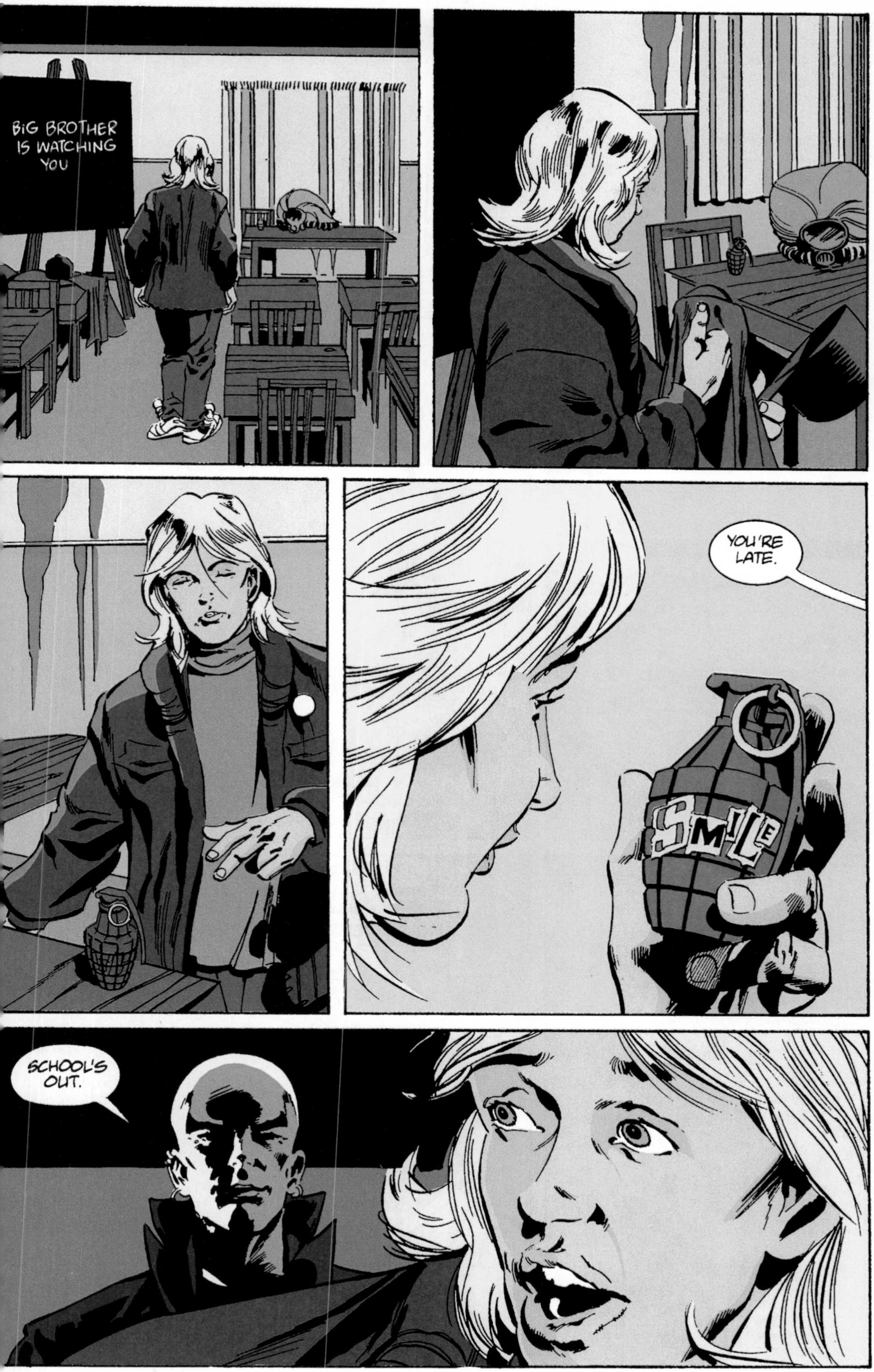
BIG BROTHER IS WATCHING YOU
YOU'RE LATE.
SMILE
SCHOOL'S OUT.

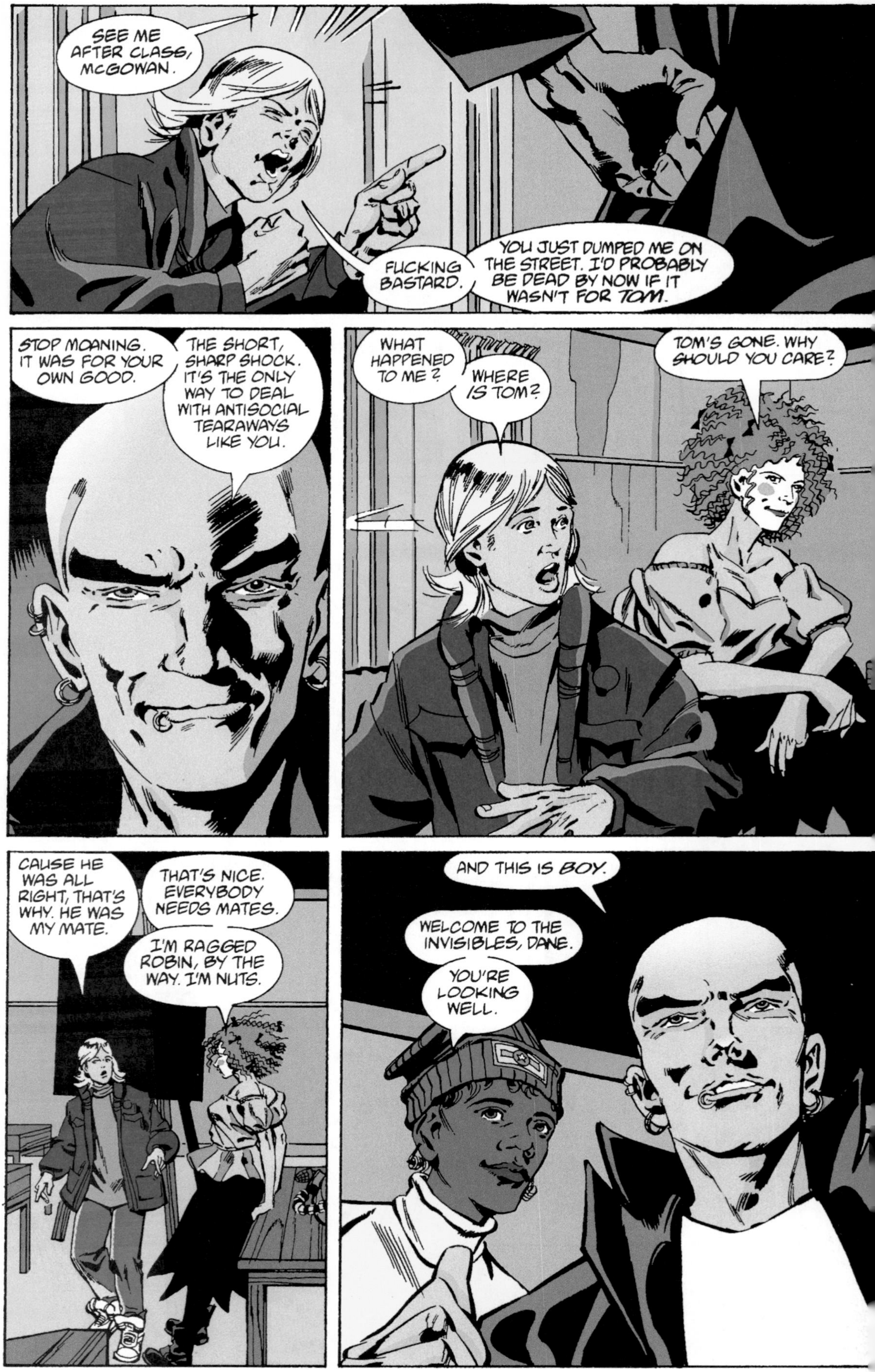
SEE ME AFTER CLASS, McGOWAN.
FUCKING BASTARD.
YOU JUST DUMPED ME ON THE STREET. I'D PROBABLY BE DEAD BY NOW IF IT WASN'T FOR TOM.
STOP MOANING. IT WAS FOR YOUR OWN GOOD.
THE SHORT, SHARP SHOCK. IT'S THE ONLY WAY TO DEAL WITH ANTISOCIAL TEARAWAYS LIKE YOU.
WHAT HAPPENED TO ME?
WHERE IS TOM?
TOM'S GONE. WHY SHOULD YOU CARE?
CAUSE HE WAS ALL RIGHT, THAT'S WHY. HE WAS MY MATE.
THAT'S NICE. EVERYBODY NEEDS MATES.
I'M RAGGED ROBIN, BY THE WAY. I'M NUTS.
AND THIS IS BOY.
WELCOME TO THE INVISIBLES, DANE.
YOU'RE LOOKING WELL.

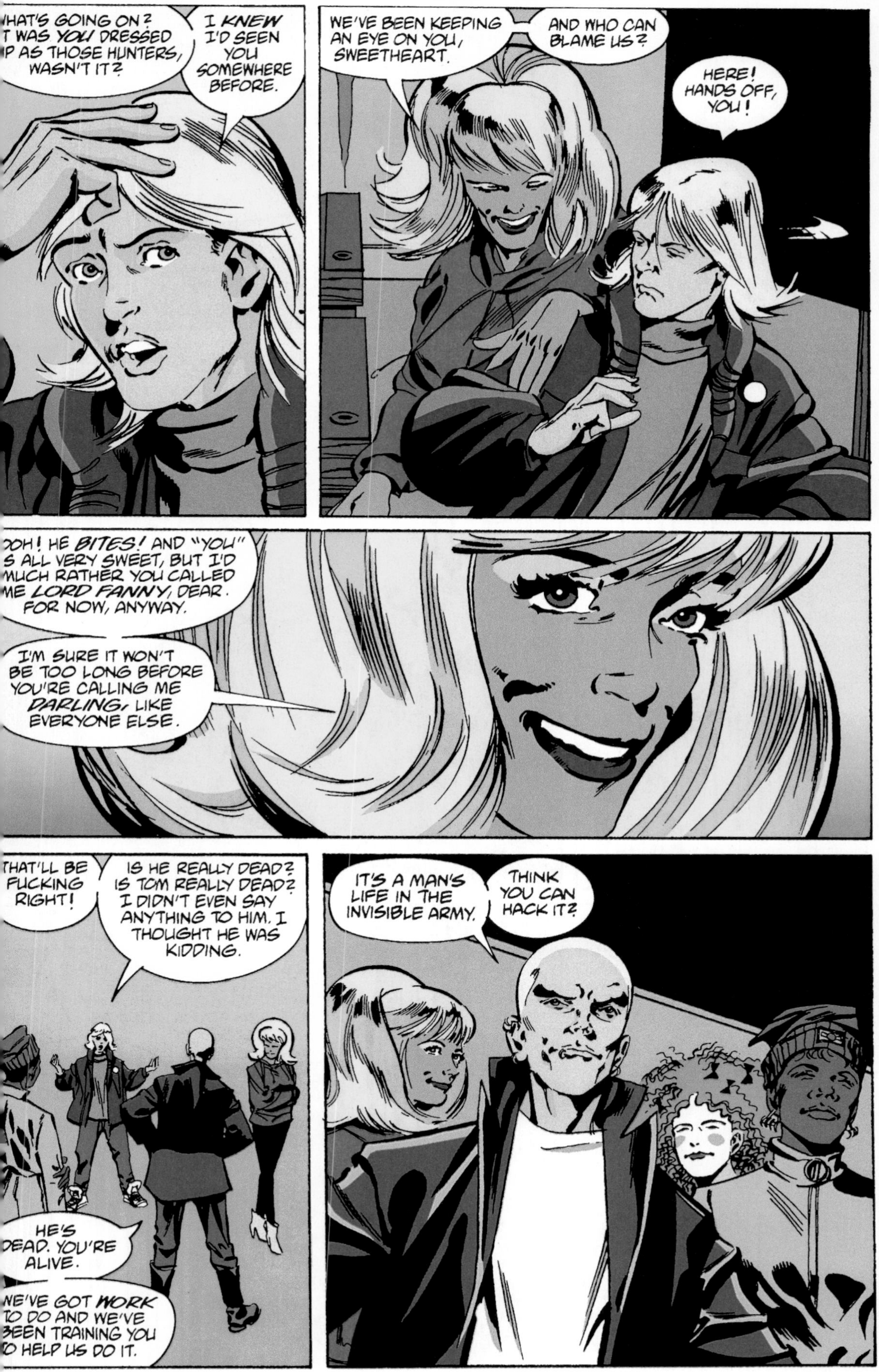

WHAT'S GOING ON? IT WAS YOU! DRESSED UP AS THOSE HUNTERS, WASN'T IT?
I KNEW I'D SEEN YOU SOMEWHERE BEFORE.
WE'VE BEEN KEEPING AN EYE ON YOU, SWEETHEART.
AND WHO CAN BLAME US?
HERE! HANDS OFF, YOU!
OOH! HE BITES! AND "YOU" IS ALL VERY SWEET, BUT I'D MUCH RATHER YOU CALLED ME LORD FANNY, DEAR. FOR NOW, ANYWAY.
I'M SURE IT WON'T BE TOO LONG BEFORE YOU'RE CALLING ME DARLING, LIKE EVERYONE ELSE.
THAT'LL BE FUCKING RIGHT!
IS HE REALLY DEAD? IS TOM REALLY DEAD? I DIDN'T EVEN SAY ANYTHING TO HIM. I THOUGHT HE WAS KIDDING.
HE'S DEAD. YOU'RE ALIVE.
WE'VE GOT WORK TO DO AND WE'VE BEEN TRAINING YOU TO HELP US DO IT.
IT'S A MAN'S LIFE IN THE INVISIBLE ARMY.
THINK YOU CAN HACK IT?

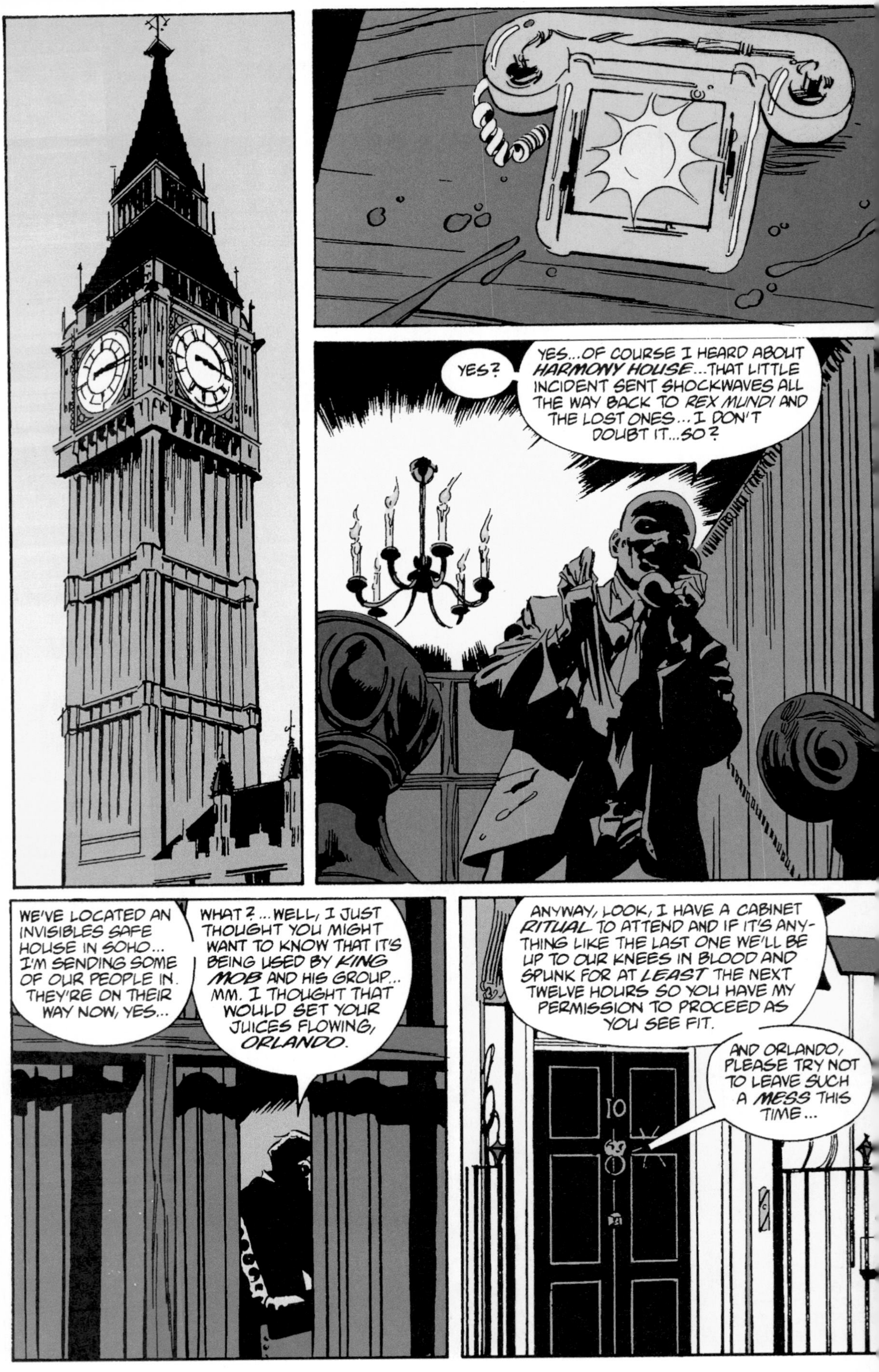
YES?
YES...OF COURSE I HEARD ABOUT HARMONY HOUSE...THAT LITTLE INCIDENT SENT SHOCKWAVES ALL THE WAY BACK TO REX MUNDI AND THE LOST ONES... I DON'T DOUBT IT...SO?
WE'VE LOCATED AN INVISIBLES SAFE HOUSE IN SOHO... I'M SENDING SOME OF OUR PEOPLE IN. THEY'RE ON THEIR WAY NOW, YES...
WHAT? ...WELL, I JUST THOUGHT YOU MIGHT WANT TO KNOW THAT IT'S BEING USED BY KING MOB AND HIS GROUP... MM. I THOUGHT THAT WOULD SET YOUR JUICES FLOWING, ORLANDO.
ANYWAY, LOOK, I HAVE A CABINET RITUAL TO ATTEND AND IF IT'S ANYTHING LIKE THE LAST ONE WE'LL BE UP TO OUR KNEES IN BLOOD AND SPUNK FOR AT LEAST THE NEXT TWELVE HOURS SO YOU HAVE MY PERMISSION TO PROCEED AS YOU SEE FIT.
AND ORLANDO, PLEASE TRY NOT TO LEAVE SUCH A MESS THIS TIME...

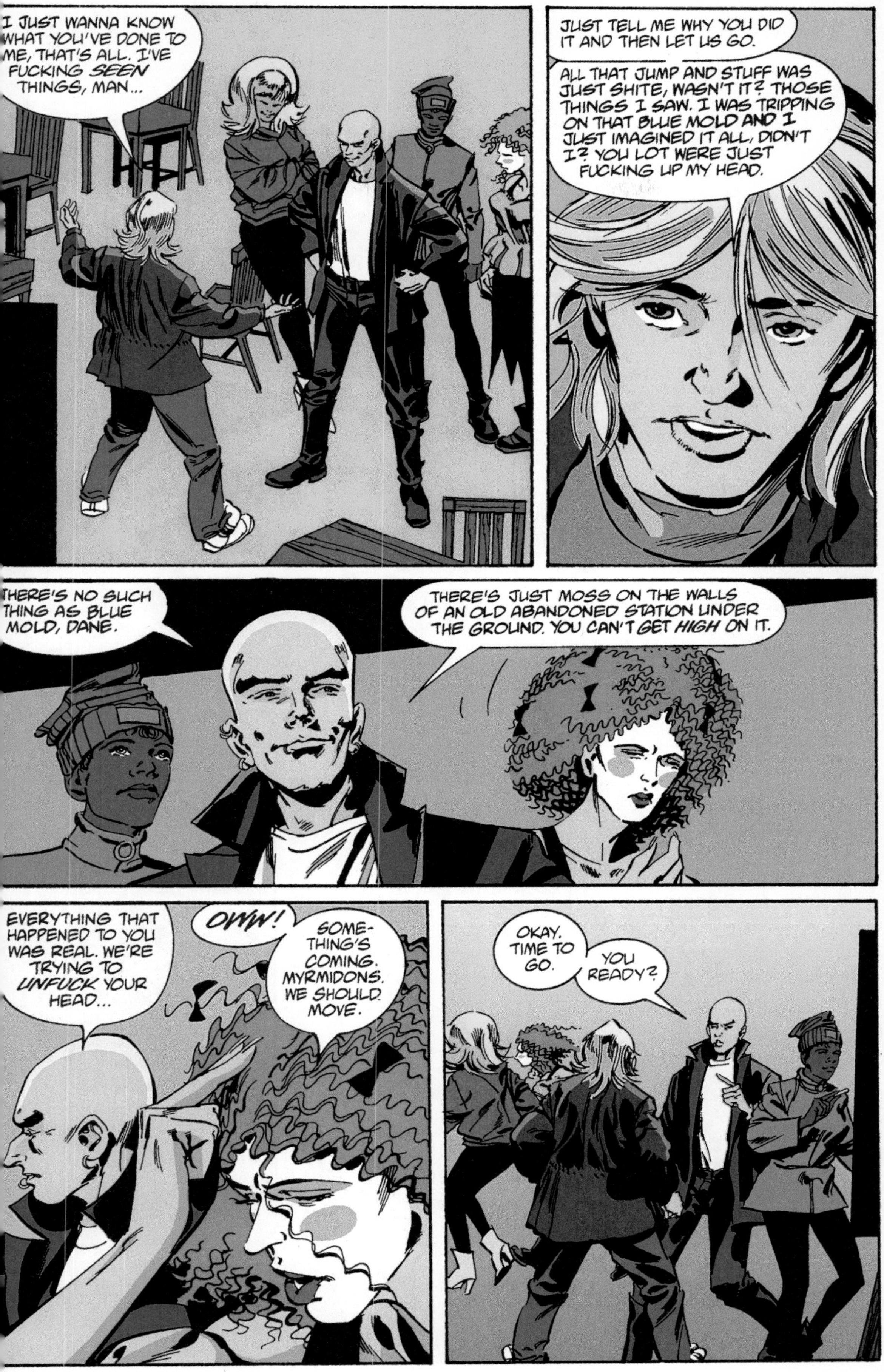
I JUST WANNA KNOW WHAT YOU'VE DONE TO ME, THAT'S ALL. I'VE FUCKING *SEEN* THINGS, MAN...
JUST TELL ME WHY YOU DID IT AND THEN LET US GO.
ALL THAT JUMP AND STUFF WAS JUST SHITE, WASN'T IT? THOSE THINGS I SAW. I WAS TRIPPING ON THAT BLUE MOLD AND I JUST IMAGINED IT ALL, DIDN'T I? YOU LOT WERE JUST FUCKING UP MY HEAD.
THERE'S NO SUCH THING AS BLUE MOLD, DANE.
THERE'S JUST MOSS ON THE WALLS OF AN OLD ABANDONED STATION UNDER THE GROUND. YOU CAN'T GET *HIGH* ON IT.
EVERYTHING THAT HAPPENED TO YOU WAS REAL. WE'RE TRYING TO *UNFUCK* YOUR HEAD...
OWW!
SOME-THING'S COMING. MYRMIDONS. WE SHOULD MOVE.
OKAY. TIME TO GO.
YOU READY?

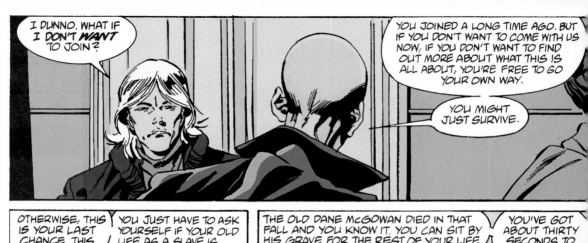

I DUNNO. WHAT IF I DON'T *WANT* TO JOIN?

YOU JOINED A LONG TIME AGO. BUT IF YOU DON'T WANT TO COME WITH US NOW, IF YOU DON'T WANT TO FIND OUT MORE ABOUT WHAT THIS IS ALL ABOUT, YOU'RE FREE TO GO YOUR OWN WAY.

YOU MIGHT JUST SURVIVE.

OTHERWISE, THIS IS YOUR LAST CHANCE. THIS DOOR ONLY OPENS ONCE.

YOU JUST HAVE TO ASK YOURSELF IF YOUR OLD LIFE AS A SLAVE IS WORTH CLINGING ON TO AND WEIGH THAT UP AGAINST THE CHANCE OF BECOMING FREE IN WAYS YOU CAN'T IMAGINE.

THE OLD DANE McGOWAN DIED IN THAT FALL AND YOU KNOW IT. YOU CAN SIT BY HIS GRAVE FOR THE REST OF YOUR LIFE OR YOU CAN JOIN US AND BE *JACK FROST.*

YOU'VE GOT ABOUT THIRTY SECONDS TO THINK IT OVER.

EVERY-BODY OUT!

GO GO GO!

EY!

HANG ON A MINUTE!

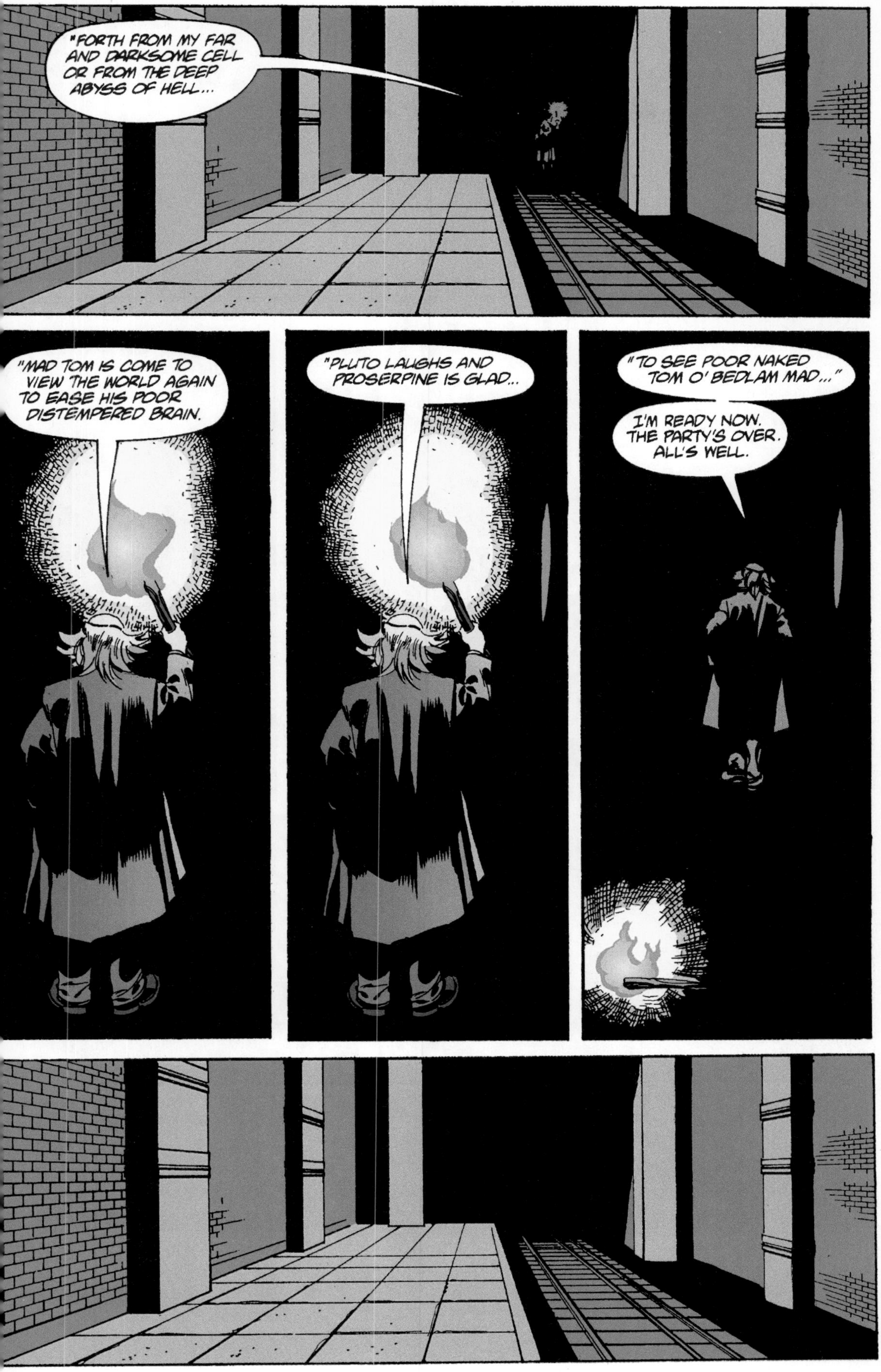
"FORTH FROM MY FAR AND DARKSOME CELL OR FROM THE DEEP ABYSS OF HELL...
"MAD TOM IS COME TO VIEW THE WORLD AGAIN TO EASE HIS POOR DISTEMPERED BRAIN.
"PLUTO LAUGHS AND PROSERPINE IS GLAD...
"TO SEE POOR NAKED TOM O' BEDLAM MAD..."
I'M READY NOW. THE PARTY'S OVER. ALL'S WELL.

SHIT!

I CAN SMELL THEM! I CAN FUCKING SMELL THEM!

SIR! THERE! ON THE DESK.

THEY CAN'T HAVE GOT FAR.

BIG BROTHER IS WATCHING YOU

LEARN TO BECOME INVISIBLE

BASTARDS! IT'S ALWAYS...SHIT...

NO PIN. SHIT! THERE'S NO PIN.

GET OUT!

SMILE

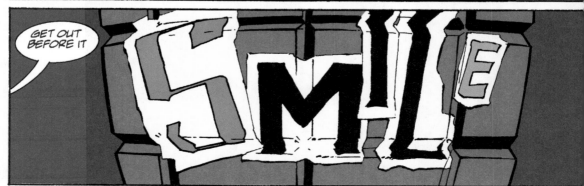

GET OUT BEFORE IT

SMILE

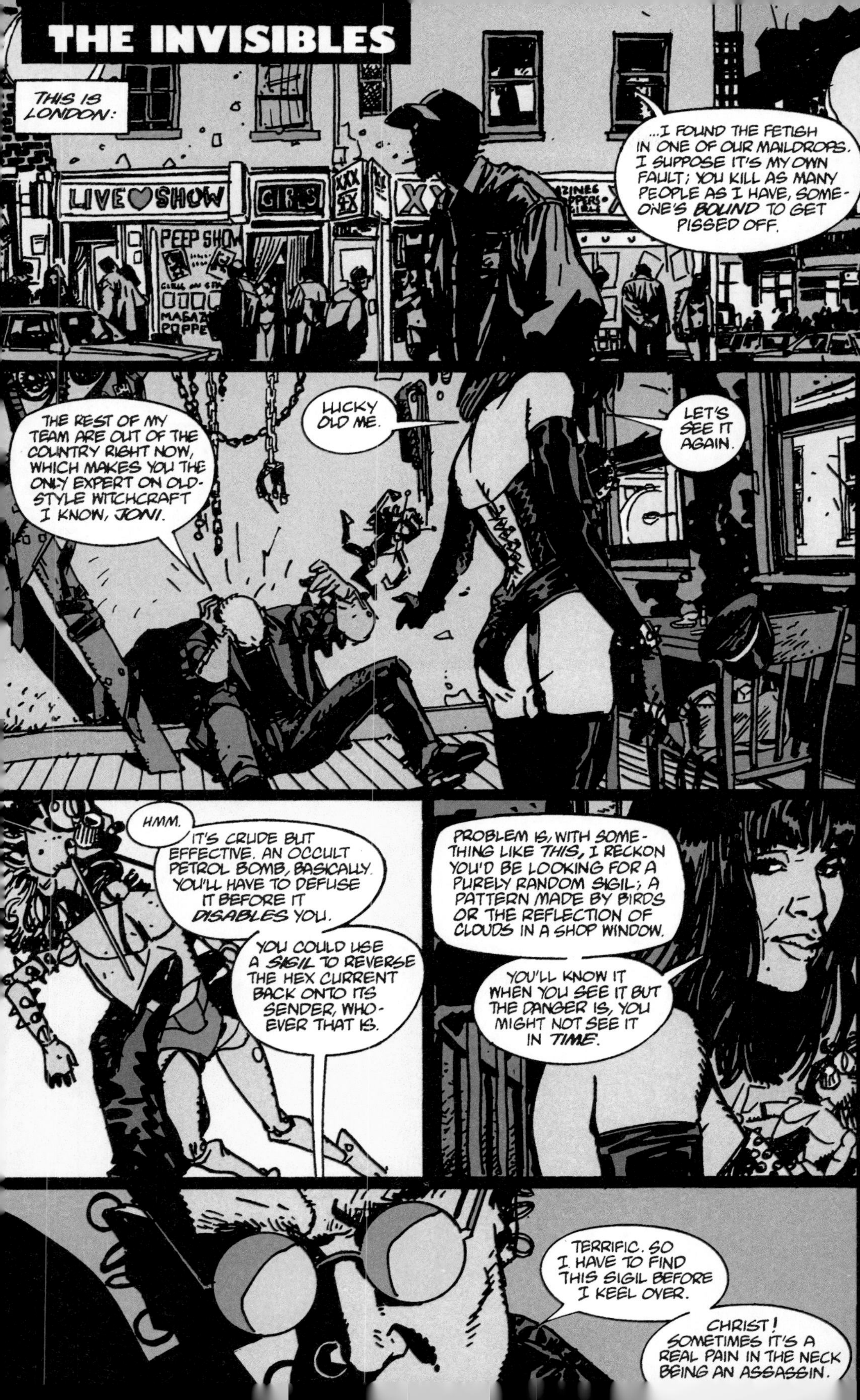
THE INVISIBLES
THIS IS LONDON:
LIVE SHOW
GIRLS
XXX SEX
PEEP SHOW
...I FOUND THE FETISH IN ONE OF OUR MAILDROPS. I SUPPOSE IT'S MY OWN FAULT; YOU KILL AS MANY PEOPLE AS I HAVE, SOMEONE'S BOUND TO GET PISSED OFF.
THE REST OF MY TEAM ARE OUT OF THE COUNTRY RIGHT NOW, WHICH MAKES YOU THE ONLY EXPERT ON OLD-STYLE WITCHCRAFT I KNOW, JONI.
LUCKY OLD ME.
LET'S SEE IT AGAIN.
HMM.
IT'S CRUDE BUT EFFECTIVE. AN OCCULT PETROL BOMB, BASICALLY. YOU'LL HAVE TO DEFUSE IT BEFORE IT DISABLES YOU.
YOU COULD USE A SIGIL TO REVERSE THE HEX CURRENT BACK ONTO ITS SENDER, WHOEVER THAT IS.
PROBLEM IS, WITH SOMETHING LIKE THIS, I RECKON YOU'D BE LOOKING FOR A PURELY RANDOM SIGIL; A PATTERN MADE BY BIRDS OR THE REFLECTION OF CLOUDS IN A SHOP WINDOW.
YOU'LL KNOW IT WHEN YOU SEE IT BUT THE DANGER IS, YOU MIGHT NOT SEE IT IN TIME.
TERRIFIC. SO I HAVE TO FIND THIS SIGIL BEFORE I KEEL OVER.
CHRIST! SOMETIMES IT'S A REAL PAIN IN THE NECK BEING AN ASSASSIN.

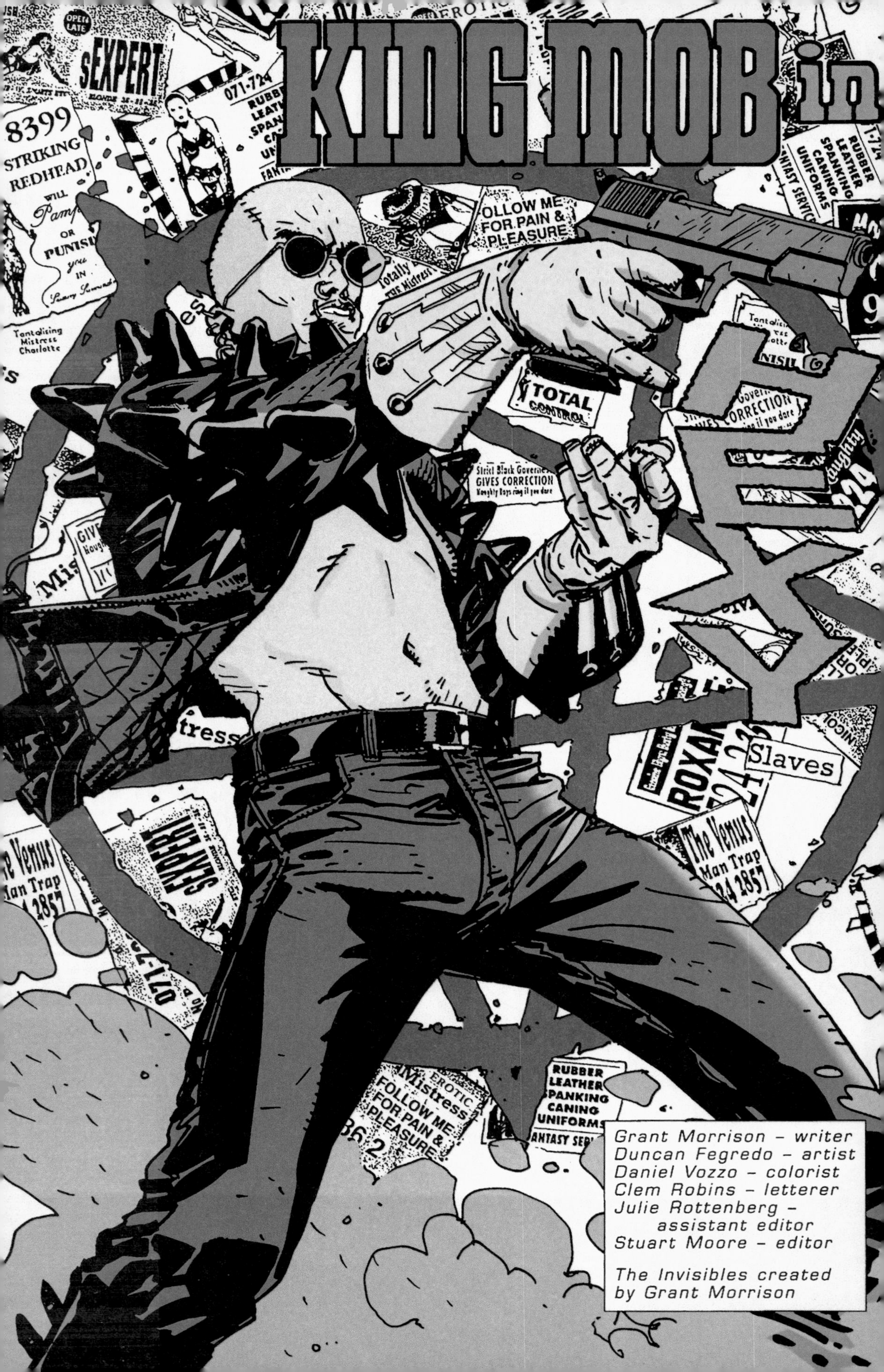
KING MOB in
Grant Morrison – writer
Duncan Fegredo – artist
Daniel Vozzo – colorist
Clem Robins – letterer
Julie Rottenberg – assistant editor
Stuart Moore – editor
The Invisibles created by Grant Morrison

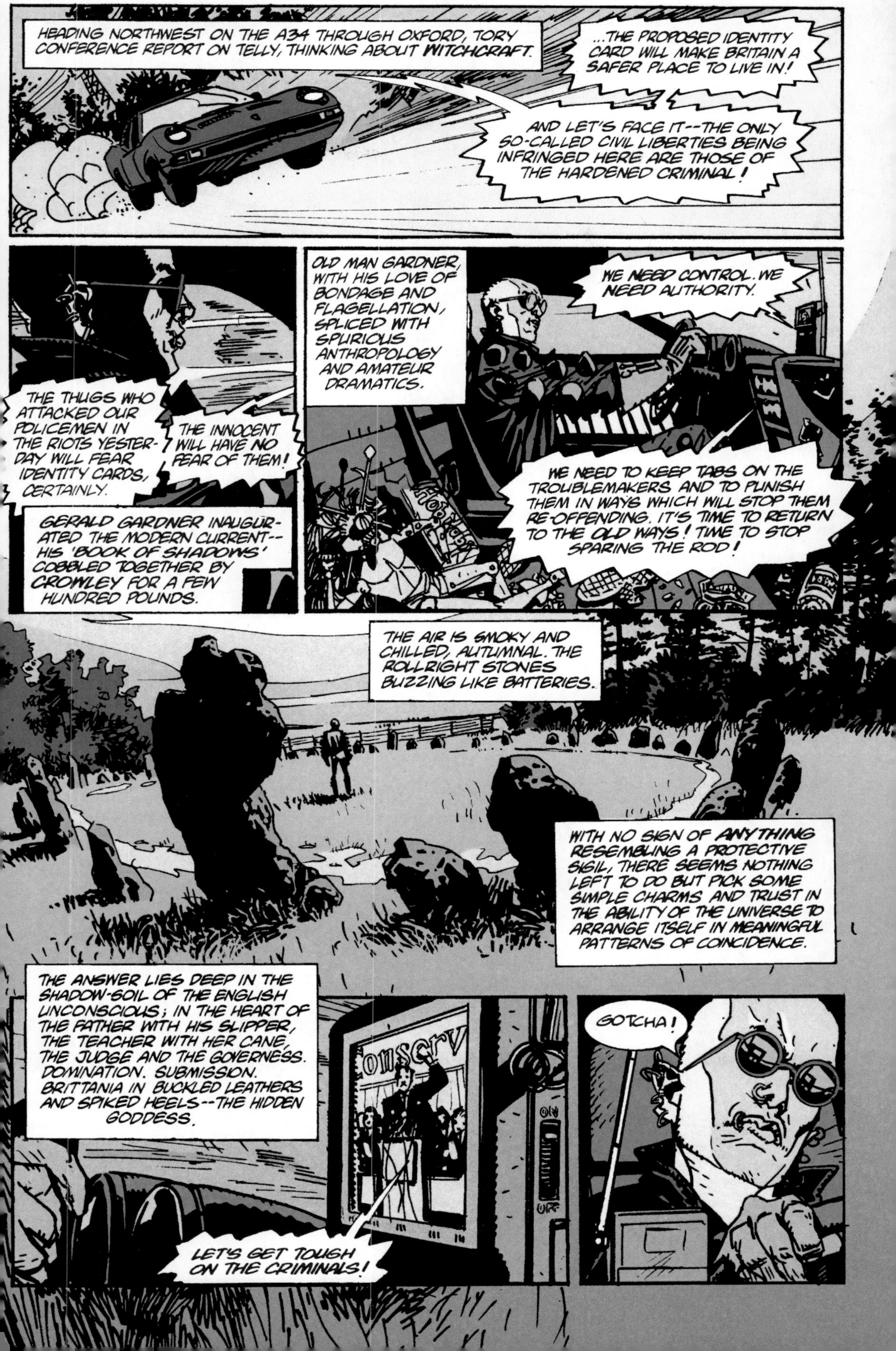
HEADING NORTHWEST ON THE A34 THROUGH OXFORD, TORY CONFERENCE REPORT ON TELLY, THINKING ABOUT WITCHCRAFT.
...THE PROPOSED IDENTITY CARD WILL MAKE BRITAIN A SAFER PLACE TO LIVE IN!
AND LET'S FACE IT--THE ONLY SO-CALLED CIVIL LIBERTIES BEING INFRINGED HERE ARE THOSE OF THE HARDENED CRIMINAL!
THE THUGS WHO ATTACKED OUR POLICEMEN IN THE RIOTS YESTERDAY WILL FEAR IDENTITY CARDS, CERTAINLY.
THE INNOCENT WILL HAVE NO FEAR OF THEM!
GERALD GARDNER INAUGURATED THE MODERN CURRENT-- HIS 'BOOK OF SHADOWS' COBBLED TOGETHER BY CROWLEY FOR A FEW HUNDRED POUNDS.
OLD MAN GARDNER, WITH HIS LOVE OF BONDAGE AND FLAGELLATION, SPLICED WITH SPURIOUS ANTHROPOLOGY AND AMATEUR DRAMATICS.
WE NEED CONTROL. WE NEED AUTHORITY.
WE NEED TO KEEP TABS ON THE TROUBLEMAKERS AND TO PUNISH THEM IN WAYS WHICH WILL STOP THEM RE-OFFENDING. IT'S TIME TO RETURN TO THE OLD WAYS! TIME TO STOP SPARING THE ROD!
THE AIR IS SMOKY AND CHILLED, AUTUMNAL. THE ROLLRIGHT STONES BUZZING LIKE BATTERIES.
WITH NO SIGN OF ANYTHING RESEMBLING A PROTECTIVE SIGIL, THERE SEEMS NOTHING LEFT TO DO BUT PICK SOME SIMPLE CHARMS AND TRUST IN THE ABILITY OF THE UNIVERSE TO ARRANGE ITSELF IN MEANINGFUL PATTERNS OF COINCIDENCE.
THE ANSWER LIES DEEP IN THE SHADOW-SOIL OF THE ENGLISH UNCONSCIOUS; IN THE HEART OF THE FATHER WITH HIS SLIPPER, THE TEACHER WITH HER CANE, THE JUDGE AND THE GOVERNESS. DOMINATION. SUBMISSION. BRITTANIA IN BUCKLED LEATHERS AND SPIKED HEELS--THE HIDDEN GODDESS.
LET'S GET TOUGH ON THE CRIMINALS!
GOTCHA!

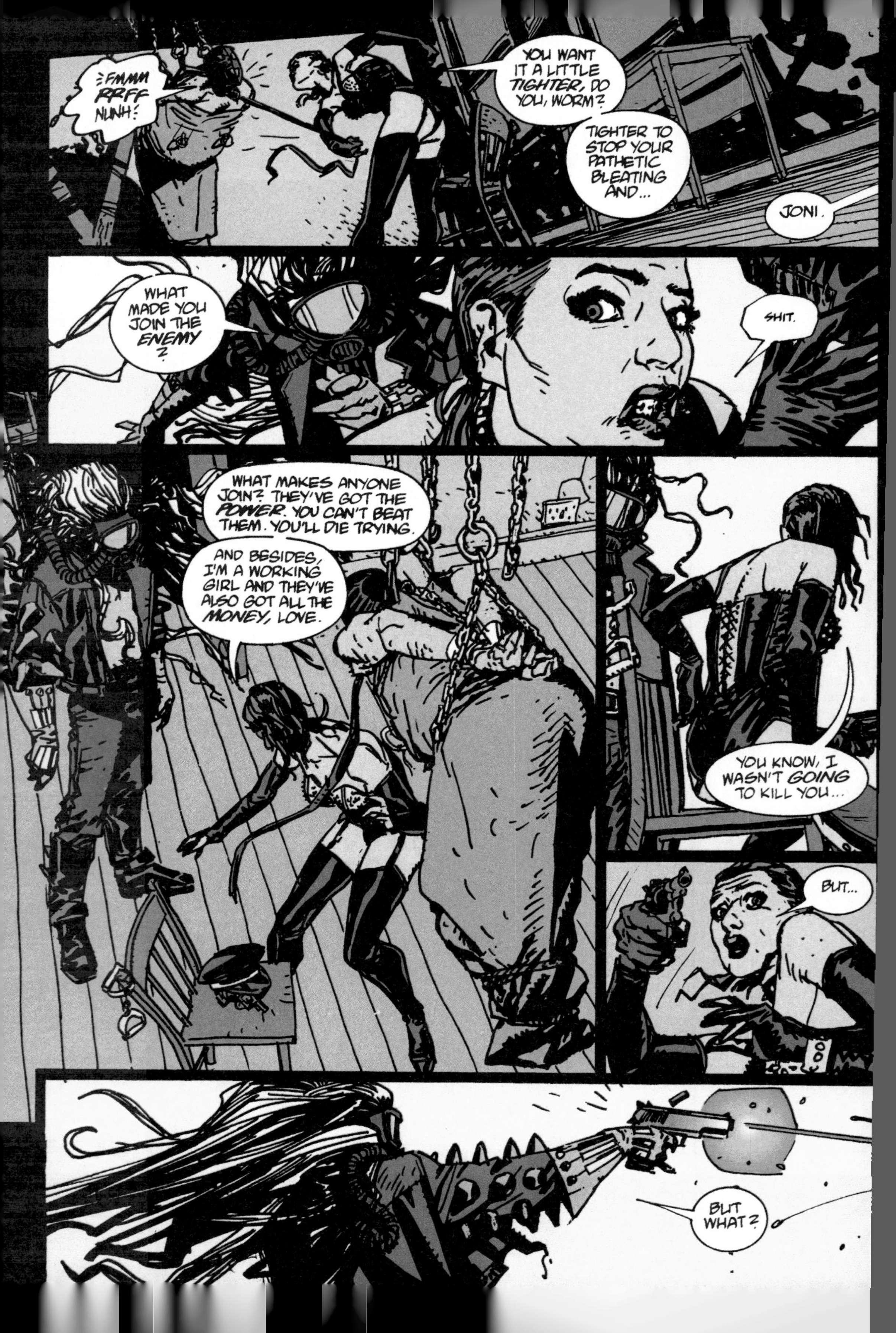
FMMM RRFF NUNH!
YOU WANT IT A LITTLE TIGHTER, DO YOU, WORM?
TIGHTER TO STOP YOUR PATHETIC BLEATING AND...
JONI.
WHAT MADE YOU JOIN THE ENEMY?
SHIT.
WHAT MAKES ANYONE JOIN? THEY'VE GOT THE POWER. YOU CAN'T BEAT THEM. YOU'LL DIE TRYING.
AND BESIDES, I'M A WORKING GIRL AND THEY'VE ALSO GOT ALL THE MONEY, LOVE.
YOU KNOW, I WASN'T GOING TO KILL YOU...
BUT...
BUT WHAT?

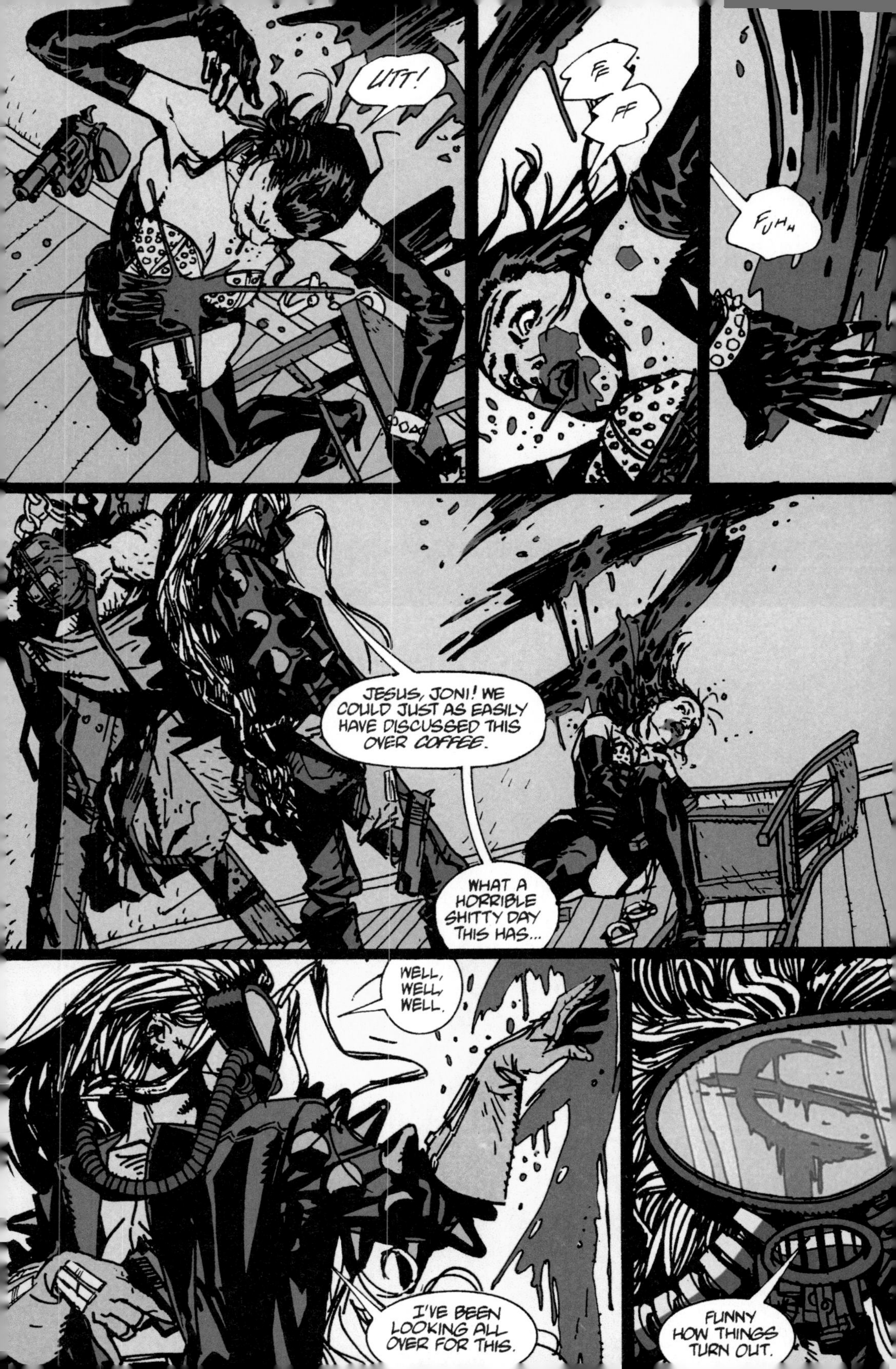
UTT!
FF
FF
FUHH
JESUS, JONI! WE COULD JUST AS EASILY HAVE DISCUSSED THIS OVER COFFEE.
WHAT A HORRIBLE SHITTY DAY THIS HAS...
WELL, WELL, WELL.
I'VE BEEN LOOKING ALL OVER FOR THIS.
FUNNY HOW THINGS TURN OUT.

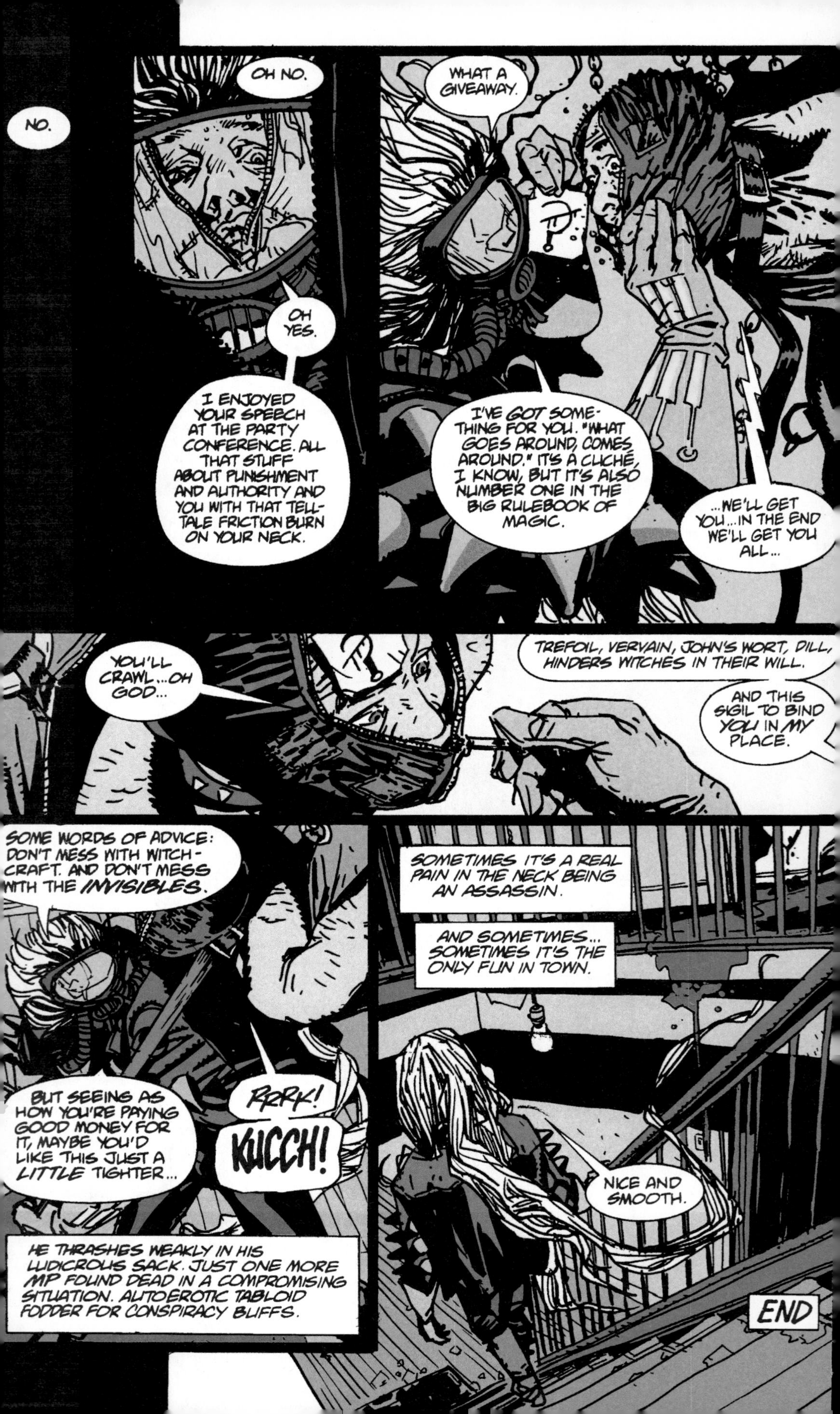
NO.
OH NO.
OH YES.
I ENJOYED YOUR SPEECH AT THE PARTY CONFERENCE. ALL THAT STUFF ABOUT PUNISHMENT AND AUTHORITY AND YOU WITH THAT TELL-TALE FRICTION BURN ON YOUR NECK.
WHAT A GIVEAWAY.
I'VE GOT SOME-THING FOR YOU. "WHAT GOES AROUND, COMES AROUND." IT'S A CLICHÉ, I KNOW, BUT IT'S ALSO NUMBER ONE IN THE BIG RULEBOOK OF MAGIC.
...WE'LL GET YOU...IN THE END WE'LL GET YOU ALL...
YOU'LL CRAWL...OH GOD...
TREFOIL, VERVAIN, JOHN'S WORT, DILL, HINDERS WITCHES IN THEIR WILL.
AND THIS SIGIL TO BIND YOU IN MY PLACE.
SOME WORDS OF ADVICE: DON'T MESS WITH WITCH-CRAFT. AND DON'T MESS WITH THE INVISIBLES.
BUT SEEING AS HOW YOU'RE PAYING GOOD MONEY FOR IT, MAYBE YOU'D LIKE THIS JUST A LITTLE TIGHTER...
RRRK!
KUCCH!
HE THRASHES WEAKLY IN HIS LUDICROUS SACK. JUST ONE MORE MP FOUND DEAD IN A COMPROMISING SITUATION. AUTOEROTIC TABLOID FODDER FOR CONSPIRACY BUFFS.
SOMETIMES IT'S A REAL PAIN IN THE NECK BEING AN ASSASSIN.
AND SOMETIMES... SOMETIMES IT'S THE ONLY FUN IN TOWN.
NICE AND SMOOTH.
END

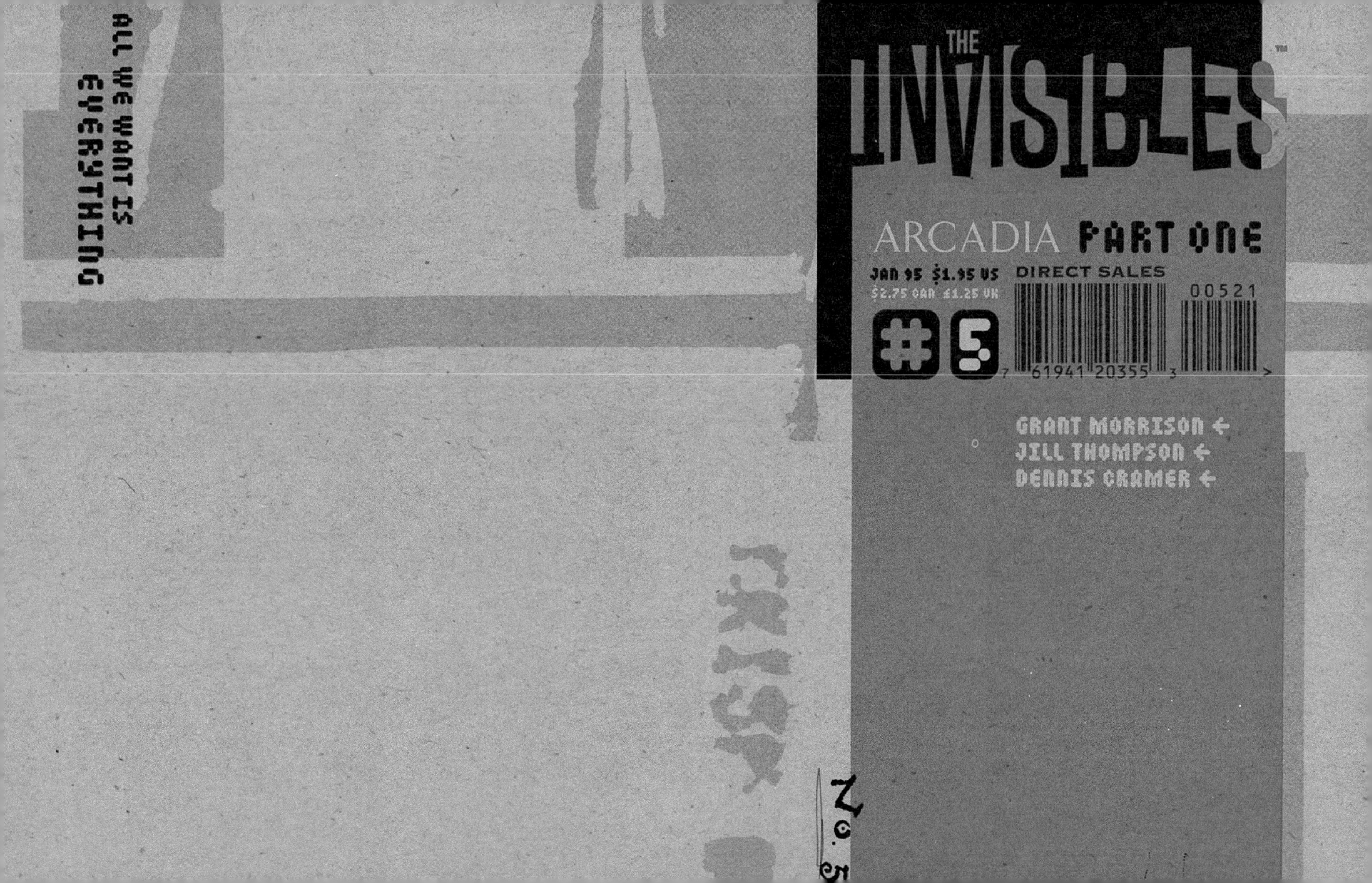
THE INVISIBLES™
ARCADIA PART ONE
JAN 95 $1.95 US
$2.75 CAN £1.25 UK
DIRECT SALES
#5
GRANT MORRISON
JILL THOMPSON
DENNIS CRAMER
ALL WE WANT IS EVERYTHING
No. 5

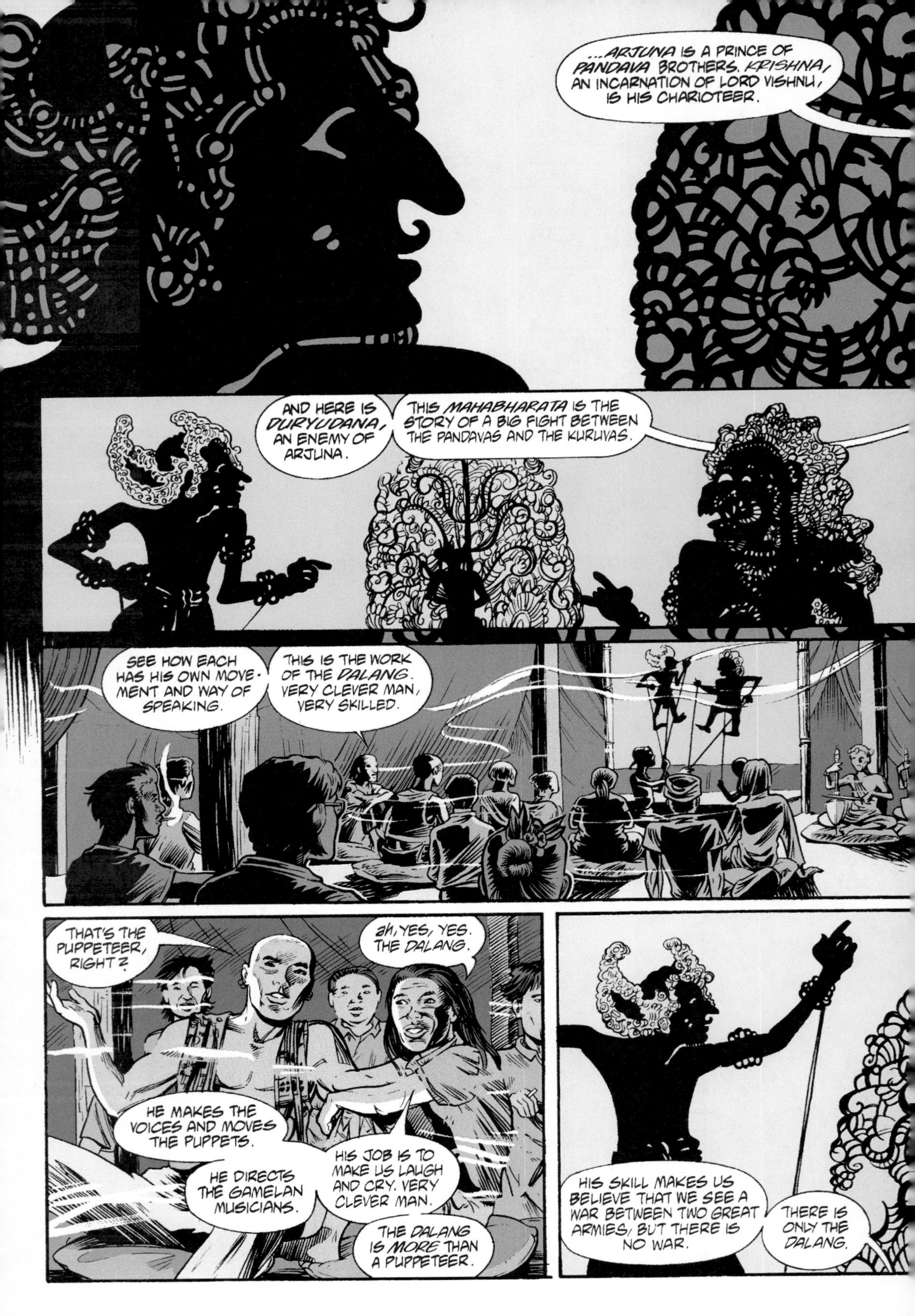
...ARJUNA IS A PRINCE OF PANDAVA BROTHERS. KRISHNA, AN INCARNATION OF LORD VISHNU, IS HIS CHARIOTEER.
AND HERE IS DURYUDANA, AN ENEMY OF ARJUNA.
THIS MAHABHARATA IS THE STORY OF A BIG FIGHT BETWEEN THE PANDAVAS AND THE KURUVAS.
SEE HOW EACH HAS HIS OWN MOVE-MENT AND WAY OF SPEAKING.
THIS IS THE WORK OF THE DALANG. VERY CLEVER MAN, VERY SKILLED.
THAT'S THE PUPPETEER, RIGHT?
AH, YES, YES. THE DALANG.
HE MAKES THE VOICES AND MOVES THE PUPPETS.
HE DIRECTS THE GAMELAN MUSICIANS.
HIS JOB IS TO MAKE US LAUGH AND CRY. VERY CLEVER MAN.
THE DALANG IS MORE THAN A PUPPETEER.
HIS SKILL MAKES US BELIEVE THAT WE SEE A WAR BETWEEN TWO GREAT ARMIES, BUT THERE IS NO WAR.
THERE IS ONLY THE DALANG.

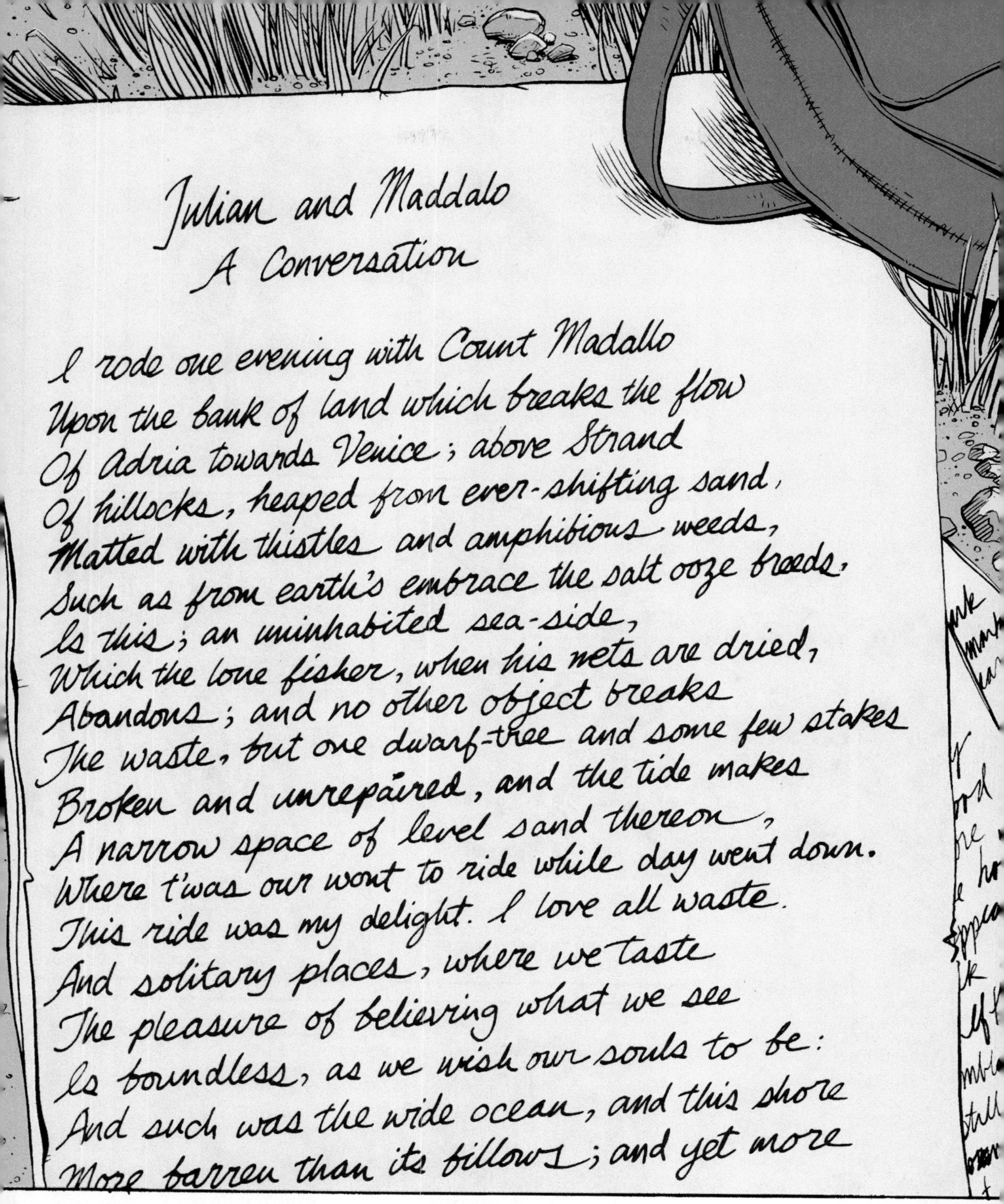
Julian and Maddalo
A Conversation
I rode one evening with Count Madallo
Upon the bank of land which breaks the flow
Of Adria towards Venice; above Strand
Of hillocks, heaped from ever-shifting sand,
Matted with thistles and amphibious weeds,
Such as from earth's embrace the salt ooze breeds,
Is this; an uninhabited sea-side,
Which the lone fisher, when his nets are dried,
Abandons; and no other object breaks
The waste, but one dwarf-tree and some few stakes
Broken and unrepaired, and the tide makes
A narrow space of level sand thereon,
Where t'was our wont to ride while day went down.
This ride was my delight. I love all waste.
And solitary places, where we taste
The pleasure of believing what we see
Is boundless, as we wish our souls to be:
And such was the wide ocean, and this shore
More barren than its billows; and yet more

ARCADIA PART 1 BLOODY POETRY

GRANT MORRISON → WRITER JILL THOMPSON → PENCILS DENNIS CRAMER → INKS
DANIEL VOZZO → COLORS CLEM ROBINS → LETTERS
JULIE ROTTENBERG → ASSISTANT EDITOR STUART MOORE → EDITOR
THE INVISIBLES CREATED BY GRANT MORRISON

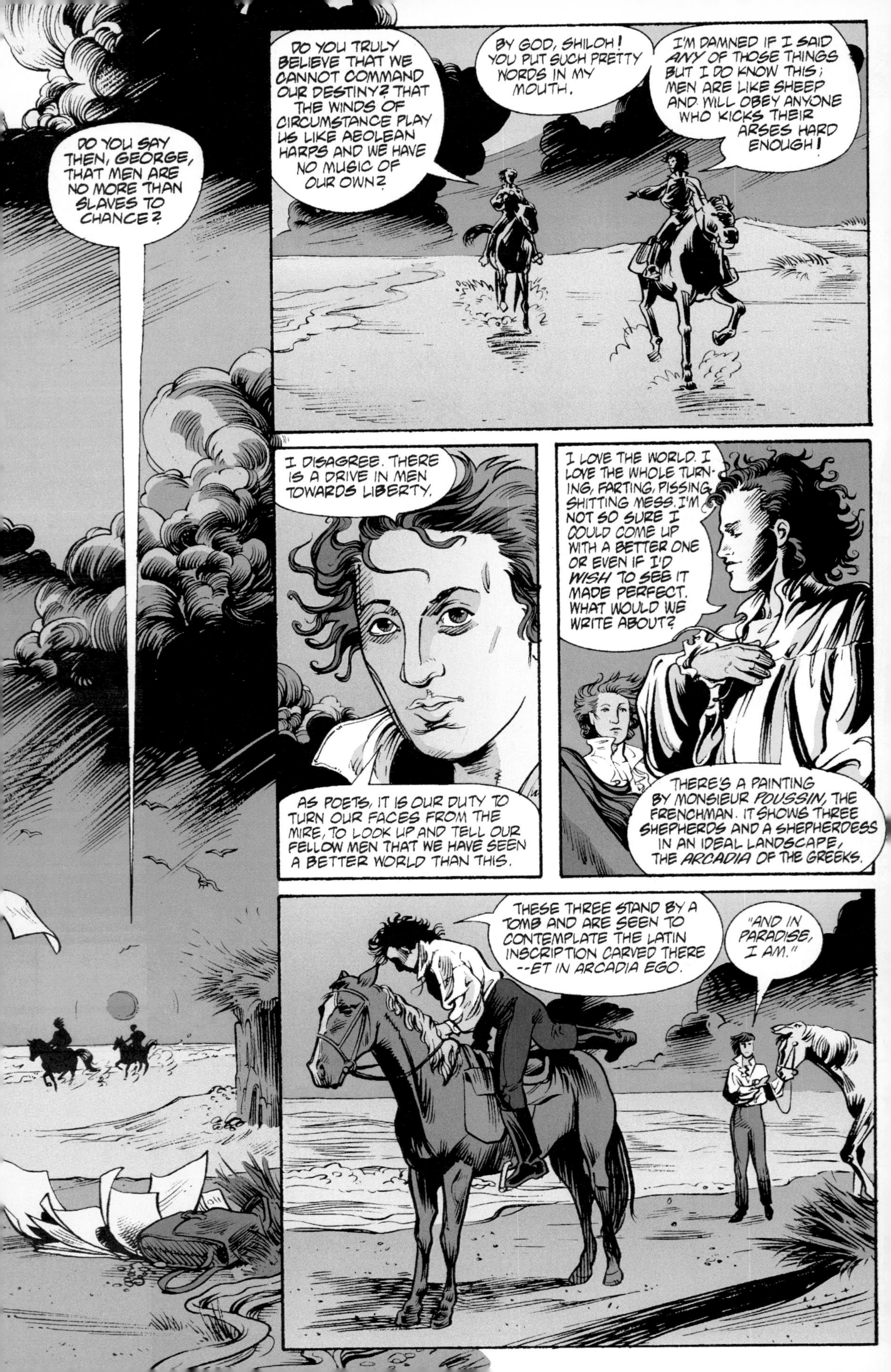
DO YOU SAY THEN, GEORGE, THAT MEN ARE NO MORE THAN SLAVES TO CHANCE?
DO YOU TRULY BELIEVE THAT WE CANNOT COMMAND OUR DESTINY? THAT THE WINDS OF CIRCUMSTANCE PLAY US LIKE AEOLEAN HARPS AND WE HAVE NO MUSIC OF OUR OWN?
BY GOD, SHILOH! YOU PUT SUCH PRETTY WORDS IN MY MOUTH.
I'M DAMNED IF I SAID ANY OF THOSE THINGS BUT I DO KNOW THIS; MEN ARE LIKE SHEEP AND WILL OBEY ANYONE WHO KICKS THEIR ARSES HARD ENOUGH!
I DISAGREE. THERE IS A DRIVE IN MEN TOWARDS LIBERTY.
AS POETS, IT IS OUR DUTY TO TURN OUR FACES FROM THE MIRE, TO LOOK UP AND TELL OUR FELLOW MEN THAT WE HAVE SEEN A BETTER WORLD THAN THIS.
I LOVE THE WORLD. I LOVE THE WHOLE TURNING, FARTING, PISSING SHITTING MESS. I'M NOT SO SURE I COULD COME UP WITH A BETTER ONE OR EVEN IF I'D WISH TO SEE IT MADE PERFECT. WHAT WOULD WE WRITE ABOUT?
THERE'S A PAINTING BY MONSIEUR POUSSIN, THE FRENCHMAN. IT SHOWS THREE SHEPHERDS AND A SHEPHERDESS IN AN IDEAL LANDSCAPE, THE ARCADIA OF THE GREEKS.
THESE THREE STAND BY A TOMB AND ARE SEEN TO CONTEMPLATE THE LATIN INSCRIPTION CARVED THERE --ET IN ARCADIA EGO.
"AND IN PARADISE, I AM."

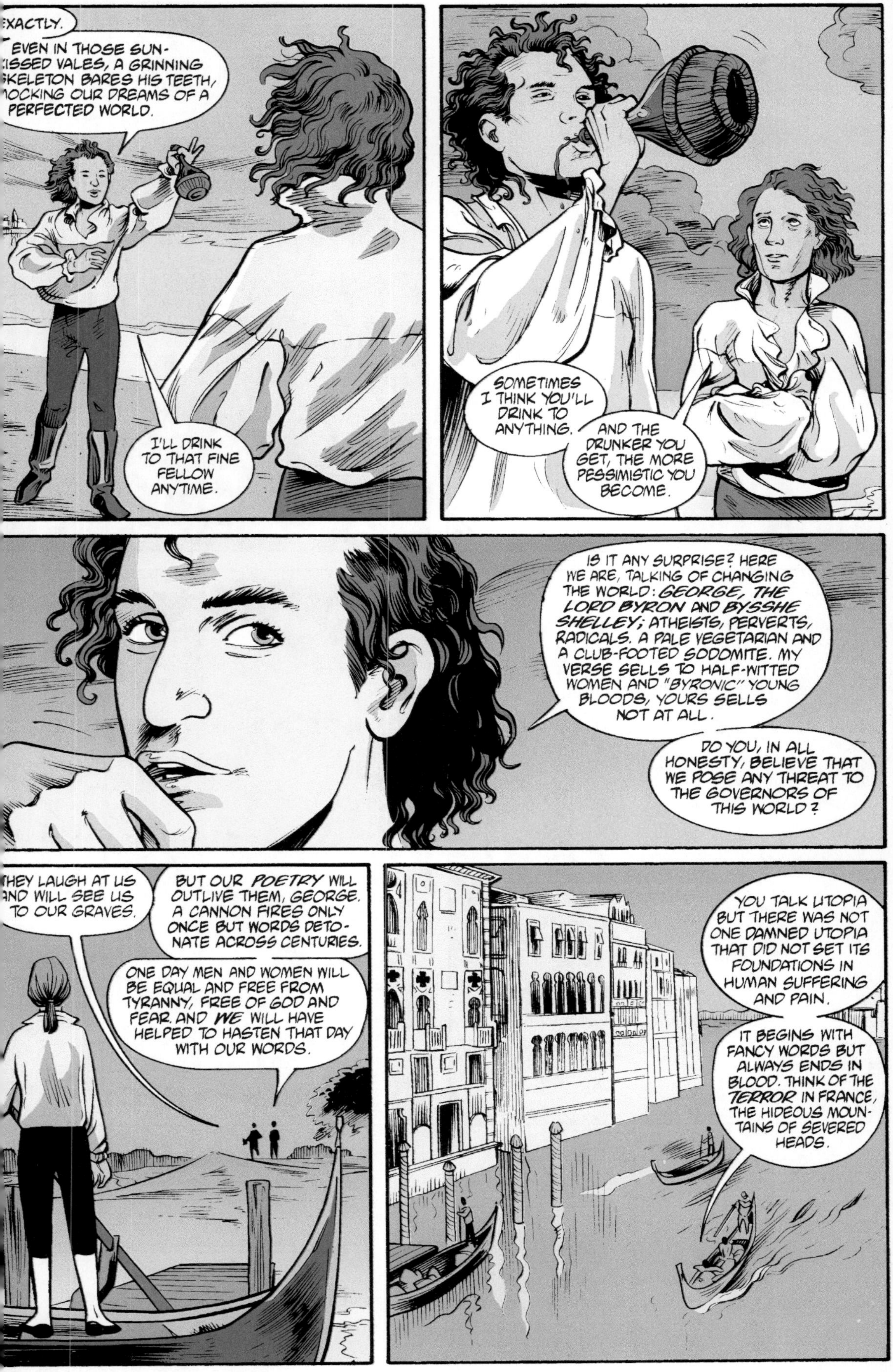
EXACTLY.
EVEN IN THOSE SUN-KISSED VALES, A GRINNING SKELETON BARES HIS TEETH, MOCKING OUR DREAMS OF A PERFECTED WORLD.
I'LL DRINK TO THAT FINE FELLOW ANYTIME.
SOMETIMES I THINK YOU'LL DRINK TO ANYTHING.
AND THE DRUNKER YOU GET, THE MORE PESSIMISTIC YOU BECOME.
IS IT ANY SURPRISE? HERE WE ARE, TALKING OF CHANGING THE WORLD: GEORGE, THE LORD BYRON AND BYSSHE SHELLEY; ATHEISTS, PERVERTS, RADICALS. A PALE VEGETARIAN AND A CLUB-FOOTED SODOMITE. MY VERSE SELLS TO HALF-WITTED WOMEN AND "BYRONIC" YOUNG BLOODS, YOURS SELLS NOT AT ALL.
DO YOU, IN ALL HONESTY, BELIEVE THAT WE POSE ANY THREAT TO THE GOVERNORS OF THIS WORLD?
THEY LAUGH AT US AND WILL SEE US TO OUR GRAVES.
BUT OUR POETRY WILL OUTLIVE THEM, GEORGE. A CANNON FIRES ONLY ONCE BUT WORDS DETONATE ACROSS CENTURIES.
ONE DAY MEN AND WOMEN WILL BE EQUAL AND FREE FROM TYRANNY, FREE OF GOD AND FEAR. AND WE WILL HAVE HELPED TO HASTEN THAT DAY WITH OUR WORDS.
YOU TALK UTOPIA BUT THERE WAS NOT ONE DAMNED UTOPIA THAT DID NOT SET ITS FOUNDATIONS IN HUMAN SUFFERING AND PAIN.
IT BEGINS WITH FANCY WORDS BUT ALWAYS ENDS IN BLOOD. THINK OF THE TERROR IN FRANCE, THE HIDEOUS MOUNTAINS OF SEVERED HEADS.

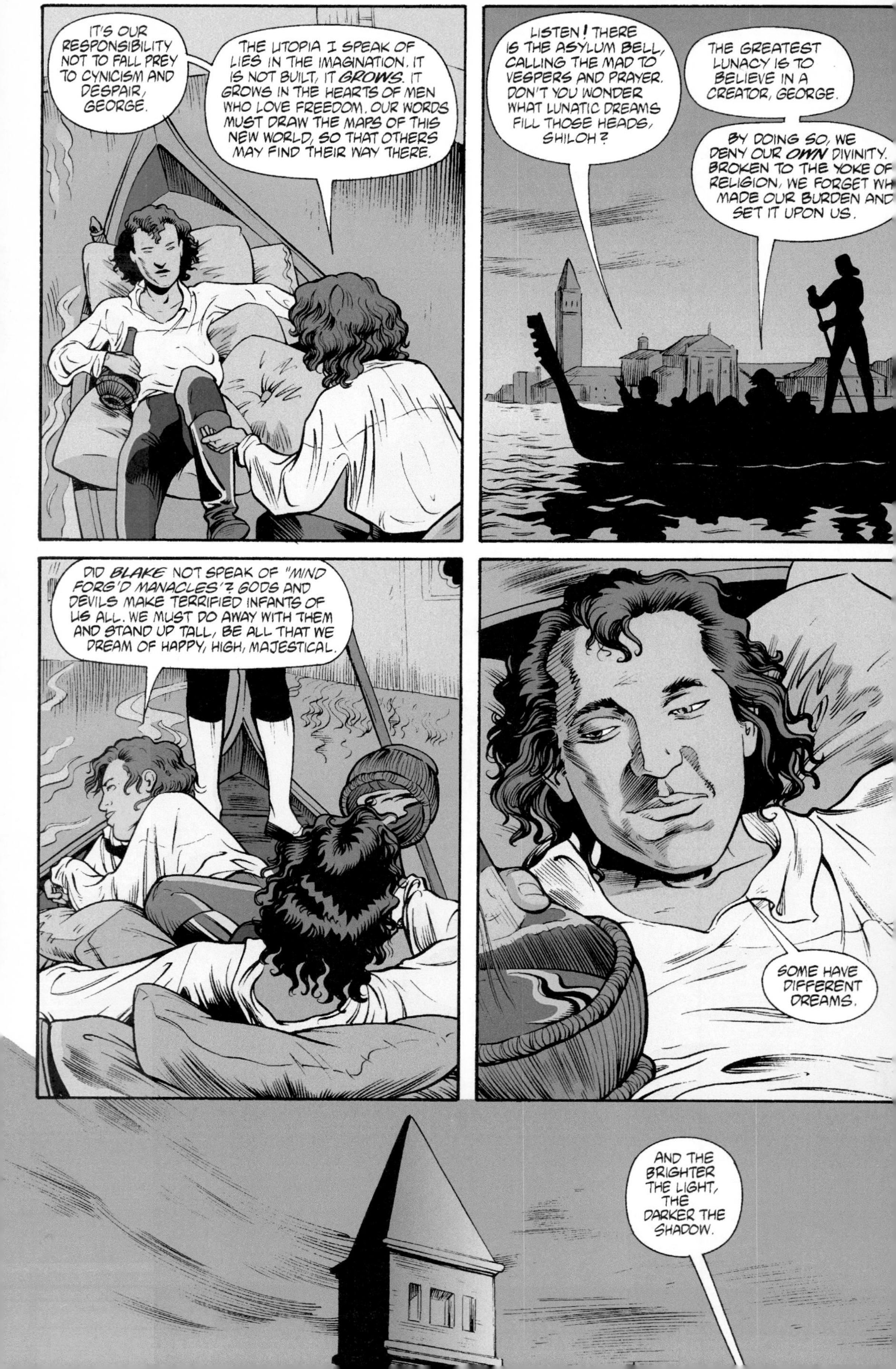
IT'S OUR RESPONSIBILITY NOT TO FALL PREY TO CYNICISM AND DESPAIR, GEORGE.
THE UTOPIA I SPEAK OF LIES IN THE IMAGINATION. IT IS NOT BUILT, IT GROWS. IT GROWS IN THE HEARTS OF MEN WHO LOVE FREEDOM. OUR WORDS MUST DRAW THE MAPS OF THIS NEW WORLD, SO THAT OTHERS MAY FIND THEIR WAY THERE.
LISTEN! THERE IS THE ASYLUM BELL, CALLING THE MAD TO VESPERS AND PRAYER. DON'T YOU WONDER WHAT LUNATIC DREAMS FILL THOSE HEADS, SHILOH?
THE GREATEST LUNACY IS TO BELIEVE IN A CREATOR, GEORGE.
BY DOING SO, WE DENY OUR OWN DIVINITY. BROKEN TO THE YOKE OF RELIGION, WE FORGET WH MADE OUR BURDEN AND SET IT UPON US.
DID BLAKE NOT SPEAK OF "MIND FORG'D MANACLES"? GODS AND DEVILS MAKE TERRIFIED INFANTS OF US ALL. WE MUST DO AWAY WITH THEM AND STAND UP TALL, BE ALL THAT WE DREAM OF HAPPY, HIGH, MAJESTICAL.
SOME HAVE DIFFERENT DREAMS.
AND THE BRIGHTER THE LIGHT, THE DARKER THE SHADOW.

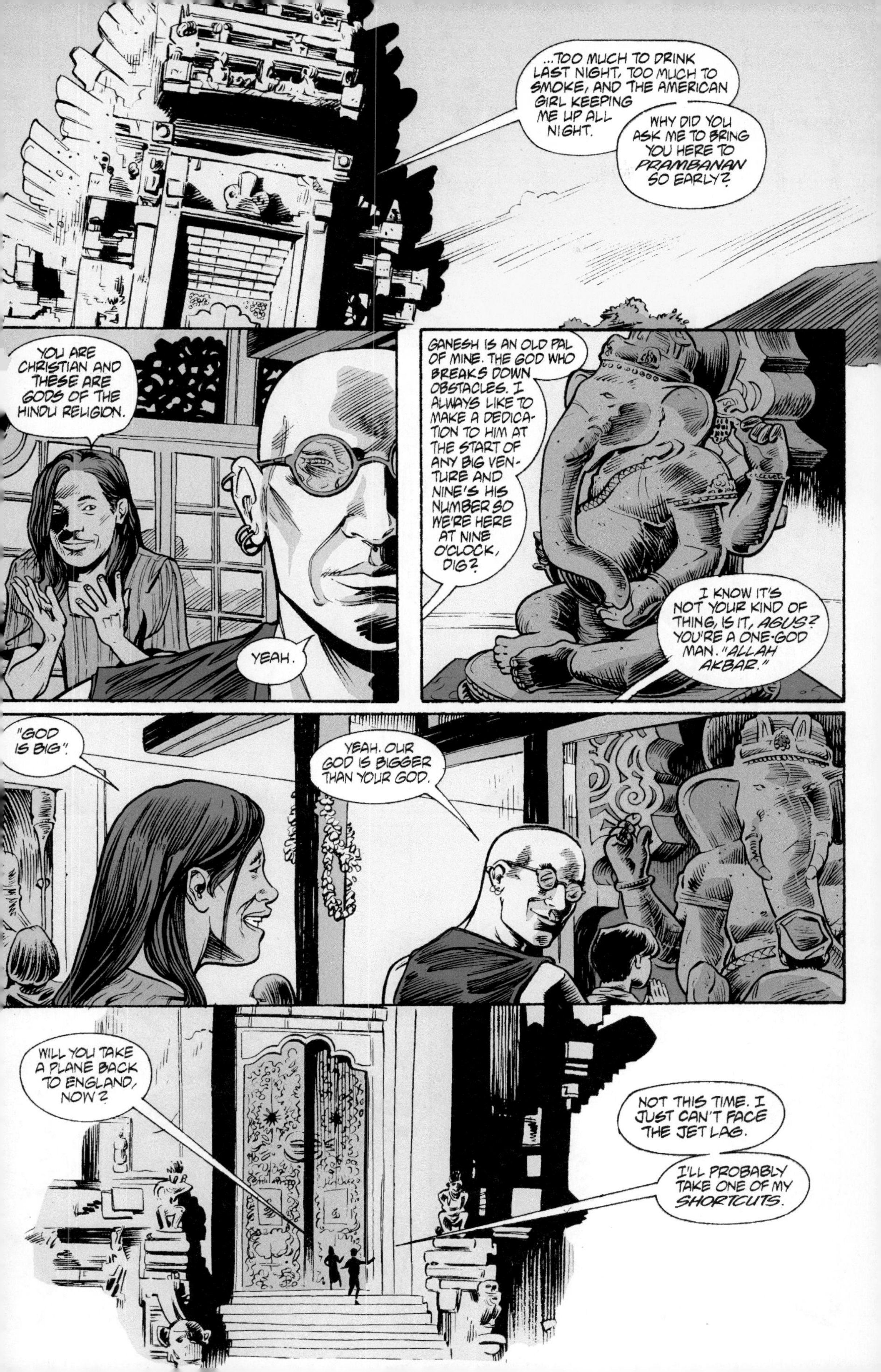
...TOO MUCH TO DRINK LAST NIGHT, TOO MUCH TO SMOKE, AND THE AMERICAN GIRL KEEPING ME UP ALL NIGHT.
WHY DID YOU ASK ME TO BRING YOU HERE TO PRAMBANAN SO EARLY?
YOU ARE CHRISTIAN AND THESE ARE GODS OF THE HINDU RELIGION.
YEAH.
GANESH IS AN OLD PAL OF MINE. THE GOD WHO BREAKS DOWN OBSTACLES. I ALWAYS LIKE TO MAKE A DEDICATION TO HIM AT THE START OF ANY BIG VENTURE AND NINE'S HIS NUMBER SO WE'RE HERE AT NINE O'CLOCK, DIG?
I KNOW IT'S NOT YOUR KIND OF THING, IS IT, AGUS? YOU'RE A ONE-GOD MAN. "ALLAH AKBAR."
"GOD IS BIG".
YEAH. OUR GOD IS BIGGER THAN YOUR GOD.
WILL YOU TAKE A PLANE BACK TO ENGLAND, NOW?
NOT THIS TIME. I JUST CAN'T FACE THE JET LAG.
I'LL PROBABLY TAKE ONE OF MY SHORTCUTS.

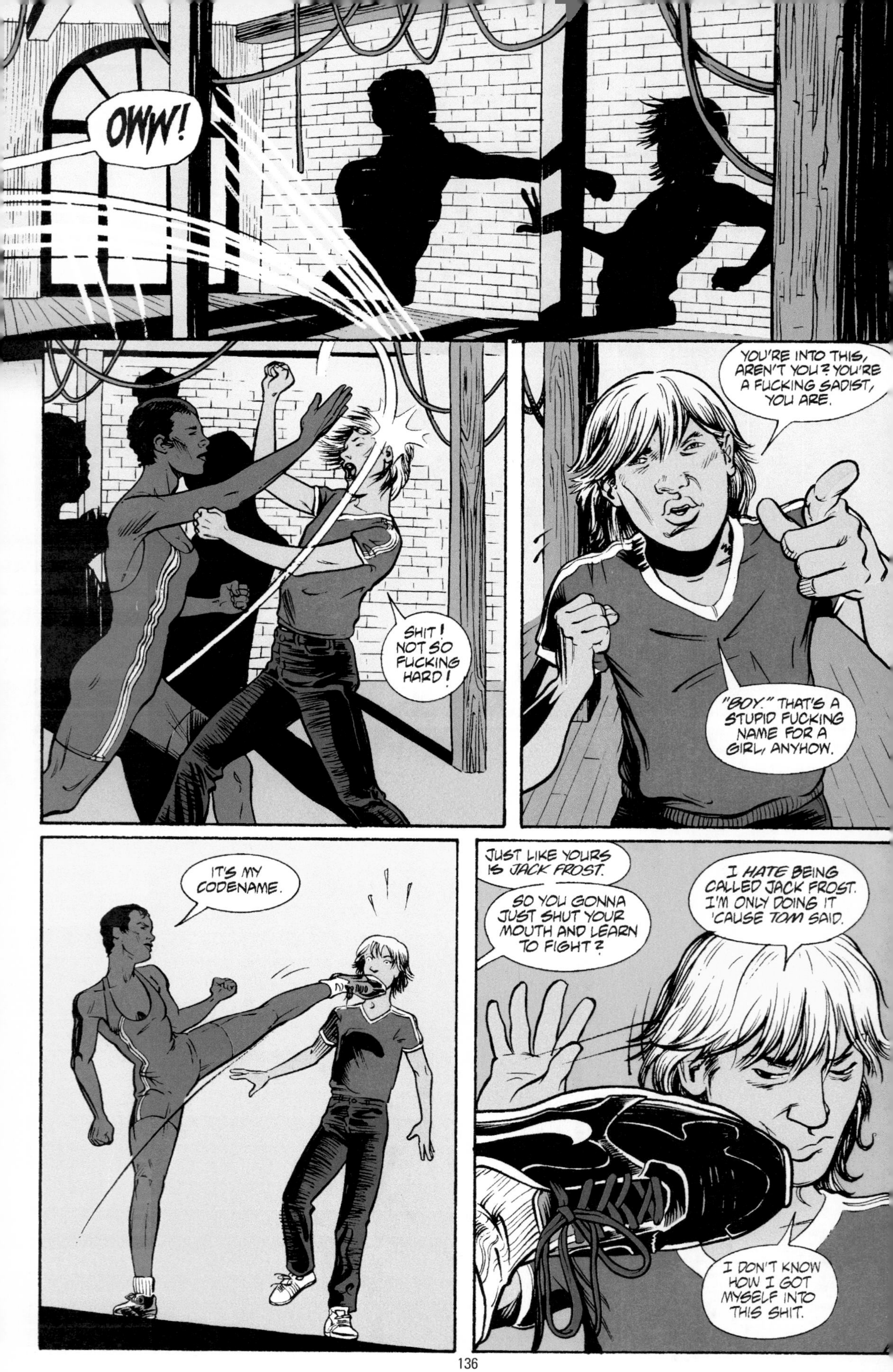
OWW!
SHIT! NOT SO FUCKING HARD!
YOU'RE INTO THIS, AREN'T YOU? YOU'RE A FUCKING SADIST, YOU ARE.
"BOY." THAT'S A STUPID FUCKING NAME FOR A GIRL, ANYHOW.
IT'S MY CODENAME.
JUST LIKE YOURS IS JACK FROST.
SO YOU GONNA JUST SHUT YOUR MOUTH AND LEARN TO FIGHT?
I HATE BEING CALLED JACK FROST. I'M ONLY DOING IT 'CAUSE TOM SAID.
I DON'T KNOW HOW I GOT MYSELF INTO THIS SHIT.

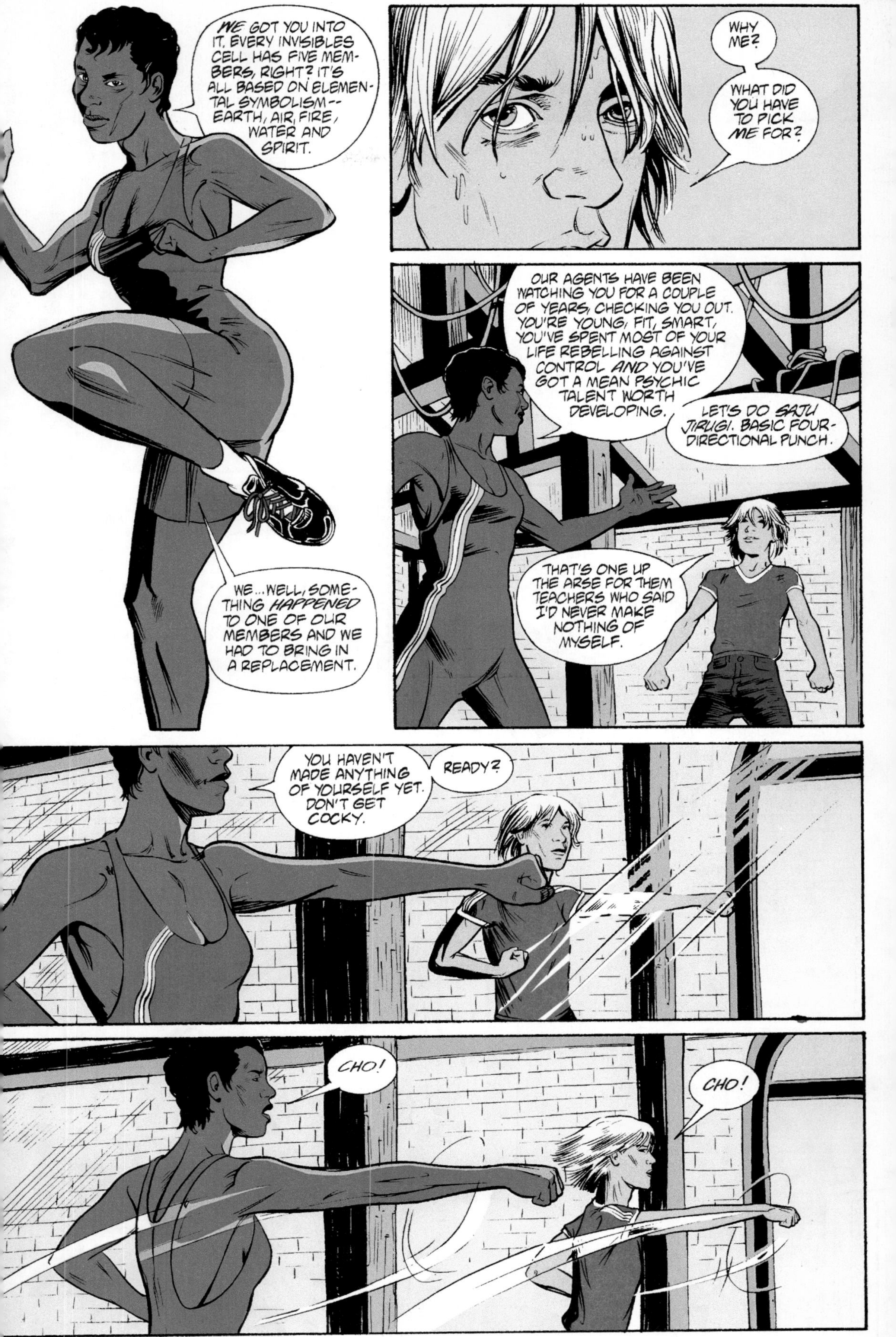
WE GOT YOU INTO IT. EVERY INVISIBLES CELL HAS FIVE MEMBERS, RIGHT? IT'S ALL BASED ON ELEMENTAL SYMBOLISM -- EARTH, AIR, FIRE, WATER AND SPIRIT.
WE... WELL, SOMETHING HAPPENED TO ONE OF OUR MEMBERS AND WE HAD TO BRING IN A REPLACEMENT.
WHY ME?
WHAT DID YOU HAVE TO PICK ME FOR?
OUR AGENTS HAVE BEEN WATCHING YOU FOR A COUPLE OF YEARS, CHECKING YOU OUT. YOU'RE YOUNG, FIT, SMART, YOU'VE SPENT MOST OF YOUR LIFE REBELLING AGAINST CONTROL AND YOU'VE GOT A MEAN PSYCHIC TALENT WORTH DEVELOPING.
LET'S DO SAJU JIRUGI. BASIC FOUR-DIRECTIONAL PUNCH.
THAT'S ONE UP THE ARSE FOR THEM TEACHERS WHO SAID I'D NEVER MAKE NOTHING OF MYSELF.
YOU HAVEN'T MADE ANYTHING OF YOURSELF YET. DON'T GET COCKY.
READY?
CHO!
CHO!

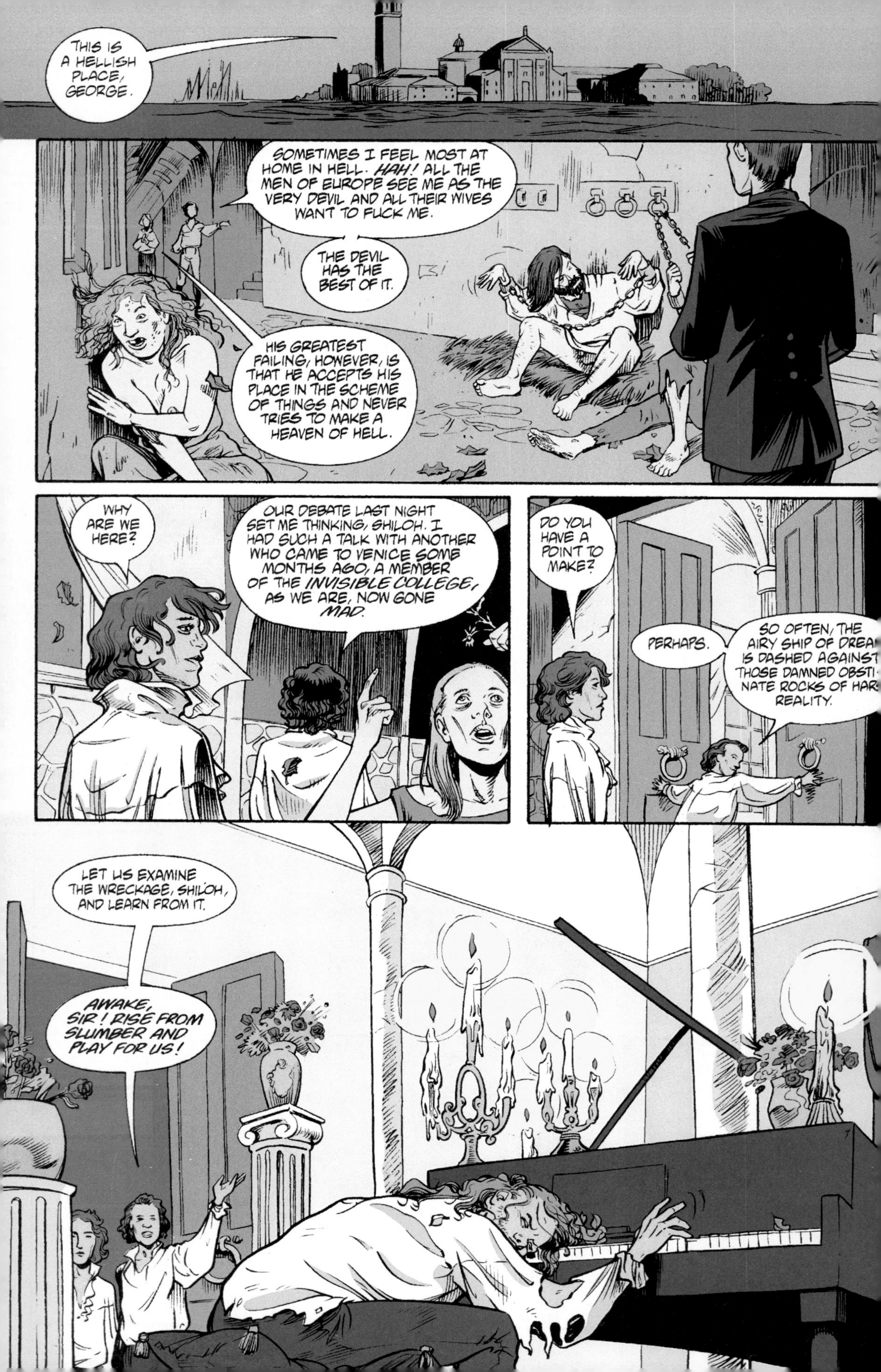
THIS IS A HELLISH PLACE, GEORGE.
SOMETIMES I FEEL MOST AT HOME IN HELL. HAH! ALL THE MEN OF EUROPE SEE ME AS THE VERY DEVIL AND ALL THEIR WIVES WANT TO FUCK ME.
THE DEVIL HAS THE BEST OF IT.
HIS GREATEST FAILING, HOWEVER, IS THAT HE ACCEPTS HIS PLACE IN THE SCHEME OF THINGS AND NEVER TRIES TO MAKE A HEAVEN OF HELL.
WHY ARE WE HERE?
OUR DEBATE LAST NIGHT SET ME THINKING, SHILOH. I HAD SUCH A TALK WITH ANOTHER WHO CAME TO VENICE SOME MONTHS AGO, A MEMBER OF THE INVISIBLE COLLEGE, AS WE ARE, NOW GONE MAD.
DO YOU HAVE A POINT TO MAKE?
PERHAPS.
SO OFTEN, THE AIRY SHIP OF DREA IS DASHED AGAINST THOSE DAMNED OBSTI-NATE ROCKS OF HAR REALITY.
LET US EXAMINE THE WRECKAGE, SHILOH, AND LEARN FROM IT.
AWAKE, SIR! RISE FROM SLUMBER AND PLAY FOR US!

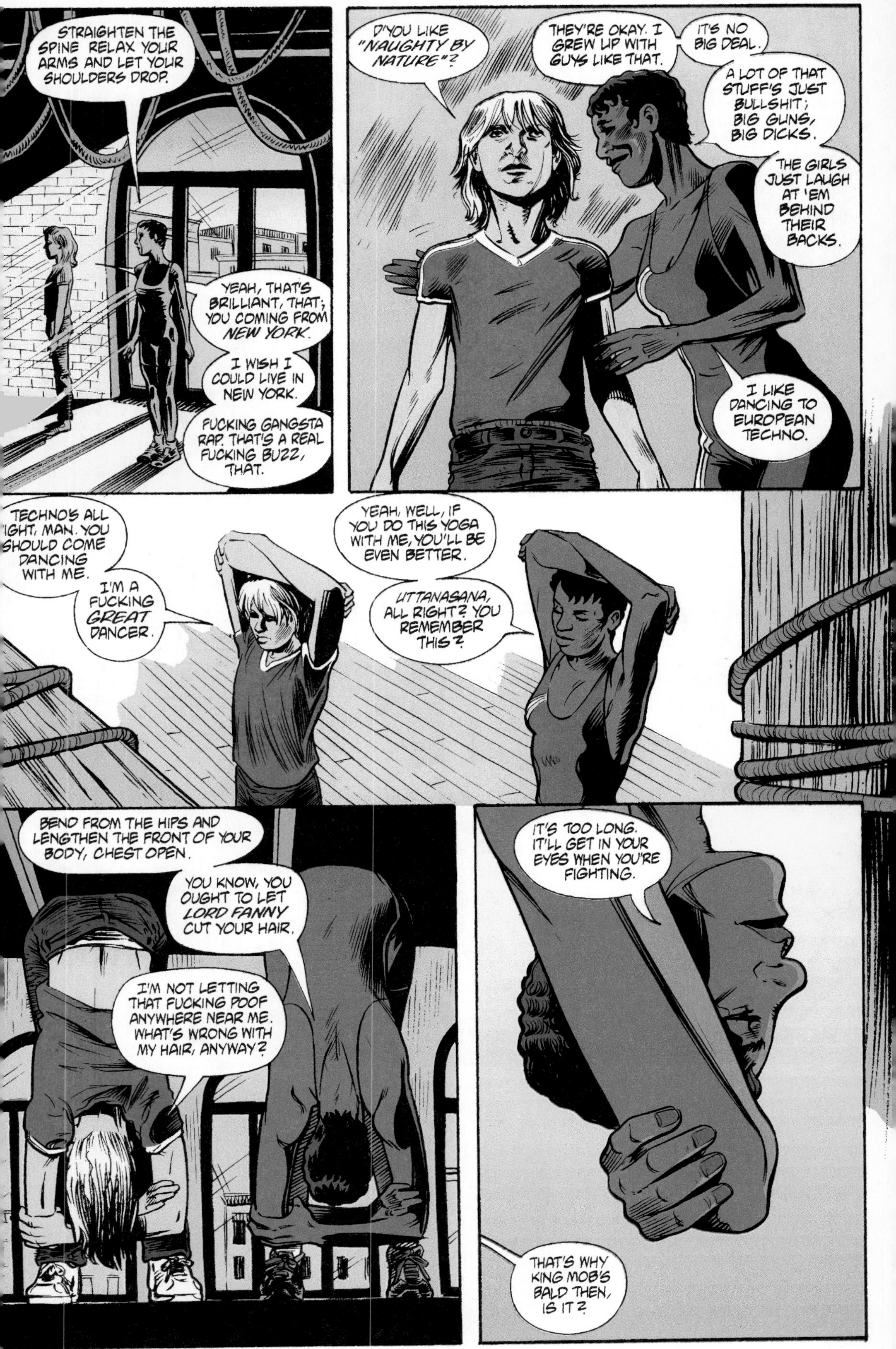
STRAIGHTEN THE SPINE RELAX YOUR ARMS AND LET YOUR SHOULDERS DROP.
YEAH, THAT'S BRILLIANT, THAT; YOU COMING FROM NEW YORK.
I WISH I COULD LIVE IN NEW YORK.
FUCKING GANGSTA RAP. THAT'S A REAL FUCKING BUZZ, THAT.
D'YOU LIKE "NAUGHTY BY NATURE"?
THEY'RE OKAY. I GREW UP WITH GUYS LIKE THAT.
IT'S NO BIG DEAL.
A LOT OF THAT STUFF'S JUST BULLSHIT; BIG GUNS, BIG DICKS.
THE GIRLS JUST LAUGH AT 'EM BEHIND THEIR BACKS.
I LIKE DANCING TO EUROPEAN TECHNO.
TECHNO'S ALL IGHT, MAN. YOU SHOULD COME DANCING WITH ME.
I'M A FUCKING GREAT DANCER.
YEAH, WELL, IF YOU DO THIS YOGA WITH ME, YOU'LL BE EVEN BETTER.
UTTANASANA, ALL RIGHT? YOU REMEMBER THIS?
BEND FROM THE HIPS AND LENGTHEN THE FRONT OF YOUR BODY, CHEST OPEN.
YOU KNOW, YOU OUGHT TO LET LORD FANNY CUT YOUR HAIR.
I'M NOT LETTING THAT FUCKING POOF ANYWHERE NEAR ME. WHAT'S WRONG WITH MY HAIR, ANYWAY?
IT'S TOO LONG. IT'LL GET IN YOUR EYES WHEN YOU'RE FIGHTING.
THAT'S WHY KING MOB'S BALD THEN, IS IT?

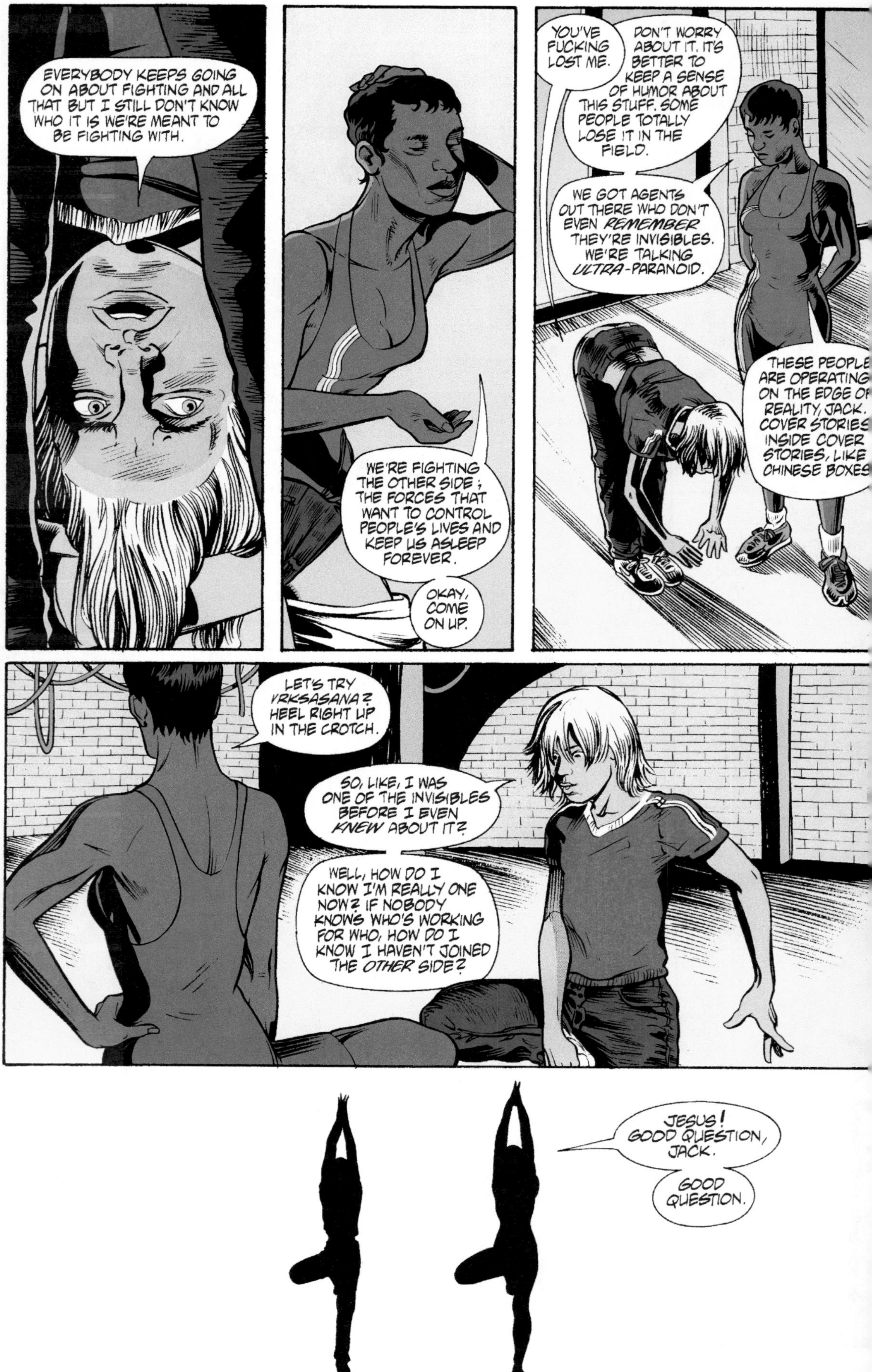
EVERYBODY KEEPS GOING ON ABOUT FIGHTING AND ALL THAT BUT I STILL DON'T KNOW WHO IT IS WE'RE MEANT TO BE FIGHTING WITH.
WE'RE FIGHTING THE OTHER SIDE; THE FORCES THAT WANT TO CONTROL PEOPLE'S LIVES AND KEEP US ASLEEP FOREVER.
OKAY, COME ON UP.
YOU'VE FUCKING LOST ME.
DON'T WORRY ABOUT IT. IT'S BETTER TO KEEP A SENSE OF HUMOR ABOUT THIS STUFF. SOME PEOPLE TOTALLY LOSE IT IN THE FIELD.
WE GOT AGENTS OUT THERE WHO DON'T EVEN *REMEMBER* THEY'RE INVISIBLES. WE'RE TALKING *ULTRA*-PARANOID.
THESE PEOPLE ARE OPERATING ON THE EDGE OF REALITY, JACK. COVER STORIES INSIDE COVER STORIES, LIKE CHINESE BOXES.
LET'S TRY *VRKSASANA*? HEEL RIGHT UP IN THE CROTCH.
SO, LIKE, I WAS ONE OF THE INVISIBLES BEFORE I EVEN *KNEW* ABOUT IT?
WELL, HOW DO I KNOW I'M REALLY ONE NOW? IF NOBODY KNOWS WHO'S WORKING FOR WHO, HOW DO I KNOW I HAVEN'T JOINED THE *OTHER* SIDE?
JESUS! GOOD QUESTION, JACK.
GOOD QUESTION.

PHEW! WHAT A *SCORCHER!*

I SUPPOSE THAT'S ONE GOOD THING ABOUT THE WAR; IT'S ALWAYS SUNNY NOW.

SO WHERE DID YOU SAY YOU WERE GOING?

INTO LONDON FIRST.

PROBABLY GO BACK TO EUROPE ONCE I'M DONE. I HEAR BERLIN'S NICE NOW THAT THEY'VE REBUILT THE WALL.

THEY SAY YOU CAN SEE THE NEW ONE FROM SPACE.

I FANCY SPRAYPAINTING MY NAME ON THAT.

WAAAAA

I THINK THE BABY'S HUNGRY.

SHE STILL CRIES A LOT. I'M NOT SURE WHO HER DAD WAS. THERE WERE SO MANY OF THEM, AMERICAN SOLDIERS.

COO-EE!

I SUPPOSE I WAS LUCKY; THEY KILLED A LOT OF THE OTHER GIRLS.

I SAY 'SHE' BUT IT'S SORT OF HARD TO TELL...

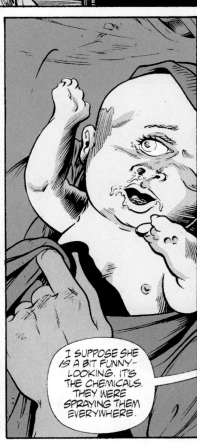

I SUPPOSE SHE *IS* A BIT FUNNY-LOOKING. IT'S THE CHEMICALS. THEY WERE SPRAYING THEM EVERYWHERE.

141

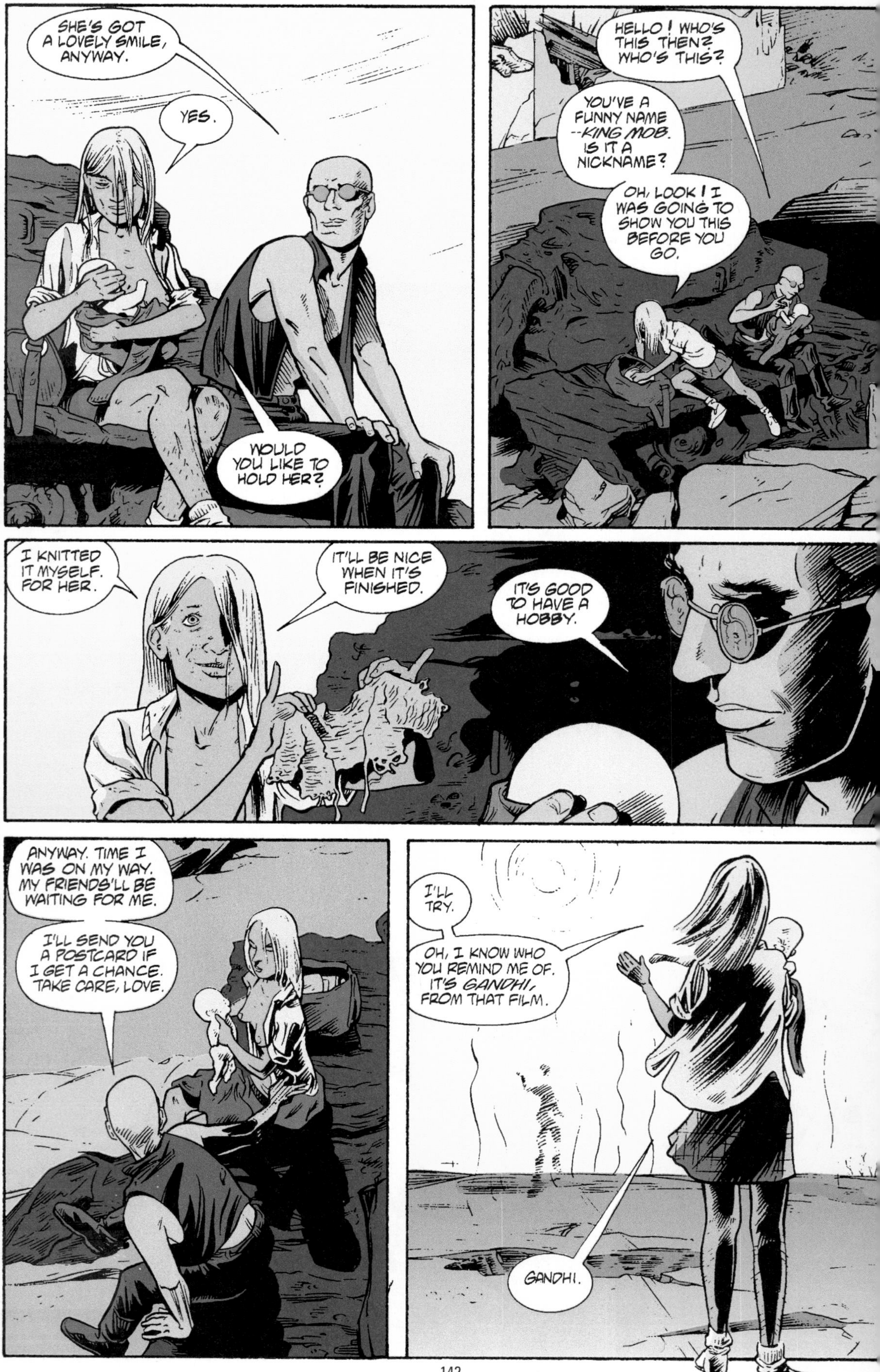
SHE'S GOT A LOVELY SMILE, ANYWAY.
YES.
WOULD YOU LIKE TO HOLD HER?
HELLO! WHO'S THIS THEN? WHO'S THIS?
YOU'VE A FUNNY NAME --KING MOB. IS IT A NICKNAME?
OH, LOOK! I WAS GOING TO SHOW YOU THIS BEFORE YOU GO.
I KNITTED IT MYSELF. FOR HER.
IT'LL BE NICE WHEN IT'S FINISHED.
IT'S GOOD TO HAVE A HOBBY.
ANYWAY. TIME I WAS ON MY WAY. MY FRIENDS'LL BE WAITING FOR ME.
I'LL SEND YOU A POSTCARD IF I GET A CHANCE. TAKE CARE, LOVE.
I'LL TRY.
OH, I KNOW WHO YOU REMIND ME OF. IT'S GANDHI, FROM THAT FILM.
GANDHI.

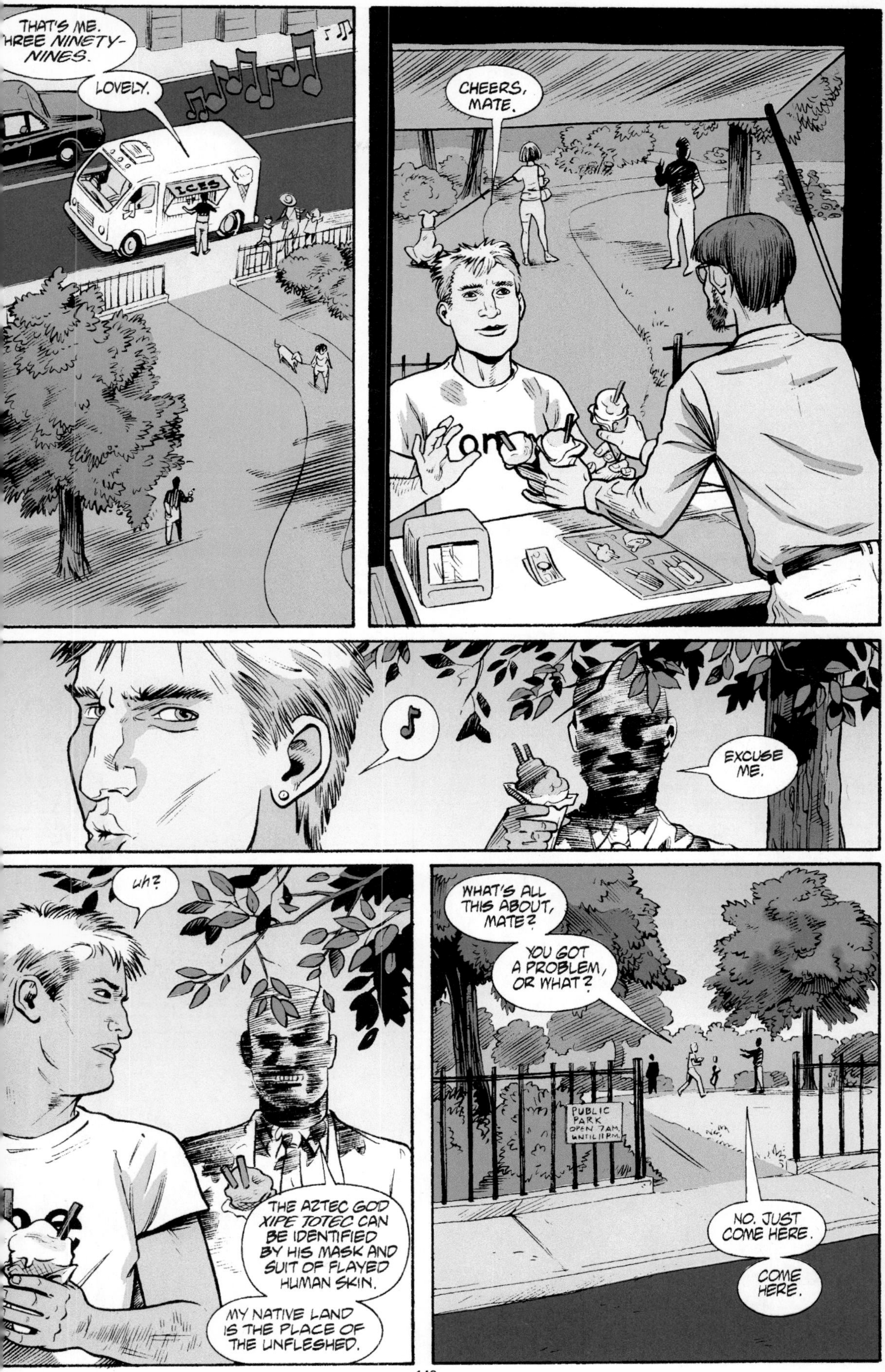
THAT'S ME. THREE NINETY-NINES.
LOVELY.
ICES
CHEERS, MATE.
EXCUSE ME.
uh?
THE AZTEC GOD XIPE TOTEC CAN BE IDENTIFIED BY HIS MASK AND SUIT OF FLAYED HUMAN SKIN.
MY NATIVE LAND IS THE PLACE OF THE UNFLESHED.
WHAT'S ALL THIS ABOUT, MATE?
YOU GOT A PROBLEM, OR WHAT?
PUBLIC PARK OPEN 7AM UNTIL 11PM.
NO. JUST COME HERE.
COME HERE.

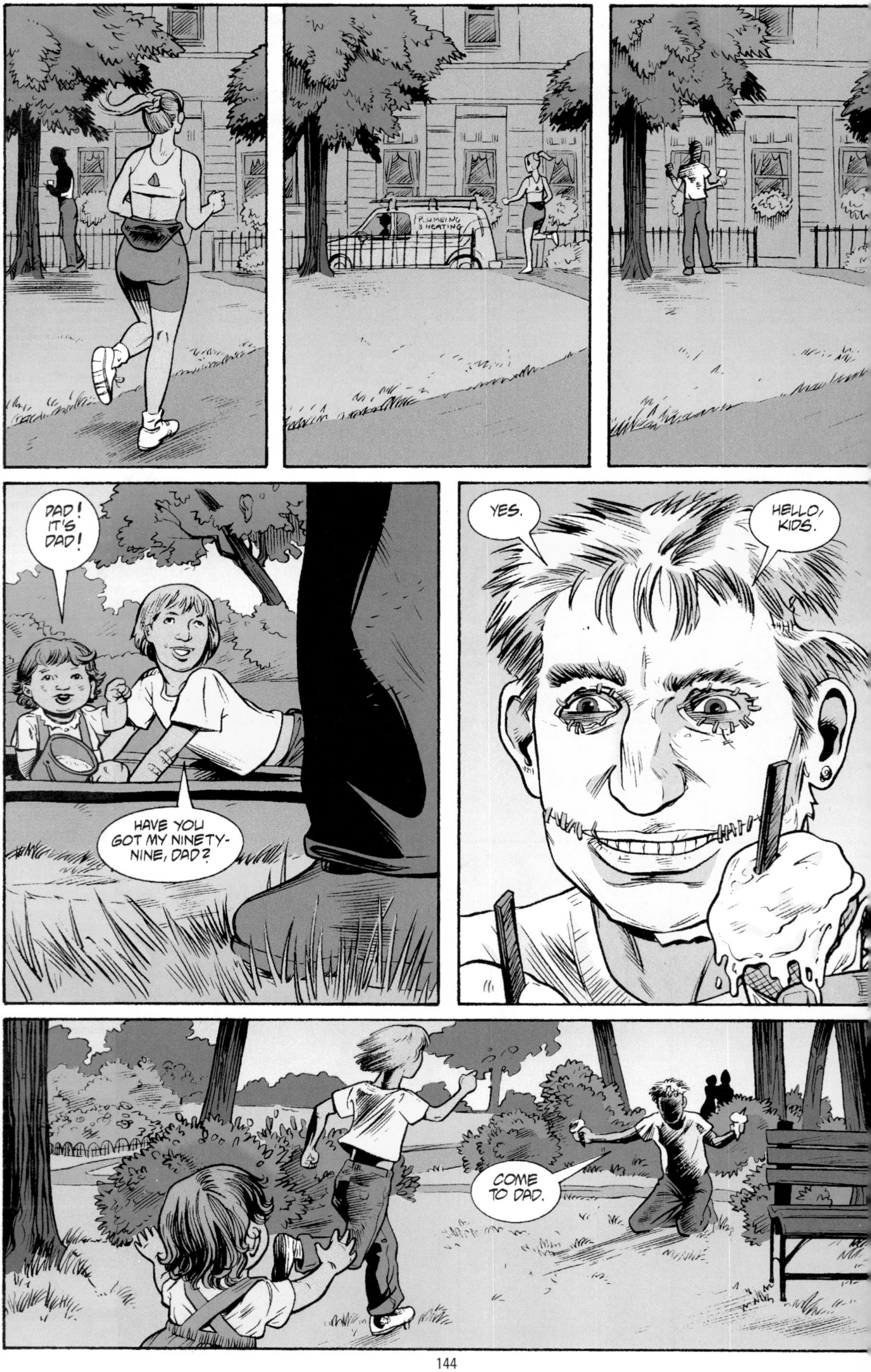
PLUMBING & HEATING
DAD! IT'S DAD!
HAVE YOU GOT MY NINETY-NINE, DAD?
YES.
HELLO, KIDS.
COME TO DAD.

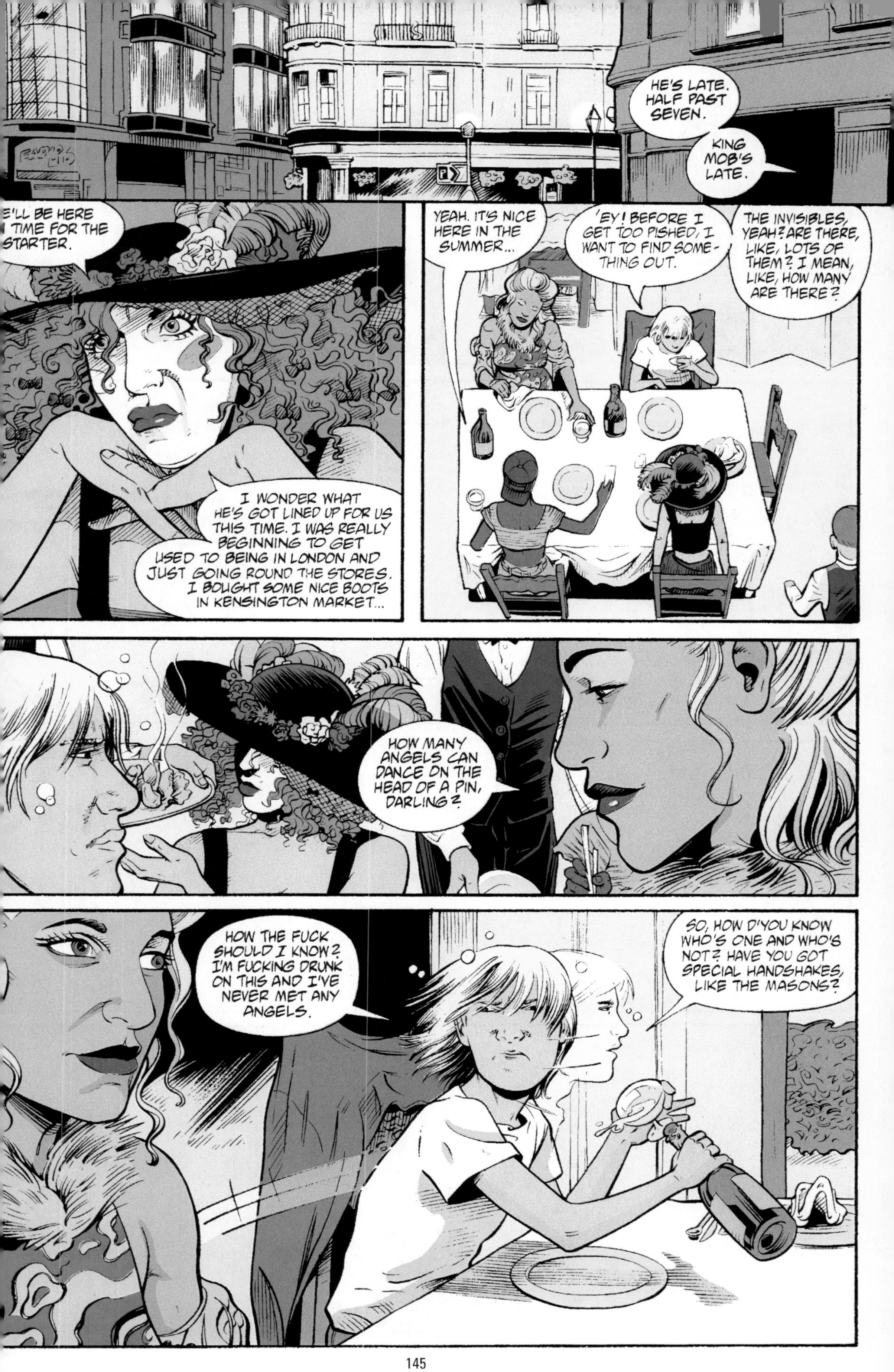
HE'S LATE. HALF PAST SEVEN.
KING MOB'S LATE.
E'LL BE HERE TIME FOR THE STARTER.
I WONDER WHAT HE'S GOT LINED UP FOR US THIS TIME. I WAS REALLY BEGINNING TO GET USED TO BEING IN LONDON AND JUST GOING ROUND THE STORES. I BOUGHT SOME NICE BOOTS IN KENSINGTON MARKET...
YEAH. IT'S NICE HERE IN THE SUMMER...
'EY! BEFORE I GET TOO PISHED, I WANT TO FIND SOMETHING OUT.
THE INVISIBLES, YEAH? ARE THERE, LIKE, LOTS OF THEM? I MEAN, LIKE, HOW MANY ARE THERE?
HOW MANY ANGELS CAN DANCE ON THE HEAD OF A PIN, DARLING?
HOW THE FUCK SHOULD I KNOW? I'M FUCKING DRUNK ON THIS AND I'VE NEVER MET ANY ANGELS.
SO, HOW D'YOU KNOW WHO'S ONE AND WHO'S NOT? HAVE YOU GOT SPECIAL HANDSHAKES, LIKE THE MASONS?

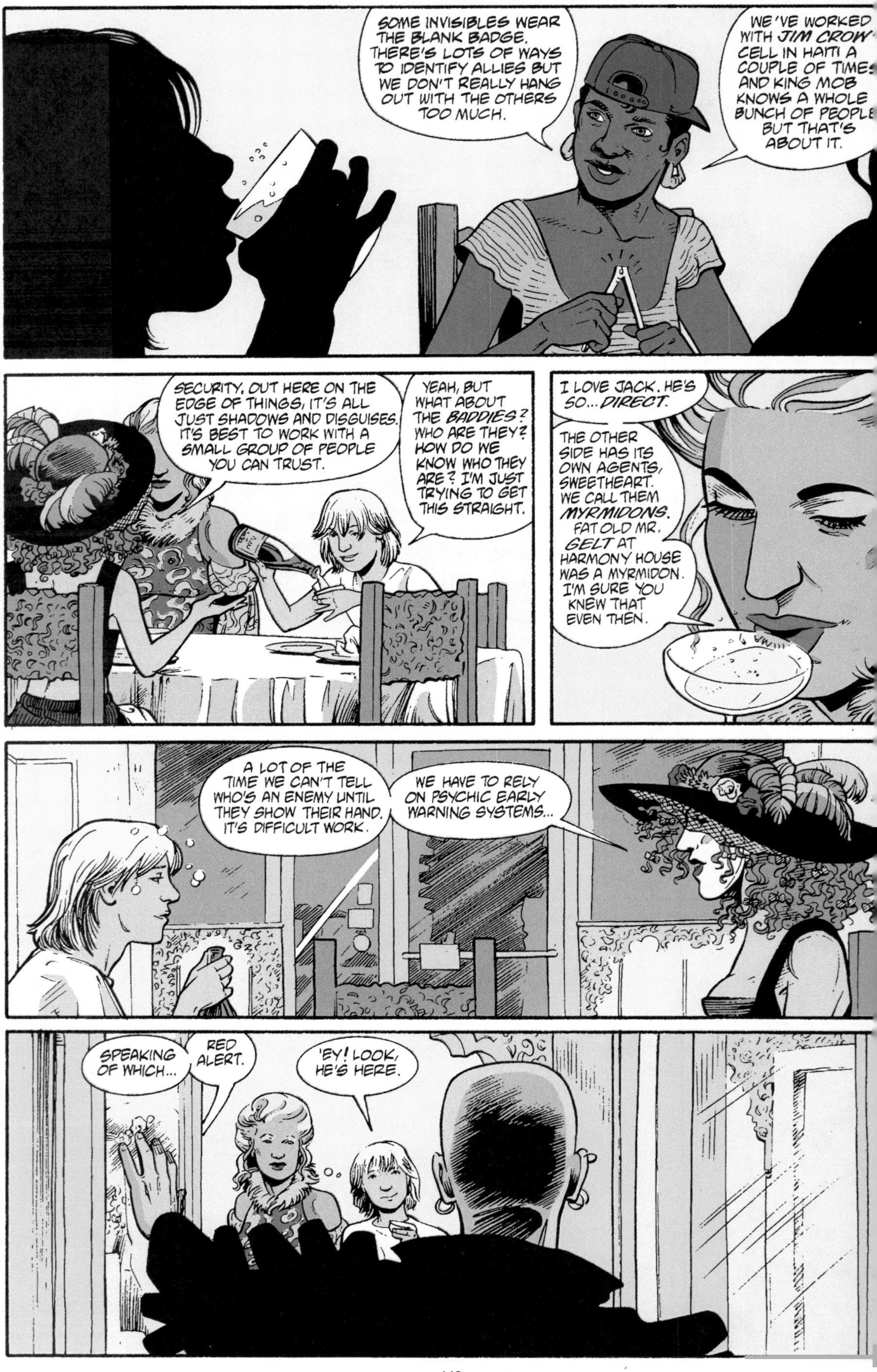
SOME INVISIBLES WEAR THE BLANK BADGE. THERE'S LOTS OF WAYS TO IDENTIFY ALLIES BUT WE DON'T REALLY HANG OUT WITH THE OTHERS TOO MUCH.
WE'VE WORKED WITH JIM CROW CELL IN HAITI A COUPLE OF TIMES AND KING MOB KNOWS A WHOLE BUNCH OF PEOPLE BUT THAT'S ABOUT IT.
SECURITY. OUT HERE ON THE EDGE OF THINGS, IT'S ALL JUST SHADOWS AND DISGUISES. IT'S BEST TO WORK WITH A SMALL GROUP OF PEOPLE YOU CAN TRUST.
YEAH, BUT WHAT ABOUT THE BADDIES? WHO ARE THEY? HOW DO WE KNOW WHO THEY ARE? I'M JUST TRYING TO GET THIS STRAIGHT.
I LOVE JACK. HE'S SO... DIRECT.
THE OTHER SIDE HAS ITS OWN AGENTS, SWEETHEART. WE CALL THEM MYRMIDONS. FAT OLD MR. GELT AT HARMONY HOUSE WAS A MYRMIDON. I'M SURE YOU KNEW THAT EVEN THEN.
A LOT OF THE TIME WE CAN'T TELL WHO'S AN ENEMY UNTIL THEY SHOW THEIR HAND. IT'S DIFFICULT WORK.
WE HAVE TO RELY ON PSYCHIC EARLY WARNING SYSTEMS...
SPEAKING OF WHICH...
RED ALERT.
'EY! LOOK, HE'S HERE.

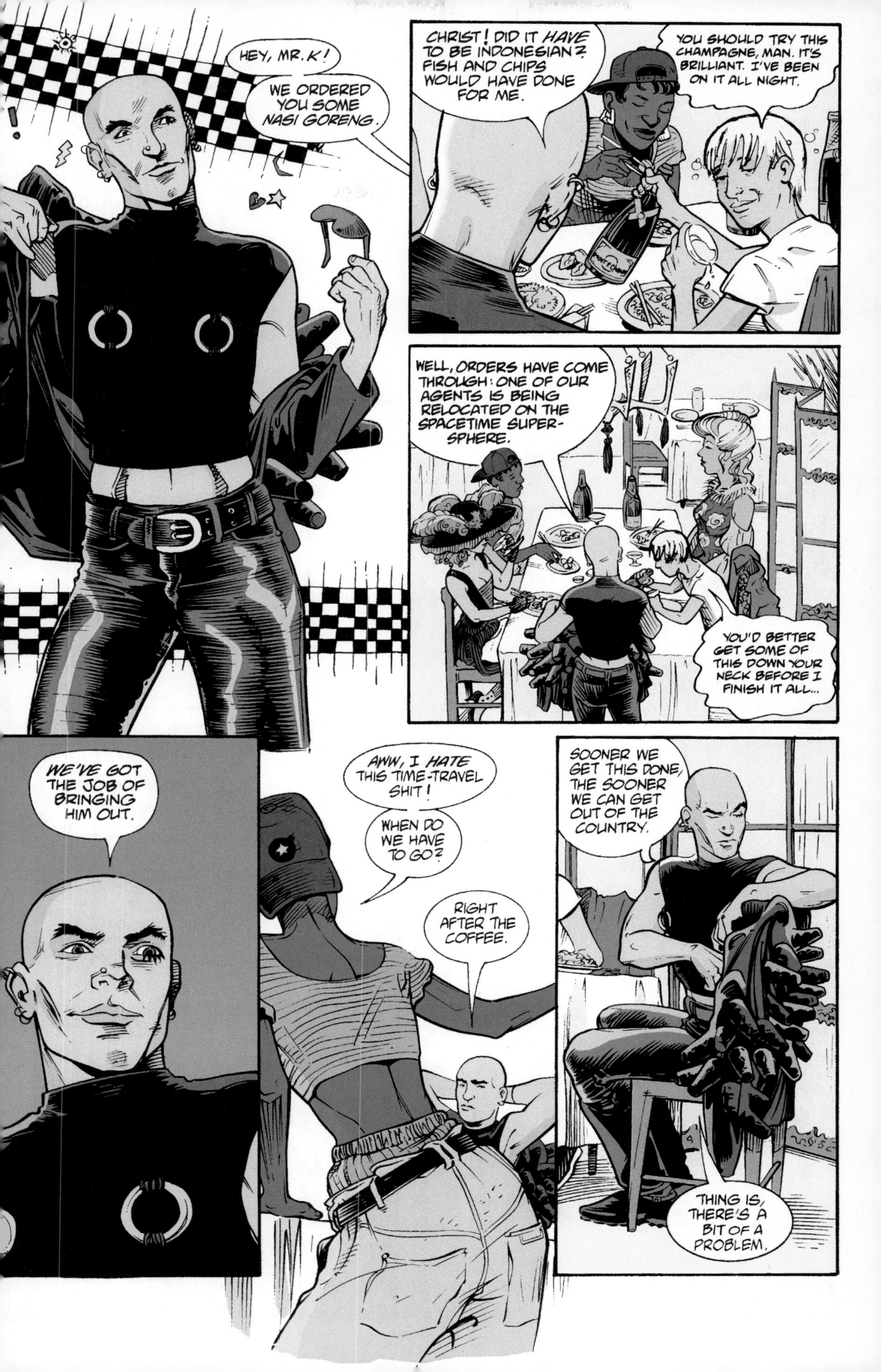
HEY, MR. K!
WE ORDERED YOU SOME NASI GORENG.
CHRIST! DID IT HAVE TO BE INDONESIAN? FISH AND CHIPS WOULD HAVE DONE FOR ME.
YOU SHOULD TRY THIS CHAMPAGNE, MAN. IT'S BRILLIANT. I'VE BEEN ON IT ALL NIGHT.
WELL, ORDERS HAVE COME THROUGH: ONE OF OUR AGENTS IS BEING RELOCATED ON THE SPACETIME SUPER-SPHERE.
YOU'D BETTER GET SOME OF THIS DOWN YOUR NECK BEFORE I FINISH IT ALL...
WE'VE GOT THE JOB OF BRINGING HIM OUT.
AWW, I HATE THIS TIME-TRAVEL SHIT!
WHEN DO WE HAVE TO GO?
RIGHT AFTER THE COFFEE.
SOONER WE GET THIS DONE, THE SOONER WE CAN GET OUT OF THE COUNTRY.
THING IS, THERE'S A BIT OF A PROBLEM.

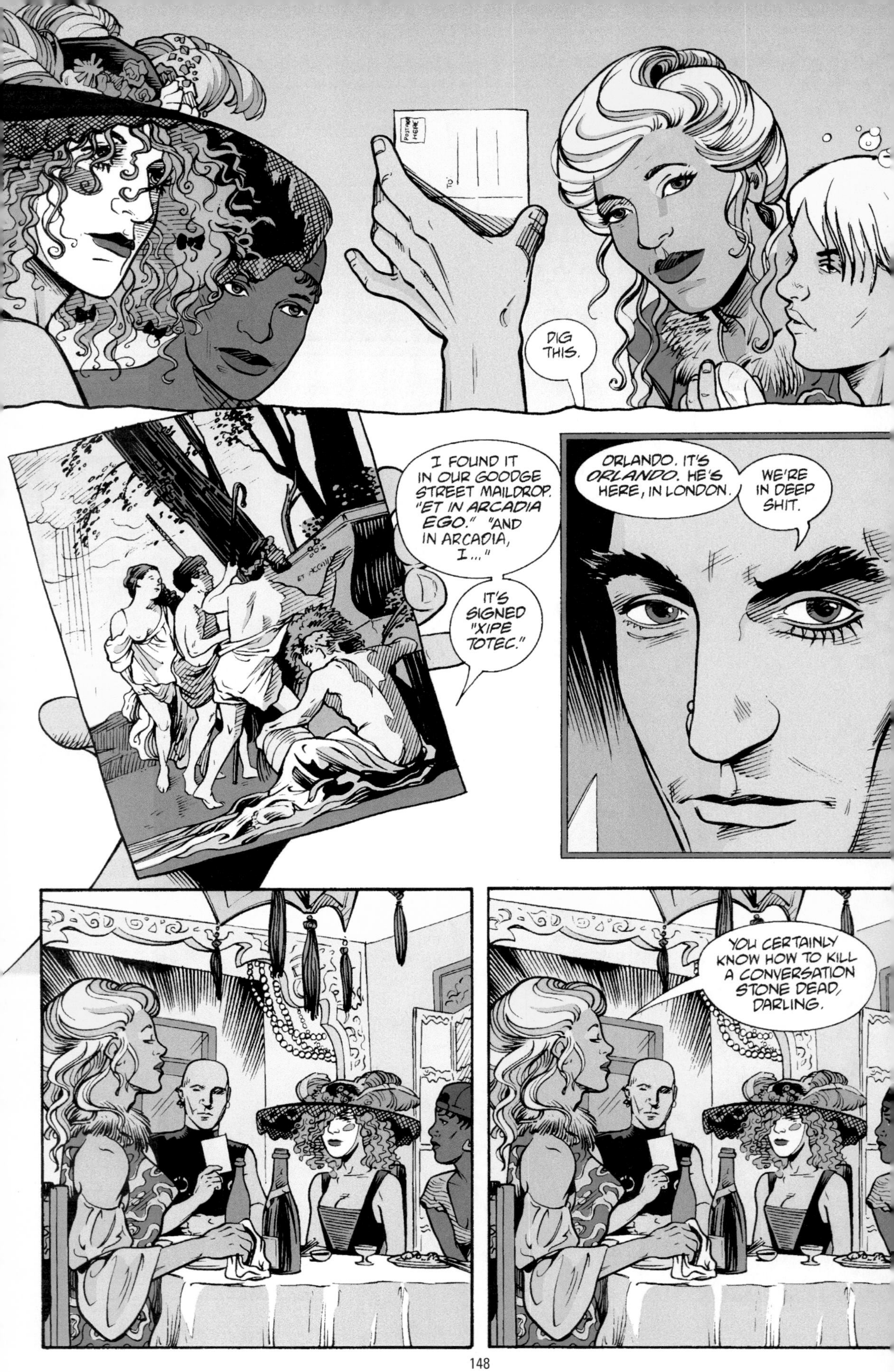
DIG THIS.
I FOUND IT IN OUR GOODGE STREET MAILDROP. "ET IN ARCADIA EGO." "AND IN ARCADIA, I..."
IT'S SIGNED "XIPE TOTEC."
ORLANDO. IT'S ORLANDO. HE'S HERE, IN LONDON.
WE'RE IN DEEP SHIT.
YOU CERTAINLY KNOW HOW TO KILL A CONVERSATION STONE DEAD, DARLING.

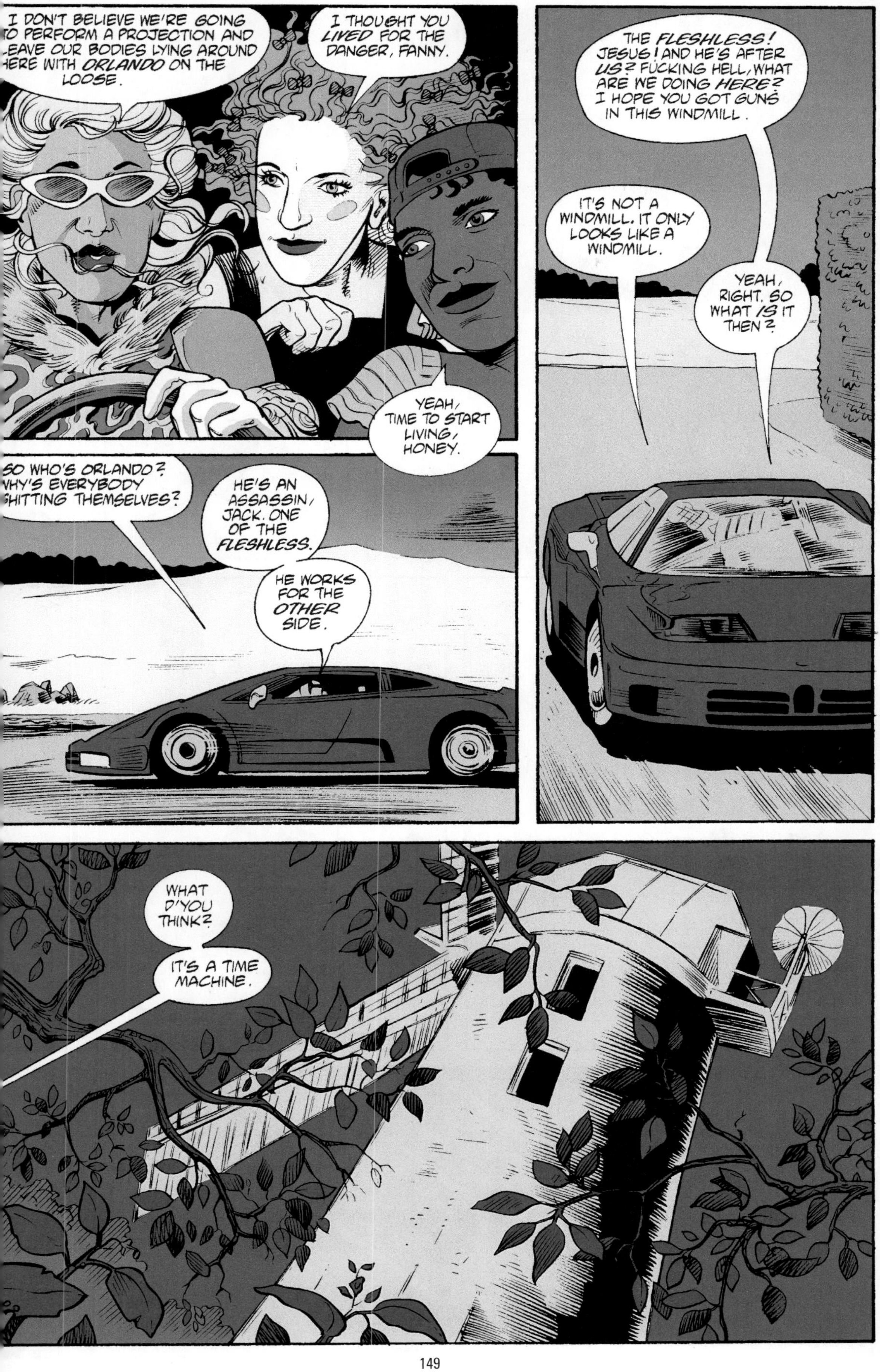

I DON'T BELIEVE WE'RE GOING TO PERFORM A PROJECTION AND LEAVE OUR BODIES LYING AROUND HERE WITH ORLANDO ON THE LOOSE.
I THOUGHT YOU LIVED FOR THE DANGER, FANNY.
YEAH, TIME TO START LIVING, HONEY.
SO WHO'S ORLANDO? WHY'S EVERYBODY SHITTING THEMSELVES?
HE'S AN ASSASSIN, JACK. ONE OF THE FLESHLESS.
HE WORKS FOR THE OTHER SIDE.
THE FLESHLESS! JESUS! AND HE'S AFTER US? FUCKING HELL, WHAT ARE WE DOING HERE? I HOPE YOU GOT GUNS IN THIS WINDMILL.
IT'S NOT A WINDMILL. IT ONLY LOOKS LIKE A WINDMILL.
YEAH, RIGHT. SO WHAT IS IT THEN?
WHAT D'YOU THINK?
IT'S A TIME MACHINE.

THE BANISHINGS ARE ALL DONE. I THINK WE CAN GO NOW.

EVERYBODY JOIN HANDS.

I'M NOT FUCKING HOLDING HANDS WITH HIM!

IT'S NOT MY HAND, SWEETHEART. IT'S A SATIN EVENING GLOVE FROM HARRODS.

STOP ACTING LIKE A FUCKING MORON, JACK, AND JUST DO IT.

TT!

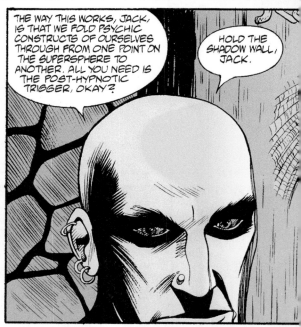

THE WAY THIS WORKS, JACK, IS THAT WE FOLD PSYCHIC CONSTRUCTS OF OURSELVES THROUGH FROM ONE POINT ON THE SUPERSPHERE TO ANOTHER. ALL YOU NEED IS THE POST-HYPNOTIC TRIGGER, OKAY?

HOLD THE SHADOW WALL, JACK.

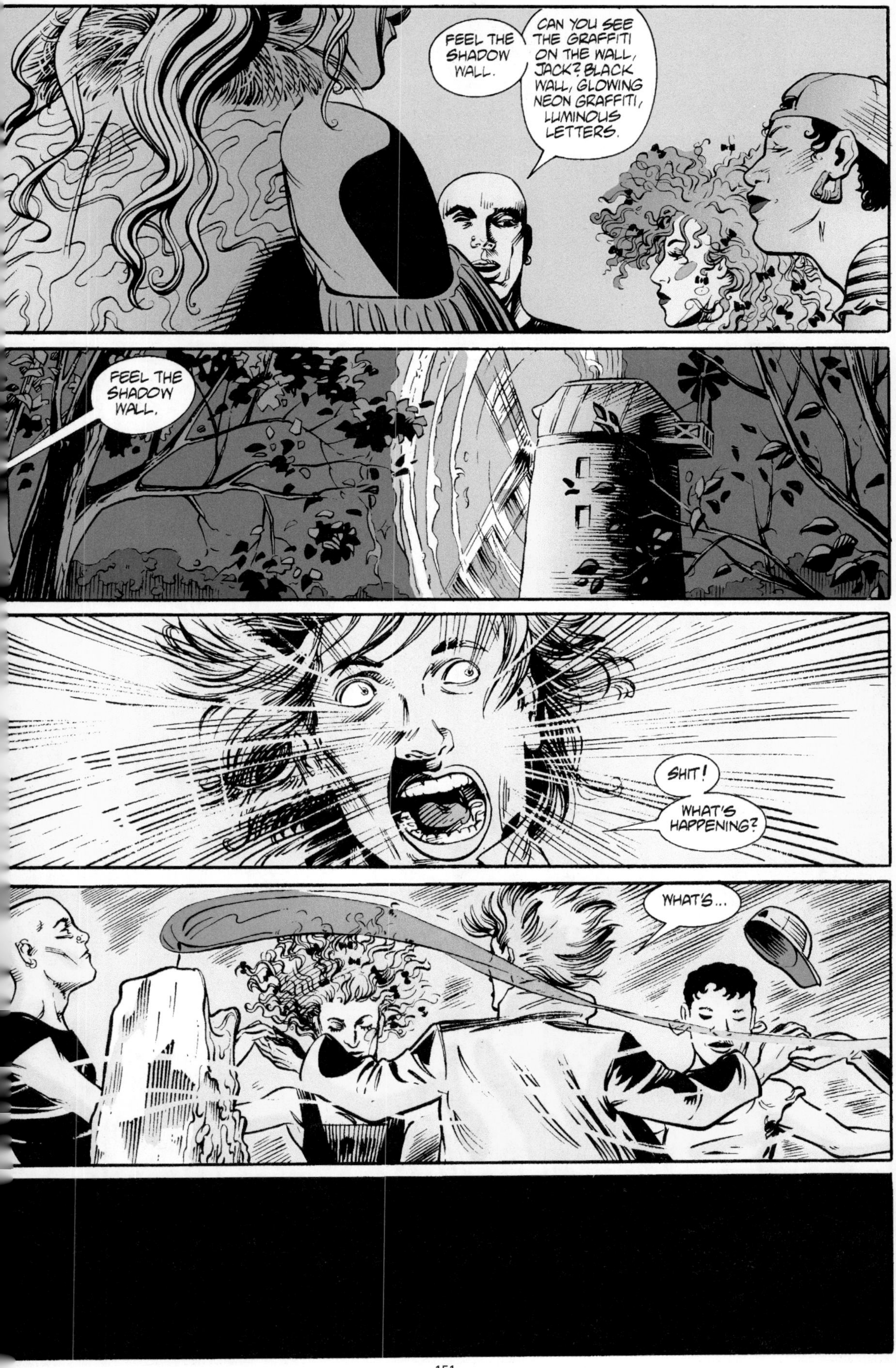
FEEL THE SHADOW WALL.
CAN YOU SEE THE GRAFFITI ON THE WALL, JACK? BLACK WALL, GLOWING NEON GRAFFITI, LUMINOUS LETTERS.
FEEL THE SHADOW WALL.
SHIT!
WHAT'S HAPPENING?
WHAT'S...

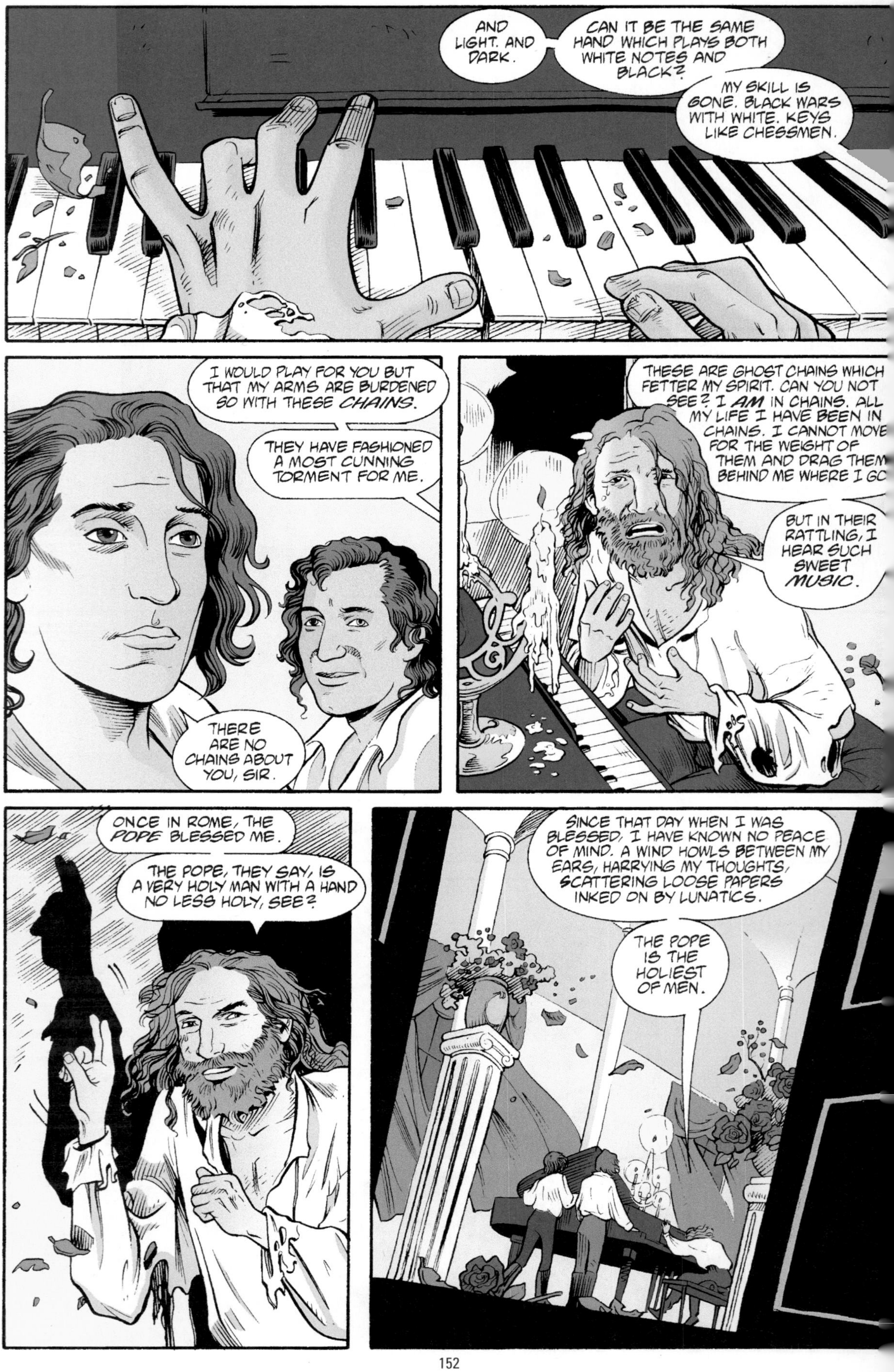
AND LIGHT. AND DARK.
CAN IT BE THE SAME HAND WHICH PLAYS BOTH WHITE NOTES AND BLACK?
MY SKILL IS GONE. BLACK WARS WITH WHITE. KEYS LIKE CHESSMEN.
I WOULD PLAY FOR YOU BUT THAT MY ARMS ARE BURDENED SO WITH THESE CHAINS.
THEY HAVE FASHIONED A MOST CUNNING TORMENT FOR ME.
THERE ARE NO CHAINS ABOUT YOU, SIR.
THESE ARE GHOST CHAINS WHICH FETTER MY SPIRIT. CAN YOU NOT SEE? I AM IN CHAINS. ALL MY LIFE I HAVE BEEN IN CHAINS. I CANNOT MOVE FOR THE WEIGHT OF THEM AND DRAG THEM BEHIND ME WHERE I GO.
BUT IN THEIR RATTLING, I HEAR SUCH SWEET MUSIC.
ONCE IN ROME, THE POPE BLESSED ME.
THE POPE, THEY SAY, IS A VERY HOLY MAN WITH A HAND NO LESS HOLY, SEE?
SINCE THAT DAY WHEN I WAS BLESSED, I HAVE KNOWN NO PEACE OF MIND. A WIND HOWLS BETWEEN MY EARS, HARRYING MY THOUGHTS, SCATTERING LOOSE PAPERS INKED ON BY LUNATICS.
THE POPE IS THE HOLIEST OF MEN.

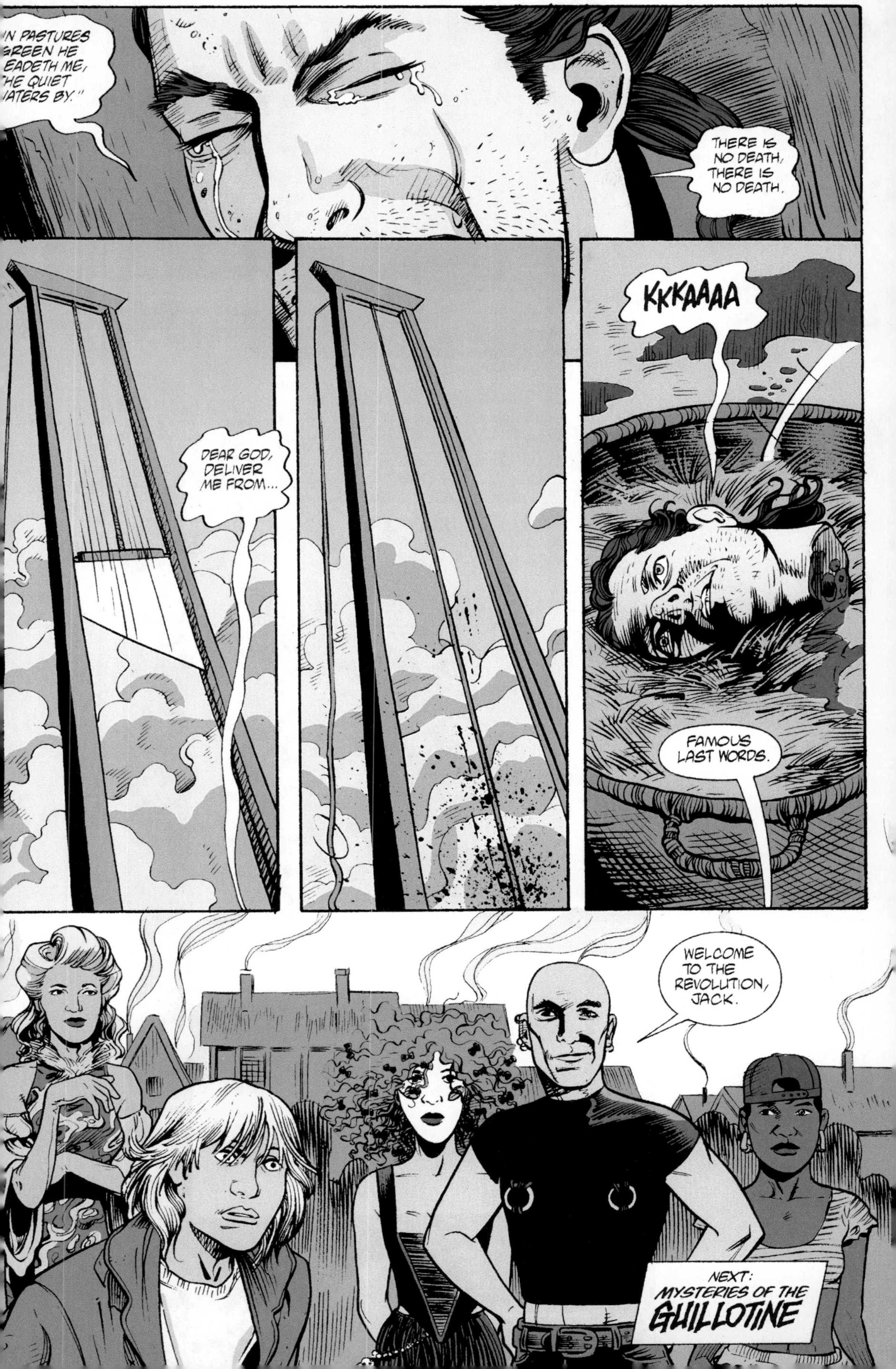

...IN PASTURES GREEN HE LEADETH ME, THE QUIET WATERS BY."
THERE IS NO DEATH, THERE IS NO DEATH.
DEAR GOD, DELIVER ME FROM...
KKKAAAA
FAMOUS LAST WORDS.
WELCOME TO THE REVOLUTION, JACK.
NEXT: MYSTERIES OF THE GUILLOTINE

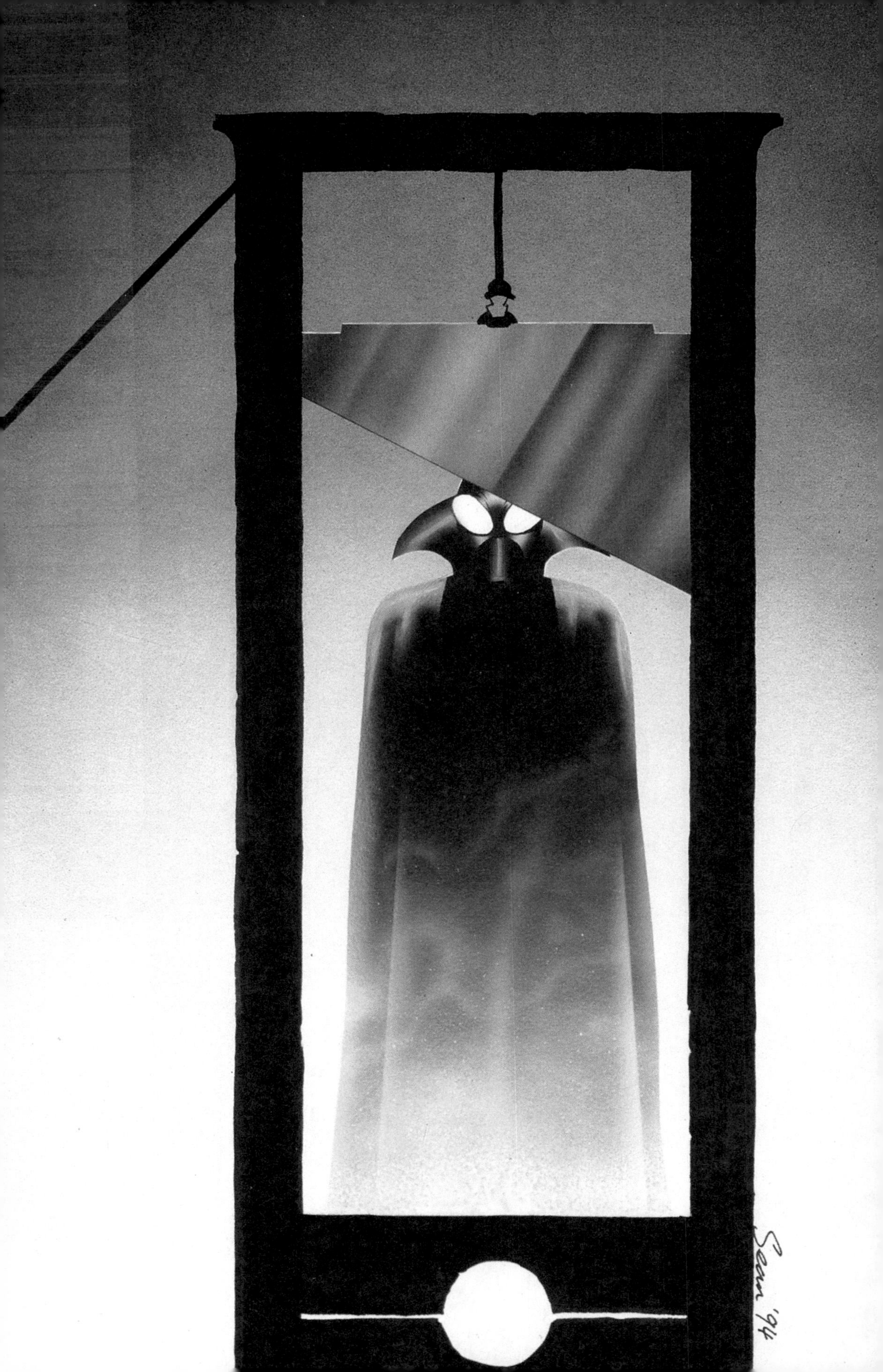
Sean '94

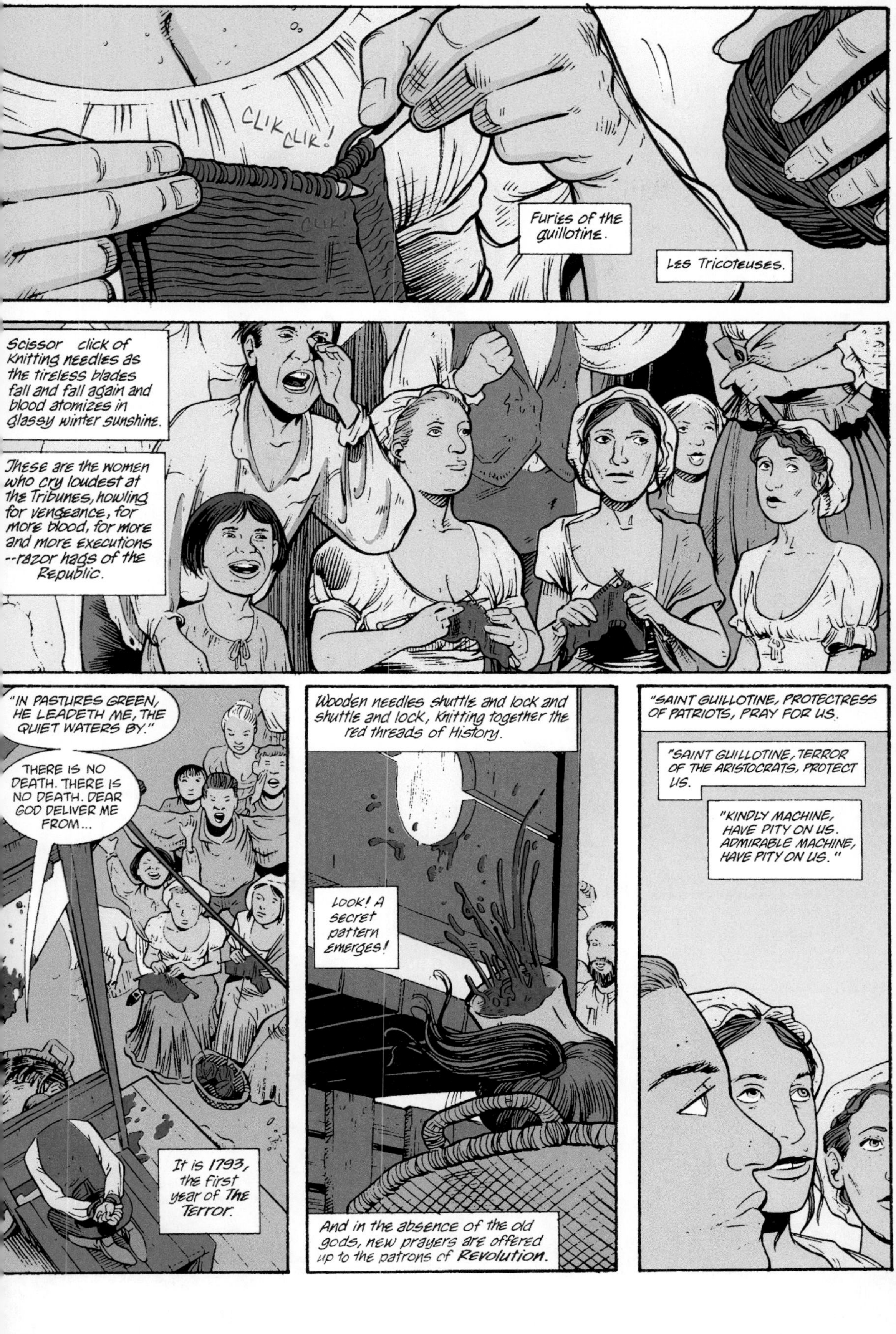
CLIK CLIK!
CLIK!
Furies of the guillotine.
Les Tricoteuses.
Scissor click of knitting needles as the tireless blades fall and fall again and blood atomizes in glassy winter sunshine.
These are the women who cry loudest at the Tribunes, howling for vengeance, for more blood, for more and more executions --razor hags of the Republic.
"IN PASTURES GREEN, HE LEADETH ME, THE QUIET WATERS BY."
THERE IS NO DEATH. THERE IS NO DEATH. DEAR GOD DELIVER ME FROM...
It is 1793, the first year of The Terror.
Wooden needles shuttle and lock and shuttle and lock, knitting together the red threads of History.
Look! A secret pattern emerges!
And in the absence of the old gods, new prayers are offered up to the patrons of Revolution.
"SAINT GUILLOTINE, PROTECTRESS OF PATRIOTS, PRAY FOR US.
"SAINT GUILLOTINE, TERROR OF THE ARISTOCRATS, PROTECT US.
"KINDLY MACHINE, HAVE PITY ON US. ADMIRABLE MACHINE, HAVE PITY ON US."

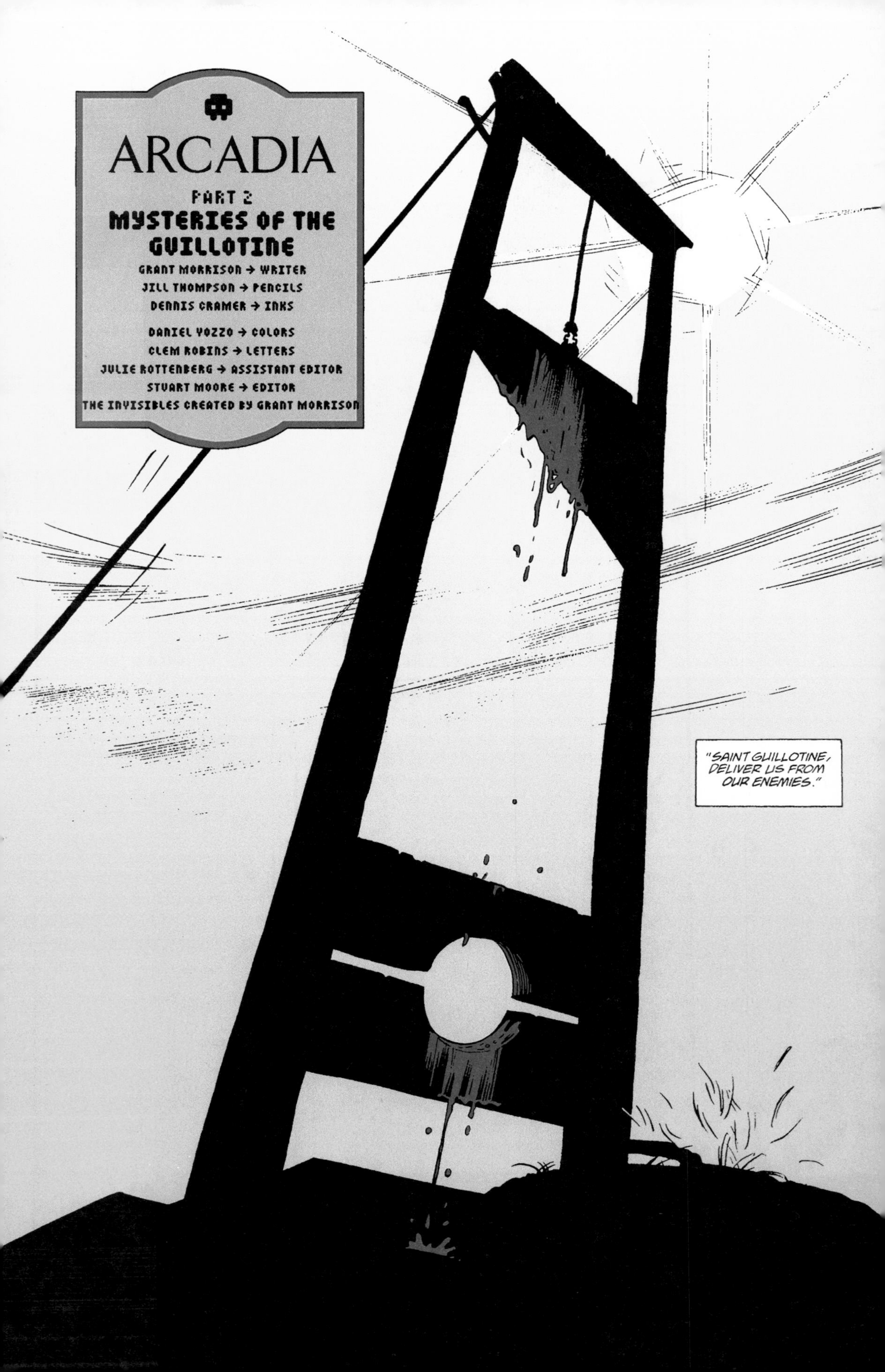
ARCADIA
PART 2
MYSTERIES OF THE GUILLOTINE
GRANT MORRISON → WRITER
JILL THOMPSON → PENCILS
DENNIS CRAMER → INKS
DANIEL VOZZO → COLORS
CLEM ROBINS → LETTERS
JULIE ROTTENBERG → ASSISTANT EDITOR
STUART MOORE → EDITOR
THE INVISIBLES CREATED BY GRANT MORRISON
"SAINT GUILLOTINE, DELIVER US FROM OUR ENEMIES."

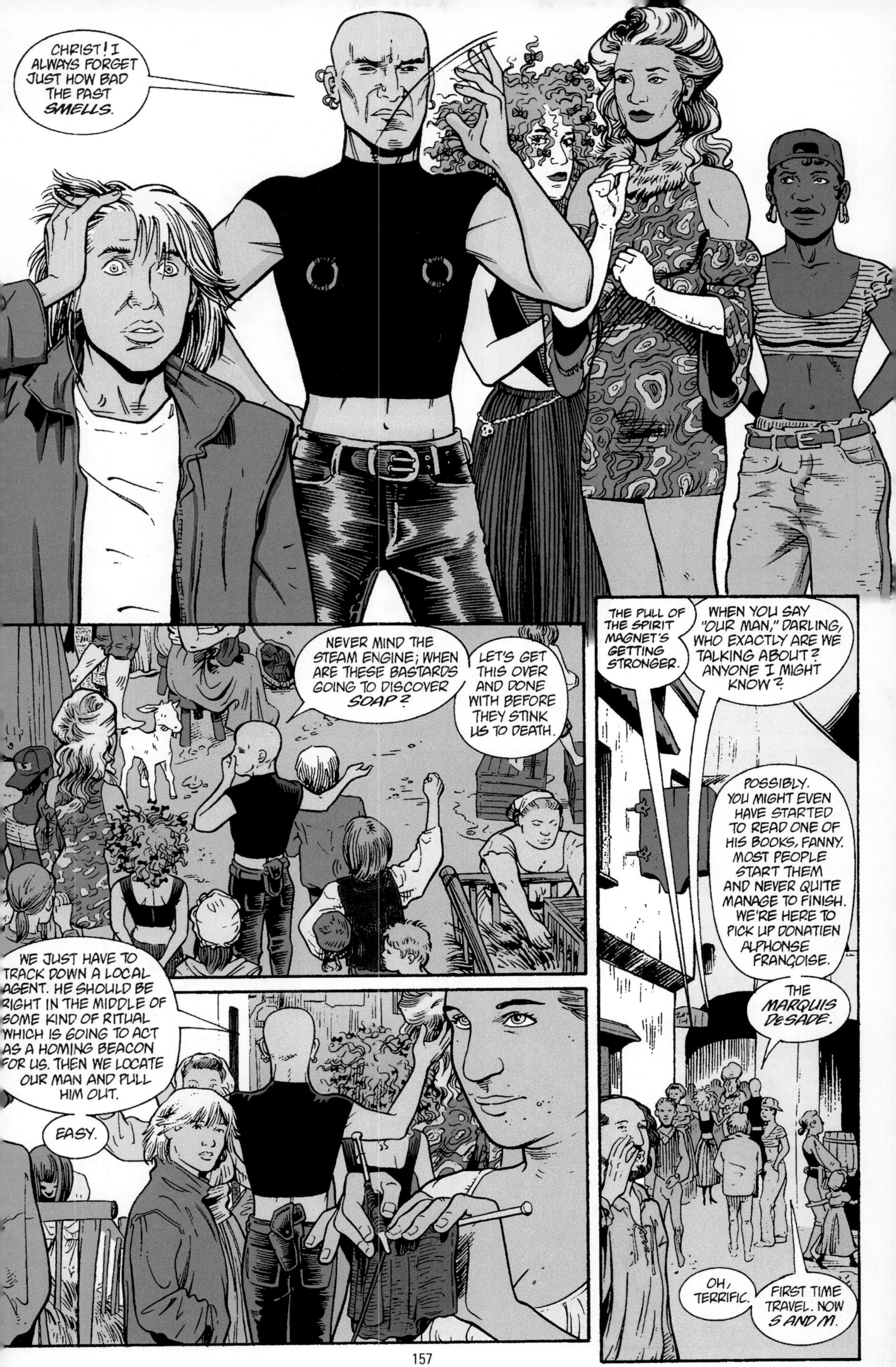
CHRIST! I ALWAYS FORGET JUST HOW BAD THE PAST SMELLS.
NEVER MIND THE STEAM ENGINE; WHEN ARE THESE BASTARDS GOING TO DISCOVER SOAP?
LET'S GET THIS OVER AND DONE WITH BEFORE THEY STINK US TO DEATH.
WE JUST HAVE TO TRACK DOWN A LOCAL AGENT. HE SHOULD BE RIGHT IN THE MIDDLE OF SOME KIND OF RITUAL WHICH IS GOING TO ACT AS A HOMING BEACON FOR US. THEN WE LOCATE OUR MAN AND PULL HIM OUT.
EASY.
THE PULL OF THE SPIRIT MAGNET'S GETTING STRONGER.
WHEN YOU SAY "OUR MAN," DARLING, WHO EXACTLY ARE WE TALKING ABOUT? ANYONE I MIGHT KNOW?
POSSIBLY. YOU MIGHT EVEN HAVE STARTED TO READ ONE OF HIS BOOKS, FANNY. MOST PEOPLE START THEM AND NEVER QUITE MANAGE TO FINISH. WE'RE HERE TO PICK UP DONATIEN ALPHONSE FRANÇOISE.
THE MARQUIS DeSADE.
OH, TERRIFIC.
FIRST TIME TRAVEL. NOW S AND M.

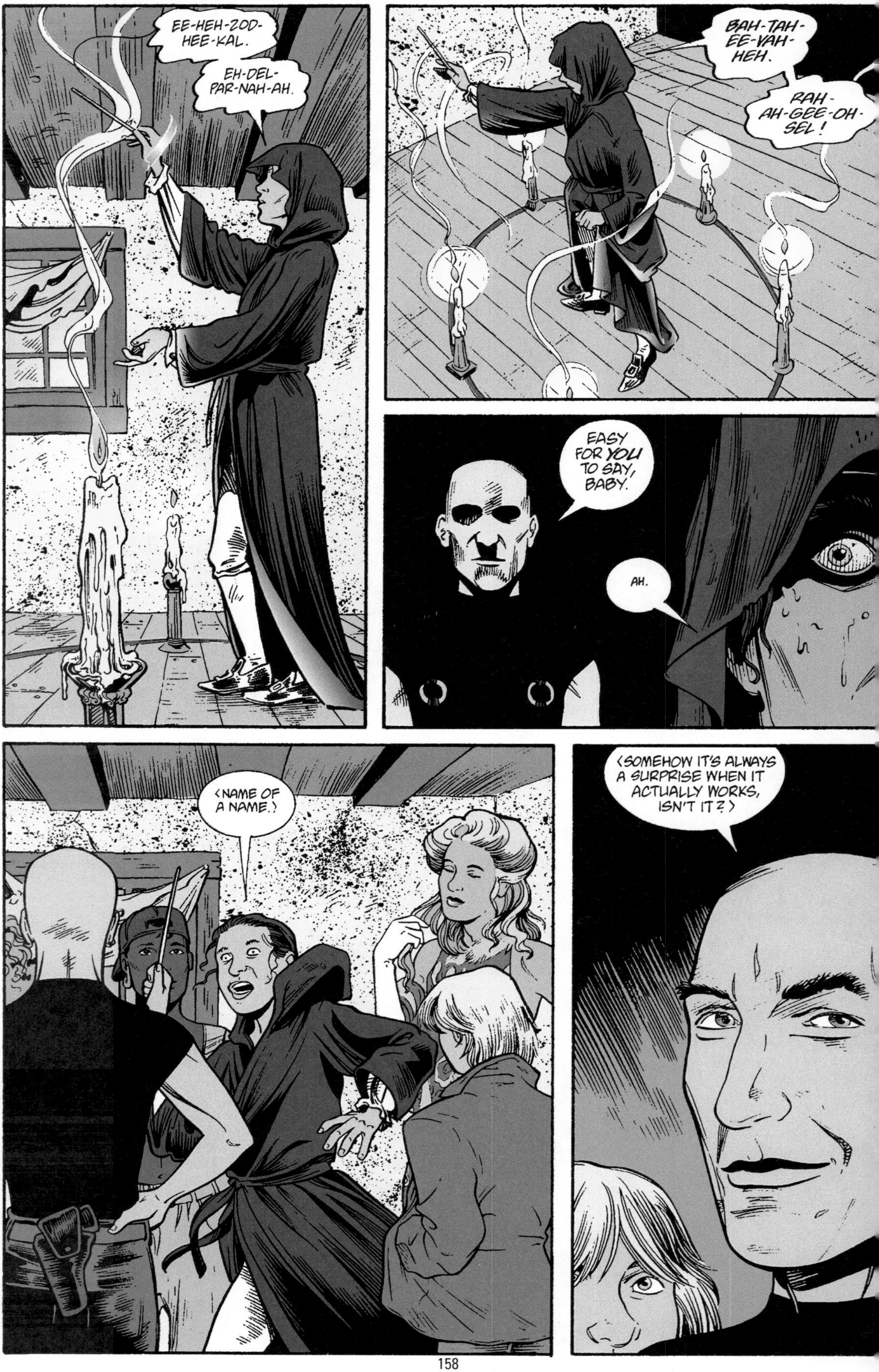
EE-HEH-ZOD-HEE-KAL.
EH-DEL-PAR-NAH-AH.
BAH-TAH EE-VAH-HEH.
RAH-AH-GEE-OH-SEL!
EASY FOR YOU TO SAY, BABY.
AH.
<NAME OF A NAME.>
<SOMEHOW IT'S ALWAYS A SURPRISE WHEN IT ACTUALLY WORKS, ISN'T IT?>

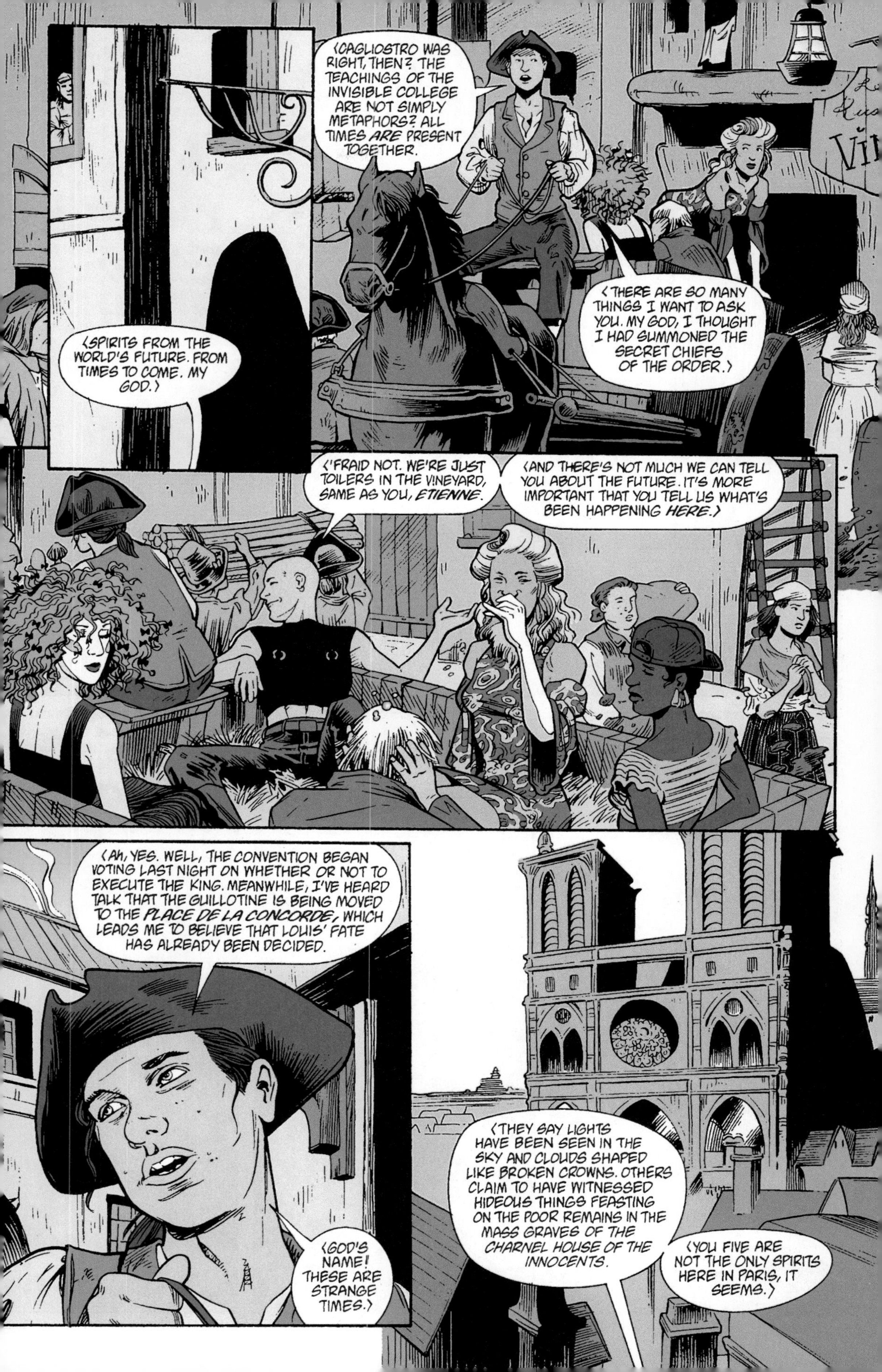

‹CAGLIOSTRO WAS RIGHT, THEN? THE TEACHINGS OF THE INVISIBLE COLLEGE ARE NOT SIMPLY METAPHORS? ALL TIMES *ARE* PRESENT TOGETHER.
‹SPIRITS FROM THE WORLD'S FUTURE. FROM TIMES TO COME. MY GOD.›
‹THERE ARE SO MANY THINGS I WANT TO ASK YOU. MY GOD, I THOUGHT I HAD SUMMONED THE SECRET CHIEFS OF THE ORDER.›
‹'FRAID NOT. WE'RE JUST TOILERS IN THE VINEYARD, SAME AS YOU, *ETIENNE*.
‹AND THERE'S NOT MUCH WE CAN TELL YOU ABOUT THE FUTURE. IT'S MORE IMPORTANT THAT YOU TELL US WHAT'S BEEN HAPPENING *HERE*.›
‹AH, YES. WELL, THE CONVENTION BEGAN VOTING LAST NIGHT ON WHETHER OR NOT TO EXECUTE THE KING. MEANWHILE, I'VE HEARD TALK THAT THE GUILLOTINE IS BEING MOVED TO THE *PLACE DE LA CONCORDE*, WHICH LEADS ME TO BELIEVE THAT LOUIS' FATE HAS ALREADY BEEN DECIDED.
‹GOD'S NAME! THESE ARE STRANGE TIMES.›
‹THEY SAY LIGHTS HAVE BEEN SEEN IN THE SKY AND CLOUDS SHAPED LIKE BROKEN CROWNS. OTHERS CLAIM TO HAVE WITNESSED HIDEOUS THINGS FEASTING ON THE POOR REMAINS IN THE MASS GRAVES OF THE CHARNEL HOUSE OF THE INNOCENTS.
‹YOU FIVE ARE NOT THE ONLY SPIRITS HERE IN PARIS, IT SEEMS.›

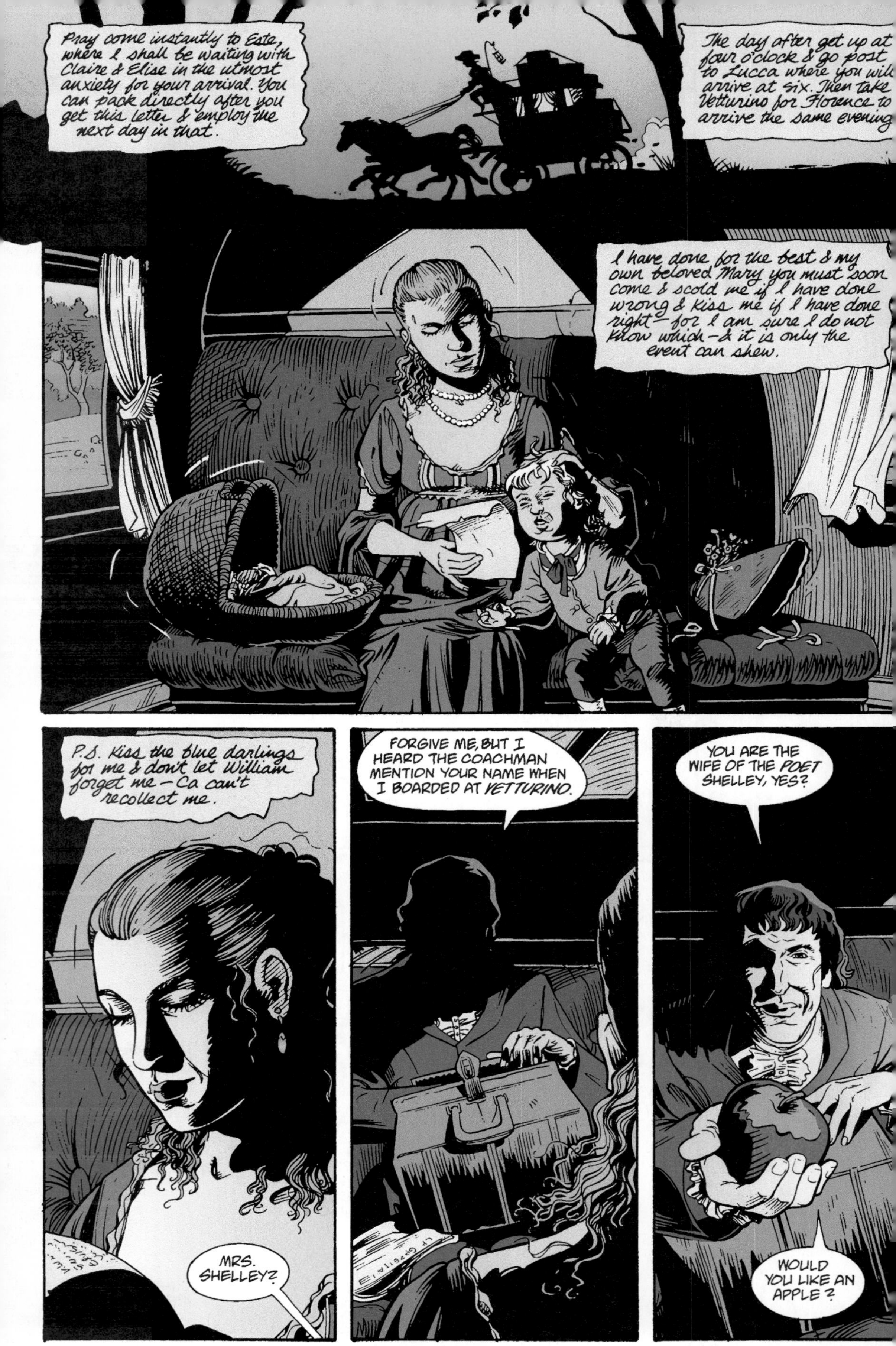

Pray come instantly to Este, where I shall be waiting with Claire & Elise in the utmost anxiety for your arrival. You can pack directly after you get this letter & employ the next day in that.
The day after get up at four o'clock & go post to Lucca where you will arrive at six. Then take Vetturino for Florence to arrive the same evening.
I have done for the best & my own beloved Mary you must soon come & scold me if I have done wrong & kiss me if I have done right—for I am sure I do not know which—& it is only the event can shew.
P.S. Kiss the blue darlings for me & don't let William forget me—Ca can't recollect me.
MRS. SHELLEY?
FORGIVE ME, BUT I HEARD THE COACHMAN MENTION YOUR NAME WHEN I BOARDED AT VETTURINO.
YOU ARE THE WIFE OF THE POET SHELLEY, YES?
WOULD YOU LIKE AN APPLE?

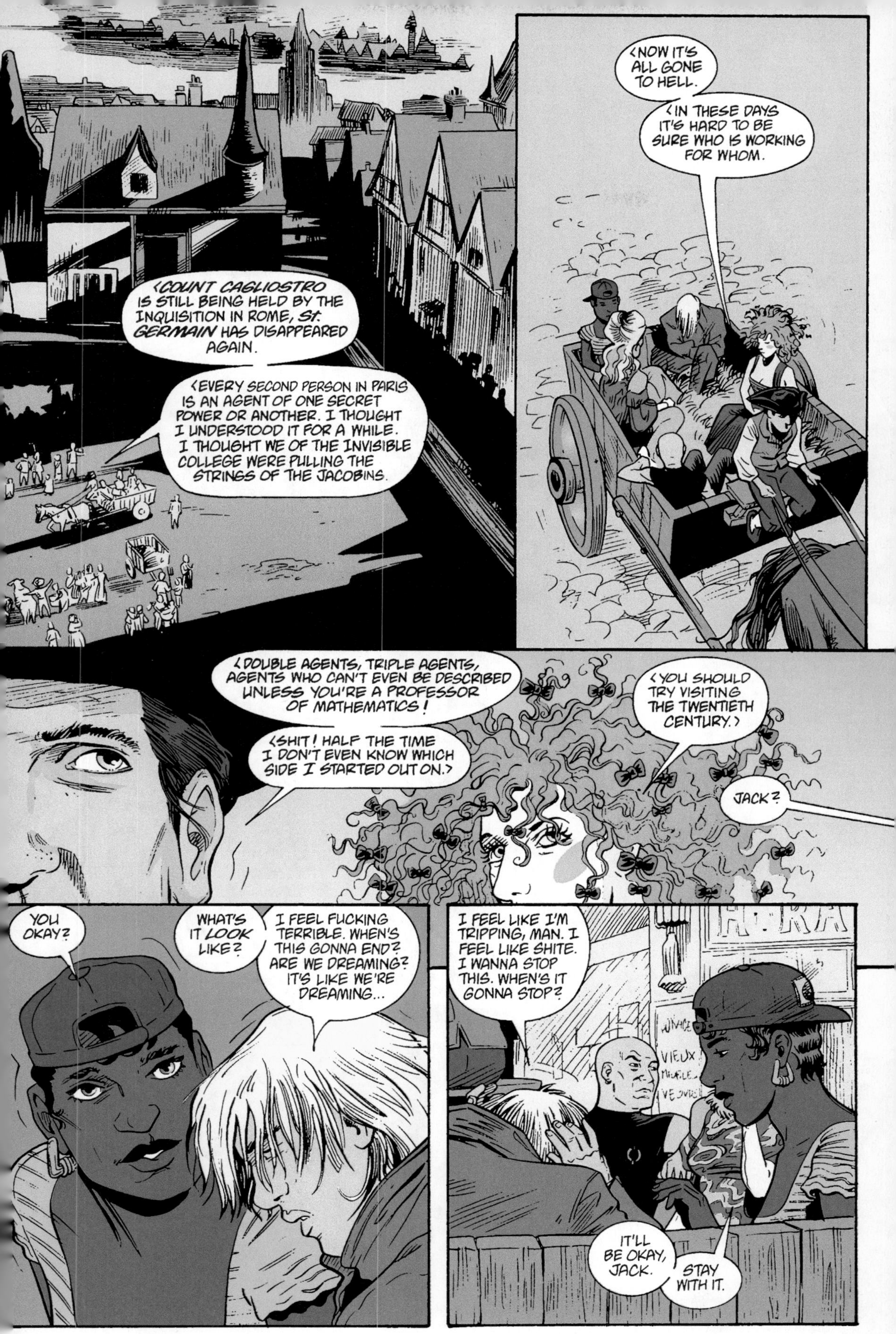
<COUNT CAGLIOSTRO IS STILL BEING HELD BY THE INQUISITION IN ROME, ST. GERMAIN HAS DISAPPEARED AGAIN.
<EVERY SECOND PERSON IN PARIS IS AN AGENT OF ONE SECRET POWER OR ANOTHER. I THOUGHT I UNDERSTOOD IT FOR A WHILE. I THOUGHT WE OF THE INVISIBLE COLLEGE WERE PULLING THE STRINGS OF THE JACOBINS.
<NOW IT'S ALL GONE TO HELL.
<IN THESE DAYS IT'S HARD TO BE SURE WHO IS WORKING FOR WHOM.
<DOUBLE AGENTS, TRIPLE AGENTS, AGENTS WHO CAN'T EVEN BE DESCRIBED UNLESS YOU'RE A PROFESSOR OF MATHEMATICS!
<SHIT! HALF THE TIME I DON'T EVEN KNOW WHICH SIDE I STARTED OUT ON.>
<YOU SHOULD TRY VISITING THE TWENTIETH CENTURY.>
JACK?
YOU OKAY?
WHAT'S IT LOOK LIKE?
I FEEL FUCKING TERRIBLE. WHEN'S THIS GONNA END? ARE WE DREAMING? IT'S LIKE WE'RE DREAMING...
I FEEL LIKE I'M TRIPPING, MAN. I FEEL LIKE SHITE. I WANNA STOP THIS. WHEN'S IT GONNA STOP?
VIEUX
IT'LL BE OKAY, JACK.
STAY WITH IT.

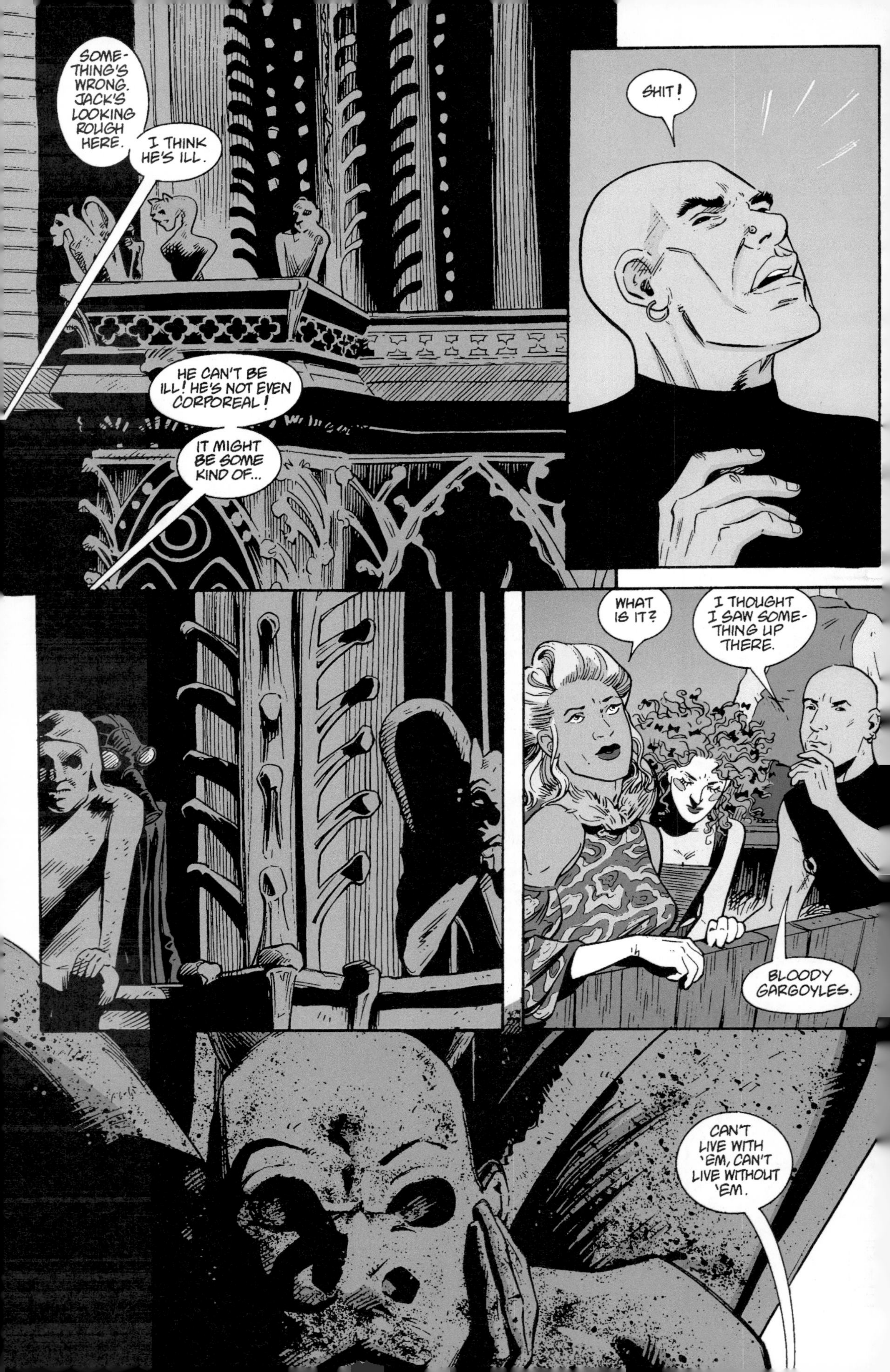
SOMETHING'S WRONG. JACK'S LOOKING ROUGH HERE.
I THINK HE'S ILL.
HE CAN'T BE ILL! HE'S NOT EVEN CORPOREAL!
IT MIGHT BE SOME KIND OF...
SHIT!
WHAT IS IT?
I THOUGHT I SAW SOMETHING UP THERE.
BLOODY GARGOYLES.
CAN'T LIVE WITH 'EM, CAN'T LIVE WITHOUT 'EM.

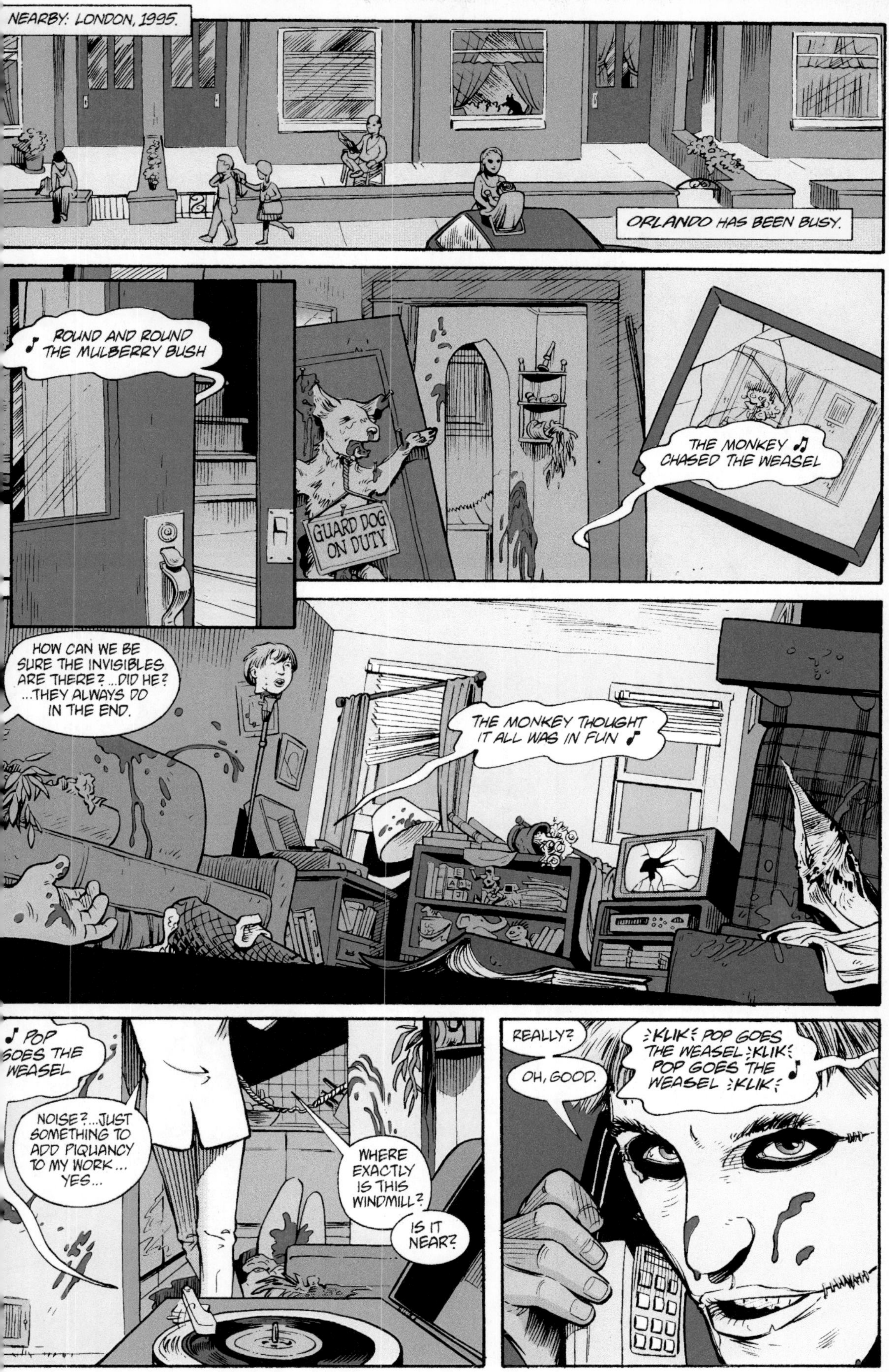

NEARBY: LONDON, 1995.
ORLANDO HAS BEEN BUSY.
♪ ROUND AND ROUND THE MULBERRY BUSH
GUARD DOG ON DUTY
THE MONKEY ♫ CHASED THE WEASEL
HOW CAN WE BE SURE THE INVISIBLES ARE THERE? ...DID HE? ...THEY ALWAYS DO IN THE END.
THE MONKEY THOUGHT IT ALL WAS IN FUN ♪
♪ POP GOES THE WEASEL
NOISE? ...JUST SOMETHING TO ADD PIQUANCY TO MY WORK... YES...
WHERE EXACTLY IS THIS WINDMILL?
IS IT NEAR?
REALLY?
OH, GOOD.
KLIK POP GOES THE WEASEL KLIK POP GOES THE WEASEL KLIK ♪

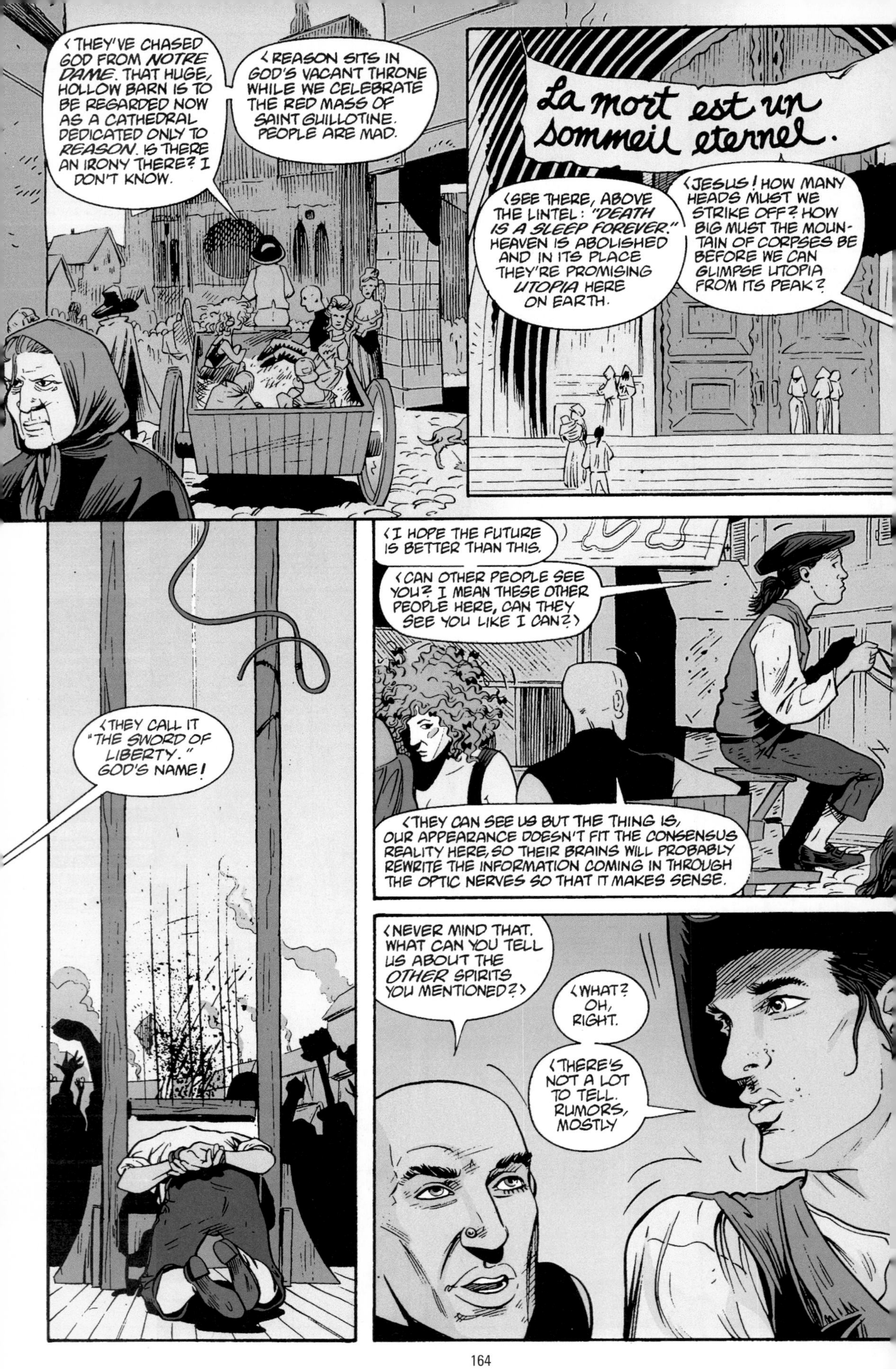
‹THEY'VE CHASED GOD FROM *NOTRE DAME*. THAT HUGE, HOLLOW BARN IS TO BE REGARDED NOW AS A CATHEDRAL DEDICATED ONLY TO *REASON*. IS THERE AN IRONY THERE? I DON'T KNOW.
‹REASON SITS IN GOD'S VACANT THRONE WHILE WE CELEBRATE THE RED MASS OF SAINT GUILLOTINE. PEOPLE ARE MAD.
La mort est un sommeil eternel.
‹SEE THERE, ABOVE THE LINTEL: *"DEATH IS A SLEEP FOREVER."* HEAVEN IS ABOLISHED AND IN ITS PLACE THEY'RE PROMISING *UTOPIA* HERE ON EARTH.
‹JESUS! HOW MANY HEADS MUST WE STRIKE OFF? HOW BIG MUST THE MOUNTAIN OF CORPSES BE BEFORE WE CAN GLIMPSE UTOPIA FROM ITS PEAK?
‹THEY CALL IT "THE *SWORD OF LIBERTY*." GOD'S NAME!
‹I HOPE THE FUTURE IS BETTER THAN THIS.
‹CAN OTHER PEOPLE SEE YOU? I MEAN THESE OTHER PEOPLE HERE, CAN THEY SEE YOU LIKE I CAN?›
‹THEY CAN SEE US BUT THE THING IS, OUR APPEARANCE DOESN'T FIT THE CONSENSUS REALITY HERE, SO THEIR BRAINS WILL PROBABLY REWRITE THE INFORMATION COMING IN THROUGH THE OPTIC NERVES SO THAT IT MAKES SENSE.
‹NEVER MIND THAT. WHAT CAN YOU TELL US ABOUT THE *OTHER* SPIRITS YOU MENTIONED?›
‹WHAT? OH, RIGHT.
‹THERE'S NOT A LOT TO TELL. RUMORS, MOSTLY

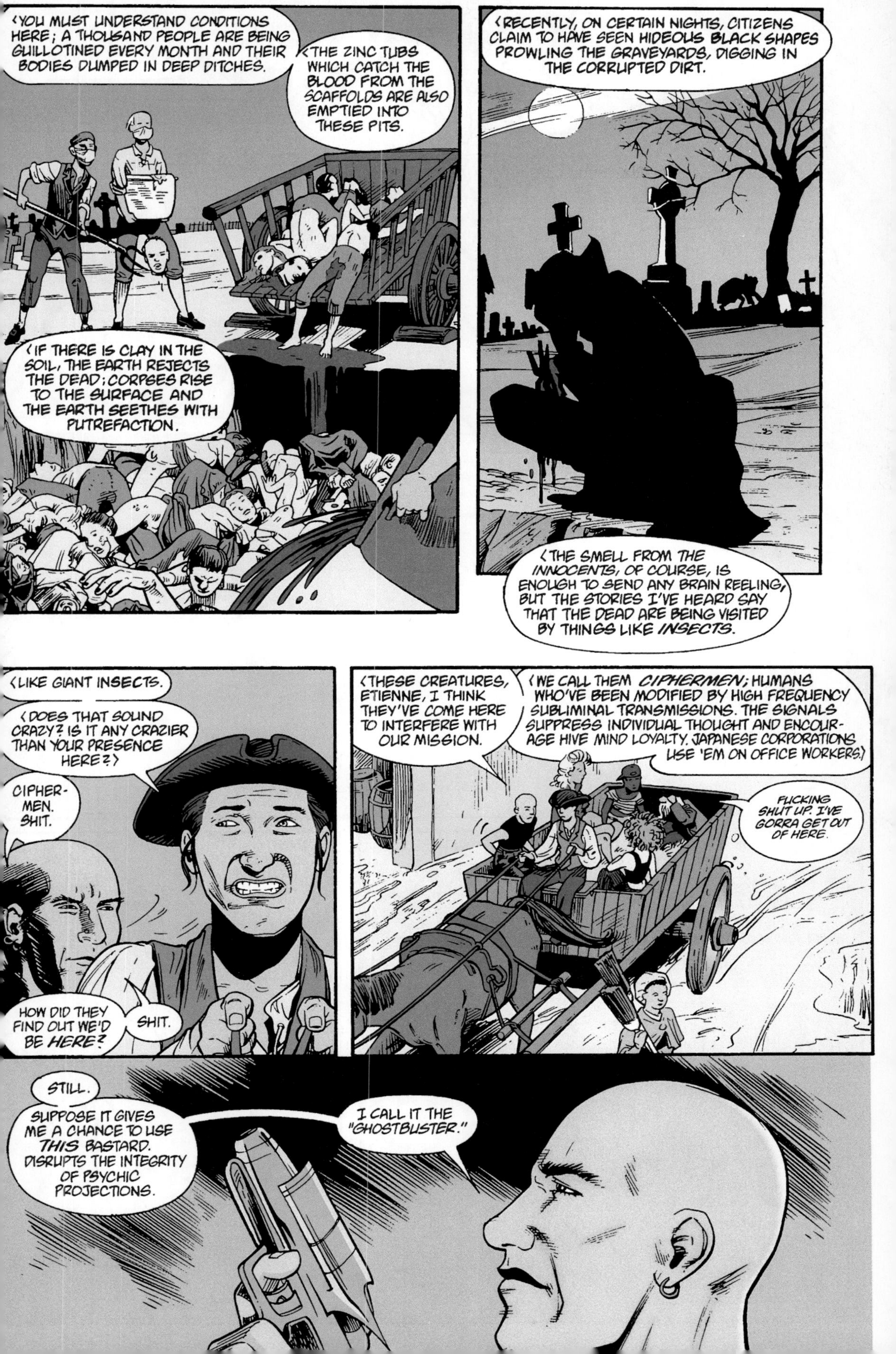

<YOU MUST UNDERSTAND CONDITIONS HERE; A THOUSAND PEOPLE ARE BEING GUILLOTINED EVERY MONTH AND THEIR BODIES DUMPED IN DEEP DITCHES.
<THE ZINC TUBS WHICH CATCH THE BLOOD FROM THE SCAFFOLDS ARE ALSO EMPTIED INTO THESE PITS.
<IF THERE IS CLAY IN THE SOIL, THE EARTH REJECTS THE DEAD; CORPSES RISE TO THE SURFACE AND THE EARTH SEETHES WITH PUTREFACTION.
<RECENTLY, ON CERTAIN NIGHTS, CITIZENS CLAIM TO HAVE SEEN HIDEOUS BLACK SHAPES PROWLING THE GRAVEYARDS, DIGGING IN THE CORRUPTED DIRT.
<THE SMELL FROM THE *INNOCENTS*, OF COURSE, IS ENOUGH TO SEND ANY BRAIN REELING, BUT THE STORIES I'VE HEARD SAY THAT THE DEAD ARE BEING VISITED BY THINGS LIKE *INSECTS*.
<LIKE GIANT INSECTS.
<DOES THAT SOUND CRAZY? IS IT ANY CRAZIER THAN YOUR PRESENCE HERE?>
CIPHER-MEN. SHIT.
HOW DID THEY FIND OUT WE'D BE *HERE*?
SHIT.
<THESE CREATURES, ETIENNE, I THINK THEY'VE COME HERE TO INTERFERE WITH OUR MISSION.
<WE CALL THEM *CIPHERMEN*; HUMANS WHO'VE BEEN MODIFIED BY HIGH FREQUENCY SUBLIMINAL TRANSMISSIONS. THE SIGNALS SUPPRESS INDIVIDUAL THOUGHT AND ENCOURAGE HIVE MIND LOYALTY. JAPANESE CORPORATIONS USE 'EM ON OFFICE WORKERS.>
FUCKING SHUT UP. I'VE GOTTA GET OUT OF HERE.
STILL.
SUPPOSE IT GIVES ME A CHANCE TO USE *THIS* BASTARD. DISRUPTS THE INTEGRITY OF PSYCHIC PROJECTIONS.
I CALL IT THE "*GHOSTBUSTER*."

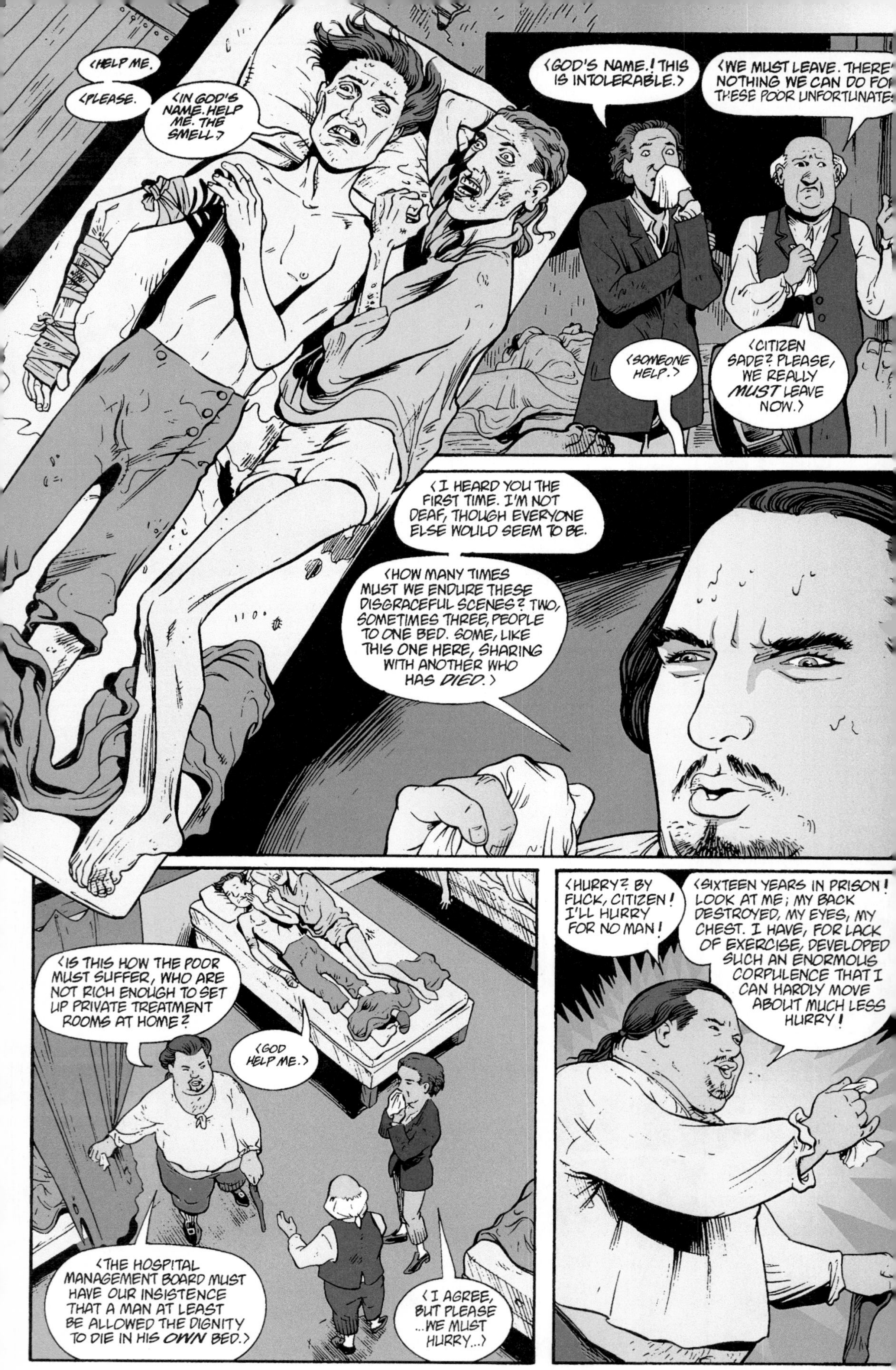

<HELP ME.
<PLEASE.
<IN GOD'S NAME. HELP ME. THE SMELL.>
<GOD'S NAME! THIS IS INTOLERABLE.>
<WE MUST LEAVE. THERE'S NOTHING WE CAN DO FOR THESE POOR UNFORTUNATES.
<SOMEONE HELP.>
<CITIZEN SADE? PLEASE, WE REALLY MUST LEAVE NOW.>
<I HEARD YOU THE FIRST TIME. I'M NOT DEAF, THOUGH EVERYONE ELSE WOULD SEEM TO BE.
<HOW MANY TIMES MUST WE ENDURE THESE DISGRACEFUL SCENES? TWO, SOMETIMES THREE, PEOPLE TO ONE BED. SOME, LIKE THIS ONE HERE, SHARING WITH ANOTHER WHO HAS DIED.>
<IS THIS HOW THE POOR MUST SUFFER, WHO ARE NOT RICH ENOUGH TO SET UP PRIVATE TREATMENT ROOMS AT HOME?
<GOD HELP ME.>
<THE HOSPITAL MANAGEMENT BOARD MUST HAVE OUR INSISTENCE THAT A MAN AT LEAST BE ALLOWED THE DIGNITY TO DIE IN HIS OWN BED.>
<I AGREE, BUT PLEASE ...WE MUST HURRY...>
<HURRY? BY FUCK, CITIZEN! I'LL HURRY FOR NO MAN!
<SIXTEEN YEARS IN PRISON! LOOK AT ME; MY BACK DESTROYED, MY EYES, MY CHEST. I HAVE, FOR LACK OF EXERCISE, DEVELOPED SUCH AN ENORMOUS CORPULENCE THAT I CAN HARDLY MOVE ABOUT MUCH LESS HURRY!

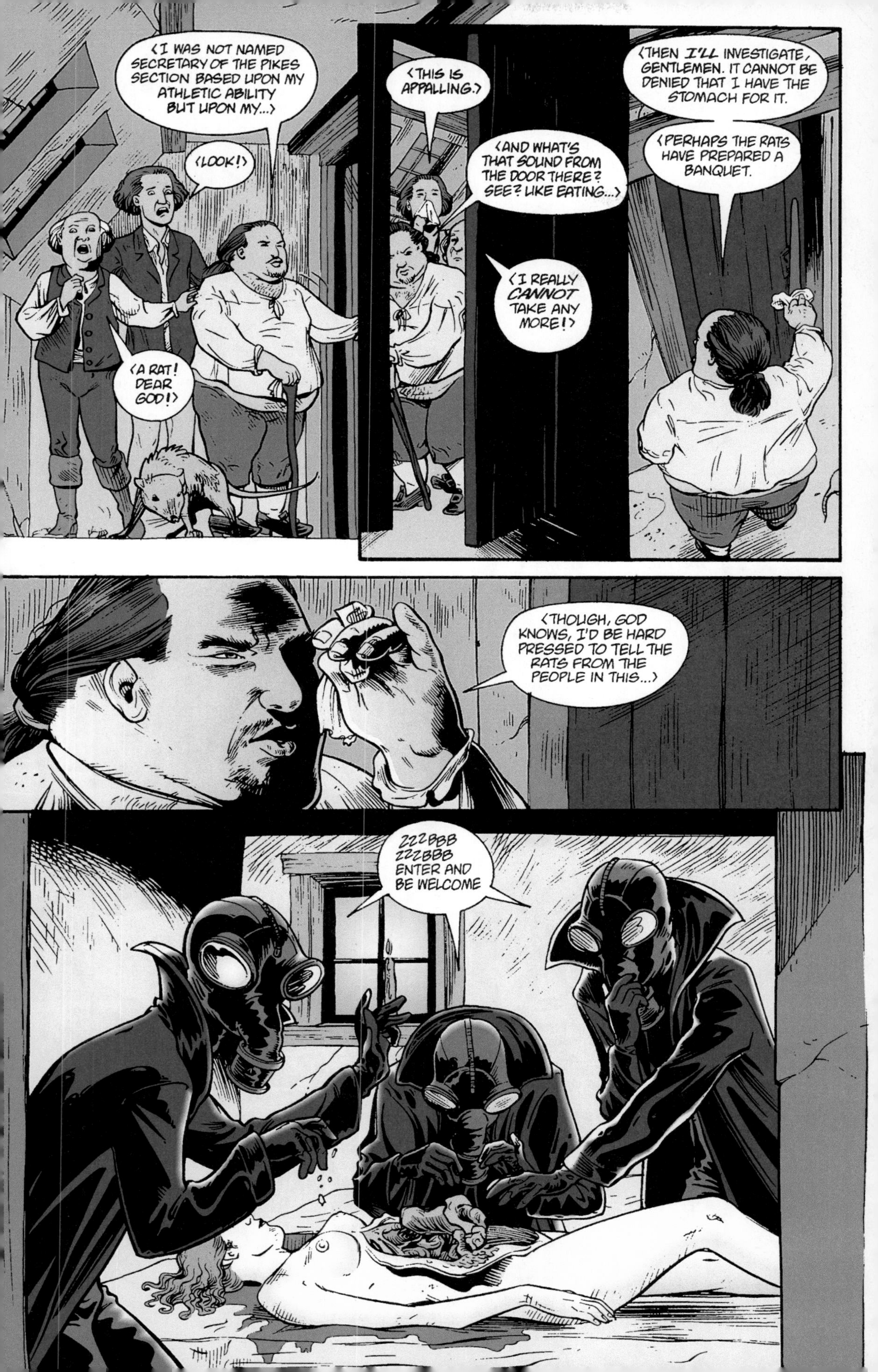
‹I WAS NOT NAMED SECRETARY OF THE PIKES SECTION BASED UPON MY ATHLETIC ABILITY BUT UPON MY...›
‹LOOK!›
‹A RAT! DEAR GOD!›
‹THIS IS APPALLING.›
‹AND WHAT'S THAT SOUND FROM THE DOOR THERE? SEE? LIKE EATING...›
‹I REALLY CANNOT TAKE ANY MORE!›
‹THEN I'LL INVESTIGATE, GENTLEMEN. IT CANNOT BE DENIED THAT I HAVE THE STOMACH FOR IT.
‹PERHAPS THE RATS HAVE PREPARED A BANQUET.
‹THOUGH, GOD KNOWS, I'D BE HARD PRESSED TO TELL THE RATS FROM THE PEOPLE IN THIS...›
ZZZBBB ZZZBBB ENTER AND BE WELCOME

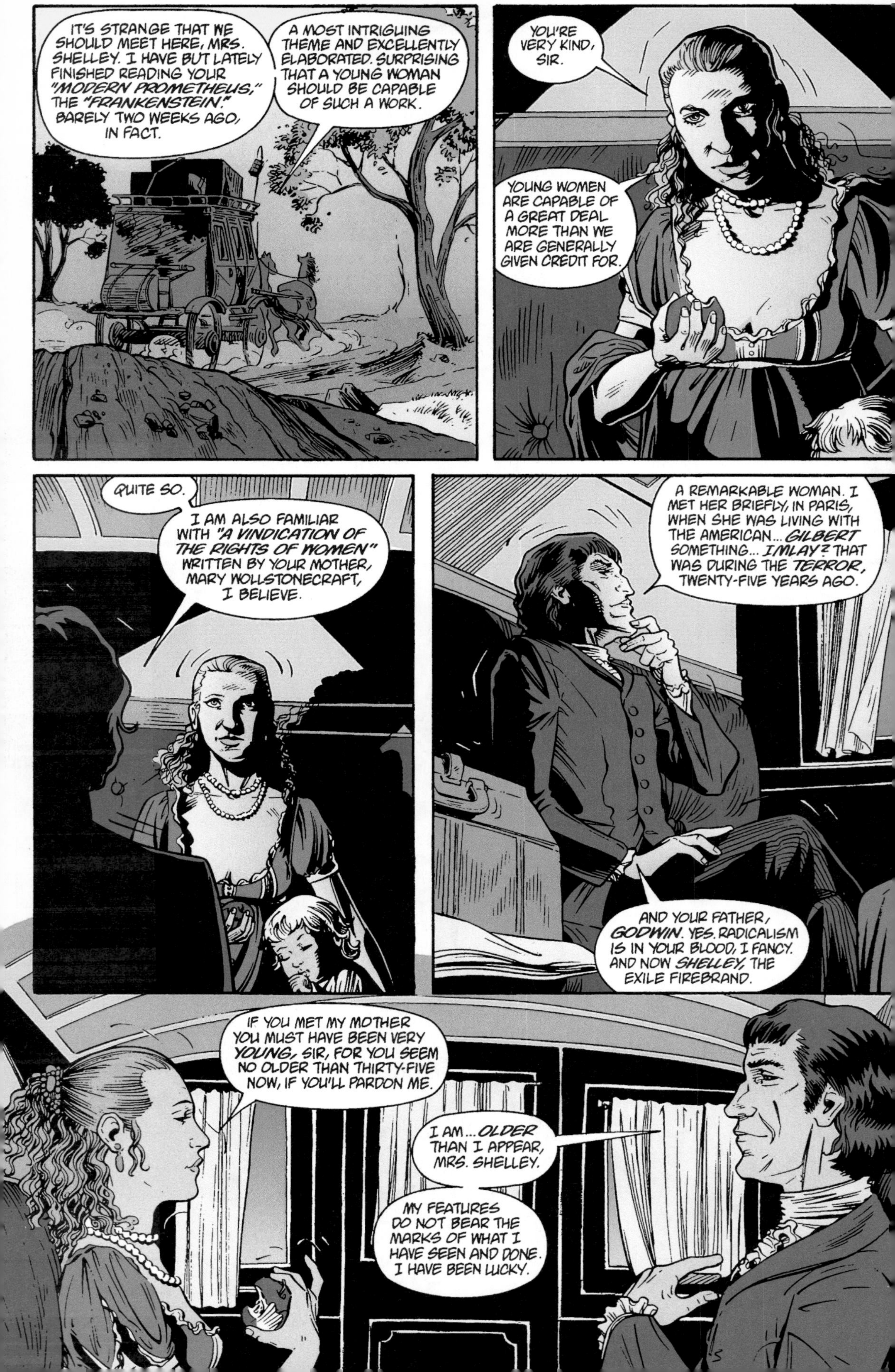
IT'S STRANGE THAT WE SHOULD MEET HERE, MRS. SHELLEY. I HAVE BUT LATELY FINISHED READING YOUR "MODERN PROMETHEUS," THE "FRANKENSTEIN." BARELY TWO WEEKS AGO, IN FACT.
A MOST INTRIGUING THEME AND EXCELLENTLY ELABORATED. SURPRISING THAT A YOUNG WOMAN SHOULD BE CAPABLE OF SUCH A WORK.
YOU'RE VERY KIND, SIR.
YOUNG WOMEN ARE CAPABLE OF A GREAT DEAL MORE THAN WE ARE GENERALLY GIVEN CREDIT FOR.
QUITE SO.
I AM ALSO FAMILIAR WITH "A VINDICATION OF THE RIGHTS OF WOMEN" WRITTEN BY YOUR MOTHER, MARY WOLLSTONECRAFT, I BELIEVE.
A REMARKABLE WOMAN. I MET HER BRIEFLY, IN PARIS, WHEN SHE WAS LIVING WITH THE AMERICAN... GILBERT SOMETHING... IMLAY? THAT WAS DURING THE TERROR, TWENTY-FIVE YEARS AGO.
AND YOUR FATHER, GODWIN. YES. RADICALISM IS IN YOUR BLOOD, I FANCY. AND NOW SHELLEY, THE EXILE FIREBRAND.
IF YOU MET MY MOTHER YOU MUST HAVE BEEN VERY YOUNG, SIR, FOR YOU SEEM NO OLDER THAN THIRTY-FIVE NOW, IF YOU'LL PARDON ME.
I AM... OLDER THAN I APPEAR, MRS. SHELLEY.
MY FEATURES DO NOT BEAR THE MARKS OF WHAT I HAVE SEEN AND DONE. I HAVE BEEN LUCKY.

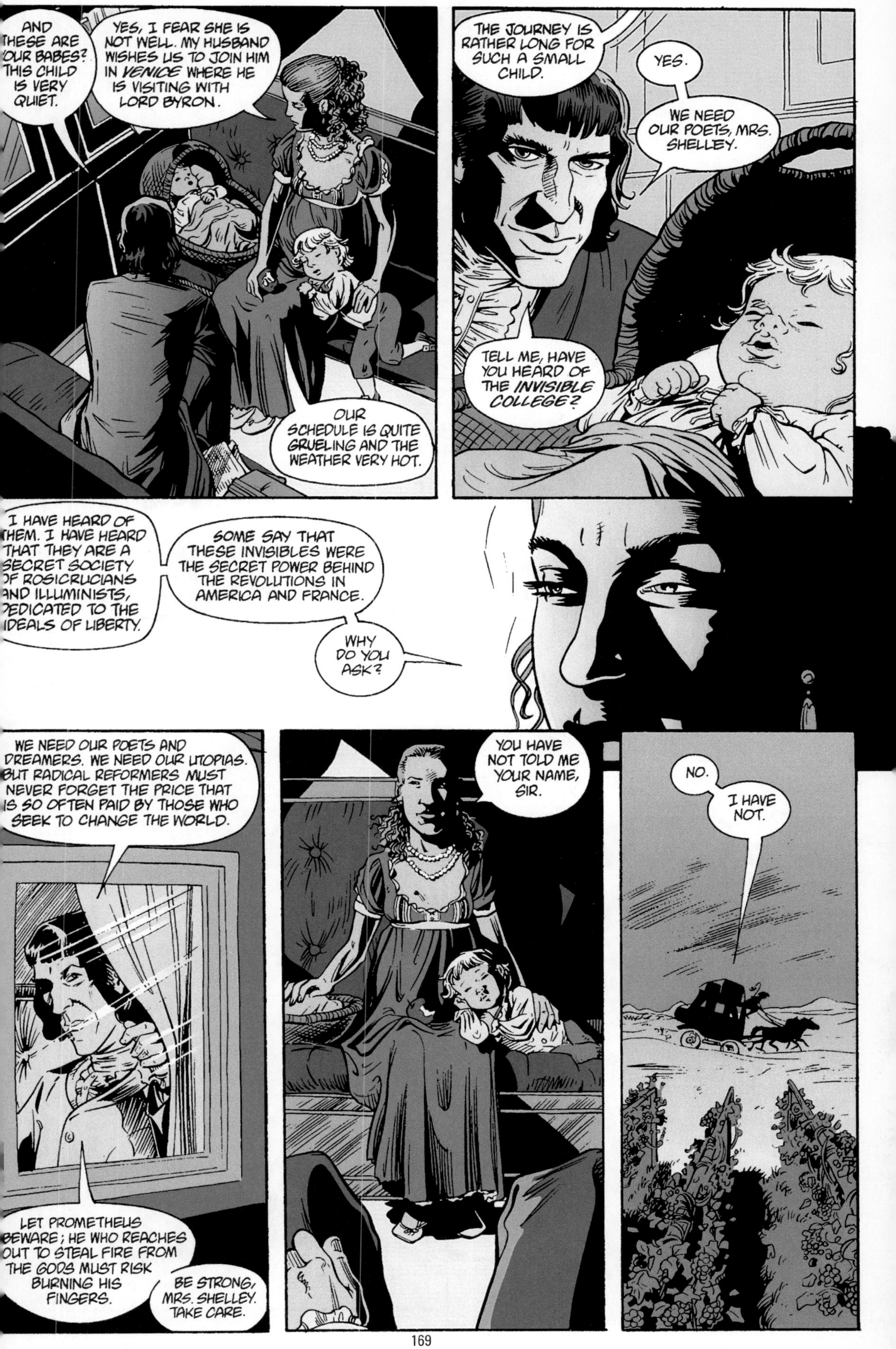

AND THESE ARE YOUR BABES? THIS CHILD IS VERY QUIET.
YES, I FEAR SHE IS NOT WELL. MY HUSBAND WISHES US TO JOIN HIM IN VENICE WHERE HE IS VISITING WITH LORD BYRON.
OUR SCHEDULE IS QUITE GRUELING AND THE WEATHER VERY HOT.
THE JOURNEY IS RATHER LONG FOR SUCH A SMALL CHILD.
YES.
WE NEED OUR POETS, MRS. SHELLEY.
TELL ME, HAVE YOU HEARD OF THE INVISIBLE COLLEGE?
I HAVE HEARD OF THEM. I HAVE HEARD THAT THEY ARE A SECRET SOCIETY OF ROSICRUCIANS AND ILLUMINISTS, DEDICATED TO THE IDEALS OF LIBERTY.
SOME SAY THAT THESE INVISIBLES WERE THE SECRET POWER BEHIND THE REVOLUTIONS IN AMERICA AND FRANCE.
WHY DO YOU ASK?
WE NEED OUR POETS AND DREAMERS. WE NEED OUR UTOPIAS. BUT RADICAL REFORMERS MUST NEVER FORGET THE PRICE THAT IS SO OFTEN PAID BY THOSE WHO SEEK TO CHANGE THE WORLD.
LET PROMETHEUS BEWARE; HE WHO REACHES OUT TO STEAL FIRE FROM THE GODS MUST RISK BURNING HIS FINGERS.
BE STRONG, MRS. SHELLEY. TAKE CARE.
YOU HAVE NOT TOLD ME YOUR NAME, SIR.
NO.
I HAVE NOT.

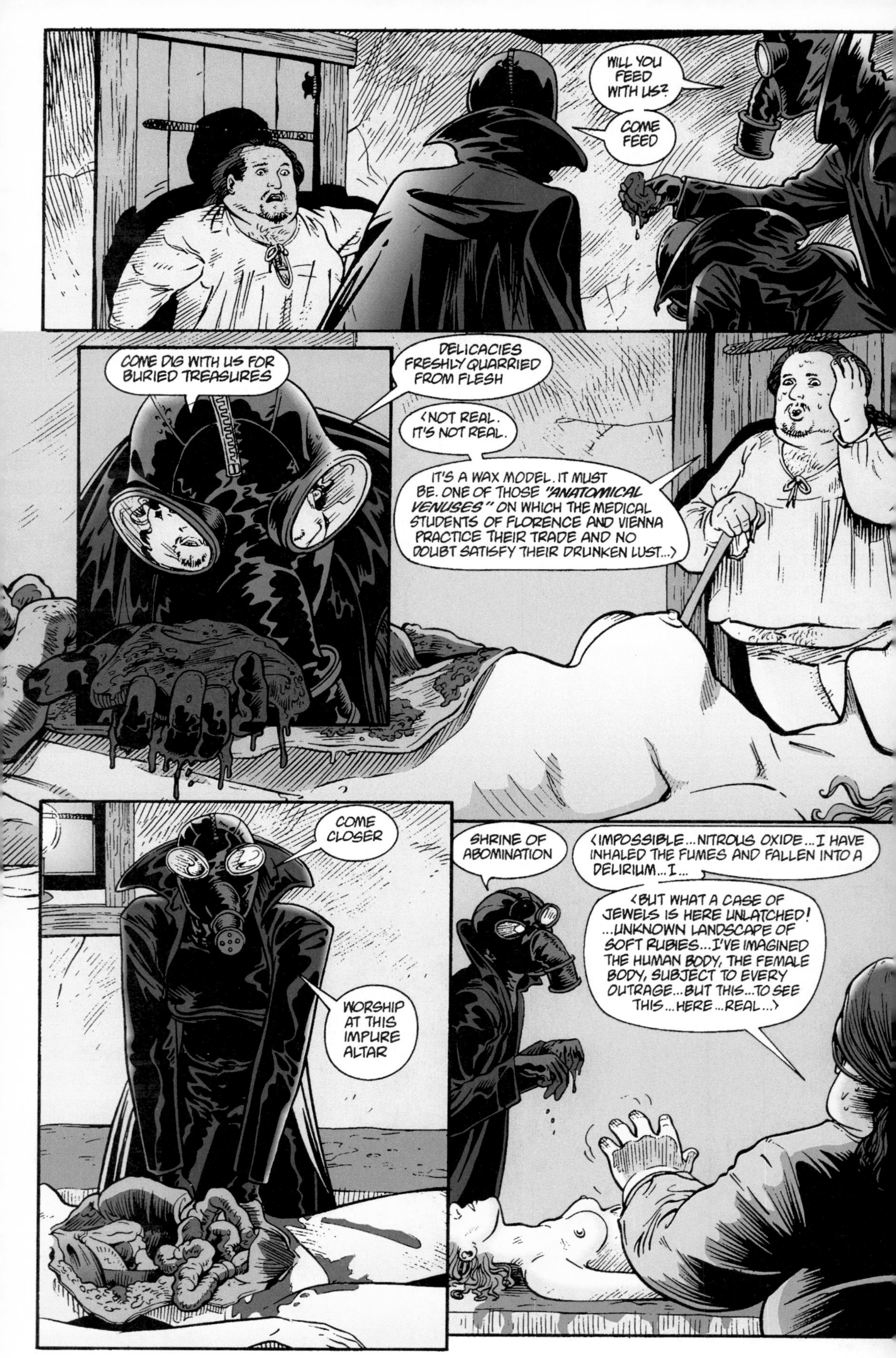

WILL YOU FEED WITH US?
COME FEED
COME DIG WITH US FOR BURIED TREASURES
DELICACIES FRESHLY QUARRIED FROM FLESH
‹NOT REAL. IT'S NOT REAL.
IT'S A WAX MODEL. IT MUST BE. ONE OF THOSE *"ANATOMICAL VENUSES"* ON WHICH THE MEDICAL STUDENTS OF FLORENCE AND VIENNA PRACTICE THEIR TRADE AND NO DOUBT SATISFY THEIR DRUNKEN LUST...›
COME CLOSER
WORSHIP AT THIS IMPURE ALTAR
SHRINE OF ABOMINATION
‹IMPOSSIBLE... NITROUS OXIDE... I HAVE INHALED THE FUMES AND FALLEN INTO A DELIRIUM... I...
‹BUT WHAT A CASE OF JEWELS IS HERE UNLATCHED! ...UNKNOWN LANDSCAPE OF SOFT RUBIES... I'VE IMAGINED THE HUMAN BODY, THE FEMALE BODY, SUBJECT TO EVERY OUTRAGE... BUT THIS... TO SEE THIS... HERE... REAL...›

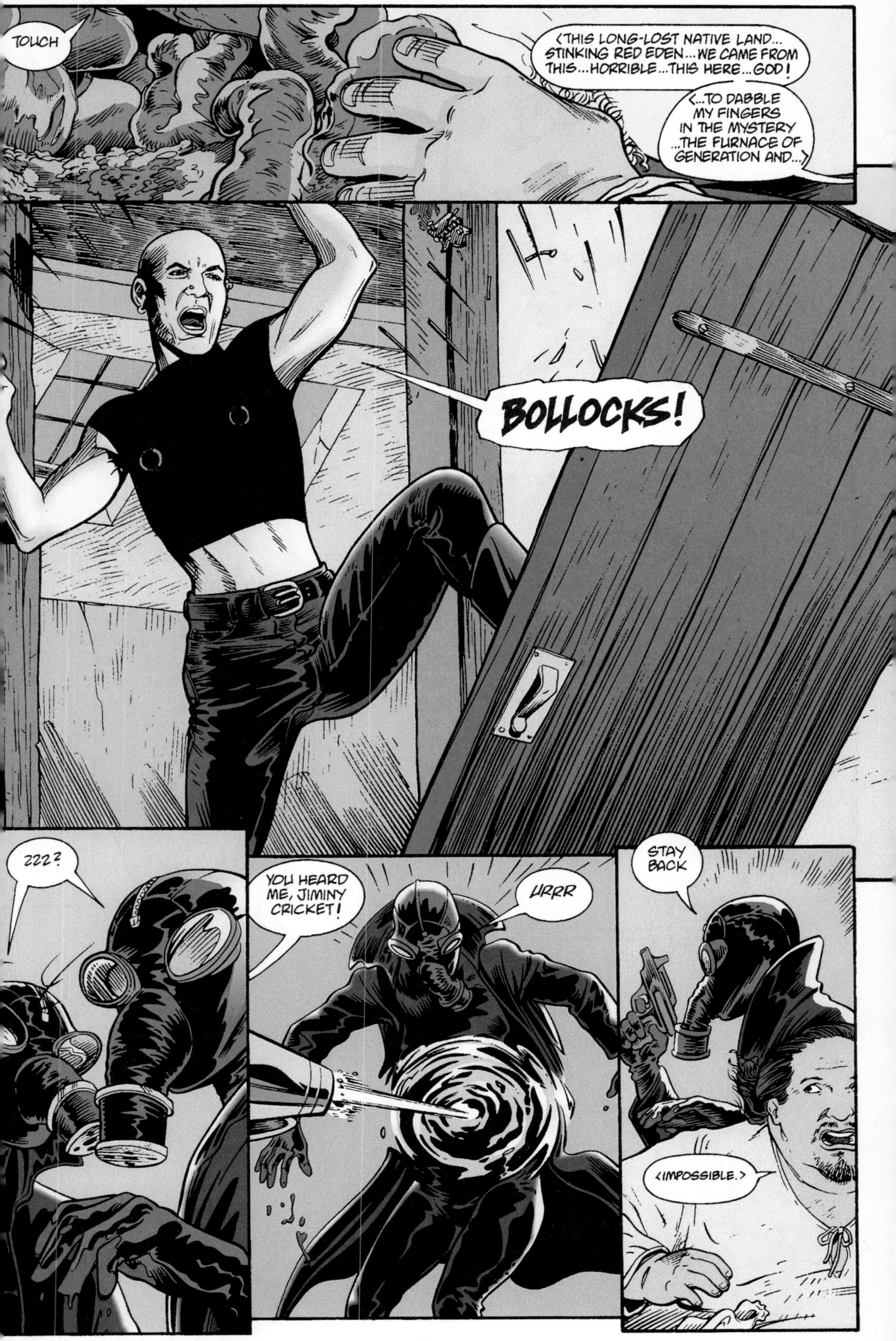
TOUCH
‹THIS LONG-LOST NATIVE LAND... STINKING RED EDEN... WE CAME FROM THIS...HORRIBLE...THIS HERE...GOD!
‹...TO DABBLE MY FINGERS IN THE MYSTERY ...THE FURNACE OF GENERATION AND...›
BOLLOCKS!
ZZZ?
YOU HEARD ME, JIMINY CRICKET!
URRR
STAY BACK
‹IMPOSSIBLE.›

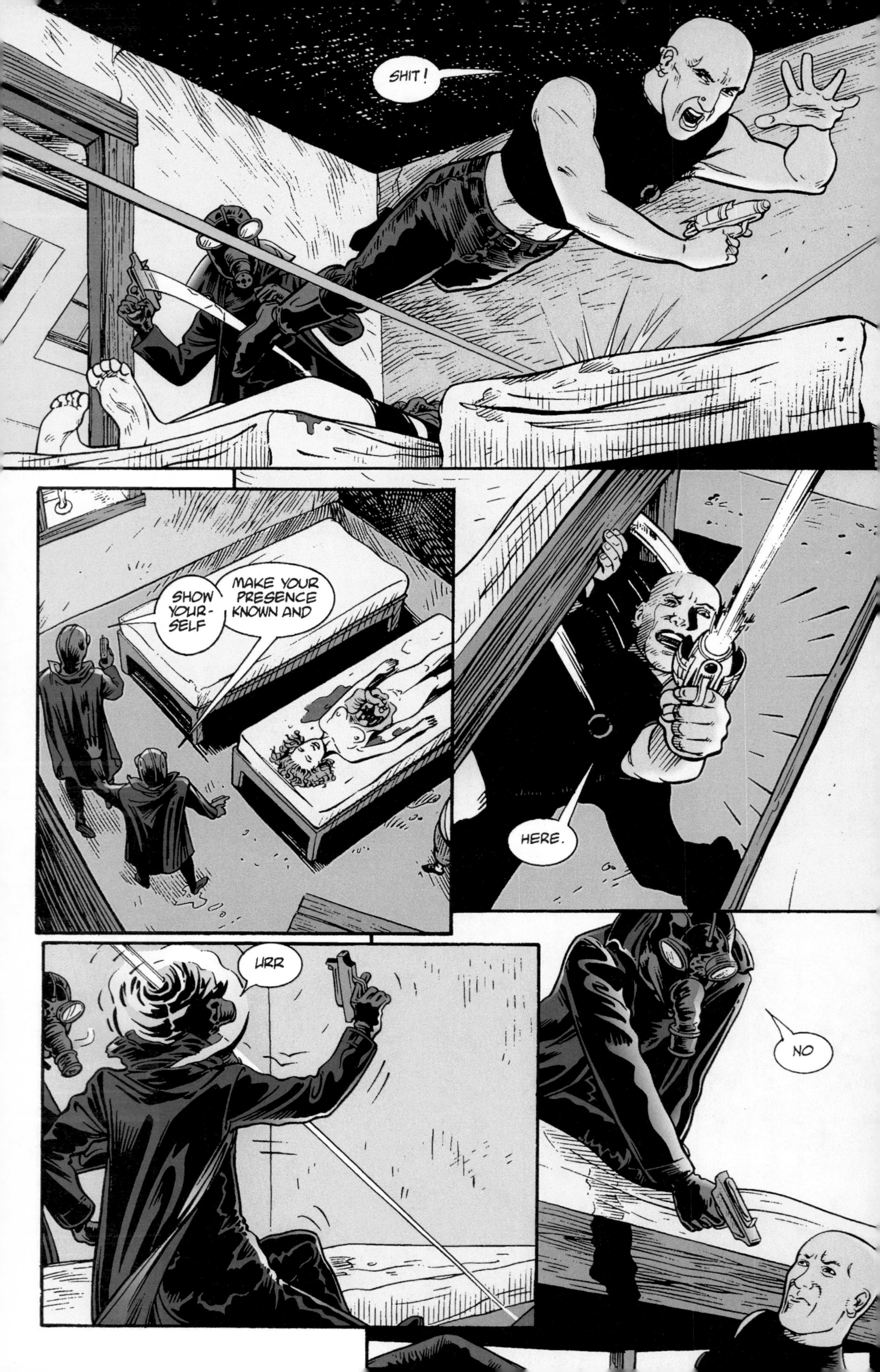
SHIT!
MAKE YOUR PRESENCE KNOWN AND
SHOW YOUR-SELF
HERE.
URR
NO

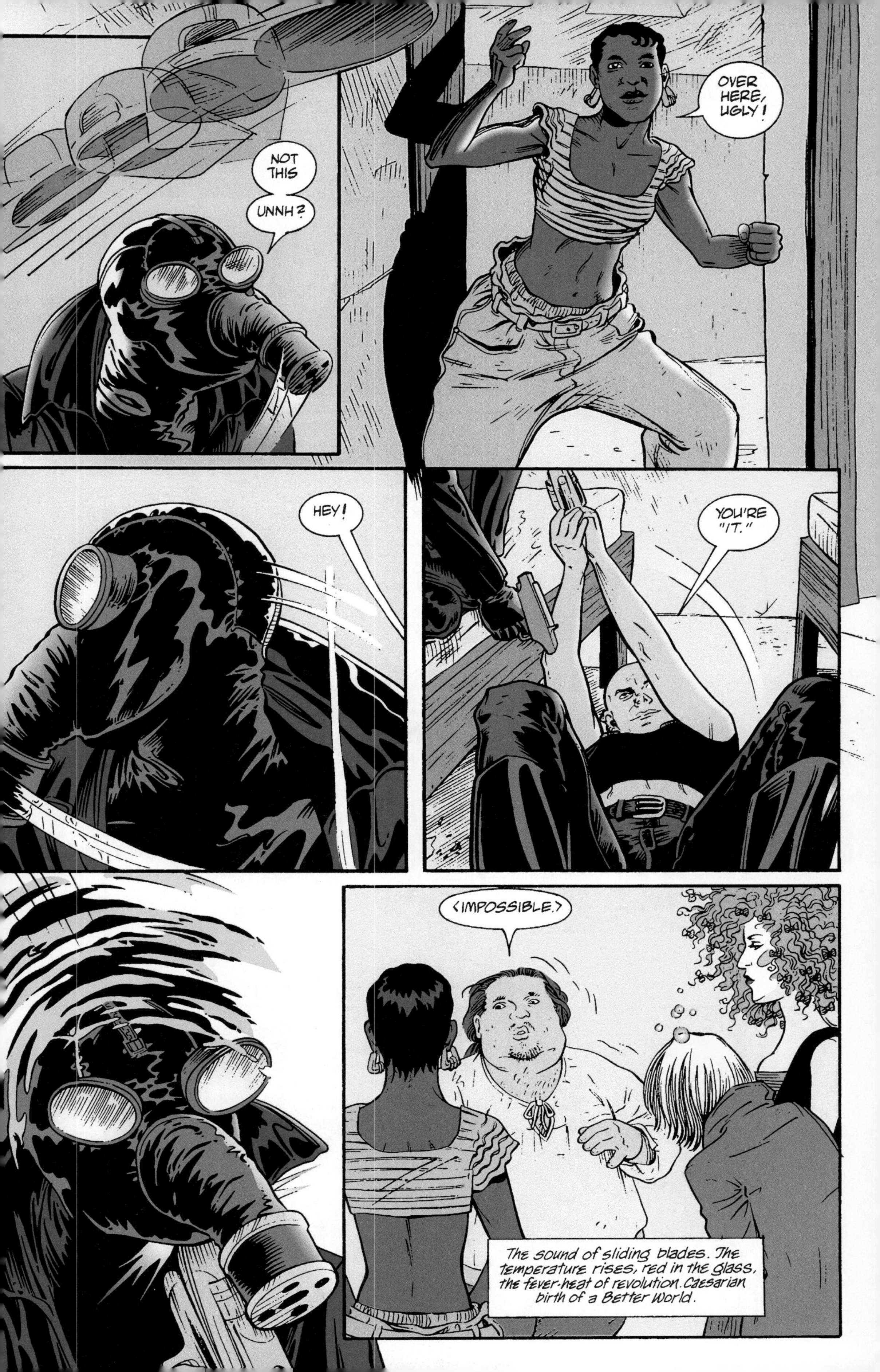

NOT THIS
UNNH?
OVER HERE, UGLY!
HEY!
YOU'RE "IT."
‹IMPOSSIBLE.›
The sound of sliding blades. The temperature rises, red in the glass, the fever-heat of revolution. Caesarian birth of a Better World.

1) The Guillotine as the prototype Murder Machine. Mass execution turned over to the bureaucrats. The living and the dead totted up as credits and debts in an accountant's ledger.

2) The Division of Head from Body. The Head of State struck from the Body Politic. Democracy of the blade.

Holy Royal Blood, sang Réal, spilled in plebeian straw, staining souvenir handkerchiefs and envelopes. Talismans. Relics.

The shadow of the scaffold cast across the Twentieth Century.

3) The Theatre of Mortality.

Disgruntled crowds call for more spectacle. The instant of amputation remains invisible; the moment of death unrecordable. The lightning stroke across the shutter; a blue-edged photograph. The severed head becomes its own frozen image in this "portrait machine".

4) The Script, the Actors. Final performances, famous last words. Madame Roland:

OH, LIBERTY, HOW MANY ARE THE CRIMES COMMITTED IN THY NAME?

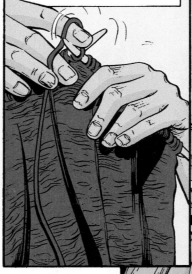

5) Les Tricoteuses.

The neck bared, the weighted razor poised.

Mysteries of the Guillotine.

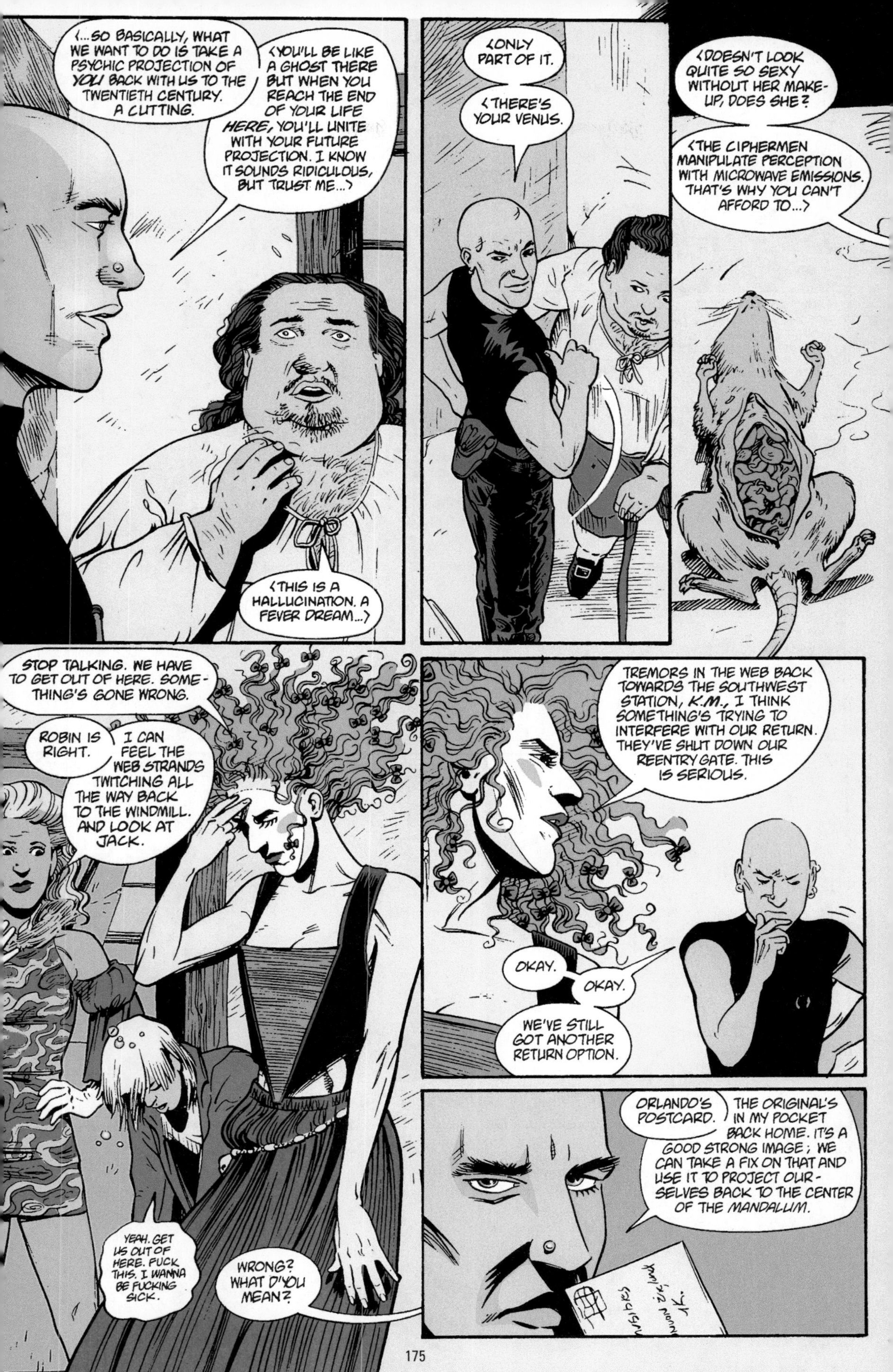
‹...SO BASICALLY, WHAT WE WANT TO DO IS TAKE A PSYCHIC PROJECTION OF YOU BACK WITH US TO THE TWENTIETH CENTURY. A CUTTING.
‹YOU'LL BE LIKE A GHOST THERE BUT WHEN YOU REACH THE END OF YOUR LIFE HERE, YOU'LL UNITE WITH YOUR FUTURE PROJECTION. I KNOW IT SOUNDS RIDICULOUS, BUT TRUST ME...›
‹THIS IS A HALLUCINATION. A FEVER DREAM...›
‹ONLY PART OF IT.
‹THERE'S YOUR VENUS.
‹DOESN'T LOOK QUITE SO SEXY WITHOUT HER MAKE-UP, DOES SHE?
‹THE CIPHERMEN MANIPULATE PERCEPTION WITH MICROWAVE EMISSIONS. THAT'S WHY YOU CAN'T AFFORD TO...›
STOP TALKING. WE HAVE TO GET OUT OF HERE. SOMETHING'S GONE WRONG.
ROBIN IS RIGHT.
I CAN FEEL THE WEB STRANDS TWITCHING ALL THE WAY BACK TO THE WINDMILL. AND LOOK AT JACK.
YEAH. GET US OUT OF HERE. FUCK THIS. I WANNA BE FUCKING SICK.
WRONG? WHAT D'YOU MEAN?
TREMORS IN THE WEB BACK TOWARDS THE SOUTHWEST STATION, K.M., I THINK SOMETHING'S TRYING TO INTERFERE WITH OUR RETURN. THEY'VE SHUT DOWN OUR REENTRY GATE. THIS IS SERIOUS.
OKAY.
OKAY.
WE'VE STILL GOT ANOTHER RETURN OPTION.
ORLANDO'S POSTCARD.
THE ORIGINAL'S IN MY POCKET BACK HOME. IT'S A GOOD STRONG IMAGE; WE CAN TAKE A FIX ON THAT AND USE IT TO PROJECT OURSELVES BACK TO THE CENTER OF THE MANDALUM.

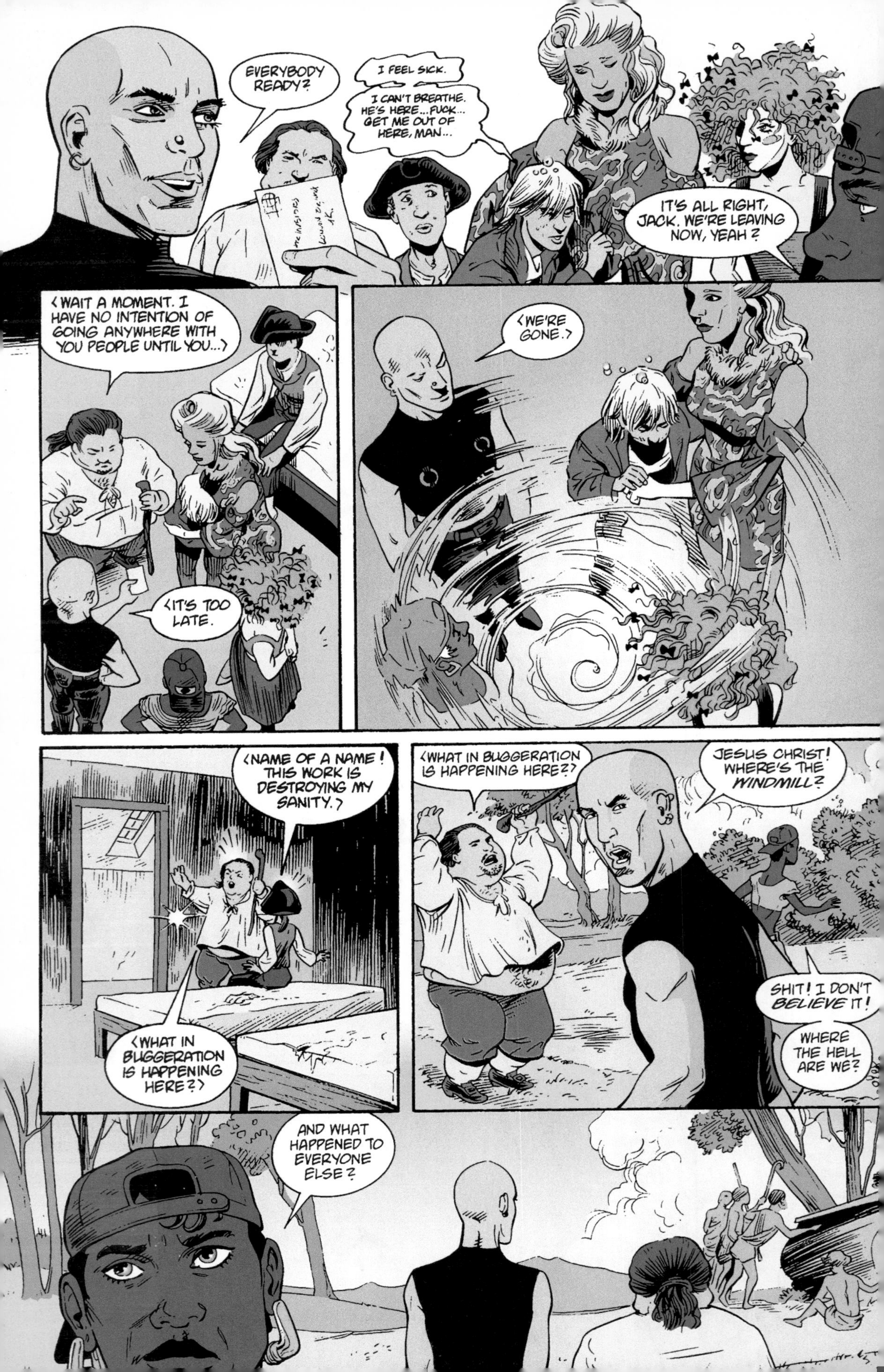
EVERYBODY READY?
I FEEL SICK.
I CAN'T BREATHE. HE'S HERE...FUCK... GET ME OUT OF HERE, MAN...
IT'S ALL RIGHT, JACK. WE'RE LEAVING NOW, YEAH?
‹WAIT A MOMENT. I HAVE NO INTENTION OF GOING ANYWHERE WITH YOU PEOPLE UNTIL YOU...›
‹IT'S TOO LATE.
‹WE'RE GONE.›
‹NAME OF A NAME! THIS WORK IS DESTROYING MY SANITY.›
‹WHAT IN BUGGERATION IS HAPPENING HERE?›
‹WHAT IN BUGGERATION IS HAPPENING HERE?›
JESUS CHRIST! WHERE'S THE WINDMILL?
SHIT! I DON'T BELIEVE IT!
WHERE THE HELL ARE WE?
AND WHAT HAPPENED TO EVERYONE ELSE?

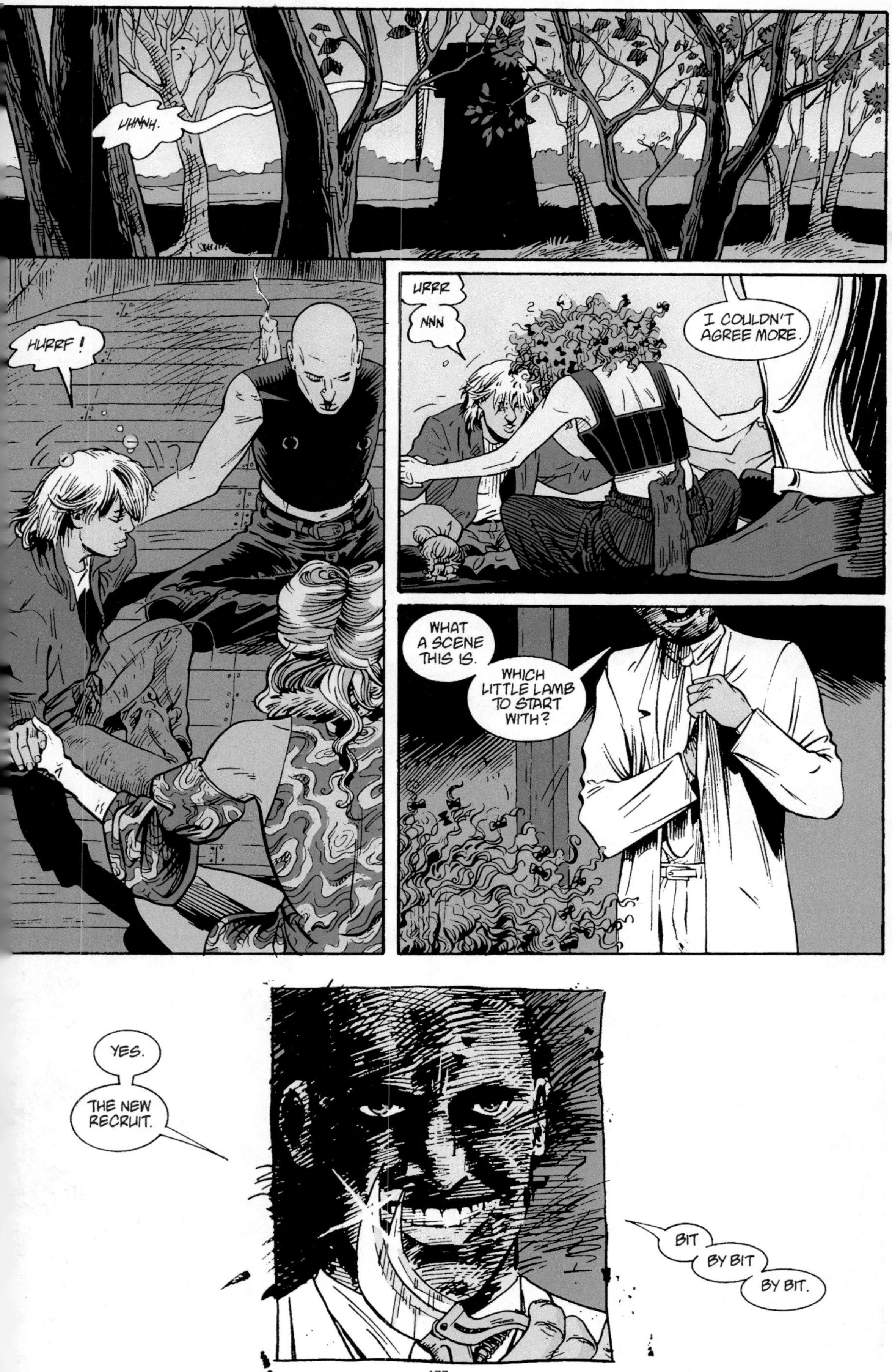
UHNNH.
HURRF!
URRR
NNN
I COULDN'T AGREE MORE.
WHAT A SCENE THIS IS.
WHICH LITTLE LAMB TO START WITH?
YES.
THE NEW RECRUIT.
BIT
BY BIT
BY BIT.

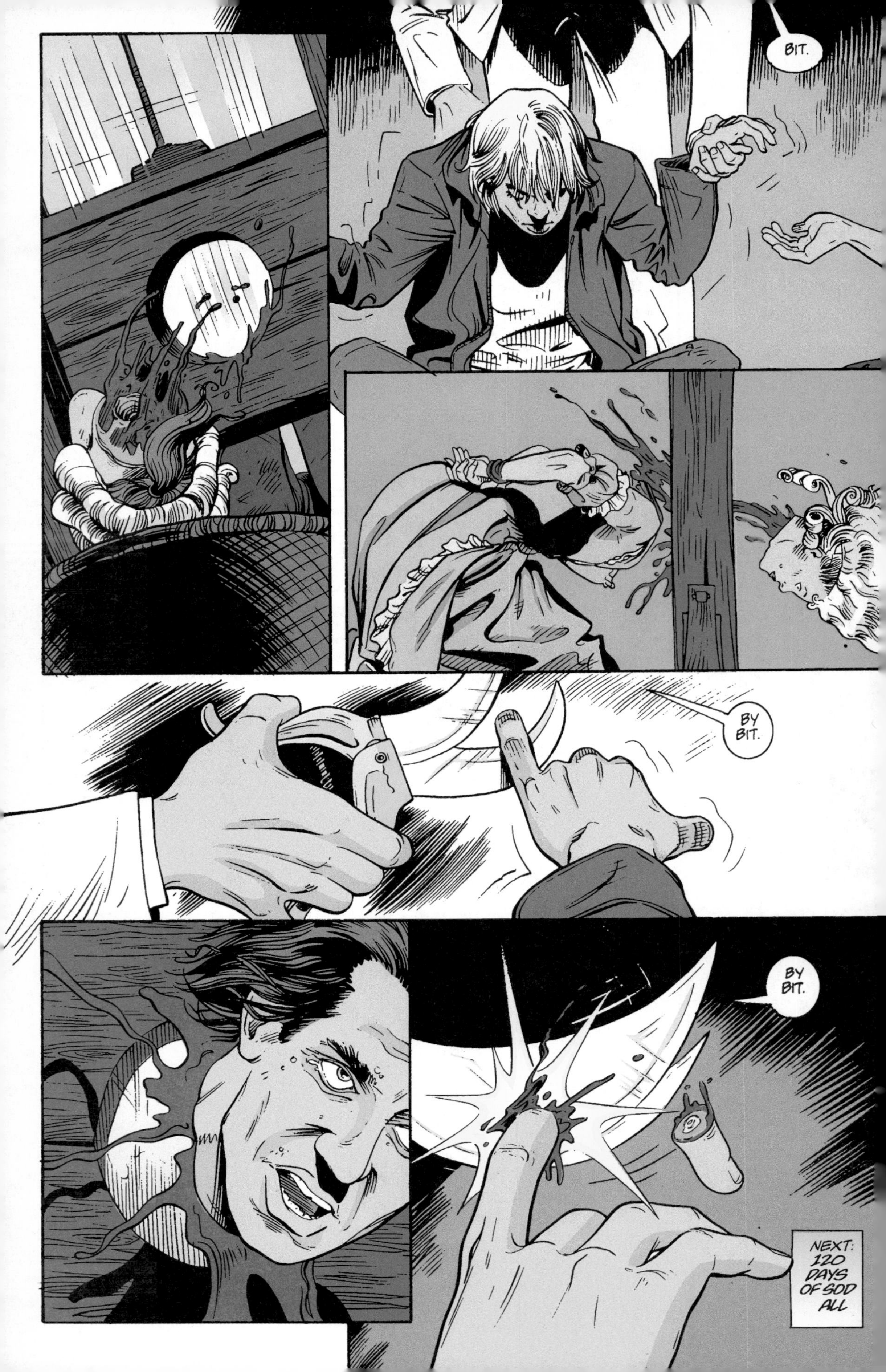
BIT.
BY BIT.
BY BIT.
NEXT: 120 DAYS OF SOD ALL

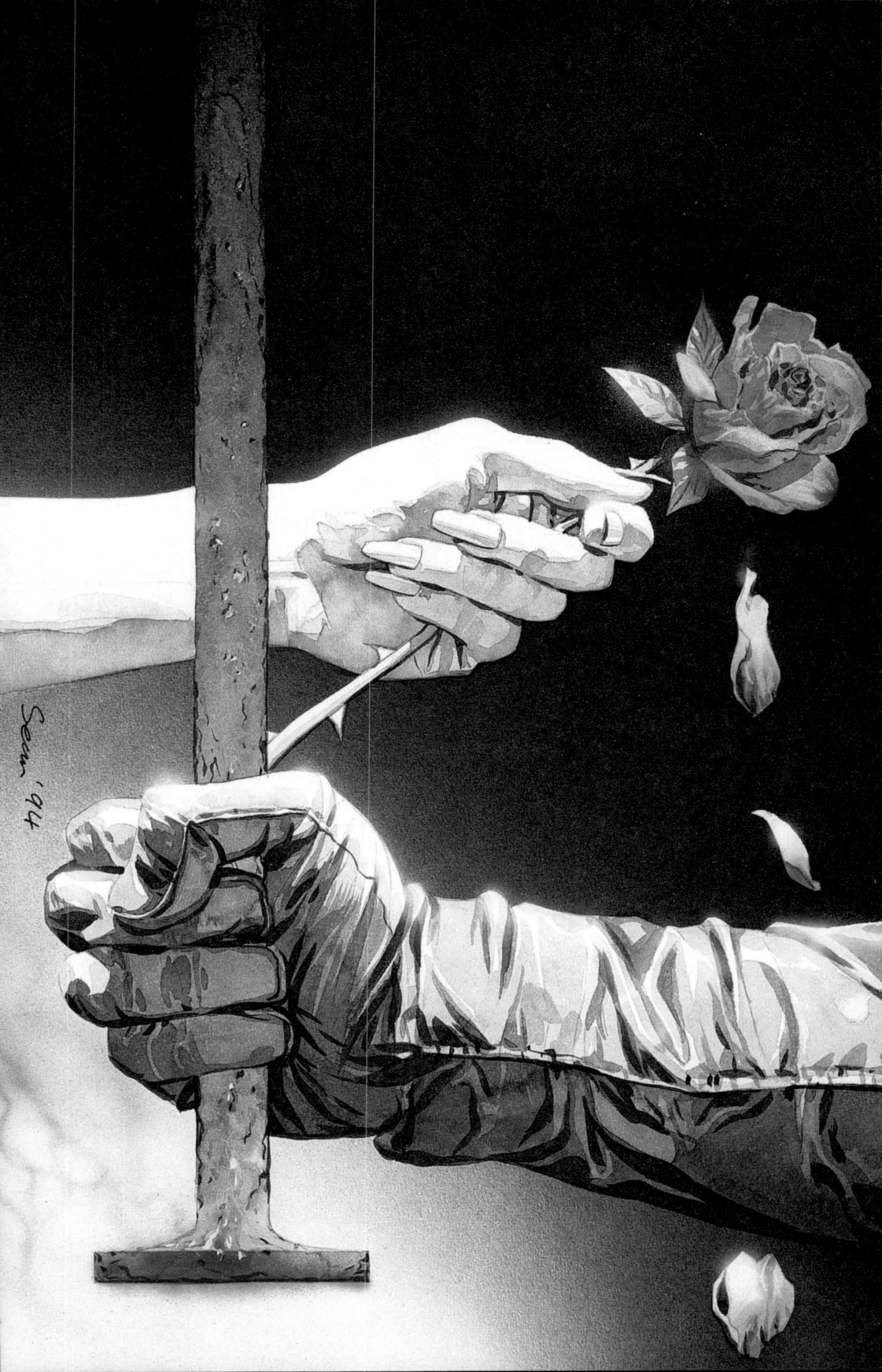
Sean '94

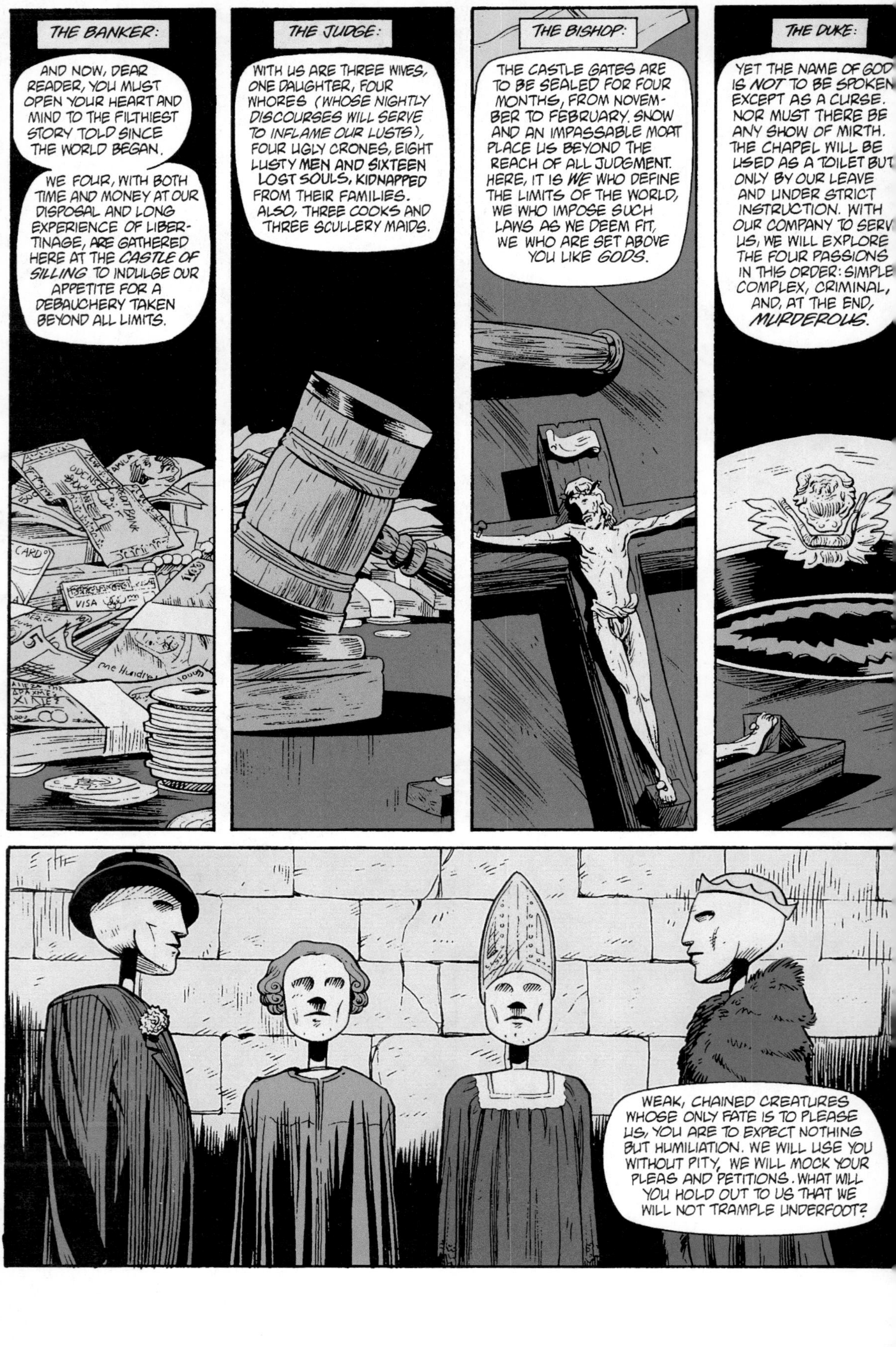
THE BANKER:
AND NOW, DEAR READER, YOU MUST OPEN YOUR HEART AND MIND TO THE FILTHIEST STORY TOLD SINCE THE WORLD BEGAN.
WE FOUR, WITH BOTH TIME AND MONEY AT OUR DISPOSAL AND LONG EXPERIENCE OF LIBERTINAGE, ARE GATHERED HERE AT THE CASTLE OF SILLING TO INDULGE OUR APPETITE FOR A DEBAUCHERY TAKEN BEYOND ALL LIMITS.
THE JUDGE:
WITH US ARE THREE WIVES, ONE DAUGHTER, FOUR WHORES (WHOSE NIGHTLY DISCOURSES WILL SERVE TO INFLAME OUR LUSTS), FOUR UGLY CRONES, EIGHT LUSTY MEN AND SIXTEEN LOST SOULS, KIDNAPPED FROM THEIR FAMILIES. ALSO, THREE COOKS AND THREE SCULLERY MAIDS.
THE BISHOP:
THE CASTLE GATES ARE TO BE SEALED FOR FOUR MONTHS, FROM NOVEMBER TO FEBRUARY. SNOW AND AN IMPASSABLE MOAT PLACE US BEYOND THE REACH OF ALL JUDGMENT. HERE, IT IS WE WHO DEFINE THE LIMITS OF THE WORLD, WE WHO IMPOSE SUCH LAWS AS WE DEEM FIT, WE WHO ARE SET ABOVE YOU LIKE GODS.
THE DUKE:
YET THE NAME OF GOD IS NOT TO BE SPOKEN EXCEPT AS A CURSE. NOR MUST THERE BE ANY SHOW OF MIRTH. THE CHAPEL WILL BE USED AS A TOILET BUT ONLY BY OUR LEAVE AND UNDER STRICT INSTRUCTION. WITH OUR COMPANY TO SERVE US, WE WILL EXPLORE THE FOUR PASSIONS IN THIS ORDER: SIMPLE, COMPLEX, CRIMINAL, AND, AT THE END, MURDEROUS.
WEAK, CHAINED CREATURES WHOSE ONLY FATE IS TO PLEASE US, YOU ARE TO EXPECT NOTHING BUT HUMILIATION. WE WILL USE YOU WITHOUT PITY, WE WILL MOCK YOUR PLEAS AND PETITIONS. WHAT WILL YOU HOLD OUT TO US THAT WE WILL NOT TRAMPLE UNDERFOOT?

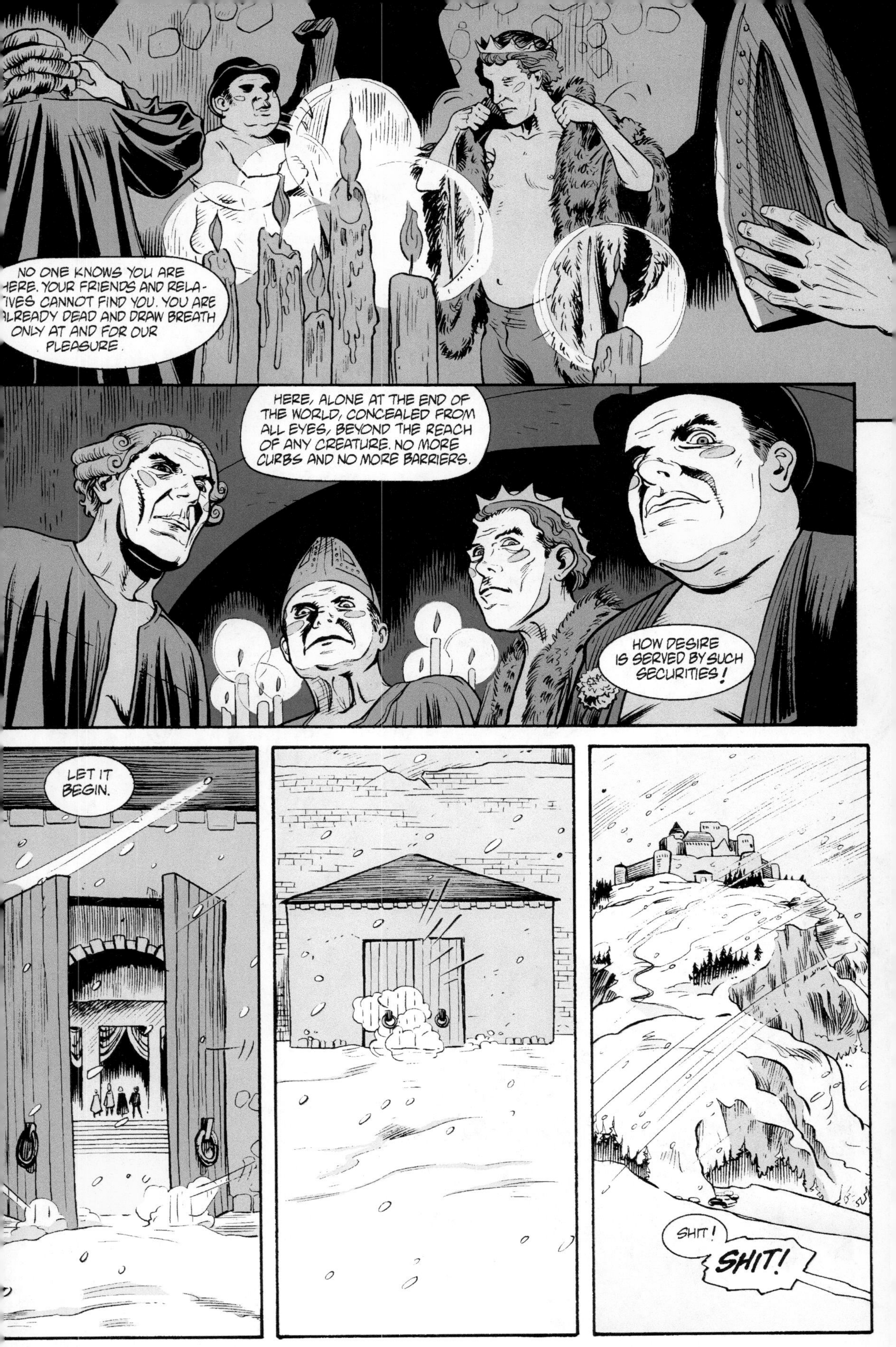
NO ONE KNOWS YOU ARE HERE. YOUR FRIENDS AND RELATIVES CANNOT FIND YOU. YOU ARE ALREADY DEAD AND DRAW BREATH ONLY AT AND FOR OUR PLEASURE.
HERE, ALONE AT THE END OF THE WORLD, CONCEALED FROM ALL EYES, BEYOND THE REACH OF ANY CREATURE. NO MORE CURBS AND NO MORE BARRIERS.
HOW DESIRE IS SERVED BY SUCH SECURITIES!
LET IT BEGIN.
SHIT!
SHIT!

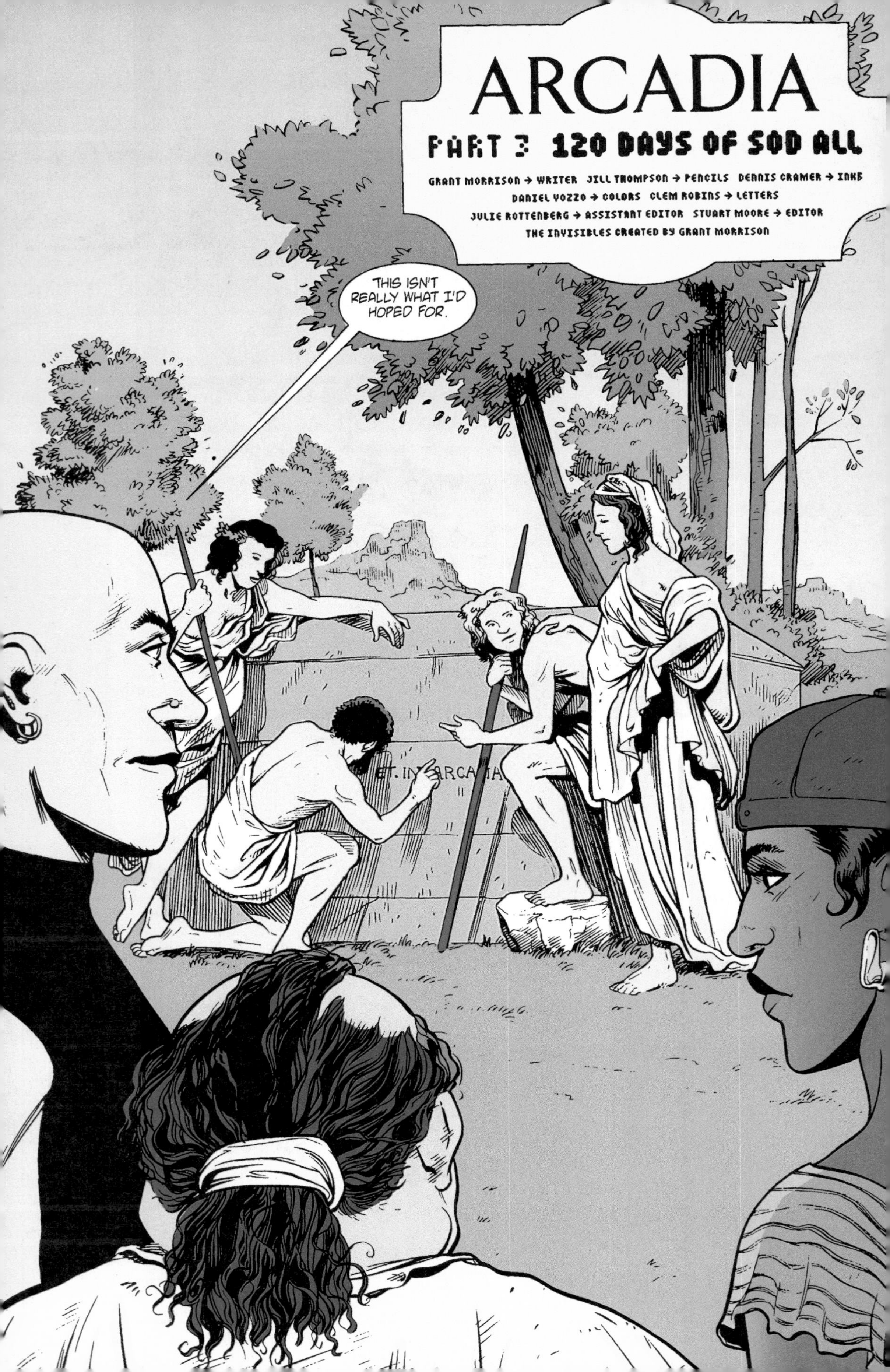

ARCADIA
PART 3 120 DAYS OF SOD ALL
GRANT MORRISON → WRITER JILL THOMPSON → PENCILS DENNIS CRAMER → INKS
DANIEL VOZZO → COLORS CLEM ROBINS → LETTERS
JULIE ROTTENBERG → ASSISTANT EDITOR STUART MOORE → EDITOR
THE INVISIBLES CREATED BY GRANT MORRISON
THIS ISN'T REALLY WHAT I'D HOPED FOR.

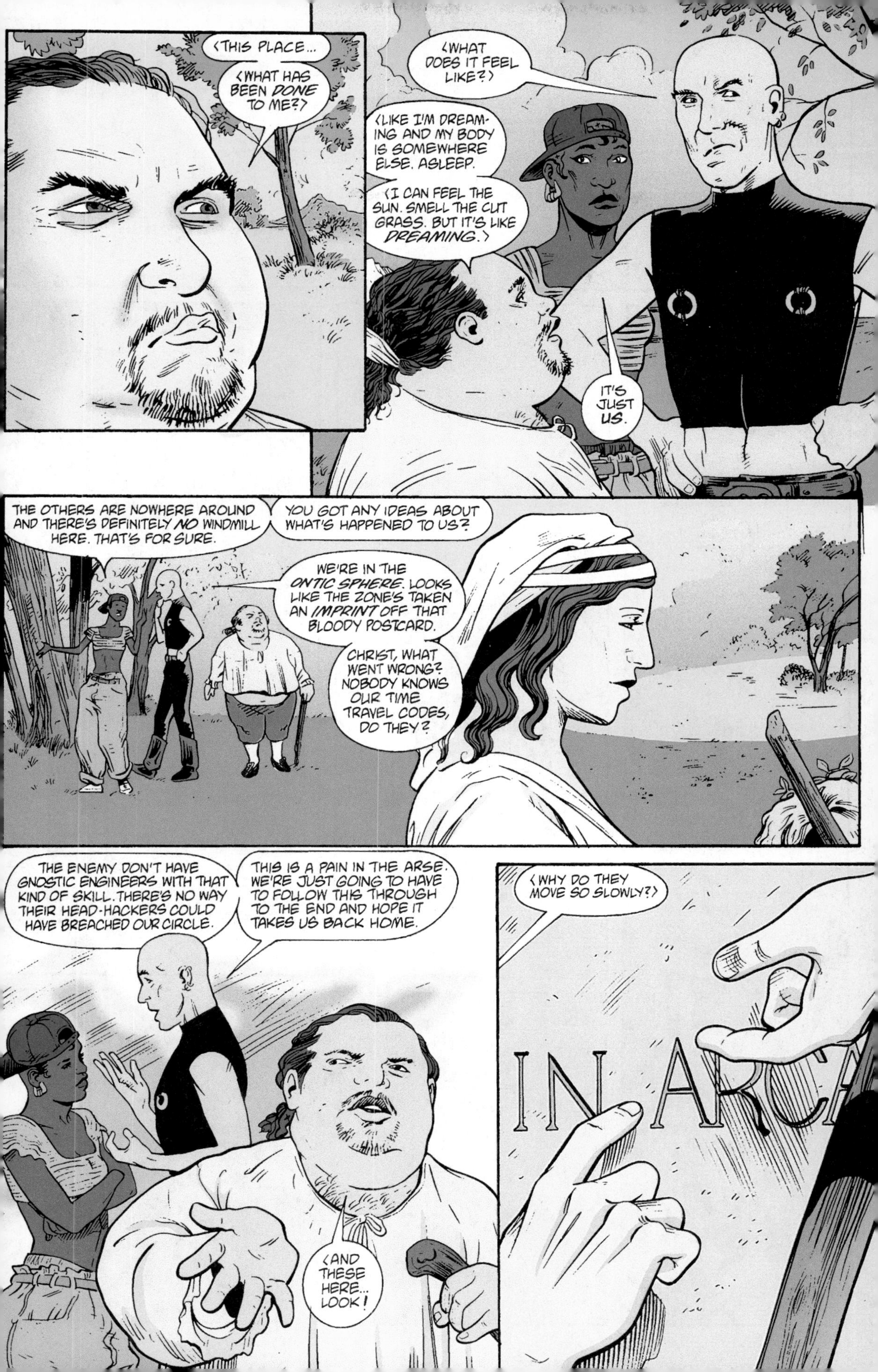
‹THIS PLACE...
‹WHAT HAS BEEN DONE TO ME?›
‹WHAT DOES IT FEEL LIKE?›
‹LIKE I'M DREAMING AND MY BODY IS SOMEWHERE ELSE. ASLEEP.
‹I CAN FEEL THE SUN. SMELL THE CUT GRASS. BUT IT'S LIKE DREAMING.›
IT'S JUST US.
THE OTHERS ARE NOWHERE AROUND AND THERE'S DEFINITELY NO WINDMILL HERE. THAT'S FOR SURE.
YOU GOT ANY IDEAS ABOUT WHAT'S HAPPENED TO US?
WE'RE IN THE ONTIC SPHERE. LOOKS LIKE THE ZONE'S TAKEN AN IMPRINT OFF THAT BLOODY POSTCARD.
CHRIST, WHAT WENT WRONG? NOBODY KNOWS OUR TIME TRAVEL CODES, DO THEY?
THE ENEMY DON'T HAVE GNOSTIC ENGINEERS WITH THAT KIND OF SKILL. THERE'S NO WAY THEIR HEAD-HACKERS COULD HAVE BREACHED OUR CIRCLE.
THIS IS A PAIN IN THE ARSE. WE'RE JUST GOING TO HAVE TO FOLLOW THIS THROUGH TO THE END AND HOPE IT TAKES US BACK HOME.
‹AND THESE HERE... LOOK!
‹WHY DO THEY MOVE SO SLOWLY?›
IN ARC

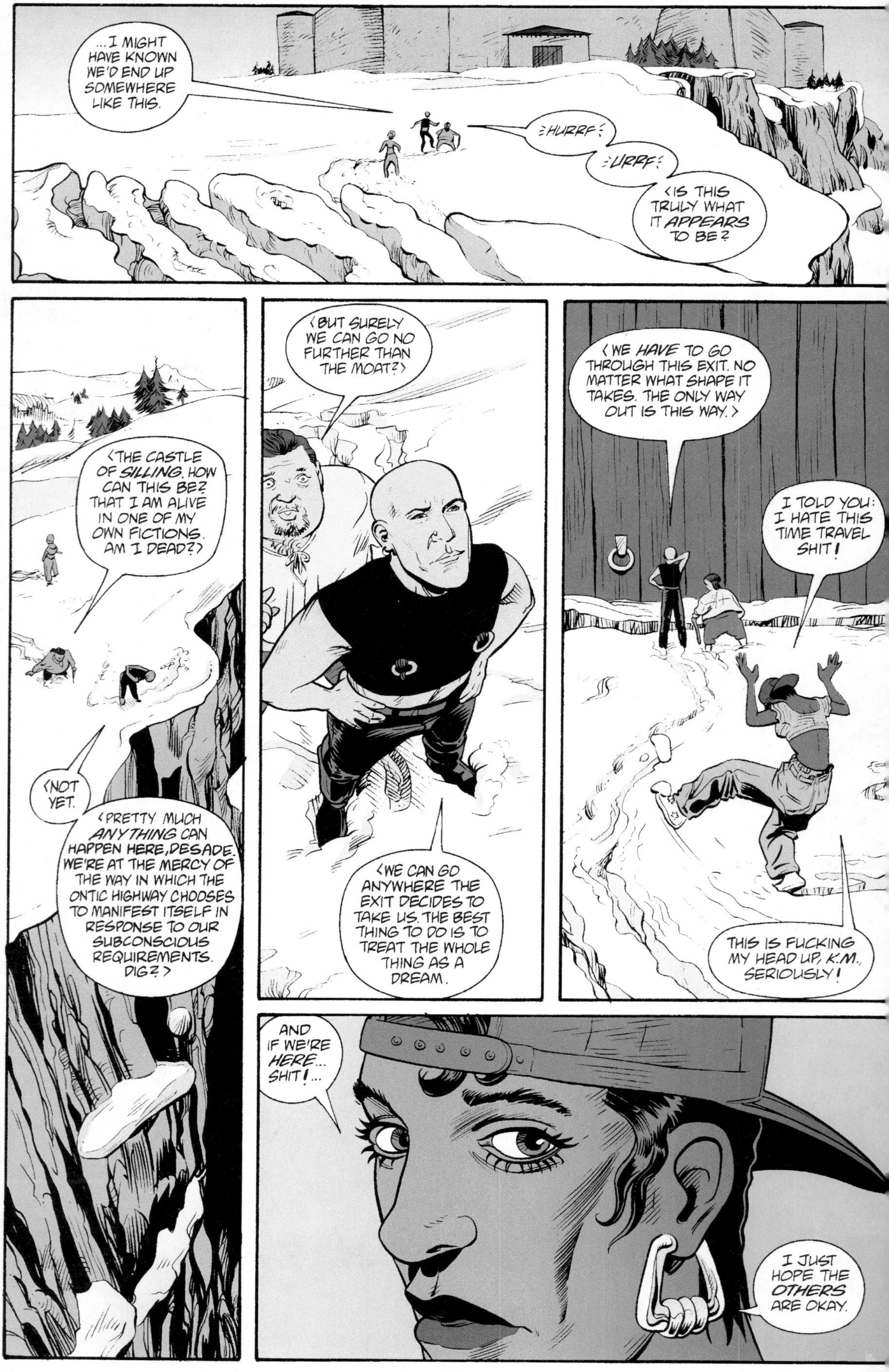

...I MIGHT HAVE KNOWN WE'D END UP SOMEWHERE LIKE THIS.
HURRF
URRF
<IS THIS TRULY WHAT IT APPEARS TO BE?
<THE CASTLE OF SILLING. HOW CAN THIS BE? THAT I AM ALIVE IN ONE OF MY OWN FICTIONS. AM I DEAD?>
<NOT YET.
<PRETTY MUCH ANYTHING CAN HAPPEN HERE, DESADE. WE'RE AT THE MERCY OF THE WAY IN WHICH THE ONTIC HIGHWAY CHOOSES TO MANIFEST ITSELF IN RESPONSE TO OUR SUBCONSCIOUS REQUIREMENTS. DIG?>
<BUT SURELY WE CAN GO NO FURTHER THAN THE MOAT?>
<WE CAN GO ANYWHERE THE EXIT DECIDES TO TAKE US. THE BEST THING TO DO IS TO TREAT THE WHOLE THING AS A DREAM.
<WE HAVE TO GO THROUGH THIS EXIT. NO MATTER WHAT SHAPE IT TAKES. THE ONLY WAY OUT IS THIS WAY.>
I TOLD YOU: I HATE THIS TIME TRAVEL SHIT!
THIS IS FUCKING MY HEAD UP, K.M., SERIOUSLY!
AND IF WE'RE HERE... SHIT!...
I JUST HOPE THE OTHERS ARE OKAY.

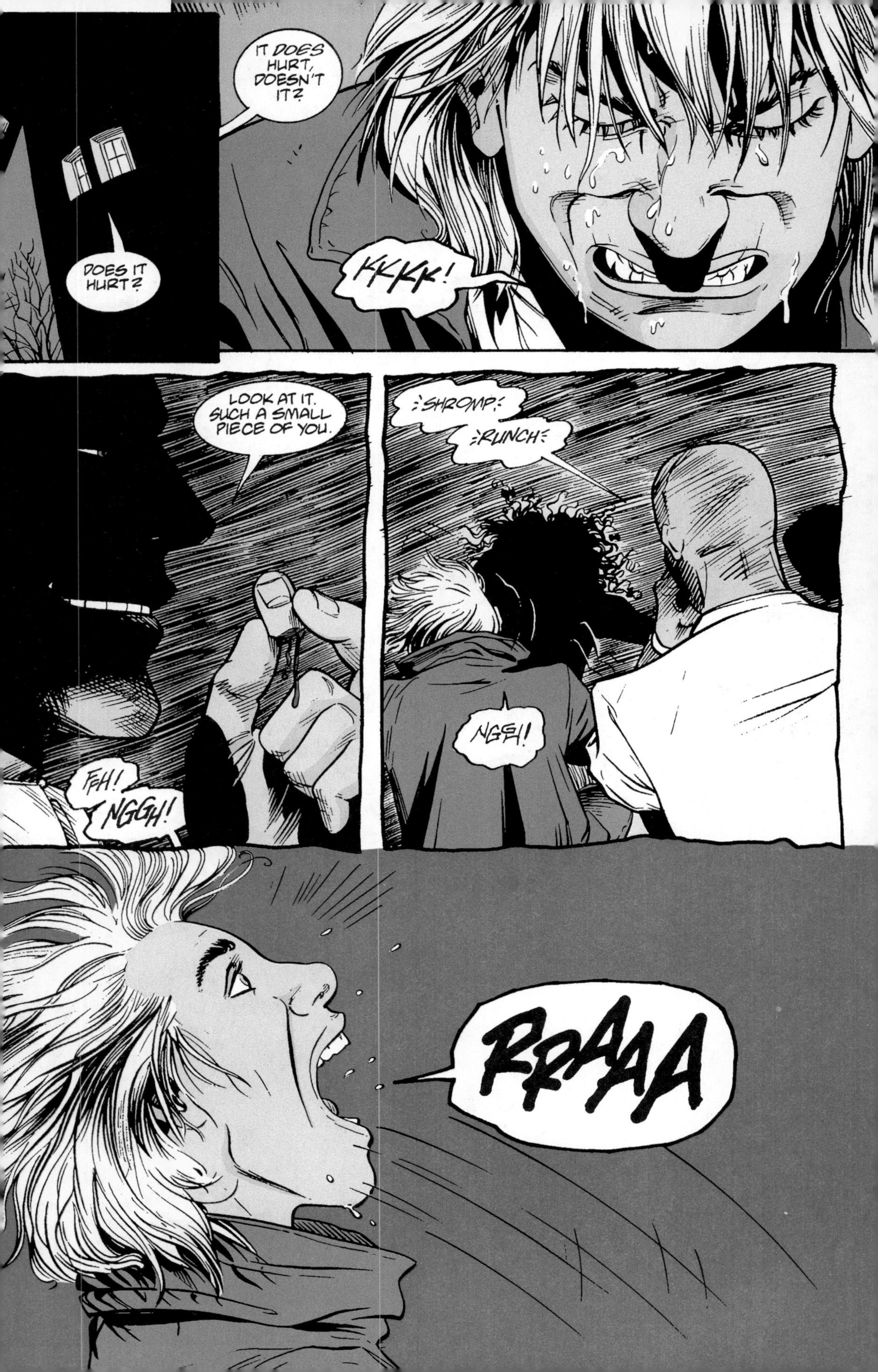
IT DOES HURT, DOESN'T IT?
DOES IT HURT?
KKKK!
LOOK AT IT. SUCH A SMALL PIECE OF YOU.
FFH!
NGGH!
SHROMP
RUNCH
NGGH!
RRAAAA

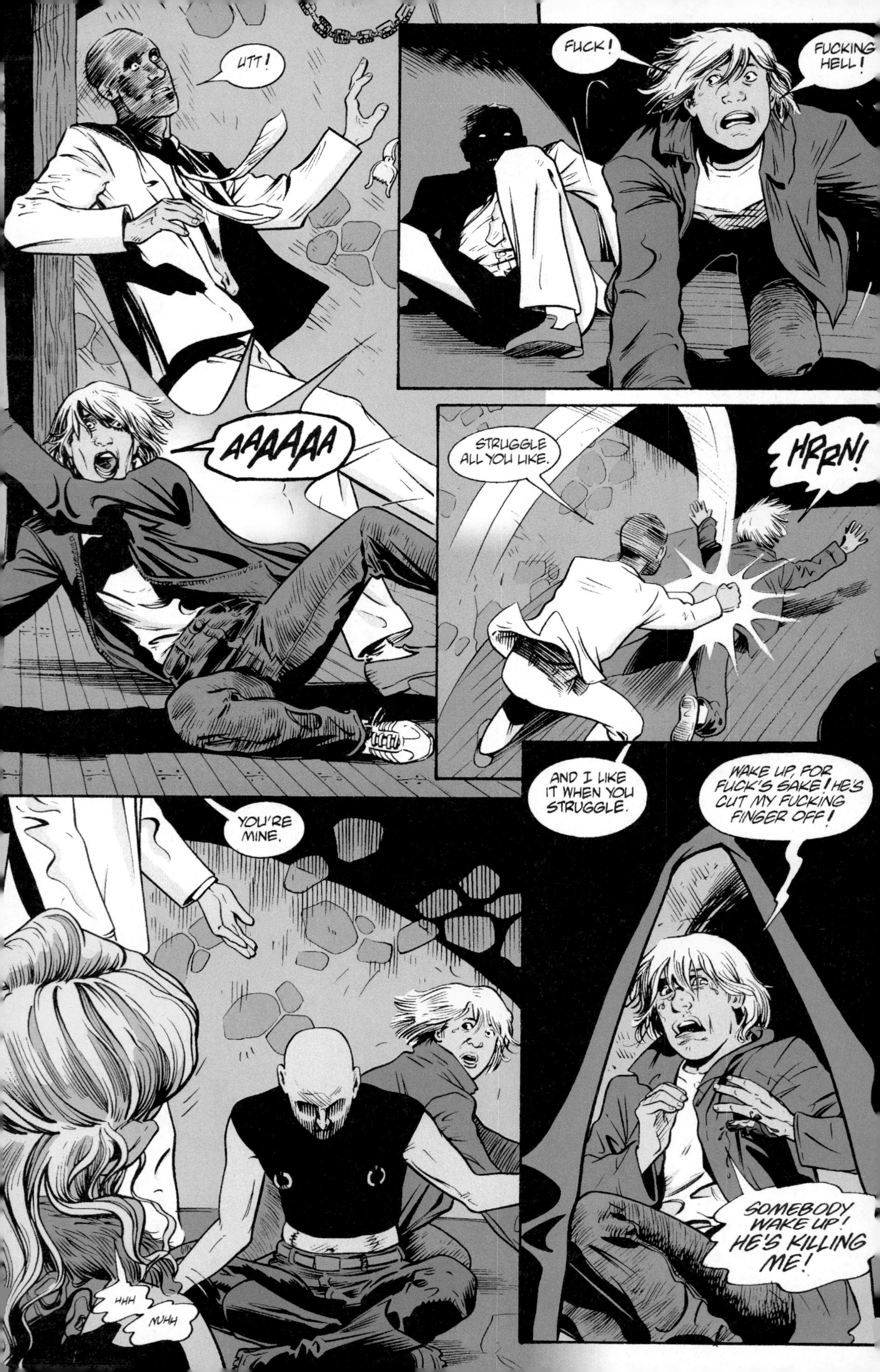
UTT!
FUCK!
FUCKING HELL!
AAAAAA
STRUGGLE ALL YOU LIKE.
HRRN!
AND I LIKE IT WHEN YOU STRUGGLE.
WAKE UP, FOR FUCK'S SAKE! HE'S CUT MY FUCKING FINGER OFF!
YOU'RE MINE.
HHH
NUHH
SOMEBODY WAKE UP! HE'S KILLING ME!

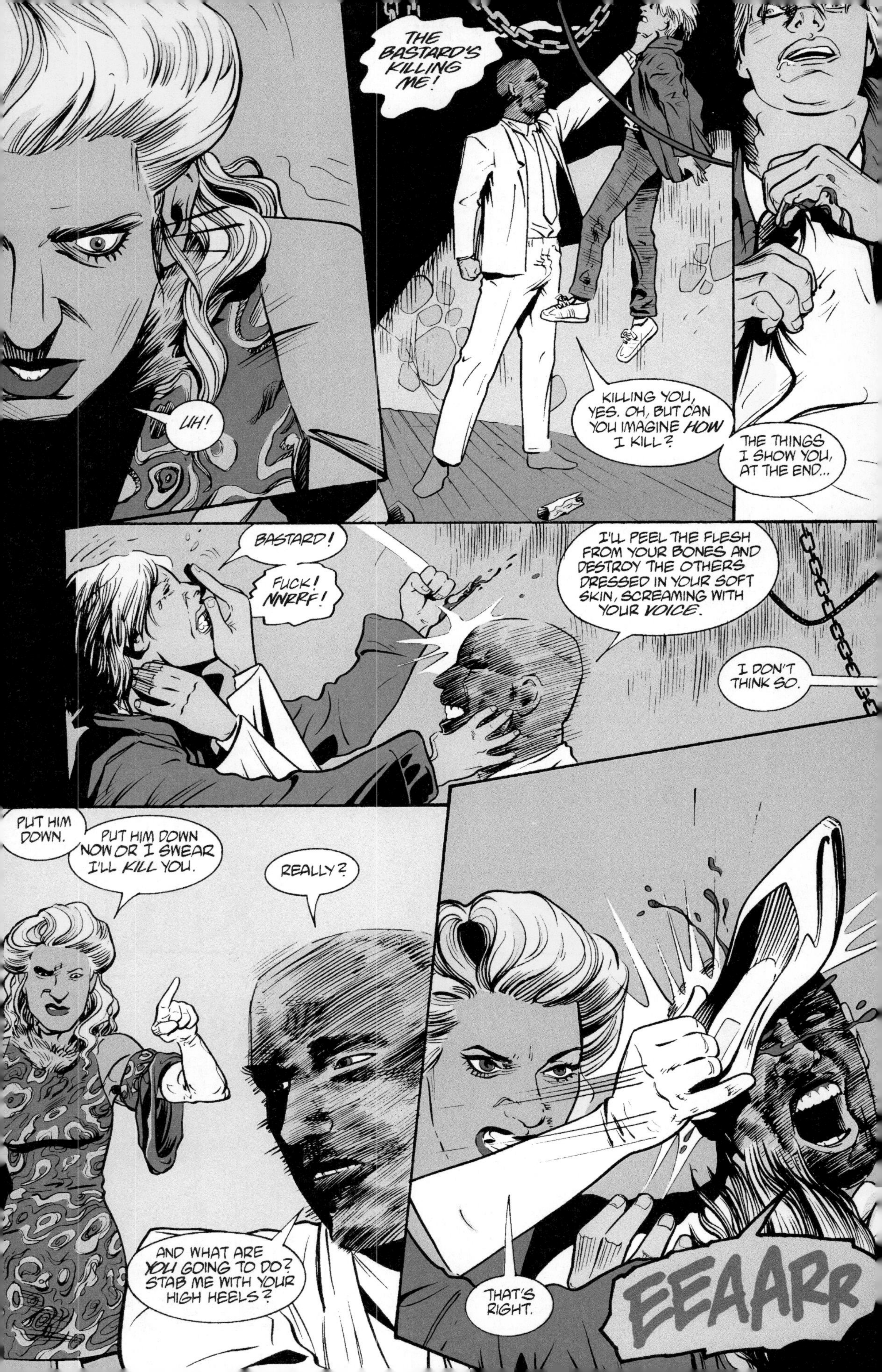
UH!
THE BASTARD'S KILLING ME!
KILLING YOU, YES. OH, BUT CAN YOU IMAGINE HOW I KILL?
THE THINGS I SHOW YOU, AT THE END...
BASTARD!
FUCK! NNRRF!
I'LL PEEL THE FLESH FROM YOUR BONES AND DESTROY THE OTHERS DRESSED IN YOUR SOFT SKIN, SCREAMING WITH YOUR VOICE.
I DON'T THINK SO.
PUT HIM DOWN.
PUT HIM DOWN NOW OR I SWEAR I'LL KILL YOU.
REALLY?
AND WHAT ARE YOU GOING TO DO? STAB ME WITH YOUR HIGH HEELS?
THAT'S RIGHT.
EEAARR

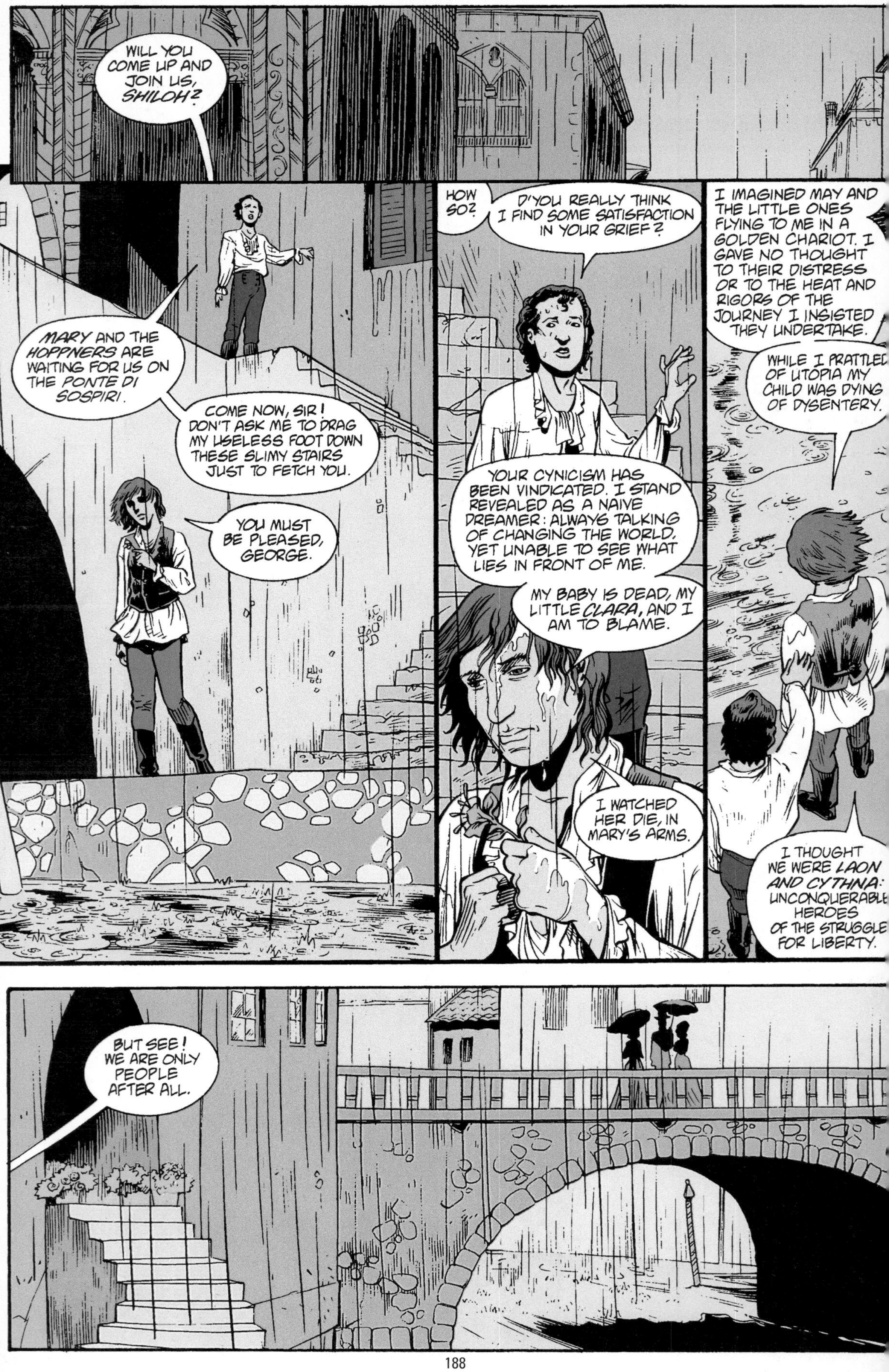
WILL YOU COME UP AND JOIN US, SHILOH?
MARY AND THE HOPPNERS ARE WAITING FOR US ON THE PONTE DI SOSPIRI.
COME NOW, SIR! DON'T ASK ME TO DRAG MY USELESS FOOT DOWN THESE SLIMY STAIRS JUST TO FETCH YOU.
YOU MUST BE PLEASED, GEORGE.
HOW SO?
D'YOU REALLY THINK I FIND SOME SATISFACTION IN YOUR GRIEF?
YOUR CYNICISM HAS BEEN VINDICATED. I STAND REVEALED AS A NAIVE DREAMER: ALWAYS TALKING OF CHANGING THE WORLD, YET UNABLE TO SEE WHAT LIES IN FRONT OF ME.
MY BABY IS DEAD, MY LITTLE CLARA, AND I AM TO BLAME.
I WATCHED HER DIE, IN MARY'S ARMS.
I IMAGINED MAY AND THE LITTLE ONES FLYING TO ME IN A GOLDEN CHARIOT. I GAVE NO THOUGHT TO THEIR DISTRESS OR TO THE HEAT AND RIGORS OF THE JOURNEY I INSISTED THEY UNDERTAKE.
WHILE I PRATTLED OF UTOPIA MY CHILD WAS DYING OF DYSENTERY.
I THOUGHT WE WERE LAON AND CYTHNA: UNCONQUERABLE HEROES OF THE STRUGGLE FOR LIBERTY.
BUT SEE! WE ARE ONLY PEOPLE AFTER ALL.

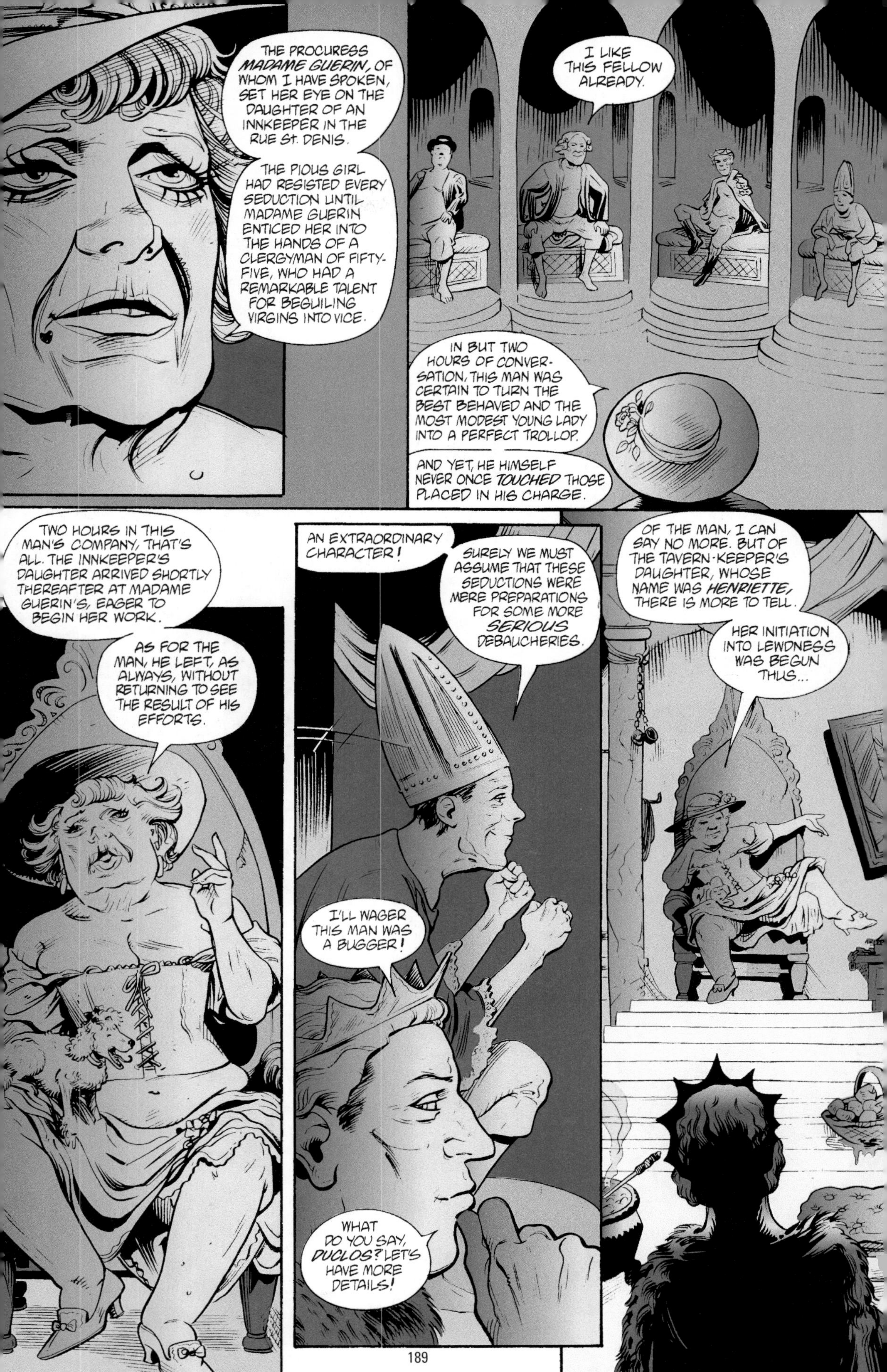

THE PROCURESS *MADAME GUERIN*, OF WHOM I HAVE SPOKEN, SET HER EYE ON THE DAUGHTER OF AN INNKEEPER IN THE RUE St. DENIS.
THE PIOUS GIRL HAD RESISTED EVERY SEDUCTION UNTIL MADAME GUERIN ENTICED HER INTO THE HANDS OF A CLERGYMAN OF FIFTY-FIVE, WHO HAD A REMARKABLE TALENT FOR BEGUILING VIRGINS INTO VICE.
I LIKE THIS FELLOW ALREADY.
IN BUT TWO HOURS OF CONVERSATION, THIS MAN WAS CERTAIN TO TURN THE BEST BEHAVED AND THE MOST MODEST YOUNG LADY INTO A PERFECT TROLLOP.
AND YET, HE HIMSELF NEVER ONCE *TOUCHED* THOSE PLACED IN HIS CHARGE.
TWO HOURS IN THIS MAN'S COMPANY, THAT'S ALL. THE INNKEEPER'S DAUGHTER ARRIVED SHORTLY THEREAFTER AT MADAME GUERIN'S, EAGER TO BEGIN HER WORK.
AS FOR THE MAN, HE LEFT, AS ALWAYS, WITHOUT RETURNING TO SEE THE RESULT OF HIS EFFORTS.
AN EXTRAORDINARY CHARACTER!
SURELY WE MUST ASSUME THAT THESE SEDUCTIONS WERE MERE PREPARATIONS FOR SOME MORE *SERIOUS* DEBAUCHERIES.
I'LL WAGER THIS MAN WAS A BUGGER!
WHAT DO YOU SAY, *DUCLOS*? LET'S HAVE MORE DETAILS!
OF THE MAN, I CAN SAY NO MORE. BUT OF THE TAVERN-KEEPER'S DAUGHTER, WHOSE NAME WAS *HENRIETTE*, THERE IS MORE TO TELL.
HER INITIATION INTO LEWDNESS WAS BEGUN THUS...

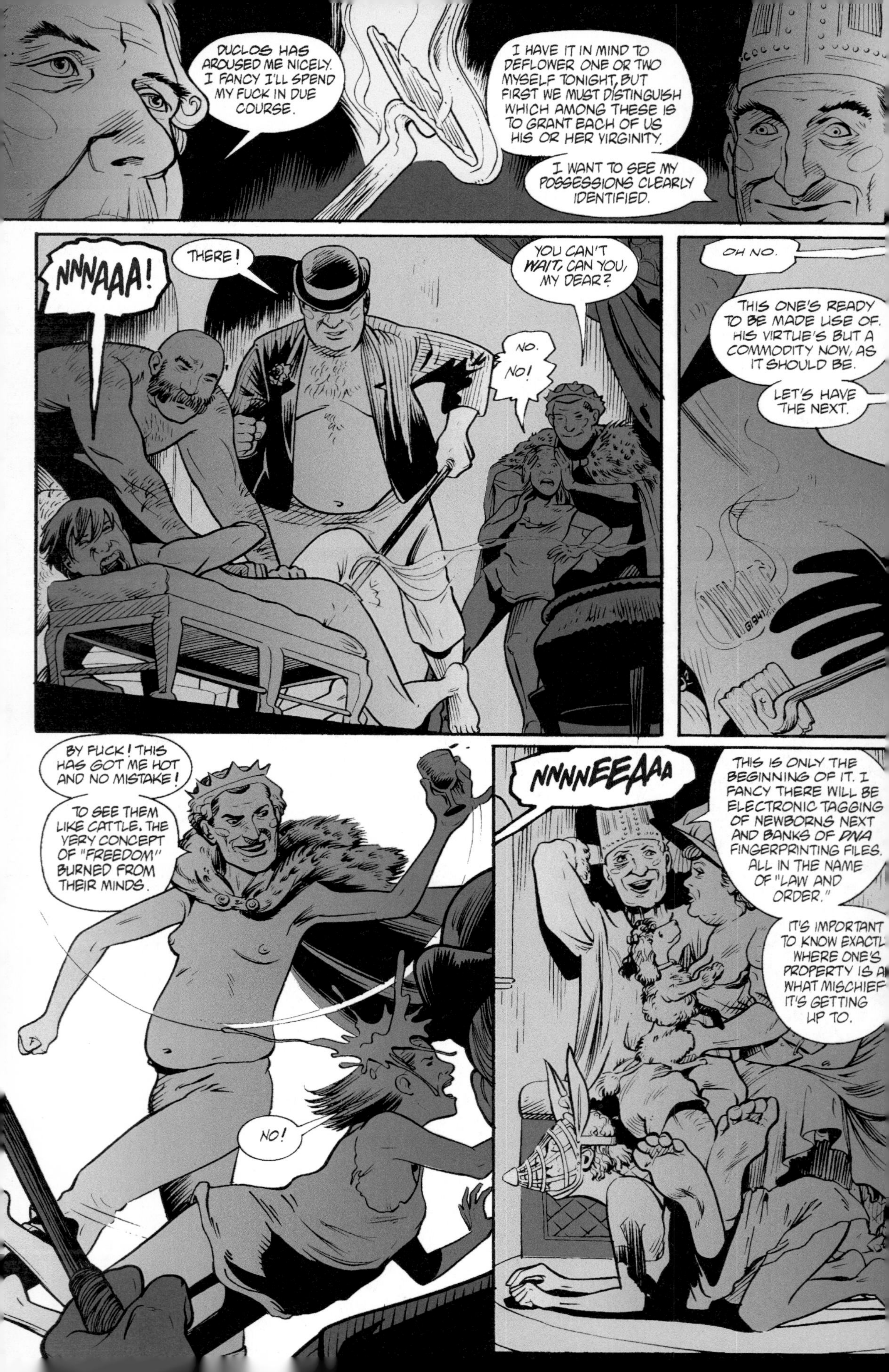
DUCLOS HAS AROUSED ME NICELY. I FANCY I'LL SPEND MY FUCK IN DUE COURSE.
I HAVE IT IN MIND TO DEFLOWER ONE OR TWO MYSELF TONIGHT, BUT FIRST WE MUST DISTINGUISH WHICH AMONG THESE IS TO GRANT EACH OF US HIS OR HER VIRGINITY.
I WANT TO SEE MY POSSESSIONS CLEARLY IDENTIFIED.
NNNAAA!
THERE!
YOU CAN'T WAIT, CAN YOU, MY DEAR?
NO.
NO!
OH NO.
THIS ONE'S READY TO BE MADE USE OF. HIS VIRTUE'S BUT A COMMODITY NOW, AS IT SHOULD BE.
LET'S HAVE THE NEXT.
BY FUCK! THIS HAS GOT ME HOT AND NO MISTAKE!
TO SEE THEM LIKE CATTLE. THE VERY CONCEPT OF "FREEDOM" BURNED FROM THEIR MINDS.
NO!
NNNNEEAAA
THIS IS ONLY THE BEGINNING OF IT. I FANCY THERE WILL BE ELECTRONIC TAGGING OF NEWBORNS NEXT AND BANKS OF DNA FINGERPRINTING FILES. ALL IN THE NAME OF "LAW AND ORDER."
IT'S IMPORTANT TO KNOW EXACTL WHERE ONE'S PROPERTY IS A WHAT MISCHIEF IT'S GETTING UP TO.

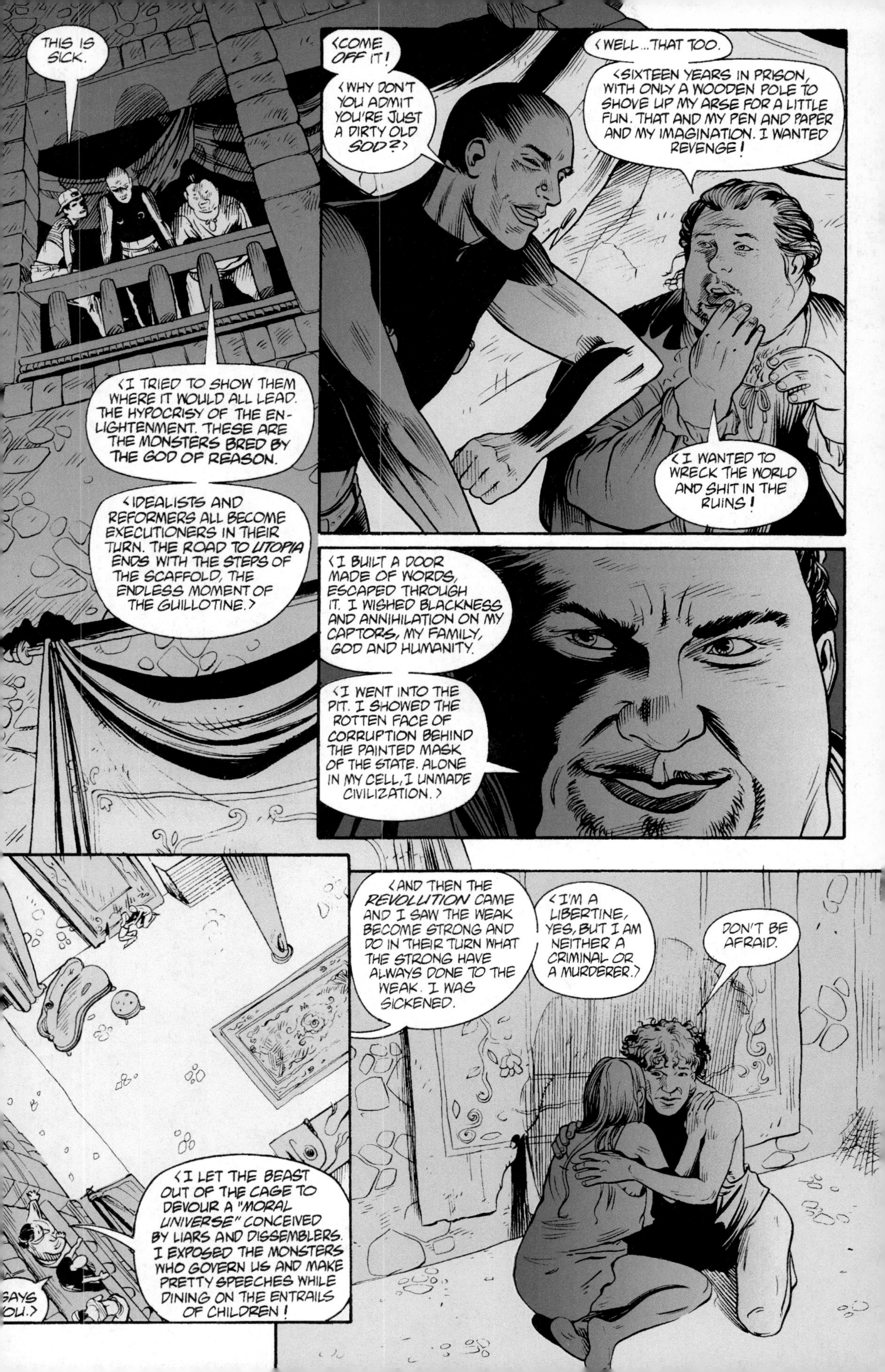

THIS IS SICK.
<I TRIED TO SHOW THEM WHERE IT WOULD ALL LEAD. THE HYPOCRISY OF THE ENLIGHTENMENT. THESE ARE THE MONSTERS BRED BY THE GOD OF REASON.
<IDEALISTS AND REFORMERS ALL BECOME EXECUTIONERS IN THEIR TURN. THE ROAD TO UTOPIA ENDS WITH THE STEPS OF THE SCAFFOLD, THE ENDLESS MOMENT OF THE GUILLOTINE.>
<COME OFF IT!
<WHY DON'T YOU ADMIT YOU'RE JUST A DIRTY OLD SOD?>
<WELL...THAT TOO.
<SIXTEEN YEARS IN PRISON, WITH ONLY A WOODEN POLE TO SHOVE UP MY ARSE FOR A LITTLE FUN. THAT AND MY PEN AND PAPER AND MY IMAGINATION. I WANTED REVENGE!
<I WANTED TO WRECK THE WORLD AND SHIT IN THE RUINS!
<I BUILT A DOOR MADE OF WORDS, ESCAPED THROUGH IT. I WISHED BLACKNESS AND ANNIHILATION ON MY CAPTORS, MY FAMILY, GOD AND HUMANITY.
<I WENT INTO THE PIT. I SHOWED THE ROTTEN FACE OF CORRUPTION BEHIND THE PAINTED MASK OF THE STATE. ALONE IN MY CELL, I UNMADE CIVILIZATION.>
<I LET THE BEAST OUT OF THE CAGE TO DEVOUR A "MORAL UNIVERSE" CONCEIVED BY LIARS AND DISSEMBLERS. I EXPOSED THE MONSTERS WHO GOVERN US AND MAKE PRETTY SPEECHES WHILE DINING ON THE ENTRAILS OF CHILDREN!
SAYS OU.>
<AND THEN THE REVOLUTION CAME AND I SAW THE WEAK BECOME STRONG AND DO IN THEIR TURN WHAT THE STRONG HAVE ALWAYS DONE TO THE WEAK. I WAS SICKENED.
<I'M A LIBERTINE, YES, BUT I AM NEITHER A CRIMINAL OR A MURDERER.>
DON'T BE AFRAID.

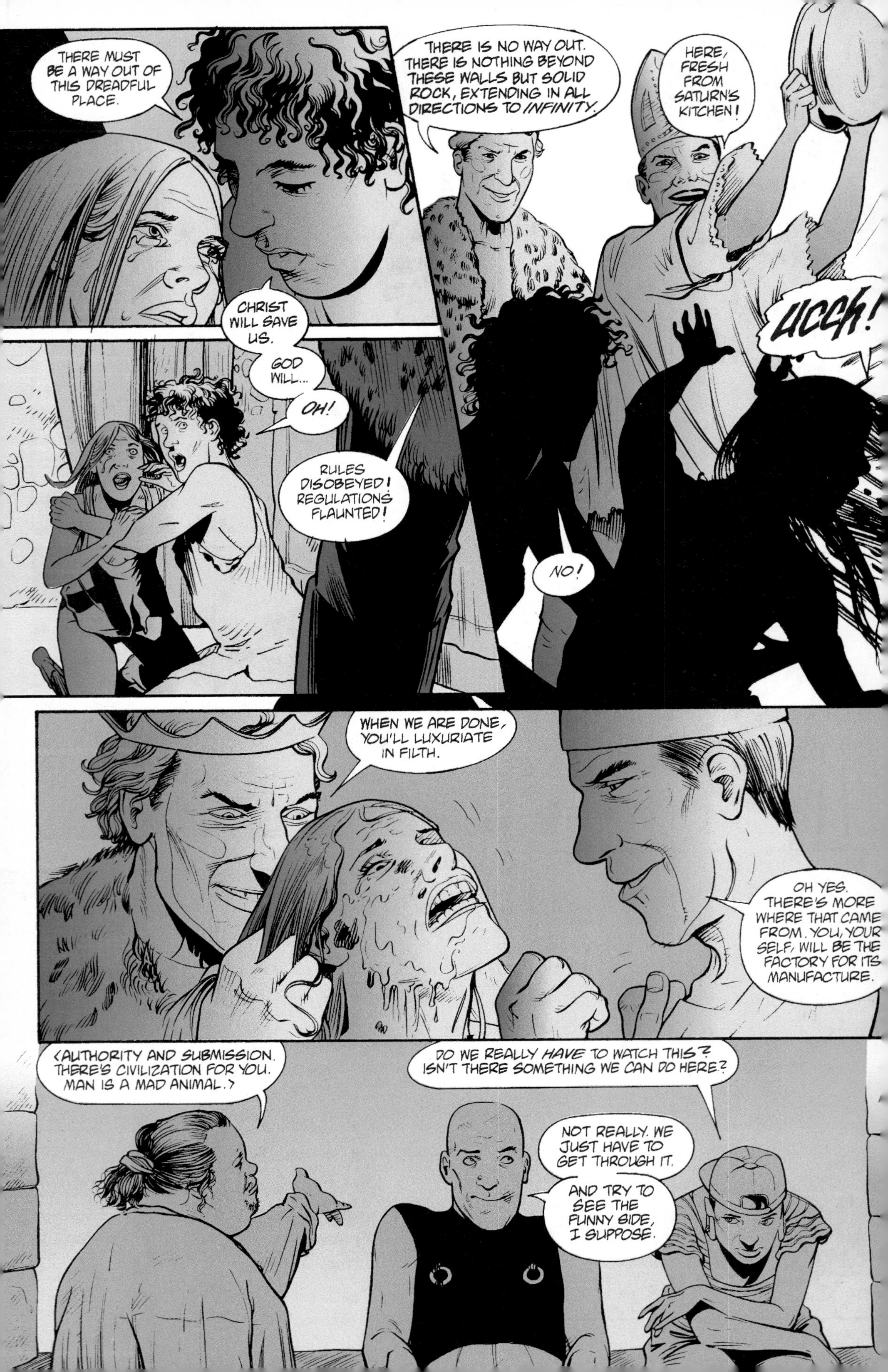
THERE MUST BE A WAY OUT OF THIS DREADFUL PLACE.
CHRIST WILL SAVE US.
THERE IS NO WAY OUT. THERE IS NOTHING BEYOND THESE WALLS BUT SOLID ROCK, EXTENDING IN ALL DIRECTIONS TO *INFINITY*.
HERE, FRESH FROM SATURN'S KITCHEN!
GOD WILL...
OH!
RULES DISOBEYED! REGULATIONS FLAUNTED!
UCCH!
NO!
WHEN WE ARE DONE, YOU'LL LUXURIATE IN FILTH.
OH YES. THERE'S MORE WHERE THAT CAME FROM. YOU, YOUR SELF, WILL BE THE FACTORY FOR ITS MANUFACTURE.
<AUTHORITY AND SUBMISSION. THERE'S CIVILIZATION FOR YOU. MAN IS A MAD ANIMAL.>
DO WE REALLY *HAVE* TO WATCH THIS? ISN'T THERE SOMETHING WE CAN DO HERE?
NOT REALLY. WE JUST HAVE TO GET THROUGH IT.
AND TRY TO SEE THE FUNNY SIDE, I SUPPOSE.

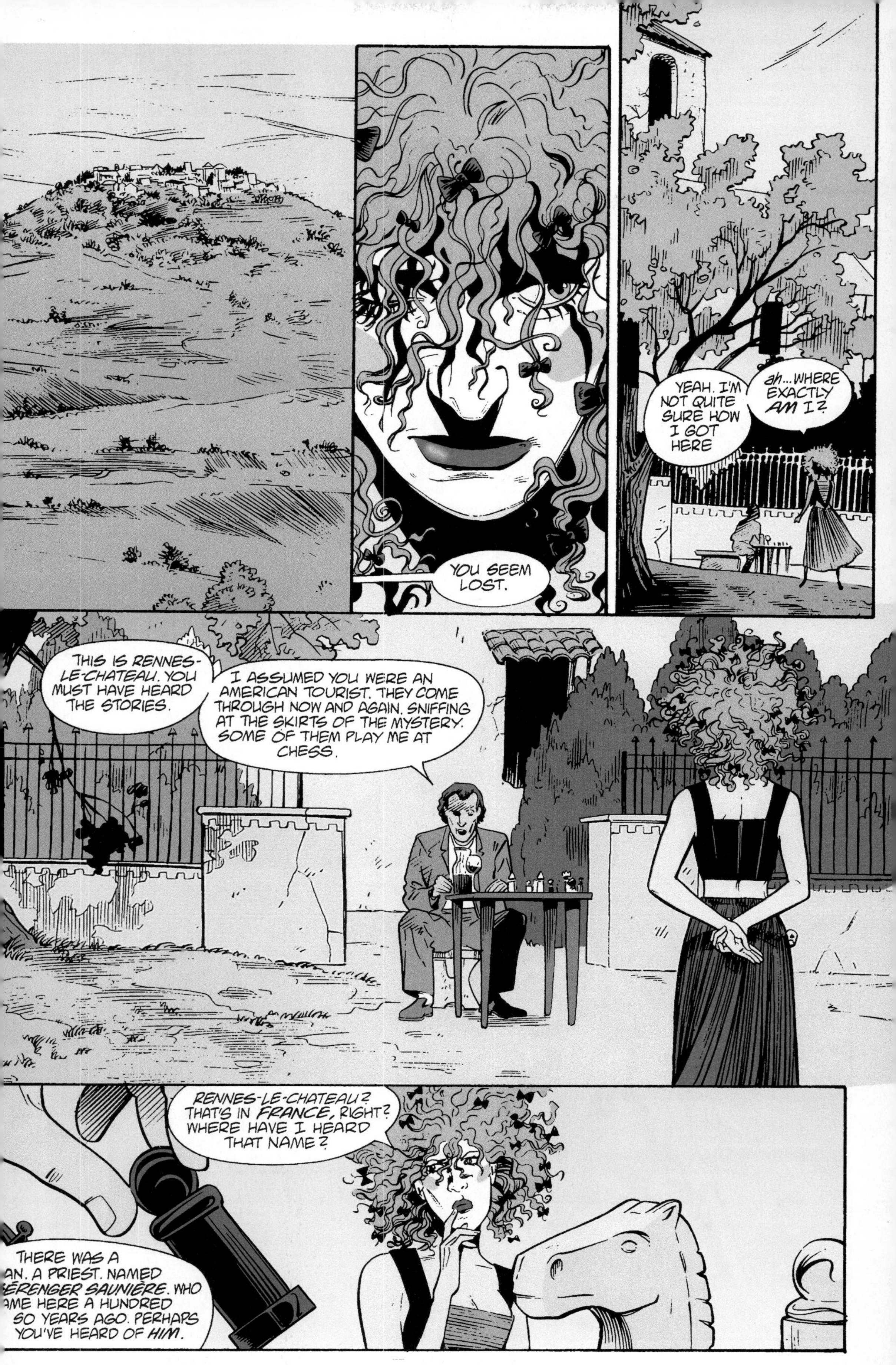
YOU SEEM LOST.
YEAH. I'M NOT QUITE SURE HOW I GOT HERE
ah... WHERE EXACTLY AM I?
THIS IS RENNES-LE-CHATEAU. YOU MUST HAVE HEARD THE STORIES.
I ASSUMED YOU WERE AN AMERICAN TOURIST. THEY COME THROUGH NOW AND AGAIN. SNIFFING AT THE SKIRTS OF THE MYSTERY. SOME OF THEM PLAY ME AT CHESS.
RENNES-LE-CHATEAU? THAT'S IN FRANCE, RIGHT? WHERE HAVE I HEARD THAT NAME?
THERE WAS A AN. A PRIEST. NAMED ÉRENGER SAUNIÈRE. WHO AME HERE A HUNDRED SO YEARS AGO. PERHAPS YOU'VE HEARD OF HIM.

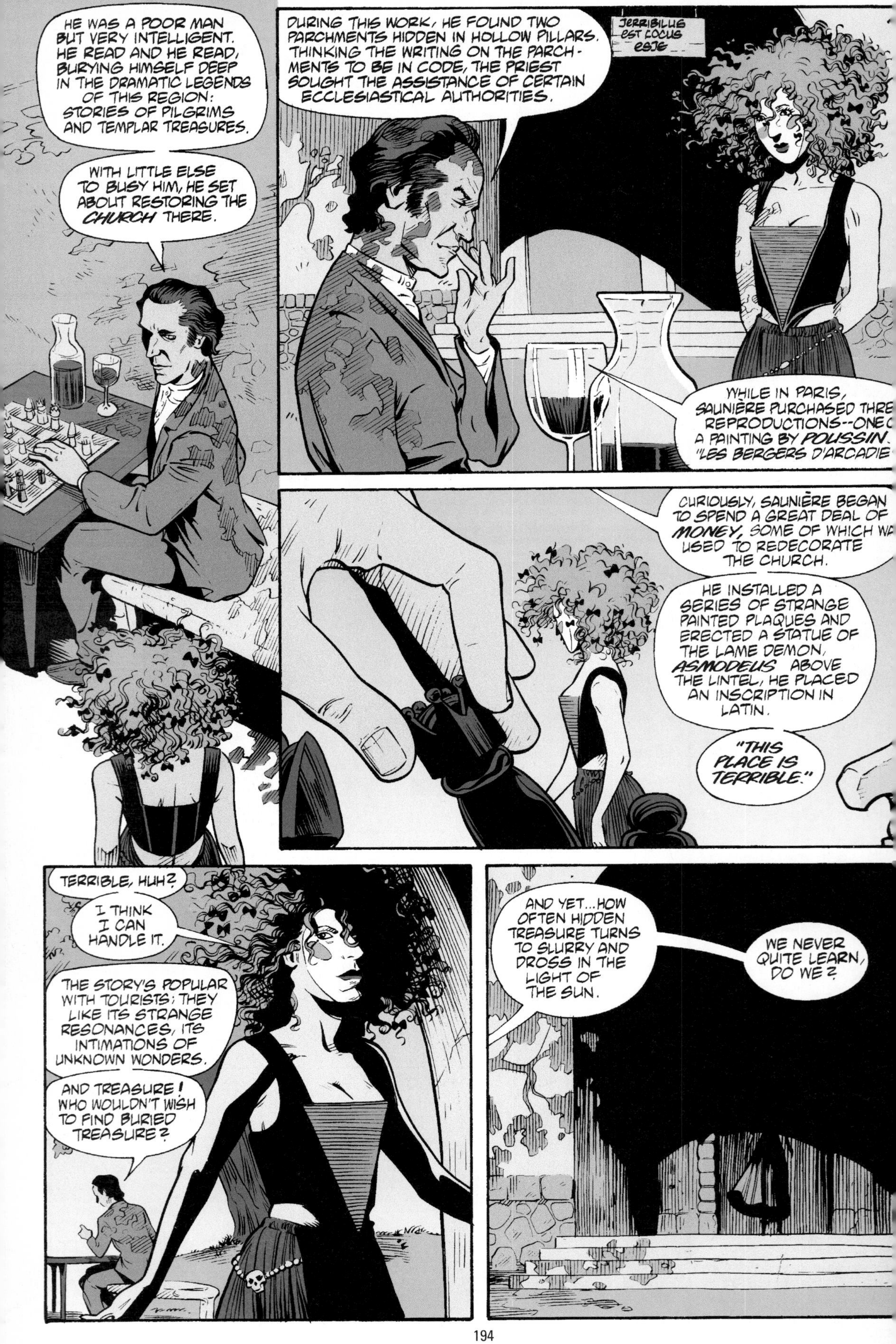
HE WAS A POOR MAN BUT VERY INTELLIGENT. HE READ AND HE READ, BURYING HIMSELF DEEP IN THE DRAMATIC LEGENDS OF THIS REGION: STORIES OF PILGRIMS AND TEMPLAR TREASURES.
WITH LITTLE ELSE TO BUSY HIM, HE SET ABOUT RESTORING THE *CHURCH* THERE.
DURING THIS WORK, HE FOUND TWO PARCHMENTS HIDDEN IN HOLLOW PILLARS. THINKING THE WRITING ON THE PARCH-MENTS TO BE IN CODE, THE PRIEST SOUGHT THE ASSISTANCE OF CERTAIN ECCLESIASTICAL AUTHORITIES.
TERRIBILIS EST LOCUS ISTE
WHILE IN PARIS, SAUNIÈRE PURCHASED THRE REPRODUCTIONS--ONE A PAINTING BY *POUSSIN*. "LES BERGERS D'ARCADIE
CURIOUSLY, SAUNIÈRE BEGAN TO SPEND A GREAT DEAL OF *MONEY*, SOME OF WHICH WA USED TO REDECORATE THE CHURCH.
HE INSTALLED A SERIES OF STRANGE PAINTED PLAQUES AND ERECTED A STATUE OF THE LAME DEMON, *ASMODEUS* ABOVE THE LINTEL, HE PLACED AN INSCRIPTION IN LATIN.
"THIS PLACE IS TERRIBLE."
TERRIBLE, HUH?
I THINK I CAN HANDLE IT.
THE STORY'S POPULAR WITH TOURISTS; THEY LIKE ITS STRANGE RESONANCES, ITS INTIMATIONS OF UNKNOWN WONDERS.
AND TREASURE! WHO WOULDN'T WISH TO FIND BURIED TREASURE?
AND YET... HOW OFTEN HIDDEN TREASURE TURNS TO SLURRY AND DROSS IN THE LIGHT OF THE SUN.
WE NEVER QUITE LEARN, DO WE?

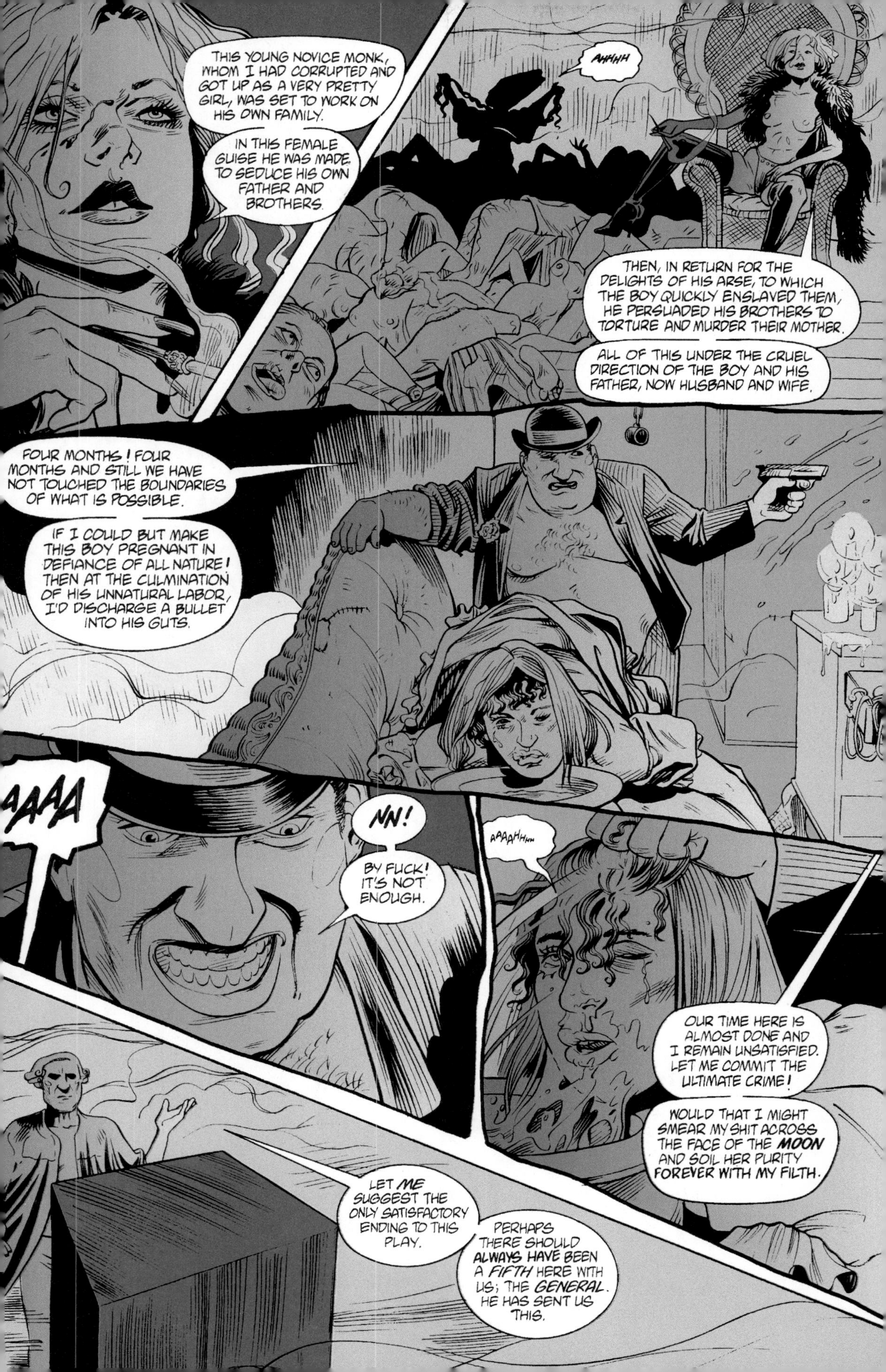

THIS YOUNG NOVICE MONK, WHOM I HAD CORRUPTED AND GOT UP AS A VERY PRETTY GIRL, WAS SET TO WORK ON HIS OWN FAMILY.
IN THIS FEMALE GUISE HE WAS MADE TO SEDUCE HIS OWN FATHER AND BROTHERS.
AHHHH
THEN, IN RETURN FOR THE DELIGHTS OF HIS ARSE, TO WHICH THE BOY QUICKLY ENSLAVED THEM, HE PERSUADED HIS BROTHERS TO TORTURE AND MURDER THEIR MOTHER.
ALL OF THIS UNDER THE CRUEL DIRECTION OF THE BOY AND HIS FATHER, NOW HUSBAND AND WIFE.
FOUR MONTHS! FOUR MONTHS AND STILL WE HAVE NOT TOUCHED THE BOUNDARIES OF WHAT IS POSSIBLE.
IF I COULD BUT MAKE THIS BOY PREGNANT IN DEFIANCE OF ALL NATURE! THEN AT THE CULMINATION OF HIS UNNATURAL LABOR, I'D DISCHARGE A BULLET INTO HIS GUTS.
AAAA
NN!
BY FUCK! IT'S NOT ENOUGH.
AAAAHHHH
OUR TIME HERE IS ALMOST DONE AND I REMAIN UNSATISFIED. LET ME COMMIT THE ULTIMATE CRIME!
WOULD THAT I MIGHT SMEAR MY SHIT ACROSS THE FACE OF THE MOON AND SOIL HER PURITY FOREVER WITH MY FILTH.
LET ME SUGGEST THE ONLY SATISFACTORY ENDING TO THIS PLAY.
PERHAPS THERE SHOULD ALWAYS HAVE BEEN A FIFTH HERE WITH US; THE GENERAL. HE HAS SENT US THIS.

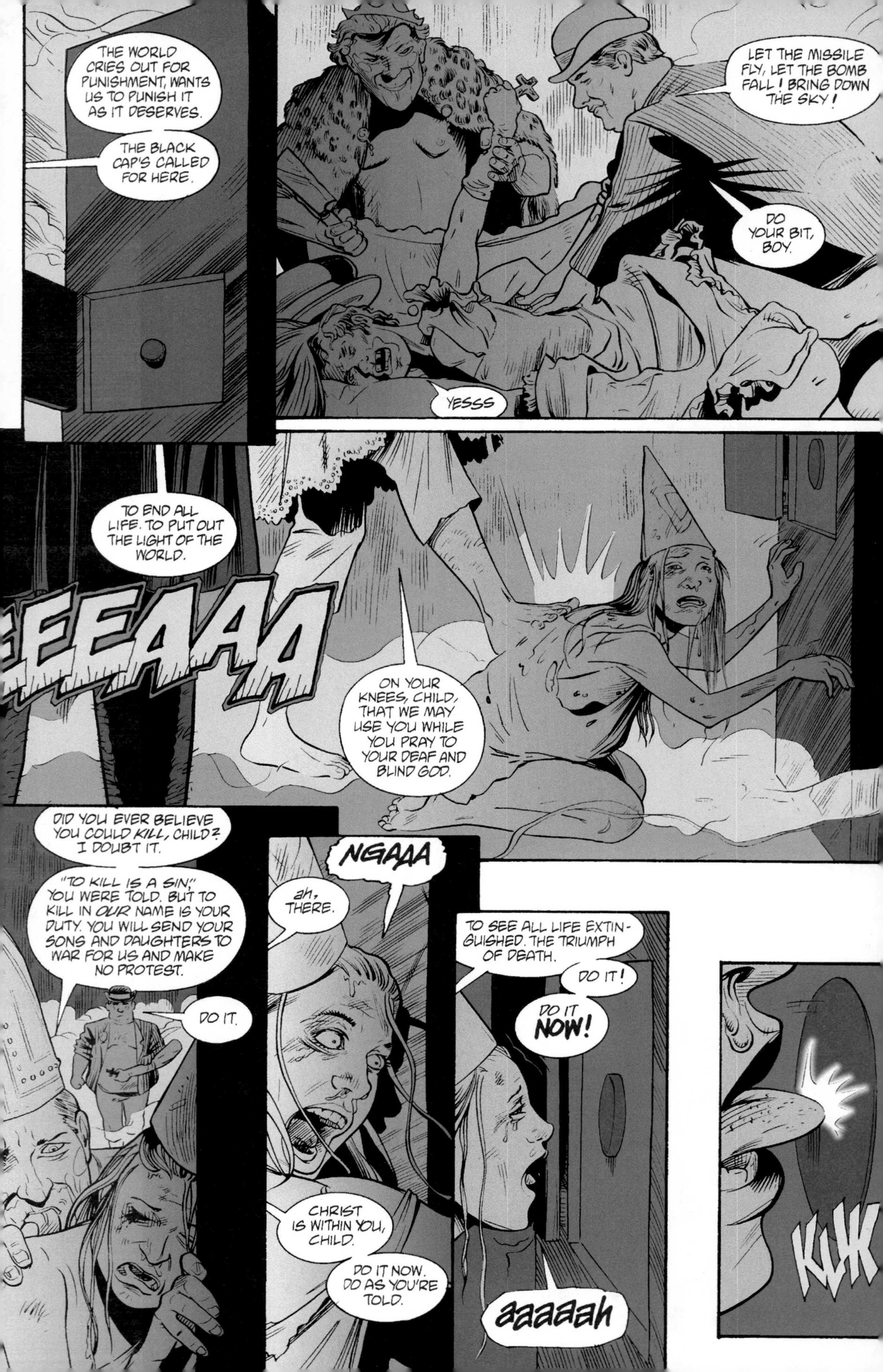

THE WORLD CRIES OUT FOR PUNISHMENT, WANTS US TO PUNISH IT AS IT DESERVES.
THE BLACK CAP'S CALLED FOR HERE.
LET THE MISSILE FLY, LET THE BOMB FALL! BRING DOWN THE SKY!
DO YOUR BIT, BOY.
YESSS
TO END ALL LIFE. TO PUT OUT THE LIGHT OF THE WORLD.
EEAAA
ON YOUR KNEES, CHILD, THAT WE MAY USE YOU WHILE YOU PRAY TO YOUR DEAF AND BLIND GOD.
DID YOU EVER BELIEVE YOU COULD KILL, CHILD? I DOUBT IT.
"TO KILL IS A SIN," YOU WERE TOLD. BUT TO KILL IN OUR NAME IS YOUR DUTY. YOU WILL SEND YOUR SONS AND DAUGHTERS TO WAR FOR US AND MAKE NO PROTEST.
DO IT.
NGAAA
ah, THERE.
CHRIST IS WITHIN YOU, CHILD.
DO IT NOW. DO AS YOU'RE TOLD.
TO SEE ALL LIFE EXTINGUISHED. THE TRIUMPH OF DEATH.
DO IT!
DO IT NOW!
aaaaah
KLIK

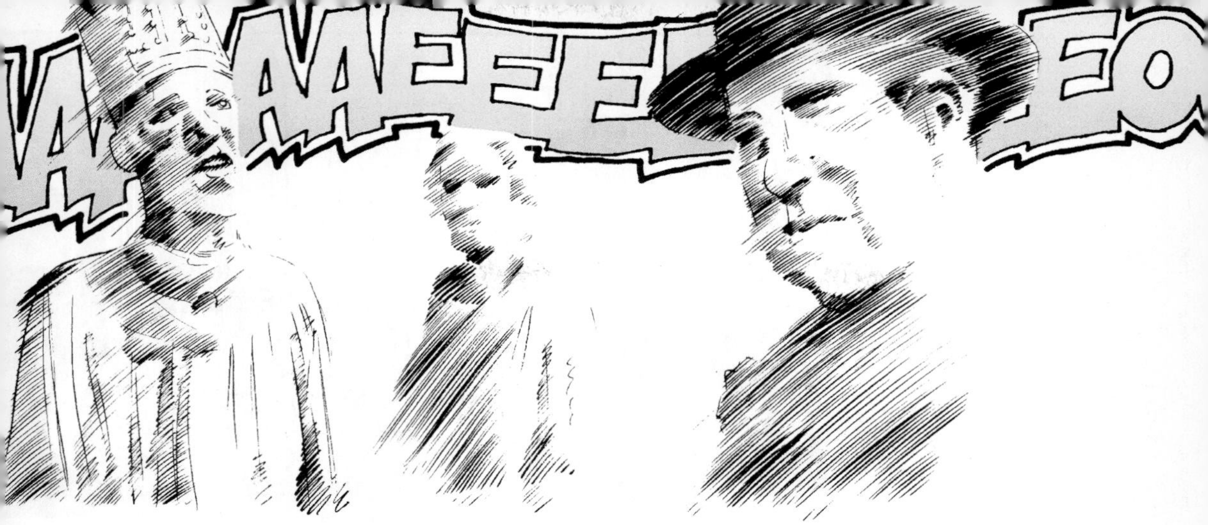

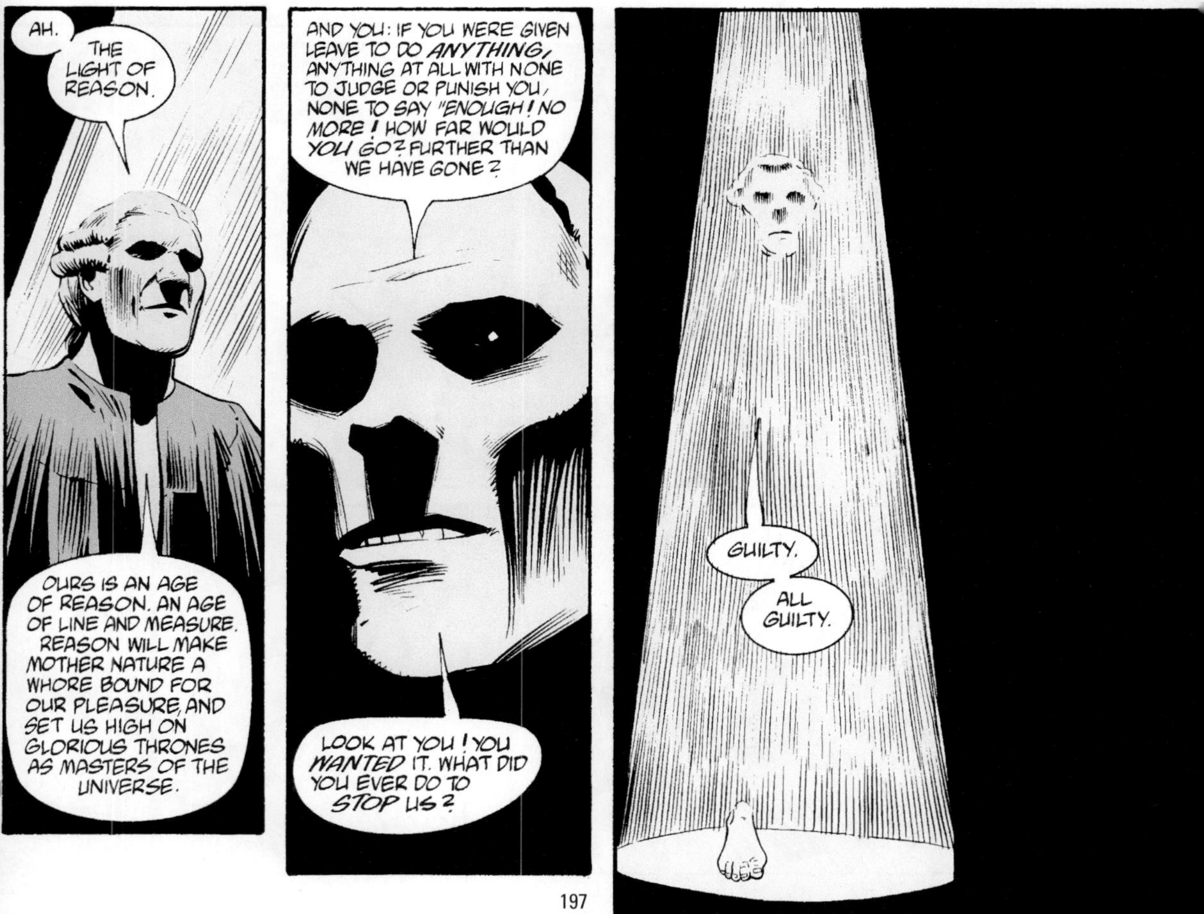
AH.
THE LIGHT OF REASON.
OURS IS AN AGE OF REASON. AN AGE OF LINE AND MEASURE. REASON WILL MAKE MOTHER NATURE A WHORE BOUND FOR OUR PLEASURE, AND SET US HIGH ON GLORIOUS THRONES AS MASTERS OF THE UNIVERSE.
AND YOU: IF YOU WERE GIVEN LEAVE TO DO *ANYTHING*, ANYTHING AT ALL WITH NONE TO JUDGE OR PUNISH YOU, NONE TO SAY "ENOUGH! NO MORE! HOW FAR WOULD YOU GO? FURTHER THAN WE HAVE GONE?
LOOK AT YOU! YOU *WANTED* IT. WHAT DID YOU EVER DO TO *STOP* US?
GUILTY.
ALL GUILTY.

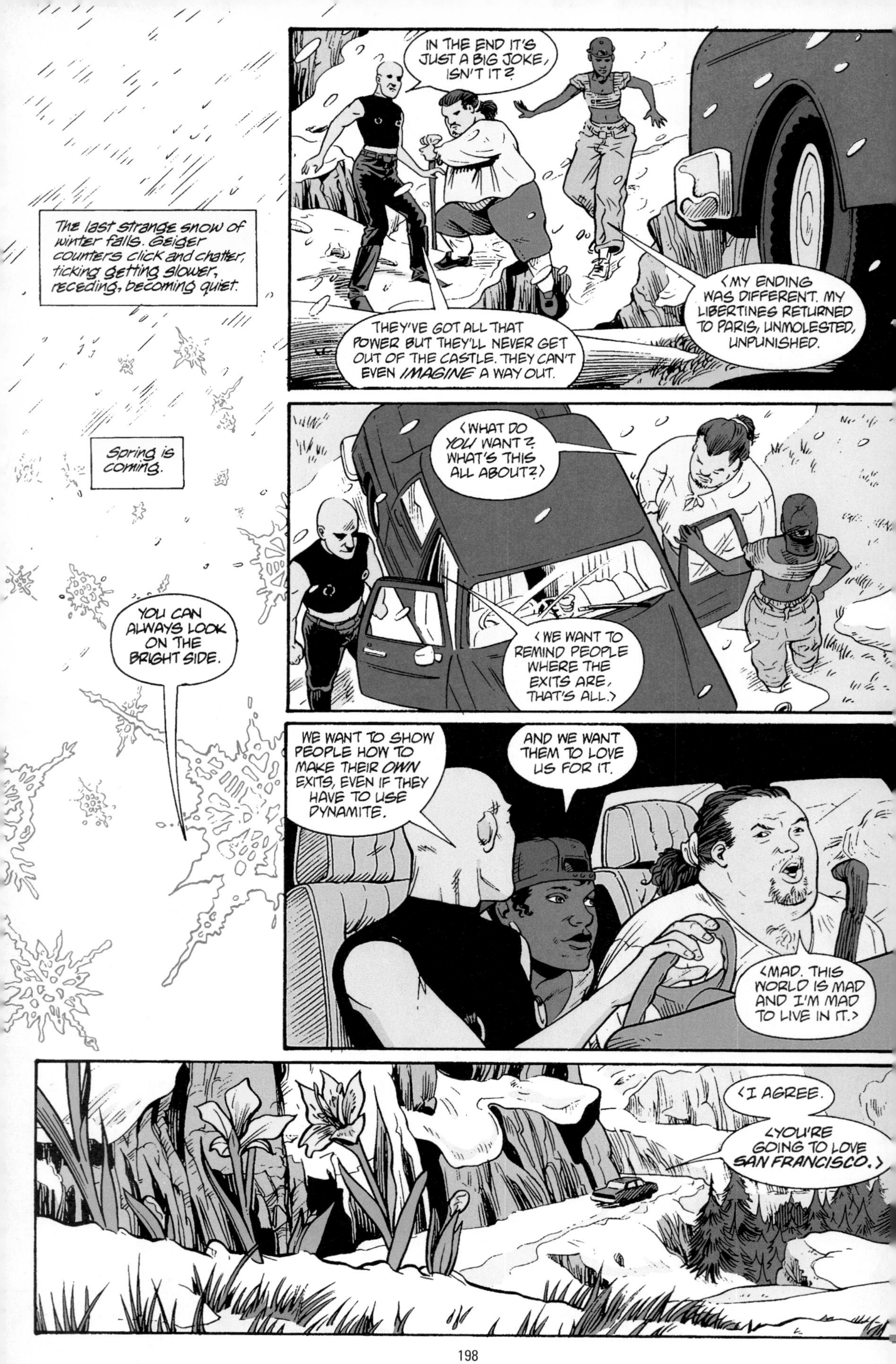
The last strange snow of winter falls. Geiger counters click and chatter, ticking getting slower, receding, becoming quiet.
IN THE END IT'S JUST A BIG JOKE, ISN'T IT?
THEY'VE GOT ALL THAT POWER BUT THEY'LL NEVER GET OUT OF THE CASTLE. THEY CAN'T EVEN *IMAGINE* A WAY OUT.
‹MY ENDING WAS DIFFERENT. MY LIBERTINES RETURNED TO PARIS, UNMOLESTED, UNPUNISHED.
Spring is coming.
‹WHAT DO *YOU* WANT? WHAT'S THIS ALL ABOUT?›
‹WE WANT TO REMIND PEOPLE WHERE THE EXITS ARE, THAT'S ALL.›
YOU CAN ALWAYS LOOK ON THE BRIGHT SIDE.
WE WANT TO SHOW PEOPLE HOW TO MAKE THEIR *OWN* EXITS, EVEN IF THEY HAVE TO USE DYNAMITE.
AND WE WANT THEM TO LOVE US FOR IT.
‹MAD. THIS WORLD IS MAD AND I'M MAD TO LIVE IN IT.›
‹I AGREE.
‹YOU'RE GOING TO LOVE **SAN FRANCISCO.**›

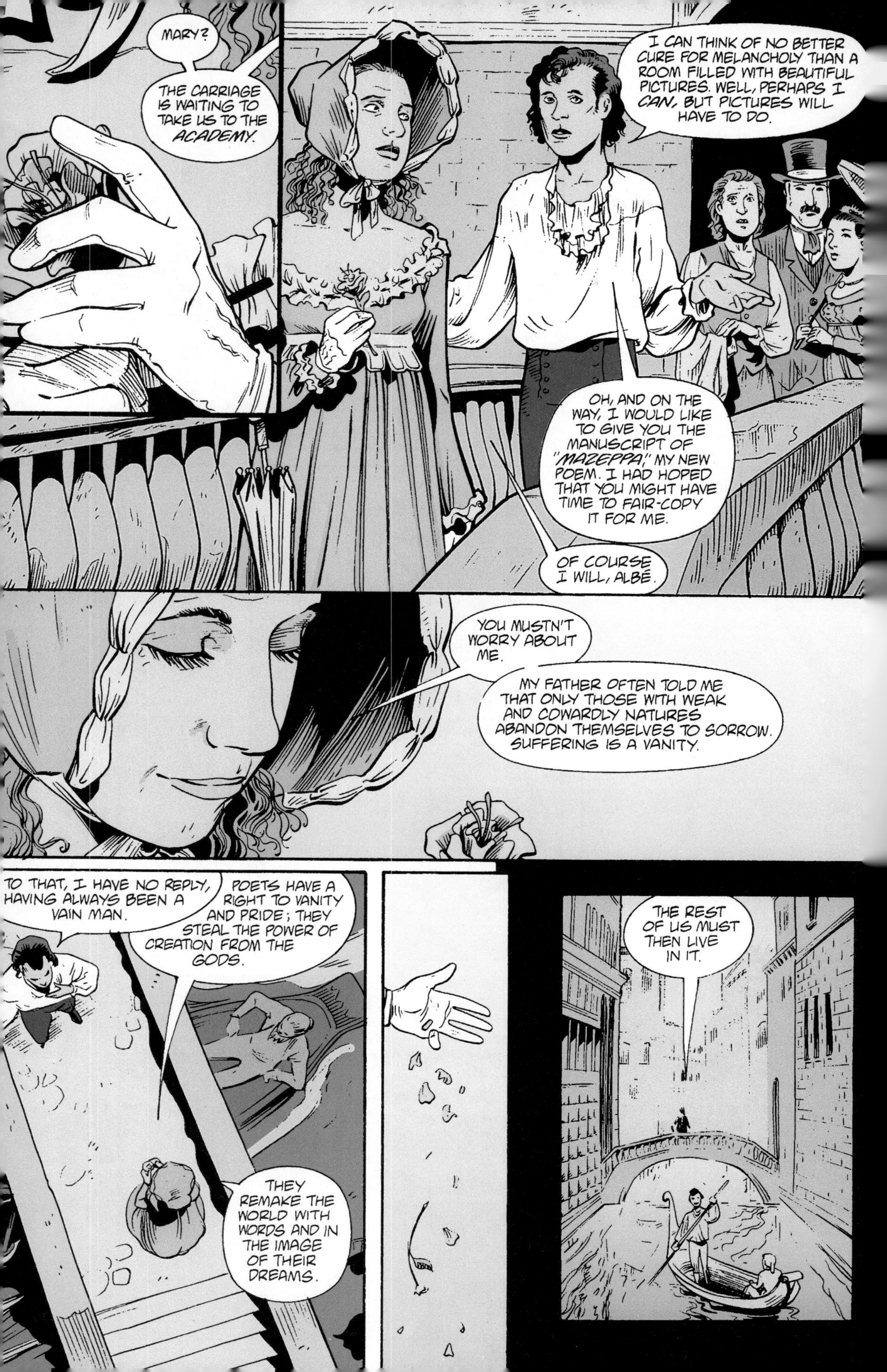
MARY?
THE CARRIAGE IS WAITING TO TAKE US TO THE ACADEMY.
I CAN THINK OF NO BETTER CURE FOR MELANCHOLY THAN A ROOM FILLED WITH BEAUTIFUL PICTURES. WELL, PERHAPS I CAN, BUT PICTURES WILL HAVE TO DO.
OH, AND ON THE WAY, I WOULD LIKE TO GIVE YOU THE MANUSCRIPT OF "MAZEPPA," MY NEW POEM. I HAD HOPED THAT YOU MIGHT HAVE TIME TO FAIR-COPY IT FOR ME.
OF COURSE I WILL, ALBÉ.
YOU MUSTN'T WORRY ABOUT ME.
MY FATHER OFTEN TOLD ME THAT ONLY THOSE WITH WEAK AND COWARDLY NATURES ABANDON THEMSELVES TO SORROW. SUFFERING IS A VANITY.
TO THAT, I HAVE NO REPLY, HAVING ALWAYS BEEN A VAIN MAN.
POETS HAVE A RIGHT TO VANITY AND PRIDE; THEY STEAL THE POWER OF CREATION FROM THE GODS.
THEY REMAKE THE WORLD WITH WORDS AND IN THE IMAGE OF THEIR DREAMS.
THE REST OF US MUST THEN LIVE IN IT.

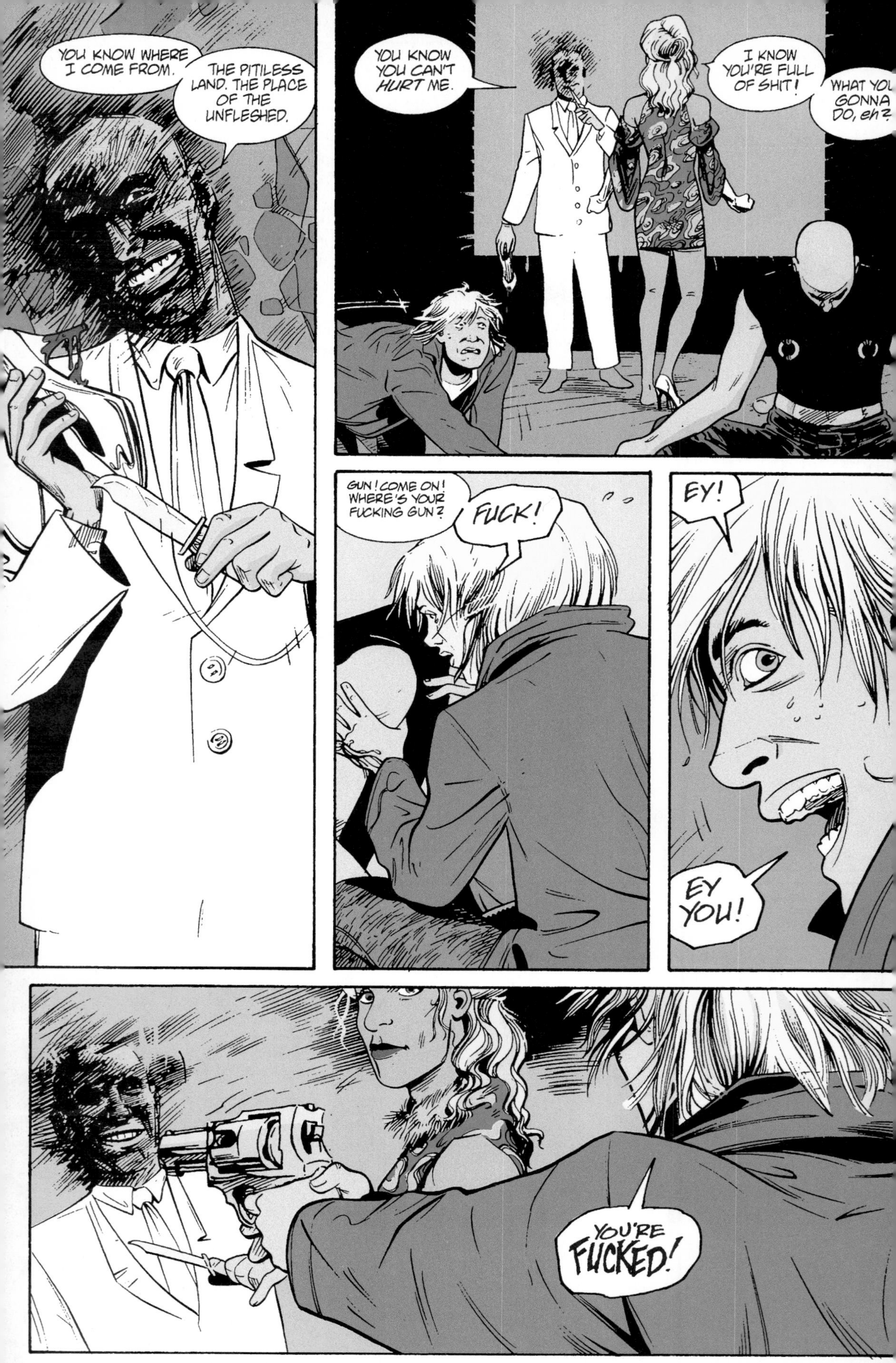

YOU KNOW WHERE I COME FROM.
THE PITILESS LAND. THE PLACE OF THE UNFLESHED.
YOU KNOW YOU CAN'T HURT ME.
I KNOW YOU'RE FULL OF SHIT!
WHAT YOU GONNA DO, eh?
GUN! COME ON! WHERE'S YOUR FUCKING GUN?
FUCK!
EY!
EY YOU!
YOU'RE FUCKED!

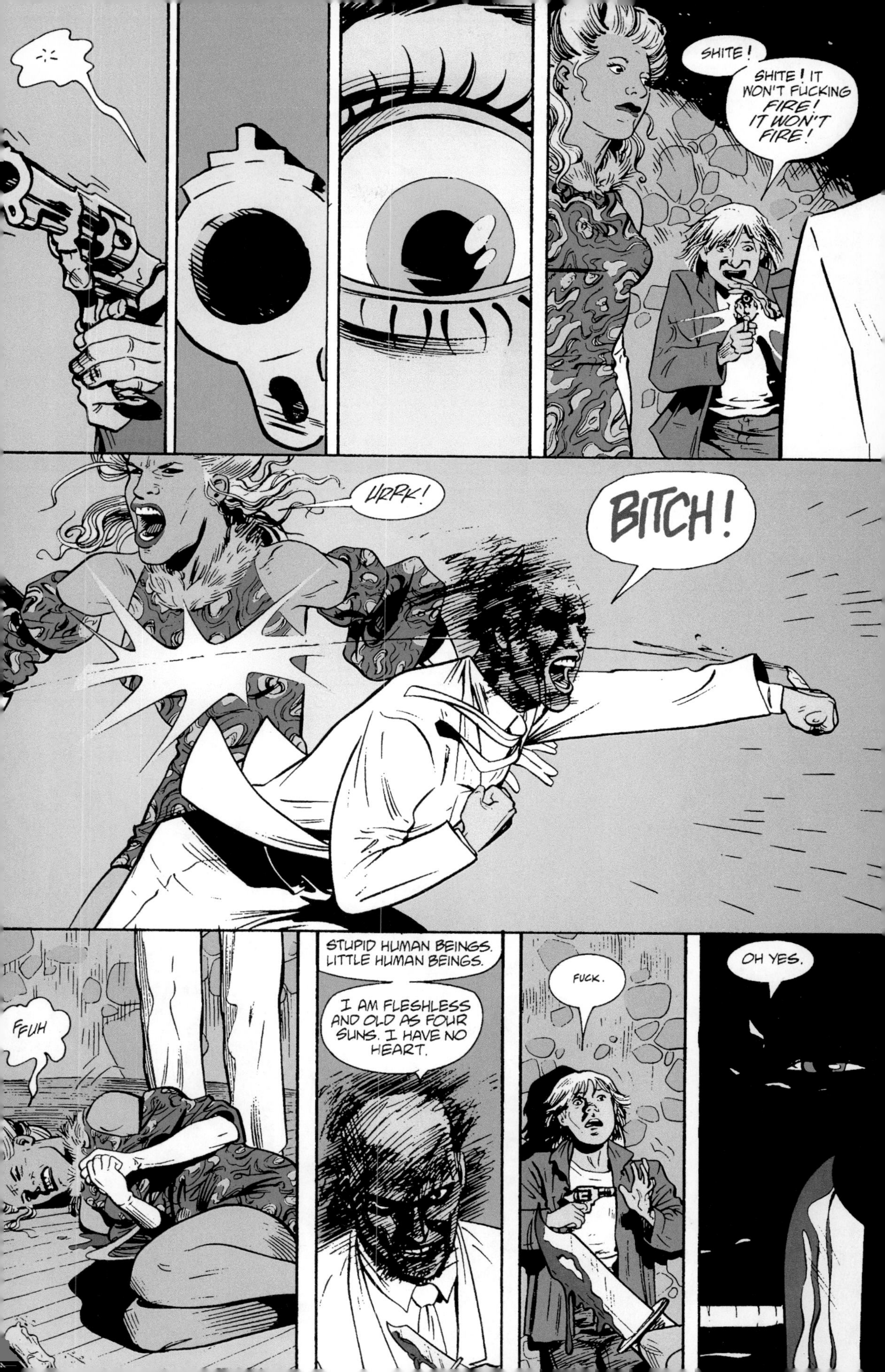

SHITE!
SHITE! IT WON'T FUCKING FIRE! IT WON'T FIRE!
URRK!
BITCH!
FFUH
STUPID HUMAN BEINGS. LITTLE HUMAN BEINGS.
I AM FLESHLESS AND OLD AS FOUR SUNS. I HAVE NO HEART.
FUCK.
OH YES.

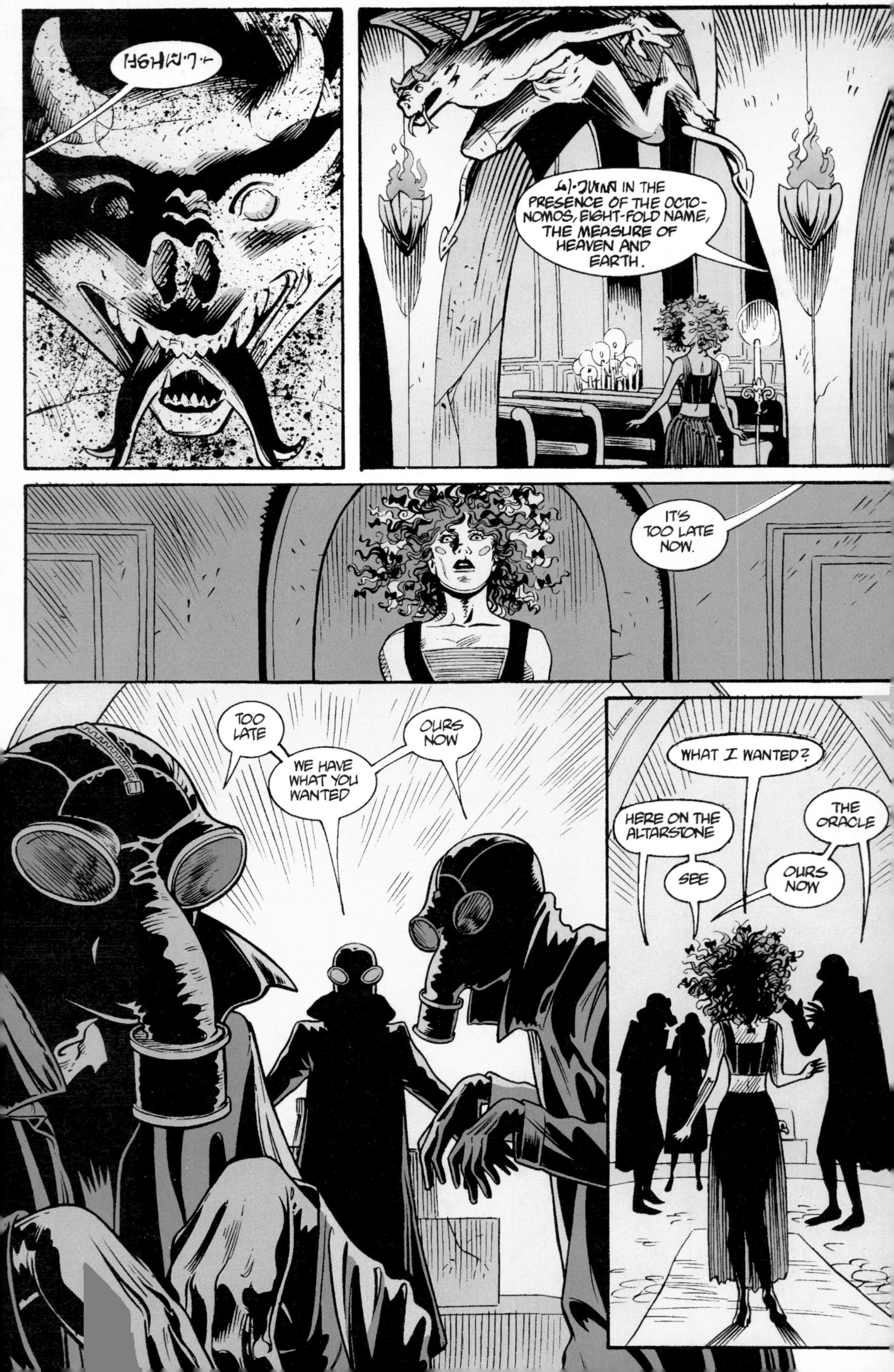
IN THE PRESENCE OF THE OCTO-NOMOS, EIGHT-FOLD NAME, THE MEASURE OF HEAVEN AND EARTH.
IT'S TOO LATE NOW.
TOO LATE
WE HAVE WHAT YOU WANTED
OURS NOW
WHAT I WANTED?
HERE ON THE ALTARSTONE
SEE
THE ORACLE
OURS NOW

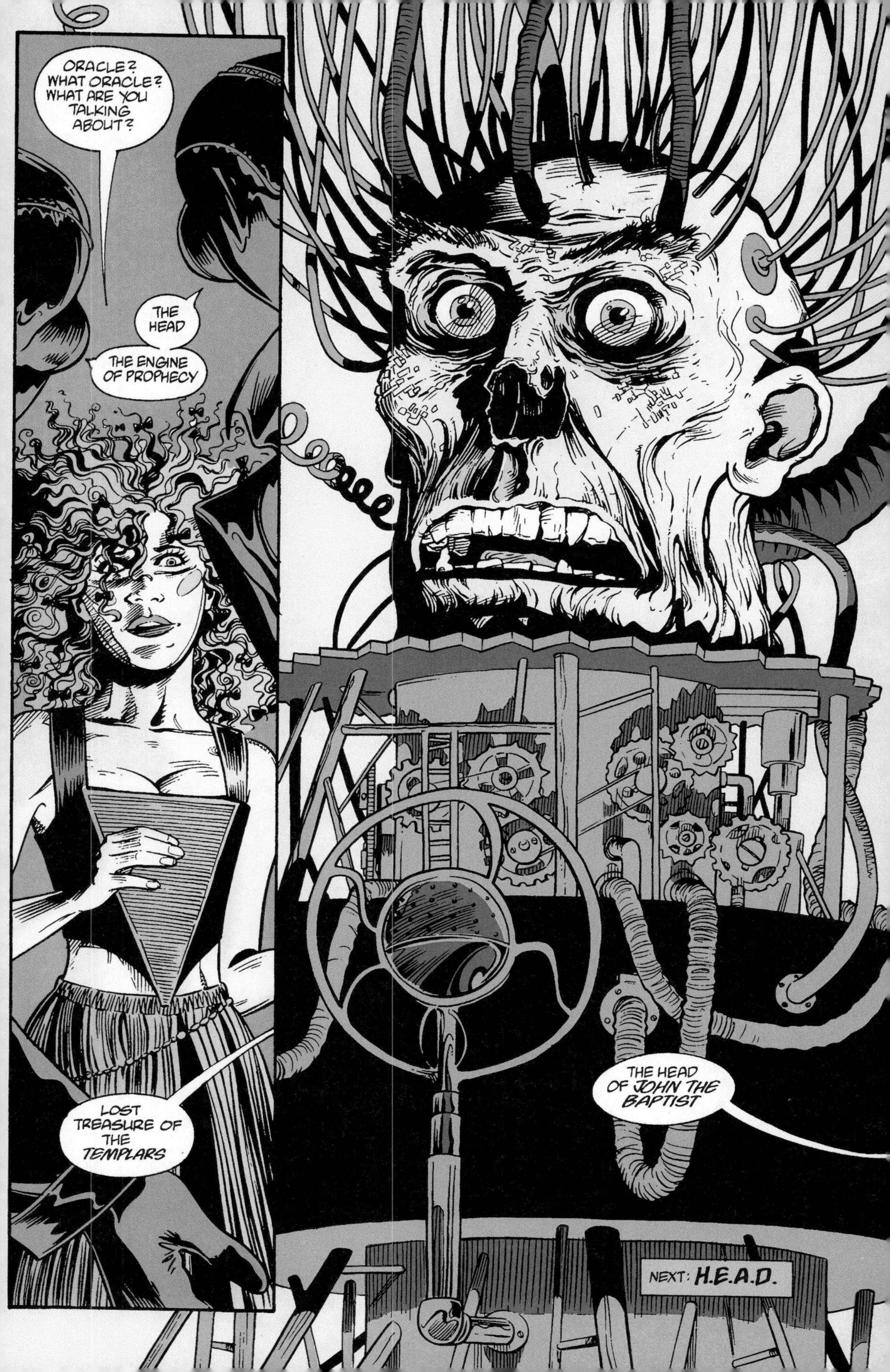
ORACLE? WHAT ORACLE? WHAT ARE YOU TALKING ABOUT?
THE HEAD
THE ENGINE OF PROPHECY
LOST TREASURE OF THE TEMPLARS
THE HEAD OF JOHN THE BAPTIST
NEXT: H.E.A.D.

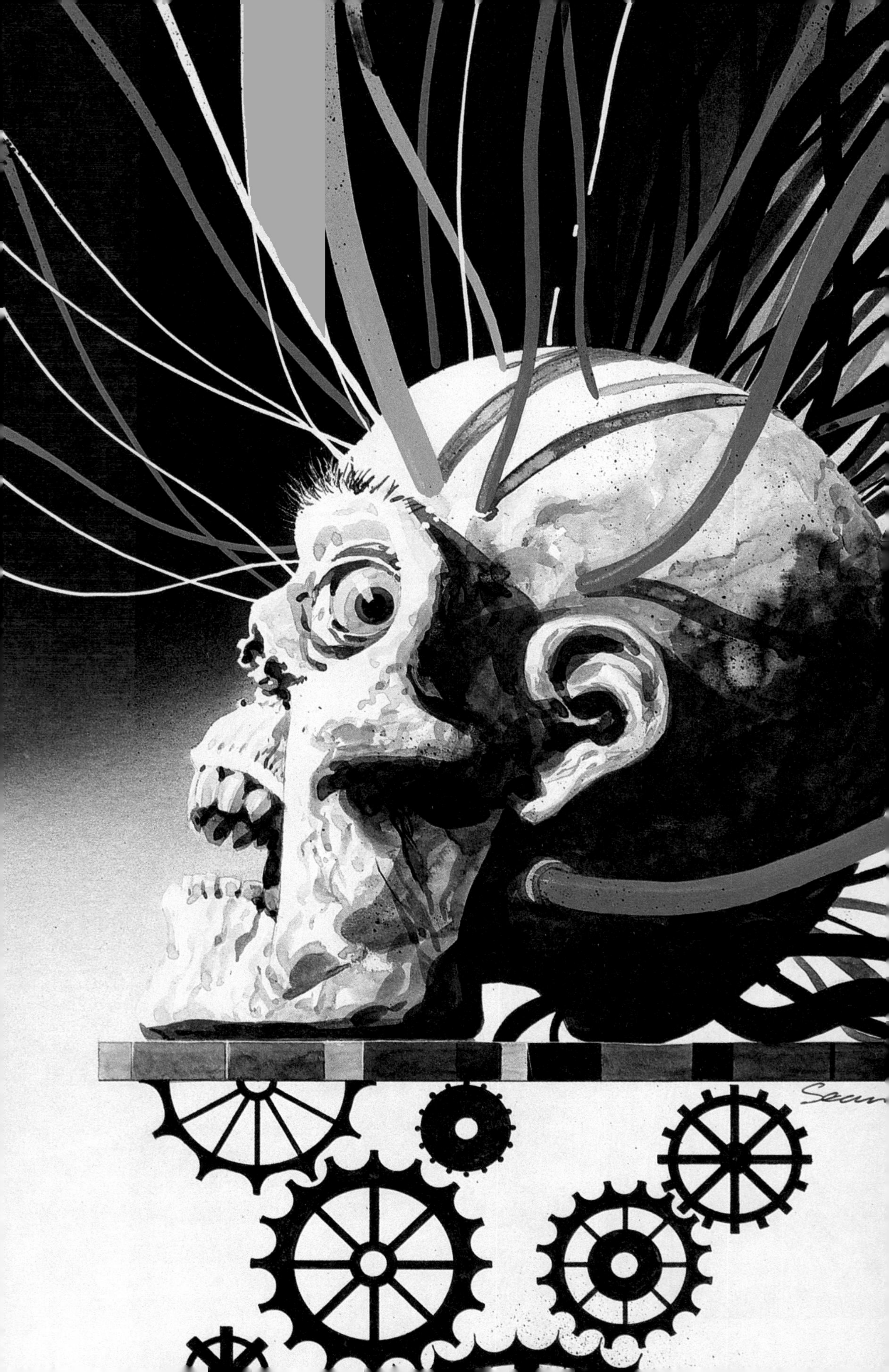

IT'S FUNNY--HERE WE ARE CAREENING TOWARDS THE CRASH BARRIER OF THE 21ST CENTURY AND SUDDENLY YOU THINK "WHO'S DRIVING THIS FUCKER?" YOU KNOW WHAT I'M SAYING?

WHO'S IN CHARGE OF THE BUS, MAN? I THINK ABOUT THAT ALL THE TIME. IN THE '60s, RIGHT?

IN THE '60s YOU HAD YOUR TIMOTHY LEARYS AND WHAT'S HIS NAME? "CUCKOO'S NEST." KESEY. ALL THOSE GUYS. THEY WERE AT THE WHEEL, THEY COULD SEE THE ROAD AHEAD, RIGHT?

THEY TOLD US ALL WE HAD TO DO WAS GET FUCKED UP ON LSD AND WE'D ALL TURN INTO SUPER-PEOPLE AND BUILD THE PROMISED LAND OUT OF RAINBOWS AND FLOWERS.

SHIT. I FELL FOR THAT SHIT. BLACK LIGHT POSTERS. I REALLY THOUGHT WE WERE CHANGING THE WORLD. IT REALLY FELT FOR A MOMENT THAT WE WERE ACTUALLY GONNA WIN, MAN.

WHEN I FINALLY CAME DOWN IT WAS 1985.

SHIT.

FROM FREE LOVE TO SAFE SEX, HUH? WHATEVER HAPPENED TO THE REVOLUTION?

LOOK, IT'S SPEAKING. WHAT DID I TELL IT?

UM. NICE TALKING TO YOU. SORRY IF I GOT CARRIED AWAY. SPEED.

GOTTA GO.

JESUS! YOU'D THINK IT HAD A MIND OF ITS OWN.

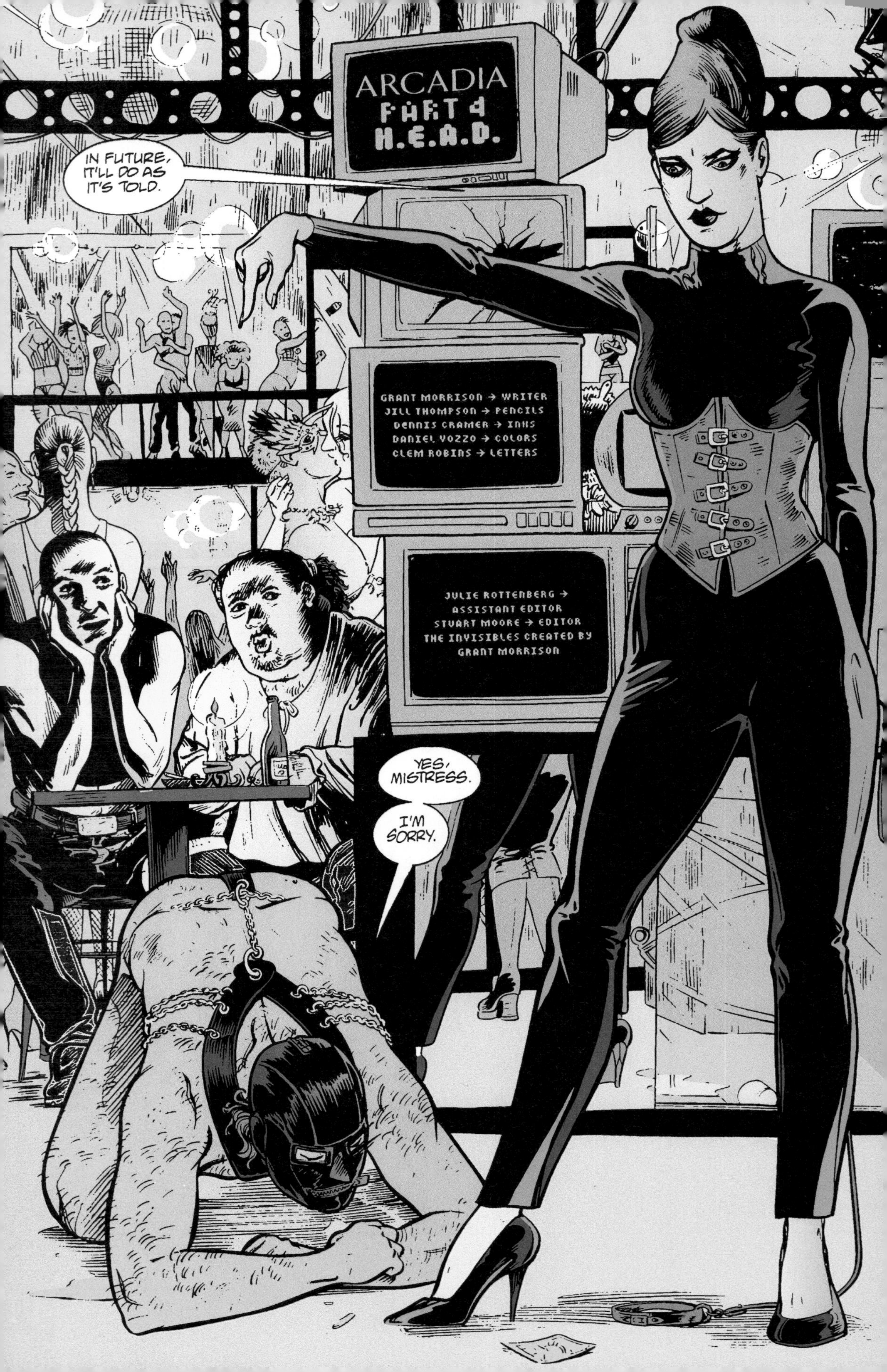
ARCADIA
PART 4
H.E.A.D.
IN FUTURE, IT'LL DO AS IT'S TOLD.
GRANT MORRISON → WRITER
JILL THOMPSON → PENCILS
DENNIS CRAMER → INKS
DANIEL VOZZO → COLORS
CLEM ROBINS → LETTERS
JULIE ROTTENBERG → ASSISTANT EDITOR
STUART MOORE → EDITOR
THE INVISIBLES CREATED BY GRANT MORRISON
YES, MISTRESS.
I'M SORRY.

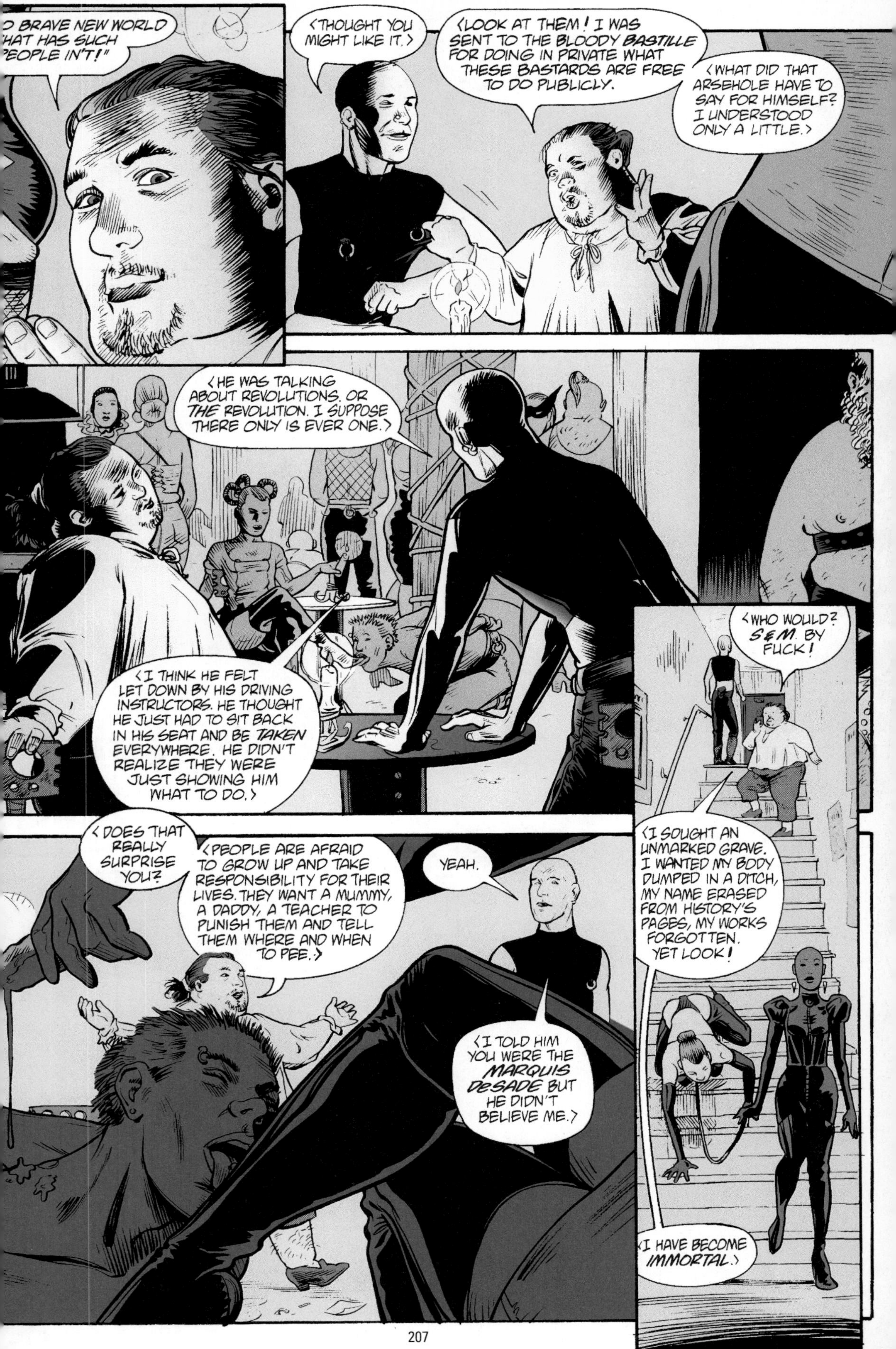
O BRAVE NEW WORLD THAT HAS SUCH PEOPLE IN'T!"
<THOUGHT YOU MIGHT LIKE IT.>
<LOOK AT THEM! I WAS SENT TO THE BLOODY BASTILLE FOR DOING IN PRIVATE WHAT THESE BASTARDS ARE FREE TO DO PUBLICLY.
<WHAT DID THAT ARSEHOLE HAVE TO SAY FOR HIMSELF? I UNDERSTOOD ONLY A LITTLE.>
<HE WAS TALKING ABOUT REVOLUTIONS. OR THE REVOLUTION. I SUPPOSE THERE ONLY IS EVER ONE.>
<I THINK HE FELT LET DOWN BY HIS DRIVING INSTRUCTORS. HE THOUGHT HE JUST HAD TO SIT BACK IN HIS SEAT AND BE TAKEN EVERYWHERE. HE DIDN'T REALIZE THEY WERE JUST SHOWING HIM WHAT TO DO.>
<WHO WOULD? S&M. BY FUCK!
<I SOUGHT AN UNMARKED GRAVE. I WANTED MY BODY DUMPED IN A DITCH, MY NAME ERASED FROM HISTORY'S PAGES, MY WORKS FORGOTTEN. YET LOOK!
<I HAVE BECOME IMMORTAL.>
<DOES THAT REALLY SURPRISE YOU?
<PEOPLE ARE AFRAID TO GROW UP AND TAKE RESPONSIBILITY FOR THEIR LIVES. THEY WANT A MUMMY, A DADDY, A TEACHER TO PUNISH THEM AND TELL THEM WHERE AND WHEN TO PEE.>
YEAH.
<I TOLD HIM YOU WERE THE MARQUIS DeSADE BUT HE DIDN'T BELIEVE ME.>

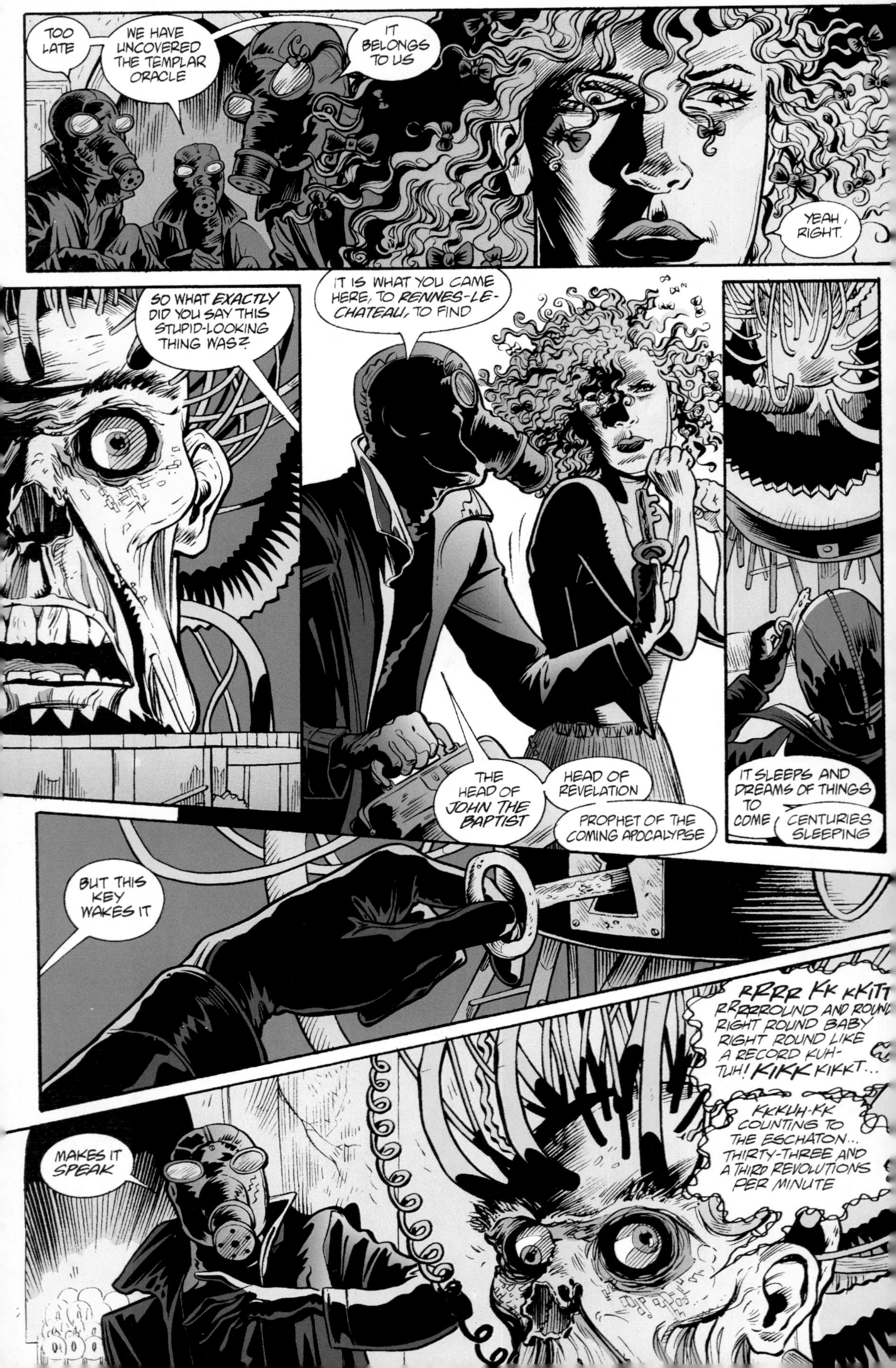
TOO LATE
WE HAVE UNCOVERED THE TEMPLAR ORACLE
IT BELONGS TO US
YEAH, RIGHT.
SO WHAT EXACTLY DID YOU SAY THIS STUPID-LOOKING THING WAS?
IT IS WHAT YOU CAME HERE, TO RENNES-LE-CHATEAU, TO FIND
THE HEAD OF JOHN THE BAPTIST
HEAD OF REVELATION
PROPHET OF THE COMING APOCALYPSE
IT SLEEPS AND DREAMS OF THINGS TO COME
CENTURIES SLEEPING
BUT THIS KEY WAKES IT
RRRR KK KKITT
RRRRROUND AND ROUND RIGHT ROUND BABY RIGHT ROUND LIKE A RECORD KUH-TUH! KIKK KIKKT...
MAKES IT SPEAK
KKKUH-KK COUNTING TO THE ESCHATON... THIRTY-THREE AND A THIRD REVOLUTIONS PER MINUTE

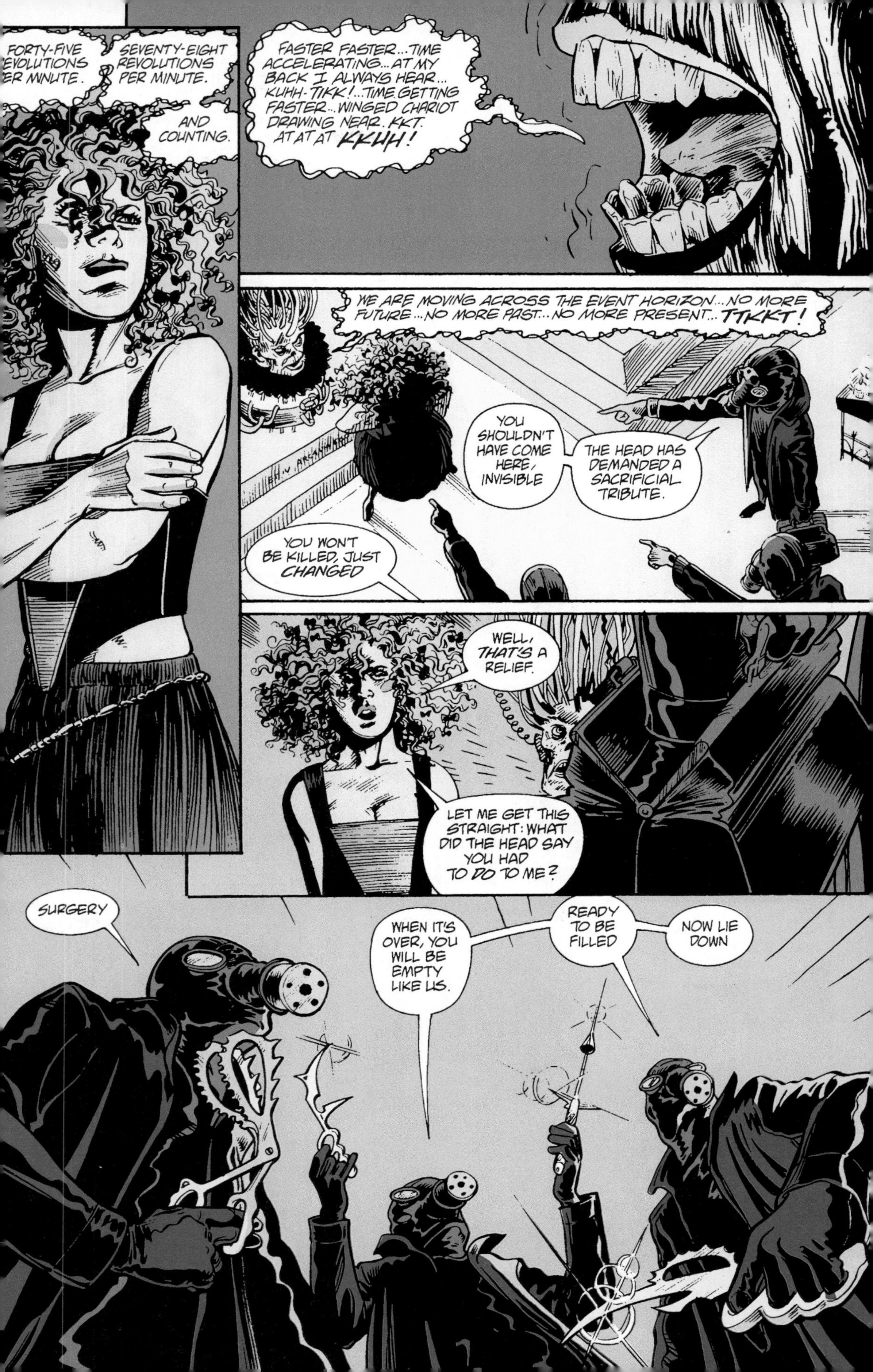
FORTY-FIVE REVOLUTIONS PER MINUTE.
SEVENTY-EIGHT REVOLUTIONS PER MINUTE.
AND COUNTING.
FASTER FASTER... TIME ACCELERATING... AT MY BACK I ALWAYS HEAR... KUHH-TIKK!... TIME GETTING FASTER... WINGED CHARIOT DRAWING NEAR. KKT. AT AT AT KKUH!
WE ARE MOVING ACROSS THE EVENT HORIZON... NO MORE FUTURE... NO MORE PAST... NO MORE PRESENT... TTKKT!
YOU SHOULDN'T HAVE COME HERE, INVISIBLE
THE HEAD HAS DEMANDED A SACRIFICIAL TRIBUTE.
YOU WON'T BE KILLED, JUST CHANGED
WELL, THAT'S A RELIEF.
LET ME GET THIS STRAIGHT: WHAT DID THE HEAD SAY YOU HAD TO DO TO ME?
SURGERY
WHEN IT'S OVER, YOU WILL BE EMPTY LIKE US.
READY TO BE FILLED
NOW LIE DOWN

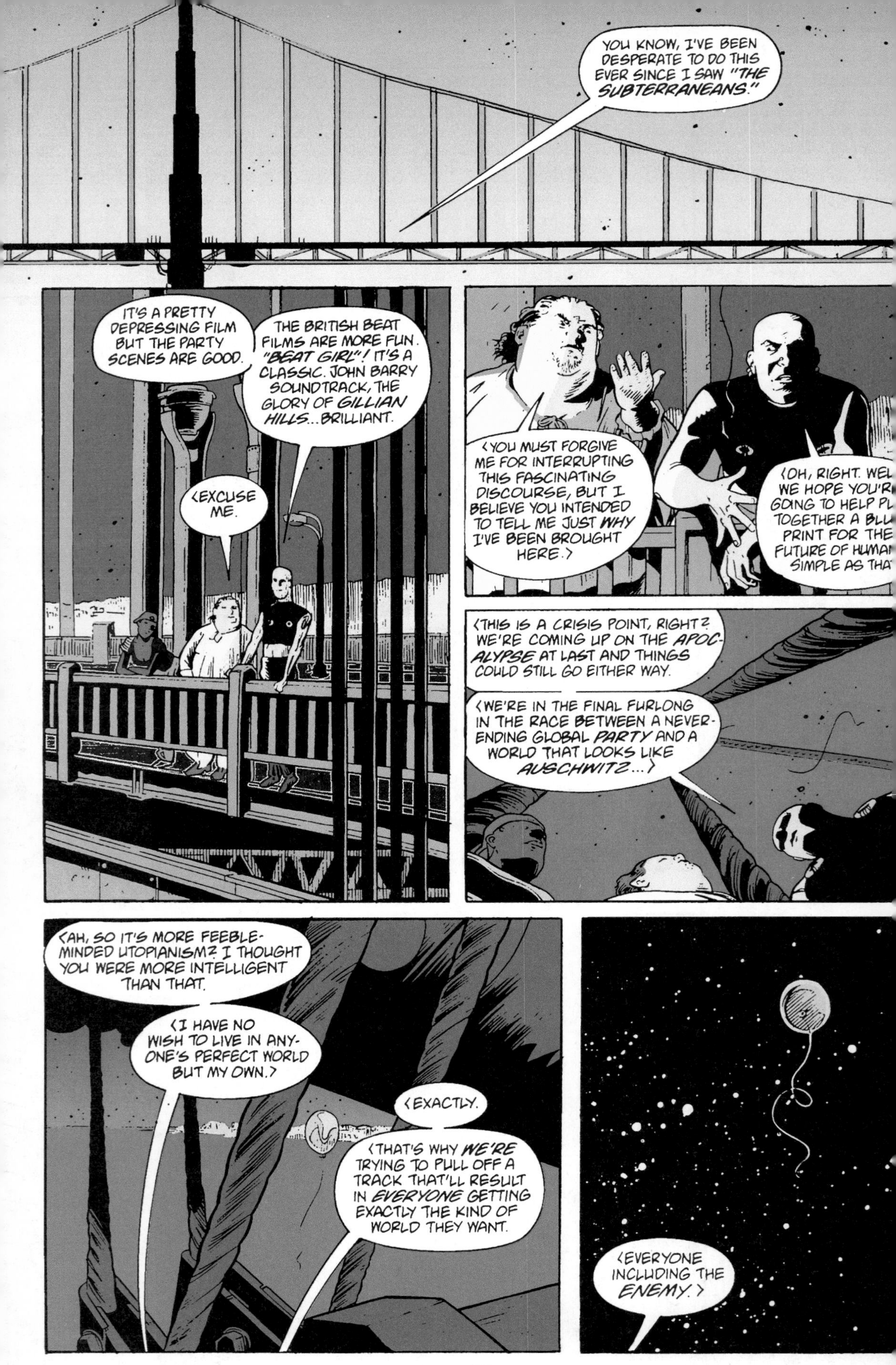
YOU KNOW, I'VE BEEN DESPERATE TO DO THIS EVER SINCE I SAW "THE SUBTERRANEANS."
IT'S A PRETTY DEPRESSING FILM BUT THE PARTY SCENES ARE GOOD.
THE BRITISH BEAT FILMS ARE MORE FUN. "BEAT GIRL"! IT'S A CLASSIC. JOHN BARRY SOUNDTRACK, THE GLORY OF GILLIAN HILLS...BRILLIANT.
‹EXCUSE ME.
‹YOU MUST FORGIVE ME FOR INTERRUPTING THIS FASCINATING DISCOURSE, BUT I BELIEVE YOU INTENDED TO TELL ME JUST WHY I'VE BEEN BROUGHT HERE.›
‹OH, RIGHT. WEL WE HOPE YOU'R GOING TO HELP PU TOGETHER A BLU PRINT FOR THE FUTURE OF HUMAN SIMPLE AS THA
‹THIS IS A CRISIS POINT, RIGHT? WE'RE COMING UP ON THE APOCALYPSE AT LAST AND THINGS COULD STILL GO EITHER WAY.
‹WE'RE IN THE FINAL FURLONG IN THE RACE BETWEEN A NEVER-ENDING GLOBAL PARTY AND A WORLD THAT LOOKS LIKE AUSCHWITZ...›
‹AH, SO IT'S MORE FEEBLE-MINDED UTOPIANISM? I THOUGHT YOU WERE MORE INTELLIGENT THAN THAT.
‹I HAVE NO WISH TO LIVE IN ANYONE'S PERFECT WORLD BUT MY OWN.›
‹EXACTLY.
‹THAT'S WHY WE'RE TRYING TO PULL OFF A TRACK THAT'LL RESULT IN EVERYONE GETTING EXACTLY THE KIND OF WORLD THEY WANT.
‹EVERYONE INCLUDING THE ENEMY.›

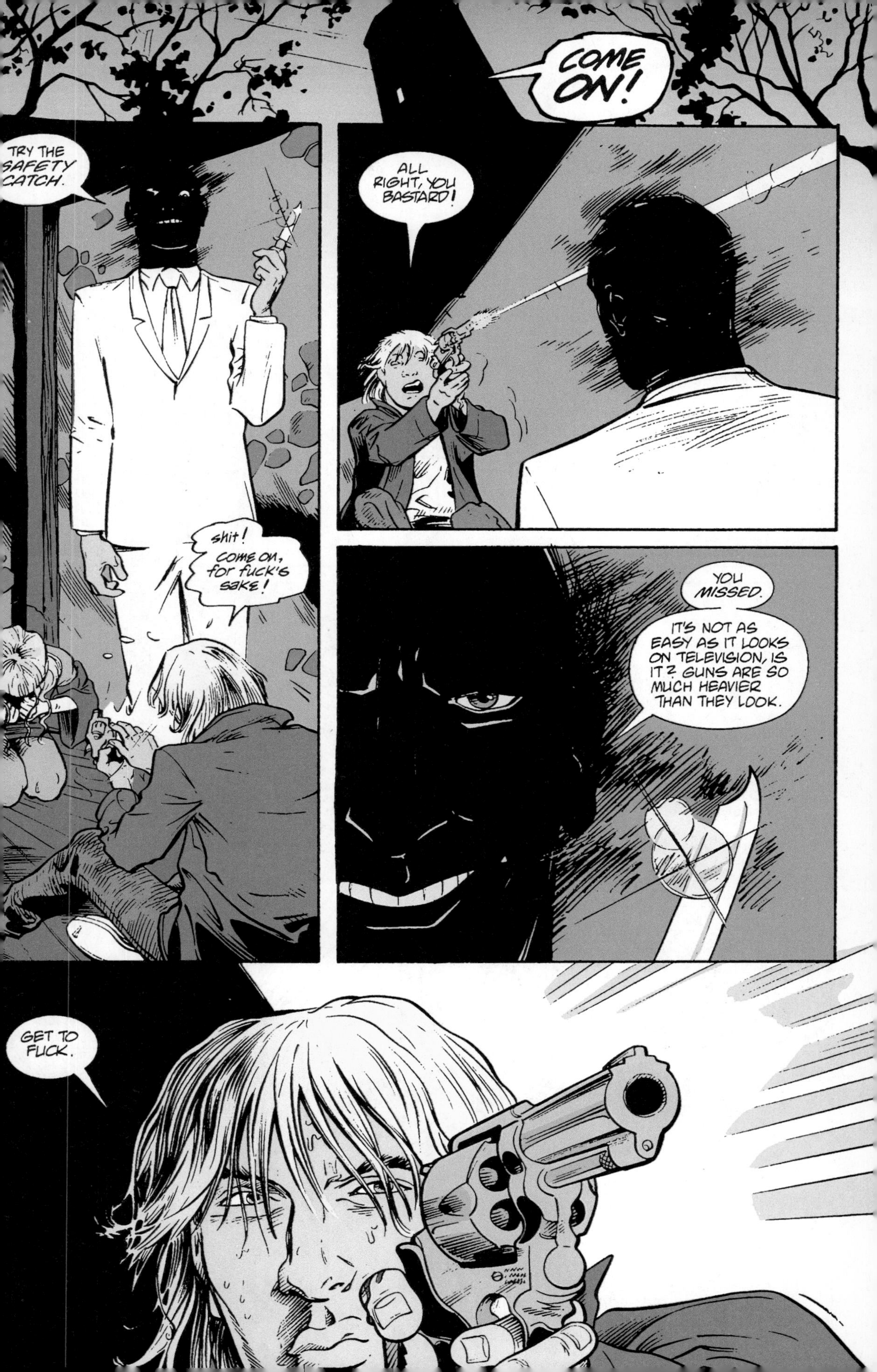
COME ON!
TRY THE SAFETY CATCH.
shit! COME ON, for fuck's sake!
ALL RIGHT, YOU BASTARD!
YOU MISSED.
IT'S NOT AS EASY AS IT LOOKS ON TELEVISION, IS IT? GUNS ARE SO MUCH HEAVIER THAN THEY LOOK.
GET TO FUCK.

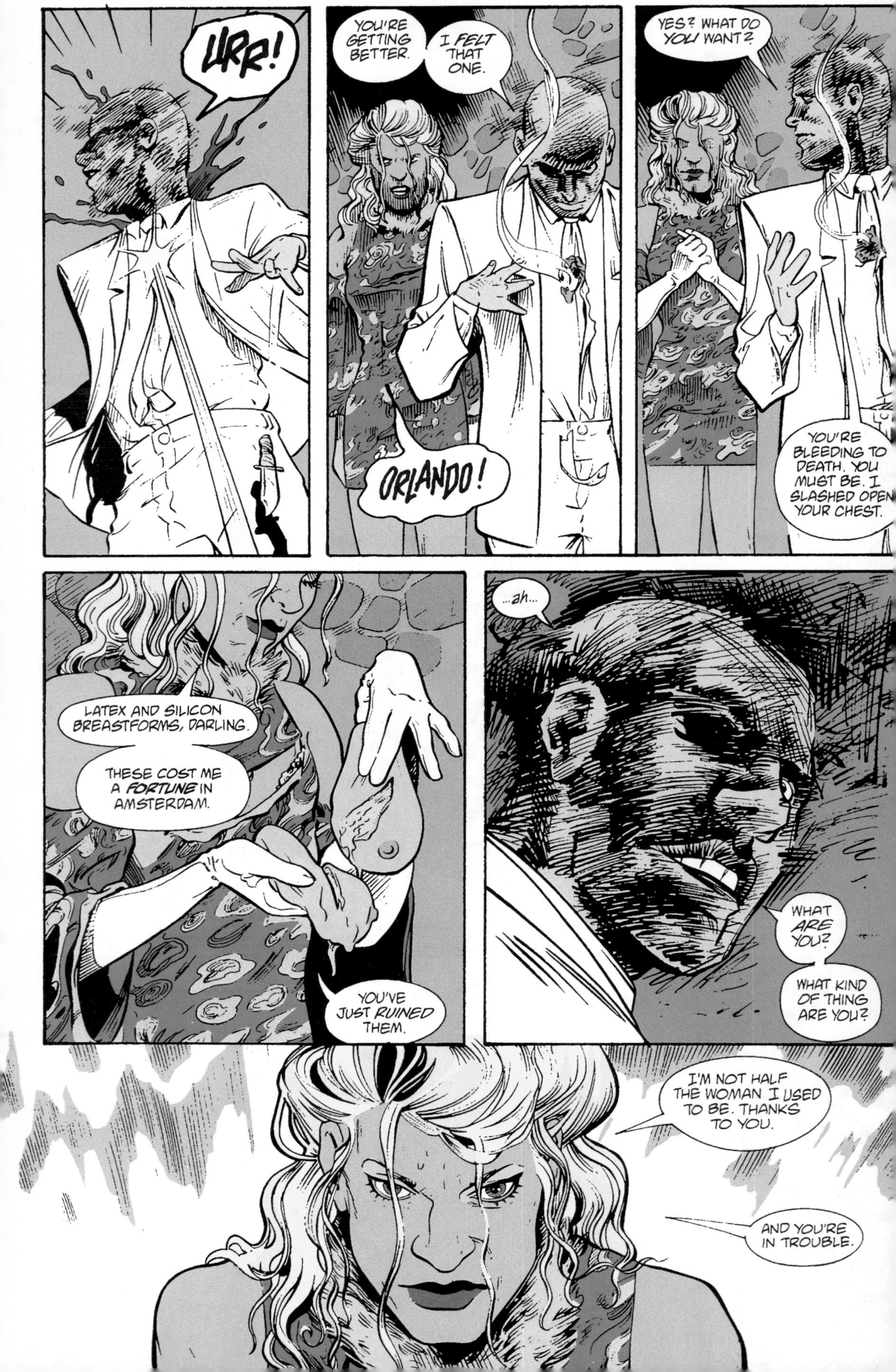
URR!
YOU'RE GETTING BETTER.
I FELT THAT ONE.
ORLANDO!
YES? WHAT DO YOU WANT?
YOU'RE BLEEDING TO DEATH. YOU MUST BE. I SLASHED OPEN YOUR CHEST.
LATEX AND SILICON BREASTFORMS, DARLING.
THESE COST ME A FORTUNE IN AMSTERDAM.
YOU'VE JUST RUINED THEM.
...ah...
WHAT ARE YOU?
WHAT KIND OF THING ARE YOU?
I'M NOT HALF THE WOMAN I USED TO BE. THANKS TO YOU.
AND YOU'RE IN TROUBLE.

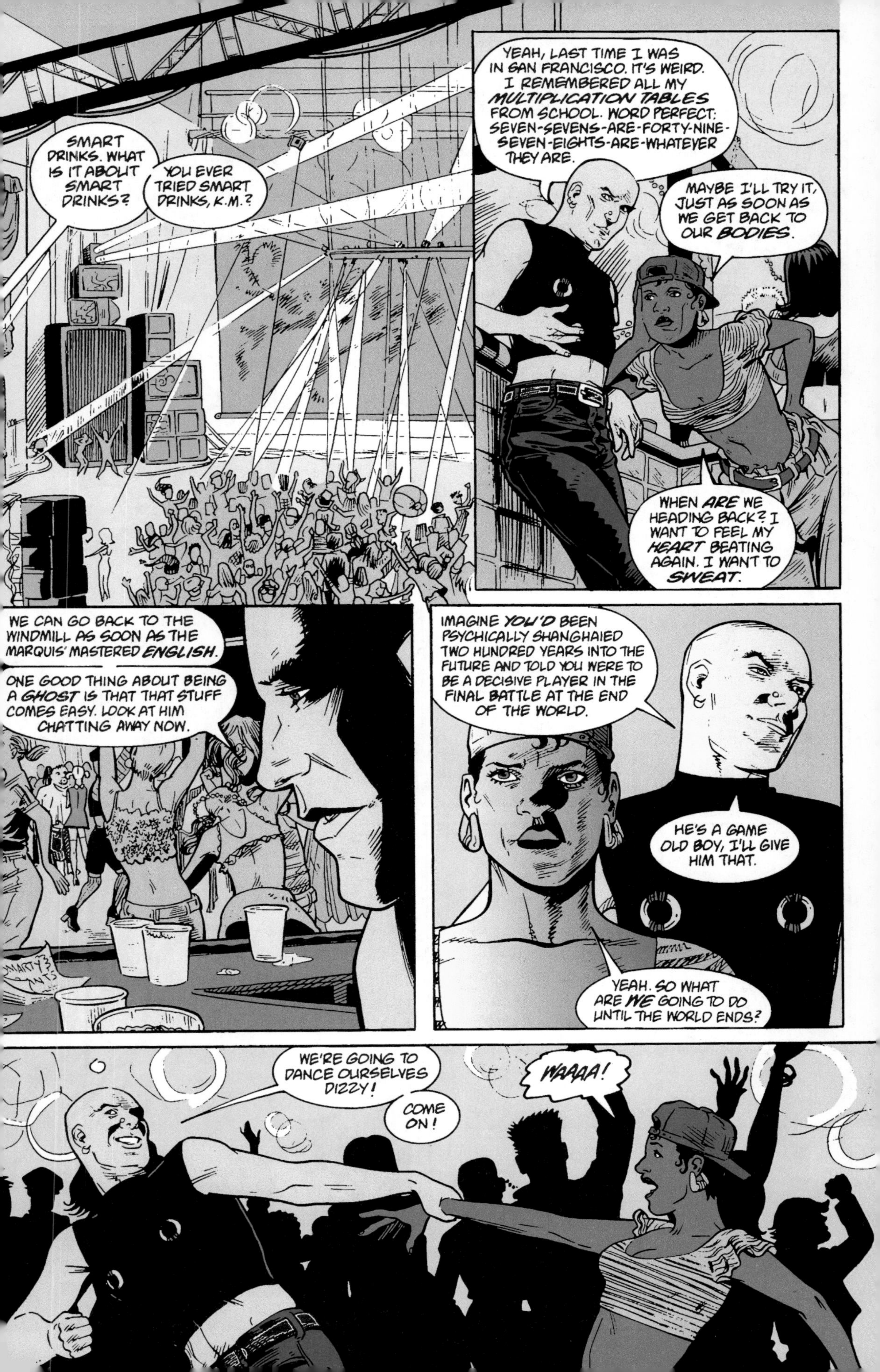
SMART DRINKS. WHAT IS IT ABOUT SMART DRINKS?
YOU EVER TRIED SMART DRINKS, K.M.?
YEAH, LAST TIME I WAS IN SAN FRANCISCO. IT'S WEIRD. I REMEMBERED ALL MY MULTIPLICATION TABLES FROM SCHOOL. WORD PERFECT: SEVEN-SEVENS-ARE-FORTY-NINE-SEVEN-EIGHTS-ARE-WHATEVER THEY ARE.
MAYBE I'LL TRY IT, JUST AS SOON AS WE GET BACK TO OUR BODIES.
WHEN ARE WE HEADING BACK? I WANT TO FEEL MY HEART BEATING AGAIN. I WANT TO SWEAT.
WE CAN GO BACK TO THE WINDMILL AS SOON AS THE MARQUIS' MASTERED ENGLISH.
ONE GOOD THING ABOUT BEING A GHOST IS THAT THAT STUFF COMES EASY. LOOK AT HIM CHATTING AWAY NOW.
IMAGINE YOU'D BEEN PSYCHICALLY SHANGHAIED TWO HUNDRED YEARS INTO THE FUTURE AND TOLD YOU WERE TO BE A DECISIVE PLAYER IN THE FINAL BATTLE AT THE END OF THE WORLD.
HE'S A GAME OLD BOY, I'LL GIVE HIM THAT.
YEAH. SO WHAT ARE WE GOING TO DO UNTIL THE WORLD ENDS?
WE'RE GOING TO DANCE OURSELVES DIZZY!
COME ON!
WAAAA!

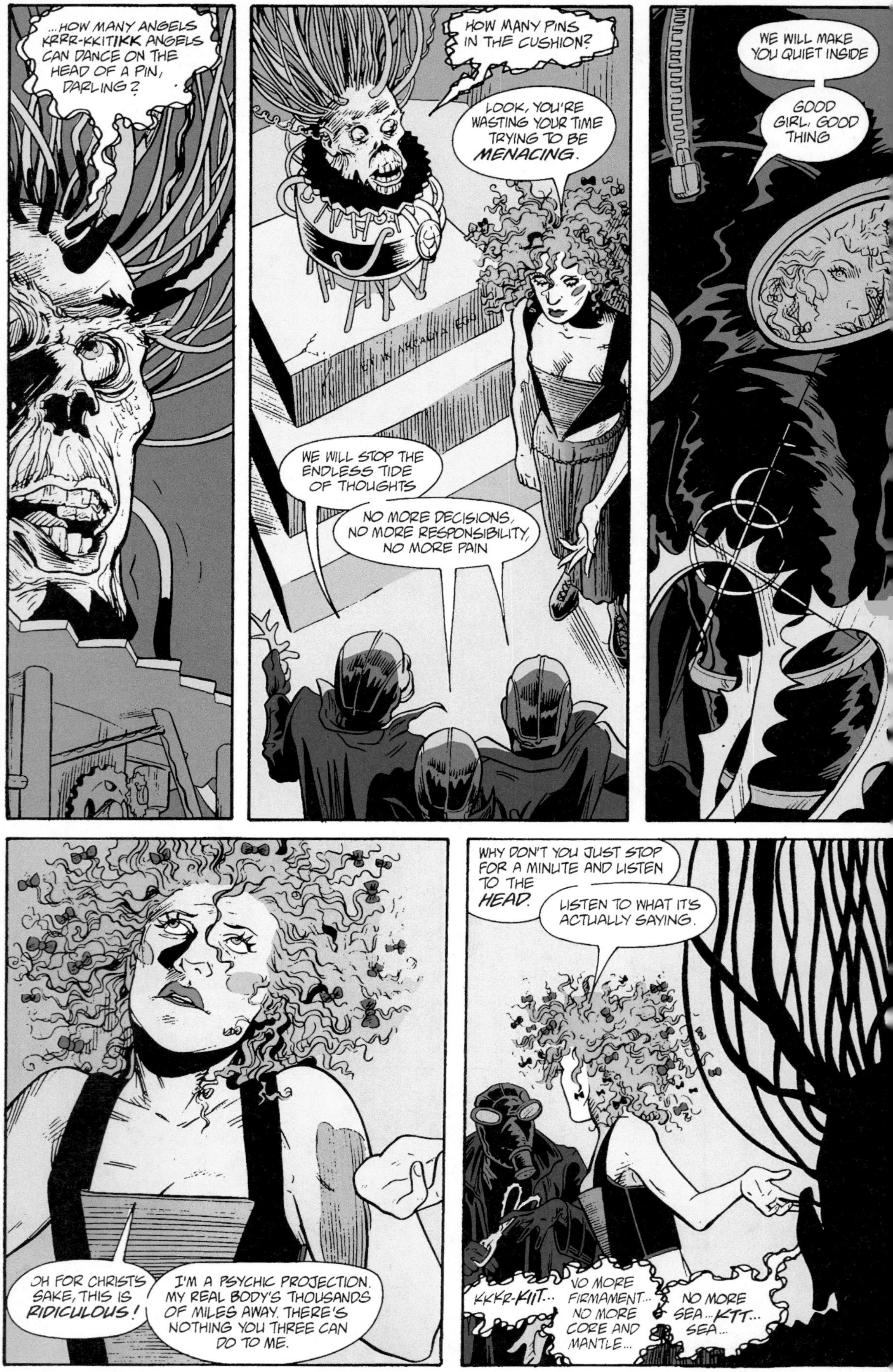
...HOW MANY ANGELS KRRR-KKITIKK ANGELS CAN DANCE ON THE HEAD OF A PIN, DARLING?
HOW MANY PINS IN THE CUSHION?
LOOK, YOU'RE WASTING YOUR TIME TRYING TO BE MENACING.
WE WILL STOP THE ENDLESS TIDE OF THOUGHTS
NO MORE DECISIONS, NO MORE RESPONSIBILITY, NO MORE PAIN
WE WILL MAKE YOU QUIET INSIDE
GOOD GIRL. GOOD THING
OH FOR CHRIST'S SAKE, THIS IS RIDICULOUS!
I'M A PSYCHIC PROJECTION. MY REAL BODY'S THOUSANDS OF MILES AWAY. THERE'S NOTHING YOU THREE CAN DO TO ME.
WHY DON'T YOU JUST STOP FOR A MINUTE AND LISTEN TO THE HEAD.
LISTEN TO WHAT IT'S ACTUALLY SAYING.
KKKR-KIIT...
NO MORE FIRMAMENT... NO MORE CORE AND MANTLE...
NO MORE SEA...KTT... SEA...

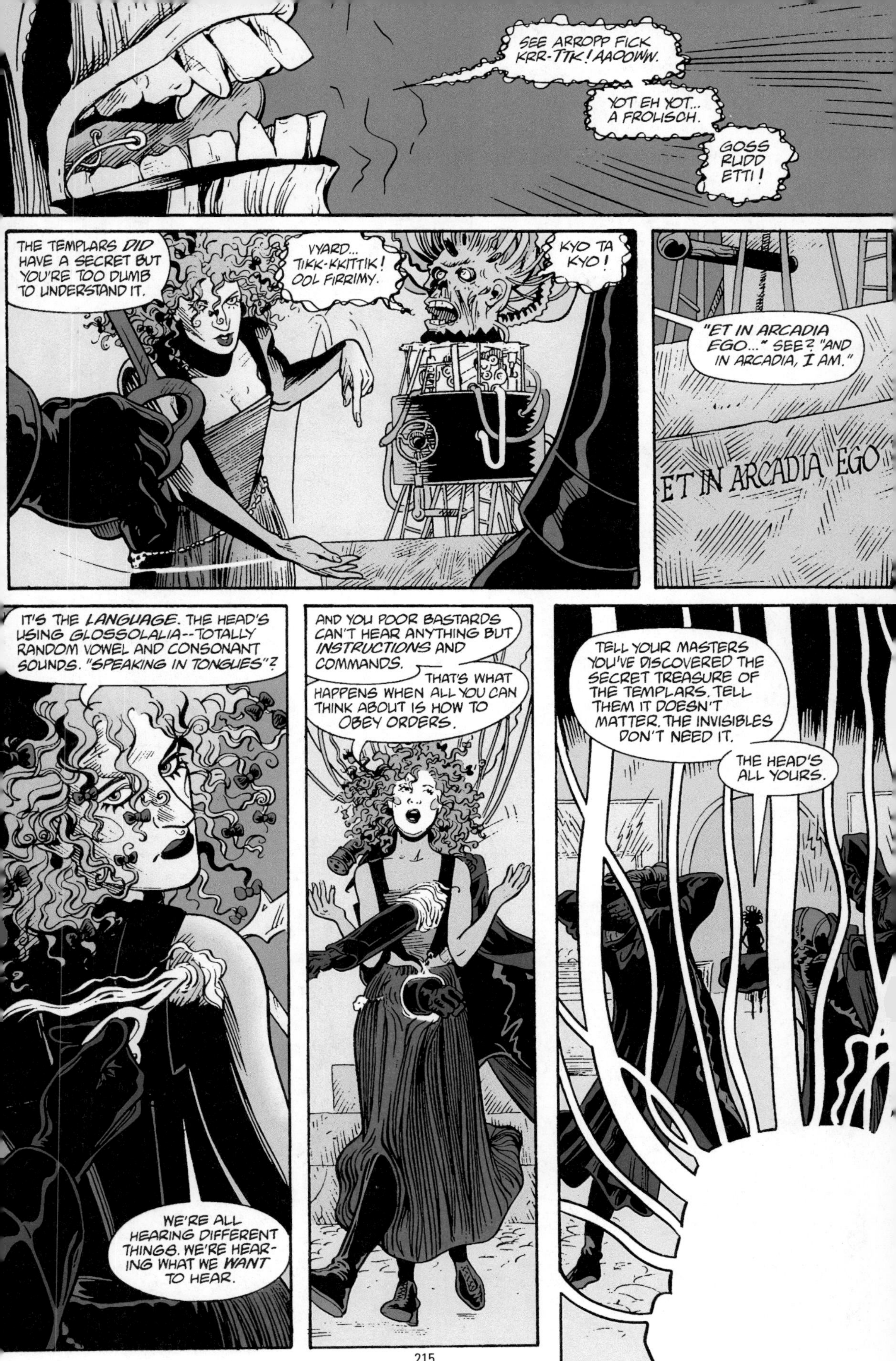
SEE ARROPP FICK KRR-TTK! AAOOWN.
YOT EH YOT... A FROLISCH.
GOSS RUDD ETTI!
THE TEMPLARS *DID* HAVE A SECRET BUT YOU'RE TOO DUMB TO UNDERSTAND IT.
VYARD... TIKK-KKITTIK! OOL FIRRIMY.
KYO TA KYO!
"ET IN ARCADIA EGO..." SEE? "AND IN ARCADIA, *I* AM."
ET IN ARCADIA EGO
IT'S THE *LANGUAGE*. THE HEAD'S USING *GLOSSOLALIA*--TOTALLY RANDOM VOWEL AND CONSONANT SOUNDS. "SPEAKING IN TONGUES"?
WE'RE ALL HEARING DIFFERENT THINGS. WE'RE HEARING WHAT WE *WANT* TO HEAR.
AND YOU POOR BASTARDS CAN'T HEAR ANYTHING BUT *INSTRUCTIONS* AND COMMANDS.
THAT'S WHAT HAPPENS WHEN ALL YOU CAN THINK ABOUT IS HOW TO OBEY ORDERS.
TELL YOUR MASTERS YOU'VE DISCOVERED THE SECRET TREASURE OF THE TEMPLARS. TELL THEM IT DOESN'T MATTER. THE INVISIBLES DON'T NEED IT.
THE HEAD'S ALL YOURS.

"Other flowering isles must be
In the sea of Life and Agony..."

SHILOH?

SHILOH? ARE YOU THERE?

WHY ARE YOU NOT WITH YOUR WIFE, SIR? MARY TELLS ME YOU HAVE BEEN CLOISTERED HERE FOR *DAYS*. SHE WANTS TO SPEAK TO YOU.

WHAT CAN WE SAY TO ONE ANOTHER, GEORGE? OUR LITTLE DAUGHTER LIES DEAD. WORK IS ALL THAT CONSOLES ME. THESE "LINES WRITTEN AMONG THE EUGANEAN HILLS."

I'VE BEEN TRYING TO PUT *OUR* RECENT DISCUSSION INTO VERSE BUT HAVE NOT THE HEART FOR IT AT PRESENT. I CAN POUR ONLY GRIEF ONTO THE PAGE.

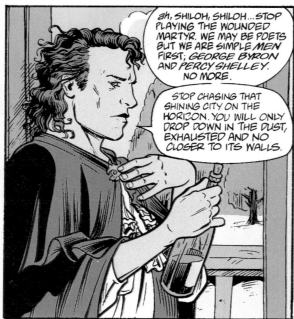

ah, SHILOH, SHILOH... STOP PLAYING THE WOUNDED MARTYR. WE MAY BE POETS BUT WE ARE SIMPLE *MEN* FIRST; *GEORGE BYRON* AND *PERCY SHELLEY.* NO MORE.

STOP CHASING THAT SHINING CITY ON THE HORIZON. YOU WILL ONLY DROP DOWN IN THE DUST, EXHAUSTED AND NO CLOSER TO ITS WALLS.

REMEMBER *PANTISOCRACY?* THAT VISION OF AN IDEAL COMMUNITY DREAMED UP BY *SOUTHEY* AND *COLERIDGE,* IN WHICH ALL PROPERTY WAS TO BE SHARED AND MEN AND WOMEN WOULD LIVE TOGETHER AS EQUALS IN PASTORAL BLISS?

HA!

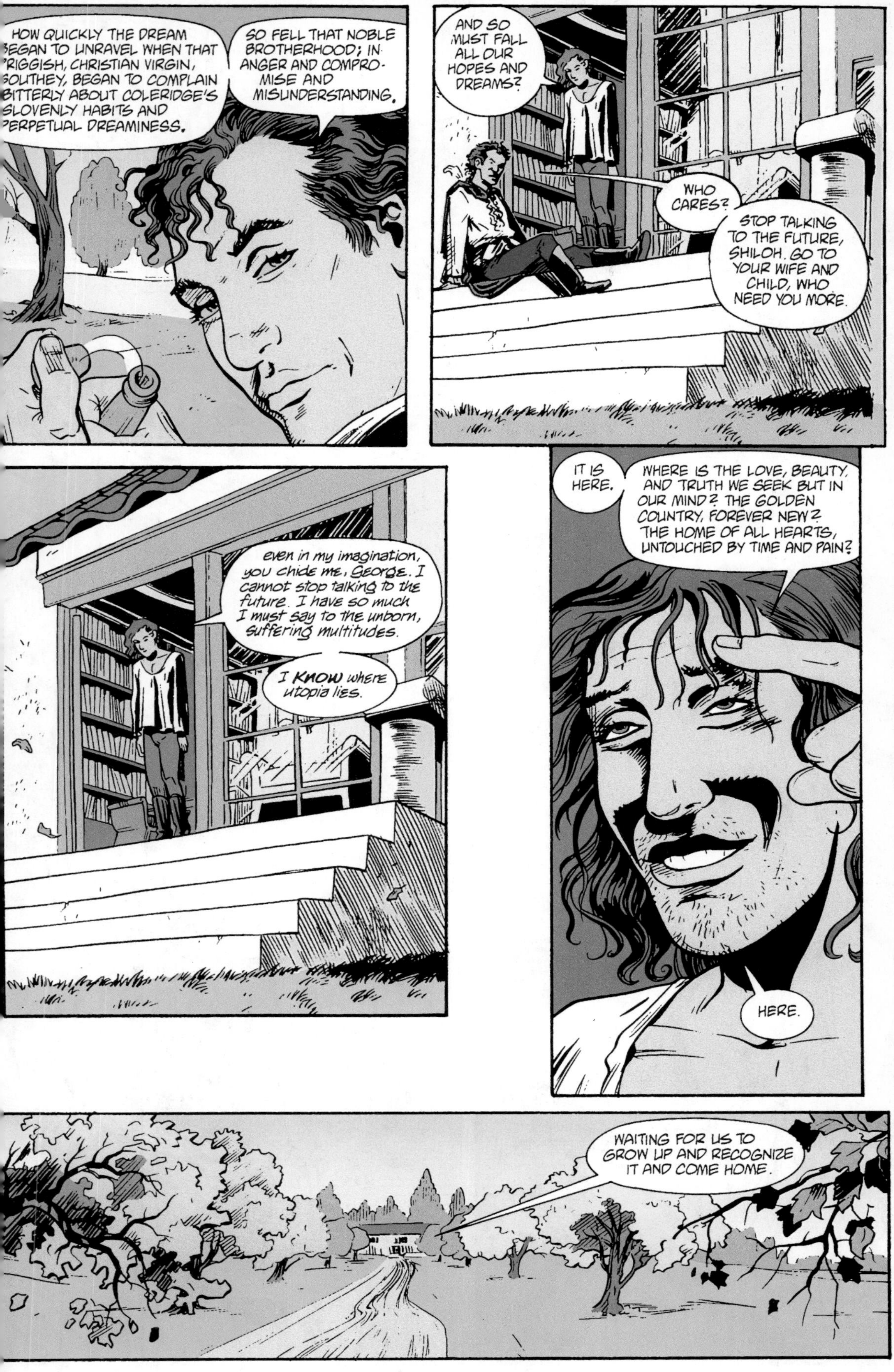
HOW QUICKLY THE DREAM BEGAN TO UNRAVEL WHEN THAT PRIGGISH, CHRISTIAN VIRGIN, SOUTHEY, BEGAN TO COMPLAIN BITTERLY ABOUT COLERIDGE'S SLOVENLY HABITS AND PERPETUAL DREAMINESS.
SO FELL THAT NOBLE BROTHERHOOD; IN ANGER AND COMPROMISE AND MISUNDERSTANDING.
AND SO MUST FALL ALL OUR HOPES AND DREAMS?
WHO CARES?
STOP TALKING TO THE FUTURE, SHILOH. GO TO YOUR WIFE AND CHILD, WHO NEED YOU MORE.
even in my imagination, you chide me, George. I cannot stop talking to the future. I have so much I must say to the unborn, suffering multitudes.
I KNOW where utopia lies.
IT IS HERE.
WHERE IS THE LOVE, BEAUTY, AND TRUTH WE SEEK BUT IN OUR MIND? THE GOLDEN COUNTRY, FOREVER NEW? THE HOME OF ALL HEARTS, UNTOUCHED BY TIME AND PAIN?
HERE.
WAITING FOR US TO GROW UP AND RECOGNIZE IT AND COME HOME.

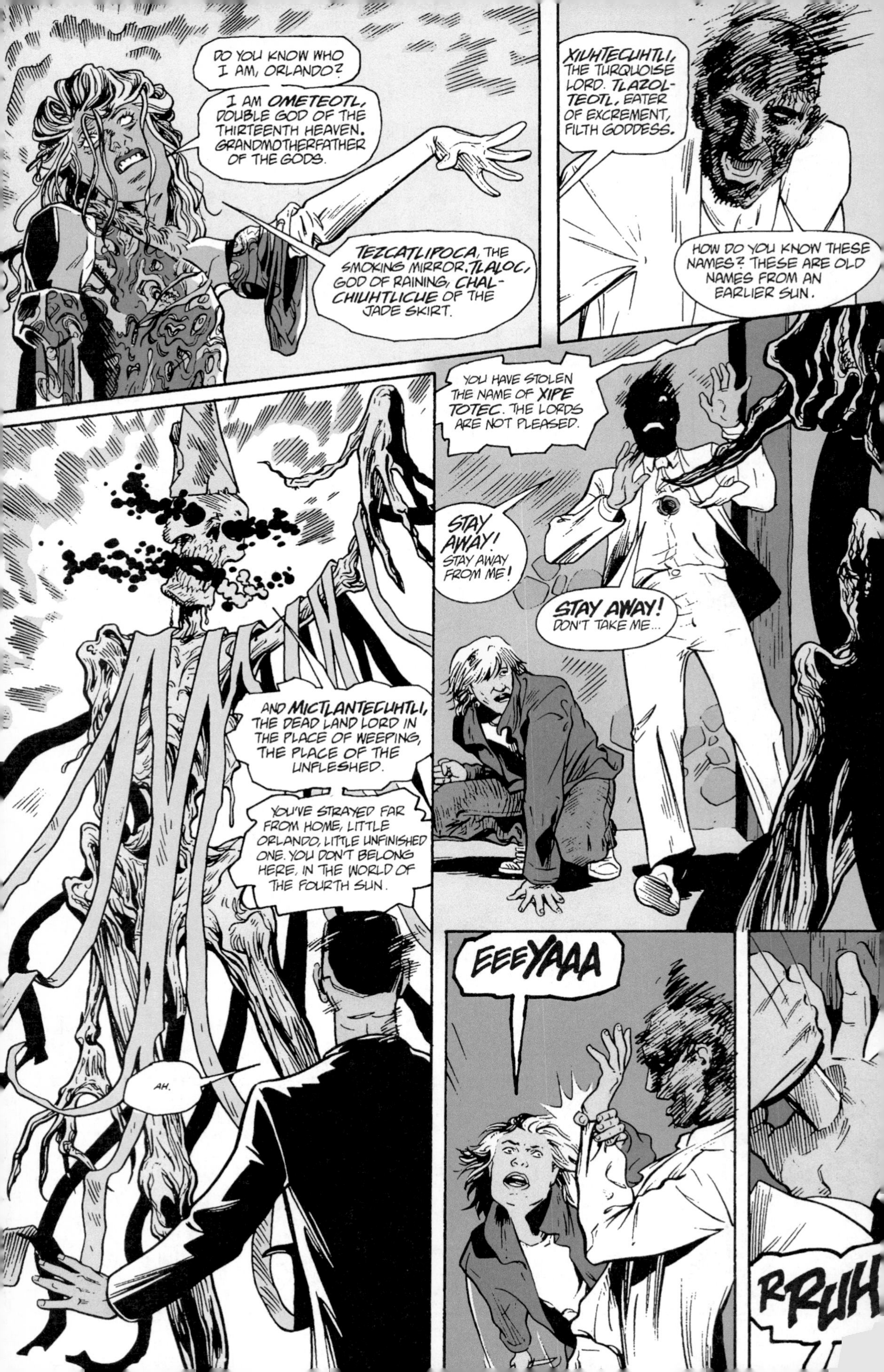
DO YOU KNOW WHO I AM, ORLANDO?
I AM OMETEOTL, DOUBLE GOD OF THE THIRTEENTH HEAVEN. GRANDMOTHERFATHER OF THE GODS.
TEZCATLIPOCA, THE SMOKING MIRROR. TLALOC, GOD OF RAINING, CHALCHIUHTLICUE OF THE JADE SKIRT.
XIUHTECUHTLI, THE TURQUOISE LORD. TLAZOLTEOTL, EATER OF EXCREMENT, FILTH GODDESS.
HOW DO YOU KNOW THESE NAMES? THESE ARE OLD NAMES FROM AN EARLIER SUN.
AND MICTLANTECUHTLI, THE DEAD LAND LORD IN THE PLACE OF WEEPING, THE PLACE OF THE UNFLESHED.
YOU'VE STRAYED FAR FROM HOME, LITTLE ORLANDO, LITTLE UNFINISHED ONE. YOU DON'T BELONG HERE, IN THE WORLD OF THE FOURTH SUN.
AH.
YOU HAVE STOLEN THE NAME OF XIPE TOTEC. THE LORDS ARE NOT PLEASED.
STAY AWAY! STAY AWAY FROM ME!
STAY AWAY! DON'T TAKE ME...
EEEYAAA
RRUH

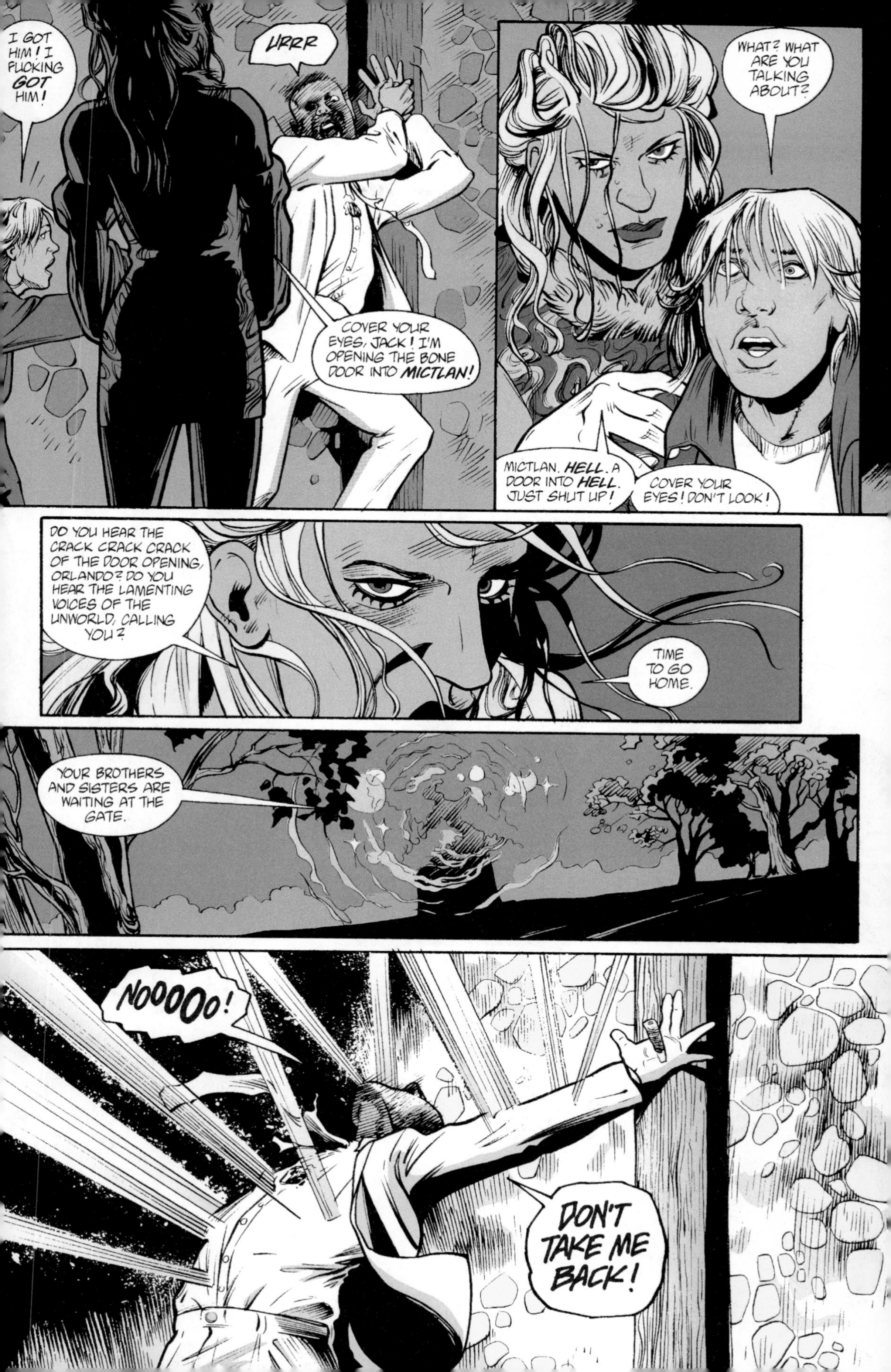
I GOT HIM! I FUCKING GOT HIM!
URRR
COVER YOUR EYES, JACK! I'M OPENING THE BONE DOOR INTO MICTLAN!
WHAT? WHAT ARE YOU TALKING ABOUT?
MICTLAN. HELL. A DOOR INTO HELL. JUST SHUT UP!
COVER YOUR EYES! DON'T LOOK!
DO YOU HEAR THE CRACK CRACK CRACK OF THE DOOR OPENING, ORLANDO? DO YOU HEAR THE LAMENTING VOICES OF THE UNWORLD, CALLING YOU?
TIME TO GO HOME.
YOUR BROTHERS AND SISTERS ARE WAITING AT THE GATE.
NOOOOo!
DON'T TAKE ME BACK!

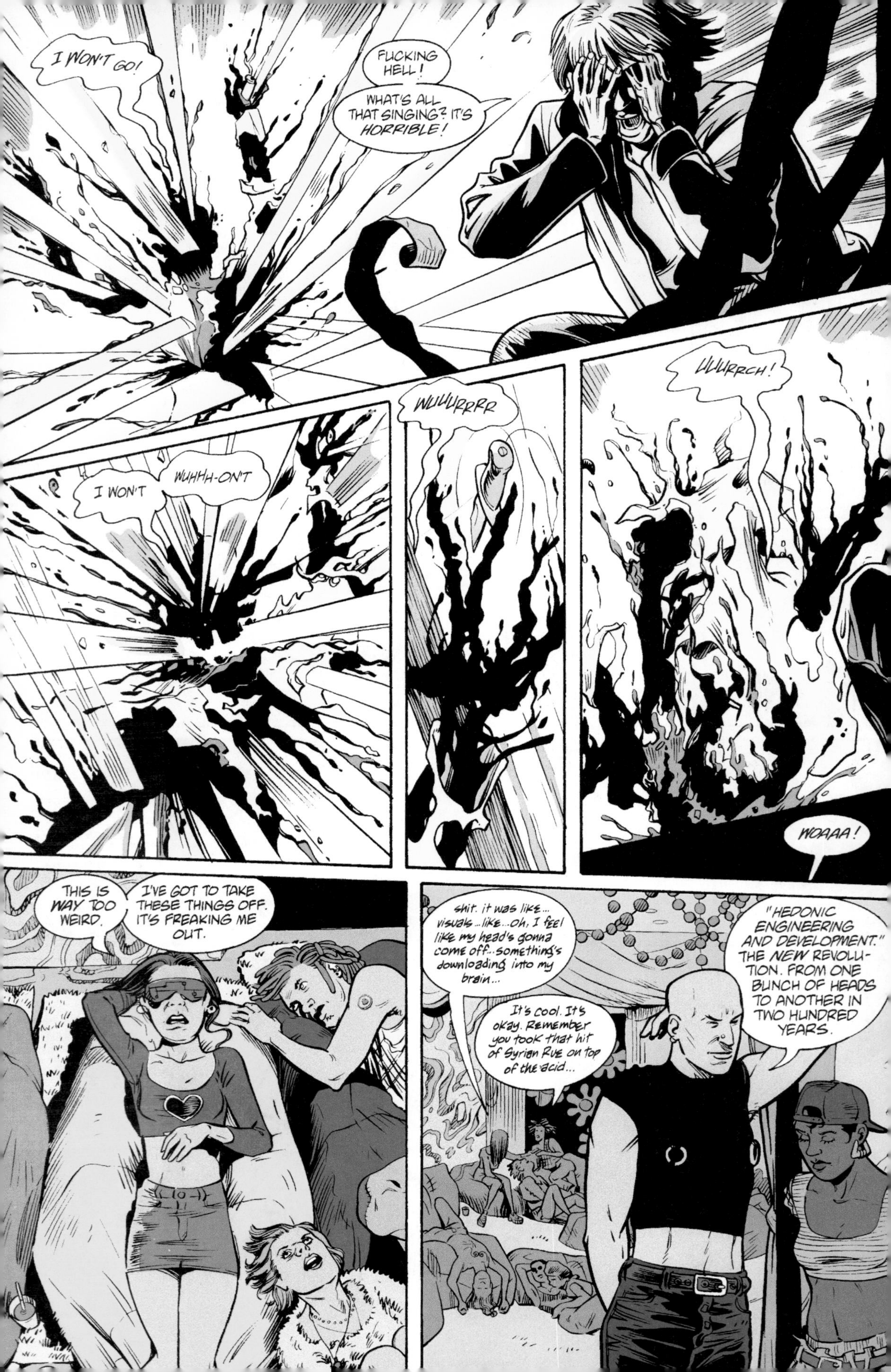
I WON'T GO!
FUCKING HELL!
WHAT'S ALL THAT SINGING? IT'S HORRIBLE!
I WON'T
WUHHH-ON'T
WUUURRRR
UUURRCH!
WOAAA!
THIS IS WAY TOO WEIRD.
I'VE GOT TO TAKE THESE THINGS OFF. IT'S FREAKING ME OUT.
shit. it was like... visuals... like... oh, I feel like my head's gonna come off... something's downloading into my brain...
It's cool. It's okay. Remember you took that hit of Syrian Rue on top of the acid...
"HEDONIC ENGINEERING AND DEVELOPMENT." THE NEW REVOLUTION. FROM ONE BUNCH OF HEADS TO ANOTHER IN TWO HUNDRED YEARS.

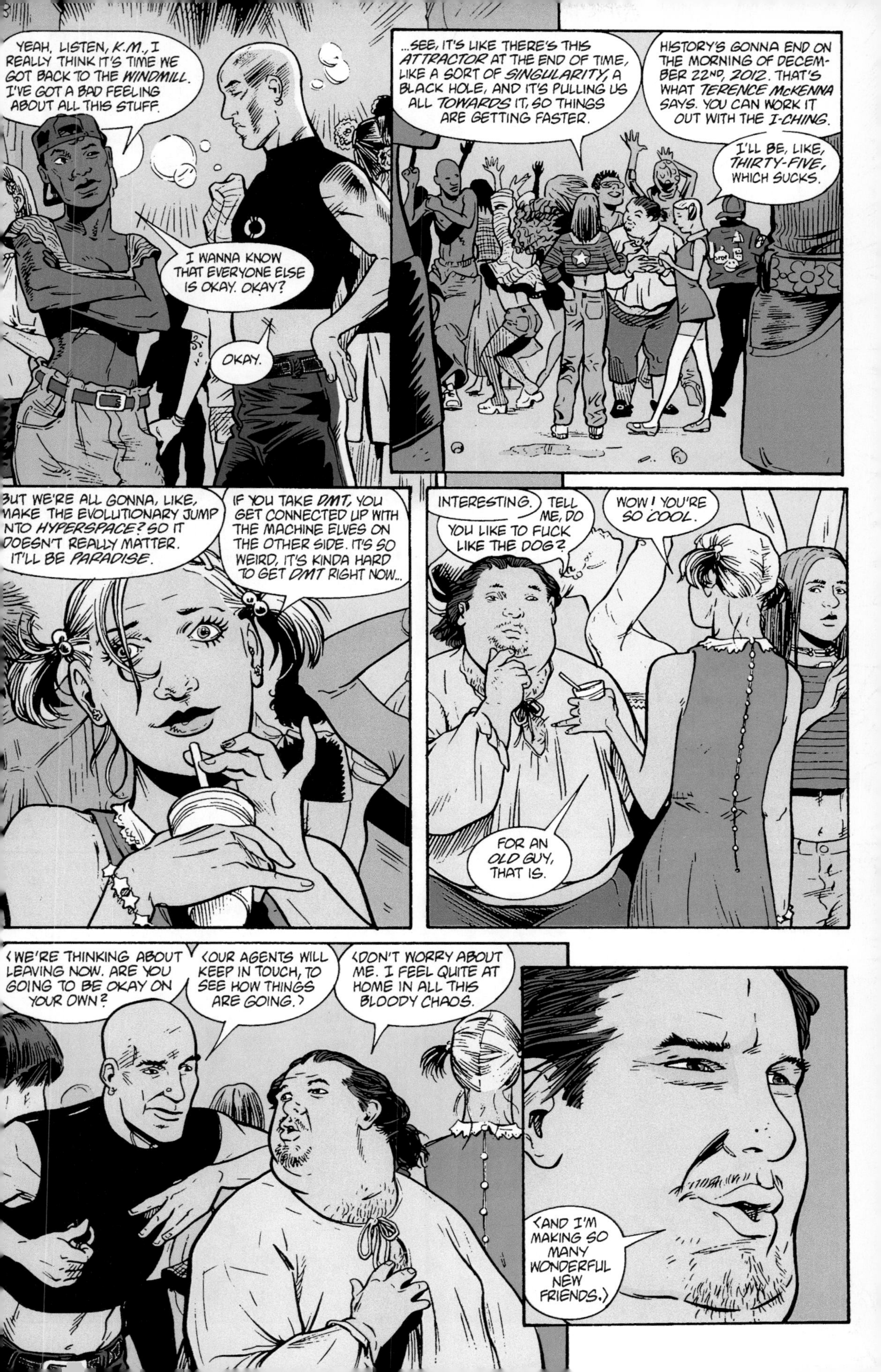

YEAH, LISTEN, K.M., I REALLY THINK IT'S TIME WE GOT BACK TO THE WINDMILL. I'VE GOT A BAD FEELING ABOUT ALL THIS STUFF.
I WANNA KNOW THAT EVERYONE ELSE IS OKAY. OKAY?
OKAY.
...SEE, IT'S LIKE THERE'S THIS ATTRACTOR AT THE END OF TIME, LIKE A SORT OF SINGULARITY, A BLACK HOLE, AND IT'S PULLING US ALL TOWARDS IT, SO THINGS ARE GETTING FASTER.
HISTORY'S GONNA END ON THE MORNING OF DECEMBER 22ND, 2012. THAT'S WHAT TERENCE McKENNA SAYS. YOU CAN WORK IT OUT WITH THE I-CHING.
I'LL BE, LIKE, THIRTY-FIVE, WHICH SUCKS.
BUT WE'RE ALL GONNA, LIKE, MAKE THE EVOLUTIONARY JUMP INTO HYPERSPACE? SO IT DOESN'T REALLY MATTER. IT'LL BE PARADISE.
IF YOU TAKE DMT, YOU GET CONNECTED UP WITH THE MACHINE ELVES ON THE OTHER SIDE. IT'S SO WEIRD, IT'S KINDA HARD TO GET DMT RIGHT NOW...
INTERESTING.
TELL ME, DO YOU LIKE TO FUCK LIKE THE DOG?
WOW! YOU'RE SO COOL.
FOR AN OLD GUY, THAT IS.
<WE'RE THINKING ABOUT LEAVING NOW. ARE YOU GOING TO BE OKAY ON YOUR OWN?
<OUR AGENTS WILL KEEP IN TOUCH, TO SEE HOW THINGS ARE GOING.>
<DON'T WORRY ABOUT ME. I FEEL QUITE AT HOME IN ALL THIS BLOODY CHAOS.
<AND I'M MAKING SO MANY WONDERFUL NEW FRIENDS.>

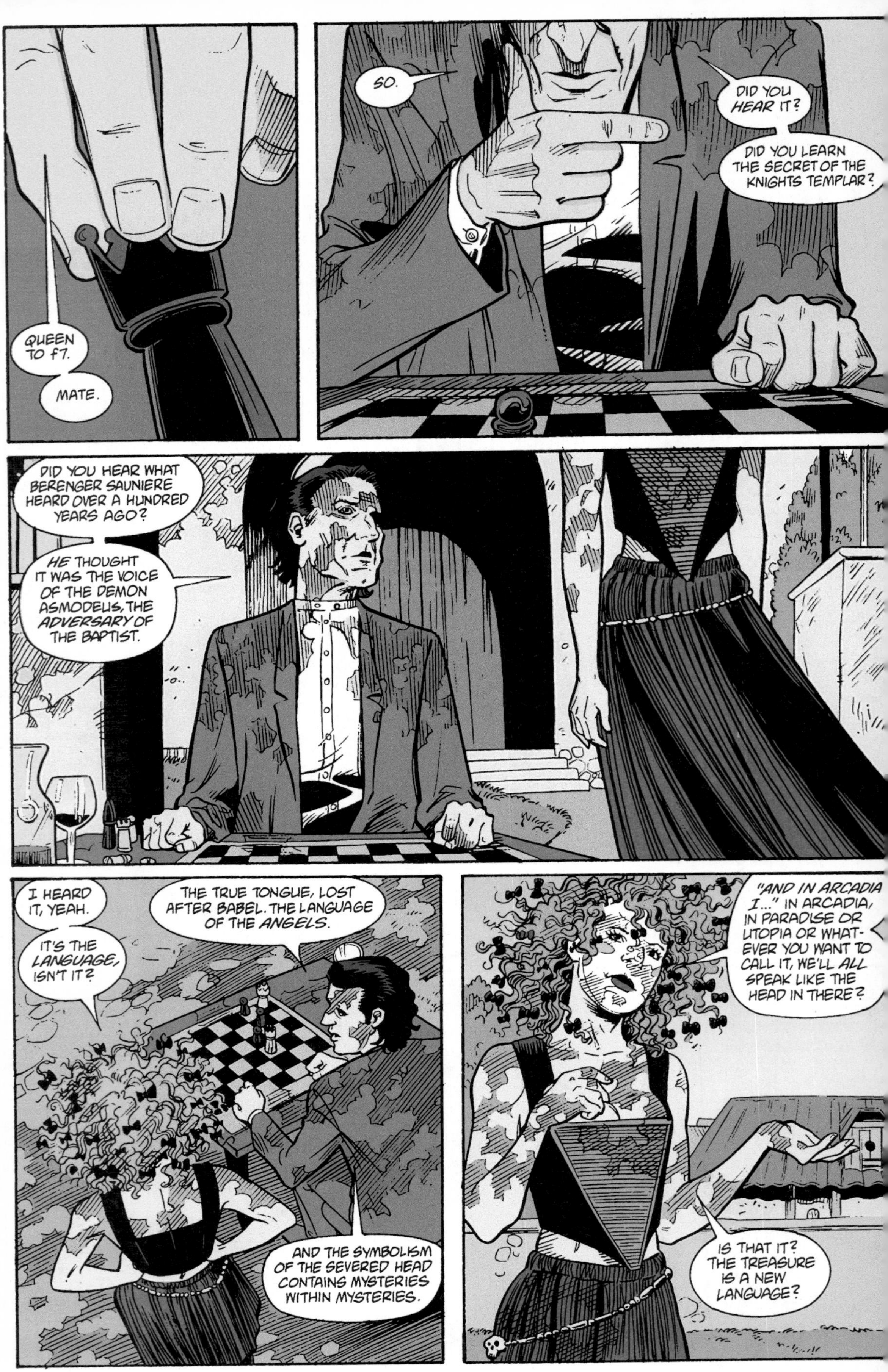
QUEEN TO f7.
MATE.
SO.
DID YOU *HEAR* IT?
DID YOU LEARN THE SECRET OF THE KNIGHTS TEMPLAR?
DID YOU HEAR WHAT BERENGER SAUNIERE HEARD OVER A HUNDRED YEARS AGO?
HE THOUGHT IT WAS THE VOICE OF THE DEMON ASMODEUS, THE *ADVERSARY* OF THE BAPTIST.
I HEARD IT, YEAH.
IT'S THE *LANGUAGE,* ISN'T IT?
THE TRUE TONGUE, LOST AFTER BABEL. THE LANGUAGE OF THE *ANGELS*.
AND THE SYMBOLISM OF THE SEVERED HEAD CONTAINS MYSTERIES WITHIN MYSTERIES.
"AND IN ARCADIA I..." IN ARCADIA, IN PARADISE OR UTOPIA OR WHAT-EVER YOU WANT TO CALL IT, WE'LL *ALL* SPEAK LIKE THE HEAD IN THERE?
IS THAT IT? THE TREASURE IS A NEW LANGUAGE?

NOT NEW. *ETERNAL*. GLOSSOLALIA IS THE LANGUAGE OF *ECSTASY* AND DREAMS. THE PRIMAL TONGUE OF FIRE.

IT IS THE ORIGINAL VOICE OF THE UNCONSCIOUS MIND, AND EVERYONE WHO HEARS IT INTERPRETS IT DIFFERENTLY. EVERYONE HEARS WHAT THEY *NEED* TO HEAR.

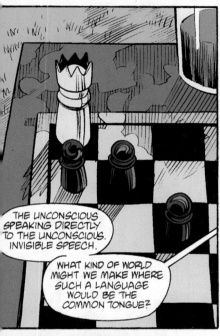

THE UNCONSCIOUS SPEAKING DIRECTLY TO THE UNCONSCIOUS. INVISIBLE SPEECH.

WHAT KIND OF WORLD MIGHT WE MAKE WHERE SUCH A LANGUAGE WOULD BE THE COMMON TONGUE?

I'M PLANNING ON BEING AROUND TO SEE IT.

LOTS OF PEOPLE WANT TO STOP US GETTING THERE...

LIKE THOSE POOR CREATURES IN THE CHURCH?

WHEN ONE REACHES MY AGE, ONE SEES THROUGH THE STRUGGLE, ONE SEES IT ALL FOR WHAT IT TRULY IS.

JUST A GAME.

WOULD YOU LIKE TO PLAY?

I'VE PLAYED ENOUGH TODAY, THANKS ANYWAY.

YOU DON'T LOOK *THAT* OLD.

NO.

I NEVER HAVE.

223

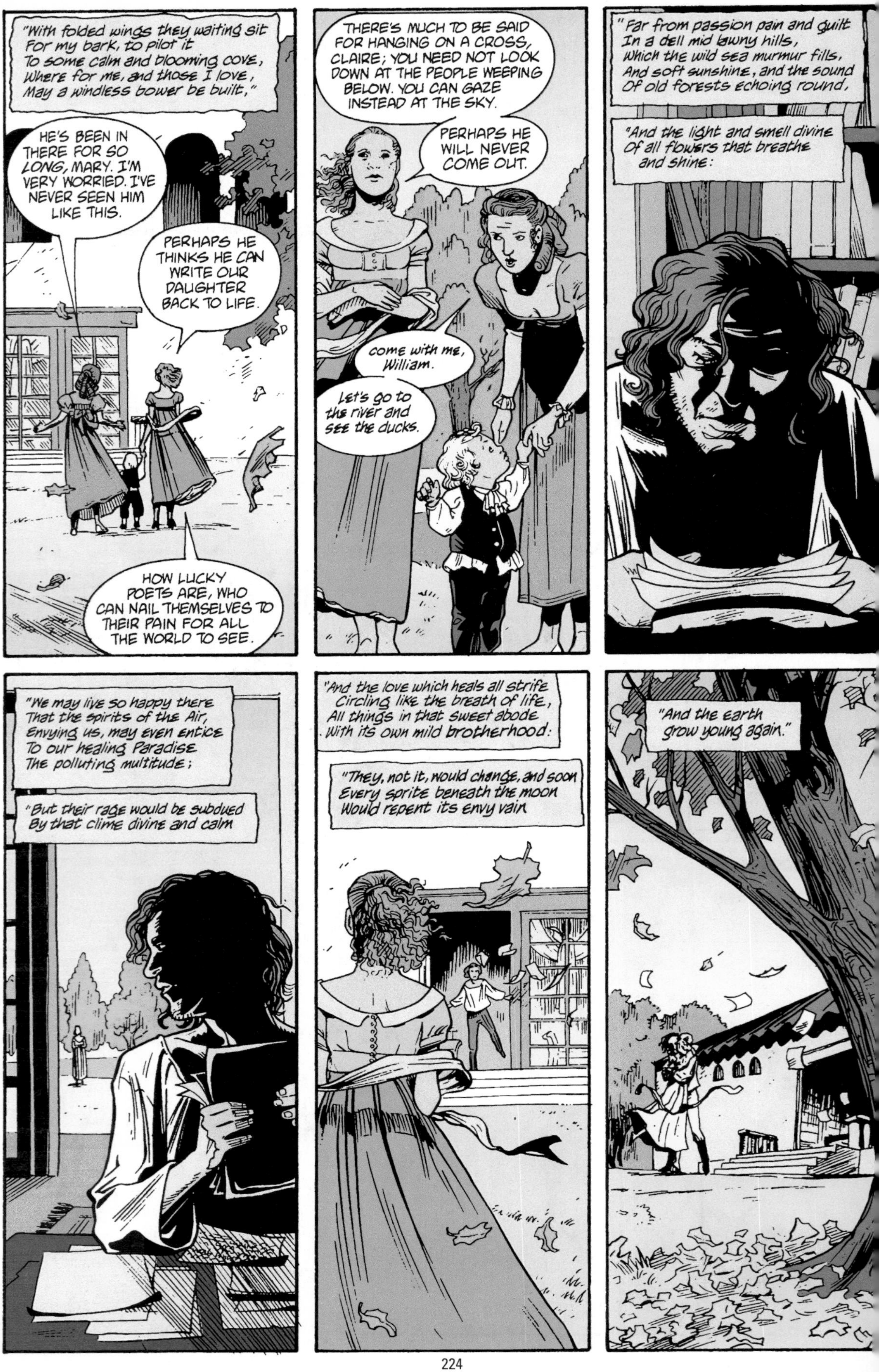
"With folded wings they waiting sit
For my bark, to pilot it
To some calm and blooming cove,
Where for me, and those I love,
May a windless bower be built,"
HE'S BEEN IN THERE FOR SO LONG, MARY. I'M VERY WORRIED. I'VE NEVER SEEN HIM LIKE THIS.
PERHAPS HE THINKS HE CAN WRITE OUR DAUGHTER BACK TO LIFE.
HOW LUCKY POETS ARE, WHO CAN NAIL THEMSELVES TO THEIR PAIN FOR ALL THE WORLD TO SEE.
THERE'S MUCH TO BE SAID FOR HANGING ON A CROSS, CLAIRE; YOU NEED NOT LOOK DOWN AT THE PEOPLE WEEPING BELOW. YOU CAN GAZE INSTEAD AT THE SKY.
PERHAPS HE WILL NEVER COME OUT.
Come with me, William.
Let's go to the river and see the ducks.
"Far from passion pain and guilt
In a dell mid lawny hills,
Which the wild sea murmur fills,
And soft sunshine, and the sound
Of old forests echoing round,
"And the light and smell divine
Of all flowers that breathe
and shine:
"We may live so happy there
That the spirits of the Air,
Envying us, may even entice
To our healing Paradise
The polluting multitude;
"But their rage would be subdued
By that clime divine and calm
"And the love which heals all strife
Circling like the breath of life,
All things in that sweet abode
With its own mild brotherhood:
"They, not it, would change, and soon
Every sprite beneath the moon
Would repent its envy vain
"And the earth
grow young again."

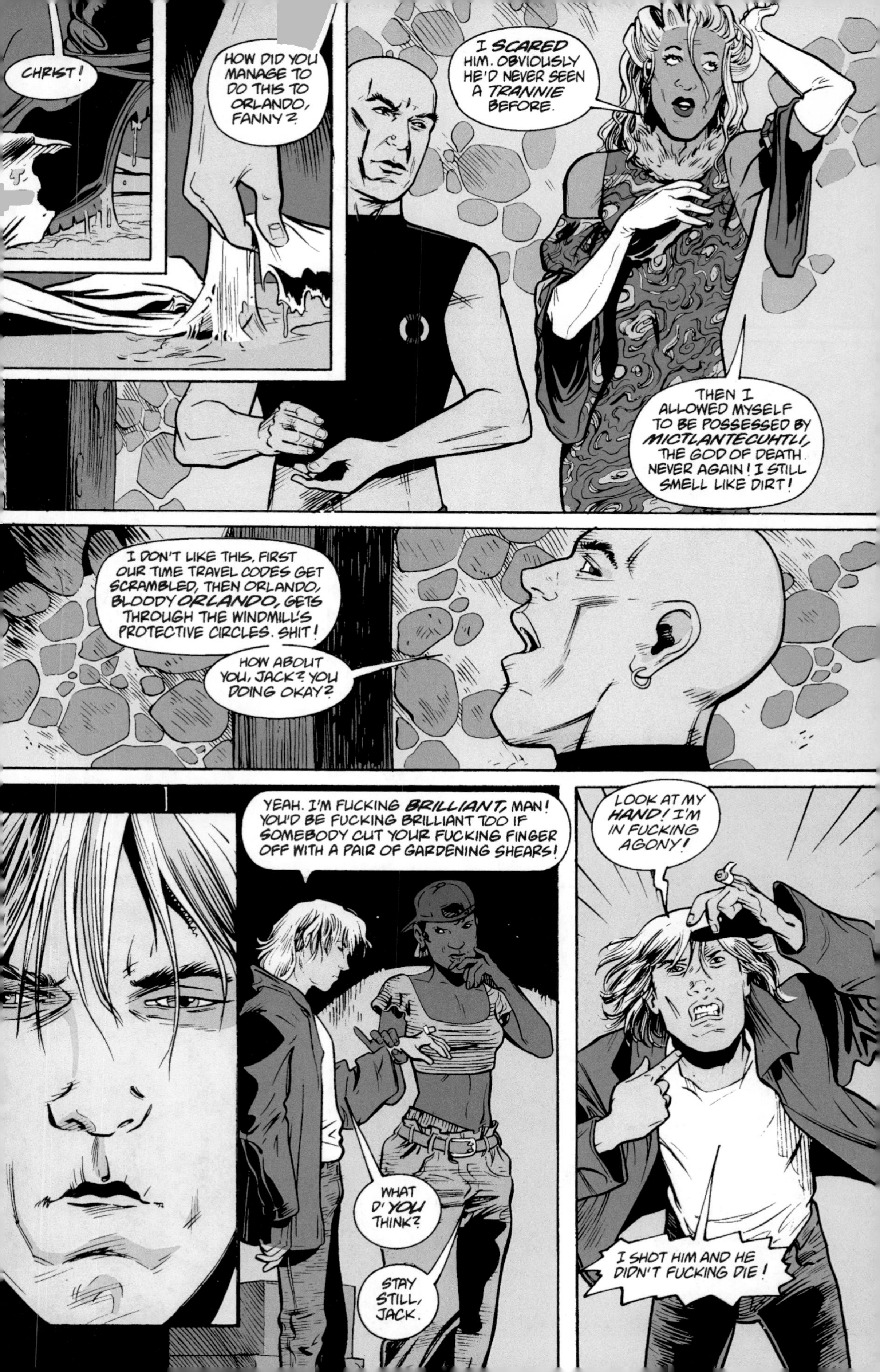
CHRIST!
HOW DID YOU MANAGE TO DO THIS TO ORLANDO, FANNY?
I SCARED HIM. OBVIOUSLY HE'D NEVER SEEN A TRANNIE BEFORE.
THEN I ALLOWED MYSELF TO BE POSSESSED BY MICTLANTECUHTLI, THE GOD OF DEATH. NEVER AGAIN! I STILL SMELL LIKE DIRT!
I DON'T LIKE THIS. FIRST OUR TIME TRAVEL CODES GET SCRAMBLED, THEN ORLANDO, BLOODY ORLANDO, GETS THROUGH THE WINDMILL'S PROTECTIVE CIRCLES. SHIT!
HOW ABOUT YOU, JACK? YOU DOING OKAY?
YEAH. I'M FUCKING BRILLIANT, MAN! YOU'D BE FUCKING BRILLIANT TOO IF SOMEBODY CUT YOUR FUCKING FINGER OFF WITH A PAIR OF GARDENING SHEARS!
WHAT D' YOU THINK?
STAY STILL, JACK.
LOOK AT MY HAND! I'M IN FUCKING AGONY!
I SHOT HIM AND HE DIDN'T FUCKING DIE!

ORLANDO'S NOT HUMAN. HE'S A *DEMON*. THIS IS THE INVISIBLES, JACK; WEIRD SHIT GOES ON ALL THE TIME.

THERE'S NO WAY HE SHOULD HAVE BEEN ABLE TO GET NEAR US, THOUGH...

WELL, HE GOT NEAR *ME* ALL RIGHT!

FIRST I HAVE A FUCKING DREAM WHERE I'M IN THE PAST AND THEN I WAKE UP WITH *HIM* CUTTING OFF MY FINGER!

I HAD A NORMAL LIFE BEFORE *YOU* FUCKED IT UP. I HAD A FUCKING *FINGER* FOR A START!

YOU LOT ARE USELESS! SITTING THERE SLEEPING! THE ONLY ONE WHO DID ANYTHING WAS THAT POOF IN A DRESS.

WILL YOU PLEASE STAY STILL?...

WE'RE GOING TO HAVE TO CONSIDER THE POSSIBILITY THAT SOME-ONE'S GIVING THE ENEMY INFORMATION ABOUT OUR EVERY MOVE.

THIS COULD MEAN SERIOUS TROUBLE.

NOT FOR *ME*, MAN. I'VE GOT NOTHING TO DO WITH YOU.

I'VE HAD IT, RIGHT?

YOU CAN TAKE YOUR FUCKING INVISIBLES AND SHOVE THEM UP YOUR ARSE!

I'M GOING HOME.

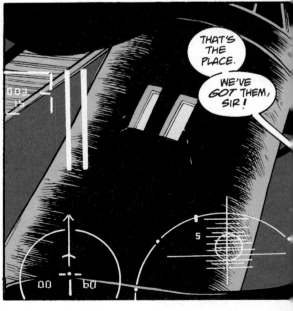

THAT'S THE PLACE.

WE'VE *GOT* THEM, SIR!

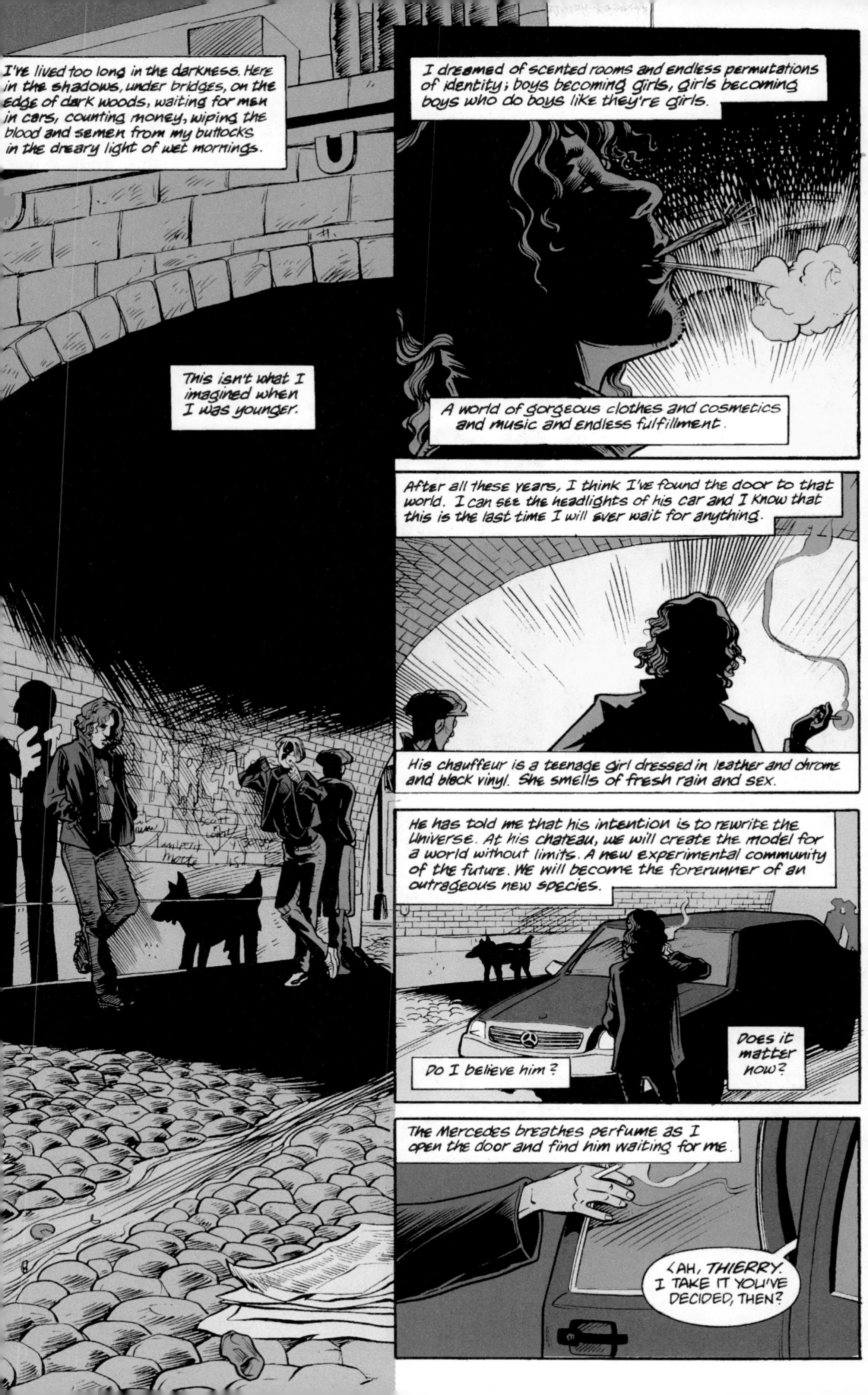

I've lived too long in the darkness. Here in the shadows, under bridges, on the edge of dark woods, waiting for men in cars, counting money, wiping the blood and semen from my buttocks in the dreary light of wet mornings.
This isn't what I imagined when I was younger.
I dreamed of scented rooms and endless permutations of identity; boys becoming girls, girls becoming boys who do boys like they're girls.
A world of gorgeous clothes and cosmetics and music and endless fulfillment.
After all these years, I think I've found the door to that world. I can see the headlights of his car and I know that this is the last time I will ever wait for anything.
His chauffeur is a teenage girl dressed in leather and chrome and black vinyl. She smells of fresh rain and sex.
He has told me that his intention is to rewrite the Universe. At his chateau, we will create the model for a world without limits. A new experimental community of the future. We will become the forerunner of an outrageous new species.
Do I believe him?
Does it matter now?
The Mercedes breathes perfume as I open the door and find him waiting for me.
<AH, THIERRY. I TAKE IT YOU'VE DECIDED, THEN?

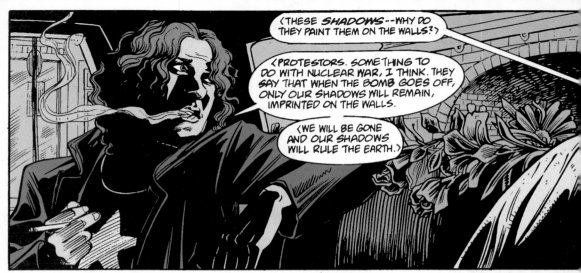

‹THESE *SHADOWS*--WHY DO THEY PAINT THEM ON THE WALLS?›

‹PROTESTORS. SOMETHING TO DO WITH NUCLEAR WAR, I THINK. THEY SAY THAT WHEN THE BOMB GOES OFF, ONLY OUR SHADOWS WILL REMAIN, IMPRINTED ON THE WALLS.›

‹WE WILL BE GONE AND OUR SHADOWS WILL RULE THE EARTH.›

‹I THOUGHT THEY ALREADY DID.›

‹BUT WE WILL GIVE THEM PAUSE. YES INDEED. WE WILL *DROWN* THEM IN THE RAGING TORRENT OF THEIR OWN UNACKNOWLEDGED FEARS AND DESIRES.›

He tells me that I have left the houses of the dead and entered the land of the truly living. I am to be no particular age, no particular sex. I am to be fluid, mercurial. He tells me I must slough my name and my past as a snake sheds its skin.

He pins a blank white badge to the collar of my jacket. I sit in my seat, nameless, invisible, untouchable, breathing blue smoke. I ask him what I should call him.

‹I AM THE DIVINE MARQUIS. I AM DeSADE.›

‹AND I AM FREE AT LAST.›

BOW WOW *WOW!*

The engine starts up.

I settle back in the leather seat, becoming weightless and transparent. There is no more time. I close my eyes.

And in my mind, I see the sun rise on a new and better world.

THE END

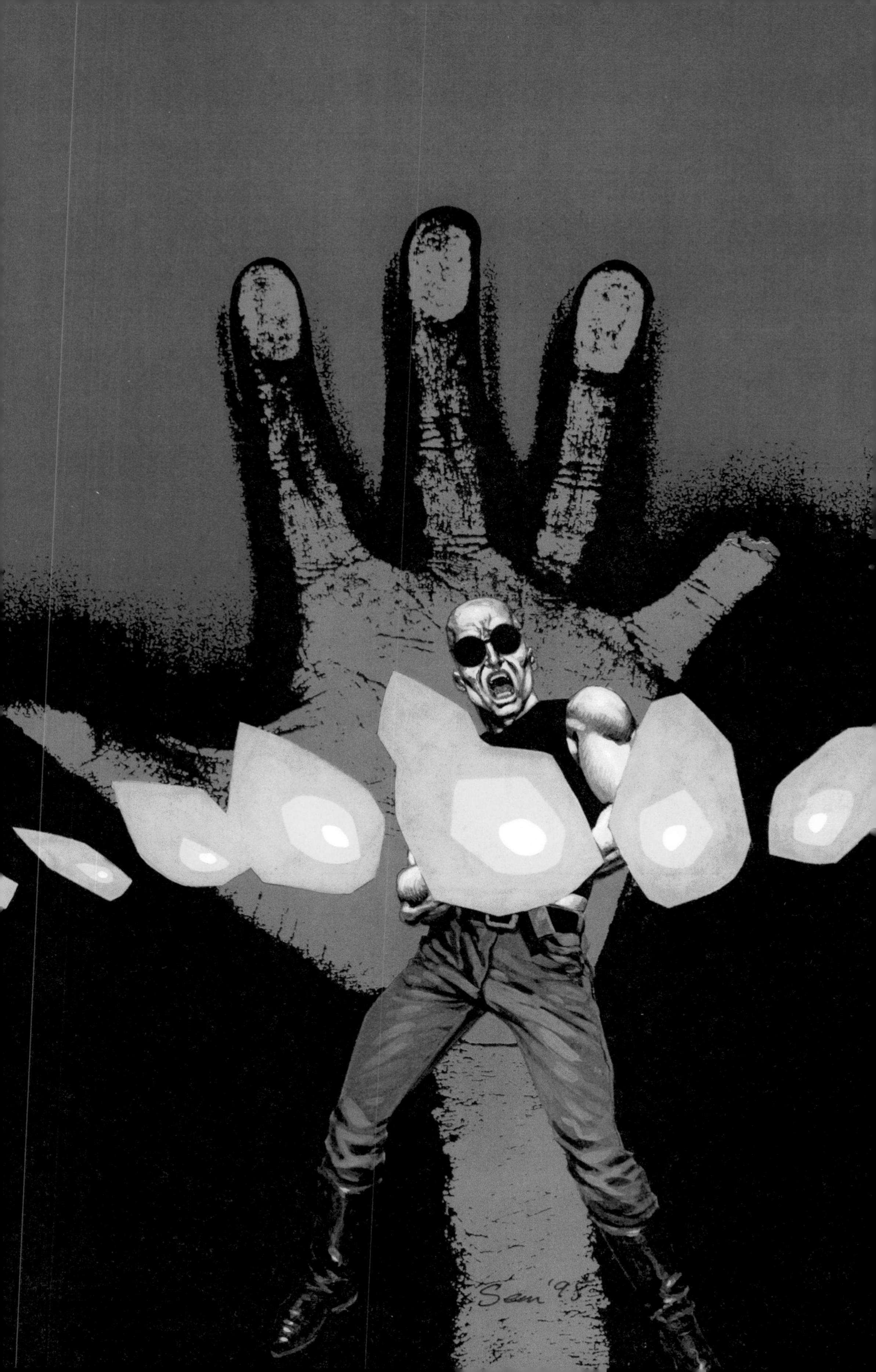

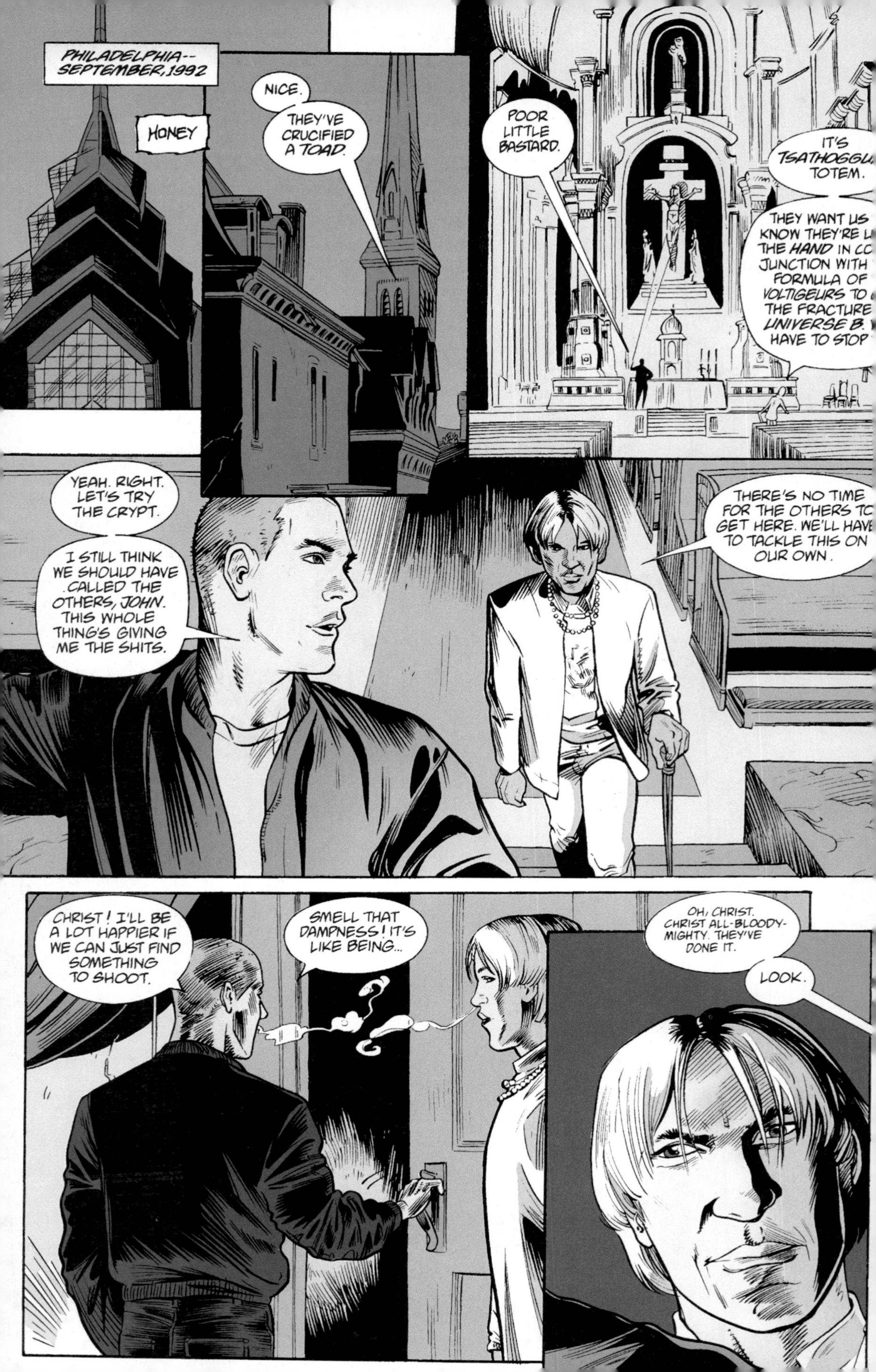
PHILADELPHIA-- SEPTEMBER, 1992
HONEY
NICE.
THEY'VE CRUCIFIED A TOAD.
POOR LITTLE BASTARD.
IT'S TSATHOGGU TOTEM.
THEY WANT US KNOW THEY'RE THE HAND IN CO JUNCTION WITH FORMULA OF VOLTIGEURS TO THE FRACTURE UNIVERSE B. HAVE TO STOP
YEAH. RIGHT. LET'S TRY THE CRYPT.
I STILL THINK WE SHOULD HAVE CALLED THE OTHERS, JOHN. THIS WHOLE THING'S GIVING ME THE SHITS.
THERE'S NO TIME FOR THE OTHERS TO GET HERE. WE'LL HAVE TO TACKLE THIS ON OUR OWN.
CHRIST! I'LL BE A LOT HAPPIER IF WE CAN JUST FIND SOMETHING TO SHOOT.
SMELL THAT DAMPNESS! IT'S LIKE BEING...
OH, CHRIST. CHRIST ALL-BLOODY-MIGHTY. THEY'VE DONE IT.
LOOK.

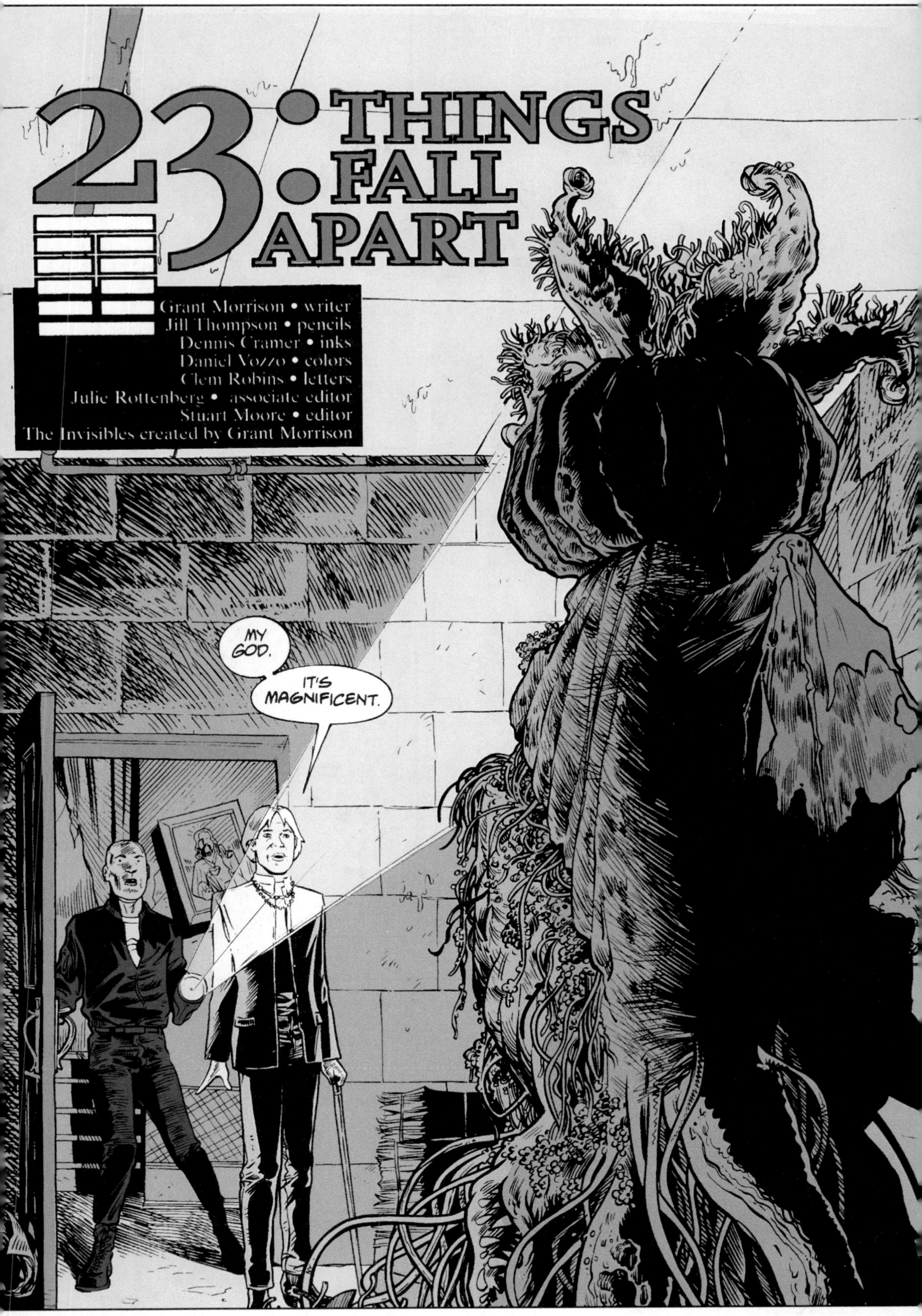
23: THINGS FALL APART
Grant Morrison • writer
Jill Thompson • pencils
Dennis Cramer • inks
Daniel Vozzo • colors
Clem Robins • letters
Julie Rottenberg • associate editor
Stuart Moore • editor
The Invisibles created by Grant Morrison
MY GOD.
IT'S MAGNIFICENT.

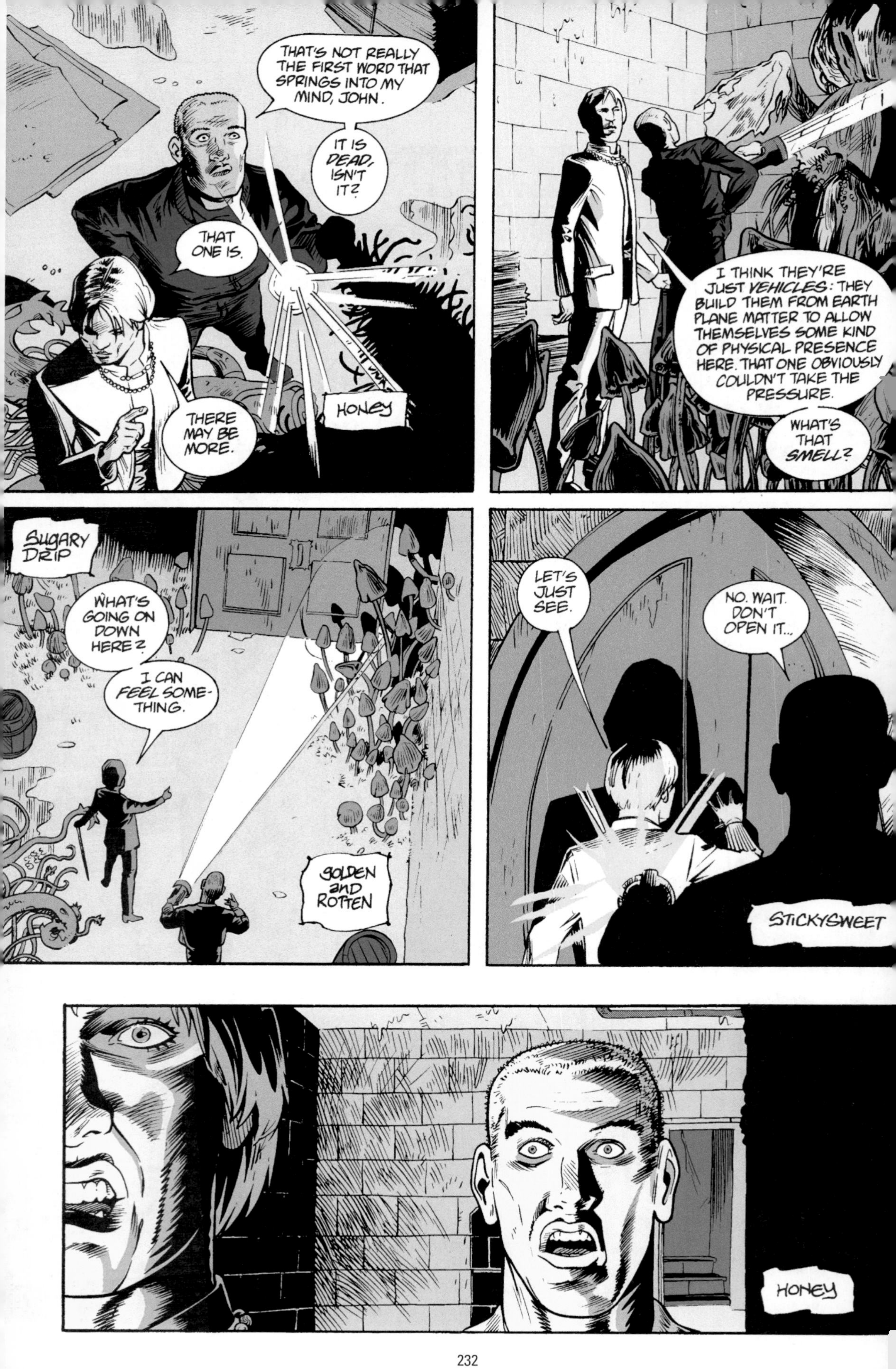

THAT'S NOT REALLY THE FIRST WORD THAT SPRINGS INTO MY MIND, JOHN.
IT IS DEAD, ISN'T IT?
THAT ONE IS.
THERE MAY BE MORE.
HONEY
I THINK THEY'RE JUST VEHICLES: THEY BUILD THEM FROM EARTH PLANE MATTER TO ALLOW THEMSELVES SOME KIND OF PHYSICAL PRESENCE HERE. THAT ONE OBVIOUSLY COULDN'T TAKE THE PRESSURE.
WHAT'S THAT SMELL?
SUGARY DRIP
WHAT'S GOING ON DOWN HERE?
I CAN FEEL SOME-THING.
GOLDEN and ROTTEN
LET'S JUST SEE.
NO. WAIT. DON'T OPEN IT...
STICKYSWEET
HONEY

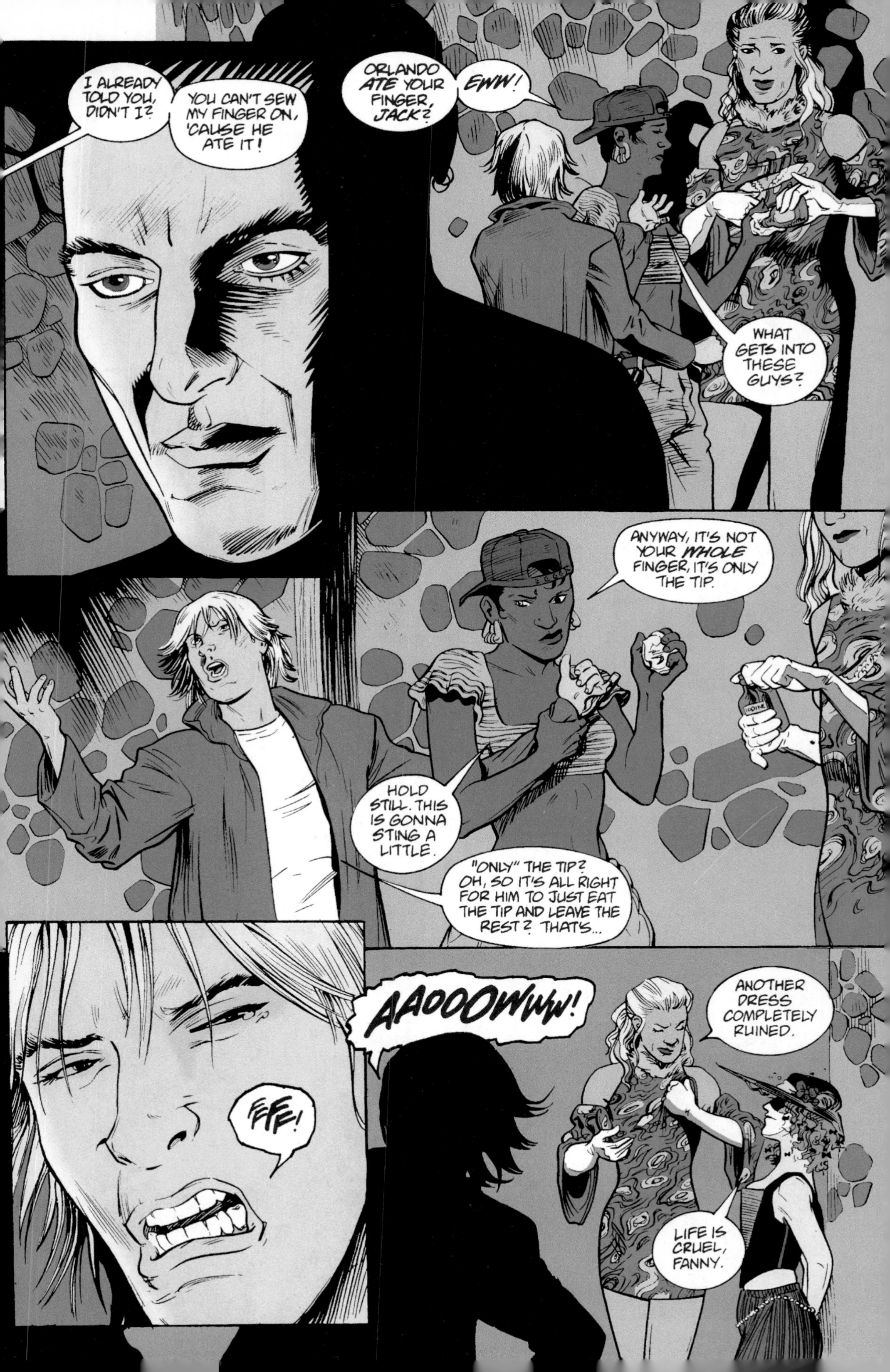
I ALREADY TOLD YOU, DIDN'T I?
YOU CAN'T SEW MY FINGER ON, 'CAUSE HE ATE IT!
ORLANDO ATE YOUR FINGER, JACK?
EWW!
WHAT GETS INTO THESE GUYS?
ANYWAY, IT'S NOT YOUR WHOLE FINGER, IT'S ONLY THE TIP.
HOLD STILL. THIS IS GONNA STING A LITTLE.
"ONLY" THE TIP? OH, SO IT'S ALL RIGHT FOR HIM TO JUST EAT THE TIP AND LEAVE THE REST? THAT'S...
FFF!
AAOOOWWW!
ANOTHER DRESS COMPLETELY RUINED.
LIFE IS CRUEL, FANNY.

I'VE JUST BEEN THINKING.

I THINK WE'RE IN TROUBLE, MUCH WORSE TROUBLE THAN WE IMAGINED.

WELL, IT'S *YOUR* TROUBLE, MAN, NOT MINE! AND YOU CAN KEEP YOUR FUCKING TROUBLE TO YOURSELF MAYBE IT'LL BE *YOU* THAT GETS CUT UP NEXT TIME!

I'M FINISHED WITH THIS! I'M GOING HOME!

LOOK AT THAT!

LOOK AT MY FUCKING HAND!

THAT'S WHAT I CALL TROUBLE!

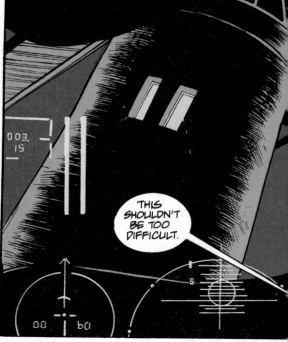

THIS SHOULDN'T BE TOO DIFFICULT.

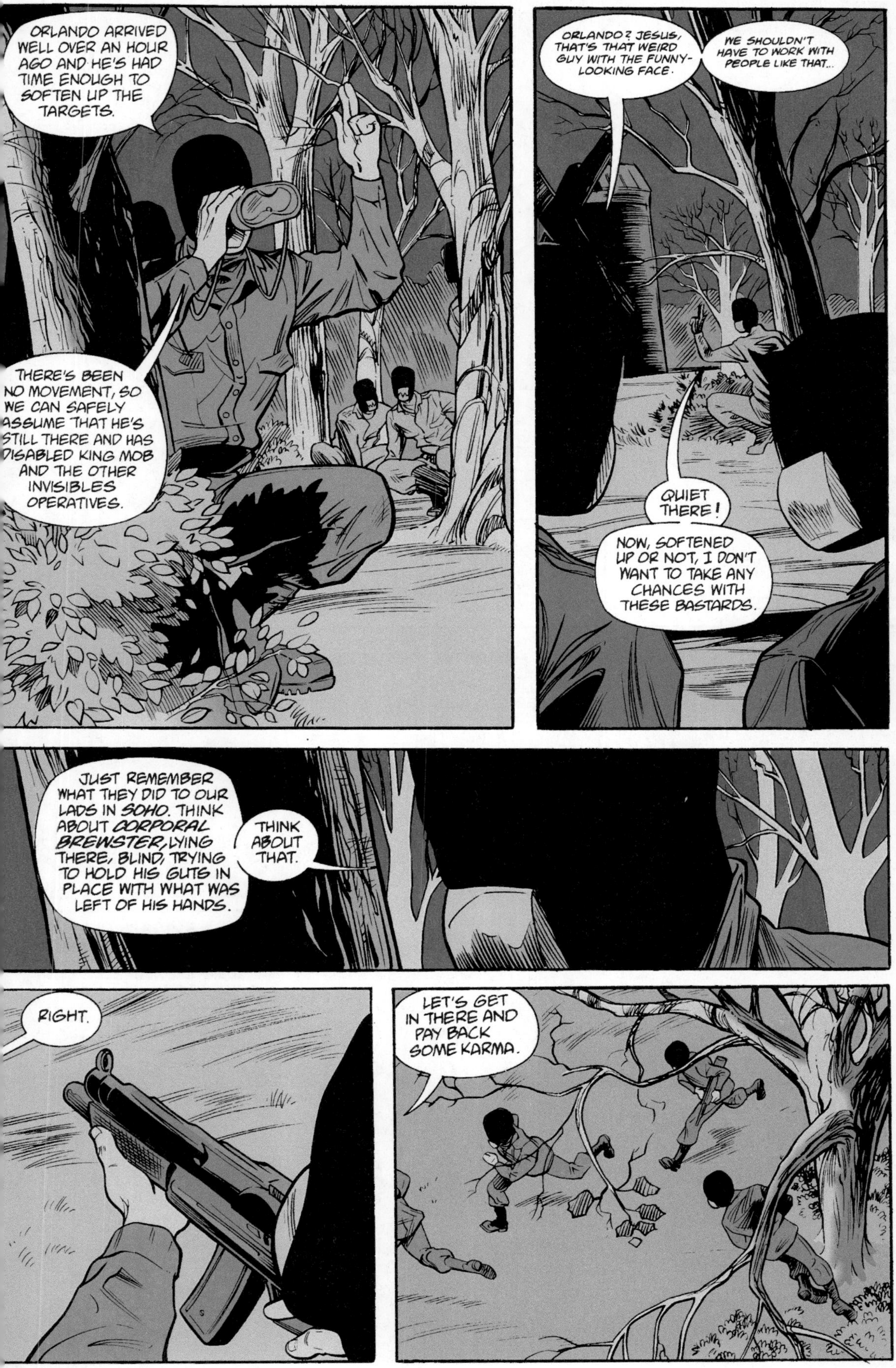
ORLANDO ARRIVED WELL OVER AN HOUR AGO AND HE'S HAD TIME ENOUGH TO SOFTEN UP THE TARGETS.
THERE'S BEEN NO MOVEMENT, SO WE CAN SAFELY ASSUME THAT HE'S STILL THERE AND HAS DISABLED KING MOB AND THE OTHER INVISIBLES OPERATIVES.
ORLANDO? JESUS, THAT'S THAT WEIRD GUY WITH THE FUNNY-LOOKING FACE.
WE SHOULDN'T HAVE TO WORK WITH PEOPLE LIKE THAT...
QUIET THERE!
NOW, SOFTENED UP OR NOT, I DON'T WANT TO TAKE ANY CHANCES WITH THESE BASTARDS.
JUST REMEMBER WHAT THEY DID TO OUR LADS IN SOHO. THINK ABOUT CORPORAL BREWSTER, LYING THERE, BLIND, TRYING TO HOLD HIS GUTS IN PLACE WITH WHAT WAS LEFT OF HIS HANDS.
THINK ABOUT THAT.
RIGHT.
LET'S GET IN THERE AND PAY BACK SOME KARMA.

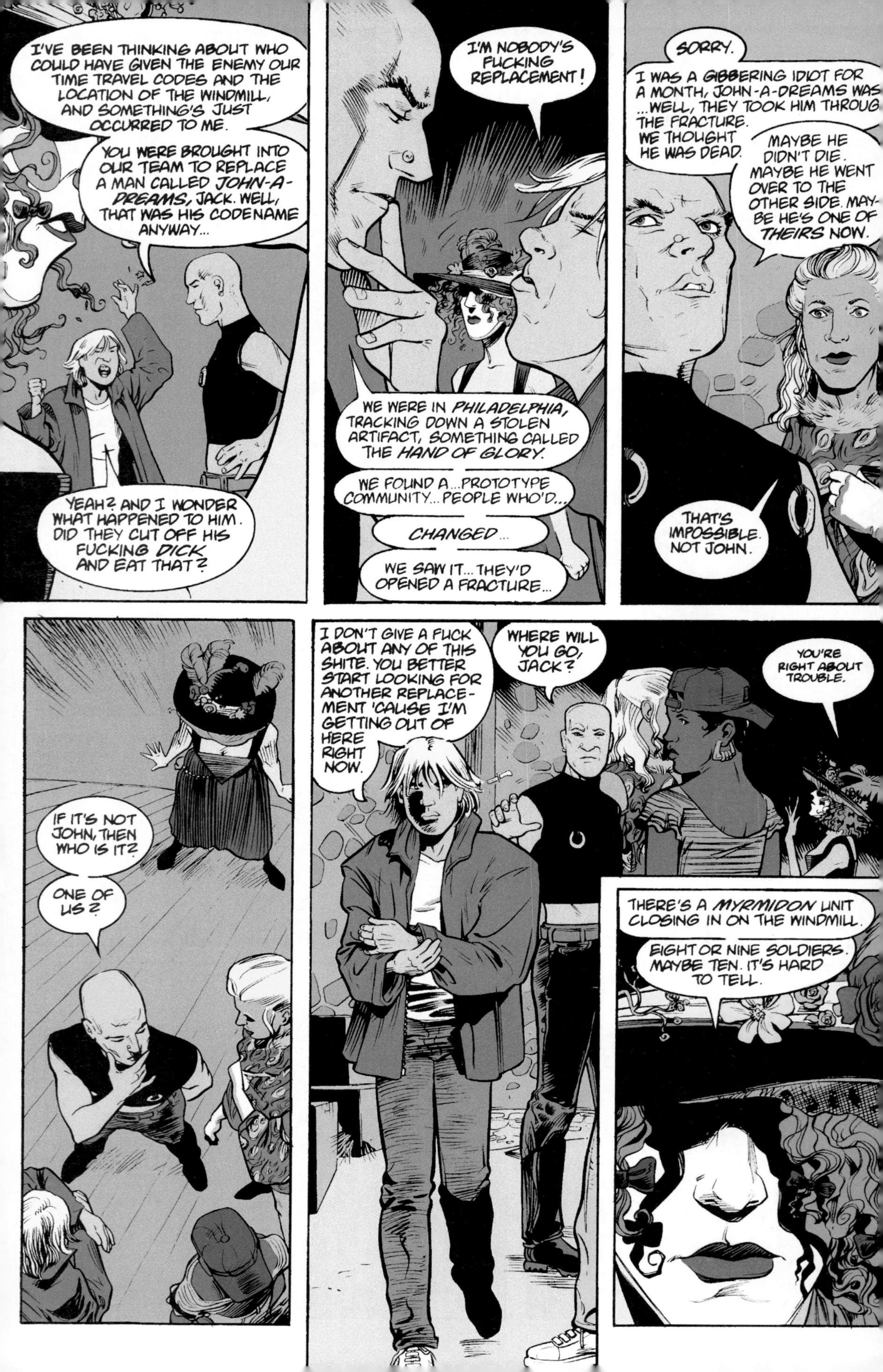
I'VE BEEN THINKING ABOUT WHO COULD HAVE GIVEN THE ENEMY OUR TIME TRAVEL CODES AND THE LOCATION OF THE WINDMILL, AND SOMETHING'S JUST OCCURRED TO ME.
YOU WERE BROUGHT INTO OUR TEAM TO REPLACE A MAN CALLED JOHN-A-DREAMS, JACK. WELL, THAT WAS HIS CODENAME ANYWAY...
YEAH? AND I WONDER WHAT HAPPENED TO HIM. DID THEY CUT OFF HIS FUCKING DICK AND EAT THAT?
I'M NOBODY'S FUCKING REPLACEMENT!
WE WERE IN PHILADELPHIA, TRACKING DOWN A STOLEN ARTIFACT, SOMETHING CALLED THE HAND OF GLORY.
WE FOUND A...PROTOTYPE COMMUNITY...PEOPLE WHO'D...
CHANGED...
WE SAW IT... THEY'D OPENED A FRACTURE...
SORRY.
I WAS A GIBBERING IDIOT FOR A MONTH, JOHN-A-DREAMS WAS ...WELL, THEY TOOK HIM THROUG THE FRACTURE.
WE THOUGHT HE WAS DEAD.
MAYBE HE DIDN'T DIE. MAYBE HE WENT OVER TO THE OTHER SIDE. MAY-BE HE'S ONE OF THEIRS NOW.
THAT'S IMPOSSIBLE. NOT JOHN.
IF IT'S NOT JOHN, THEN WHO IS IT?
ONE OF US?
I DON'T GIVE A FUCK ABOUT ANY OF THIS SHITE. YOU BETTER START LOOKING FOR ANOTHER REPLACE-MENT 'CAUSE I'M GETTING OUT OF HERE RIGHT NOW.
WHERE WILL YOU GO, JACK?
YOU'RE RIGHT ABOUT TROUBLE.
THERE'S A MYRMIDON UNIT CLOSING IN ON THE WINDMILL.
EIGHT OR NINE SOLDIERS. MAYBE TEN. IT'S HARD TO TELL.

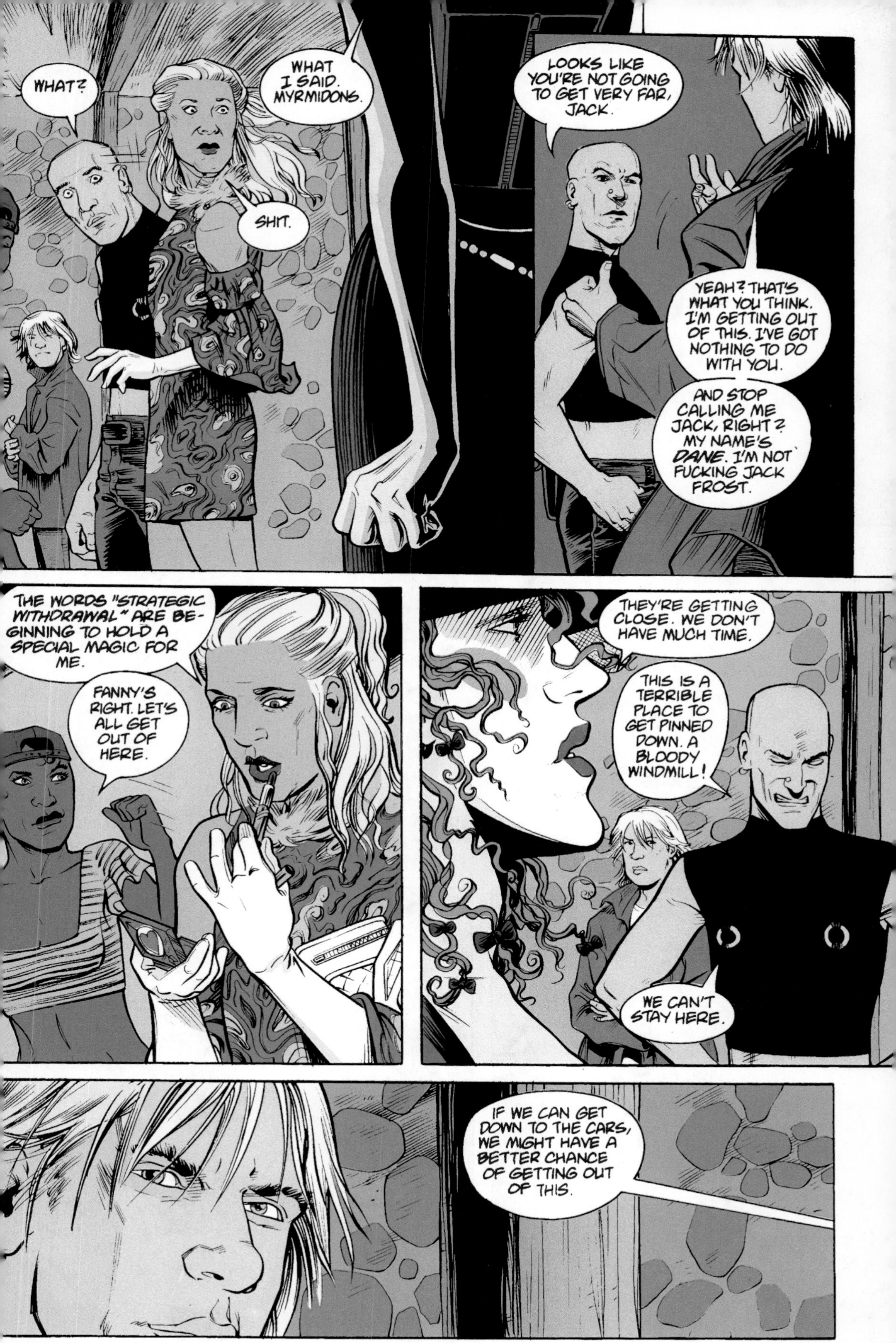
WHAT?
WHAT I SAID. MYRMIDONS.
SHIT.
LOOKS LIKE YOU'RE NOT GOING TO GET VERY FAR, JACK.
YEAH? THAT'S WHAT YOU THINK. I'M GETTING OUT OF THIS. I'VE GOT NOTHING TO DO WITH YOU.
AND STOP CALLING ME JACK, RIGHT? MY NAME'S DANE. I'M NOT FUCKING JACK FROST.
THE WORDS "STRATEGIC WITHDRAWAL" ARE BEGINNING TO HOLD A SPECIAL MAGIC FOR ME.
FANNY'S RIGHT. LET'S ALL GET OUT OF HERE.
THEY'RE GETTING CLOSE. WE DON'T HAVE MUCH TIME.
THIS IS A TERRIBLE PLACE TO GET PINNED DOWN. A BLOODY WINDMILL!
WE CAN'T STAY HERE.
IF WE CAN GET DOWN TO THE CARS, WE MIGHT HAVE A BETTER CHANCE OF GETTING OUT OF THIS.

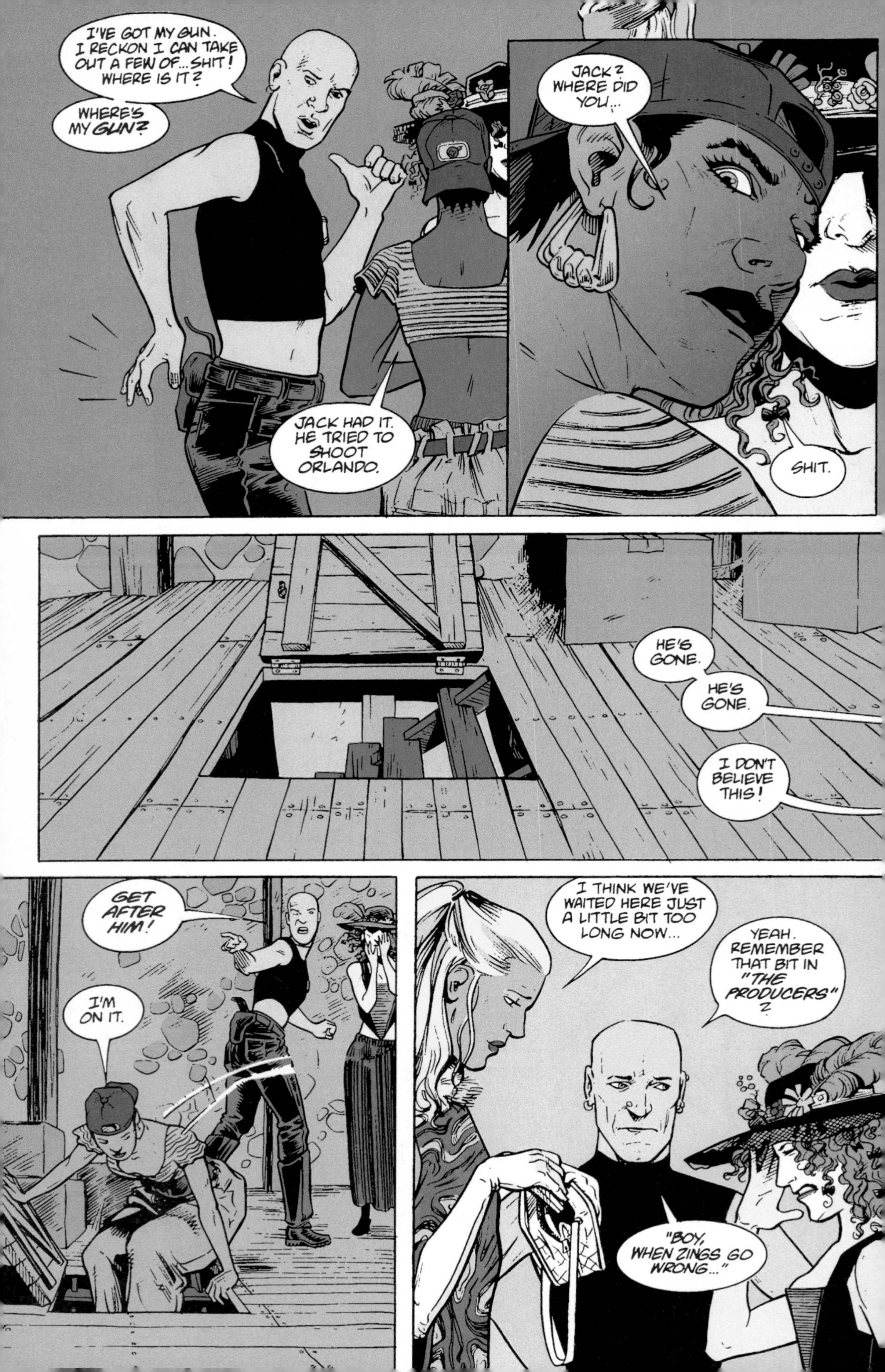
I'VE GOT MY GUN. I RECKON I CAN TAKE OUT A FEW OF... SHIT! WHERE IS IT?
WHERE'S MY GUN?
JACK HAD IT. HE TRIED TO SHOOT ORLANDO.
JACK? WHERE DID YOU...
SHIT.
HE'S GONE.
HE'S GONE.
I DON'T BELIEVE THIS!
GET AFTER HIM!
I'M ON IT.
I THINK WE'VE WAITED HERE JUST A LITTLE BIT TOO LONG NOW...
YEAH. REMEMBER THAT BIT IN "THE PRODUCERS"?
"BOY, WHEN ZINGS GO WRONG..."

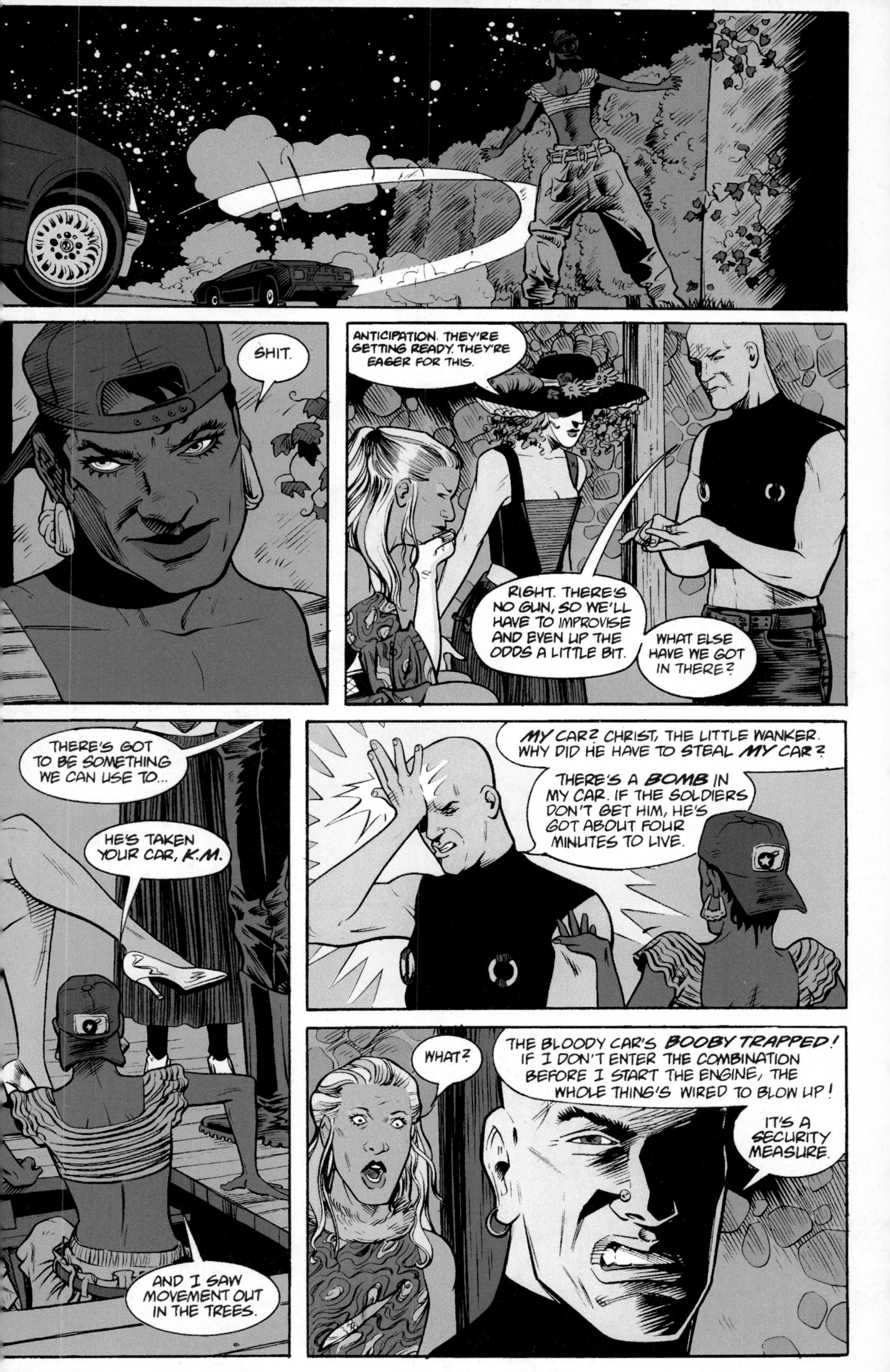
SHIT.
ANTICIPATION. THEY'RE GETTING READY. THEY'RE EAGER FOR THIS.
RIGHT. THERE'S NO GUN, SO WE'LL HAVE TO IMPROVISE AND EVEN UP THE ODDS A LITTLE BIT.
WHAT ELSE HAVE WE GOT IN THERE?
THERE'S GOT TO BE SOMETHING WE CAN USE TO...
HE'S TAKEN YOUR CAR, K.M.
AND I SAW MOVEMENT OUT IN THE TREES.
MY CAR? CHRIST, THE LITTLE WANKER. WHY DID HE HAVE TO STEAL MY CAR?
THERE'S A BOMB IN MY CAR. IF THE SOLDIERS DON'T GET HIM, HE'S GOT ABOUT FOUR MINUTES TO LIVE.
WHAT?
THE BLOODY CAR'S BOOBY TRAPPED! IF I DON'T ENTER THE COMBINATION BEFORE I START THE ENGINE, THE WHOLE THING'S WIRED TO BLOW UP!
IT'S A SECURITY MEASURE.

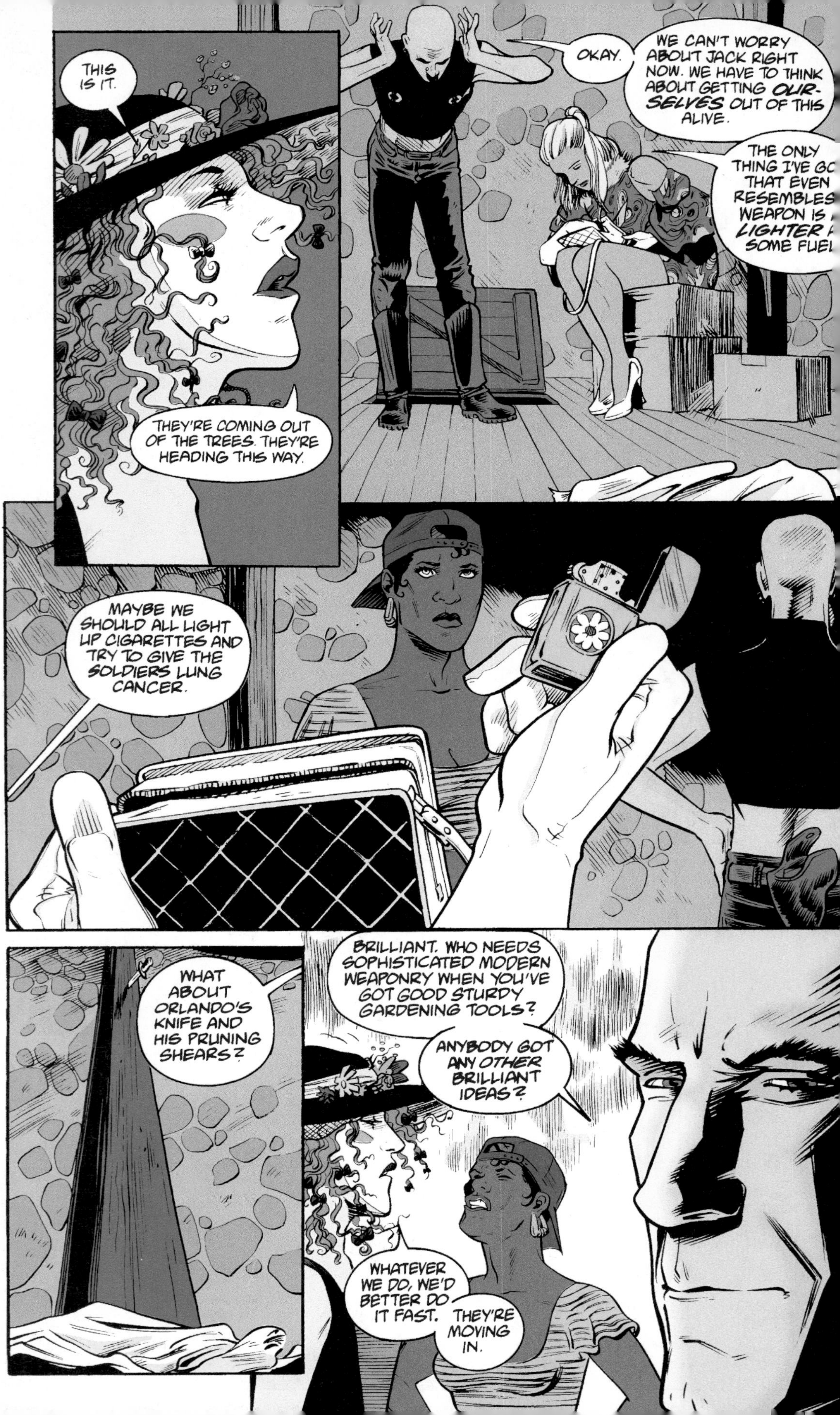
THIS IS IT.
THEY'RE COMING OUT OF THE TREES. THEY'RE HEADING THIS WAY.
OKAY.
WE CAN'T WORRY ABOUT JACK RIGHT NOW. WE HAVE TO THINK ABOUT GETTING OURSELVES OUT OF THIS ALIVE.
MAYBE WE SHOULD ALL LIGHT UP CIGARETTES AND TRY TO GIVE THE SOLDIERS LUNG CANCER.
WHAT ABOUT ORLANDO'S KNIFE AND HIS PRUNING SHEARS?
BRILLIANT. WHO NEEDS SOPHISTICATED MODERN WEAPONRY WHEN YOU'VE GOT GOOD STURDY GARDENING TOOLS?
ANYBODY GOT ANY OTHER BRILLIANT IDEAS?
WHATEVER WE DO, WE'D BETTER DO IT FAST.
THEY'RE MOVING IN.

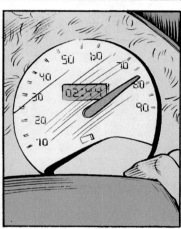

SHITE.

I DON'T THINK HE'S GONNA SLOW DOWN.

IT'S ONE OF THEM!

GET READY FOR HIM!

HE'S ACCELERATING!

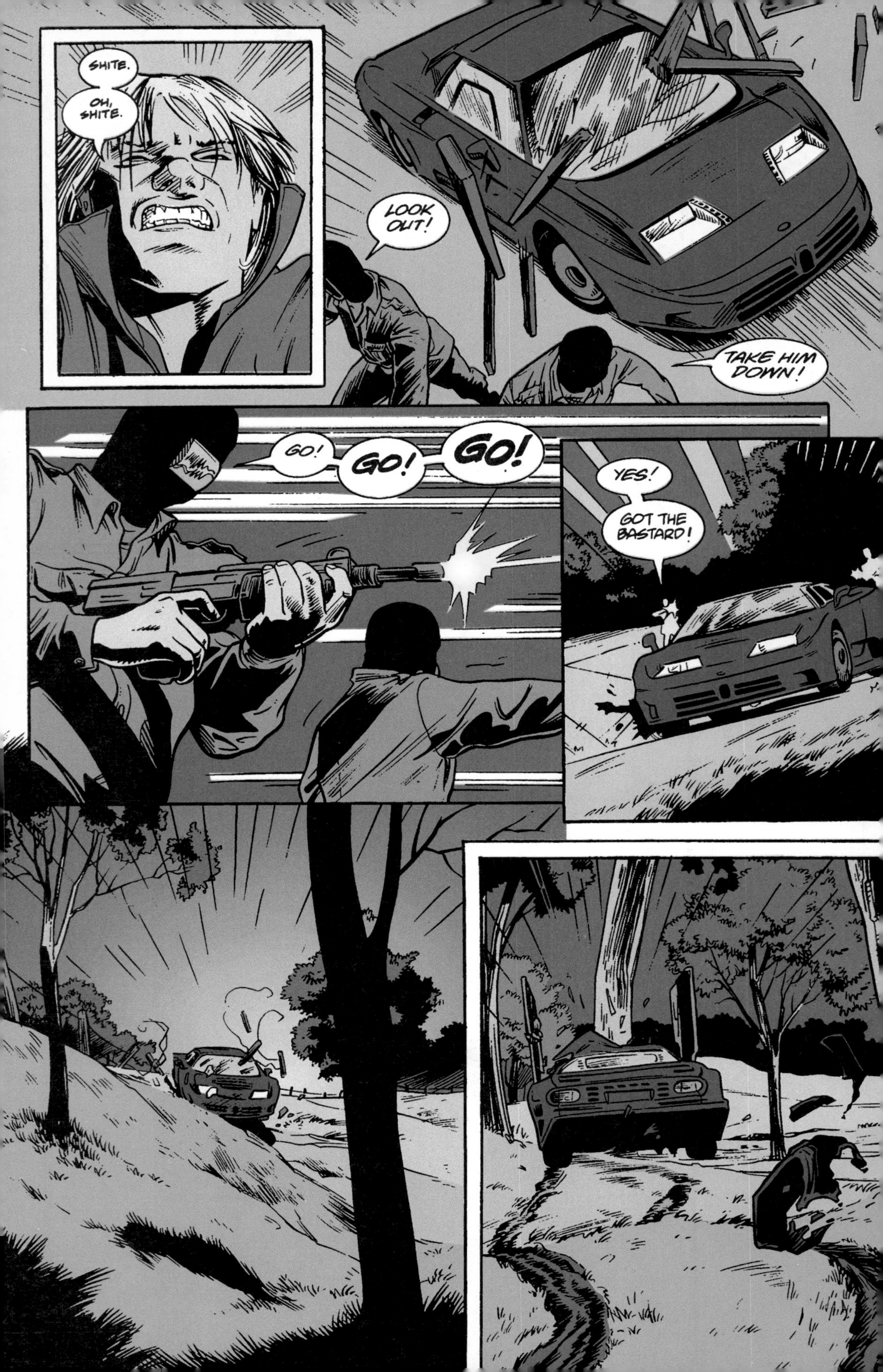
SHITE.
OH, SHITE.
LOOK OUT!
TAKE HIM DOWN!
GO!
GO!
GO!
YES!
GOT THE BASTARD!

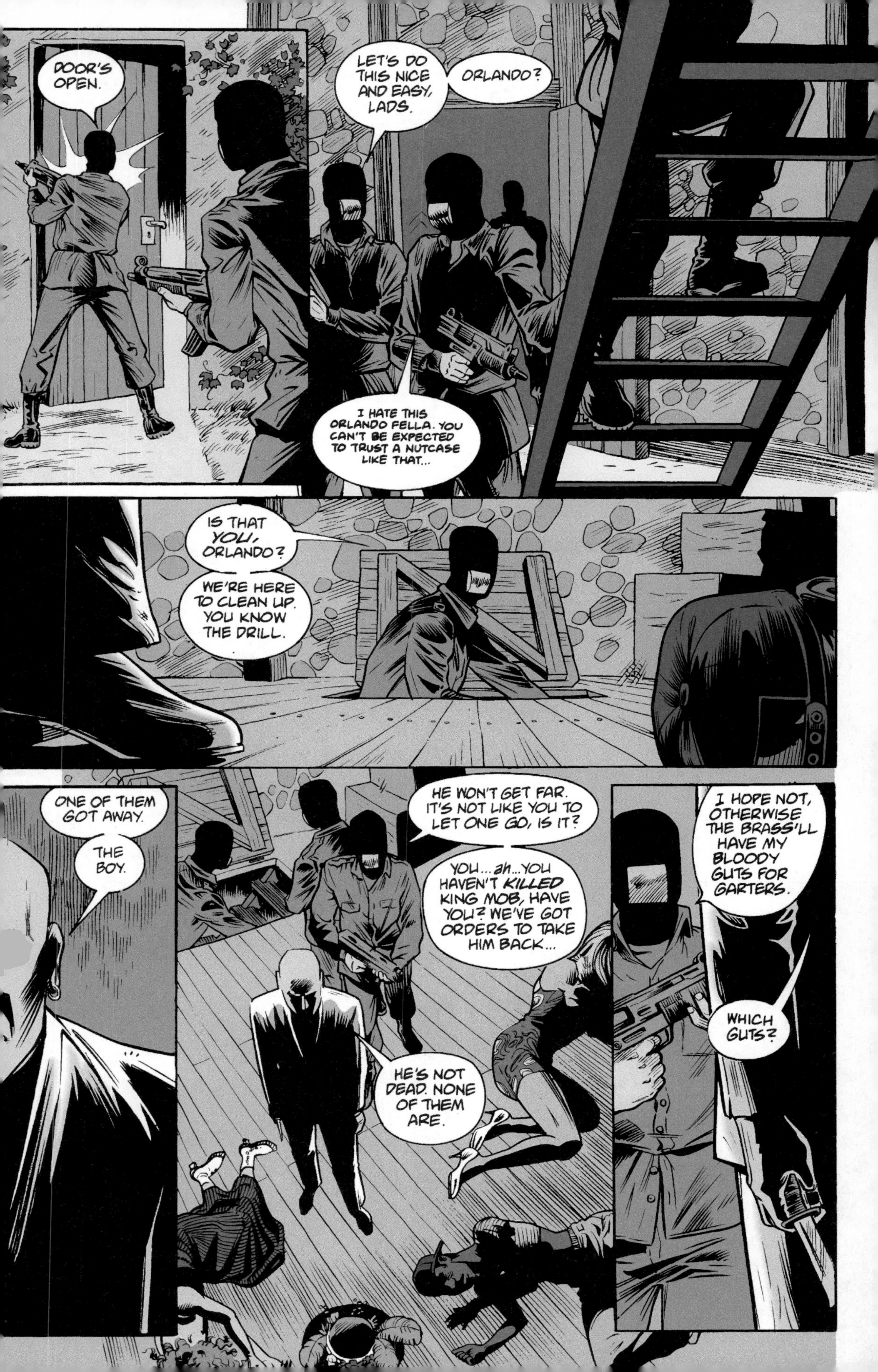
DOOR'S OPEN.
LET'S DO THIS NICE AND EASY, LADS.
ORLANDO?
I HATE THIS ORLANDO FELLA. YOU CAN'T BE EXPECTED TO TRUST A NUTCASE LIKE THAT...
IS THAT *YOU*, ORLANDO?
WE'RE HERE TO CLEAN UP. YOU KNOW THE DRILL.
ONE OF THEM GOT AWAY.
THE BOY.
HE WON'T GET FAR. IT'S NOT LIKE YOU TO LET ONE GO, IS IT?
YOU... *ah*... YOU HAVEN'T ***KILLED*** KING MOB, HAVE YOU? WE'VE GOT ORDERS TO TAKE HIM BACK...
HE'S NOT DEAD. NONE OF THEM ARE.
I HOPE NOT, OTHERWISE THE BRASS'LL HAVE MY BLOODY GUTS FOR GARTERS.
WHICH GUTS?

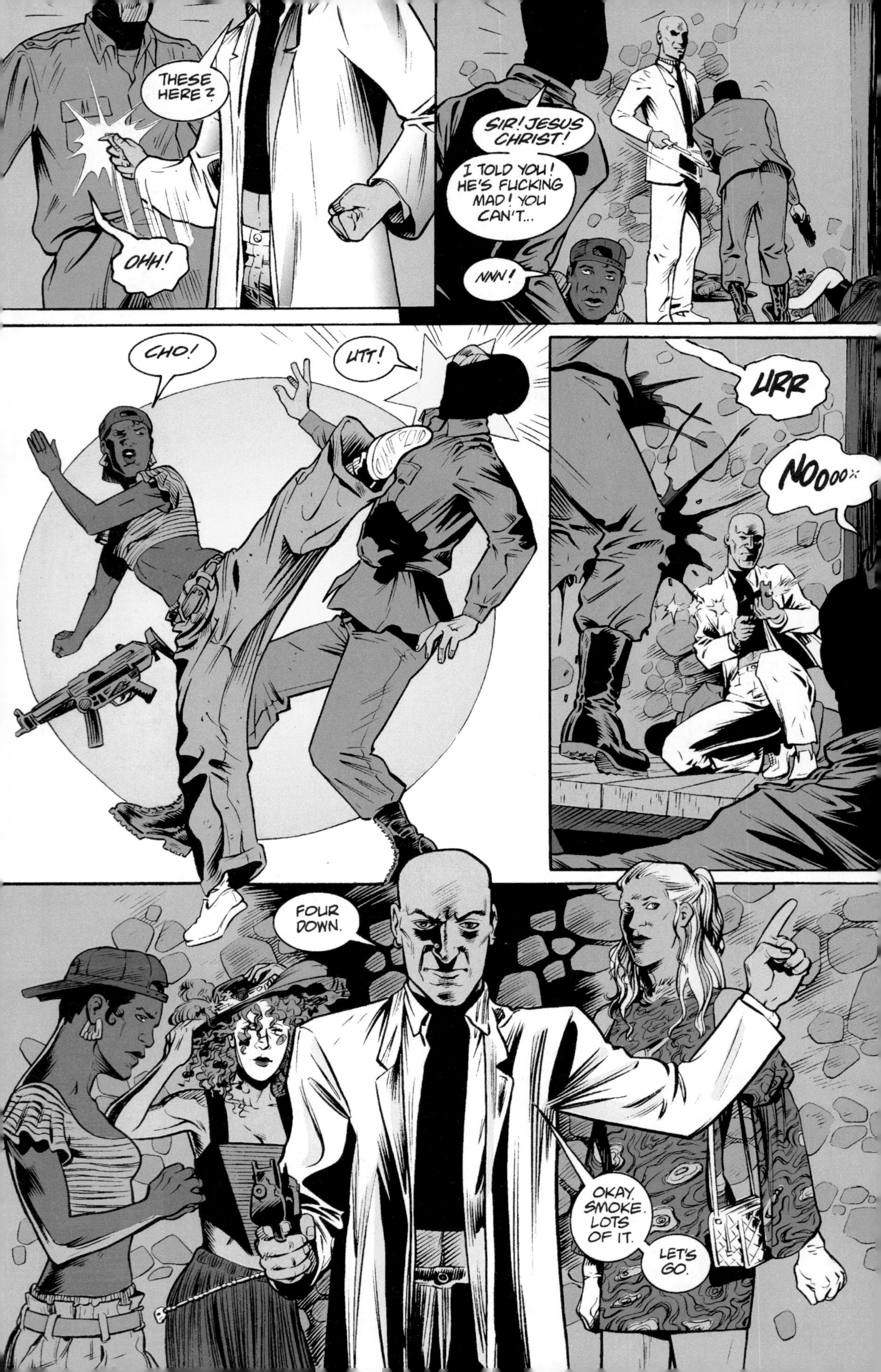
THESE HERE?
OHH!
SIR! JESUS CHRIST!
I TOLD YOU! HE'S FUCKING MAD! YOU CAN'T...
NNN!
CHO!
UTT!
URR
NOOOO
FOUR DOWN.
OKAY. SMOKE. LOTS OF IT.
LET'S GO.

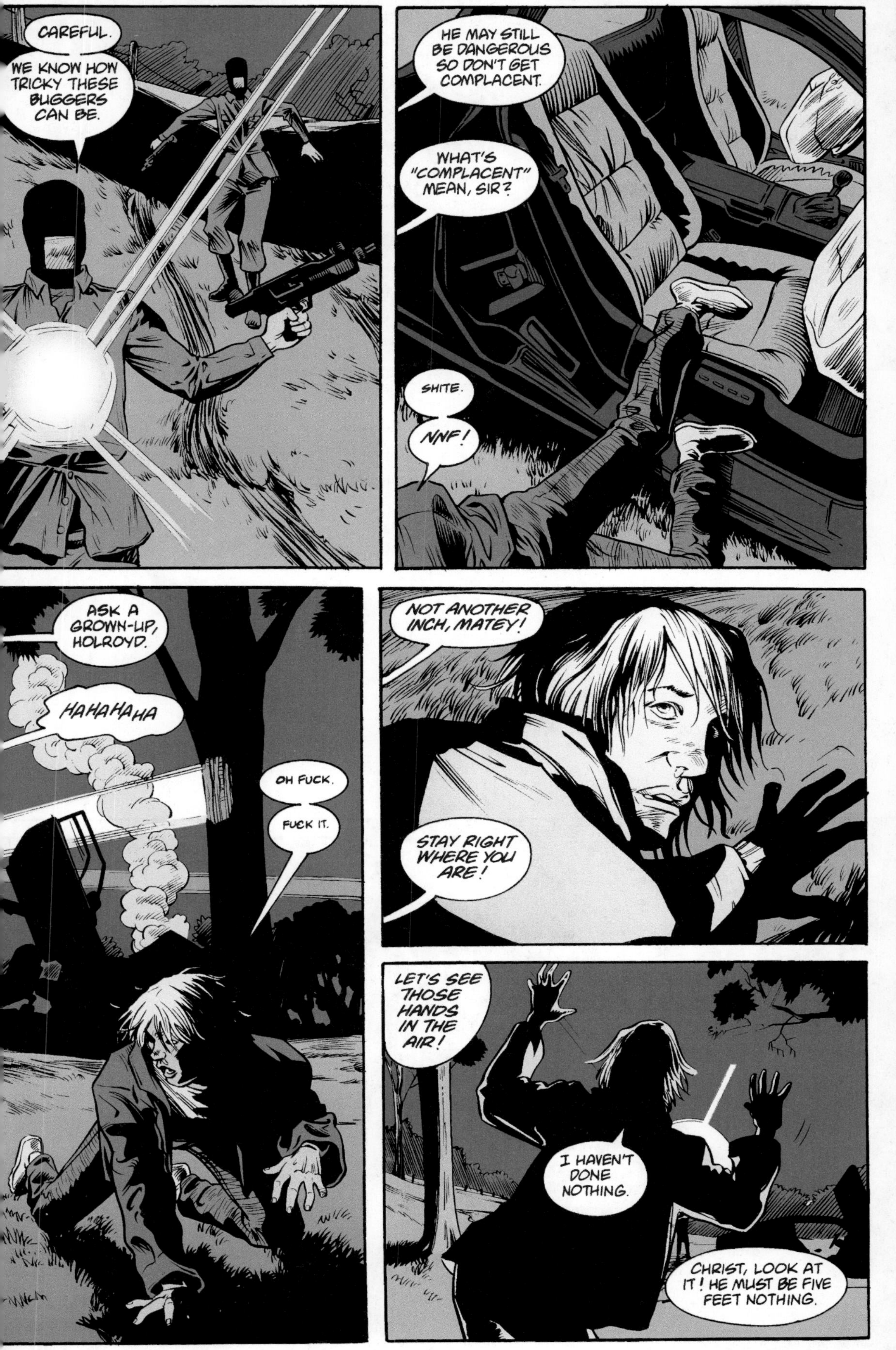
CAREFUL.
WE KNOW HOW TRICKY THESE BUGGERS CAN BE.
HE MAY STILL BE DANGEROUS SO DON'T GET COMPLACENT.
WHAT'S "COMPLACENT" MEAN, SIR?
SHITE.
NNF!
ASK A GROWN-UP, HOLROYD.
HAHAHAHAHA
OH FUCK.
FUCK IT.
NOT ANOTHER INCH, MATEY!
STAY RIGHT WHERE YOU ARE!
LET'S SEE THOSE HANDS IN THE AIR!
I HAVEN'T DONE NOTHING.
CHRIST, LOOK AT IT! HE MUST BE FIVE FEET NOTHING.

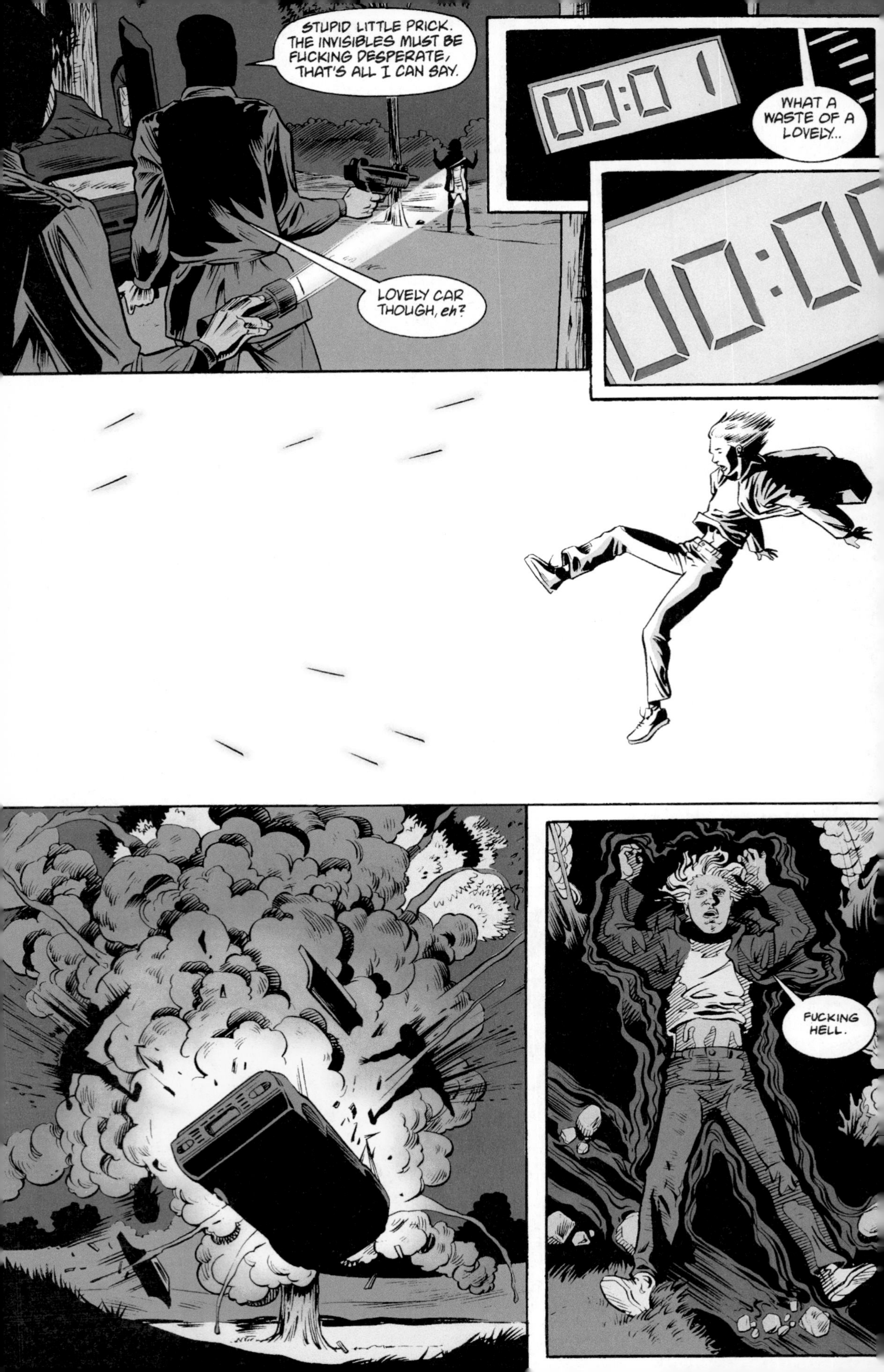
STUPID LITTLE PRICK. THE INVISIBLES MUST BE FUCKING DESPERATE, THAT'S ALL I CAN SAY.
LOVELY CAR THOUGH, *eh?*
00:01
WHAT A WASTE OF A LOVELY...
00:00
FUCKING HELL.

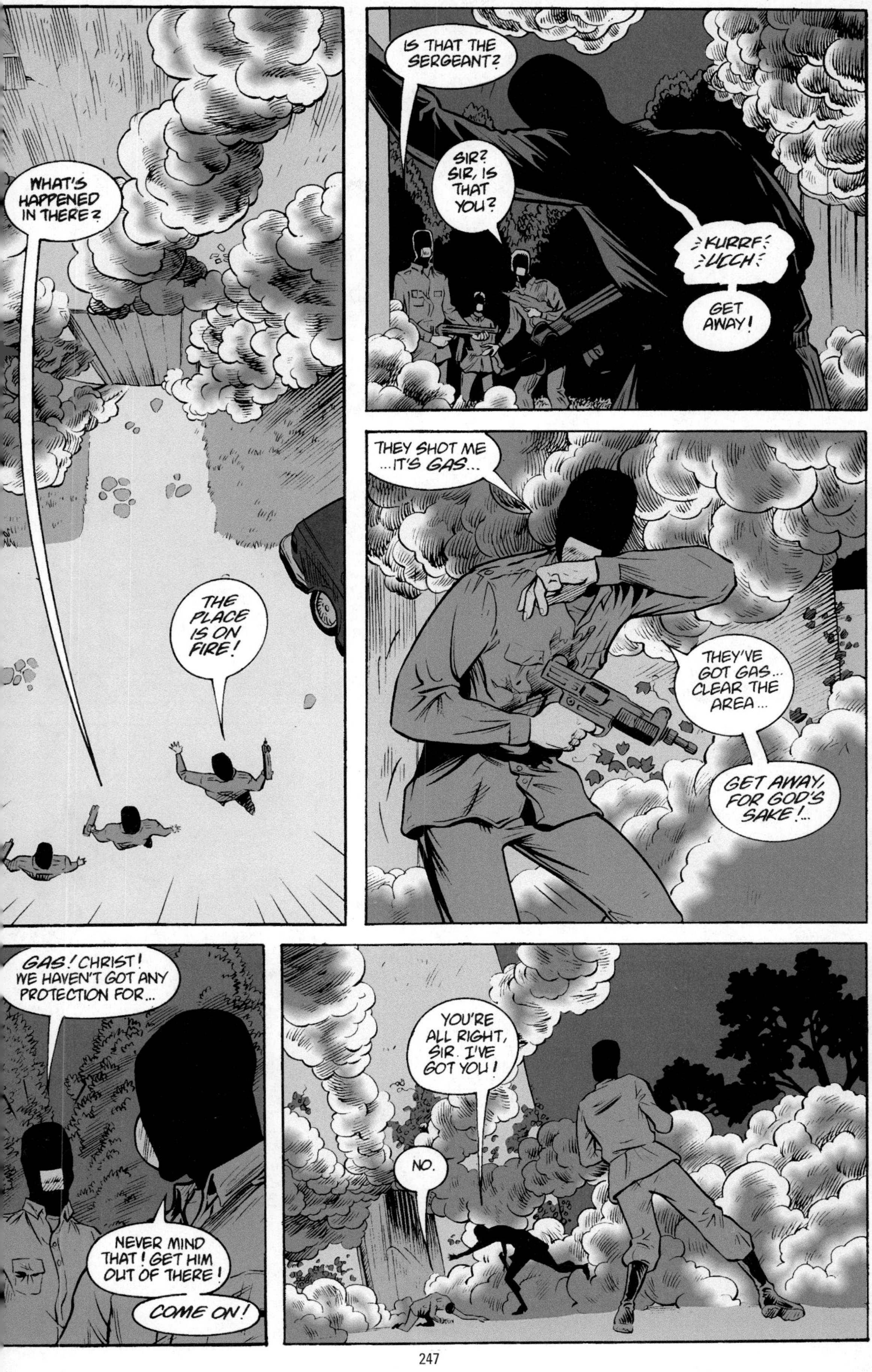
IS THAT THE SERGEANT?
SIR? SIR, IS THAT YOU?
KURRF UCCH
GET AWAY!
WHAT'S HAPPENED IN THERE?
THE PLACE IS ON FIRE!
THEY SHOT ME ...IT'S GAS...
THEY'VE GOT GAS... CLEAR THE AREA...
GET AWAY, FOR GOD'S SAKE!...
GAS! CHRIST! WE HAVEN'T GOT ANY PROTECTION FOR...
NEVER MIND THAT! GET HIM OUT OF THERE!
COME ON!
YOU'RE ALL RIGHT, SIR. I'VE GOT YOU!
NO.

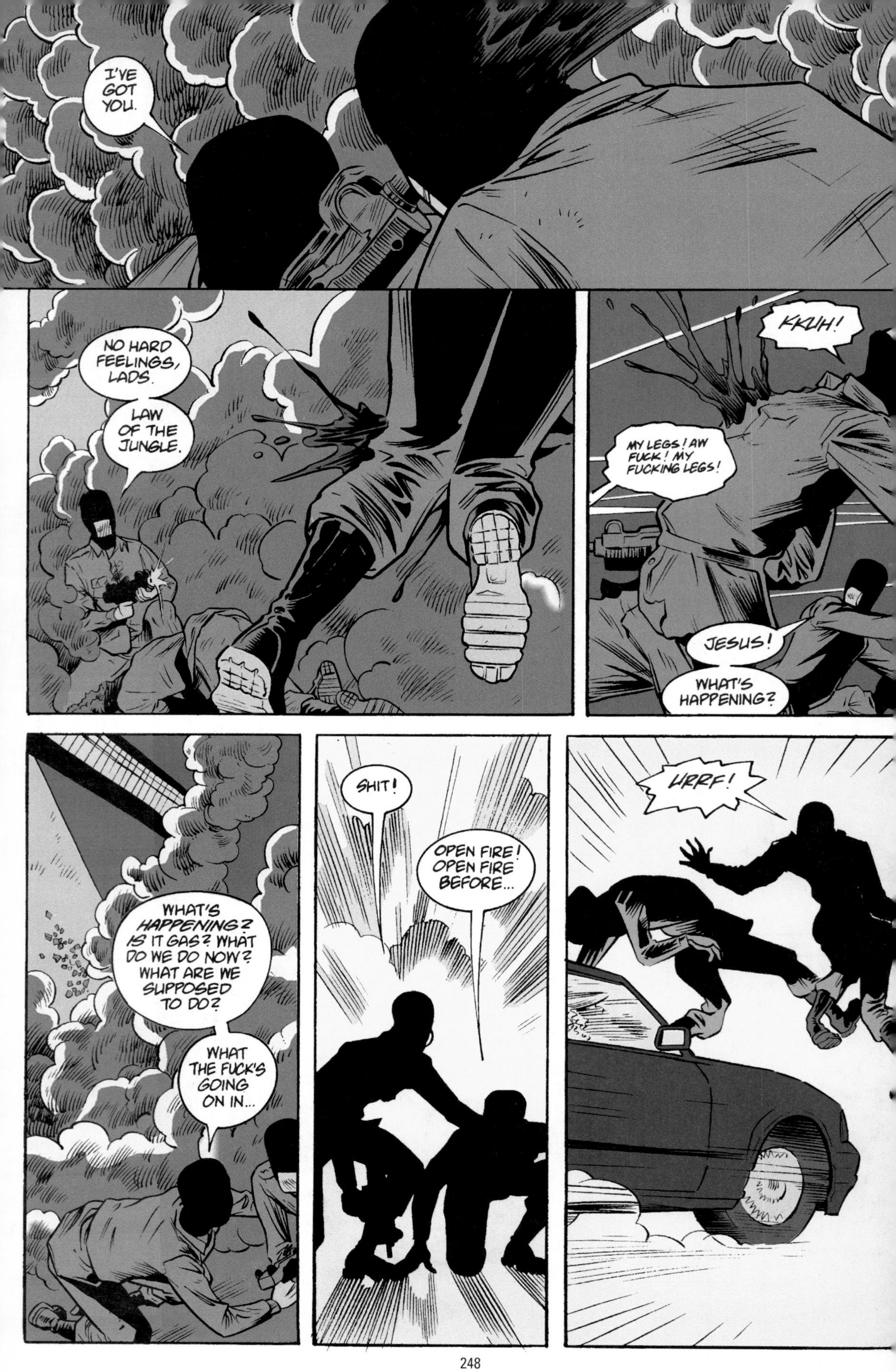
I'VE GOT YOU.
NO HARD FEELINGS, LADS.
LAW OF THE JUNGLE.
KKUH!
MY LEGS! AW FUCK! MY FUCKING LEGS!
JESUS!
WHAT'S HAPPENING?
WHAT'S HAPPENING? IS IT GAS? WHAT DO WE DO NOW? WHAT ARE WE SUPPOSED TO DO?
WHAT THE FUCK'S GOING ON IN...
SHIT!
OPEN FIRE! OPEN FIRE BEFORE...
URRF!

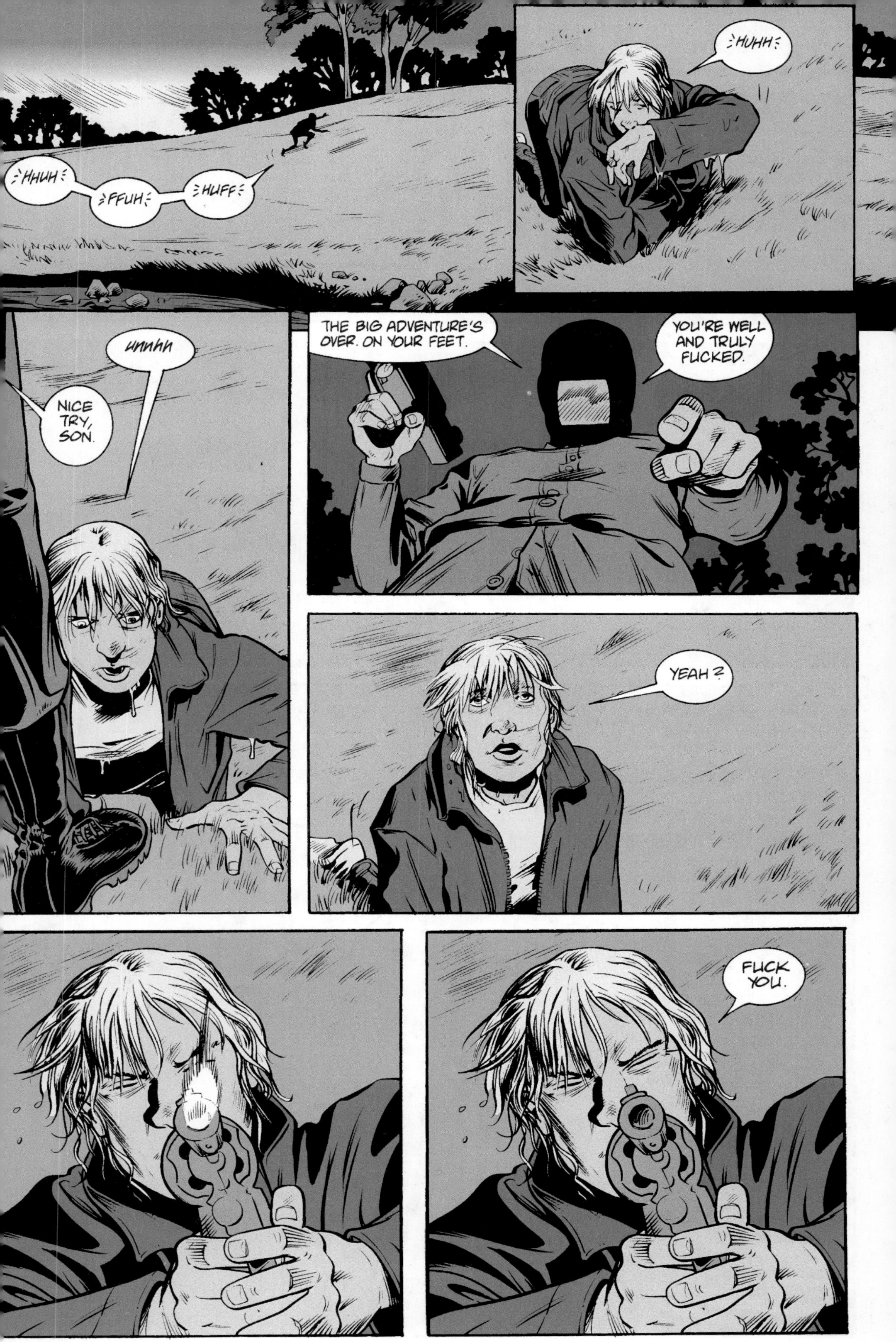
HHUH
FFUH
HUFF
HUHH
unnhh
NICE TRY, SON.
THE BIG ADVENTURE'S OVER. ON YOUR FEET.
YOU'RE WELL AND TRULY FUCKED.
YEAH?
FUCK YOU.

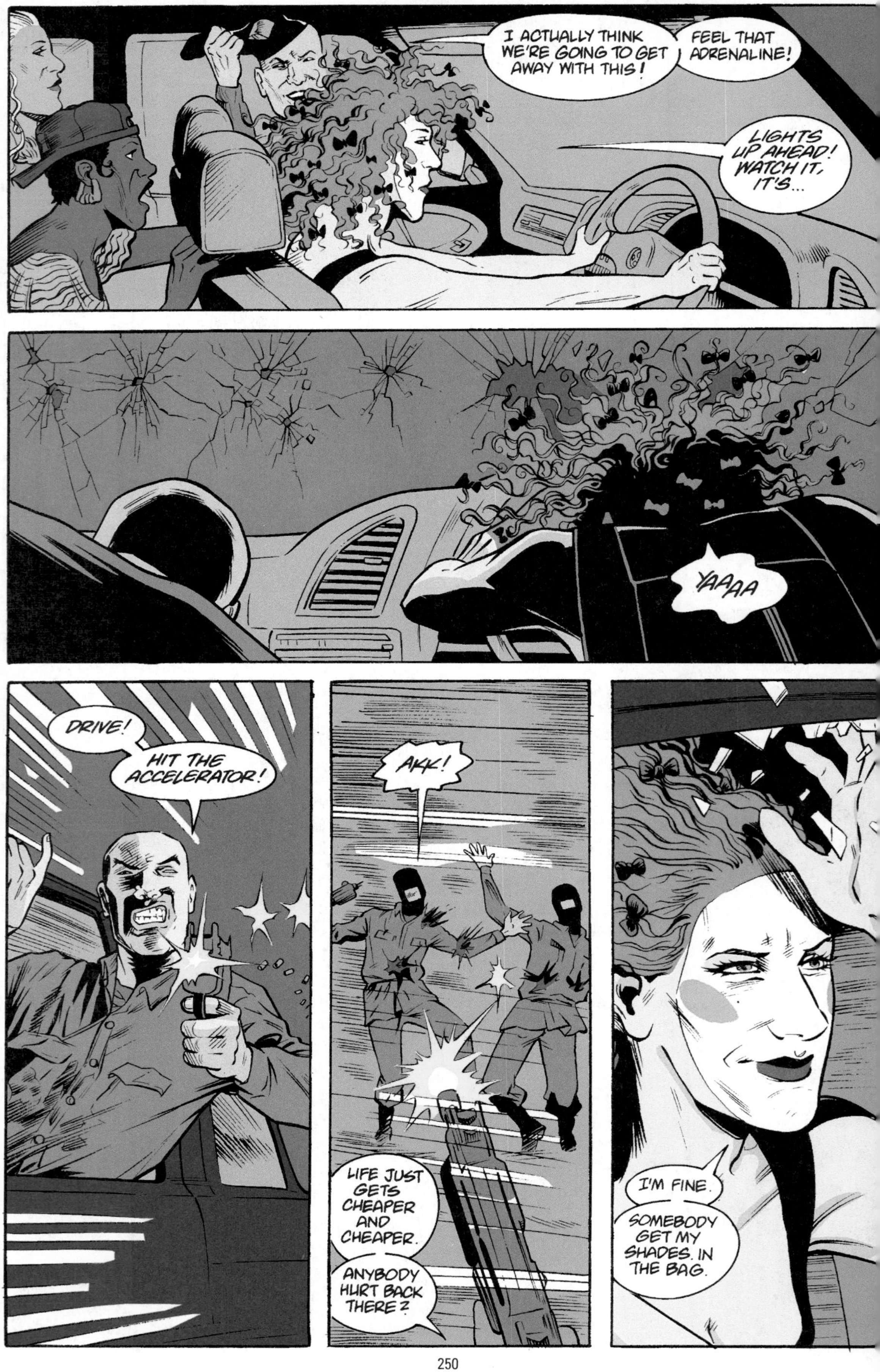
I ACTUALLY THINK WE'RE GOING TO GET AWAY WITH THIS!
FEEL THAT ADRENALINE!
LIGHTS UP AHEAD! WATCH IT, IT'S...
YAAAA
DRIVE!
HIT THE ACCELERATOR!
AKK!
LIFE JUST GETS CHEAPER AND CHEAPER.
ANYBODY HURT BACK THERE?
I'M FINE.
SOMEBODY GET MY SHADES. IN THE BAG.

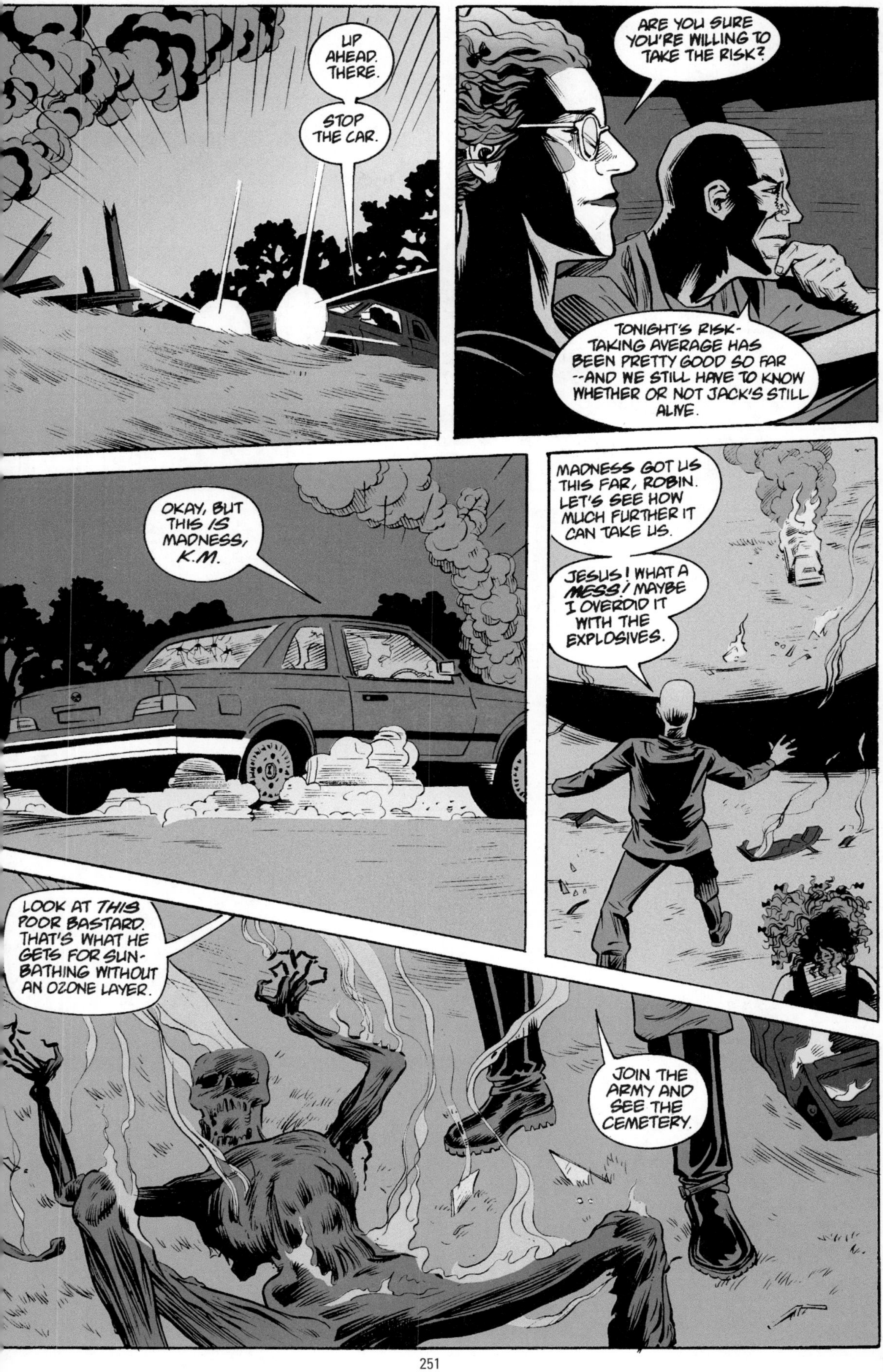
UP AHEAD. THERE.
STOP THE CAR.
ARE YOU SURE YOU'RE WILLING TO TAKE THE RISK?
TONIGHT'S RISK-TAKING AVERAGE HAS BEEN PRETTY GOOD SO FAR --AND WE STILL HAVE TO KNOW WHETHER OR NOT JACK'S STILL ALIVE.
OKAY, BUT THIS IS MADNESS, K.M.
MADNESS GOT US THIS FAR, ROBIN. LET'S SEE HOW MUCH FURTHER IT CAN TAKE US.
JESUS! WHAT A MESS! MAYBE I OVERDID IT WITH THE EXPLOSIVES.
LOOK AT THIS POOR BASTARD. THAT'S WHAT HE GETS FOR SUN-BATHING WITHOUT AN OZONE LAYER.
JOIN THE ARMY AND SEE THE CEMETERY.

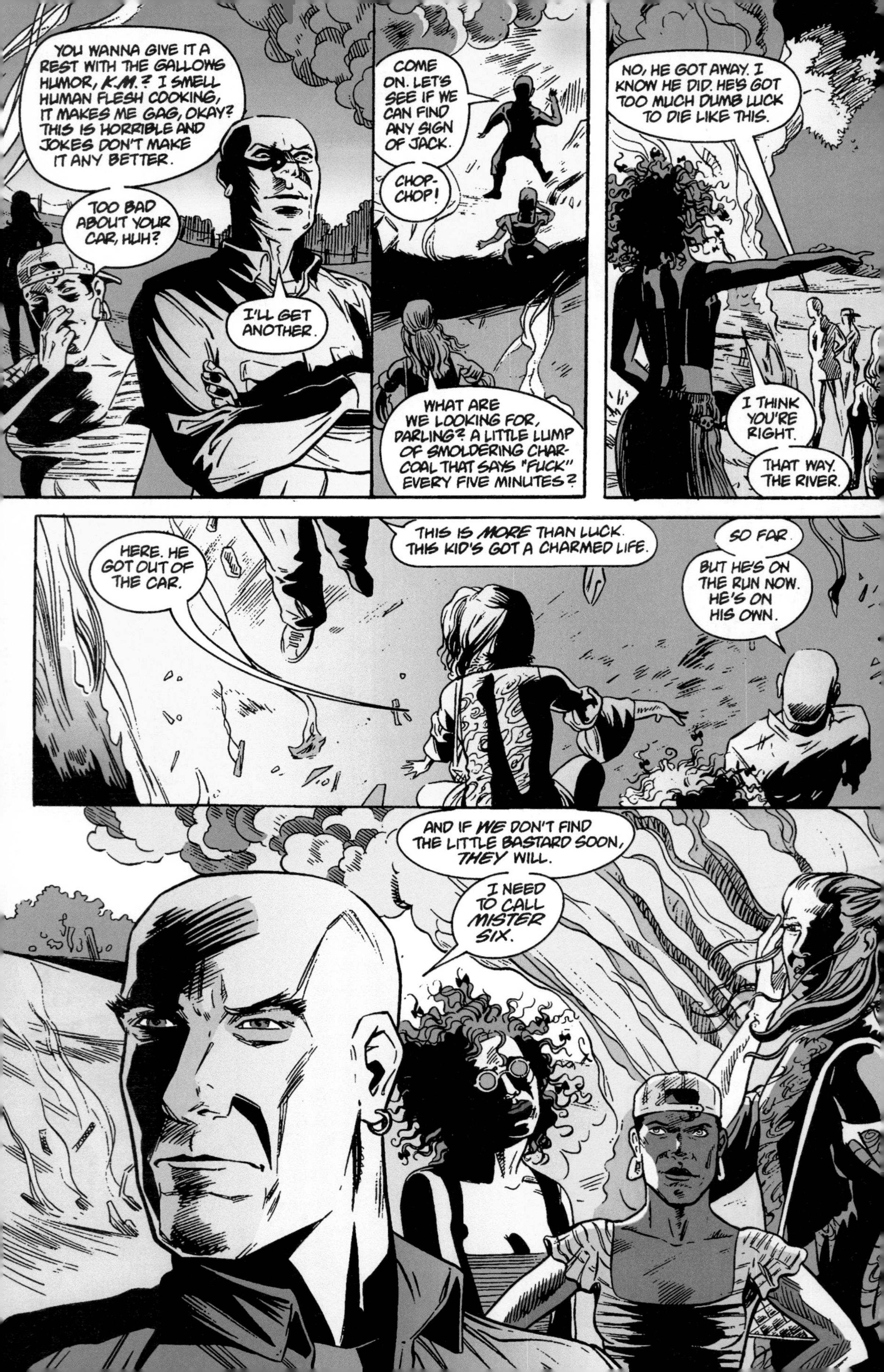
YOU WANNA GIVE IT A REST WITH THE GALLOWS HUMOR, K.M.? I SMELL HUMAN FLESH COOKING, IT MAKES ME GAG, OKAY? THIS IS HORRIBLE AND JOKES DON'T MAKE IT ANY BETTER.
TOO BAD ABOUT YOUR CAR, HUH?
I'LL GET ANOTHER.
COME ON. LET'S SEE IF WE CAN FIND ANY SIGN OF JACK.
CHOP-CHOP!
WHAT ARE WE LOOKING FOR, DARLING? A LITTLE LUMP OF SMOLDERING CHAR-COAL THAT SAYS "FUCK" EVERY FIVE MINUTES?
NO, HE GOT AWAY. I KNOW HE DID. HE'S GOT TOO MUCH DUMB LUCK TO DIE LIKE THIS.
I THINK YOU'RE RIGHT.
THAT WAY. THE RIVER.
HERE. HE GOT OUT OF THE CAR.
THIS IS MORE THAN LUCK. THIS KID'S GOT A CHARMED LIFE.
SO FAR.
BUT HE'S ON THE RUN NOW. HE'S ON HIS OWN.
AND IF WE DON'T FIND THE LITTLE BASTARD SOON, THEY WILL.
I NEED TO CALL MISTER SIX.

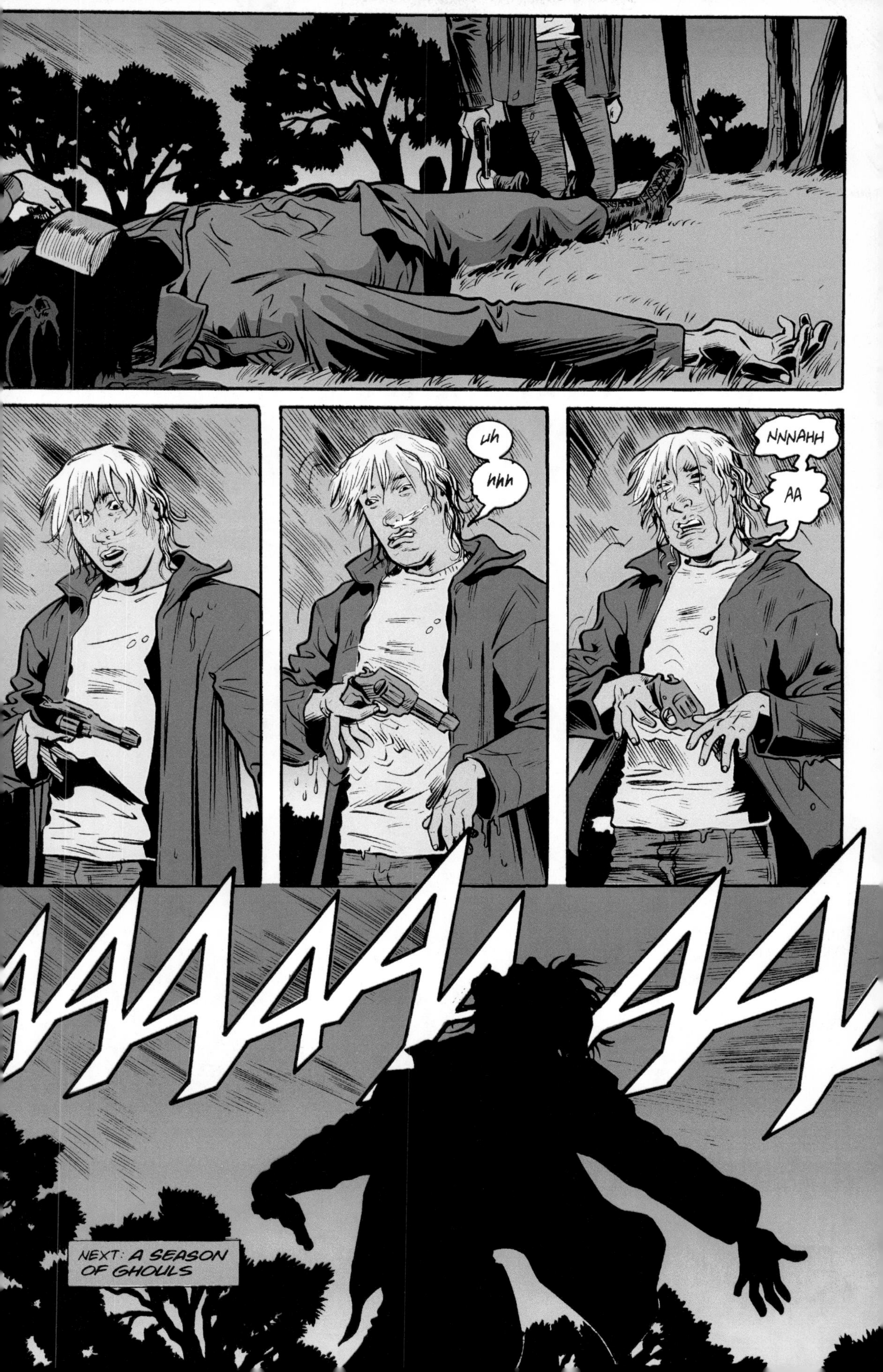
uh
hhh
NNNAHH
AA
AAAAAAAAAA
NEXT: A SEASON OF GHOULS

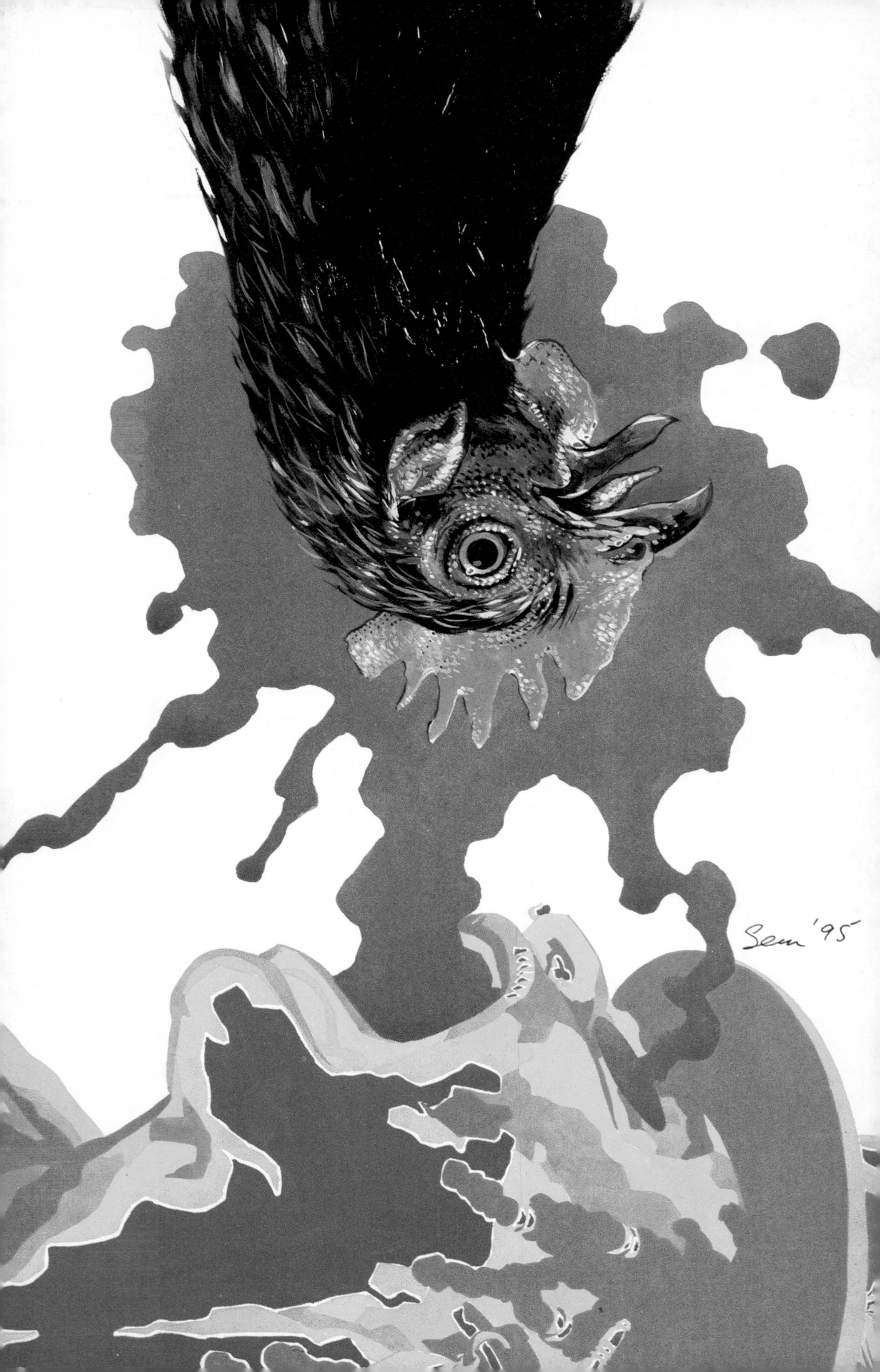
Sem '95

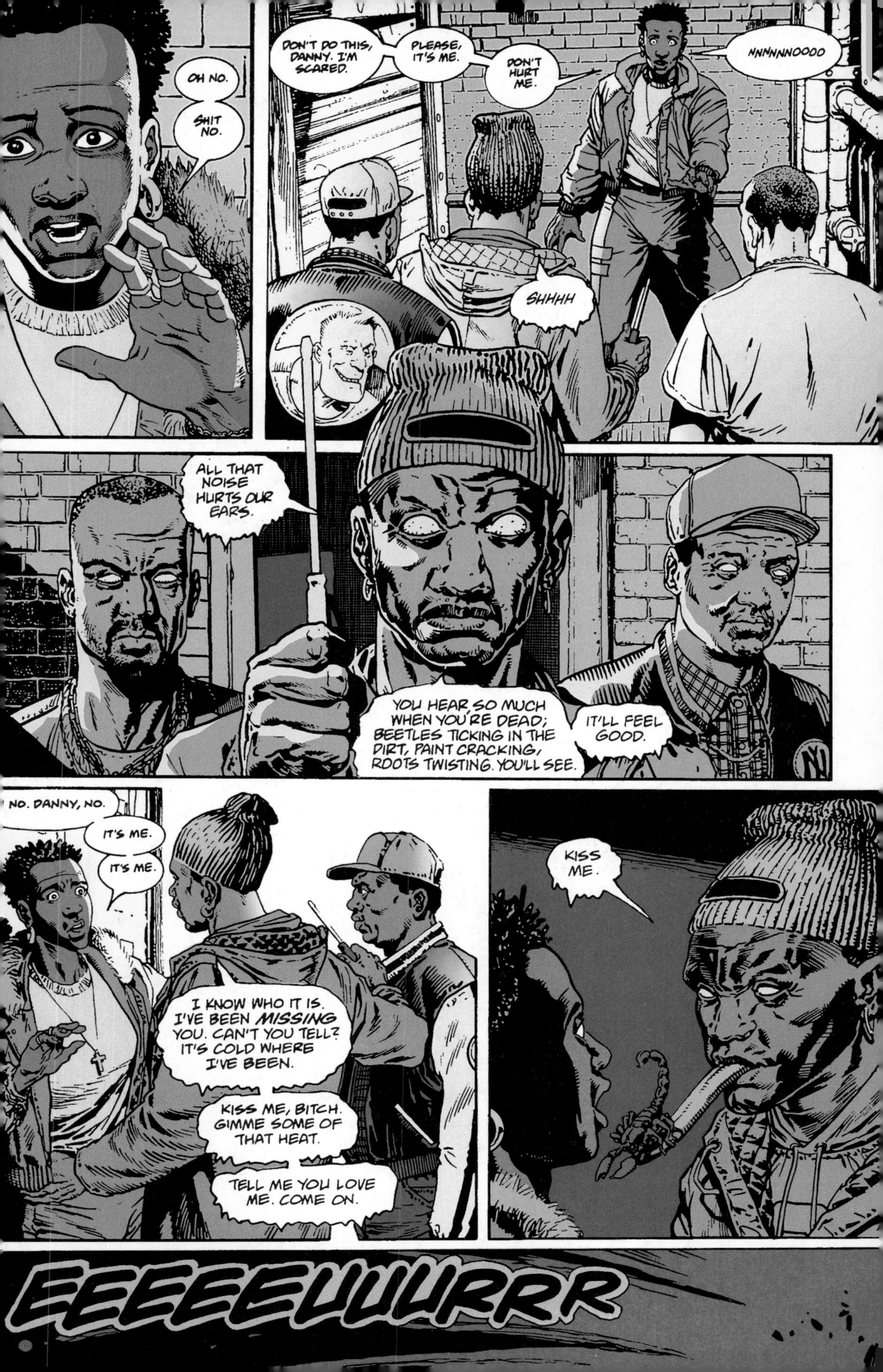
OH NO.
SHIT NO.
DON'T DO THIS, DANNY. I'M SCARED.
PLEASE, IT'S ME.
DON'T HURT ME.
NNNNNNOOOO
SHHHH
ALL THAT NOISE HURTS OUR EARS.
YOU HEAR SO MUCH WHEN YOU'RE DEAD; BEETLES TICKING IN THE DIRT, PAINT CRACKING, ROOTS TWISTING. YOU'LL SEE.
IT'LL FEEL GOOD.
NO. DANNY, NO.
IT'S ME.
IT'S ME.
I KNOW WHO IT IS. I'VE BEEN *MISSING* YOU. CAN'T YOU TELL? IT'S COLD WHERE I'VE BEEN.
KISS ME, BITCH. GIMME SOME OF THAT HEAT.
TELL ME YOU LOVE ME. COME ON.
KISS ME.
EEEEEUUURRR

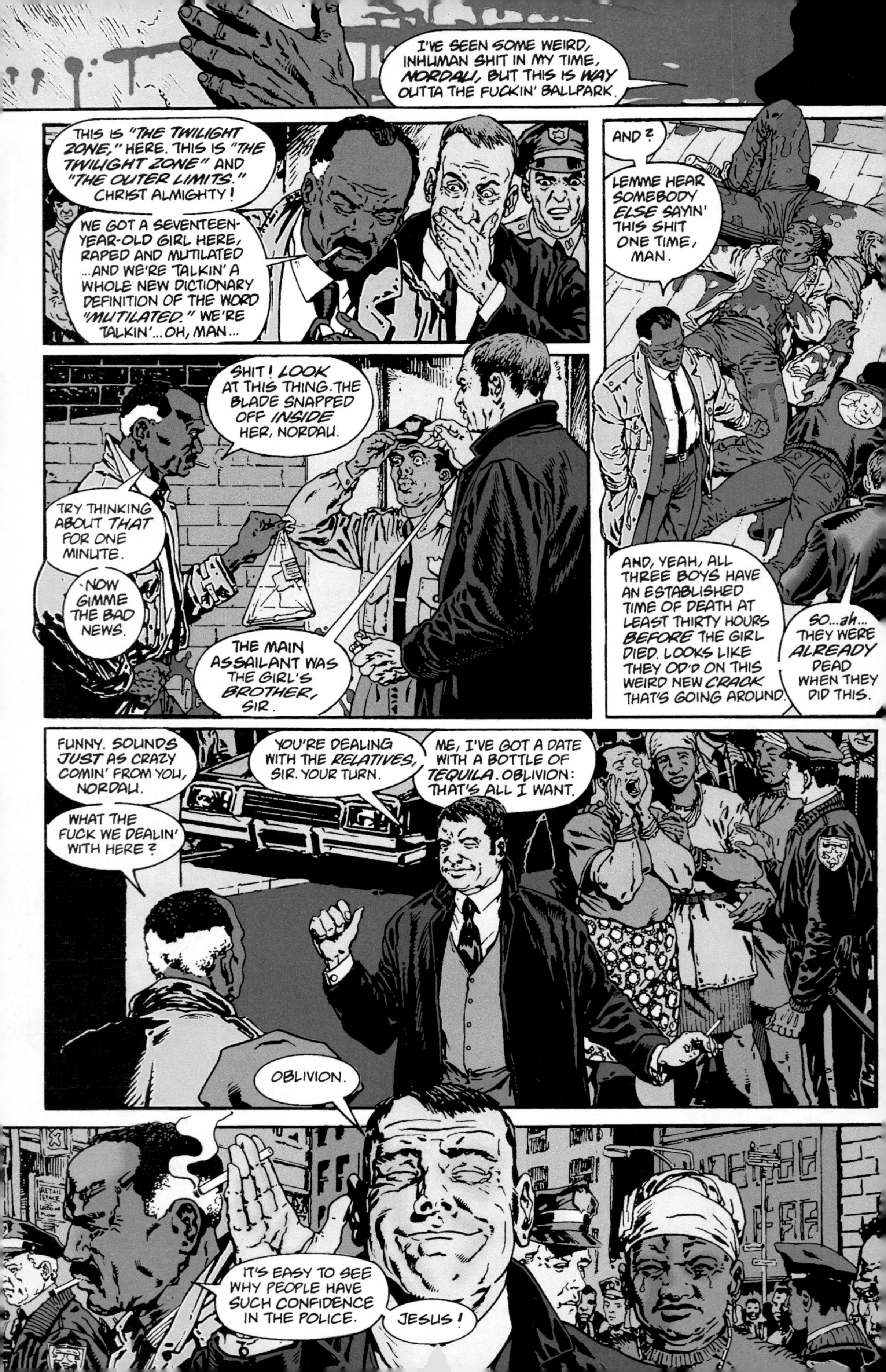
I'VE SEEN SOME WEIRD, INHUMAN SHIT IN MY TIME, NORDAU, BUT THIS IS WAY OUTTA THE FUCKIN' BALLPARK.
THIS IS "THE TWILIGHT ZONE," HERE. THIS IS "THE TWILIGHT ZONE" AND "THE OUTER LIMITS." CHRIST ALMIGHTY!
WE GOT A SEVENTEEN-YEAR-OLD GIRL HERE, RAPED AND MUTILATED ...AND WE'RE TALKIN' A WHOLE NEW DICTIONARY DEFINITION OF THE WORD "MUTILATED." WE'RE TALKIN'...OH, MAN...
AND?
LEMME HEAR SOMEBODY ELSE SAYIN' THIS SHIT ONE TIME, MAN.
SHIT! LOOK AT THIS THING. THE BLADE SNAPPED OFF INSIDE HER, NORDAU.
TRY THINKING ABOUT THAT FOR ONE MINUTE.
NOW GIMME THE BAD NEWS.
THE MAIN ASSAILANT WAS THE GIRL'S BROTHER, SIR.
AND, YEAH, ALL THREE BOYS HAVE AN ESTABLISHED TIME OF DEATH AT LEAST THIRTY HOURS BEFORE THE GIRL DIED. LOOKS LIKE THEY OD'D ON THIS WEIRD NEW CRACK THAT'S GOING AROUND.
SO...ah... THEY WERE ALREADY DEAD WHEN THEY DID THIS.
FUNNY. SOUNDS JUST AS CRAZY COMIN' FROM YOU, NORDAU.
WHAT THE FUCK WE DEALIN' WITH HERE?
YOU'RE DEALING WITH THE RELATIVES, SIR. YOUR TURN.
ME, I'VE GOT A DATE WITH A BOTTLE OF TEQUILA. OBLIVION: THAT'S ALL I WANT.
OBLIVION.
IT'S EASY TO SEE WHY PEOPLE HAVE SUCH CONFIDENCE IN THE POLICE.
JESUS!

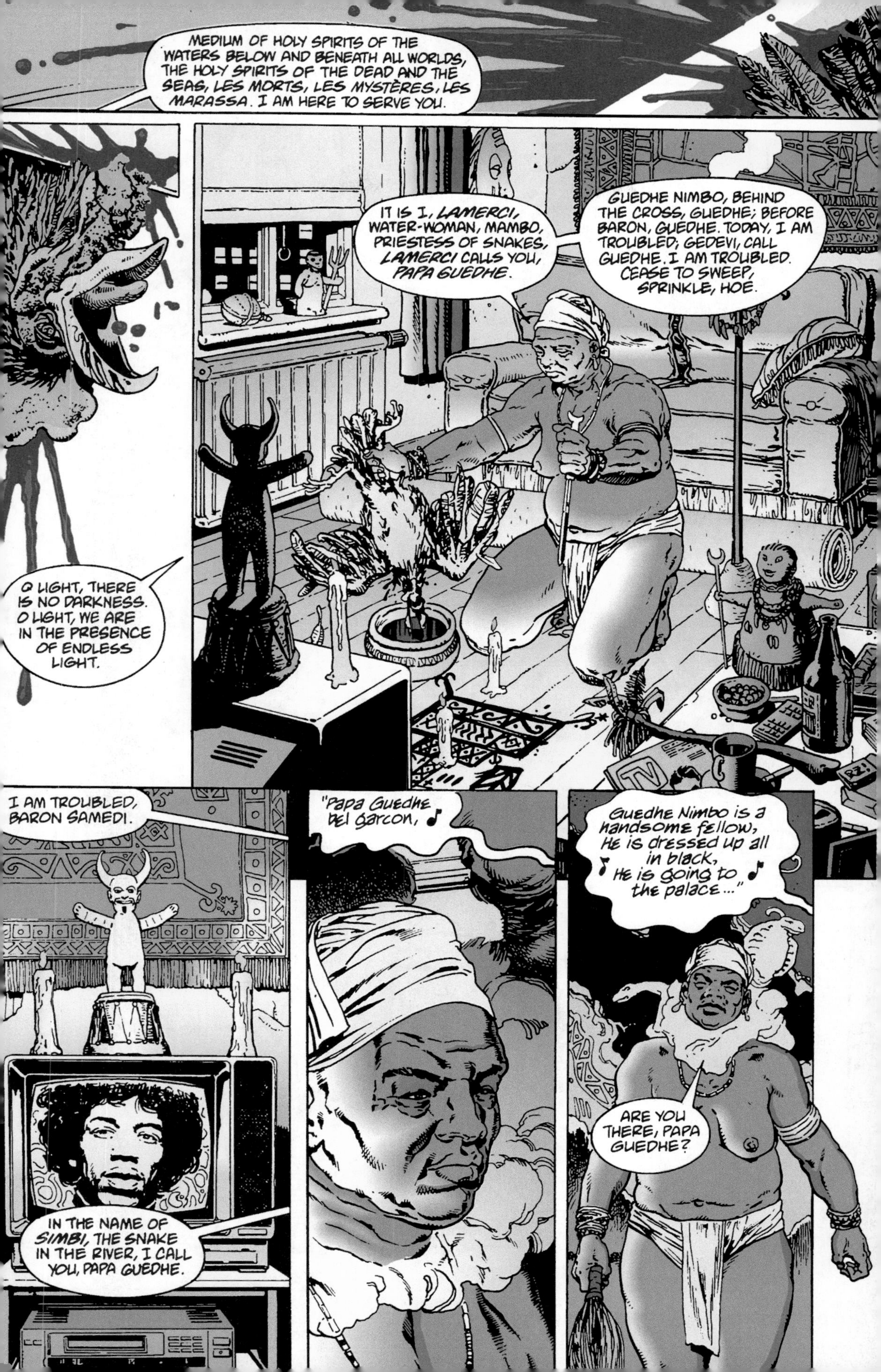
MEDIUM OF HOLY SPIRITS OF THE WATERS BELOW AND BENEATH ALL WORLDS, THE HOLY SPIRITS OF THE DEAD AND THE SEAS, LES MORTS, LES MYSTÈRES, LES MARASSA. I AM HERE TO SERVE YOU.
IT IS I, LAMERCI, WATER-WOMAN, MAMBO, PRIESTESS OF SNAKES, LAMERCI CALLS YOU, PAPA GUEDHE.
GUEDHE NIMBO, BEHIND THE CROSS, GUEDHE; BEFORE BARON, GUEDHE. TODAY, I AM TROUBLED; GEDEVI, CALL GUEDHE. I AM TROUBLED. CEASE TO SWEEP, SPRINKLE, HOE.
O LIGHT, THERE IS NO DARKNESS. O LIGHT, WE ARE IN THE PRESENCE OF ENDLESS LIGHT.
I AM TROUBLED, BARON SAMEDI.
IN THE NAME OF SIMBI, THE SNAKE IN THE RIVER, I CALL YOU, PAPA GUEDHE.
"Papa Guedhe bel garcon,
Guedhe Nimbo is a handsome fellow, He is dressed up all in black, He is going to the palace..."
ARE YOU THERE, PAPA GUEDHE?

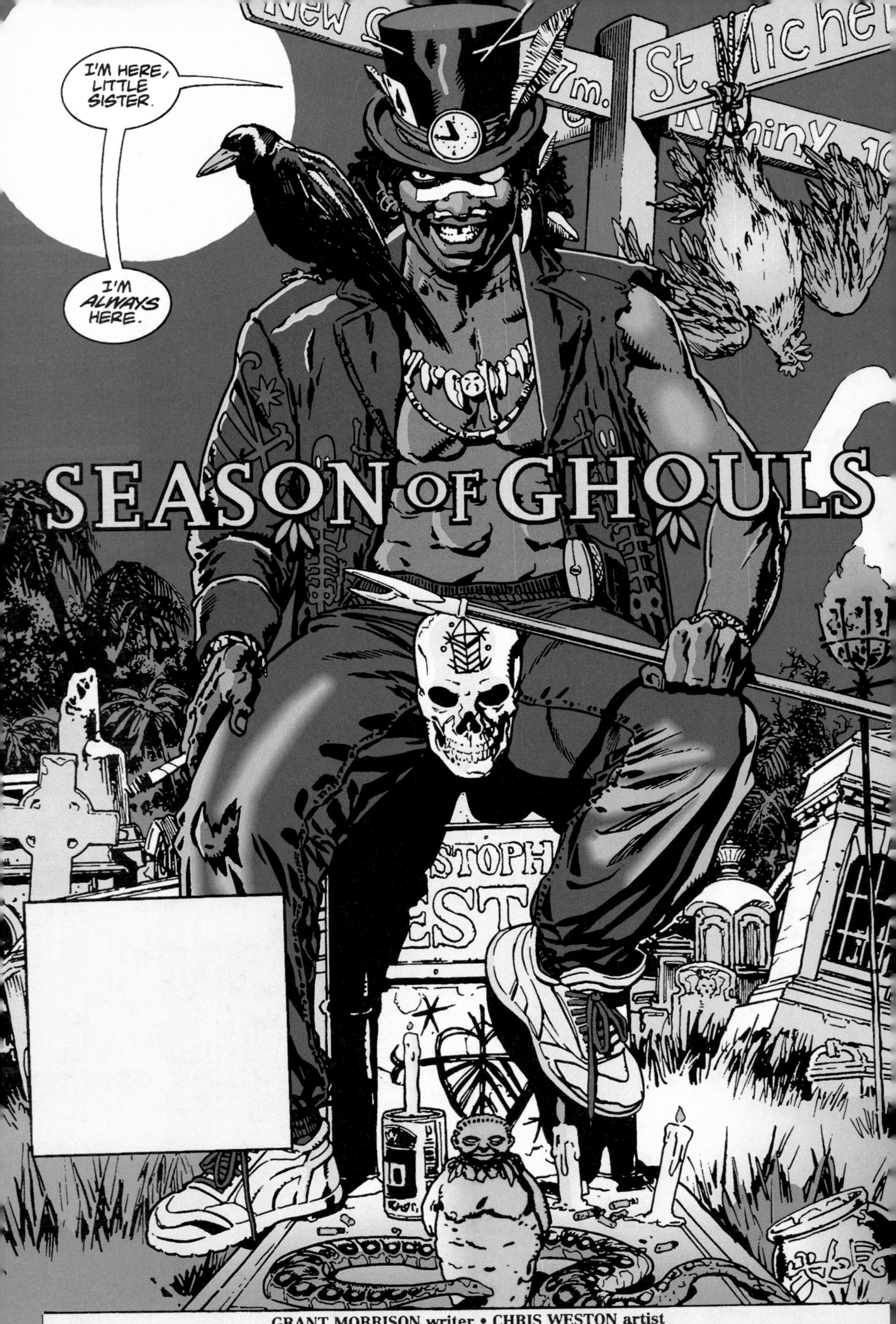
New
St. Michel
7m.
I'M HERE, LITTLE SISTER.
I'M *ALWAYS* HERE.
SEASON OF GHOULS
STOPH
EST

GRANT MORRISON writer • CHRIS WESTON artist
DANIEL VOZZO colorist • CLEM ROBINS letterer • JULIE ROTTENBERG associate editor • STUART MOORE editor
The Invisibles created by GRANT MORRISON

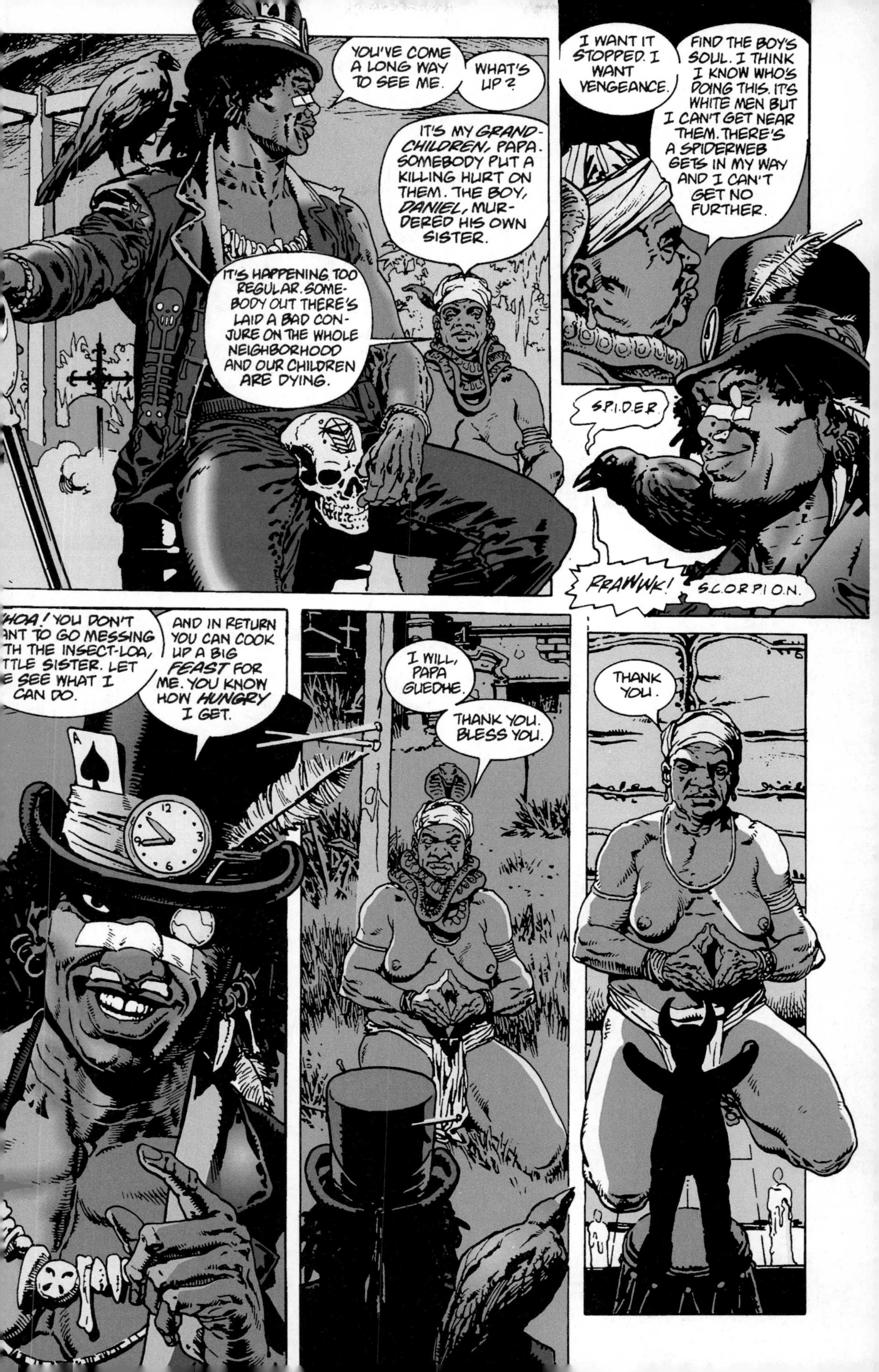
YOU'VE COME A LONG WAY TO SEE ME.
WHAT'S UP?
IT'S MY GRAND-CHILDREN, PAPA. SOMEBODY PUT A KILLING HURT ON THEM. THE BOY, DANIEL, MUR-DERED HIS OWN SISTER.
IT'S HAPPENING TOO REGULAR. SOME-BODY OUT THERE'S LAID A BAD CON-JURE ON THE WHOLE NEIGHBORHOOD AND OUR CHILDREN ARE DYING.
I WANT IT STOPPED. I WANT VENGEANCE.
FIND THE BOY'S SOUL. I THINK I KNOW WHO'S DOING THIS. IT'S WHITE MEN BUT I CAN'T GET NEAR THEM. THERE'S A SPIDERWEB GETS IN MY WAY AND I CAN'T GET NO FURTHER.
S.P.I.D.E.R.
RRAWWK!
S.C.O.R.P.I.O.N.
HOA! YOU DON'T ANT TO GO MESSING TH THE INSECT-LOA, TTLE SISTER. LET E SEE WHAT I CAN DO.
AND IN RETURN YOU CAN COOK UP A BIG FEAST FOR ME. YOU KNOW HOW HUNGRY I GET.
I WILL, PAPA GUEDHE.
THANK YOU. BLESS YOU.
THANK YOU.

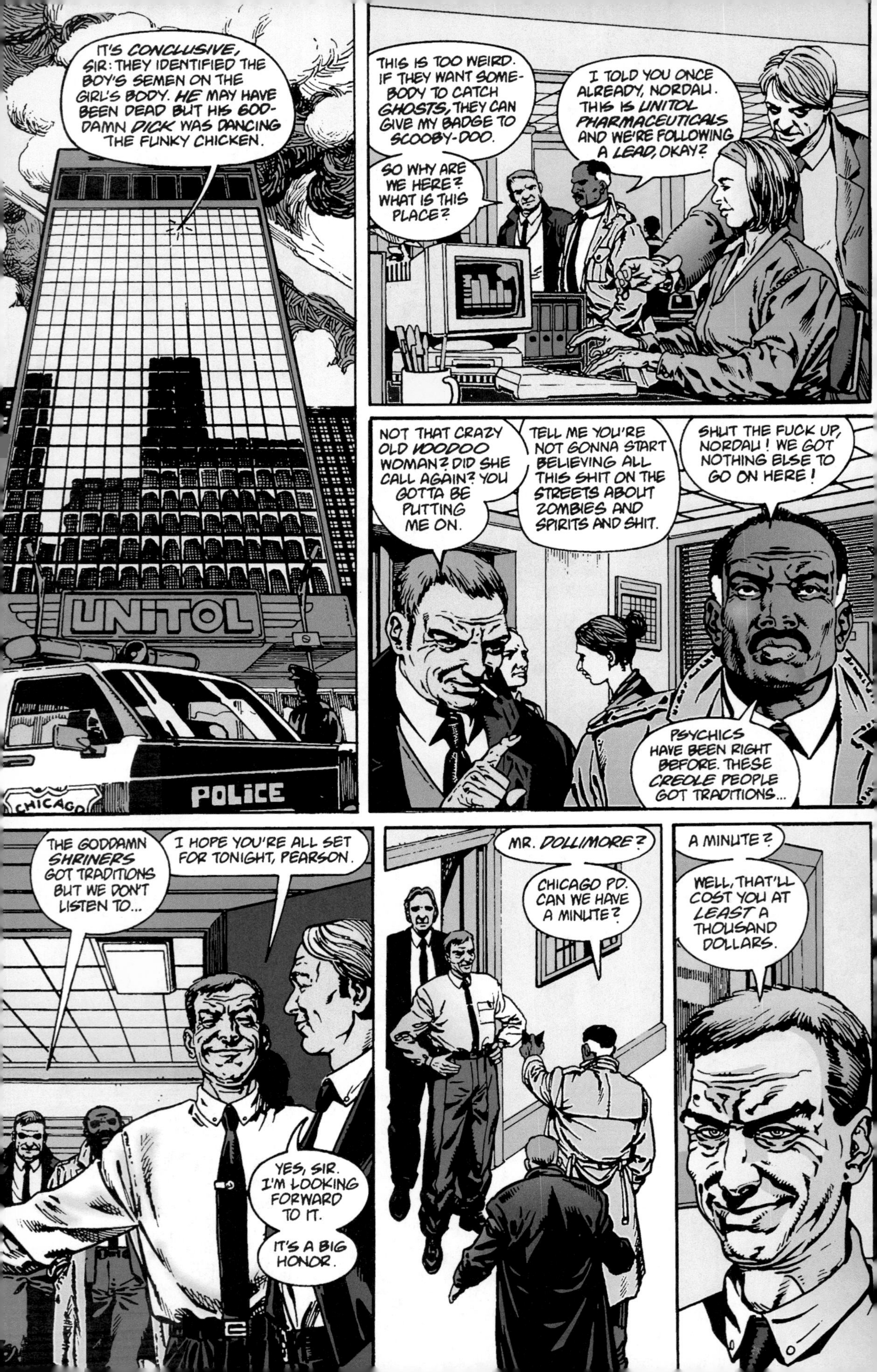
IT'S CONCLUSIVE, SIR: THEY IDENTIFIED THE BOY'S SEMEN ON THE GIRL'S BODY. HE MAY HAVE BEEN DEAD BUT HIS GOD-DAMN DICK WAS DANCING THE FUNKY CHICKEN.
UNITOL
POLICE
CHICAGO
THIS IS TOO WEIRD. IF THEY WANT SOME-BODY TO CATCH GHOSTS, THEY CAN GIVE MY BADGE TO SCOOBY-DOO.
SO WHY ARE WE HERE? WHAT IS THIS PLACE?
I TOLD YOU ONCE ALREADY, NORDAU. THIS IS UNITOL PHARMACEUTICALS AND WE'RE FOLLOWING A LEAD, OKAY?
NOT THAT CRAZY OLD VOODOO WOMAN? DID SHE CALL AGAIN? YOU GOTTA BE PUTTING ME ON.
TELL ME YOU'RE NOT GONNA START BELIEVING ALL THIS SHIT ON THE STREETS ABOUT ZOMBIES AND SPIRITS AND SHIT.
SHUT THE FUCK UP, NORDAU! WE GOT NOTHING ELSE TO GO ON HERE!
PSYCHICS HAVE BEEN RIGHT BEFORE. THESE CREOLE PEOPLE GOT TRADITIONS...
THE GODDAMN SHRINERS GOT TRADITIONS BUT WE DON'T LISTEN TO...
I HOPE YOU'RE ALL SET FOR TONIGHT, PEARSON.
YES, SIR. I'M LOOKING FORWARD TO IT.
IT'S A BIG HONOR.
MR. DOLLIMORE?
CHICAGO PD. CAN WE HAVE A MINUTE?
A MINUTE?
WELL, THAT'LL COST YOU AT LEAST A THOUSAND DOLLARS.

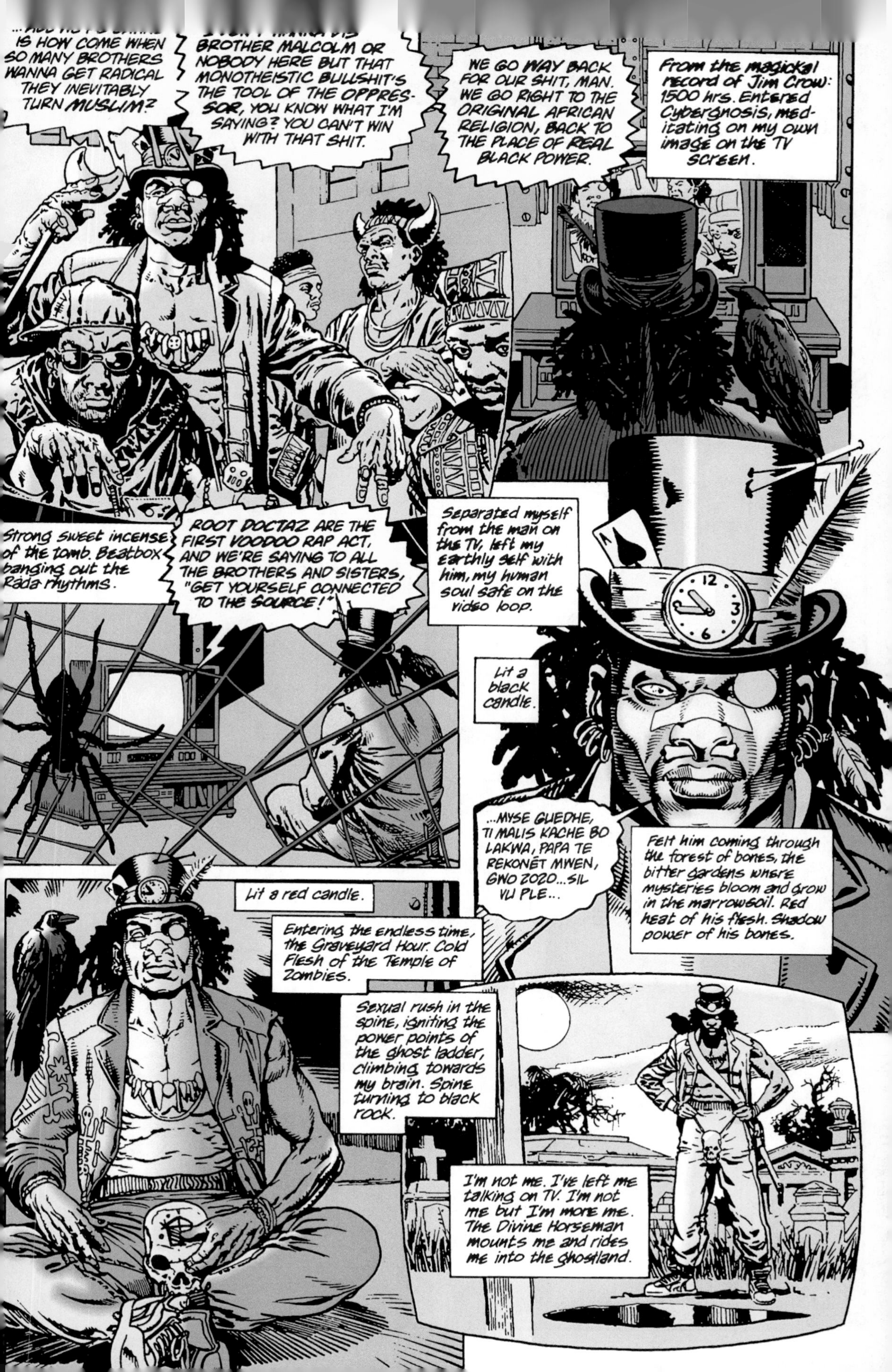
IS HOW COME WHEN SO MANY BROTHERS WANNA GET RADICAL THEY INEVITABLY TURN MUSLIM?
BROTHER MALCOLM OR NOBODY HERE BUT THAT MONOTHEISTIC BULLSHIT'S THE TOOL OF THE OPPRESSOR, YOU KNOW WHAT I'M SAYING? YOU CAN'T WIN WITH THAT SHIT.
WE GO WAY BACK FOR OUR SHIT, MAN. WE GO RIGHT TO THE ORIGINAL AFRICAN RELIGION, BACK TO THE PLACE OF REAL BLACK POWER.
From the magickal record of Jim Crow: 1500 hrs. Entered Cybergnosis, meditating on my own image on the TV screen.
Strong sweet incense of the tomb. Beatbox banging out the Rada rhythms.
ROOT DOCTAZ ARE THE FIRST VOODOO RAP ACT, AND WE'RE SAYING TO ALL THE BROTHERS AND SISTERS, "GET YOURSELF CONNECTED TO THE SOURCE!"
Separated myself from the man on the TV, left my earthly self with him, my human soul safe on the video loop.
Lit a black candle.
...MYSE GUEDHE, TI MALIS KACHE BO LAKWA, PAPA TE REKONÉT MWEN, GWO ZOZO... SIL VU PLE...
Felt him coming through the forest of bones, the bitter gardens where mysteries bloom and grow in the marrowsoil. Red heat of his flesh. Shadow power of his bones.
Lit a red candle.
Entering the endless time, the Graveyard Hour. Cold Flesh of the Temple of Zombies.
Sexual rush in the spine, igniting the power points of the ghost ladder, climbing towards my brain. Spine turning to black rock.
I'm not me. I've left me talking on TV. I'm not me but I'm more me. The Divine Horseman mounts me and rides me into the ghostland.

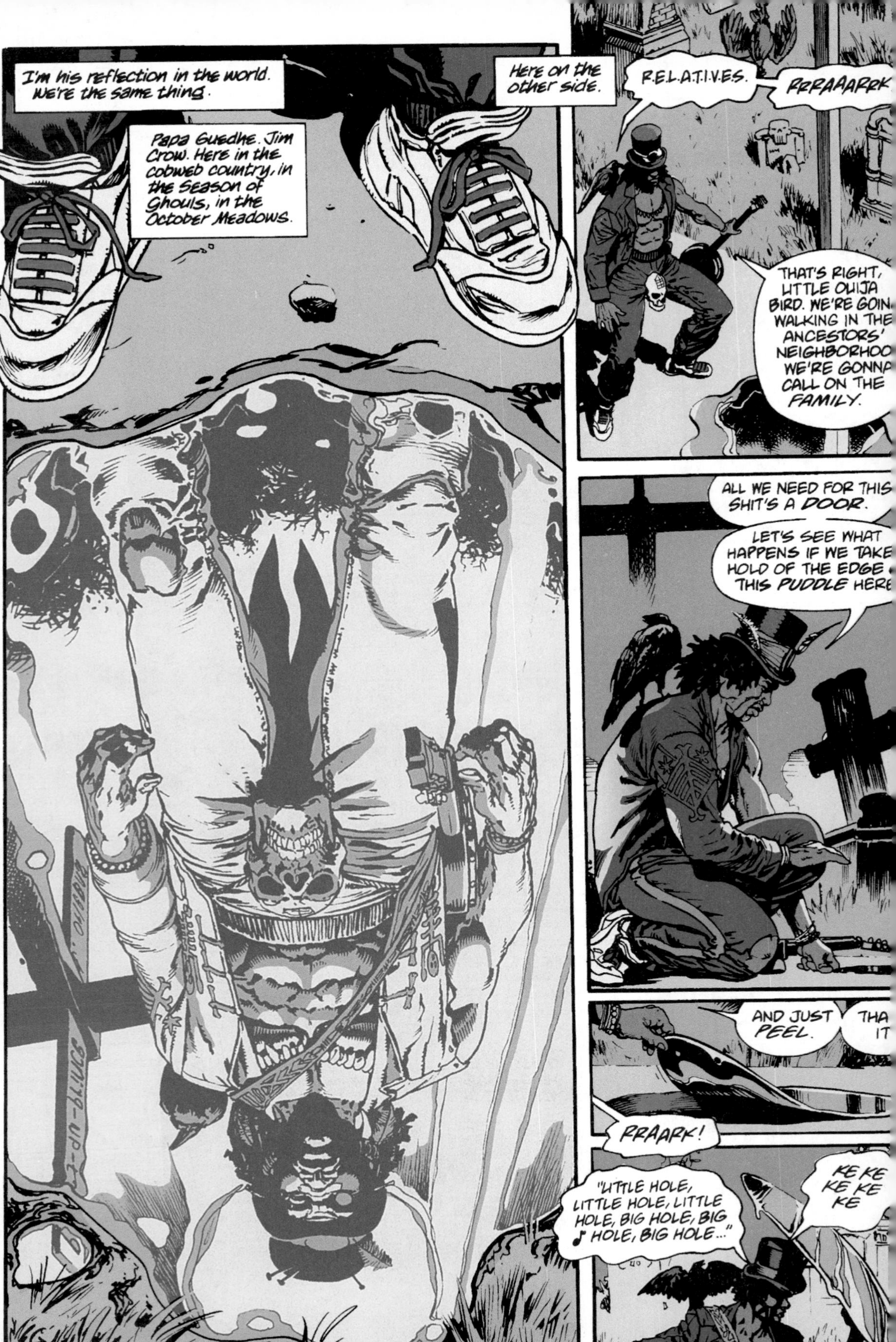
I'm his reflection in the world. We're the same thing.
Papa Guedhe. Jim Crow. Here in the cobweb country, in the Season of Ghouls, in the October Meadows.
Here on the other side.
R.E.L.A.T.I.V.E.S.
RRRAAARRK
THAT'S RIGHT, LITTLE OUIJA BIRD. WE'RE GOIN WALKING IN THE ANCESTORS' NEIGHBORHOO WE'RE GONNA CALL ON THE FAMILY.
ALL WE NEED FOR THIS SHIT'S A DOOR.
LET'S SEE WHAT HAPPENS IF WE TAKE HOLD OF THE EDGE THIS PUDDLE HERE
AND JUST PEEL.
THA IT
RRAARK!
"LITTLE HOLE, LITTLE HOLE, LITTLE HOLE, BIG HOLE, BIG ♪ HOLE, BIG HOLE..."
KE KE KE KE KE

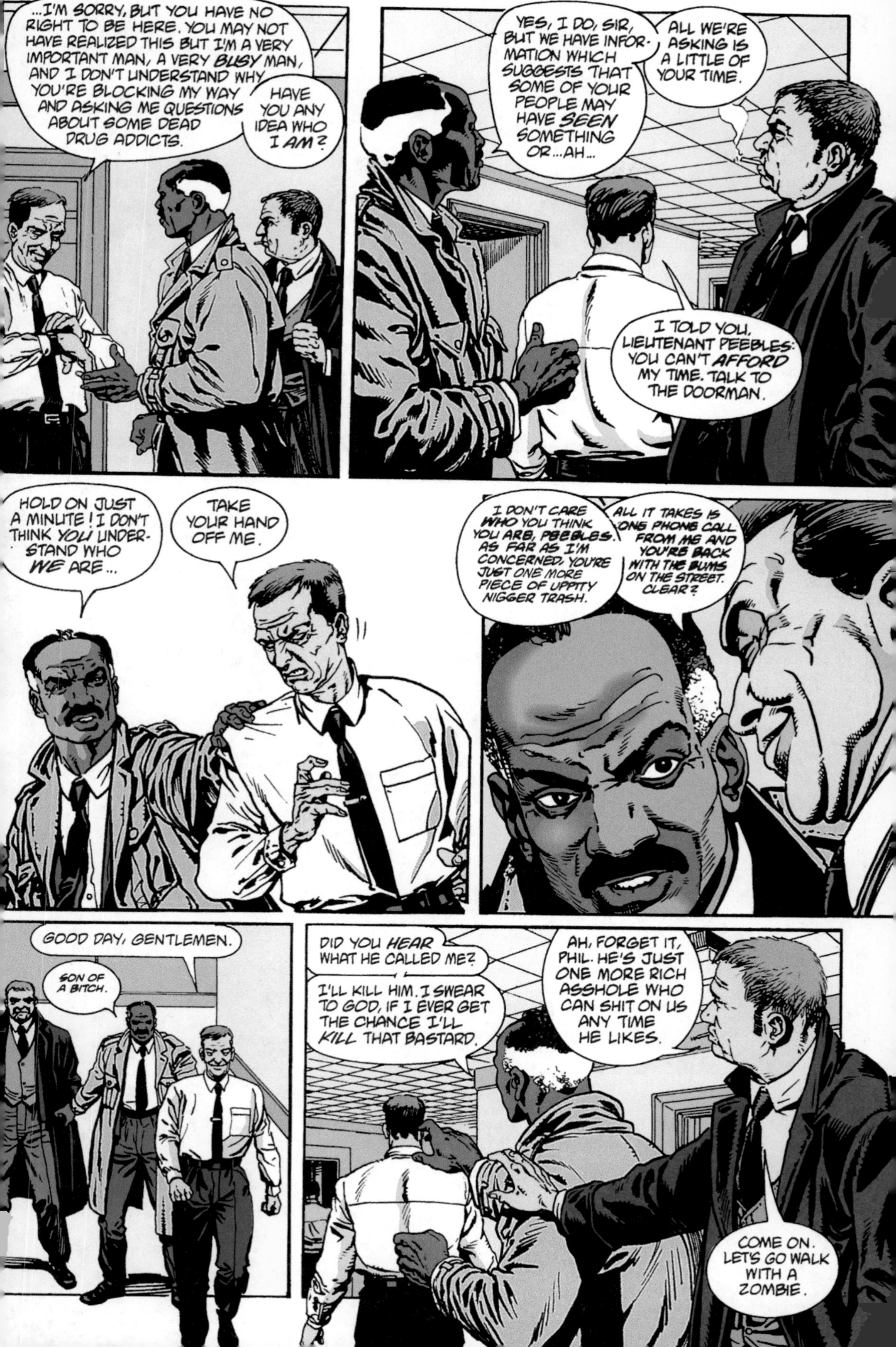
...I'M SORRY, BUT YOU HAVE NO RIGHT TO BE HERE. YOU MAY NOT HAVE REALIZED THIS BUT I'M A VERY IMPORTANT MAN, A VERY BUSY MAN, AND I DON'T UNDERSTAND WHY YOU'RE BLOCKING MY WAY AND ASKING ME QUESTIONS ABOUT SOME DEAD DRUG ADDICTS.
HAVE YOU ANY IDEA WHO I AM?
YES, I DO, SIR, BUT WE HAVE INFOR-MATION WHICH SUGGESTS THAT SOME OF YOUR PEOPLE MAY HAVE SEEN SOMETHING OR...AH...
ALL WE'RE ASKING IS A LITTLE OF YOUR TIME.
I TOLD YOU, LIEUTENANT PEEBLES: YOU CAN'T AFFORD MY TIME. TALK TO THE DOORMAN.
HOLD ON JUST A MINUTE! I DON'T THINK YOU UNDER-STAND WHO WE ARE...
TAKE YOUR HAND OFF ME.
I DON'T CARE WHO YOU THINK YOU ARE, PEEBLES. AS FAR AS I'M CONCERNED, YOU'RE JUST ONE MORE PIECE OF UPPITY NIGGER TRASH.
ALL IT TAKES IS ONE PHONE CALL FROM ME AND YOU'RE BACK WITH THE BUMS ON THE STREET. CLEAR?
GOOD DAY, GENTLEMEN.
SON OF A BITCH.
DID YOU HEAR WHAT HE CALLED ME?
I'LL KILL HIM. I SWEAR TO GOD, IF I EVER GET THE CHANCE I'LL KILL THAT BASTARD.
AH, FORGET IT, PHIL. HE'S JUST ONE MORE RICH ASSHOLE WHO CAN SHIT ON US ANY TIME HE LIKES.
COME ON. LET'S GO WALK WITH A ZOMBIE.

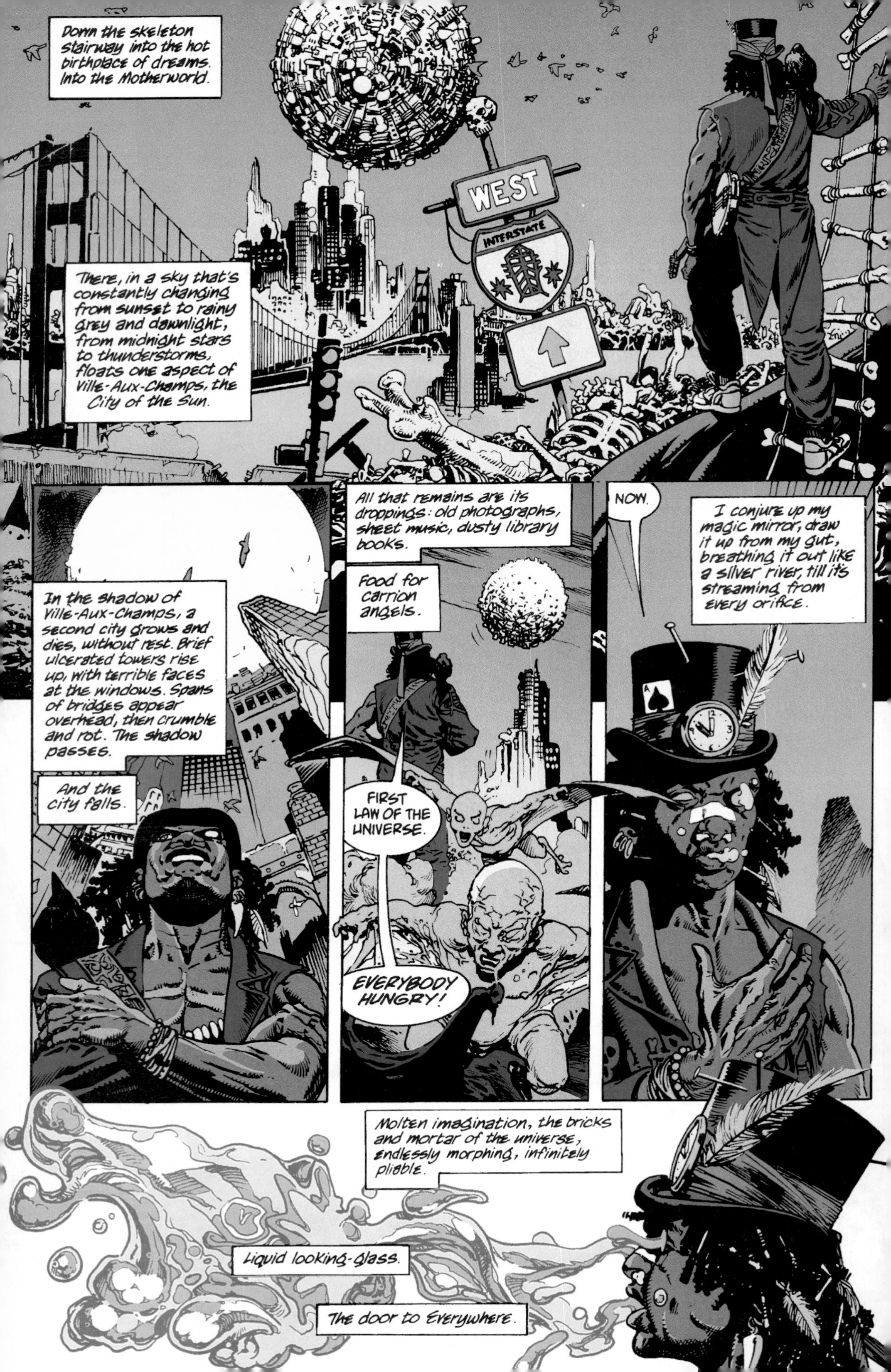

Down the skeleton stairway into the hot birthplace of dreams. Into the Motherworld.
WEST
INTERSTATE
There, in a sky that's constantly changing from sunset to rainy grey and dawnlight, from midnight stars to thunderstorms, floats one aspect of Ville-Aux-Champs, the City of the Sun.
In the shadow of Ville-Aux-Champs, a second city grows and dies, without rest. Brief ulcerated towers rise up, with terrible faces at the windows. Spans of bridges appear overhead, then crumble and rot. The shadow passes.
And the city falls.
All that remains are its droppings: old photographs, sheet music, dusty library books.
Food for carrion angels.
FIRST LAW OF THE UNIVERSE.
EVERYBODY HUNGRY!
NOW.
I conjure up my magic mirror, draw it up from my gut, breathing it out like a silver river, till it's streaming from every orifice.
Molten imagination, the bricks and mortar of the universe, endlessly morphing, infinitely pliable.
Liquid looking-glass.
The door to Everywhere.

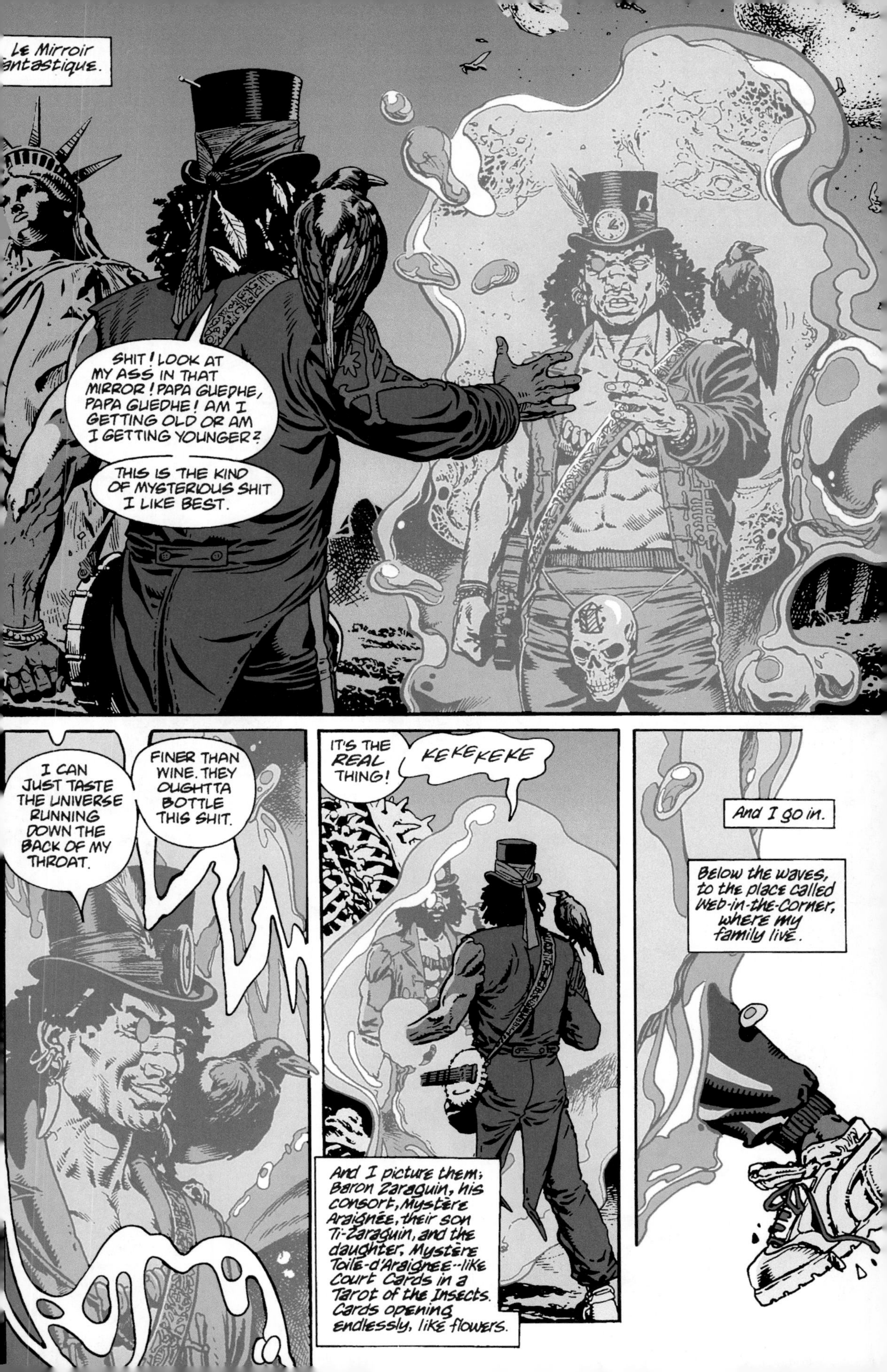
Le Mirroir Fantastique.
SHIT! LOOK AT MY ASS IN THAT MIRROR! PAPA GUEDHE, PAPA GUEDHE! AM I GETTING OLD OR AM I GETTING YOUNGER?
THIS IS THE KIND OF MYSTERIOUS SHIT I LIKE BEST.
I CAN JUST TASTE THE UNIVERSE RUNNING DOWN THE BACK OF MY THROAT.
FINER THAN WINE. THEY OUGHTTA BOTTLE THIS SHIT.
IT'S THE REAL THING!
KEKEKEKE
And I picture them; Baron Zaraguin, his consort, Mystère Araignée, their son Ti-Zaraguin, and the daughter, Mystère Toile-d'Araignee--like Court Cards in a Tarot of the Insects. Cards opening endlessly, like flowers.
And I go in.
Below the waves, to the place called Web-in-the-Corner, where my family live.

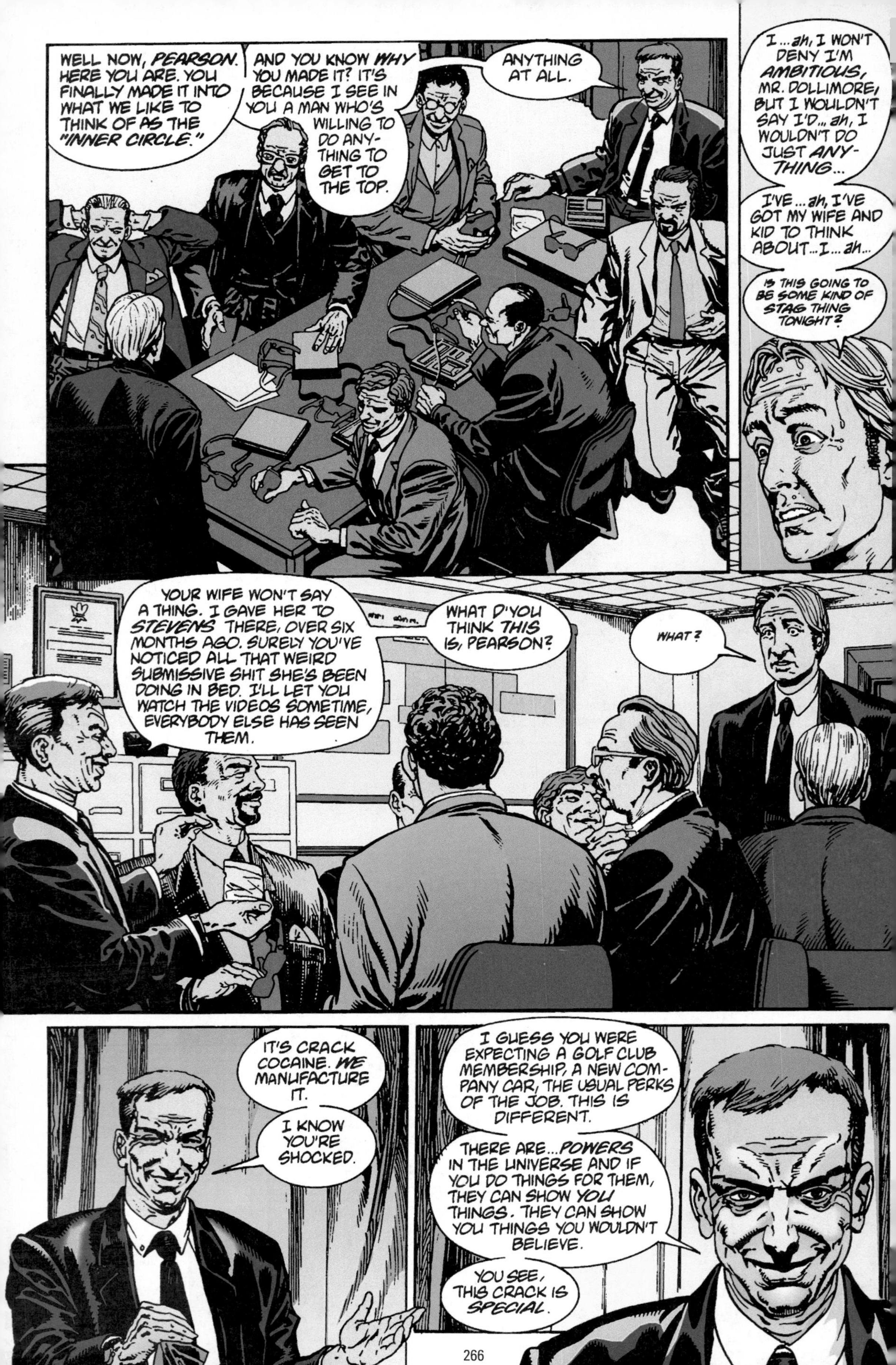
WELL NOW, PEARSON. HERE YOU ARE. YOU FINALLY MADE IT INTO WHAT WE LIKE TO THINK OF AS THE "INNER CIRCLE."
AND YOU KNOW WHY YOU MADE IT? IT'S BECAUSE I SEE IN YOU A MAN WHO'S WILLING TO DO ANY-THING TO GET TO THE TOP.
ANYTHING AT ALL.
I...ah, I WON'T DENY I'M AMBITIOUS, MR. DOLLIMORE, BUT I WOULDN'T SAY I'D... ah, I WOULDN'T DO JUST ANY-THING...
I'VE...ah, I'VE GOT MY WIFE AND KID TO THINK ABOUT...I...ah...
IS THIS GOING TO BE SOME KIND OF STAG THING TONIGHT?
YOUR WIFE WON'T SAY A THING. I GAVE HER TO STEVENS THERE, OVER SIX MONTHS AGO. SURELY YOU'VE NOTICED ALL THAT WEIRD SUBMISSIVE SHIT SHE'S BEEN DOING IN BED. I'LL LET YOU WATCH THE VIDEOS SOMETIME, EVERYBODY ELSE HAS SEEN THEM.
WHAT D'YOU THINK THIS IS, PEARSON?
WHAT?
IT'S CRACK COCAINE. WE MANUFACTURE IT.
I KNOW YOU'RE SHOCKED.
I GUESS YOU WERE EXPECTING A GOLF CLUB MEMBERSHIP, A NEW COM-PANY CAR, THE USUAL PERKS OF THE JOB. THIS IS DIFFERENT.
THERE ARE...POWERS IN THE UNIVERSE AND IF YOU DO THINGS FOR THEM, THEY CAN SHOW YOU THINGS. THEY CAN SHOW YOU THINGS YOU WOULDN'T BELIEVE.
YOU SEE, THIS CRACK IS SPECIAL.

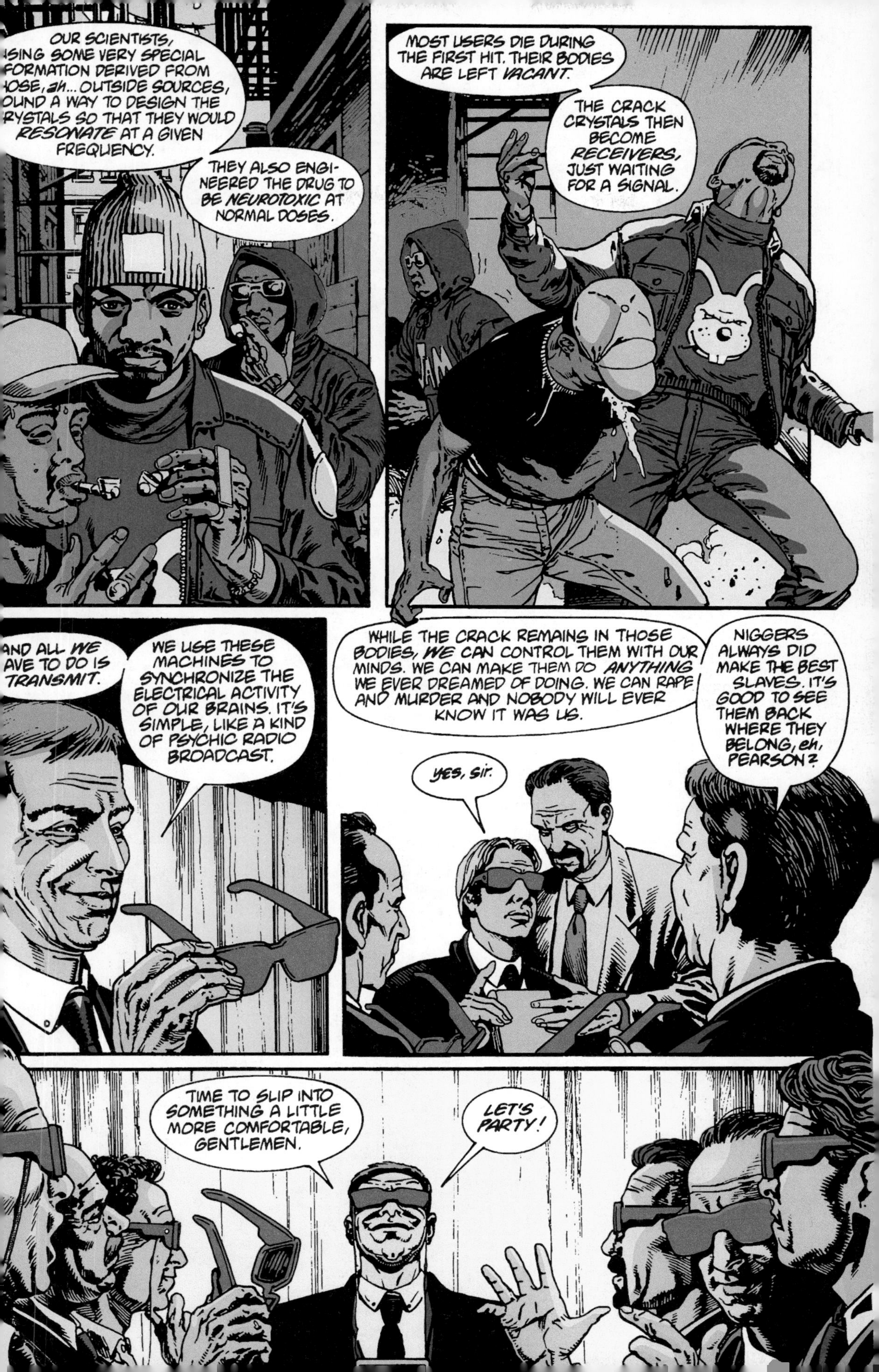

OUR SCIENTISTS, USING SOME VERY SPECIAL INFORMATION DERIVED FROM THOSE, AH... OUTSIDE SOURCES, FOUND A WAY TO DESIGN THE CRYSTALS SO THAT THEY WOULD RESONATE AT A GIVEN FREQUENCY.
THEY ALSO ENGINEERED THE DRUG TO BE NEUROTOXIC AT NORMAL DOSES.
MOST USERS DIE DURING THE FIRST HIT. THEIR BODIES ARE LEFT VACANT.
THE CRACK CRYSTALS THEN BECOME RECEIVERS, JUST WAITING FOR A SIGNAL.
AND ALL WE HAVE TO DO IS TRANSMIT.
WE USE THESE MACHINES TO SYNCHRONIZE THE ELECTRICAL ACTIVITY OF OUR BRAINS. IT'S SIMPLE, LIKE A KIND OF PSYCHIC RADIO BROADCAST.
WHILE THE CRACK REMAINS IN THOSE BODIES, WE CAN CONTROL THEM WITH OUR MINDS. WE CAN MAKE THEM DO ANYTHING WE EVER DREAMED OF DOING. WE CAN RAPE AND MURDER AND NOBODY WILL EVER KNOW IT WAS US.
NIGGERS ALWAYS DID MAKE THE BEST SLAVES. IT'S GOOD TO SEE THEM BACK WHERE THEY BELONG, EH, PEARSON?
YES, SIR.
TIME TO SLIP INTO SOMETHING A LITTLE MORE COMFORTABLE, GENTLEMEN.
LET'S PARTY!

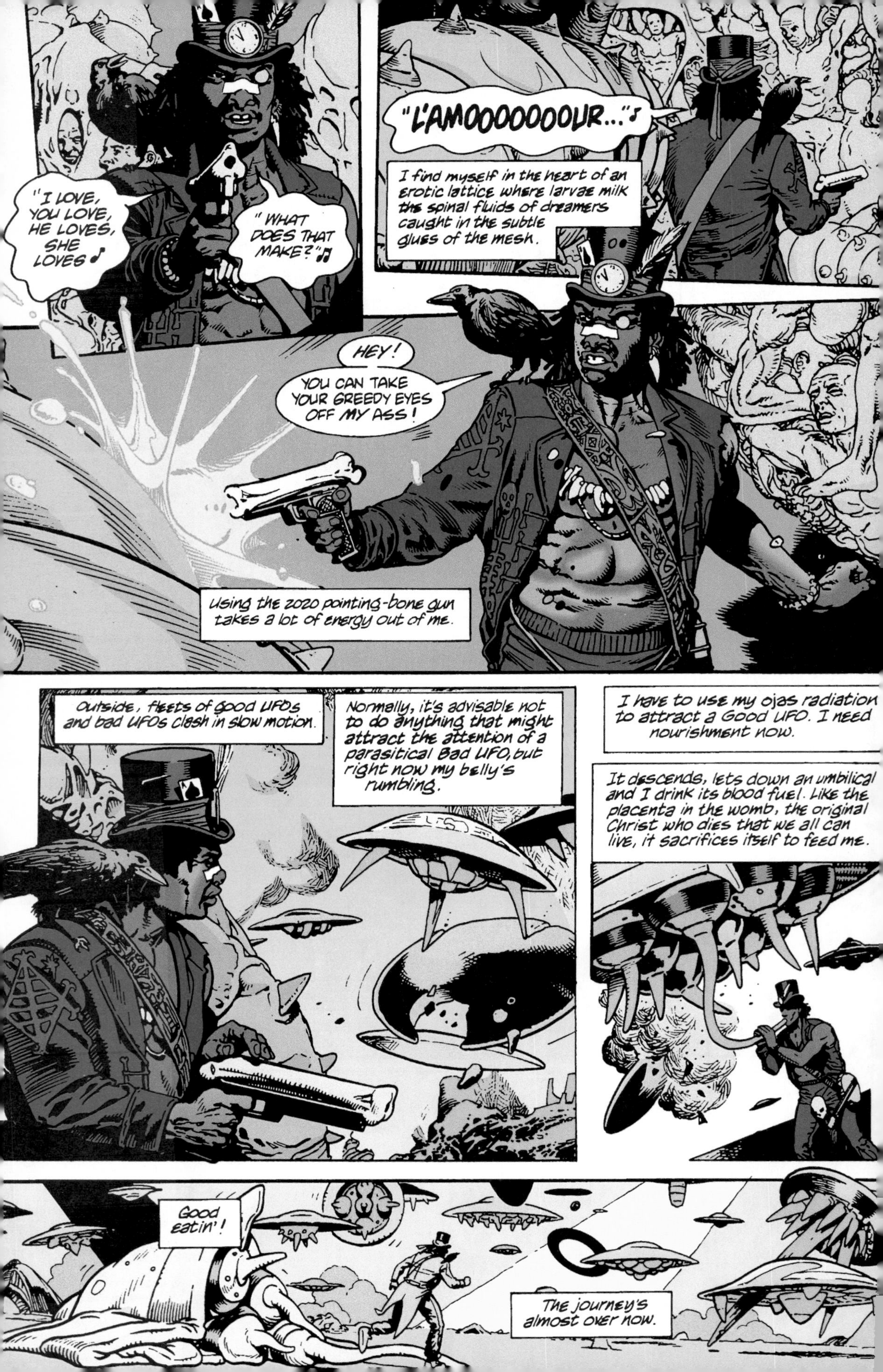
"I LOVE, YOU LOVE, HE LOVES, SHE LOVES ♪
"WHAT DOES THAT MAKE?"♫
"L'AMOOOOOOOUR..."♪
I find myself in the heart of an erotic lattice where larvae milk the spinal fluids of dreamers caught in the subtle glues of the mesh.
HEY!
YOU CAN TAKE YOUR GREEDY EYES OFF MY ASS!
Using the 2020 pointing-bone gun takes a lot of energy out of me.
Outside, fleets of Good UFOs and bad UFOs clash in slow motion.
Normally, it's advisable not to do anything that might attract the attention of a parasitical Bad UFO, but right now my belly's rumbling.
I have to use my ojas radiation to attract a Good UFO. I need nourishment now.
It descends, lets down an umbilical and I drink its blood fuel. Like the placenta in the womb, the original Christ who dies that we all can live, it sacrifices itself to feed me.
Good eatin'!
The journey's almost over now.

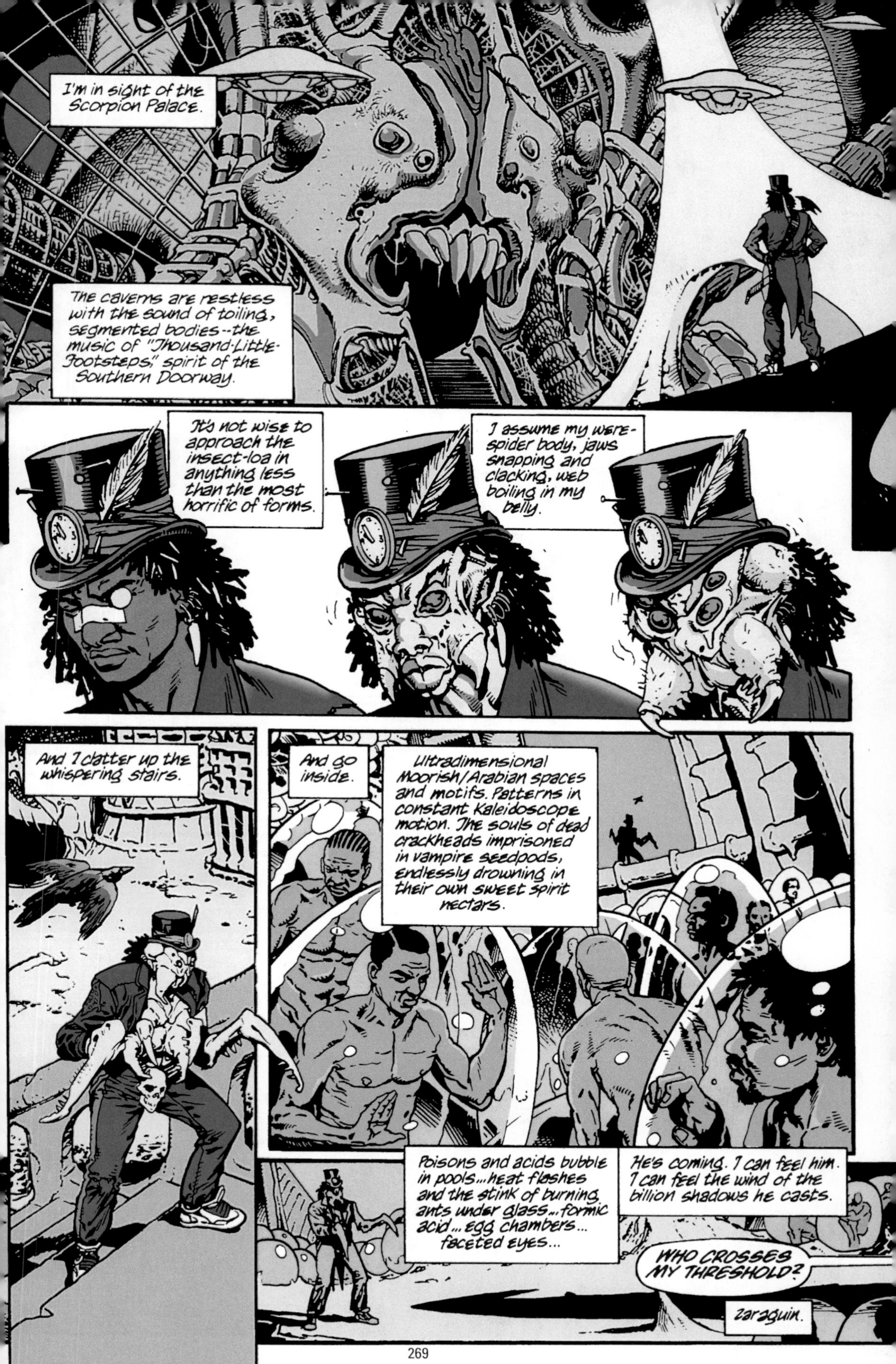

I'm in sight of the Scorpion Palace.
The caverns are restless with the sound of toiling, segmented bodies--the music of "Thousand-Little-Footsteps," spirit of the Southern Doorway.
It's not wise to approach the insect-loa in anything less than the most horrific of forms.
I assume my were-spider body, jaws snapping and clacking, web boiling in my belly.
And I clatter up the whispering stairs.
And go inside.
Ultradimensional Moorish/Arabian spaces and motifs. Patterns in constant kaleidoscope motion. The souls of dead crackheads imprisoned in vampire seedpods, endlessly drowning in their own sweet spirit nectars.
Poisons and acids bubble in pools... heat flashes and the stink of burning ants under glass... formic acid... egg chambers... faceted eyes...
He's coming. I can feel him. I can feel the wind of the billion shadows he casts.
WHO CROSSES MY THRESHOLD?
Zaraguin.

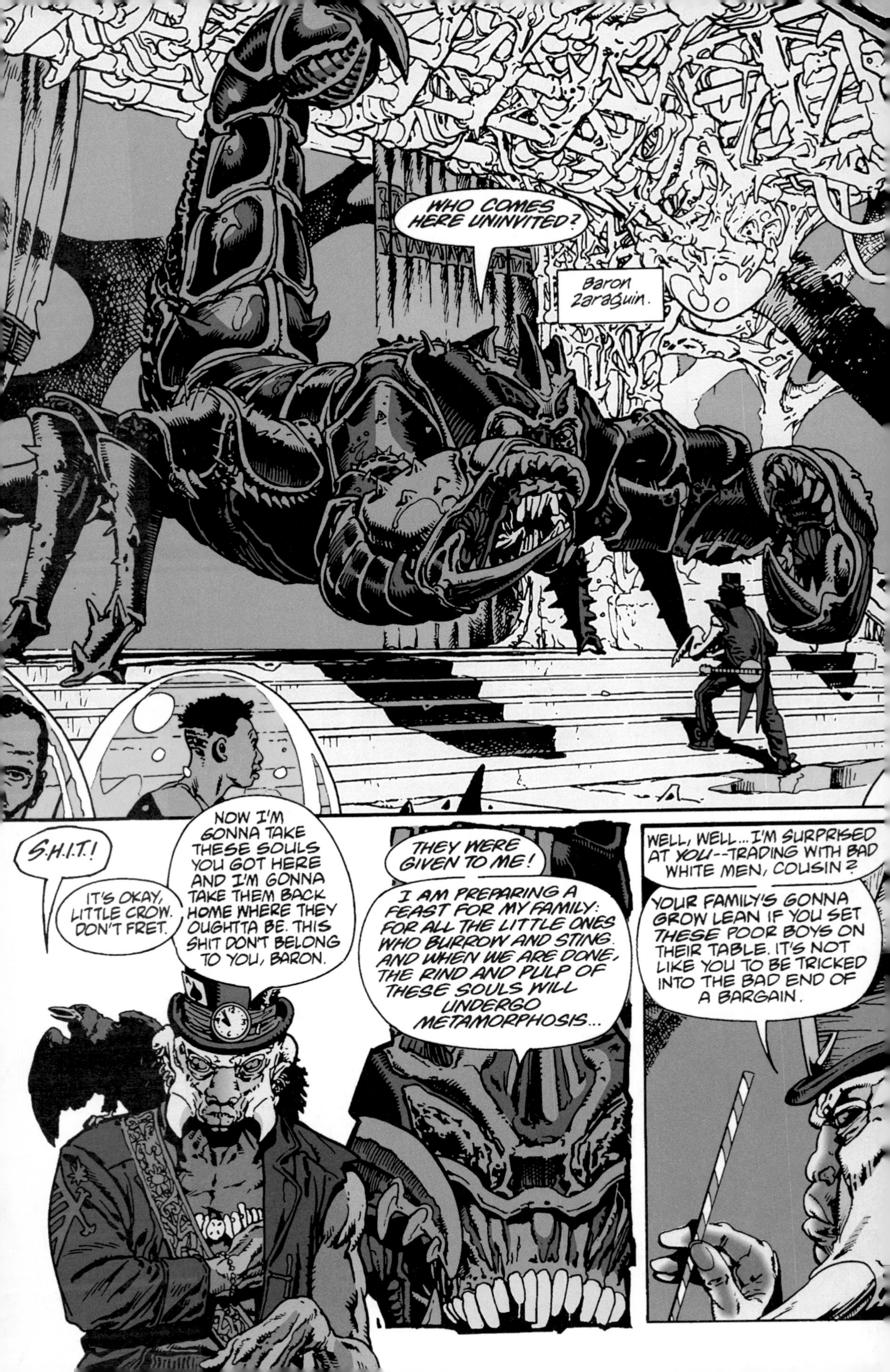
WHO COMES HERE UNINVITED?
Baron Zaraguin.
S.H.I.T.!
IT'S OKAY, LITTLE CROW. DON'T FRET.
NOW I'M GONNA TAKE THESE SOULS YOU GOT HERE AND I'M GONNA TAKE THEM BACK HOME WHERE THEY OUGHTTA BE. THIS SHIT DON'T BELONG TO YOU, BARON.
THEY WERE GIVEN TO ME!
I AM PREPARING A FEAST FOR MY FAMILY: FOR ALL THE LITTLE ONES WHO BURROW AND STING. AND WHEN WE ARE DONE, THE RIND AND PULP OF THESE SOULS WILL UNDERGO METAMORPHOSIS...
WELL, WELL... I'M SURPRISED AT YOU--TRADING WITH BAD WHITE MEN, COUSIN?
YOUR FAMILY'S GONNA GROW LEAN IF YOU SET THESE POOR BOYS ON THEIR TABLE. IT'S NOT LIKE YOU TO BE TRICKED INTO THE BAD END OF A BARGAIN.

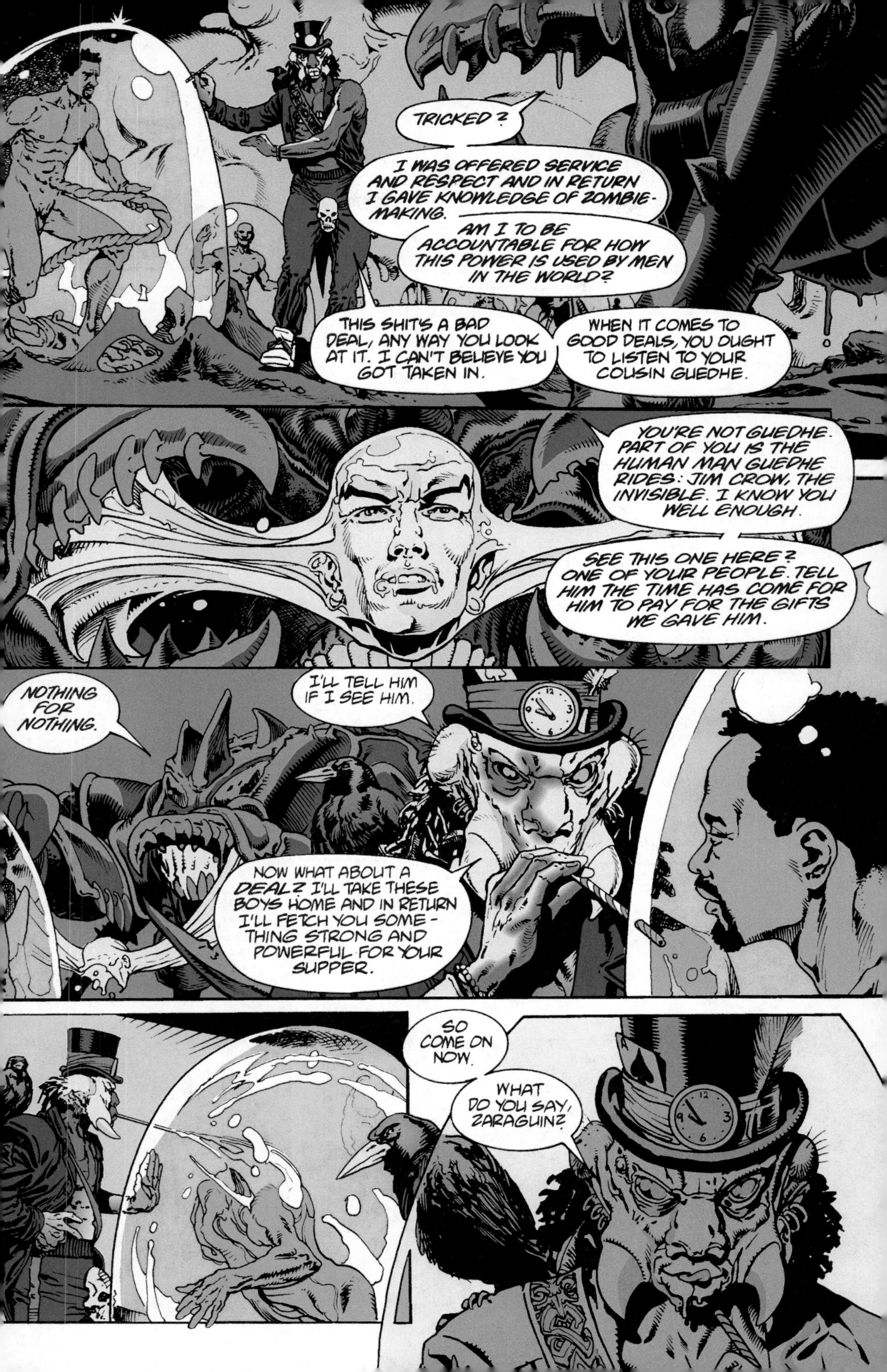
TRICKED?
I WAS OFFERED SERVICE AND RESPECT AND IN RETURN I GAVE KNOWLEDGE OF ZOMBIE-MAKING.
AM I TO BE ACCOUNTABLE FOR HOW THIS POWER IS USED BY MEN IN THE WORLD?
THIS SHIT'S A BAD DEAL, ANY WAY YOU LOOK AT IT. I CAN'T BELIEVE YOU GOT TAKEN IN.
WHEN IT COMES TO GOOD DEALS, YOU OUGHT TO LISTEN TO YOUR COUSIN GUEDHE.
YOU'RE NOT GUEDHE. PART OF YOU IS THE HUMAN MAN GUEDHE RIDES: JIM CROW, THE INVISIBLE. I KNOW YOU WELL ENOUGH.
SEE THIS ONE HERE? ONE OF YOUR PEOPLE. TELL HIM THE TIME HAS COME FOR HIM TO PAY FOR THE GIFTS WE GAVE HIM.
NOTHING FOR NOTHING.
I'LL TELL HIM IF I SEE HIM.
NOW WHAT ABOUT A DEAL? I'LL TAKE THESE BOYS HOME AND IN RETURN I'LL FETCH YOU SOME-THING STRONG AND POWERFUL FOR YOUR SUPPER.
SO COME ON NOW.
WHAT DO YOU SAY, ZARAGUIN?

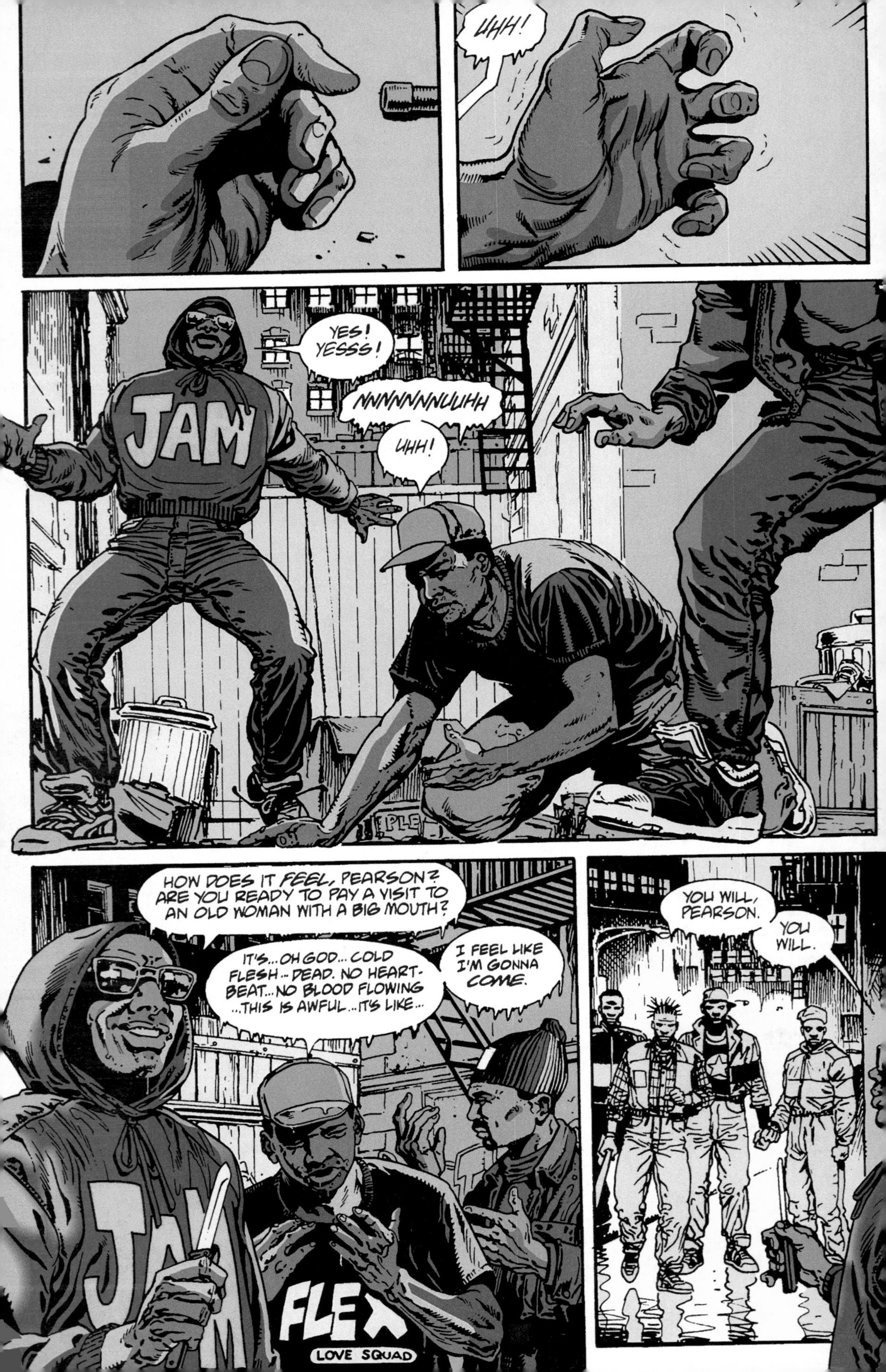
UHH!
YES! YESSS!
NNNNNNNUUHH
UHH!
JAM
HOW DOES IT FEEL, PEARSON? ARE YOU READY TO PAY A VISIT TO AN OLD WOMAN WITH A BIG MOUTH?
IT'S...OH GOD... COLD FLESH... DEAD. NO HEART-BEAT...NO BLOOD FLOWING ...THIS IS AWFUL...IT'S LIKE...
I FEEL LIKE I'M GONNA COME.
FLEX
LOVE SQUAD
YOU WILL, PEARSON.
YOU WILL.

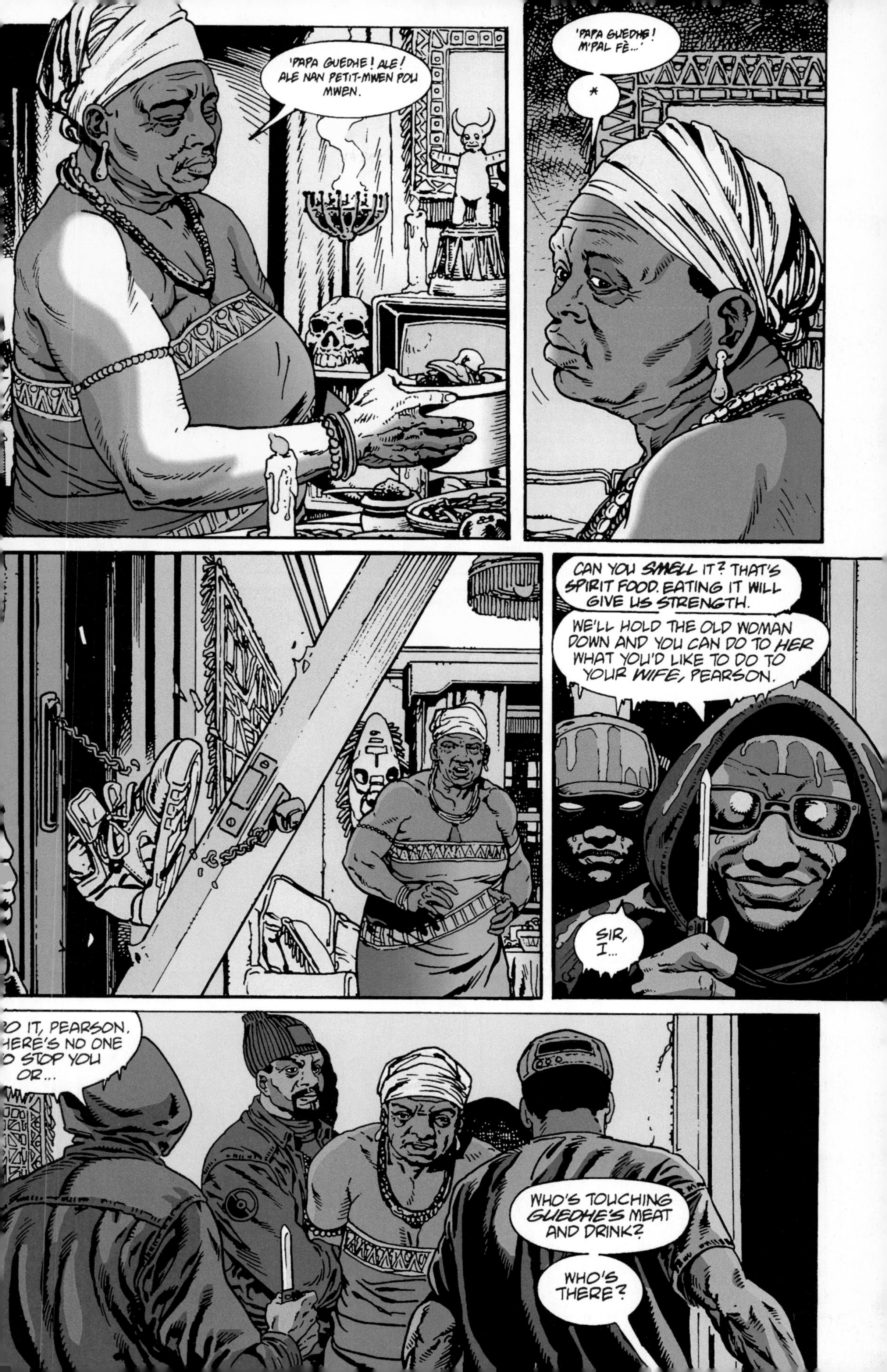'PAPA GUEDHE! ALE! ALE NAN PETIT-MWEN POU MWEN.
'PAPA GUEDHE! M'PAL FÈ...'
*
CAN YOU SMELL IT? THAT'S SPIRIT FOOD. EATING IT WILL GIVE US STRENGTH.
WE'LL HOLD THE OLD WOMAN DOWN AND YOU CAN DO TO HER WHAT YOU'D LIKE TO DO TO YOUR WIFE, PEARSON.
SIR, I...
O IT, PEARSON. HERE'S NO ONE O STOP YOU OR...
WHO'S TOUCHING GUEDHE'S MEAT AND DRINK?
WHO'S THERE?

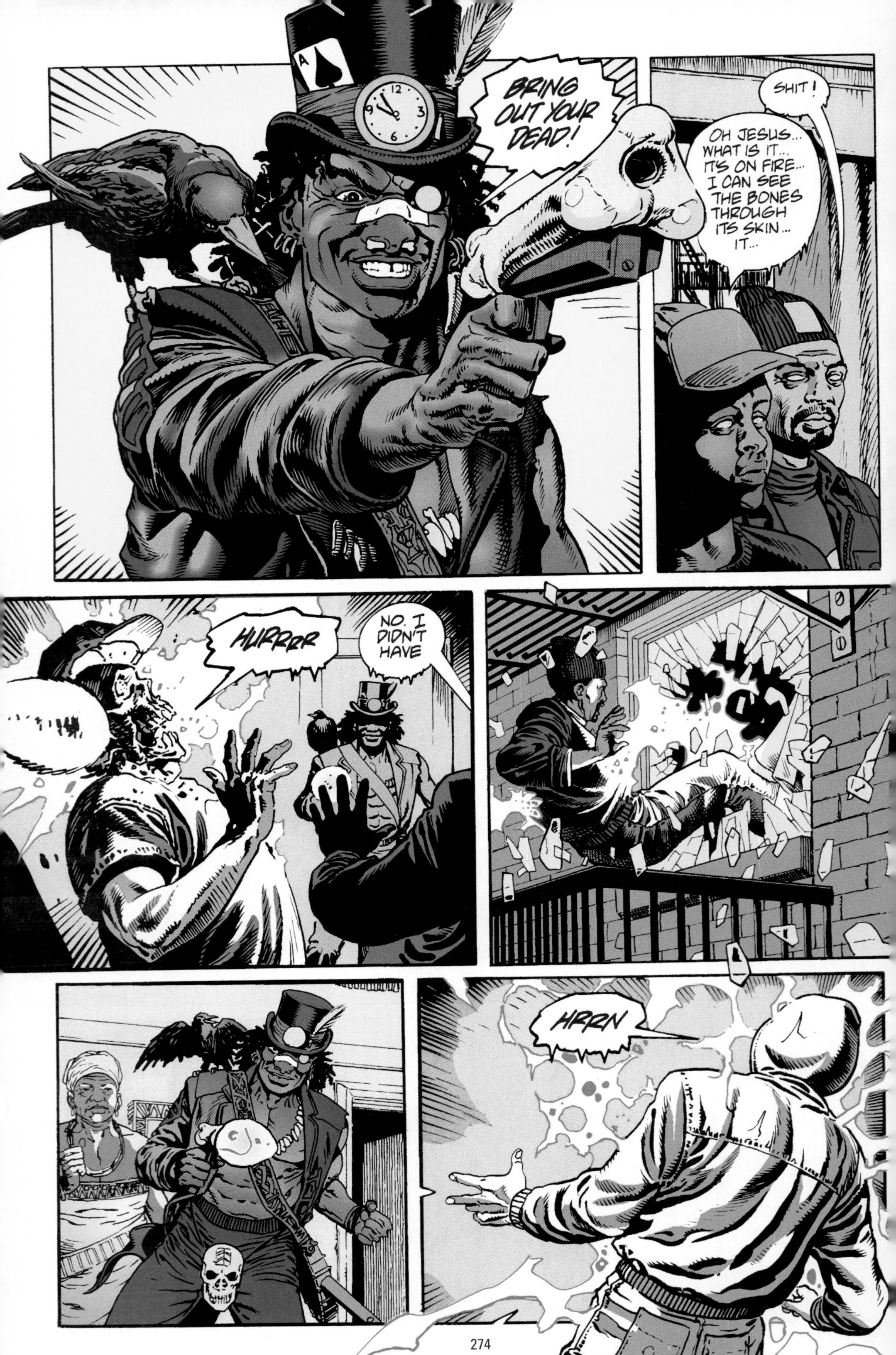
BRING OUT YOUR DEAD!
SHIT!
OH JESUS... WHAT IS IT... IT'S ON FIRE... I CAN SEE THE BONES THROUGH ITS SKIN... IT...
HURRRR
NO. I DIDN'T HAVE
HRRN

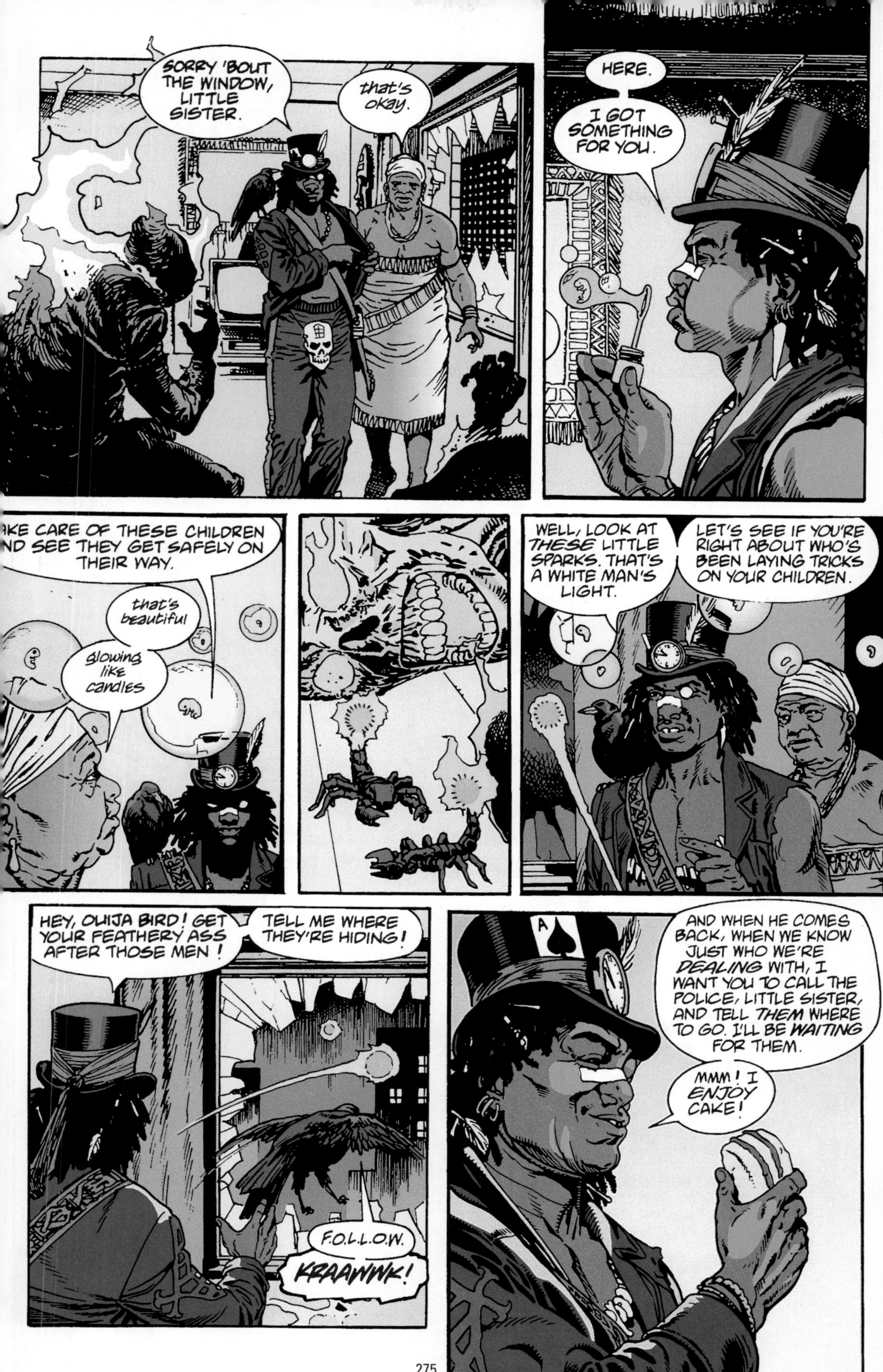
SORRY 'BOUT THE WINDOW, LITTLE SISTER.
that's okay.
HERE.
I GOT SOMETHING FOR YOU.
AKE CARE OF THESE CHILDREN ND SEE THEY GET SAFELY ON THEIR WAY.
that's beautiful
glowing like candles
WELL, LOOK AT THESE LITTLE SPARKS. THAT'S A WHITE MAN'S LIGHT.
LET'S SEE IF YOU'RE RIGHT ABOUT WHO'S BEEN LAYING TRICKS ON YOUR CHILDREN.
HEY, OUIJA BIRD! GET YOUR FEATHERY ASS AFTER THOSE MEN!
TELL ME WHERE THEY'RE HIDING!
F.O.L.L.O.W.
KRAAWWK!
AND WHEN HE COMES BACK, WHEN WE KNOW JUST WHO WE'RE DEALING WITH, I WANT YOU TO CALL THE POLICE, LITTLE SISTER, AND TELL THEM WHERE TO GO. I'LL BE WAITING FOR THEM.
MMM! I ENJOY CAKE!

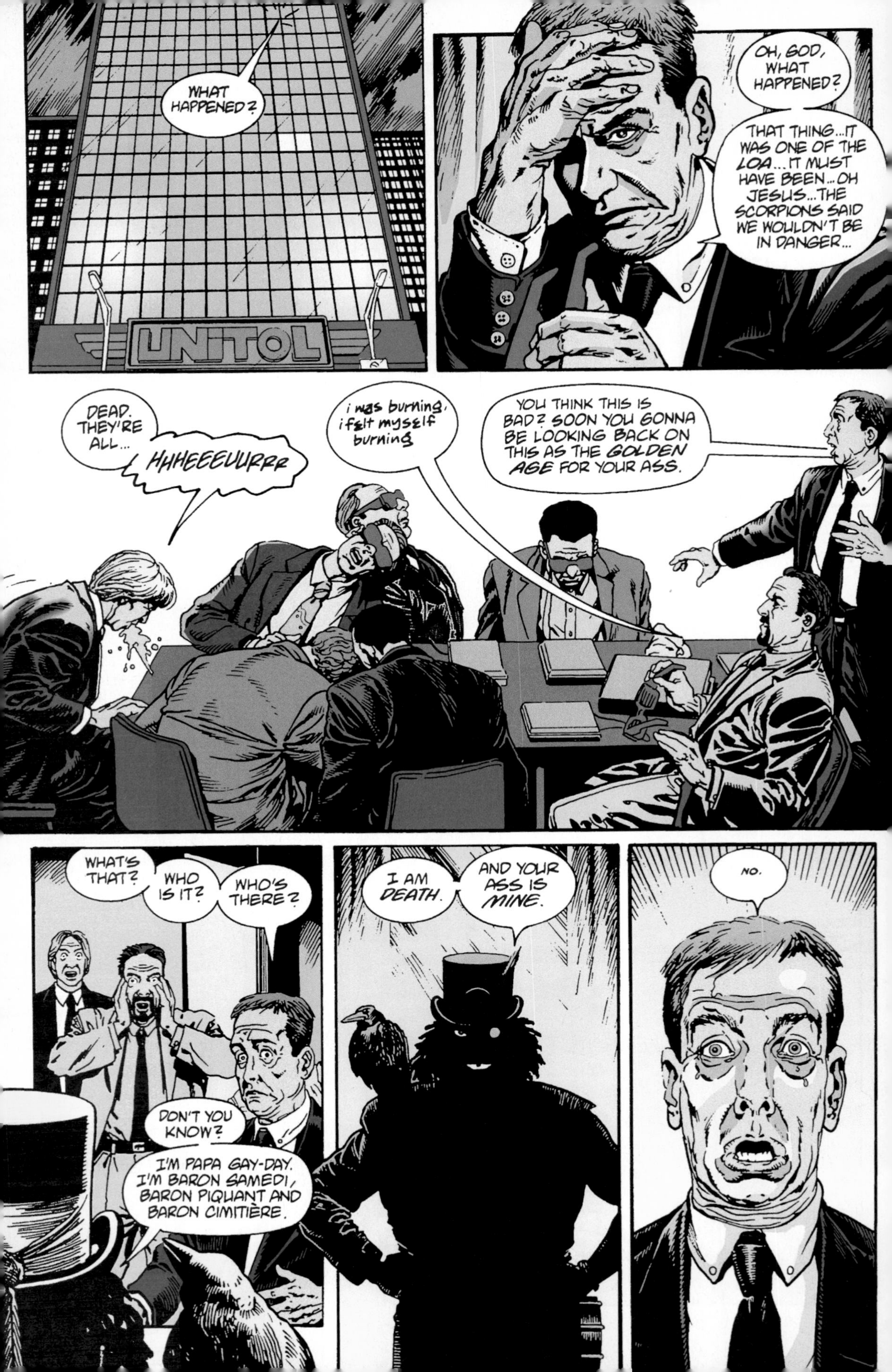
WHAT HAPPENED?
OH, GOD, WHAT HAPPENED?
THAT THING...IT WAS ONE OF THE LOA... IT MUST HAVE BEEN...OH JESUS...THE SCORPIONS SAID WE WOULDN'T BE IN DANGER...
DEAD. THEY'RE ALL...
HHHEEEUURRR
i was burning, i felt myself burning
YOU THINK THIS IS BAD? SOON YOU GONNA BE LOOKING BACK ON THIS AS THE GOLDEN AGE FOR YOUR ASS.
WHAT'S THAT?
WHO IS IT?
WHO'S THERE?
DON'T YOU KNOW?
I'M PAPA GAY-DAY. I'M BARON SAMEDI, BARON PIQUANT AND BARON CIMITIÈRE.
I AM DEATH.
AND YOUR ASS IS MINE.
NO.

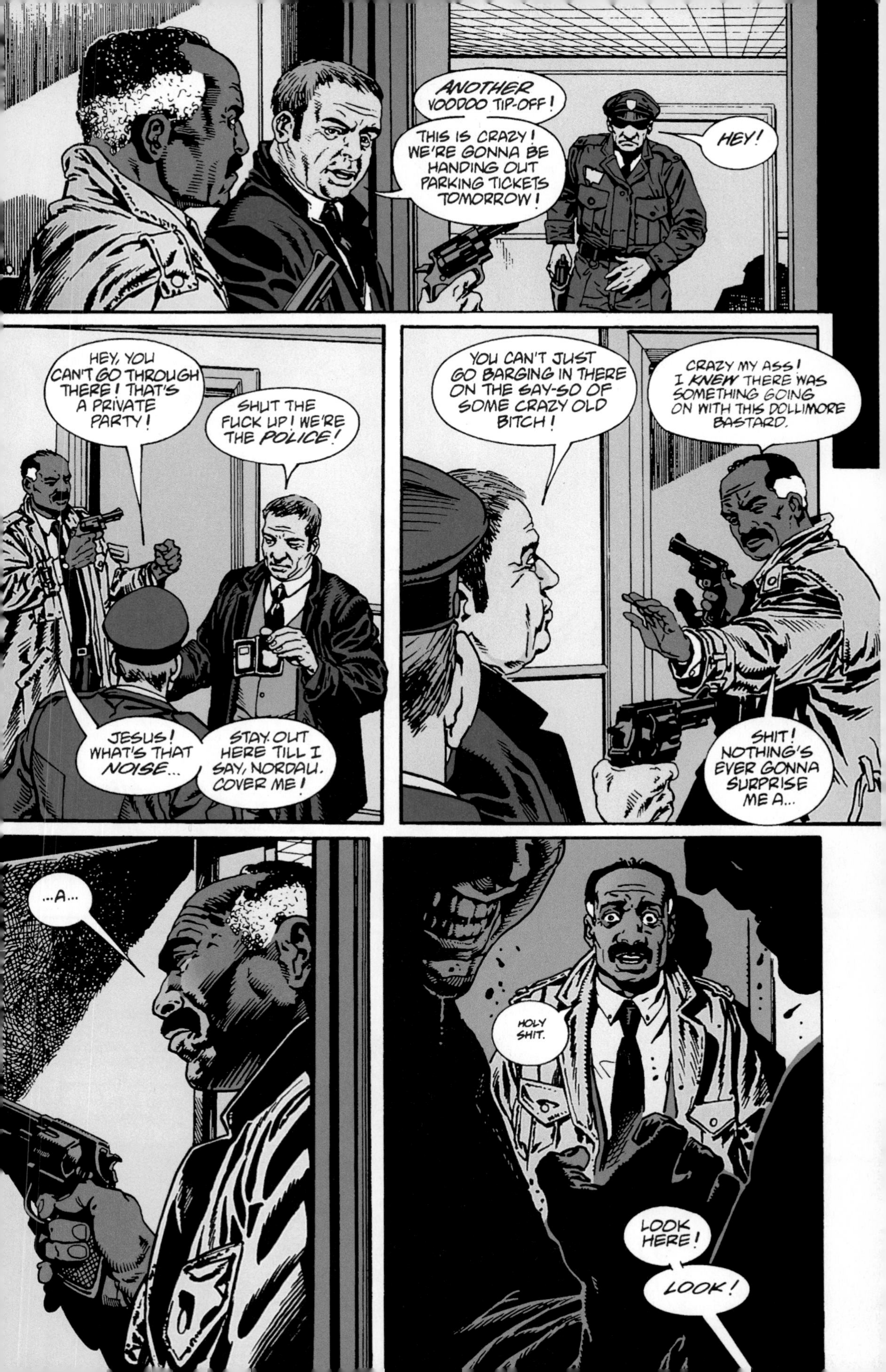
ANOTHER VOODOO TIP-OFF!
THIS IS CRAZY! WE'RE GONNA BE HANDING OUT PARKING TICKETS TOMORROW!
HEY!
HEY, YOU CAN'T GO THROUGH THERE! THAT'S A PRIVATE PARTY!
SHUT THE FUCK UP! WE'RE THE POLICE!
JESUS! WHAT'S THAT NOISE...
STAY OUT HERE TILL I SAY, NORDAU. COVER ME!
YOU CAN'T JUST GO BARGING IN THERE ON THE SAY-SO OF SOME CRAZY OLD BITCH!
CRAZY MY ASS! I KNEW THERE WAS SOMETHING GOING ON WITH THIS DOLLIMORE BASTARD.
SHIT! NOTHING'S EVER GONNA SURPRISE ME A...
...A...
HOLY SHIT.
LOOK HERE!
LOOK!

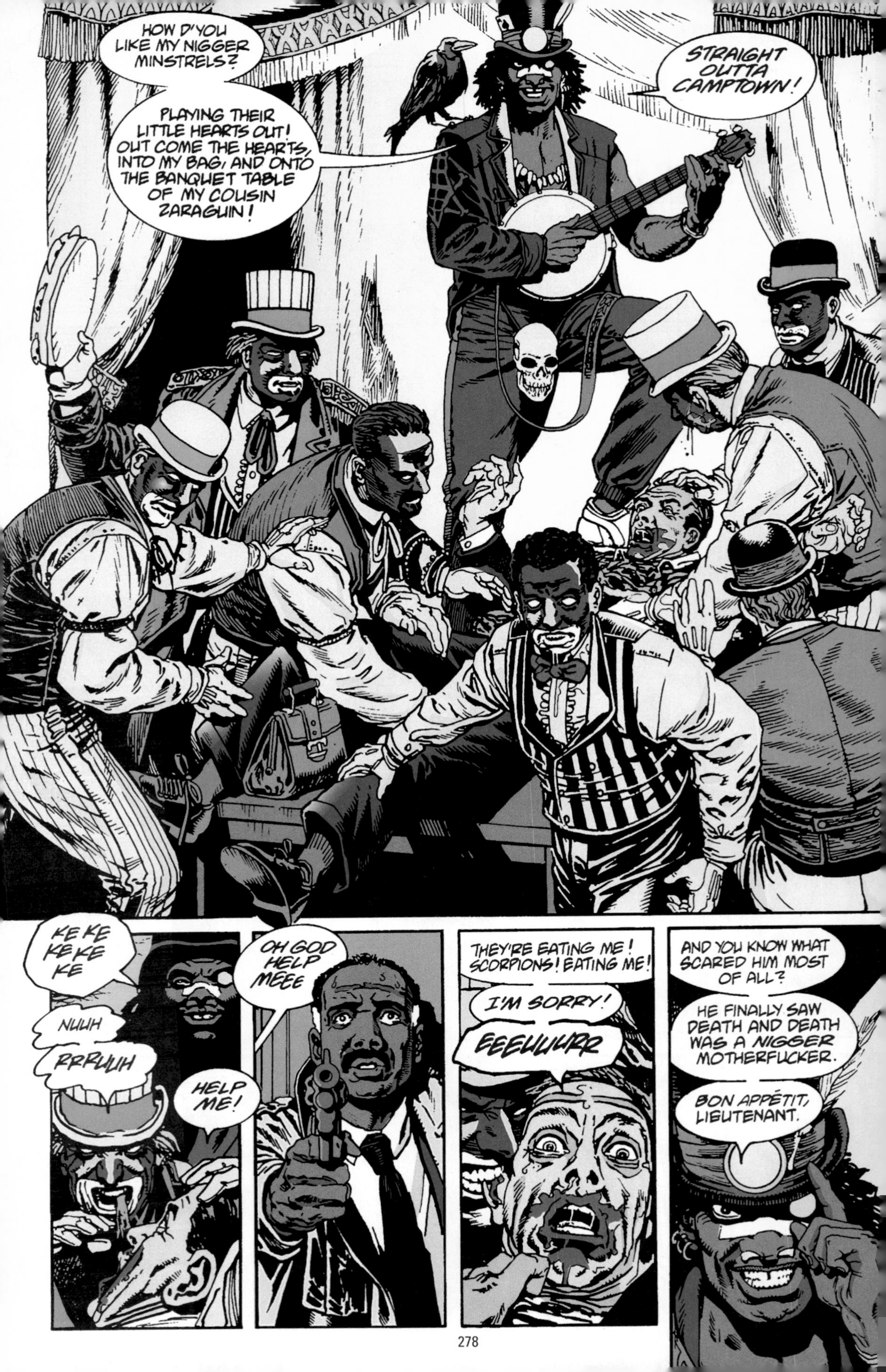

HOW D'YOU LIKE MY NIGGER MINSTRELS?
STRAIGHT OUTTA CAMPTOWN!
PLAYING THEIR LITTLE HEARTS OUT! OUT COME THE HEARTS, INTO MY BAG, AND ONTO THE BANQUET TABLE OF MY COUSIN ZARAGUIN!
KE KE KE KE KE
NUUH
RRRUUH
HELP ME!
OH GOD HELP MEEE
THEY'RE EATING ME! SCORPIONS! EATING ME!
I'M SORRY!
EEEUUURR
AND YOU KNOW WHAT SCARED HIM MOST OF ALL?
HE FINALLY SAW DEATH AND DEATH WAS A NIGGER MOTHERFUCKER.
BON APPÉTIT, LIEUTENANT.

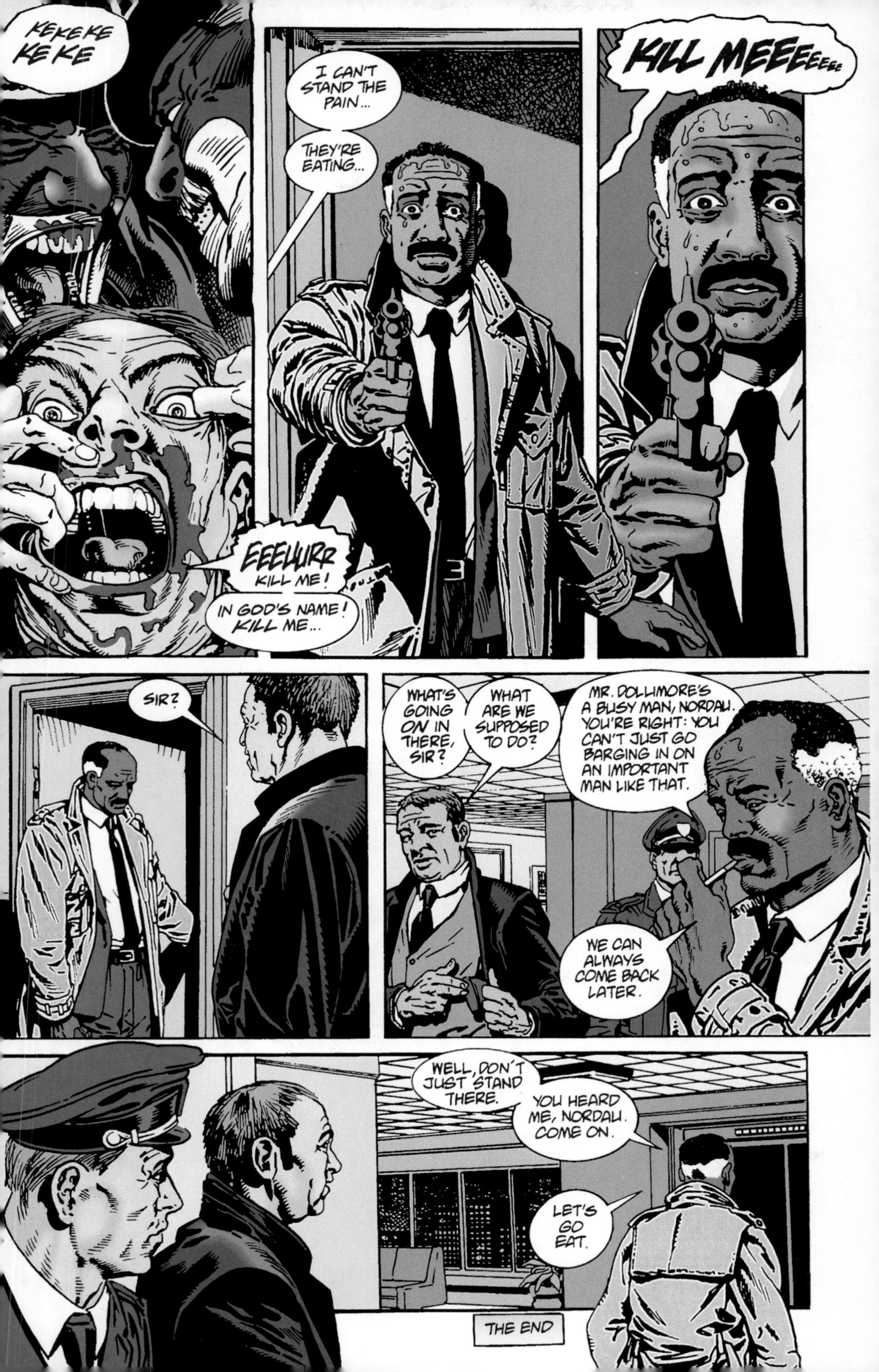
KEKEKE KE KE
I CAN'T STAND THE PAIN...
THEY'RE EATING...
KILL MEEEeeee
EEEUURR KILL ME!
IN GOD'S NAME! KILL ME...
SIR?
WHAT'S GOING ON IN THERE, SIR?
WHAT ARE WE SUPPOSED TO DO?
MR. DOLLIMORE'S A BUSY MAN, NORDAU. YOU'RE RIGHT: YOU CAN'T JUST GO BARGING IN ON AN IMPORTANT MAN LIKE THAT.
WE CAN ALWAYS COME BACK LATER.
WELL, DON'T JUST STAND THERE.
YOU HEARD ME, NORDAU. COME ON.
LET'S GO EAT.
THE END

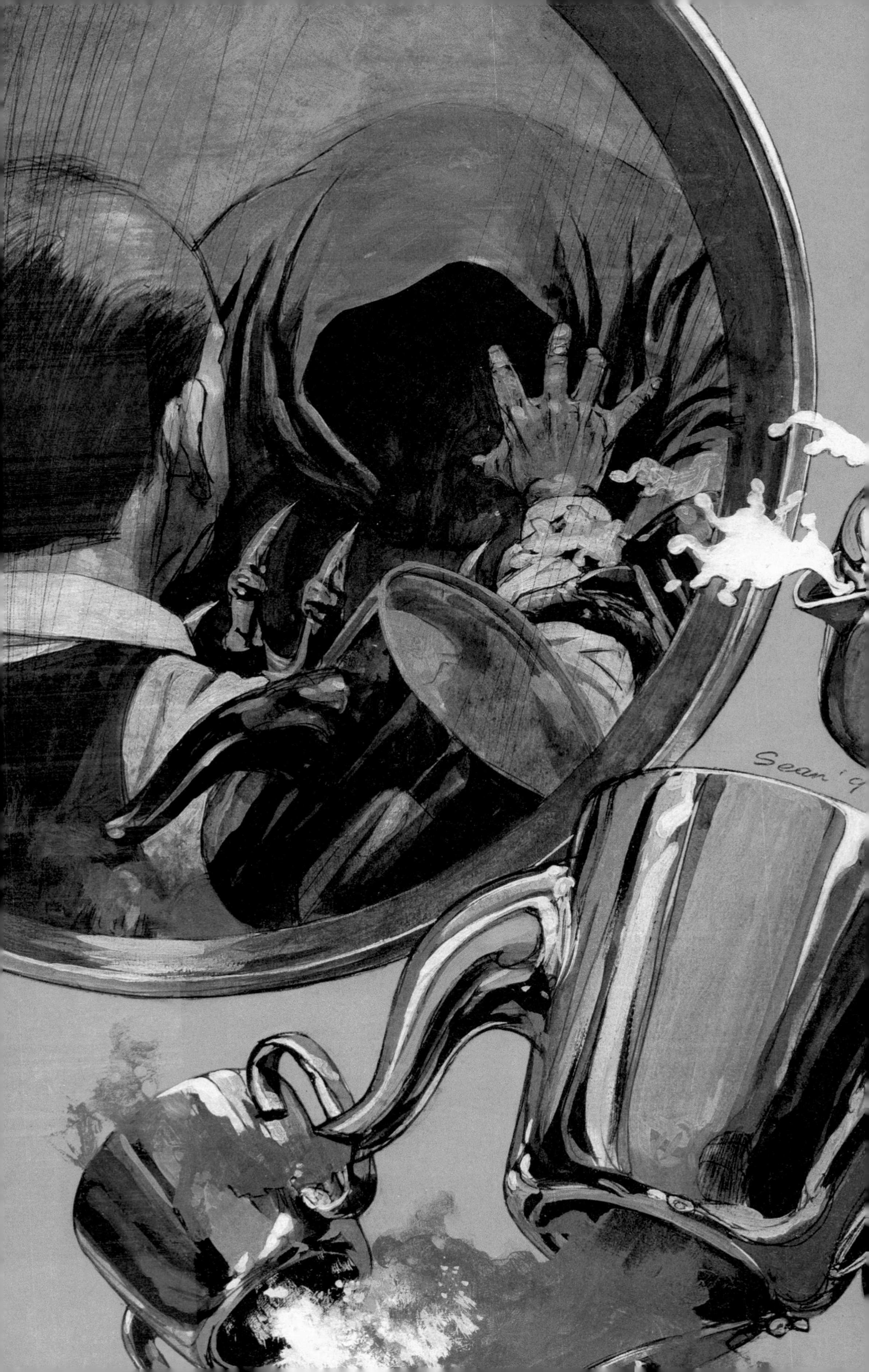
Sean '9

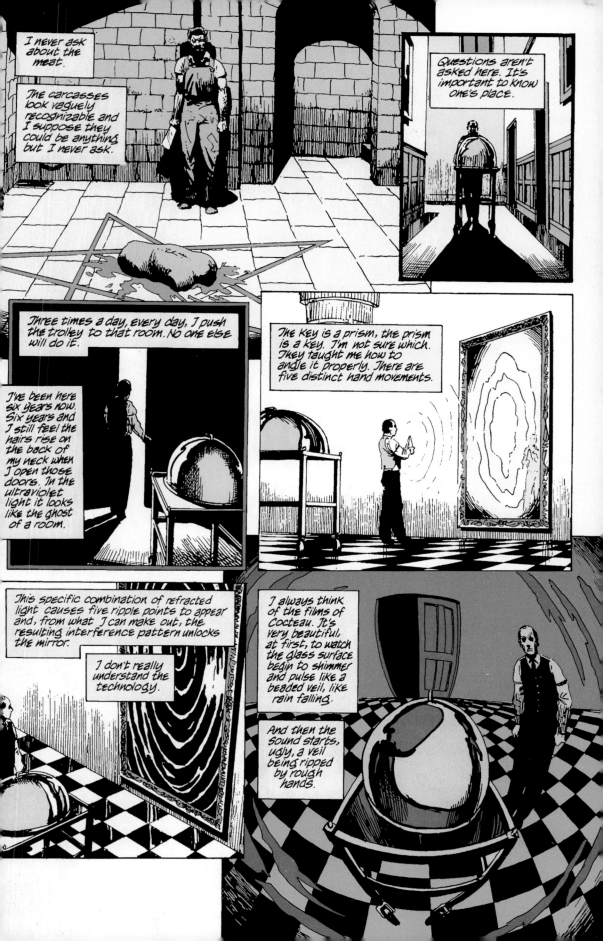

I never ask about the meat.

The carcasses look vaguely recognizable and I suppose they could be anything but I never ask.

Questions aren't asked here. It's important to know one's place.

Three times a day, every day, I push the trolley to that room. No one else will do it.

I've been here six years now. Six years and I still feel the hairs rise on the back of my neck when I open those doors. In the ultraviolet light it looks like the ghost of a room.

The key is a prism, the prism is a key. I'm not sure which. They taught me how to angle it properly. There are five distinct hand movements.

This specific combination of refracted light causes five ripple points to appear and, from what I can make out, the resulting interference pattern unlocks the mirror.

I don't really understand the technology.

I always think of the films of Cocteau. It's very beautiful, at first, to watch the glass surface begin to shimmer and pulse like a beaded veil, like rain falling.

And then the sound starts, ugly, a veil being ripped by rough hands.

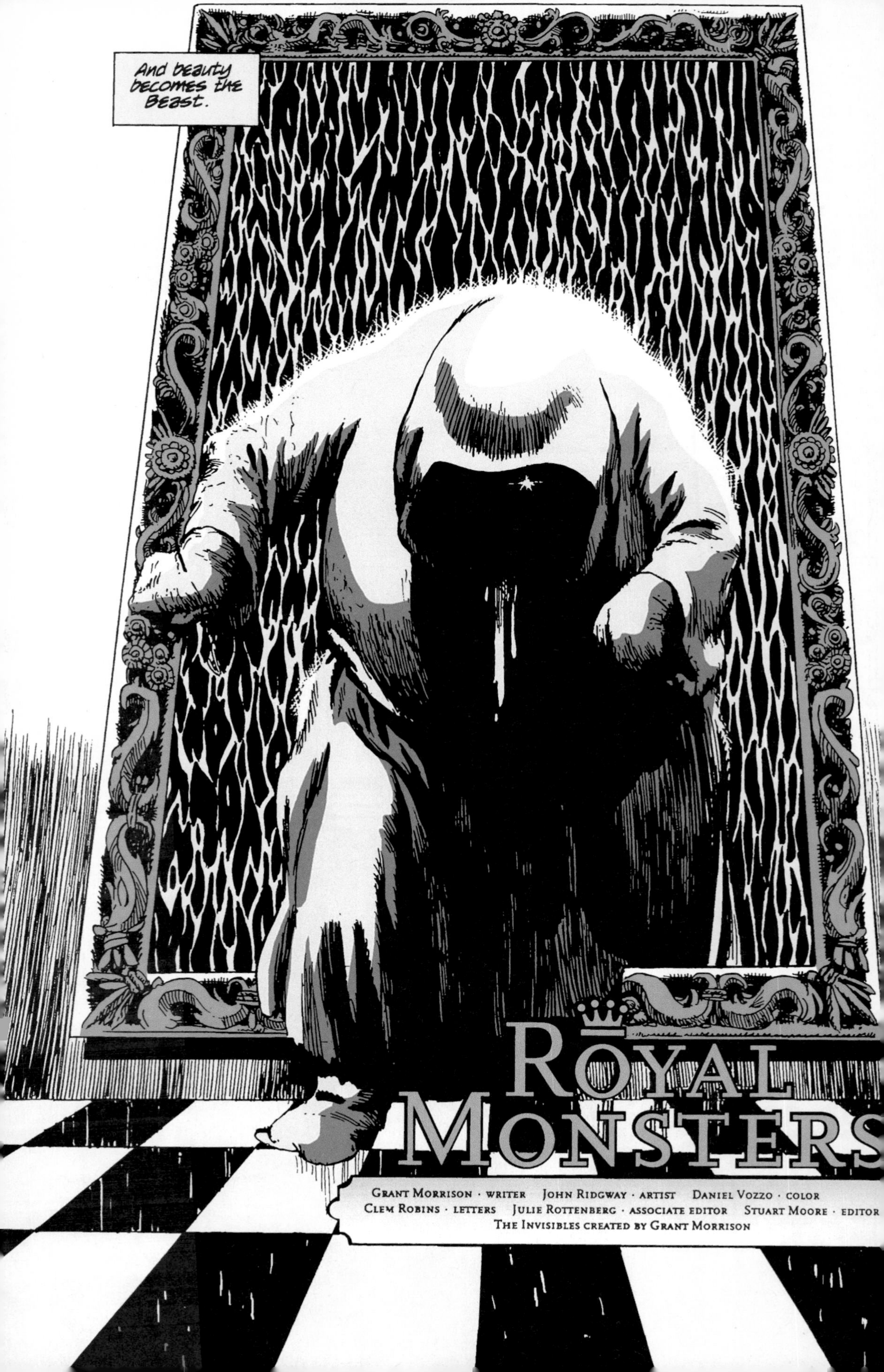

And beauty becomes the Beast.
ROYAL MONSTERS
GRANT MORRISON · WRITER JOHN RIDGWAY · ARTIST DANIEL VOZZO · COLOR
CLEM ROBINS · LETTERS JULIE ROTTENBERG · ASSOCIATE EDITOR STUART MOORE · EDITOR
THE INVISIBLES CREATED BY GRANT MORRISON

The smell is appalling and there's noise from beyond the mirror door; a relentless antiphonic clashing, and roaring. I imagine agonized women giving birth to dreadful machines.

Choirs singing in Hell might sound that way.

I don't dare consider what its world must be like, the world on the reverse of the mirror.

No, I do dare... I sometimes wonder what would be waiting if I stepped through, like Alice...

It always does the same thing --hunching over the carcass and expressing some kind of frothing, corrosive foam which softens and partially dissolves the meat.

As I said, I'm the only one who dares come in here. Everyone else is frightened.

I know the difference between fear and awe.

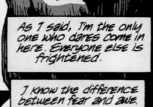

It looked at me again today. Something passed between us--an understanding, of sorts, an acknowledgment.

I'm beginning to think it likes me.

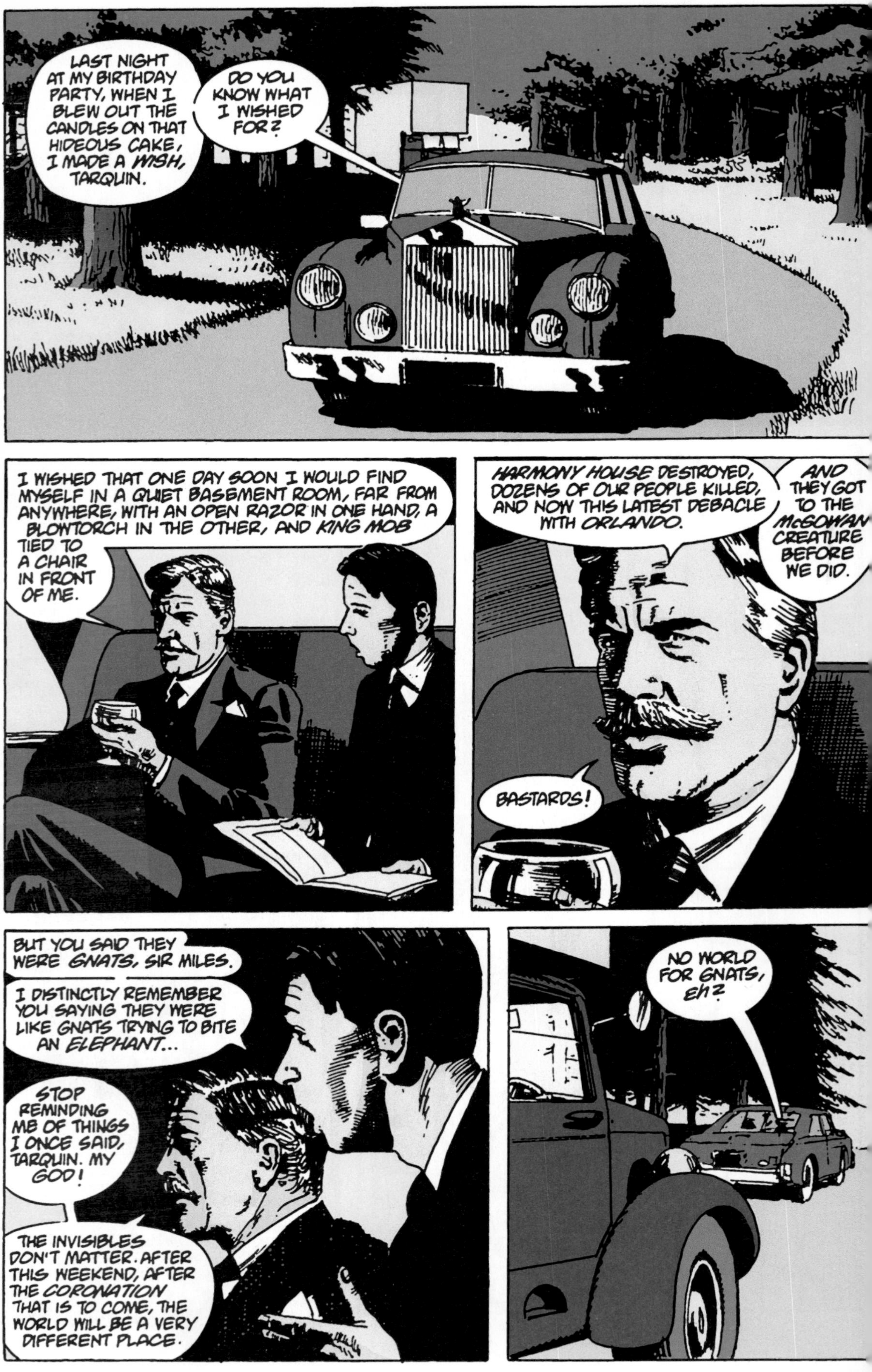

LAST NIGHT AT MY BIRTHDAY PARTY, WHEN I BLEW OUT THE CANDLES ON THAT HIDEOUS CAKE, I MADE A *WISH*, TARQUIN.
DO YOU KNOW WHAT I WISHED FOR?
I WISHED THAT ONE DAY SOON I WOULD FIND MYSELF IN A QUIET BASEMENT ROOM, FAR FROM ANYWHERE, WITH AN OPEN RAZOR IN ONE HAND, A BLOWTORCH IN THE OTHER, AND *KING MOB* TIED TO A CHAIR IN FRONT OF ME.
HARMONY HOUSE DESTROYED, DOZENS OF OUR PEOPLE KILLED, AND NOW THIS LATEST DEBACLE WITH *ORLANDO*.
AND THEY GOT TO THE *McGOWAN* CREATURE BEFORE WE DID.
BASTARDS!
BUT YOU SAID THEY WERE *GNATS*, SIR MILES.
I DISTINCTLY REMEMBER YOU SAYING THEY WERE LIKE GNATS TRYING TO BITE AN *ELEPHANT*...
STOP REMINDING ME OF THINGS I ONCE SAID, TARQUIN. MY GOD!
THE INVISIBLES DON'T MATTER. AFTER THIS WEEKEND, AFTER THE *CORONATION* THAT IS TO COME, THE WORLD WILL BE A VERY DIFFERENT PLACE.
NO WORLD FOR GNATS, EH?

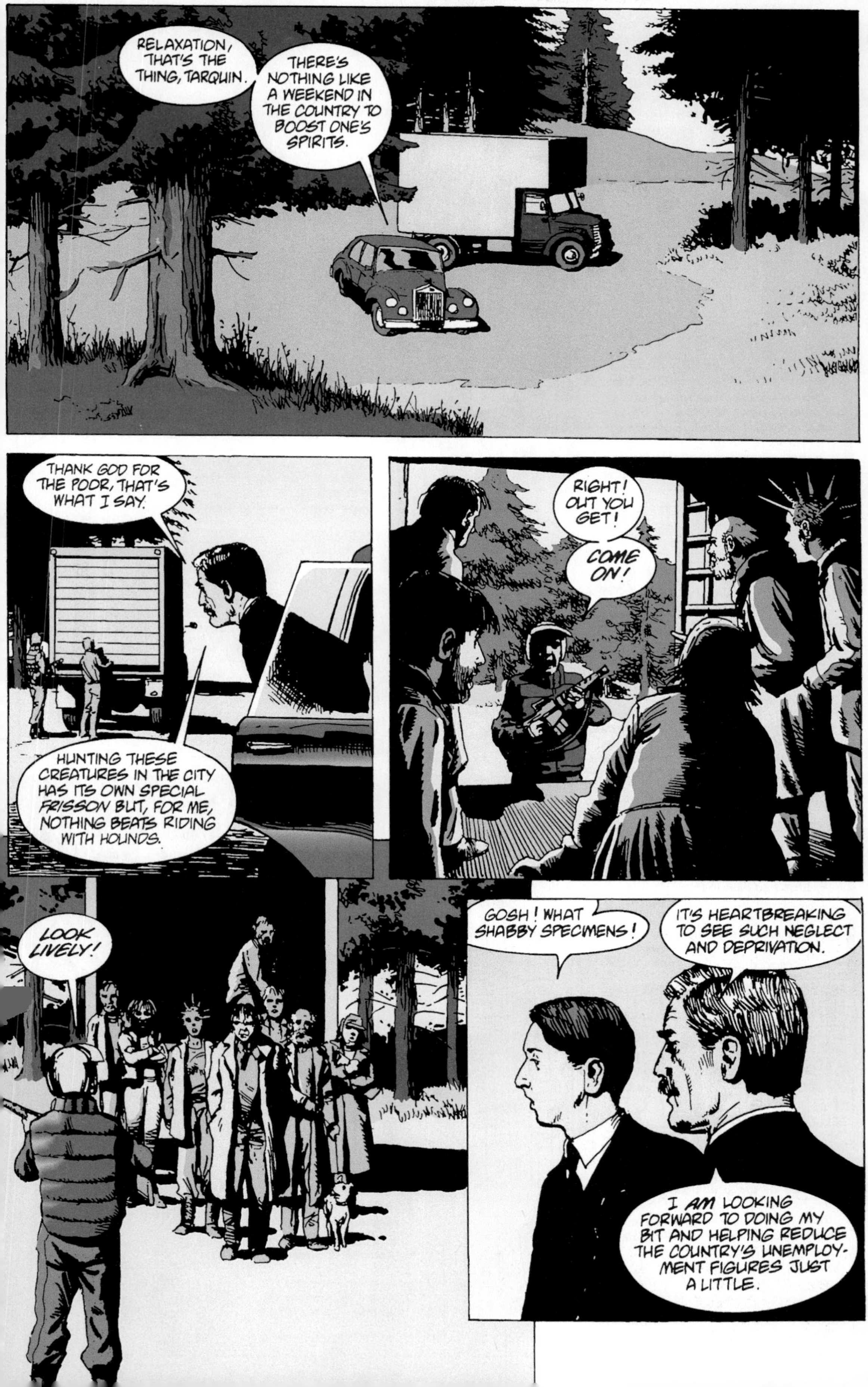
RELAXATION, THAT'S THE THING, TARQUIN.
THERE'S NOTHING LIKE A WEEKEND IN THE COUNTRY TO BOOST ONE'S SPIRITS.
THANK GOD FOR THE POOR, THAT'S WHAT I SAY.
HUNTING THESE CREATURES IN THE CITY HAS ITS OWN SPECIAL FRISSON BUT, FOR ME, NOTHING BEATS RIDING WITH HOUNDS.
RIGHT! OUT YOU GET!
COME ON!
LOOK LIVELY!
GOSH! WHAT SHABBY SPECIMENS!
IT'S HEARTBREAKING TO SEE SUCH NEGLECT AND DEPRIVATION.
I AM LOOKING FORWARD TO DOING MY BIT AND HELPING REDUCE THE COUNTRY'S UNEMPLOY-MENT FIGURES JUST A LITTLE.

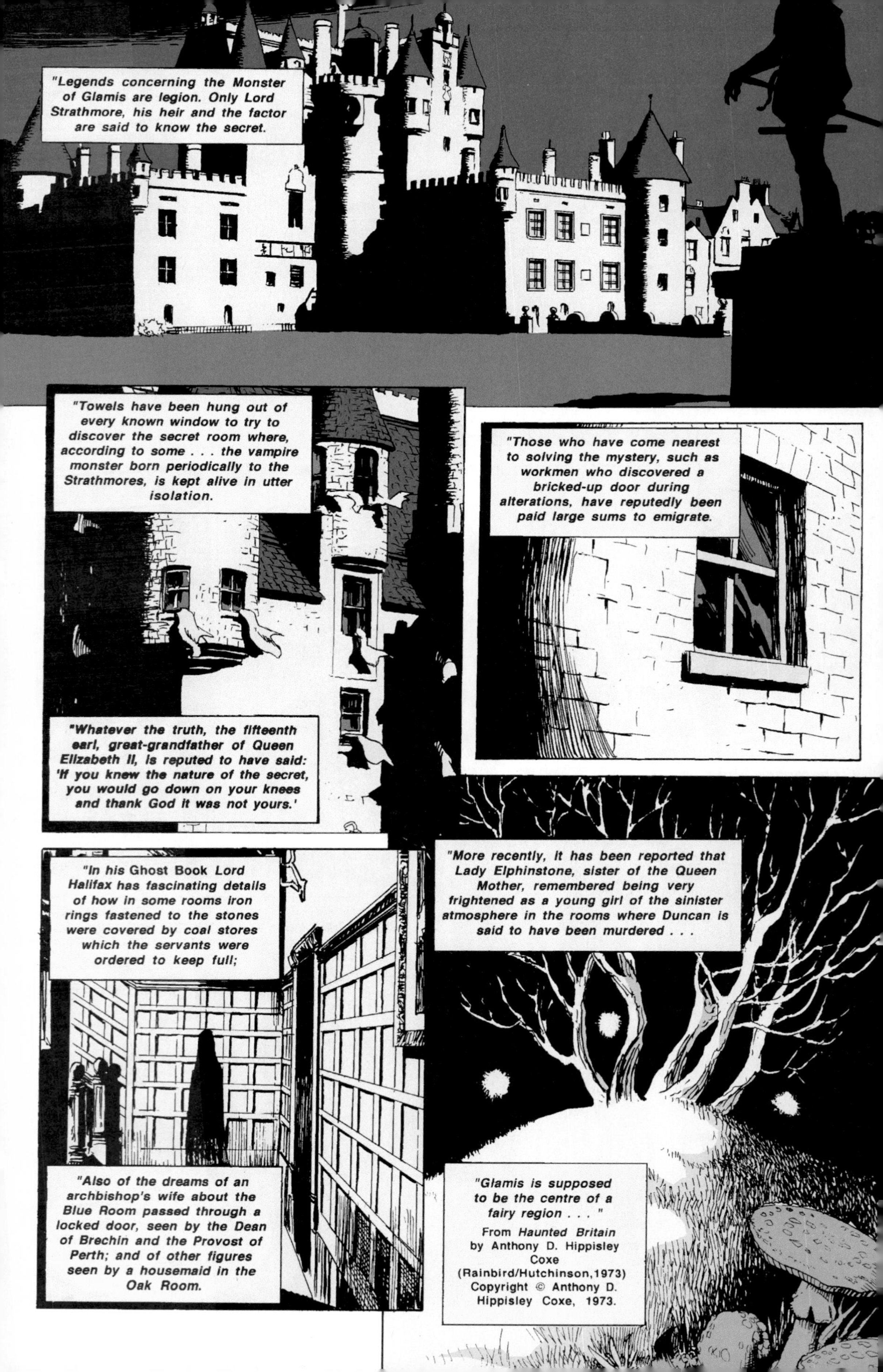
"Legends concerning the Monster of Glamis are legion. Only Lord Strathmore, his heir and the factor are said to know the secret.
"Towels have been hung out of every known window to try to discover the secret room where, according to some . . . the vampire monster born periodically to the Strathmores, is kept alive in utter isolation.
"Those who have come nearest to solving the mystery, such as workmen who discovered a bricked-up door during alterations, have reputedly been paid large sums to emigrate.
"Whatever the truth, the fifteenth earl, great-grandfather of Queen Elizabeth II, is reputed to have said: 'If you knew the nature of the secret, you would go down on your knees and thank God it was not yours.'
"In his Ghost Book Lord Halifax has fascinating details of how in some rooms iron rings fastened to the stones were covered by coal stores which the servants were ordered to keep full;
"Also of the dreams of an archbishop's wife about the Blue Room passed through a locked door, seen by the Dean of Brechin and the Provost of Perth; and of other figures seen by a housemaid in the Oak Room.
"More recently, it has been reported that Lady Elphinstone, sister of the Queen Mother, remembered being very frightened as a young girl of the sinister atmosphere in the rooms where Duncan is said to have been murdered . . .
"Glamis is supposed to be the centre of a fairy region . . . "
From Haunted Britain by Anthony D. Hippisley Coxe (Rainbird/Hutchinson, 1973) Copyright © Anthony D. Hippisley Coxe, 1973.

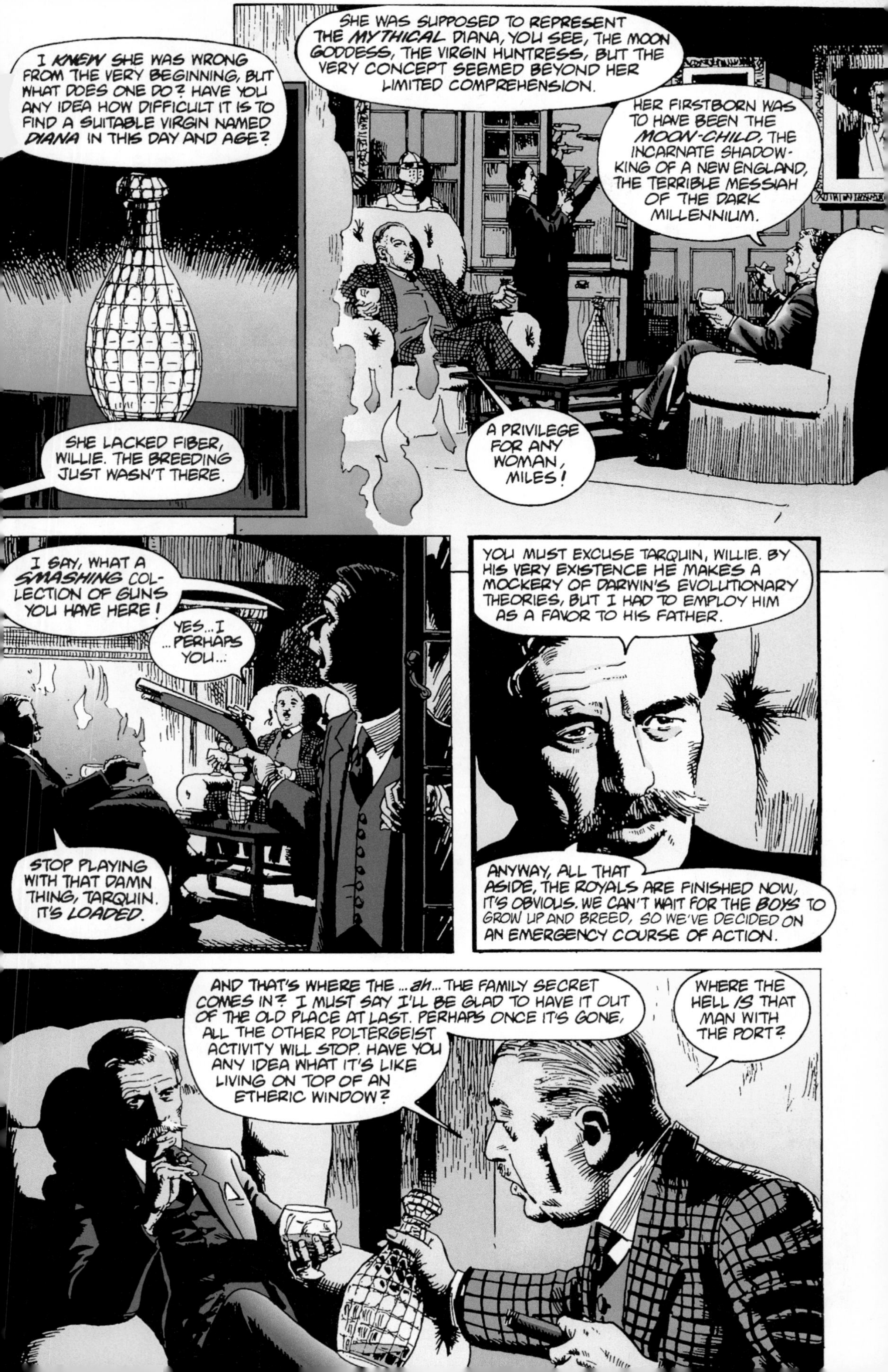
I KNEW SHE WAS WRONG FROM THE VERY BEGINNING, BUT WHAT DOES ONE DO? HAVE YOU ANY IDEA HOW DIFFICULT IT IS TO FIND A SUITABLE VIRGIN NAMED DIANA IN THIS DAY AND AGE?
SHE LACKED FIBER, WILLIE. THE BREEDING JUST WASN'T THERE.
SHE WAS SUPPOSED TO REPRESENT THE MYTHICAL DIANA, YOU SEE, THE MOON GODDESS, THE VIRGIN HUNTRESS, BUT THE VERY CONCEPT SEEMED BEYOND HER LIMITED COMPREHENSION.
HER FIRSTBORN WAS TO HAVE BEEN THE MOON-CHILD, THE INCARNATE SHADOW-KING OF A NEW ENGLAND, THE TERRIBLE MESSIAH OF THE DARK MILLENNIUM.
A PRIVILEGE FOR ANY WOMAN, MILES!
I SAY, WHAT A SMASHING COLLECTION OF GUNS YOU HAVE HERE!
YES... I ...PERHAPS YOU...
STOP PLAYING WITH THAT DAMN THING, TARQUIN. IT'S LOADED.
YOU MUST EXCUSE TARQUIN, WILLIE. BY HIS VERY EXISTENCE HE MAKES A MOCKERY OF DARWIN'S EVOLUTIONARY THEORIES, BUT I HAD TO EMPLOY HIM AS A FAVOR TO HIS FATHER.
ANYWAY, ALL THAT ASIDE, THE ROYALS ARE FINISHED NOW, IT'S OBVIOUS. WE CAN'T WAIT FOR THE BOYS TO GROW UP AND BREED, SO WE'VE DECIDED ON AN EMERGENCY COURSE OF ACTION.
AND THAT'S WHERE THE ... ah... THE FAMILY SECRET COMES IN? I MUST SAY I'LL BE GLAD TO HAVE IT OUT OF THE OLD PLACE AT LAST. PERHAPS ONCE IT'S GONE, ALL THE OTHER POLTERGEIST ACTIVITY WILL STOP. HAVE YOU ANY IDEA WHAT IT'S LIKE LIVING ON TOP OF AN ETHERIC WINDOW?
WHERE THE HELL IS THAT MAN WITH THE PORT?

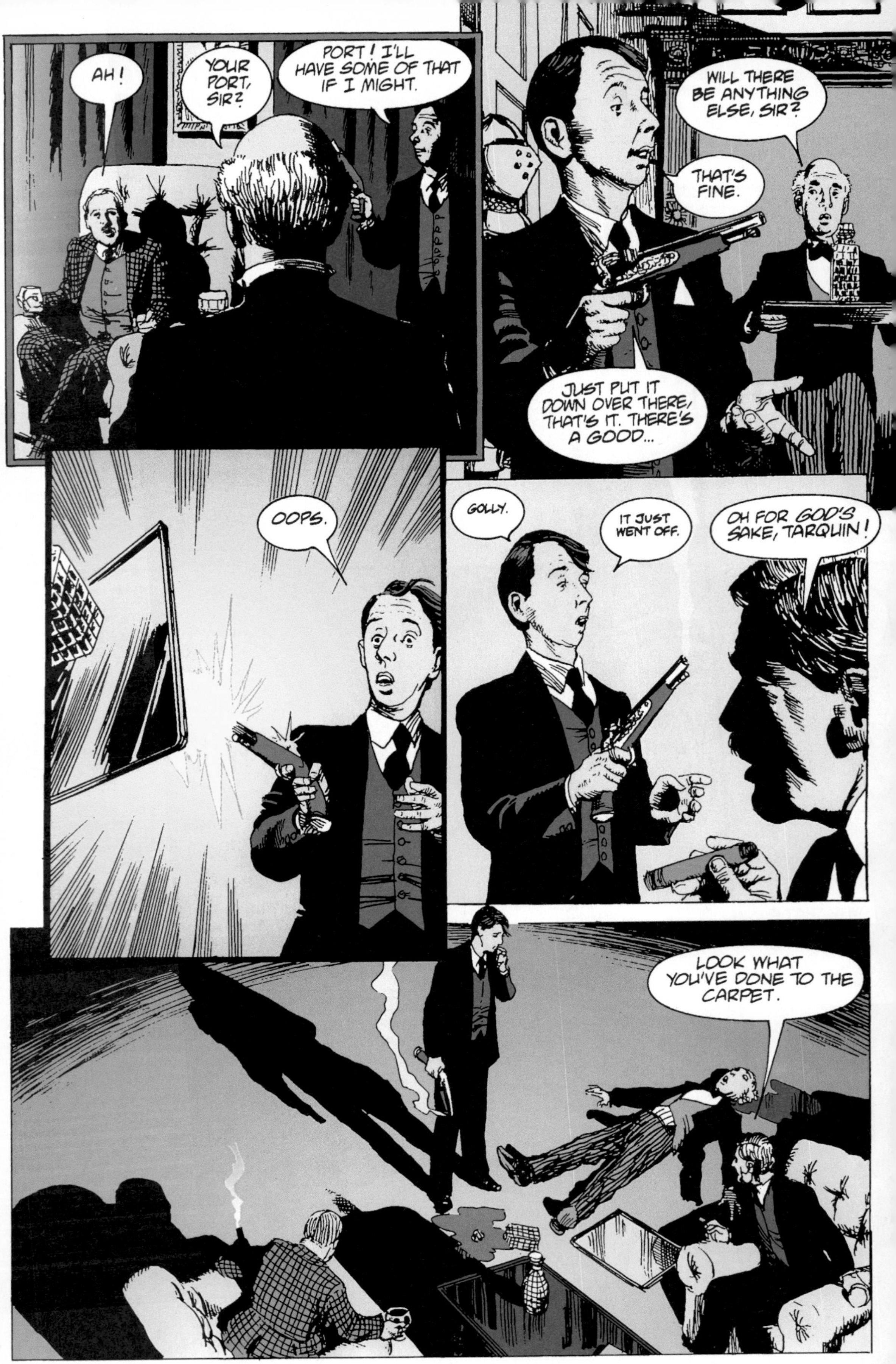
AH!
YOUR PORT, SIR?
PORT! I'LL HAVE SOME OF THAT IF I MIGHT.
WILL THERE BE ANYTHING ELSE, SIR?
THAT'S FINE.
JUST PUT IT DOWN OVER THERE, THAT'S IT. THERE'S A GOOD...
OOPS.
GOLLY.
IT JUST WENT OFF.
OH FOR GOD'S SAKE, TARQUIN!
LOOK WHAT YOU'VE DONE TO THE CARPET.

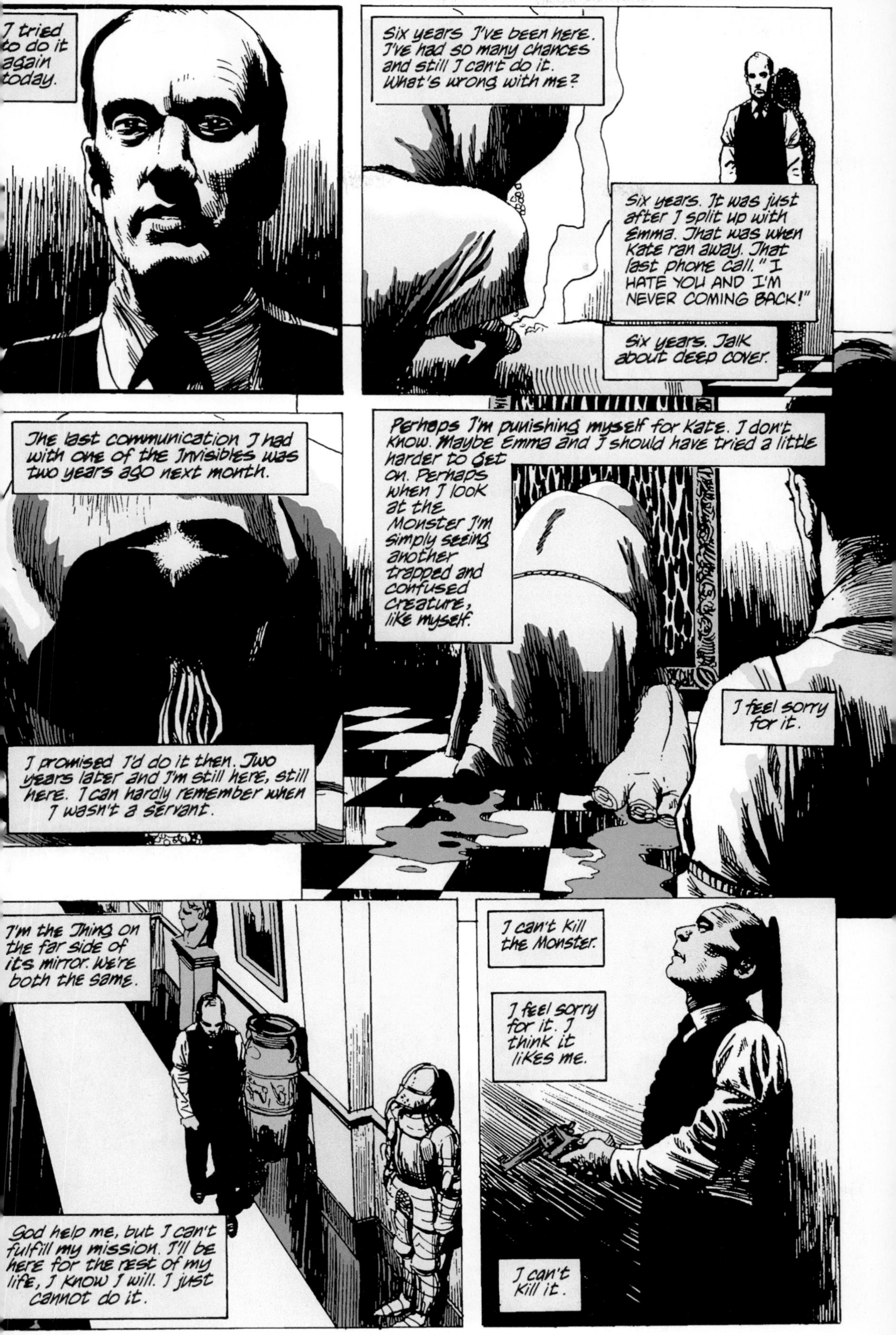
I tried to do it again today.
Six years I've been here. I've had so many chances and still I can't do it. What's wrong with me?
Six years. It was just after I split up with Emma. That was when Kate ran away. That last phone call. "I HATE YOU AND I'M NEVER COMING BACK!"
Six years. Talk about deep cover.
The last communication I had with one of the Invisibles was two years ago next month.
I promised I'd do it then. Two years later and I'm still here, still here. I can hardly remember when I wasn't a servant.
Perhaps I'm punishing myself for Kate. I don't know. Maybe Emma and I should have tried a little harder to get on. Perhaps when I look at the Monster I'm simply seeing another trapped and confused creature, like myself.
I feel sorry for it.
I'm the Thing on the far side of its mirror. We're both the same.
God help me, but I can't fulfill my mission. I'll be here for the rest of my life, I know I will. I just cannot do it.
I can't kill the Monster.
I feel sorry for it. I think it likes me.
I can't kill it.

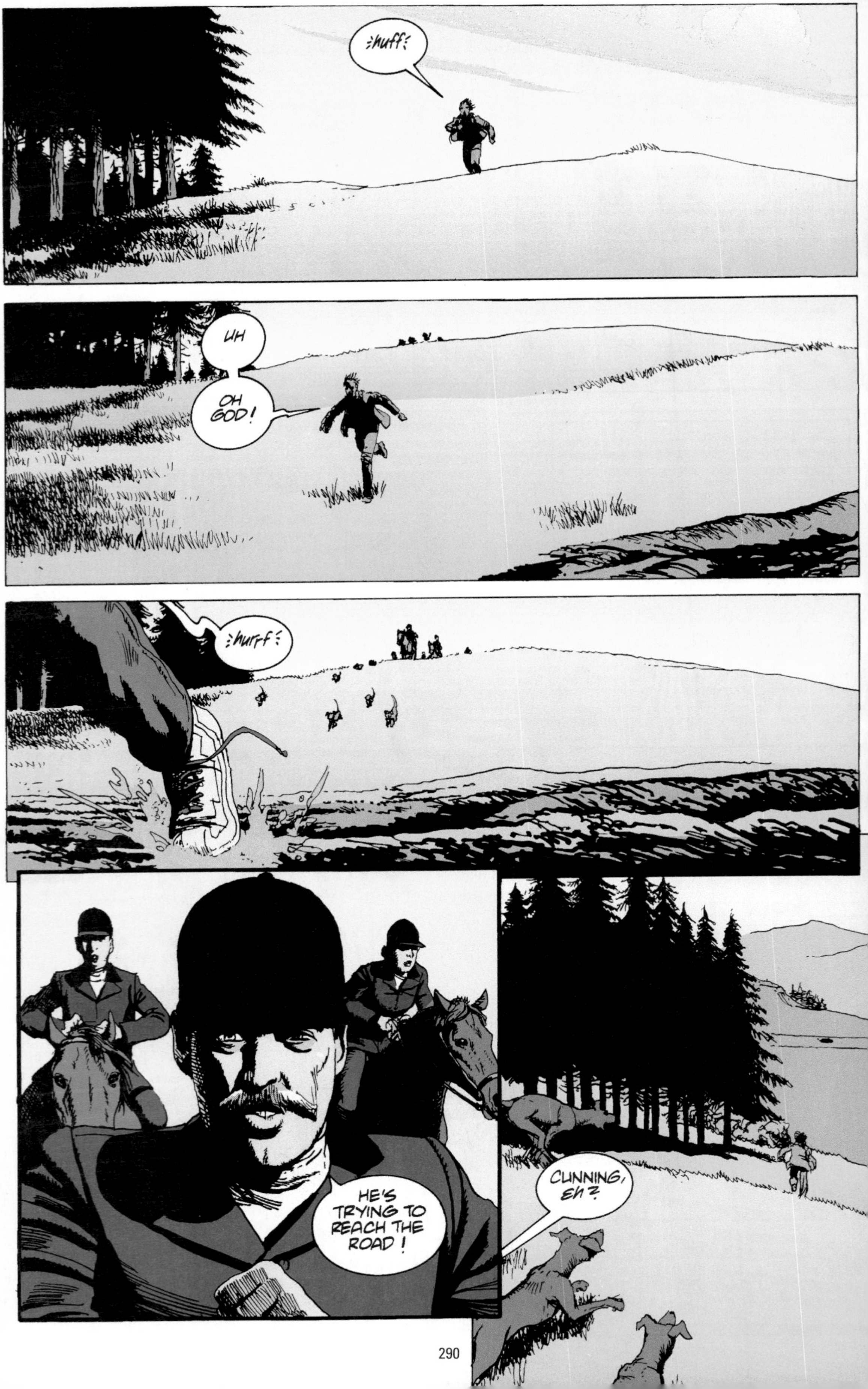
:huff:
UH
OH GOD!
:hurrf:
HE'S TRYING TO REACH THE ROAD!
CUNNING, EH?

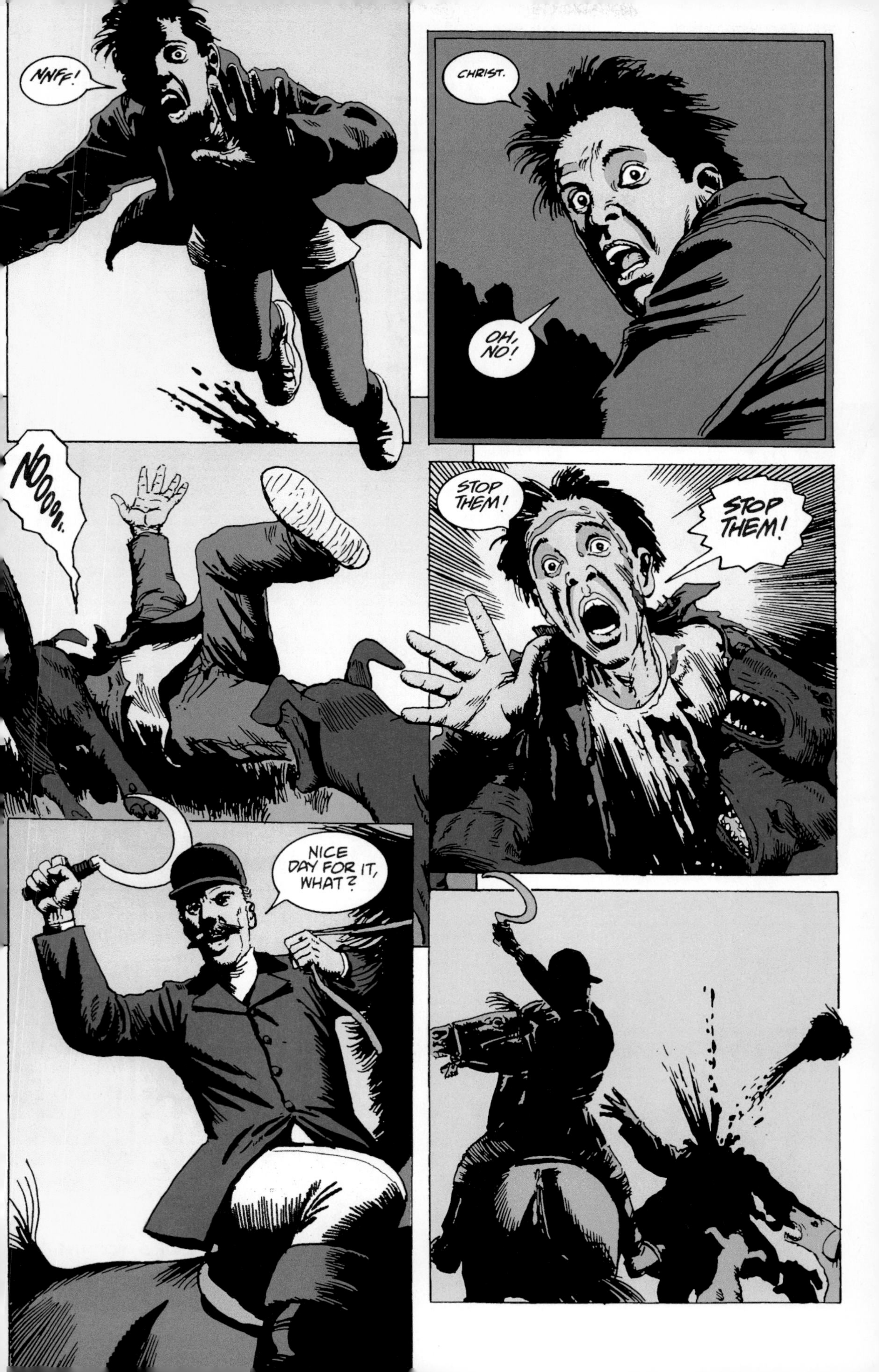
NNFF!
CHRIST.
OH, NO!
NOOOOO...
STOP THEM!
STOP THEM!
NICE DAY FOR IT, WHAT?

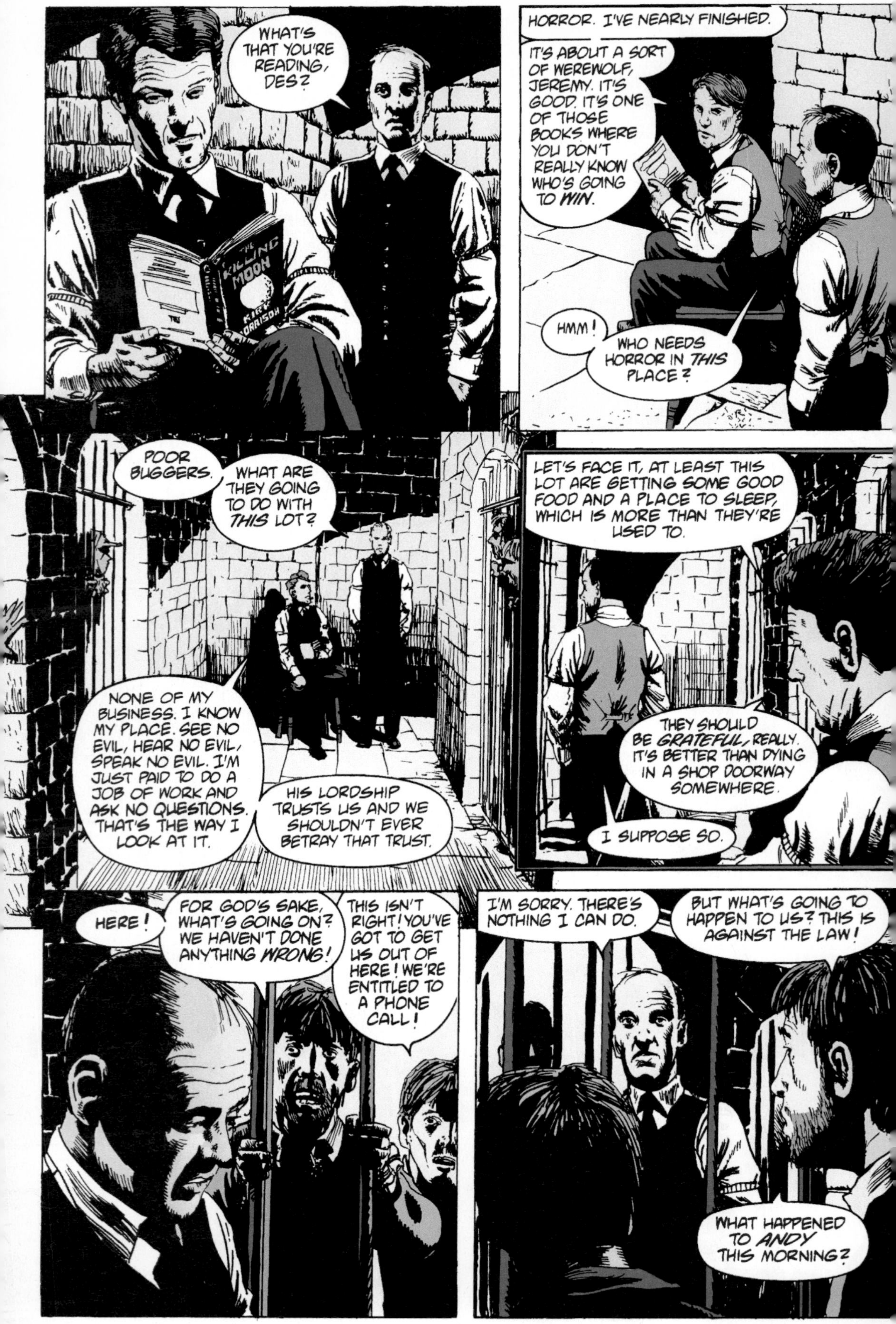

WHAT'S THAT YOU'RE READING, DES?
THE KILLING MOON
KIRK MORRISON
HORROR. I'VE NEARLY FINISHED.
IT'S ABOUT A SORT OF WEREWOLF, JEREMY. IT'S GOOD. IT'S ONE OF THOSE BOOKS WHERE YOU DON'T REALLY KNOW WHO'S GOING TO *WIN*.
HMM!
WHO NEEDS HORROR IN *THIS* PLACE?
POOR BUGGERS.
WHAT ARE THEY GOING TO DO WITH *THIS* LOT?
NONE OF MY BUSINESS. I KNOW MY PLACE. SEE NO EVIL, HEAR NO EVIL, SPEAK NO EVIL. I'M JUST PAID TO DO A JOB OF WORK AND ASK NO QUESTIONS. THAT'S THE WAY I LOOK AT IT.
HIS LORDSHIP TRUSTS US AND WE SHOULDN'T EVER BETRAY THAT TRUST.
LET'S FACE IT, AT LEAST THIS LOT ARE GETTING SOME GOOD FOOD AND A PLACE TO SLEEP, WHICH IS MORE THAN THEY'RE USED TO.
THEY SHOULD BE *GRATEFUL*, REALLY. IT'S BETTER THAN DYING IN A SHOP DOORWAY SOMEWHERE.
I SUPPOSE SO.
HERE!
FOR GOD'S SAKE, WHAT'S GOING ON? WE HAVEN'T DONE ANYTHING *WRONG*!
THIS ISN'T RIGHT! YOU'VE GOT TO GET US OUT OF HERE! WE'RE ENTITLED TO A PHONE CALL!
I'M SORRY. THERE'S NOTHING I CAN DO.
BUT WHAT'S GOING TO HAPPEN TO US? THIS IS AGAINST THE LAW!
WHAT HAPPENED TO *ANDY* THIS MORNING?

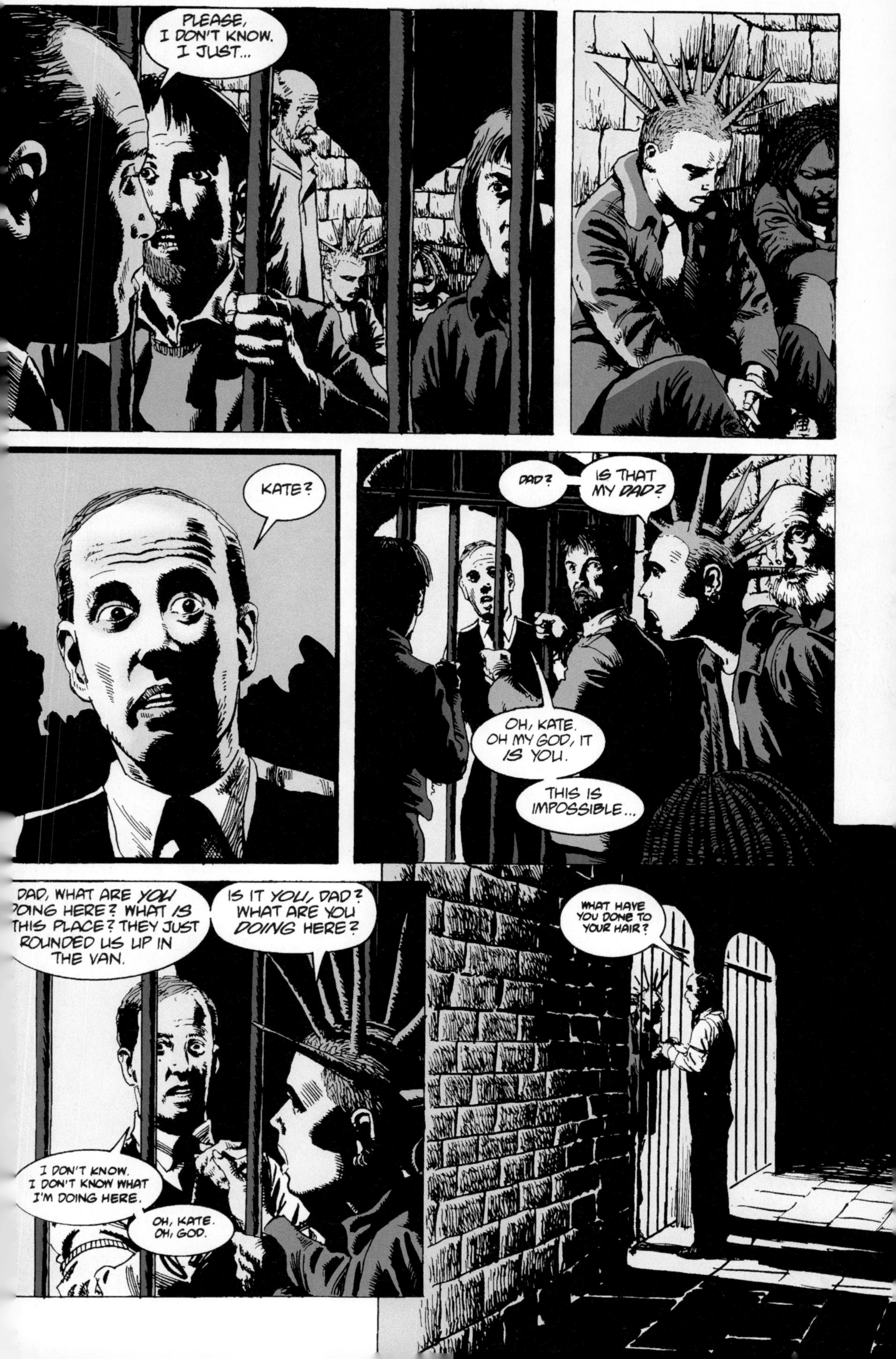
PLEASE, I DON'T KNOW. I JUST...
KATE?
DAD?
IS THAT MY DAD?
OH, KATE. OH MY GOD, IT IS YOU.
THIS IS IMPOSSIBLE...
DAD, WHAT ARE YOU DOING HERE? WHAT IS THIS PLACE? THEY JUST ROUNDED US UP IN THE VAN.
IS IT YOU, DAD? WHAT ARE YOU DOING HERE?
I DON'T KNOW. I DON'T KNOW WHAT I'M DOING HERE.
OH, KATE. OH, GOD.
WHAT HAVE YOU DONE TO YOUR HAIR?

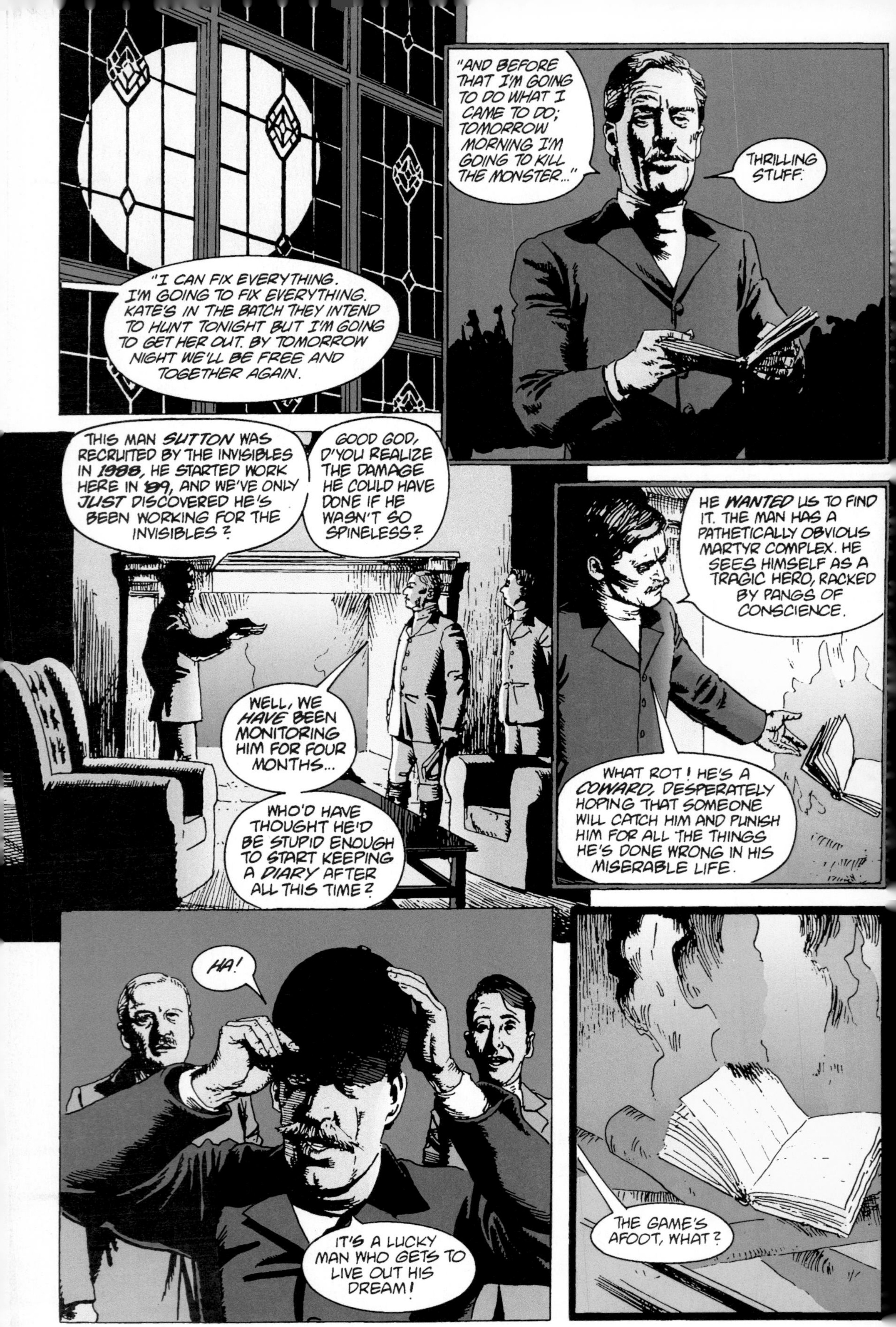
"I CAN FIX EVERYTHING. I'M GOING TO FIX EVERYTHING. KATE'S IN THE BATCH THEY INTEND TO HUNT TONIGHT BUT I'M GOING TO GET HER OUT. BY TOMORROW NIGHT WE'LL BE FREE AND TOGETHER AGAIN.
"AND BEFORE THAT I'M GOING TO DO WHAT I CAME TO DO; TOMORROW MORNING I'M GOING TO KILL THE MONSTER..."
THRILLING STUFF.
THIS MAN SUTTON WAS RECRUITED BY THE INVISIBLES IN 1988, HE STARTED WORK HERE IN '89, AND WE'VE ONLY JUST DISCOVERED HE'S BEEN WORKING FOR THE INVISIBLES?
GOOD GOD, D'YOU REALIZE THE DAMAGE HE COULD HAVE DONE IF HE WASN'T SO SPINELESS?
WELL, WE HAVE BEEN MONITORING HIM FOR FOUR MONTHS...
WHO'D HAVE THOUGHT HE'D BE STUPID ENOUGH TO START KEEPING A DIARY AFTER ALL THIS TIME?
HE WANTED US TO FIND IT. THE MAN HAS A PATHETICALLY OBVIOUS MARTYR COMPLEX. HE SEES HIMSELF AS A TRAGIC HERO, RACKED BY PANGS OF CONSCIENCE.
WHAT ROT! HE'S A COWARD, DESPERATELY HOPING THAT SOMEONE WILL CATCH HIM AND PUNISH HIM FOR ALL THE THINGS HE'S DONE WRONG IN HIS MISERABLE LIFE.
HA!
IT'S A LUCKY MAN WHO GETS TO LIVE OUT HIS DREAM!
THE GAME'S AFOOT, WHAT?

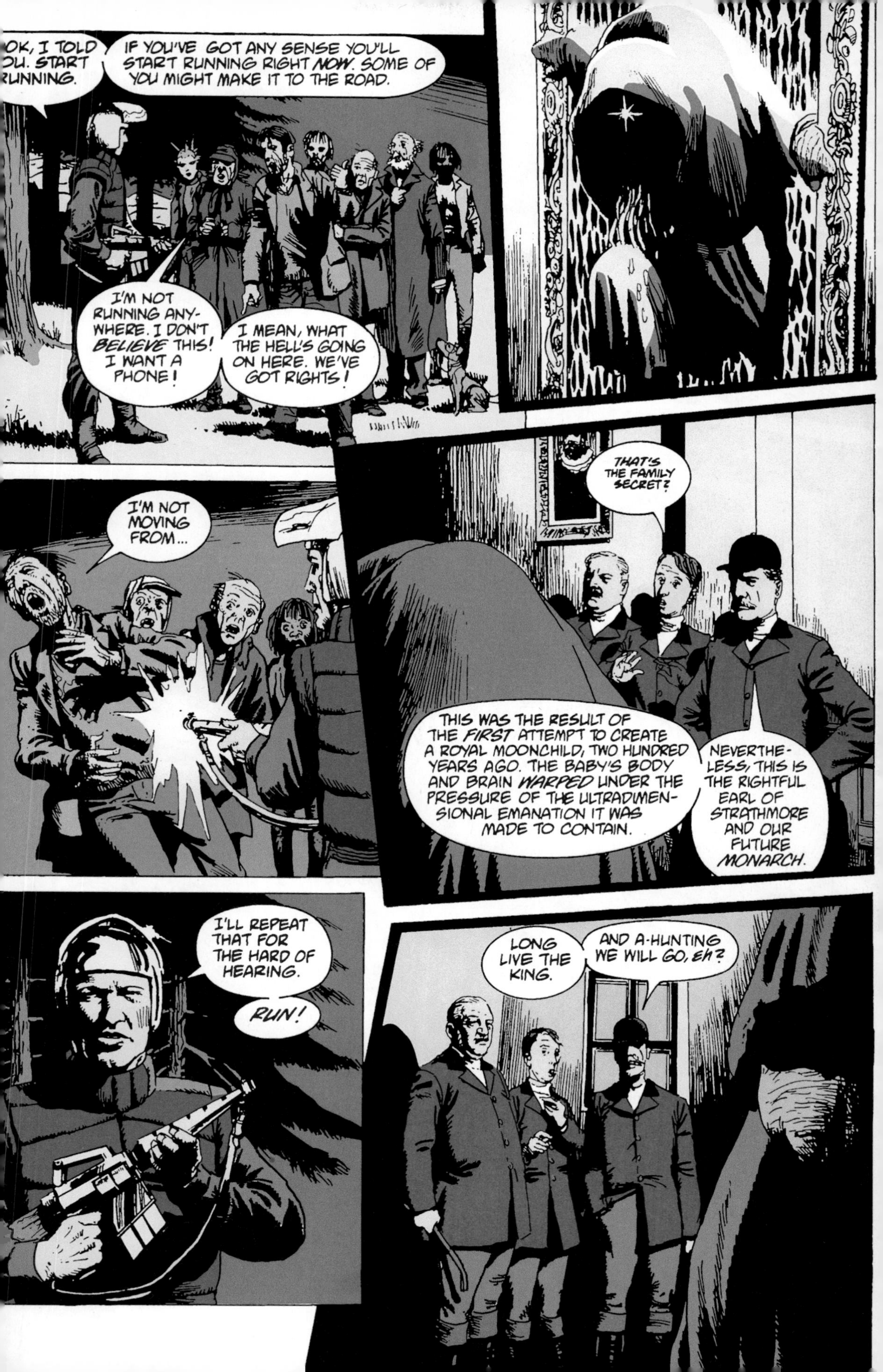

OK, I TOLD YOU. START RUNNING.
IF YOU'VE GOT ANY SENSE YOU'LL START RUNNING RIGHT NOW. SOME OF YOU MIGHT MAKE IT TO THE ROAD.
I'M NOT RUNNING ANYWHERE. I DON'T BELIEVE THIS! I WANT A PHONE!
I MEAN, WHAT THE HELL'S GOING ON HERE. WE'VE GOT RIGHTS!
THAT'S THE FAMILY SECRET?
I'M NOT MOVING FROM...
THIS WAS THE RESULT OF THE FIRST ATTEMPT TO CREATE A ROYAL MOONCHILD, TWO HUNDRED YEARS AGO. THE BABY'S BODY AND BRAIN WARPED UNDER THE PRESSURE OF THE ULTRADIMENSIONAL EMANATION IT WAS MADE TO CONTAIN.
NEVERTHELESS, THIS IS THE RIGHTFUL EARL OF STRATHMORE AND OUR FUTURE MONARCH.
I'LL REPEAT THAT FOR THE HARD OF HEARING.
RUN!
LONG LIVE THE KING.
AND A-HUNTING WE WILL GO, EH?

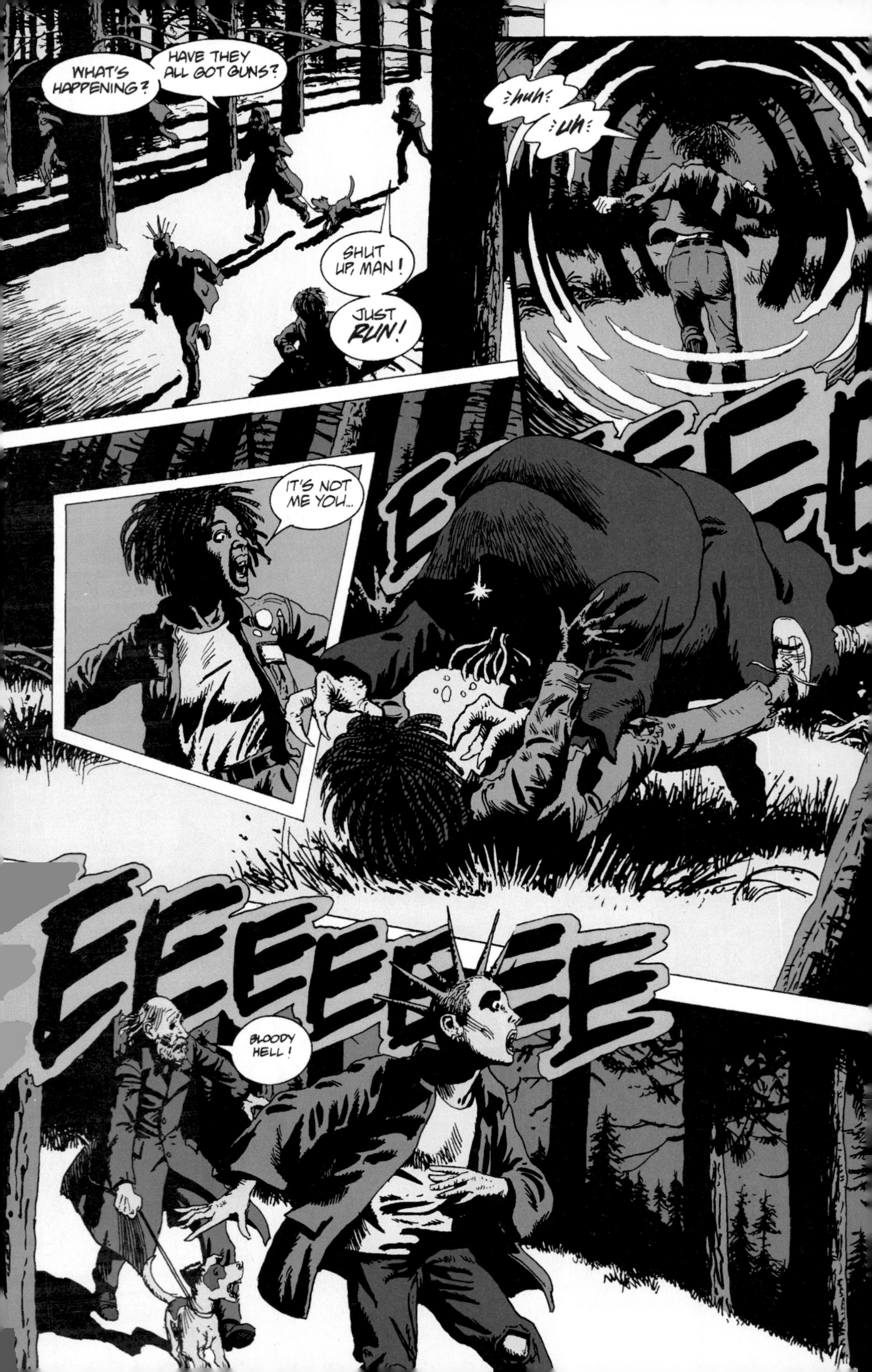
WHAT'S HAPPENING?
HAVE THEY ALL GOT GUNS?
SHUT UP, MAN!
JUST RUN!
huh
uh
IT'S NOT ME YOU...
EEEEEEEE
BLOODY HELL!

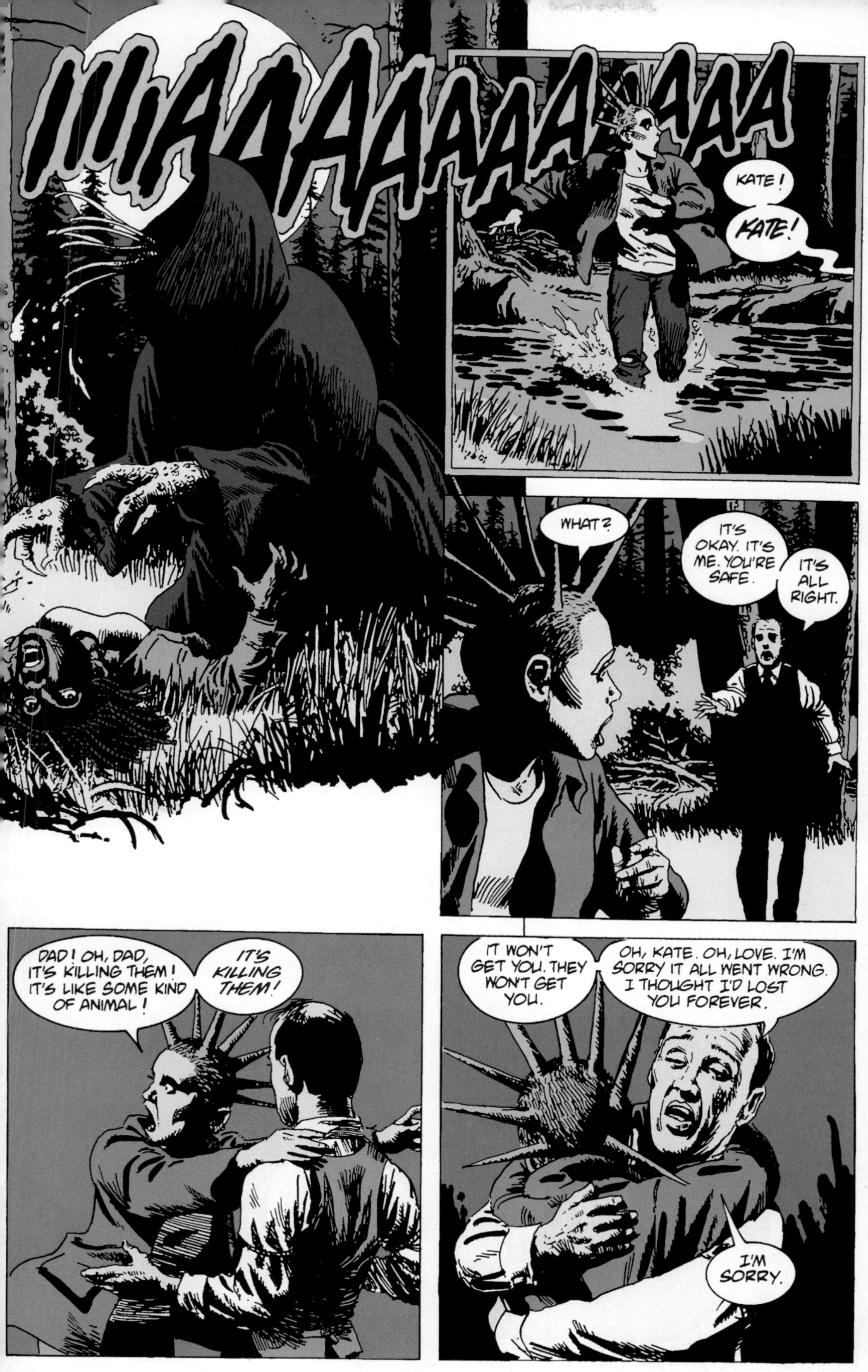
IIIAAAAAAAAAAAA
KATE!
KATE!
WHAT?
IT'S OKAY. IT'S ME. YOU'RE SAFE.
IT'S ALL RIGHT.
DAD! OH, DAD, IT'S KILLING THEM! IT'S LIKE SOME KIND OF ANIMAL!
IT'S KILLING THEM!
IT WON'T GET YOU. THEY WON'T GET YOU.
OH, KATE. OH, LOVE. I'M SORRY IT ALL WENT WRONG. I THOUGHT I'D LOST YOU FOREVER.
I'M SORRY.

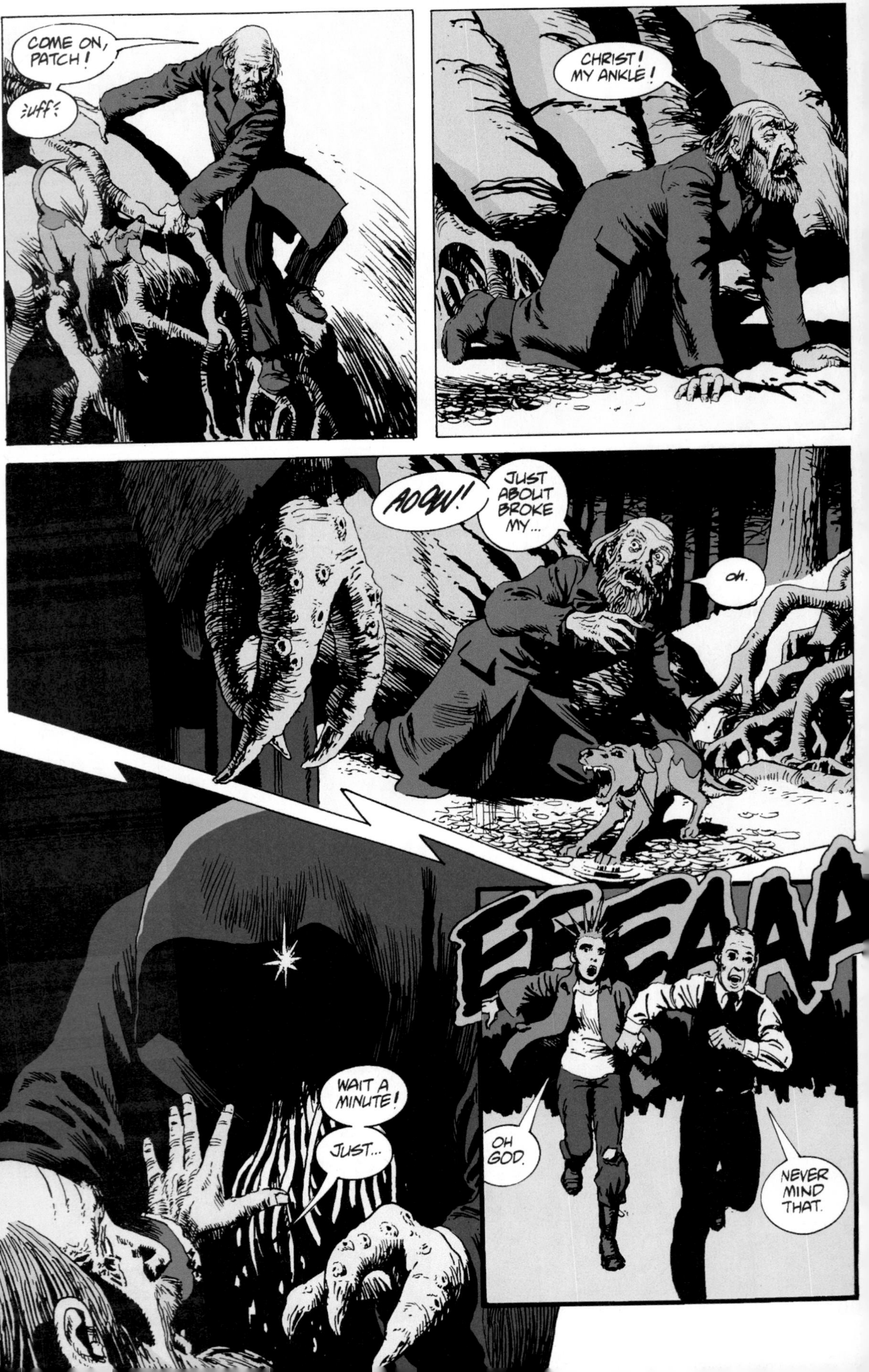
COME ON, PATCH!
:UFF:
CHRIST! MY ANKLE!
AOOW!
JUST ABOUT BROKE MY...
OH.
WAIT A MINUTE!
JUST...
OH GOD.
NEVER MIND THAT.

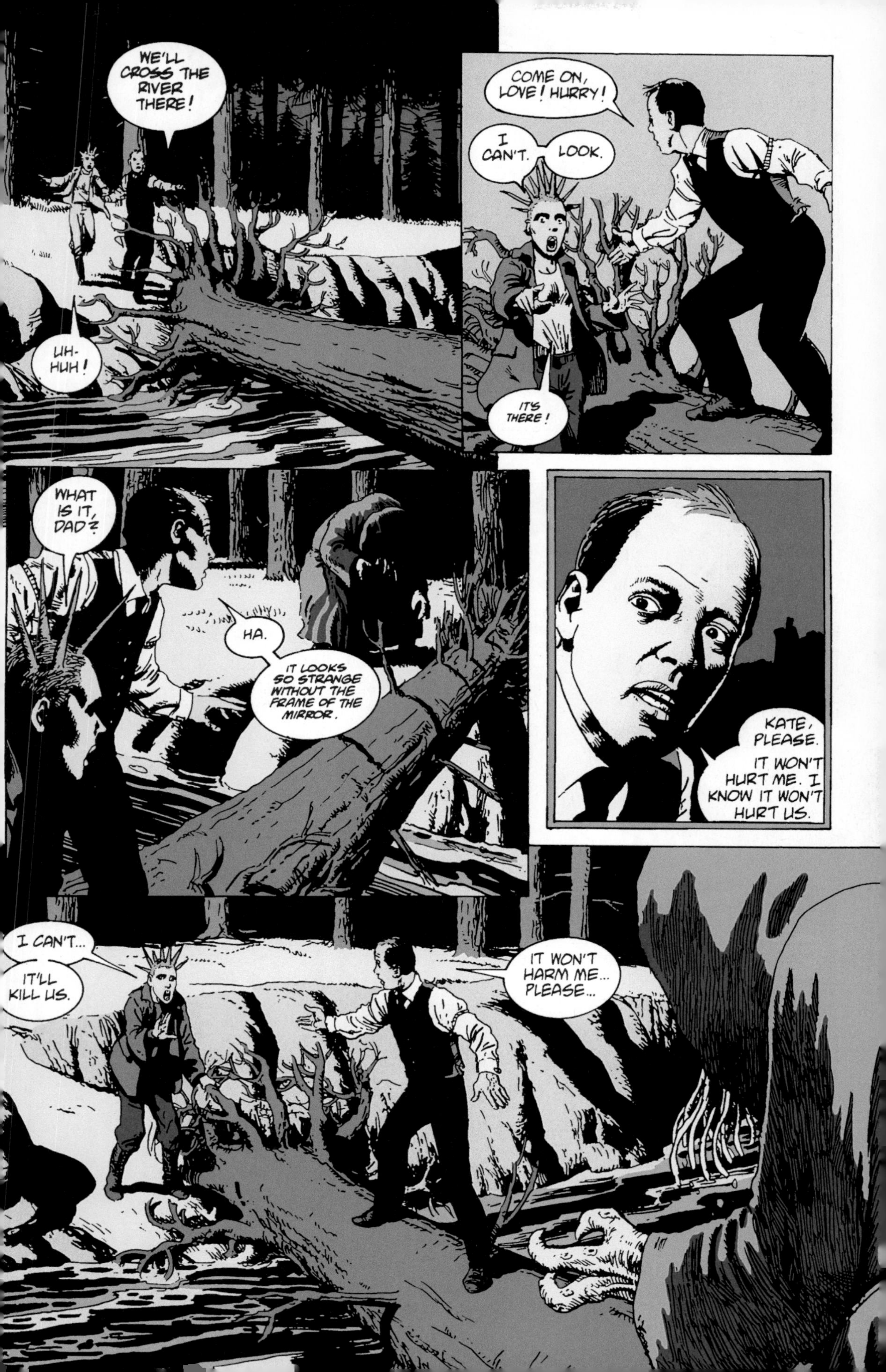
WE'LL CROSS THE RIVER THERE!
UH-HUH!
COME ON, LOVE! HURRY!
I CAN'T.
LOOK.
IT'S THERE!
WHAT IS IT, DAD?
HA.
IT LOOKS SO STRANGE WITHOUT THE FRAME OF THE MIRROR.
KATE, PLEASE.
IT WON'T HURT ME. I KNOW IT WON'T HURT US.
I CAN'T...
IT'LL KILL US.
IT WON'T HARM ME... PLEASE...

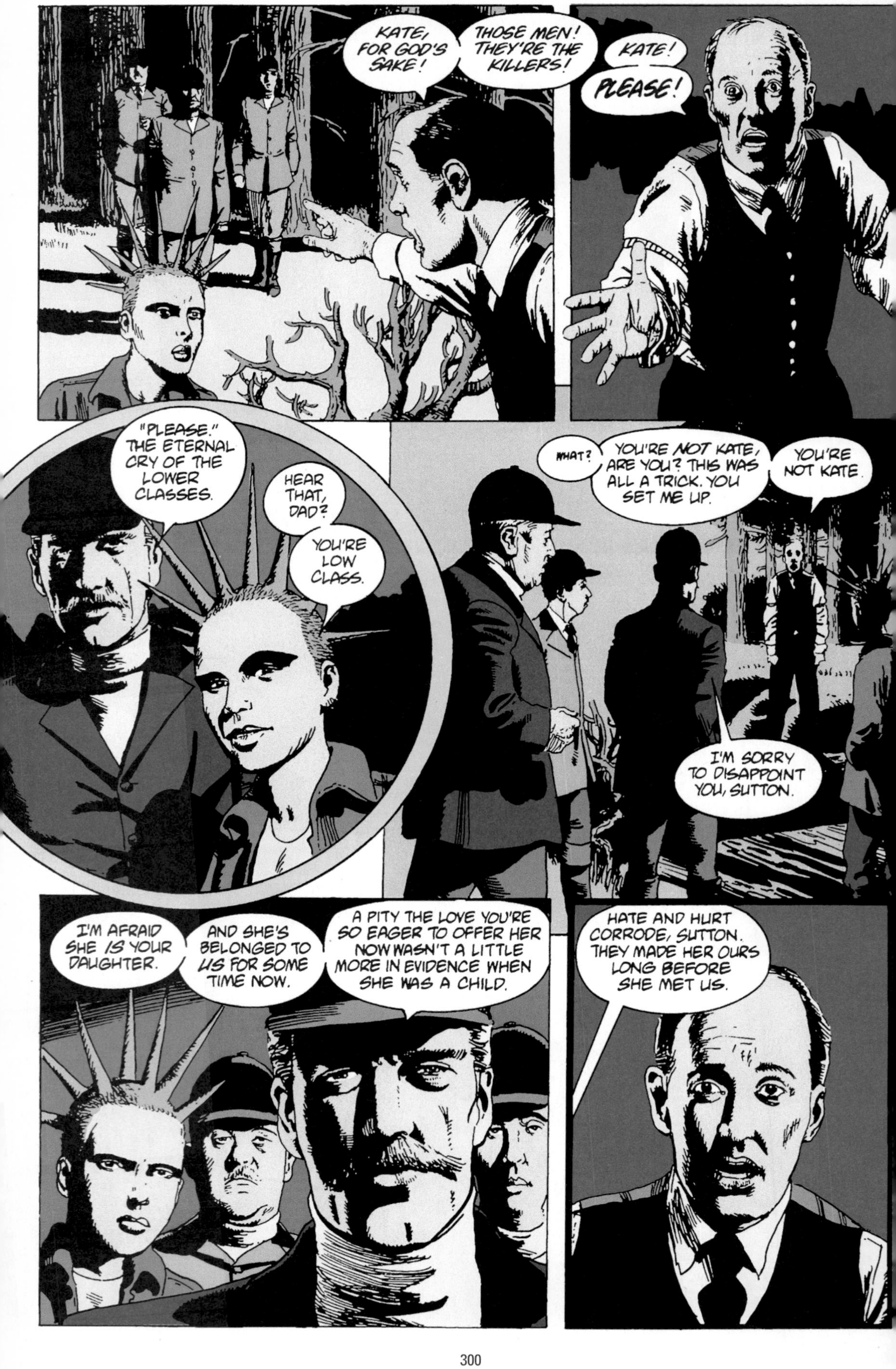
KATE, FOR GOD'S SAKE!
THOSE MEN! THEY'RE THE KILLERS!
KATE!
PLEASE!
"PLEASE." THE ETERNAL CRY OF THE LOWER CLASSES.
HEAR THAT, DAD?
YOU'RE LOW CLASS.
WHAT?
YOU'RE NOT KATE, ARE YOU? THIS WAS ALL A TRICK. YOU SET ME UP.
YOU'RE NOT KATE.
I'M SORRY TO DISAPPOINT YOU, SUTTON.
I'M AFRAID SHE IS YOUR DAUGHTER.
AND SHE'S BELONGED TO US FOR SOME TIME NOW.
A PITY THE LOVE YOU'RE SO EAGER TO OFFER HER NOW WASN'T A LITTLE MORE IN EVIDENCE WHEN SHE WAS A CHILD.
HATE AND HURT CORRODE, SUTTON. THEY MADE HER OURS LONG BEFORE SHE MET US.

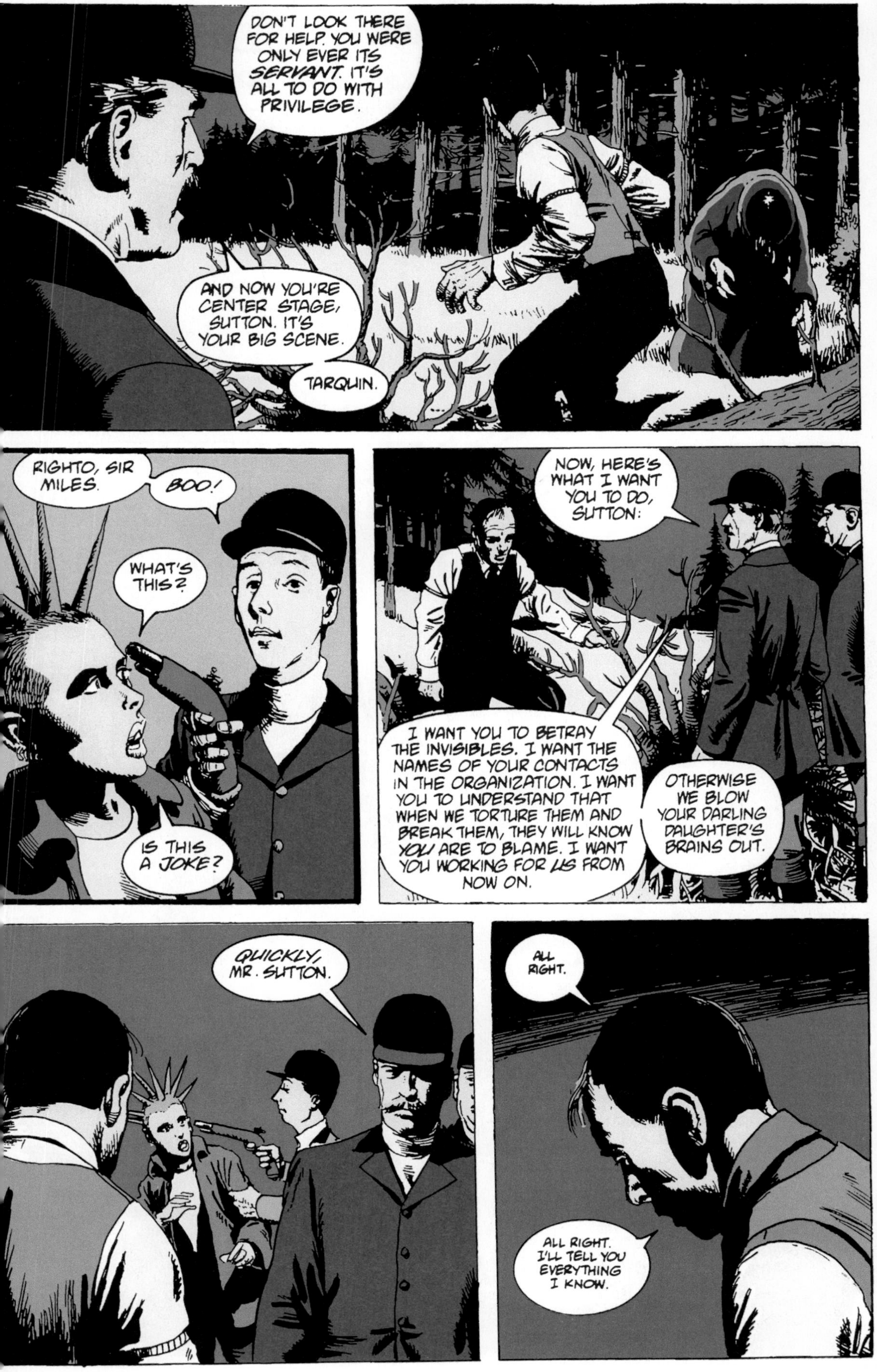
DON'T LOOK THERE FOR HELP. YOU WERE ONLY EVER ITS SERVANT. IT'S ALL TO DO WITH PRIVILEGE.
AND NOW YOU'RE CENTER STAGE, SUTTON. IT'S YOUR BIG SCENE.
TARQUIN.
RIGHTO, SIR MILES.
BOO!
WHAT'S THIS?
IS THIS A JOKE?
NOW, HERE'S WHAT I WANT YOU TO DO, SUTTON:
I WANT YOU TO BETRAY THE INVISIBLES. I WANT THE NAMES OF YOUR CONTACTS IN THE ORGANIZATION. I WANT YOU TO UNDERSTAND THAT WHEN WE TORTURE THEM AND BREAK THEM, THEY WILL KNOW YOU ARE TO BLAME. I WANT YOU WORKING FOR US FROM NOW ON.
OTHERWISE WE BLOW YOUR DARLING DAUGHTER'S BRAINS OUT.
QUICKLY, MR. SUTTON.
ALL RIGHT.
ALL RIGHT. I'LL TELL YOU EVERYTHING I KNOW.

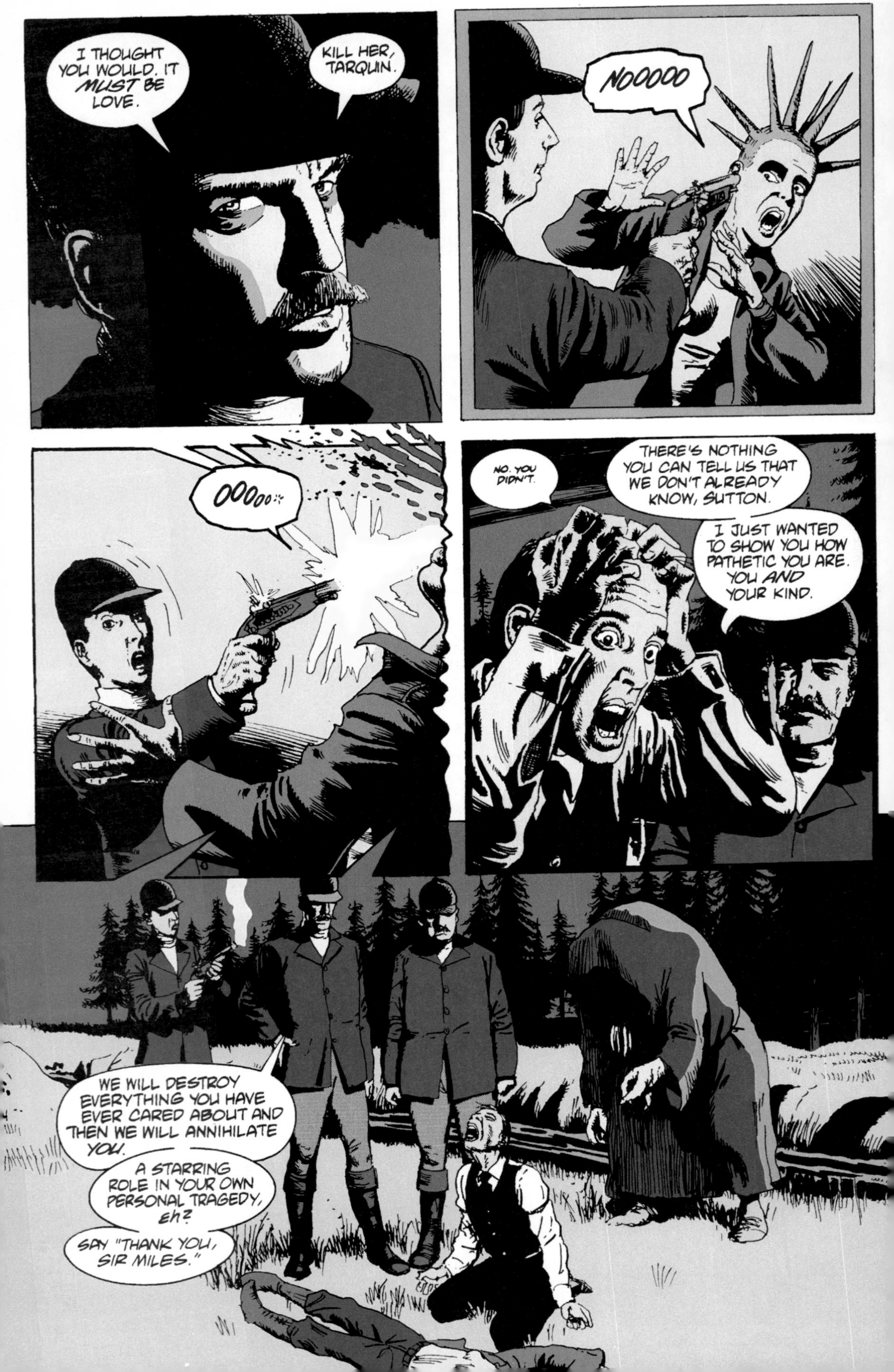

I THOUGHT YOU WOULD. IT MUST BE LOVE.
KILL HER, TARQUIN.
NOOOOO
OOOoo
NO. YOU DIDN'T.
THERE'S NOTHING YOU CAN TELL US THAT WE DON'T ALREADY KNOW, SUTTON.
I JUST WANTED TO SHOW YOU HOW PATHETIC YOU ARE. YOU AND YOUR KIND.
WE WILL DESTROY EVERYTHING YOU HAVE EVER CARED ABOUT AND THEN WE WILL ANNIHILATE YOU.
A STARRING ROLE IN YOUR OWN PERSONAL TRAGEDY, EH?
SAY "THANK YOU, SIR MILES."

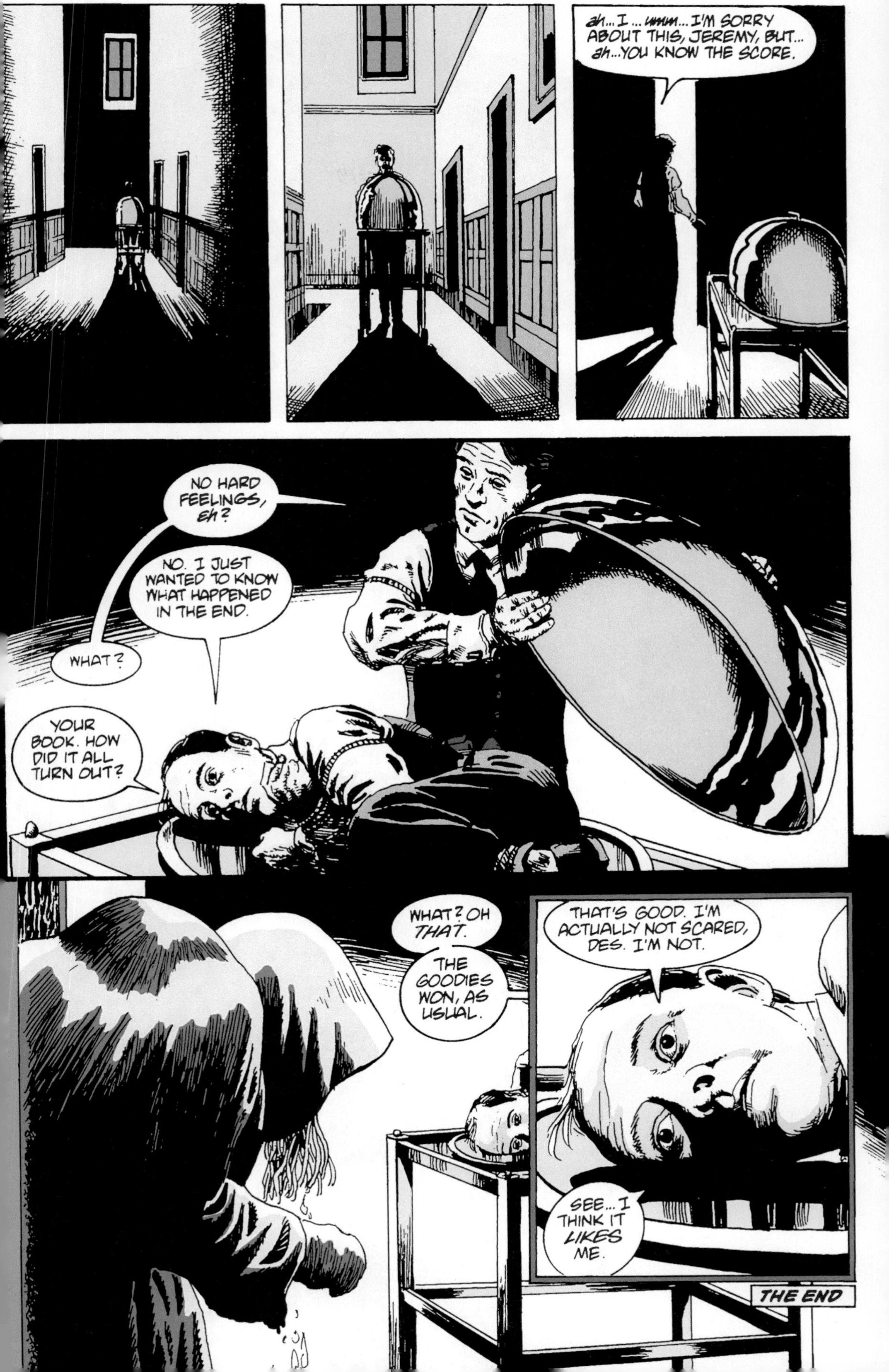
ah... I ... umm... I'M SORRY ABOUT THIS, JEREMY, BUT... ah...YOU KNOW THE SCORE.
NO HARD FEELINGS, eh?
NO. I JUST WANTED TO KNOW WHAT HAPPENED IN THE END.
WHAT?
YOUR BOOK. HOW DID IT ALL TURN OUT?
WHAT? OH THAT.
THE GOODIES WON, AS USUAL.
THAT'S GOOD. I'M ACTUALLY NOT SCARED, DES. I'M NOT.
SEE... I THINK IT LIKES ME.
THE END

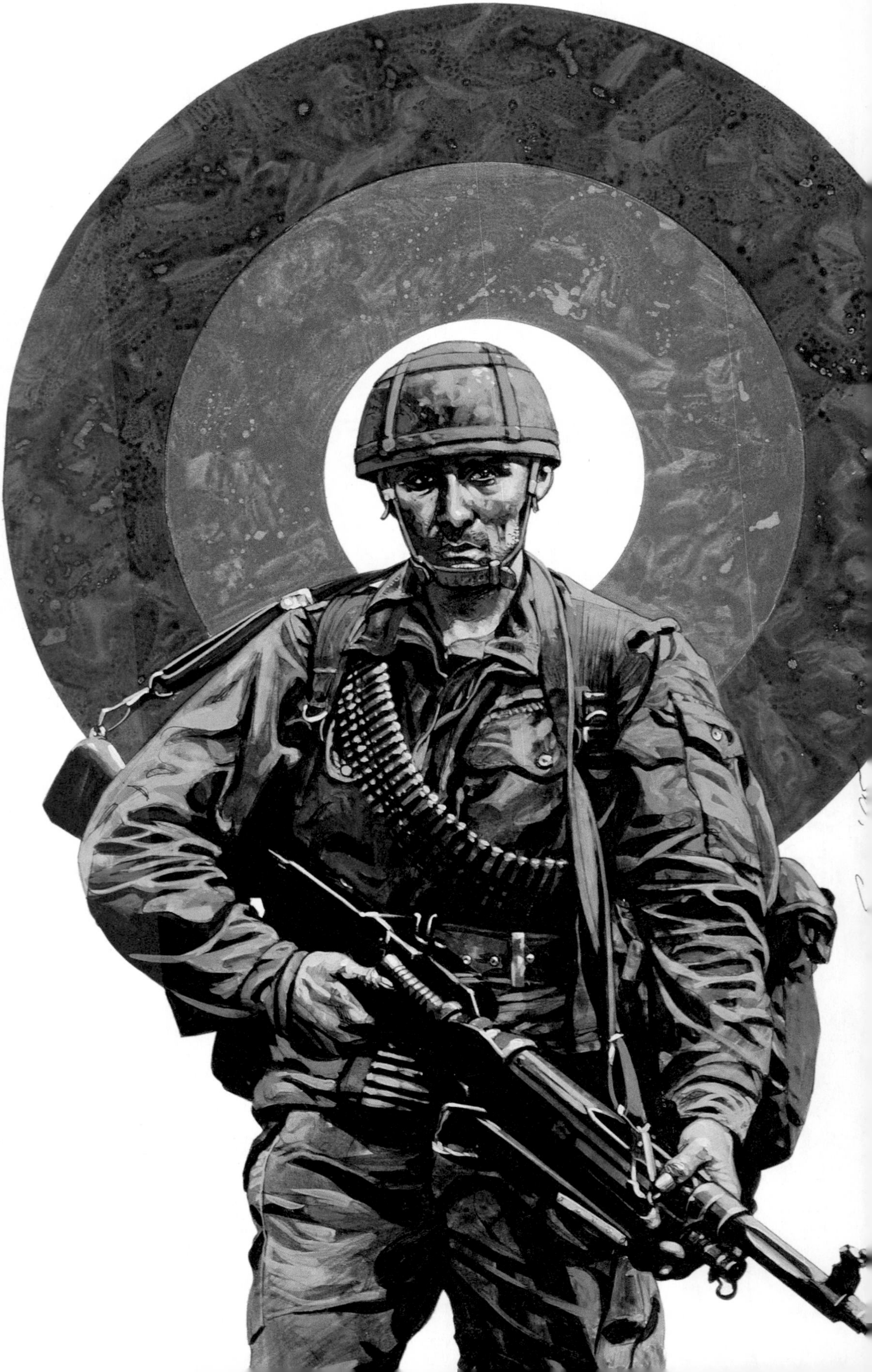

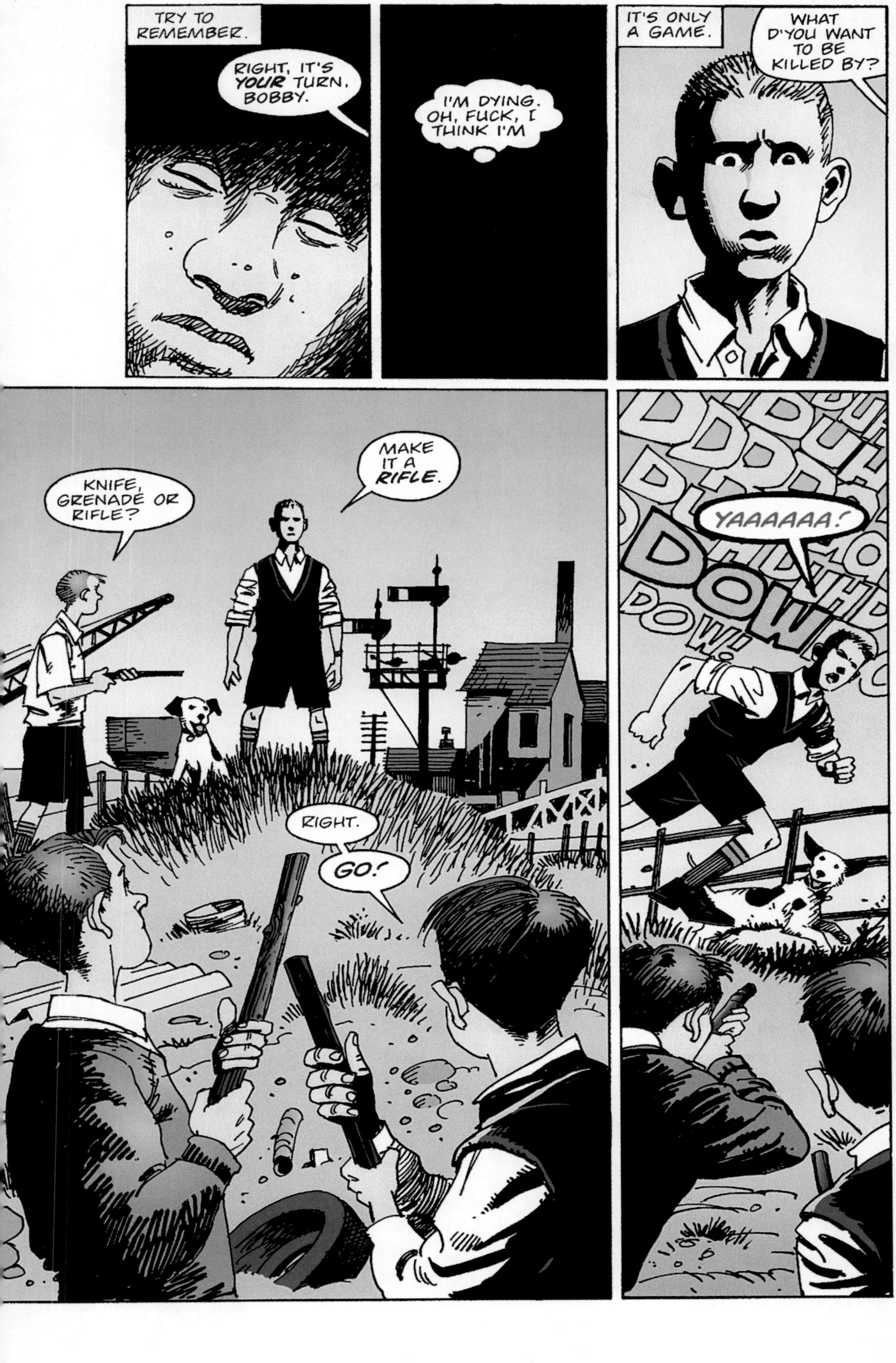
TRY TO REMEMBER.
RIGHT, IT'S YOUR TURN, BOBBY.
I'M DYING. OH, FUCK, I THINK I'M
IT'S ONLY A GAME.
WHAT D'YOU WANT TO BE KILLED BY?
KNIFE, GRENADE OR RIFLE?
MAKE IT A RIFLE.
RIGHT.
GO!
YAAAAAA!
DOW!
DOW!

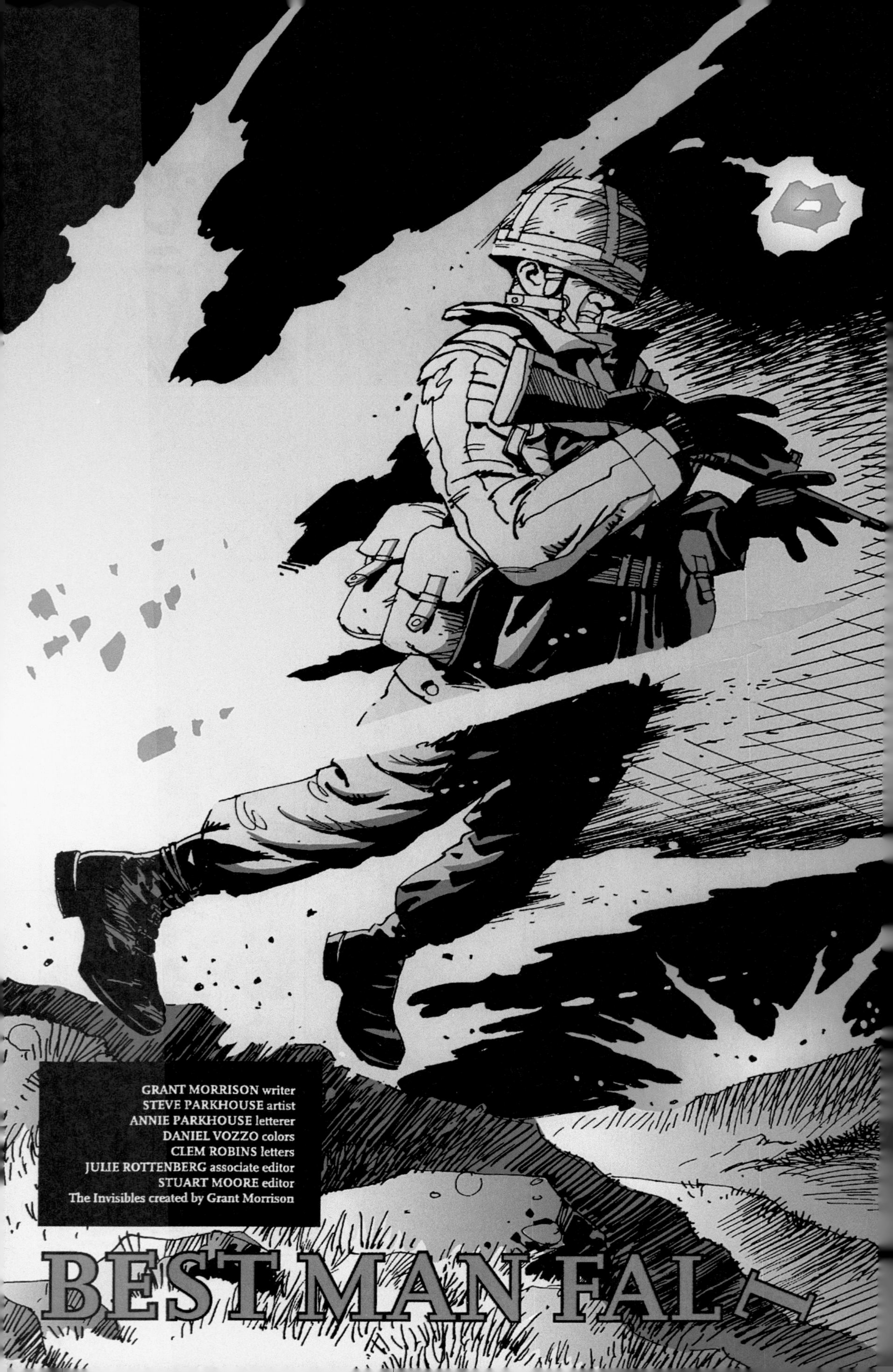

GRANT MORRISON writer
STEVE PARKHOUSE artist
ANNIE PARKHOUSE letterer
DANIEL VOZZO colors
CLEM ROBINS letters
JULIE ROTTENBERG associate editor
STUART MOORE editor
The Invisibles created by Grant Morrison
BEST MAN FALL

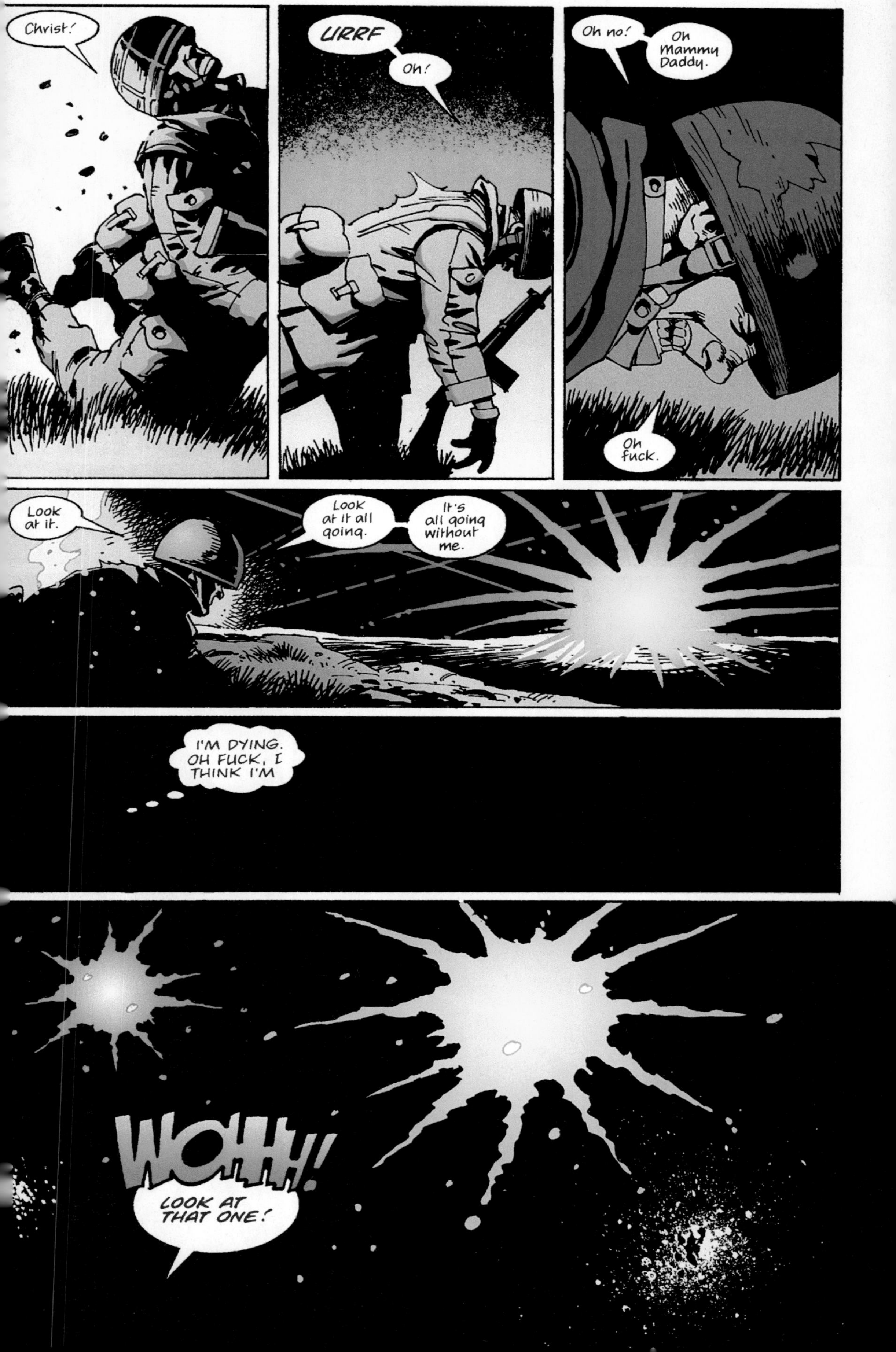
Christ!
URRF
Oh!
Oh no!
Oh Mammy Daddy.
Oh fuck.
Look at it.
Look at it all going.
It's all going without me.
I'M DYING. OH FUCK, I THINK I'M
WOHH!
LOOK AT THAT ONE!

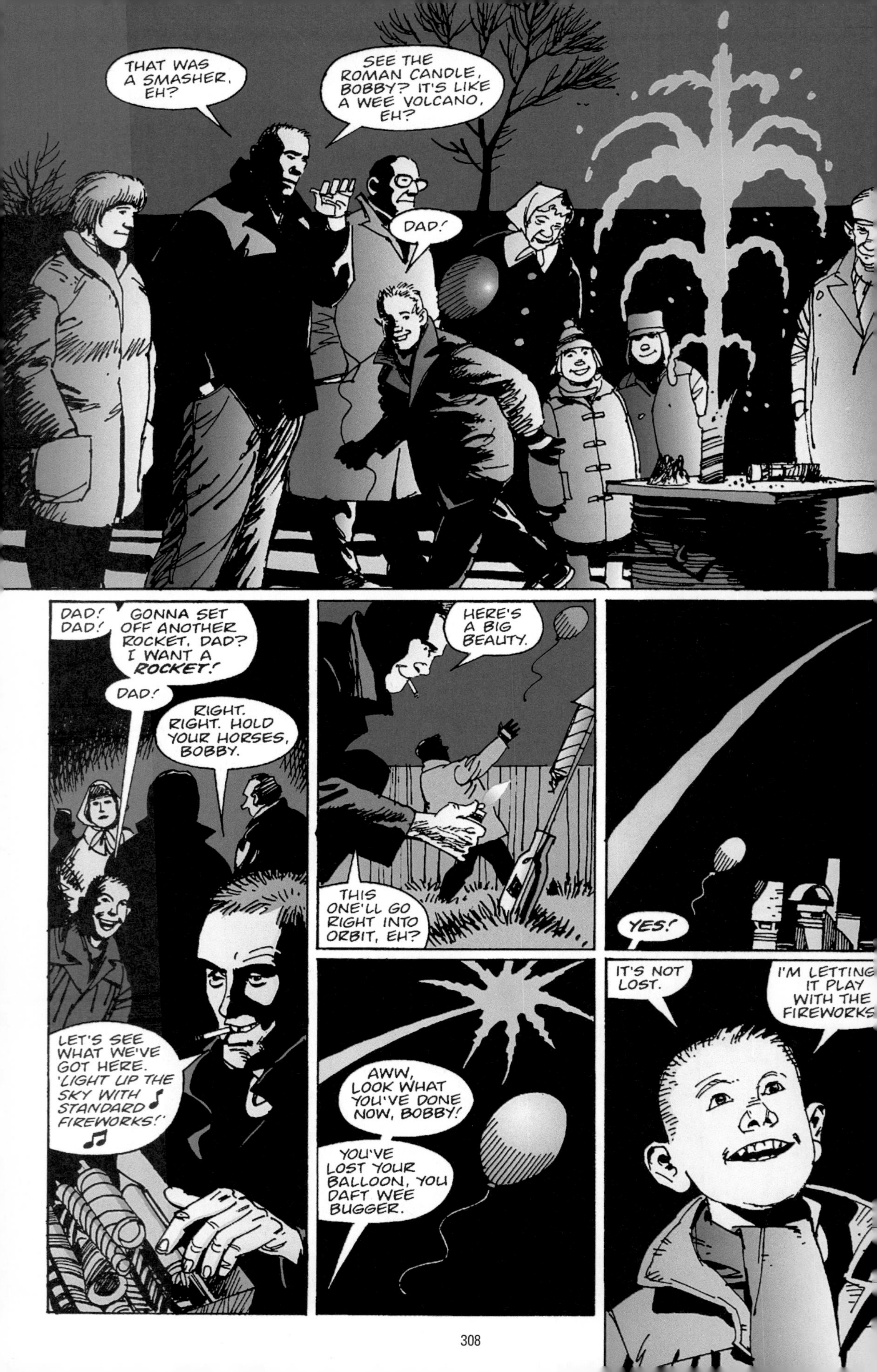
THAT WAS A SMASHER, EH?
SEE THE ROMAN CANDLE, BOBBY? IT'S LIKE A WEE VOLCANO, EH?
DAD!
DAD! DAD!
GONNA SET OFF ANOTHER ROCKET, DAD? I WANT A ROCKET!
DAD!
RIGHT. RIGHT. HOLD YOUR HORSES, BOBBY.
LET'S SEE WHAT WE'VE GOT HERE. 'LIGHT UP THE SKY WITH STANDARD FIREWORKS!'
HERE'S A BIG BEAUTY.
THIS ONE'LL GO RIGHT INTO ORBIT, EH?
YES!
AWW, LOOK WHAT YOU'VE DONE NOW, BOBBY!
YOU'VE LOST YOUR BALLOON, YOU DAFT WEE BUGGER.
IT'S NOT LOST.
I'M LETTING IT PLAY WITH THE FIREWORKS

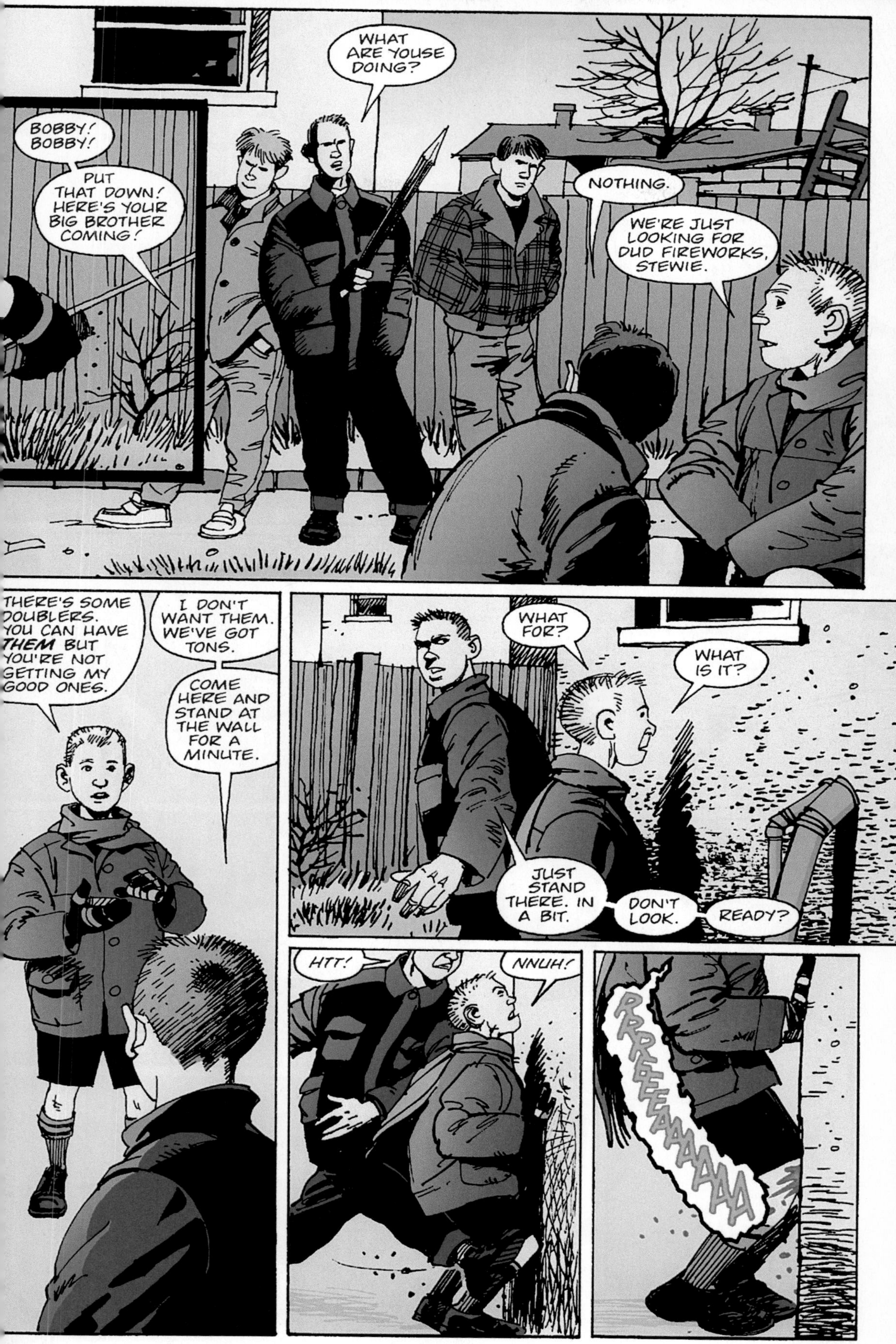
BOBBY! BOBBY!
PUT THAT DOWN! HERE'S YOUR BIG BROTHER COMING!
WHAT ARE YOUSE DOING?
NOTHING.
WE'RE JUST LOOKING FOR DUD FIREWORKS, STEWIE.
THERE'S SOME DOUBLERS. YOU CAN HAVE **THEM** BUT YOU'RE NOT GETTING MY GOOD ONES.
I DON'T WANT THEM. WE'VE GOT TONS.
COME HERE AND STAND AT THE WALL FOR A MINUTE.
WHAT FOR?
WHAT IS IT?
JUST STAND THERE. IN A BIT.
DON'T LOOK.
READY?
HTT!
NNUH!
RRREEAAAAAAA

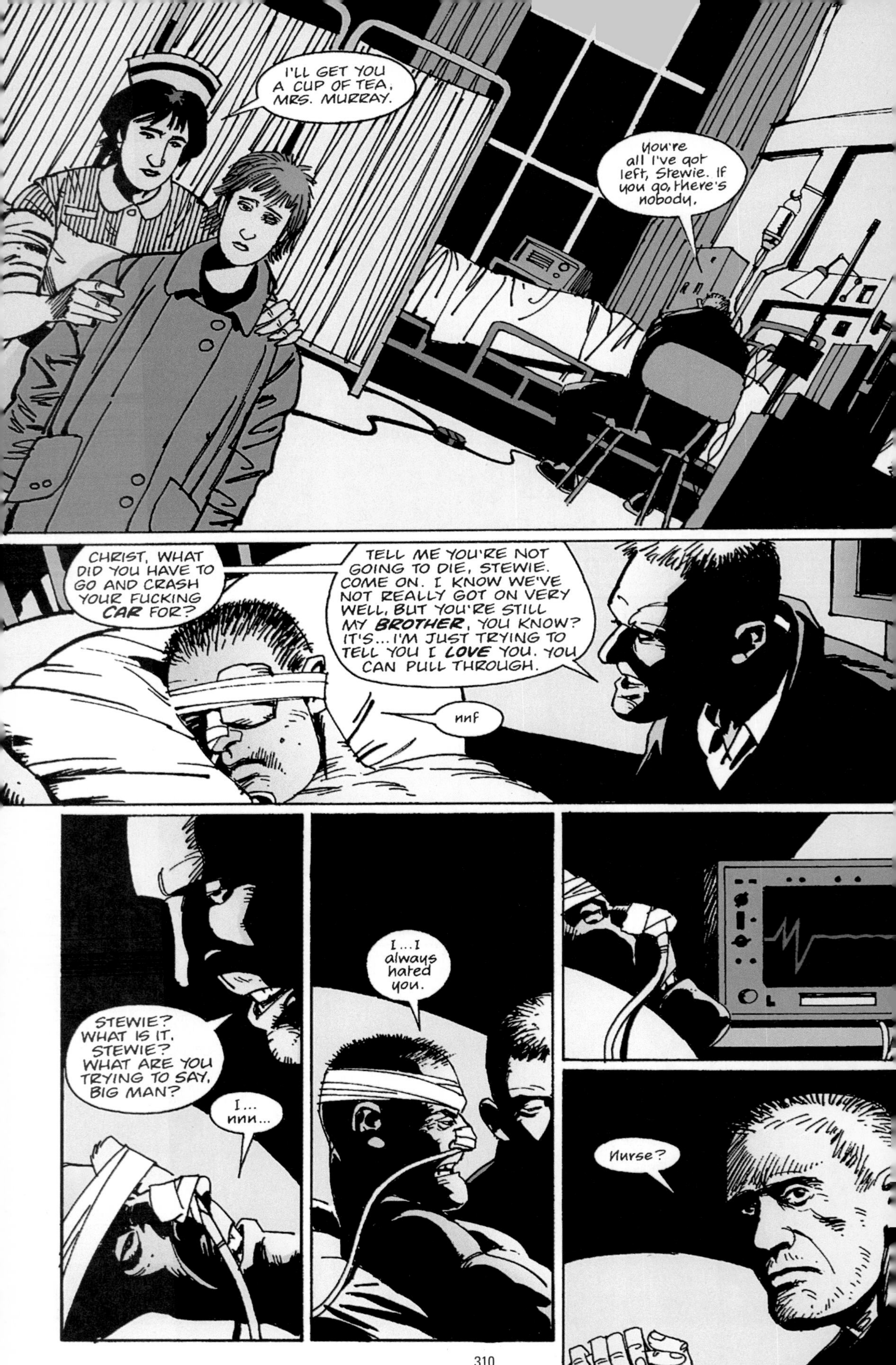
I'LL GET YOU A CUP OF TEA, MRS. MURRAY.
You're all I've got left, Stewie. If you go, there's nobody.
CHRIST, WHAT DID YOU HAVE TO GO AND CRASH YOUR FUCKING CAR FOR?
TELL ME YOU'RE NOT GOING TO DIE, STEWIE. COME ON. I KNOW WE'VE NOT REALLY GOT ON VERY WELL, BUT YOU'RE STILL MY BROTHER, YOU KNOW? IT'S... I'M JUST TRYING TO TELL YOU I LOVE YOU. YOU CAN PULL THROUGH.
nnf
STEWIE? WHAT IS IT, STEWIE? WHAT ARE YOU TRYING TO SAY, BIG MAN?
I... nnn...
I... I always hated you.
Nurse?

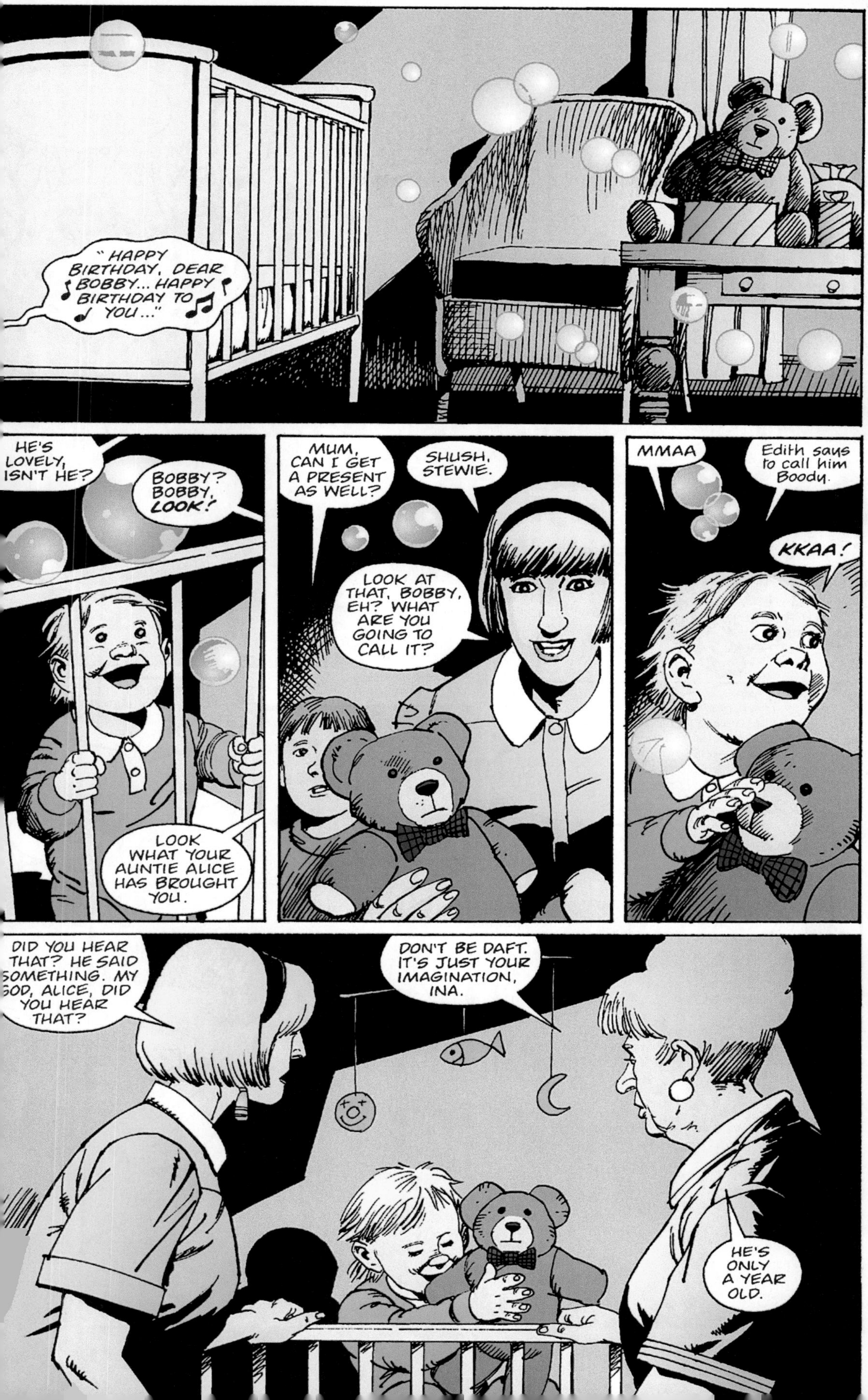
"HAPPY BIRTHDAY, DEAR BOBBY... HAPPY BIRTHDAY TO YOU..."
HE'S LOVELY, ISN'T HE?
BOBBY? BOBBY, LOOK!
LOOK WHAT YOUR AUNTIE ALICE HAS BROUGHT YOU.
MUM, CAN I GET A PRESENT AS WELL?
SHUSH, STEWIE.
LOOK AT THAT, BOBBY, EH? WHAT ARE YOU GOING TO CALL IT?
MMAA
Edith says to call him Boody.
KKAA!
DID YOU HEAR THAT? HE SAID SOMETHING. MY GOD, ALICE, DID YOU HEAR THAT?
DON'T BE DAFT. IT'S JUST YOUR IMAGINATION, INA.
HE'S ONLY A YEAR OLD.

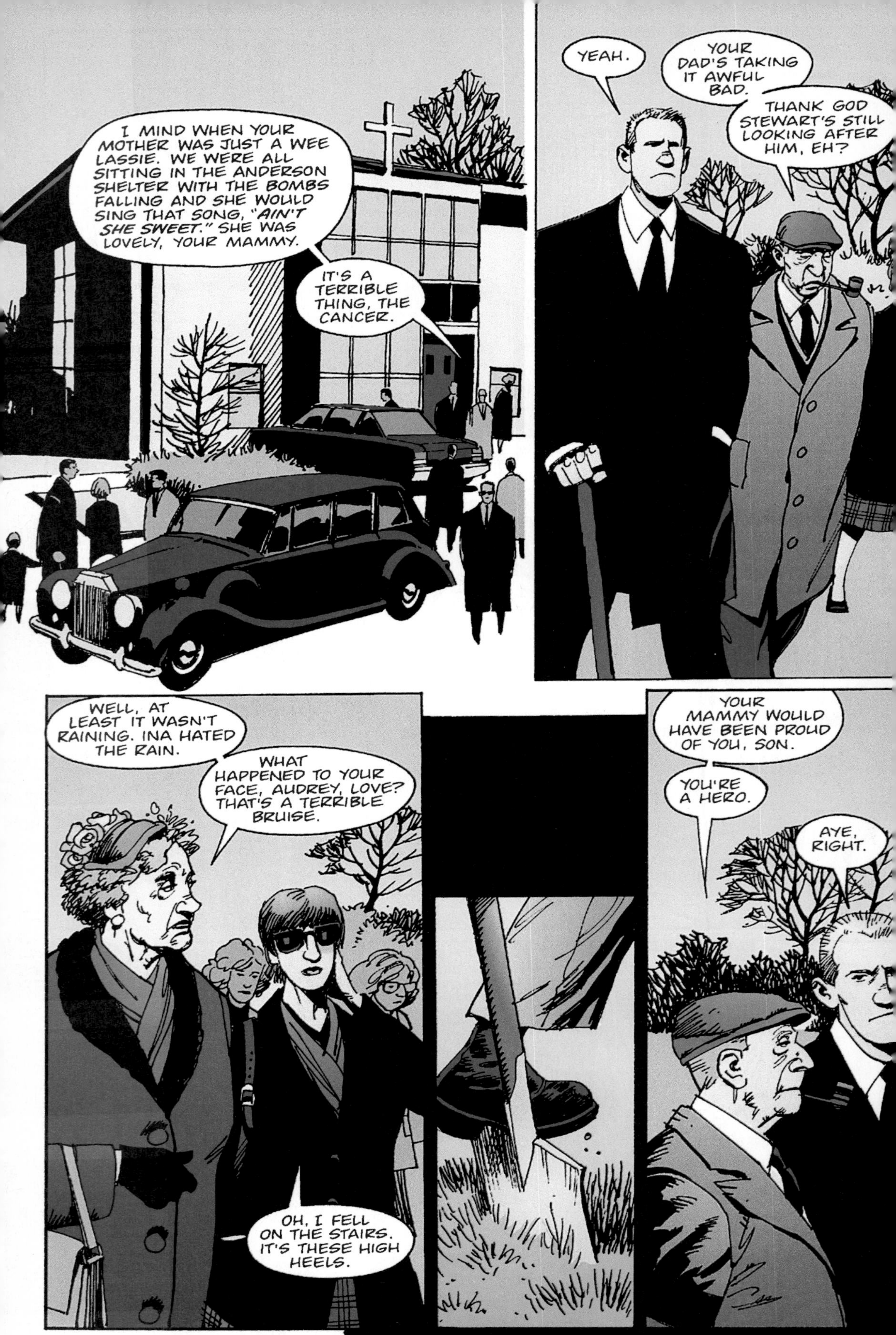
I MIND WHEN YOUR MOTHER WAS JUST A WEE LASSIE. WE WERE ALL SITTING IN THE ANDERSON SHELTER WITH THE BOMBS FALLING AND SHE WOULD SING THAT SONG, "AIN'T SHE SWEET." SHE WAS LOVELY, YOUR MAMMY.
IT'S A TERRIBLE THING, THE CANCER.
YEAH.
YOUR DAD'S TAKING IT AWFUL BAD.
THANK GOD STEWART'S STILL LOOKING AFTER HIM, EH?
WELL, AT LEAST IT WASN'T RAINING. INA HATED THE RAIN.
WHAT HAPPENED TO YOUR FACE, AUDREY, LOVE? THAT'S A TERRIBLE BRUISE.
OH, I FELL ON THE STAIRS. IT'S THESE HIGH HEELS.
YOUR MAMMY WOULD HAVE BEEN PROUD OF YOU, SON.
YOU'RE A HERO.
AYE, RIGHT.

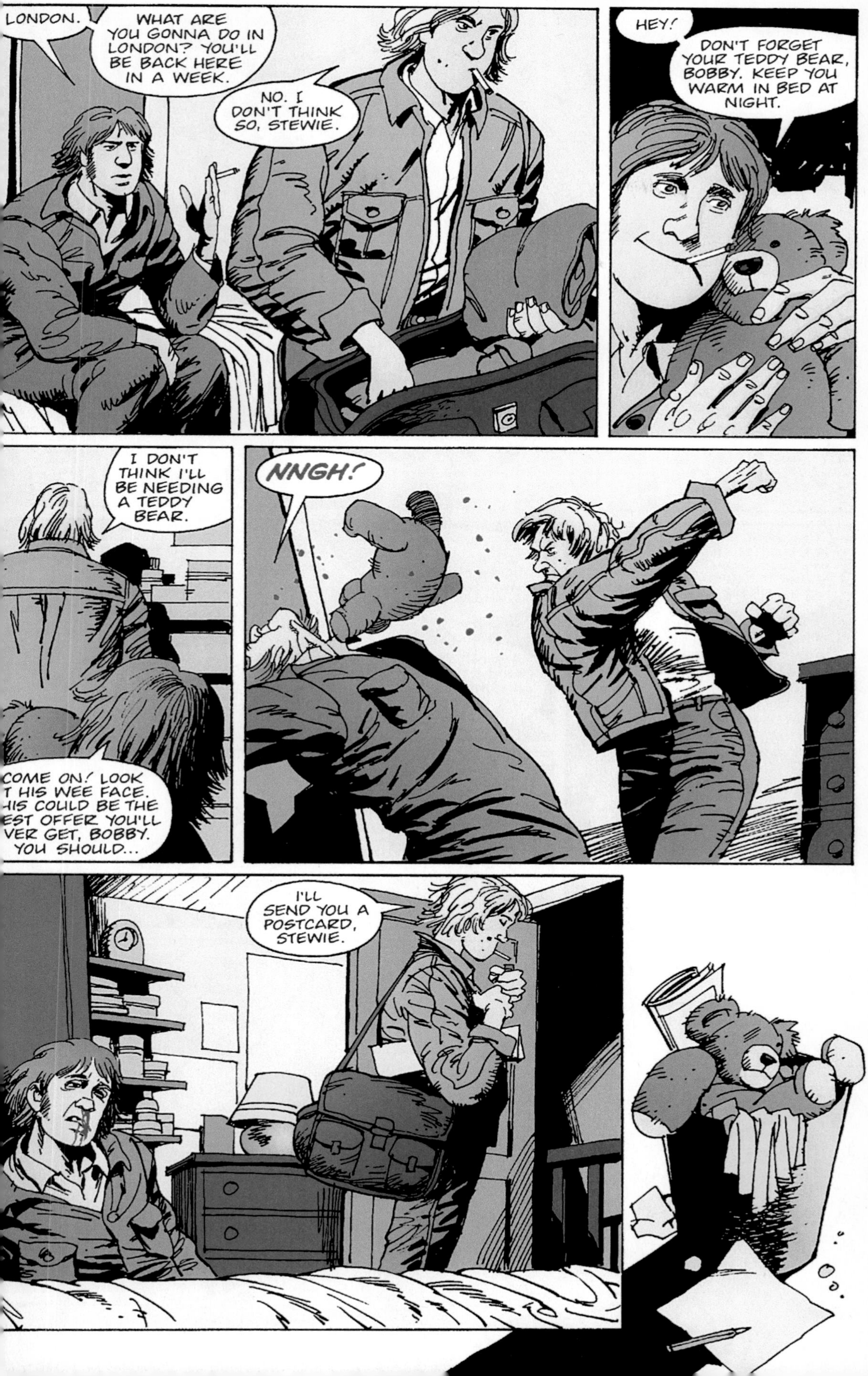
LONDON.
WHAT ARE YOU GONNA DO IN LONDON? YOU'LL BE BACK HERE IN A WEEK.
NO. I DON'T THINK SO, STEWIE.
HEY!
DON'T FORGET YOUR TEDDY BEAR, BOBBY. KEEP YOU WARM IN BED AT NIGHT.
I DON'T THINK I'LL BE NEEDING A TEDDY BEAR.
COME ON! LOOK T HIS WEE FACE. HIS COULD BE THE EST OFFER YOU'LL VER GET, BOBBY. YOU SHOULD...
NNGH!
I'LL SEND YOU A POSTCARD, STEWIE.

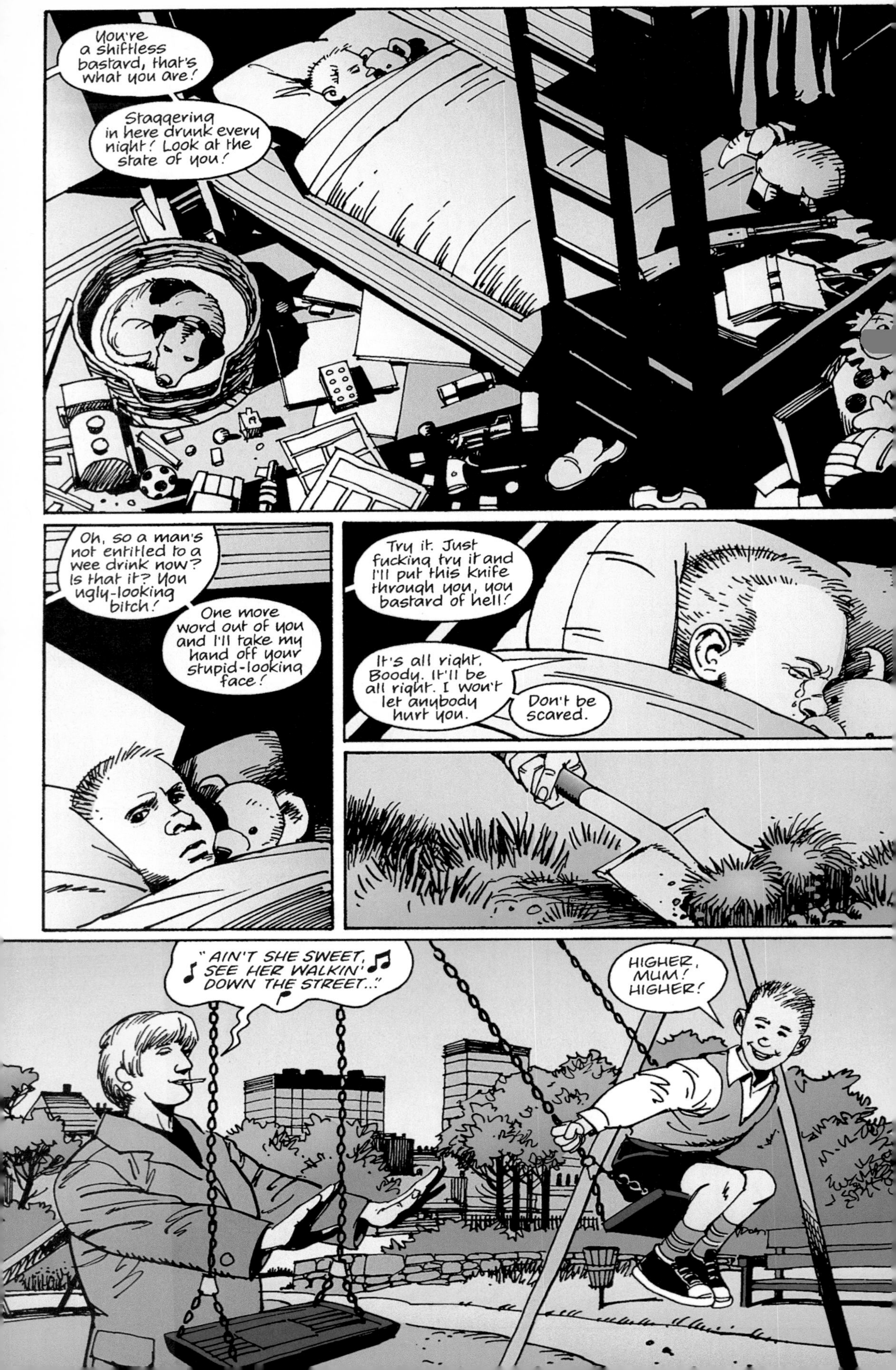
You're a shiftless bastard, that's what you are!
Staggering in here drunk every night! Look at the state of you!
Oh, so a man's not entitled to a wee drink now? Is that it? You ugly-looking bitch!
One more word out of you and I'll take my hand off your stupid-looking face!
Try it. Just fucking try it and I'll put this knife through you, you bastard of hell!
It's all right, Boody. It'll be all right. I won't let anybody hurt you.
Don't be scared.
"AIN'T SHE SWEET, SEE HER WALKIN' DOWN THE STREET..."
HIGHER, MUM! HIGHER!

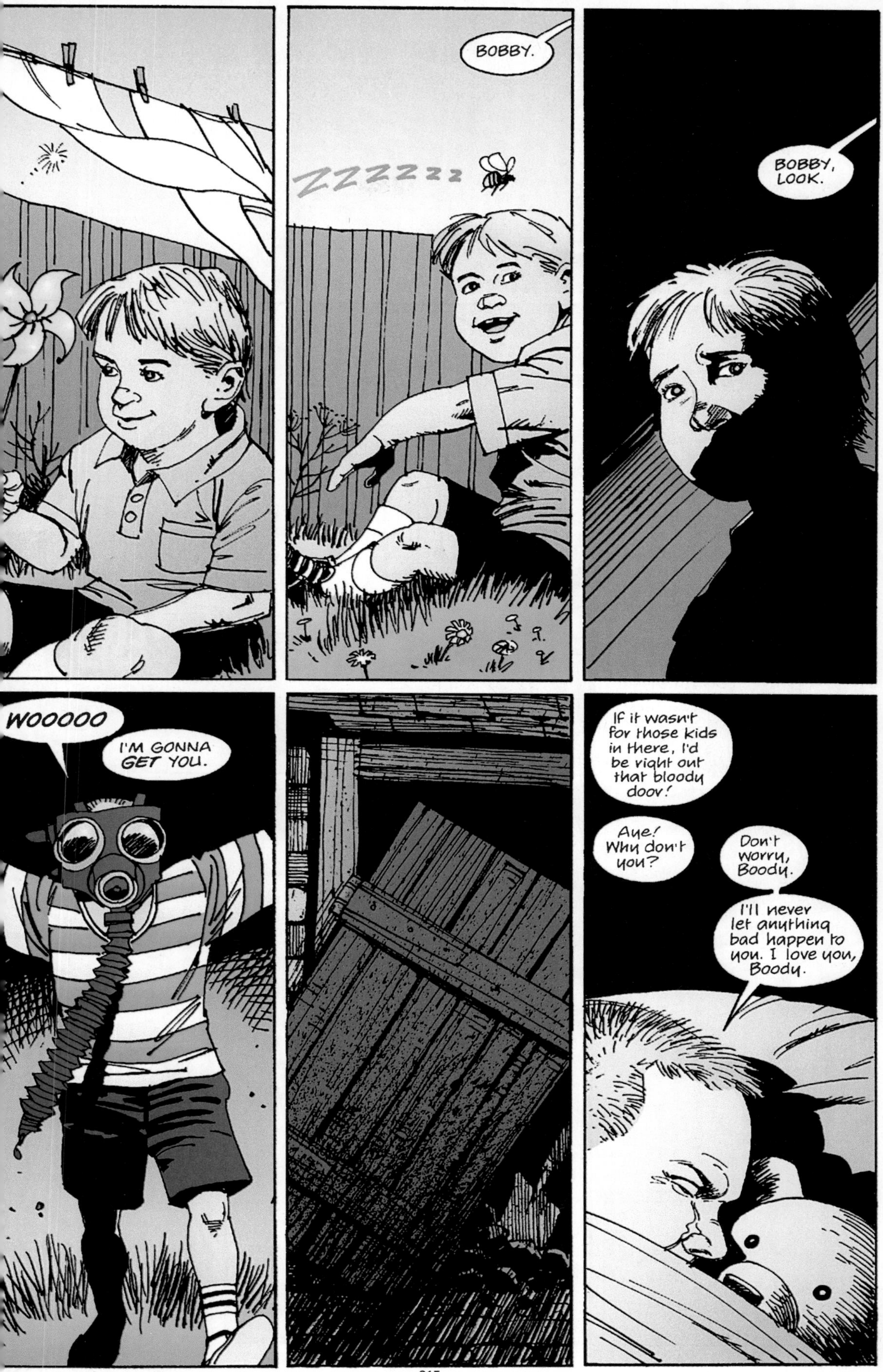
BOBBY.
ZZZZZzz
BOBBY, LOOK.
WOOOOO
I'M GONNA GET YOU.
If it wasn't for those kids in there, I'd be right out that bloody door!
Aye! Why don't you?
Don't worry, Boody.
I'll never let anything bad happen to you. I love you, Boody.

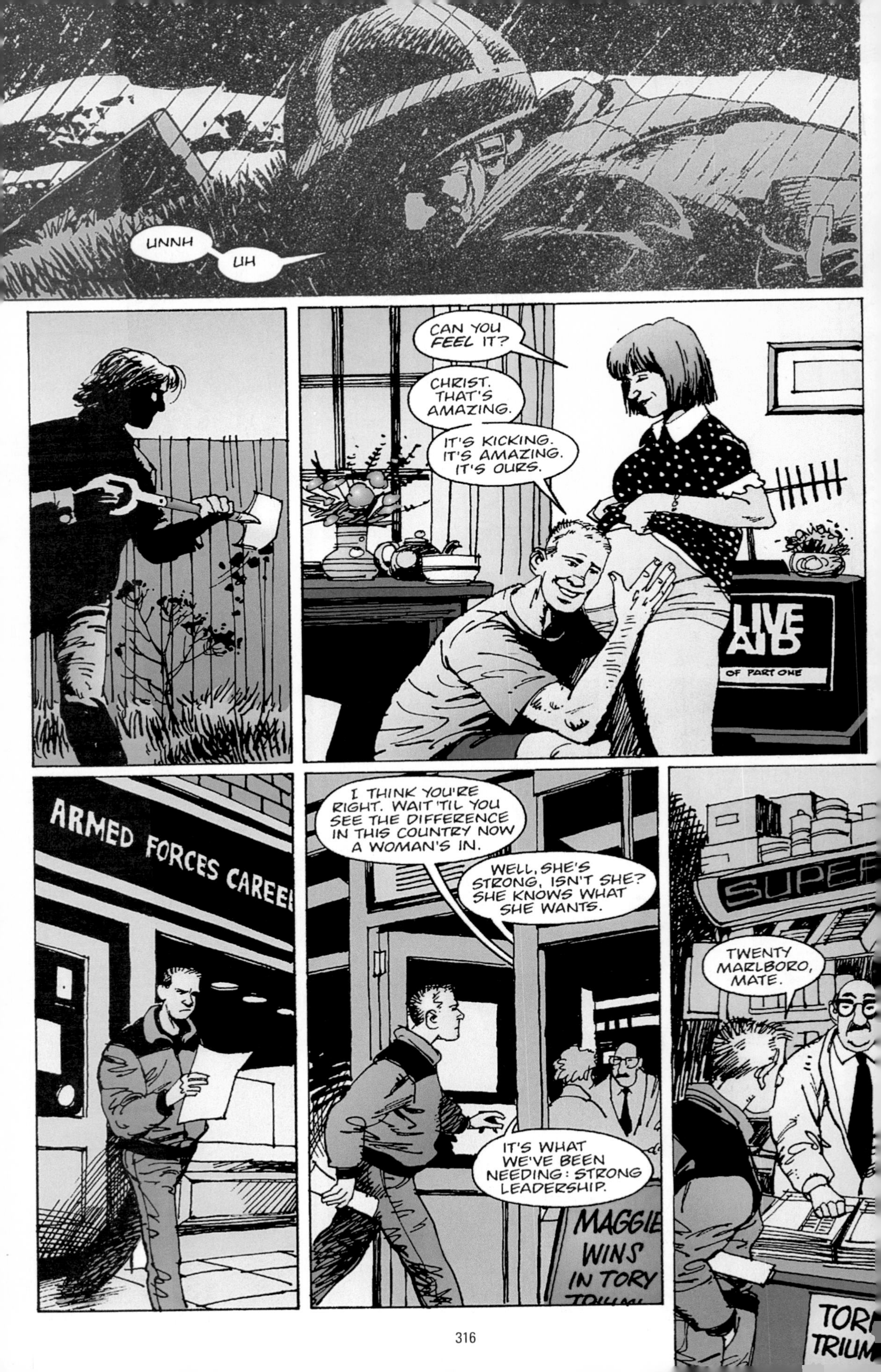
UNNH
UH
CAN YOU FEEL IT?
CHRIST. THAT'S AMAZING.
IT'S KICKING. IT'S AMAZING. IT'S OURS.
LIVE AID
OF PART ONE
ARMED FORCES CAREE
I THINK YOU'RE RIGHT. WAIT 'TIL YOU SEE THE DIFFERENCE IN THIS COUNTRY NOW A WOMAN'S IN.
WELL, SHE'S STRONG, ISN'T SHE? SHE KNOWS WHAT SHE WANTS.
IT'S WHAT WE'VE BEEN NEEDING: STRONG LEADERSHIP.
MAGGIE WINS IN TORY
TWENTY MARLBORO, MATE.
TORY TRIUM

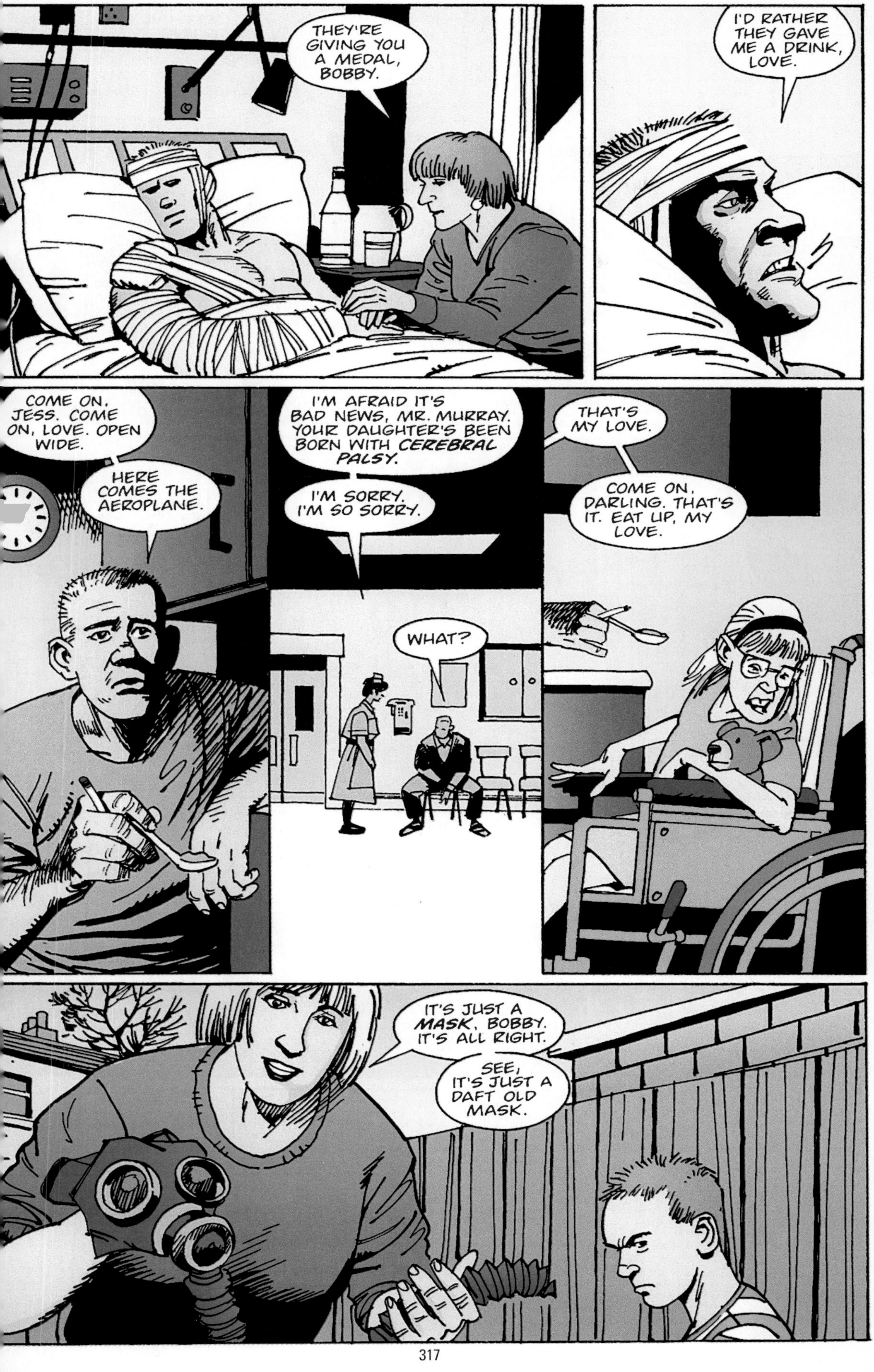
THEY'RE GIVING YOU A MEDAL, BOBBY.
I'D RATHER THEY GAVE ME A DRINK, LOVE.
COME ON, JESS. COME ON, LOVE. OPEN WIDE.
HERE COMES THE AEROPLANE.
I'M AFRAID IT'S BAD NEWS, MR. MURRAY. YOUR DAUGHTER'S BEEN BORN WITH CEREBRAL PALSY.
I'M SORRY. I'M SO SORRY.
WHAT?
THAT'S MY LOVE.
COME ON, DARLING. THAT'S IT. EAT UP, MY LOVE.
IT'S JUST A MASK, BOBBY. IT'S ALL RIGHT.
SEE, IT'S JUST A DAFT OLD MASK.

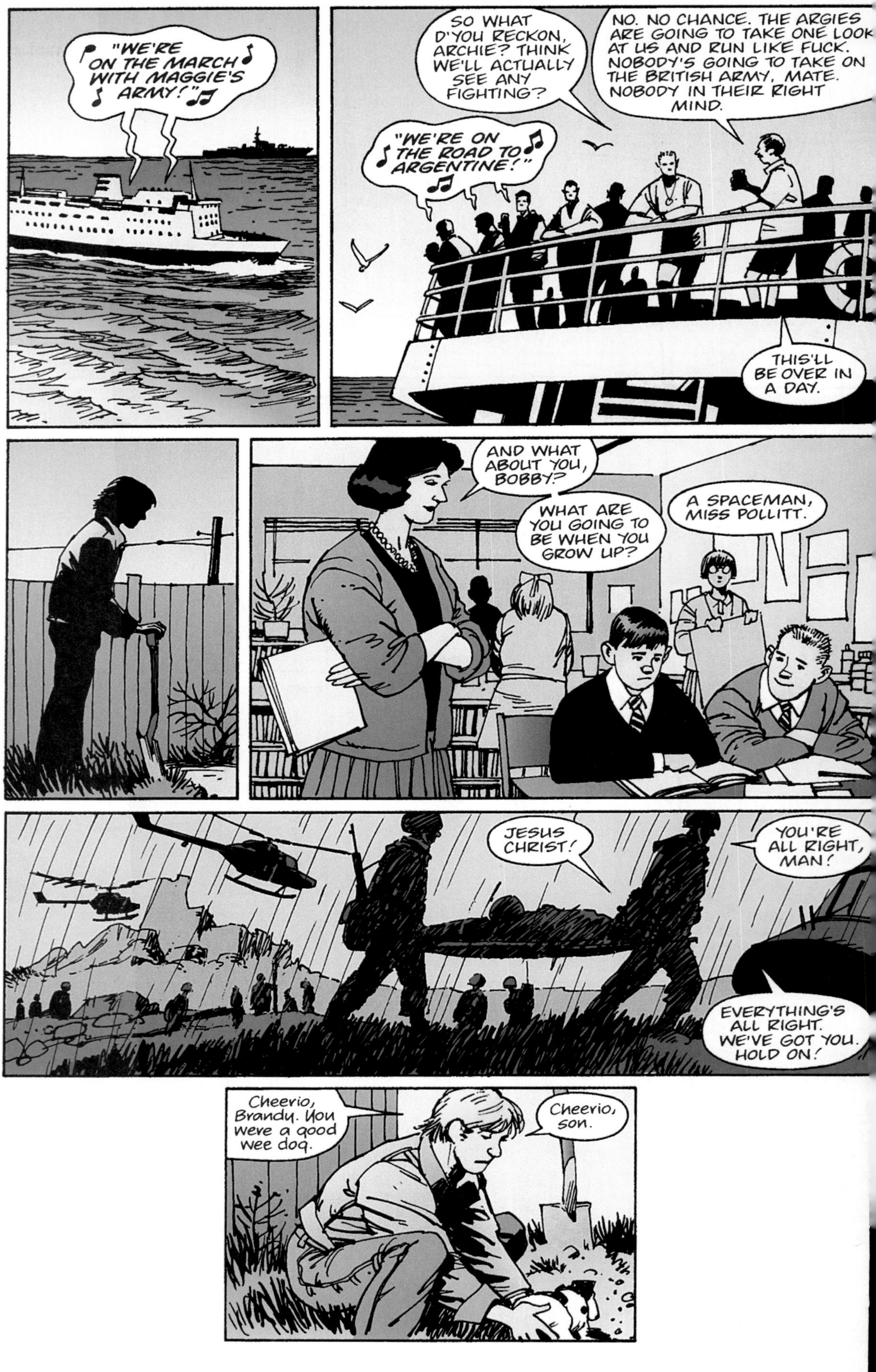
"WE'RE ON THE MARCH WITH MAGGIE'S ARMY!"
SO WHAT D'YOU RECKON, ARCHIE? THINK WE'LL ACTUALLY SEE ANY FIGHTING?
NO. NO CHANCE. THE ARGIES ARE GOING TO TAKE ONE LOOK AT US AND RUN LIKE FUCK. NOBODY'S GOING TO TAKE ON THE BRITISH ARMY, MATE. NOBODY IN THEIR RIGHT MIND.
"WE'RE ON THE ROAD TO ARGENTINE!"
THIS'LL BE OVER IN A DAY.
AND WHAT ABOUT YOU, BOBBY?
WHAT ARE YOU GOING TO BE WHEN YOU GROW UP?
A SPACEMAN, MISS POLLITT.
JESUS CHRIST!
YOU'RE ALL RIGHT, MAN!
EVERYTHING'S ALL RIGHT. WE'VE GOT YOU. HOLD ON!
Cheerio, Brandy. You were a good wee dog.
Cheerio, son.

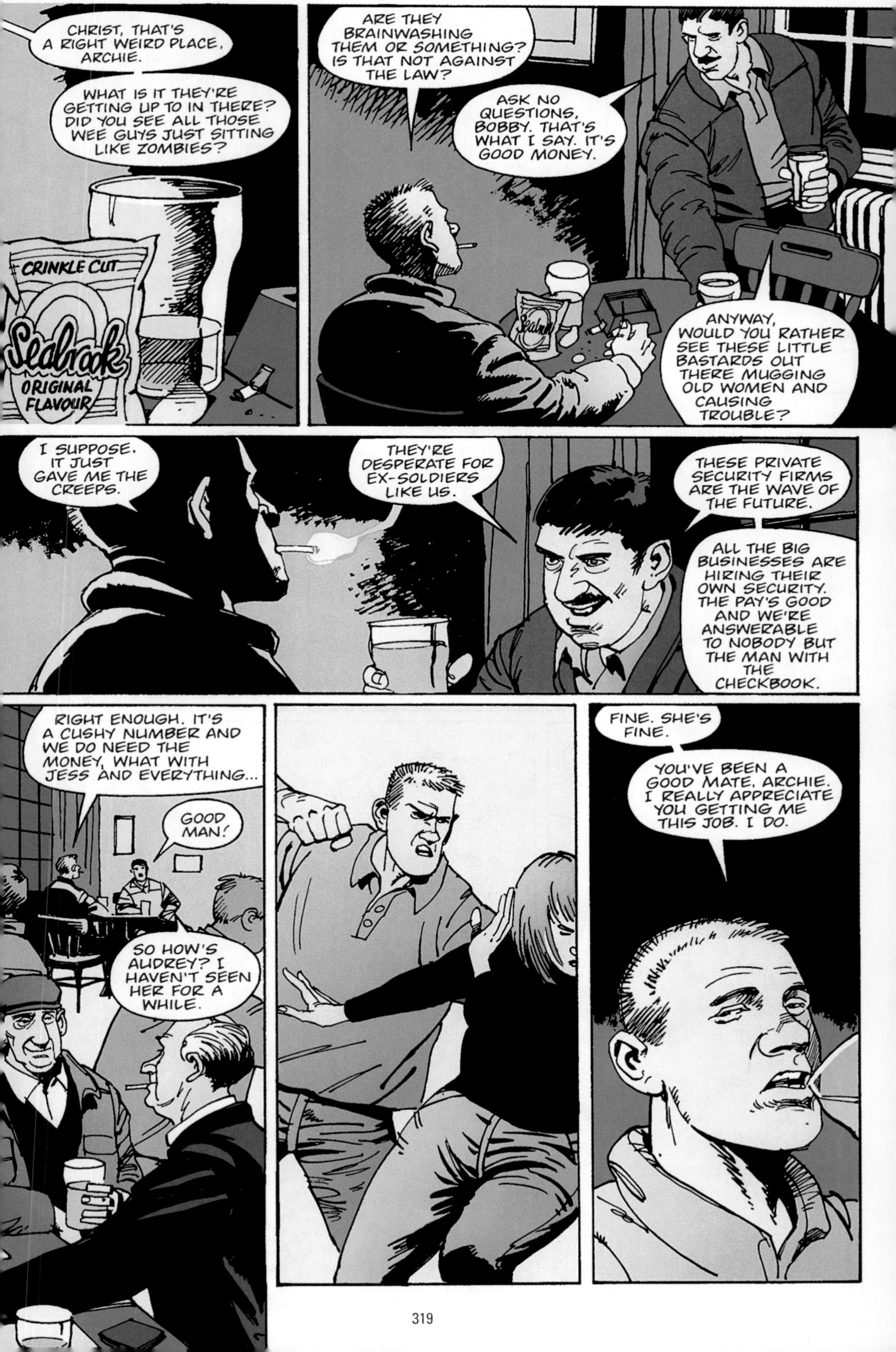
CHRIST, THAT'S A RIGHT WEIRD PLACE, ARCHIE.
WHAT IS IT THEY'RE GETTING UP TO IN THERE? DID YOU SEE ALL THOSE WEE GUYS JUST SITTING LIKE ZOMBIES?
CRINKLE CUT
Sealbrook
ORIGINAL FLAVOUR
ARE THEY BRAINWASHING THEM OR SOMETHING? IS THAT NOT AGAINST THE LAW?
ASK NO QUESTIONS, BOBBY. THAT'S WHAT I SAY. IT'S GOOD MONEY.
ANYWAY, WOULD YOU RATHER SEE THESE LITTLE BASTARDS OUT THERE MUGGING OLD WOMEN AND CAUSING TROUBLE?
I SUPPOSE. IT JUST GAVE ME THE CREEPS.
THEY'RE DESPERATE FOR EX-SOLDIERS LIKE US.
THESE PRIVATE SECURITY FIRMS ARE THE WAVE OF THE FUTURE.
ALL THE BIG BUSINESSES ARE HIRING THEIR OWN SECURITY. THE PAY'S GOOD AND WE'RE ANSWERABLE TO NOBODY BUT THE MAN WITH THE CHECKBOOK.
RIGHT ENOUGH. IT'S A CUSHY NUMBER AND WE DO NEED THE MONEY, WHAT WITH JESS AND EVERYTHING...
GOOD MAN!
SO HOW'S AUDREY? I HAVEN'T SEEN HER FOR A WHILE.
FINE. SHE'S FINE.
YOU'VE BEEN A GOOD MATE, ARCHIE. I REALLY APPRECIATE YOU GETTING ME THIS JOB. I DO.

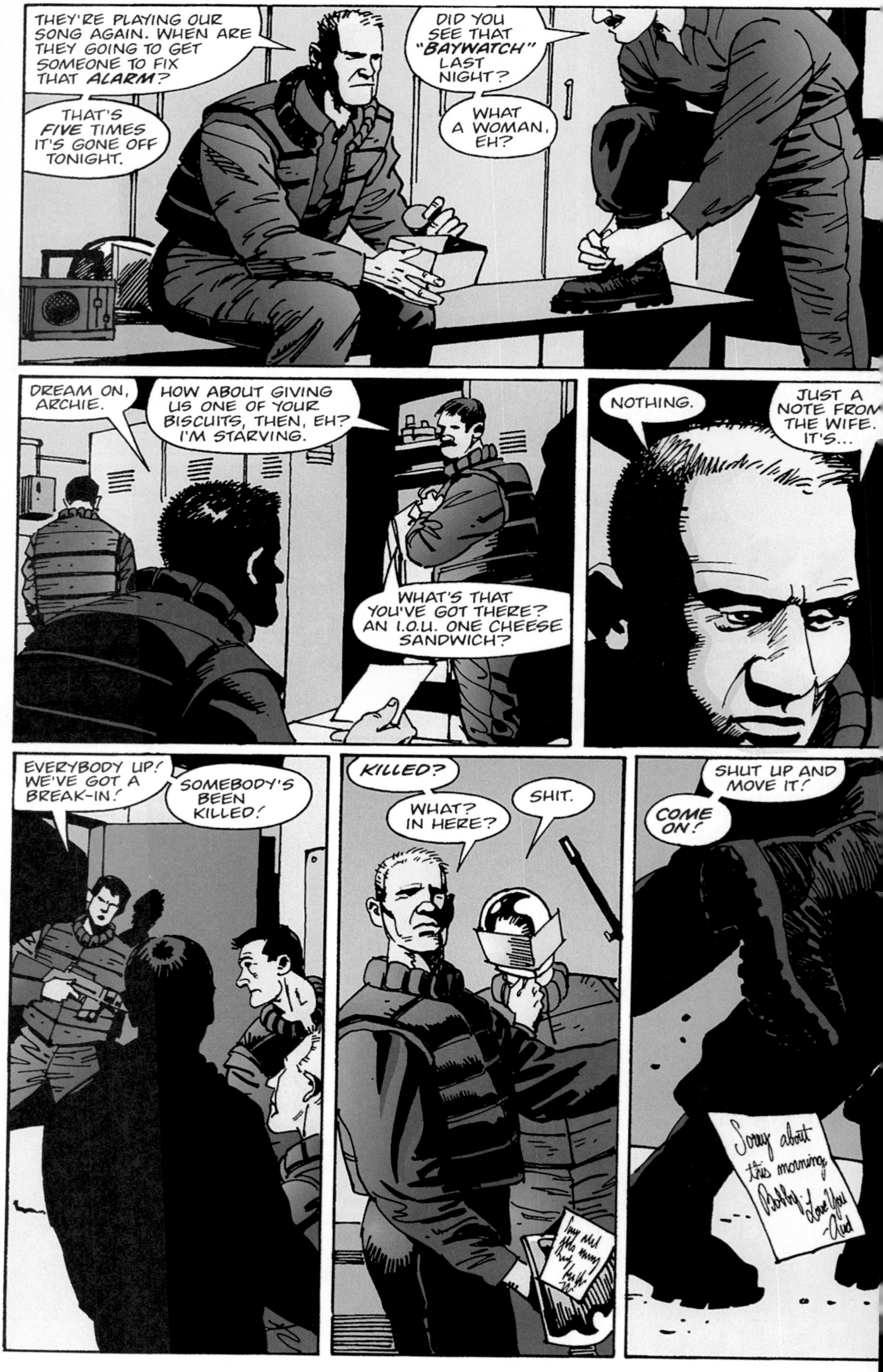
THEY'RE PLAYING OUR SONG AGAIN. WHEN ARE THEY GOING TO GET SOMEONE TO FIX THAT ALARM?
THAT'S FIVE TIMES IT'S GONE OFF TONIGHT.
DID YOU SEE THAT "BAYWATCH" LAST NIGHT?
WHAT A WOMAN, EH?
DREAM ON, ARCHIE.
HOW ABOUT GIVING US ONE OF YOUR BISCUITS, THEN, EH? I'M STARVING.
WHAT'S THAT YOU'VE GOT THERE? AN I.O.U. ONE CHEESE SANDWICH?
NOTHING.
JUST A NOTE FROM THE WIFE. IT'S...
EVERYBODY UP! WE'VE GOT A BREAK-IN!
SOMEBODY'S BEEN KILLED!
KILLED?
WHAT? IN HERE?
SHIT.
SHUT UP AND MOVE IT!
COME ON!
Sorry about this morning Bobby Love You -Aud

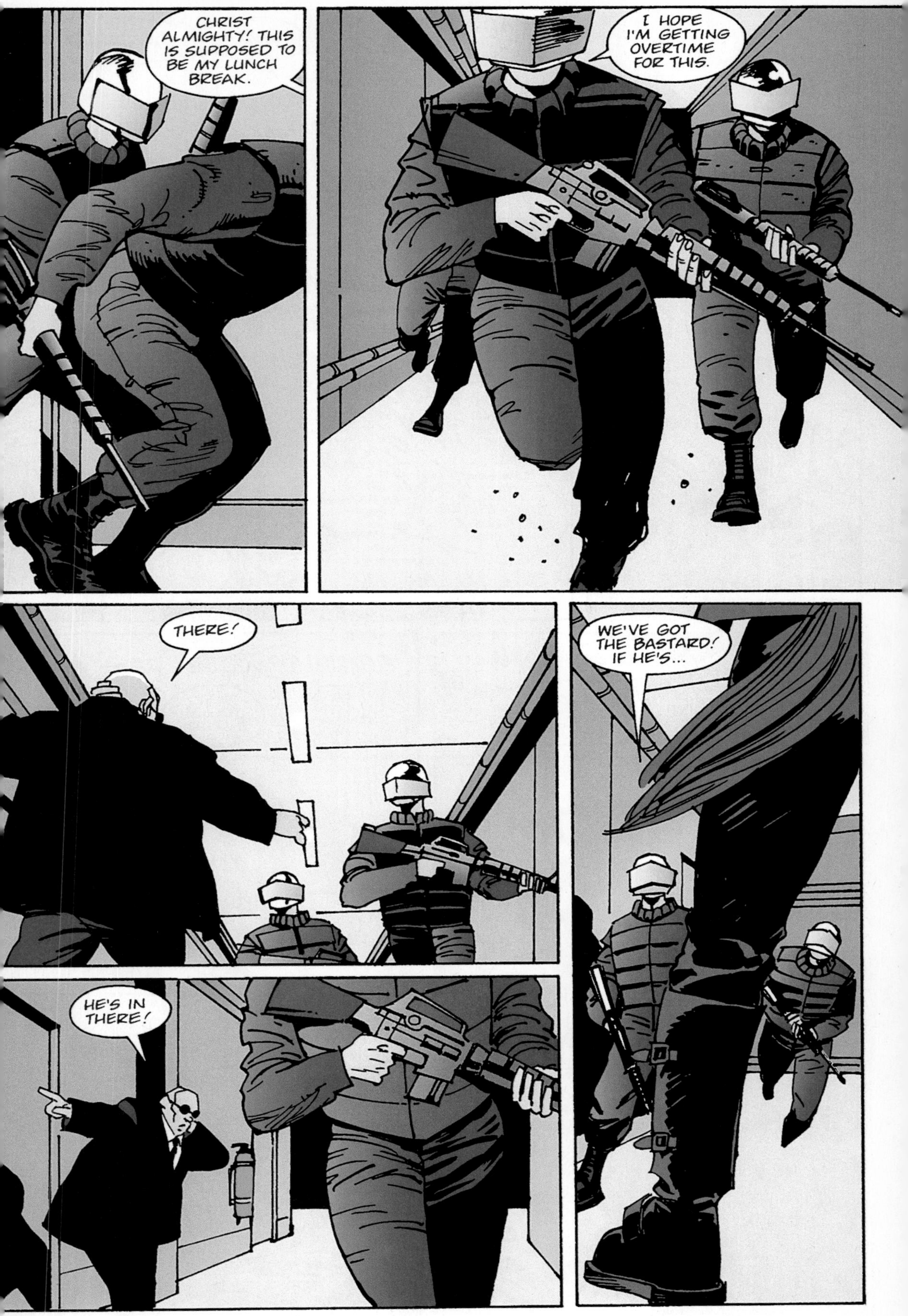
CHRIST ALMIGHTY! THIS IS SUPPOSED TO BE MY LUNCH BREAK.
I HOPE I'M GETTING OVERTIME FOR THIS.
THERE!
HE'S IN THERE!
WE'VE GOT THE BASTARD! IF HE'S...

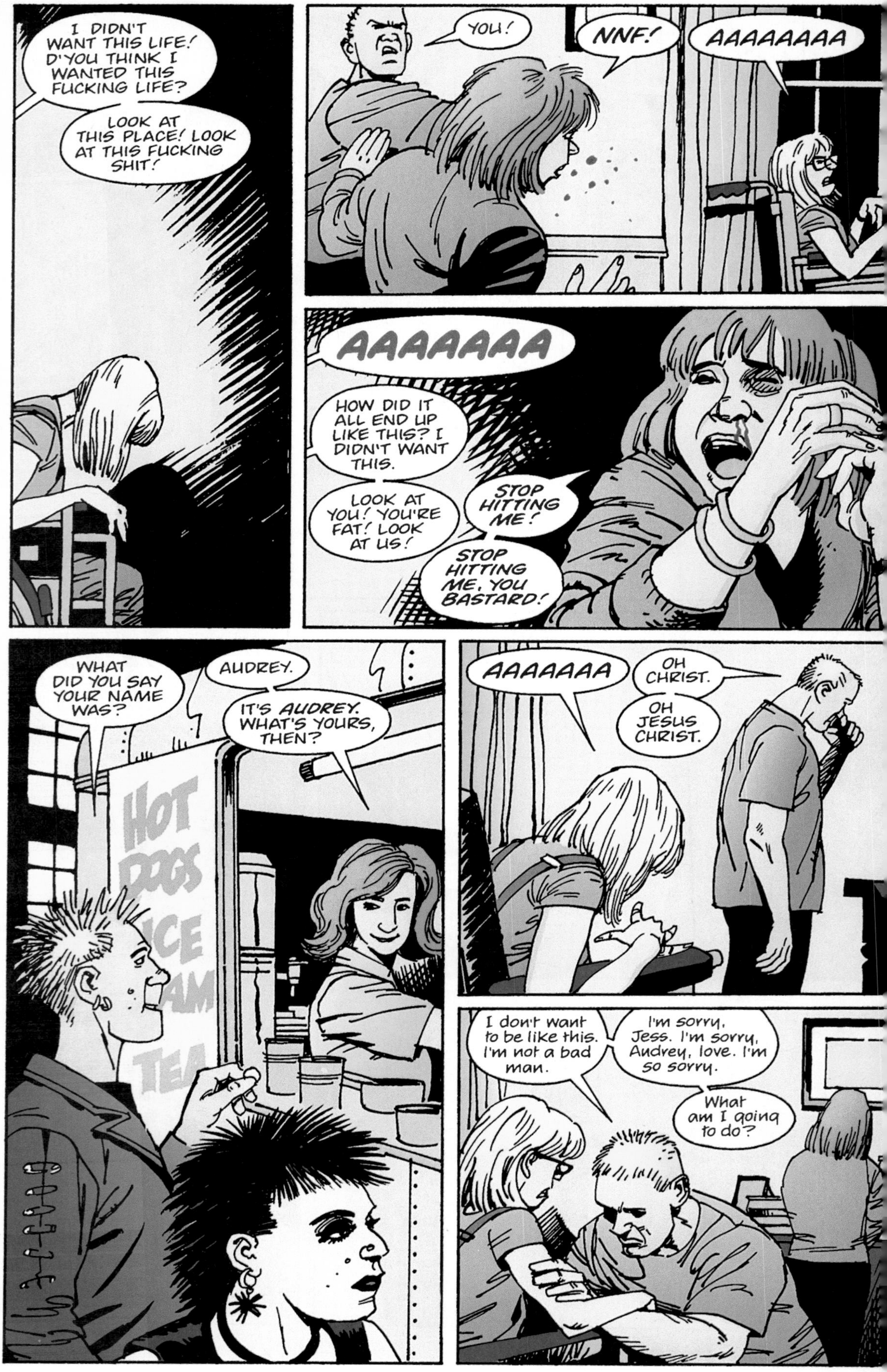
I DIDN'T WANT THIS LIFE! D'YOU THINK I WANTED THIS FUCKING LIFE?
LOOK AT THIS PLACE! LOOK AT THIS FUCKING SHIT!
YOU!
NNF!
AAAAAAAA
AAAAAAA
HOW DID IT ALL END UP LIKE THIS? I DIDN'T WANT THIS.
LOOK AT YOU! YOU'RE FAT! LOOK AT US!
STOP HITTING ME!
STOP HITTING ME, YOU BASTARD!
WHAT DID YOU SAY YOUR NAME WAS?
AUDREY.
IT'S AUDREY. WHAT'S YOURS, THEN?
HOT DOGS ICE CREAM TEA
AAAAAAA
OH CHRIST.
OH JESUS CHRIST.
I don't want to be like this. I'm not a bad man.
I'm sorry, Jess. I'm sorry, Audrey, love. I'm so sorry.
What am I going to do?

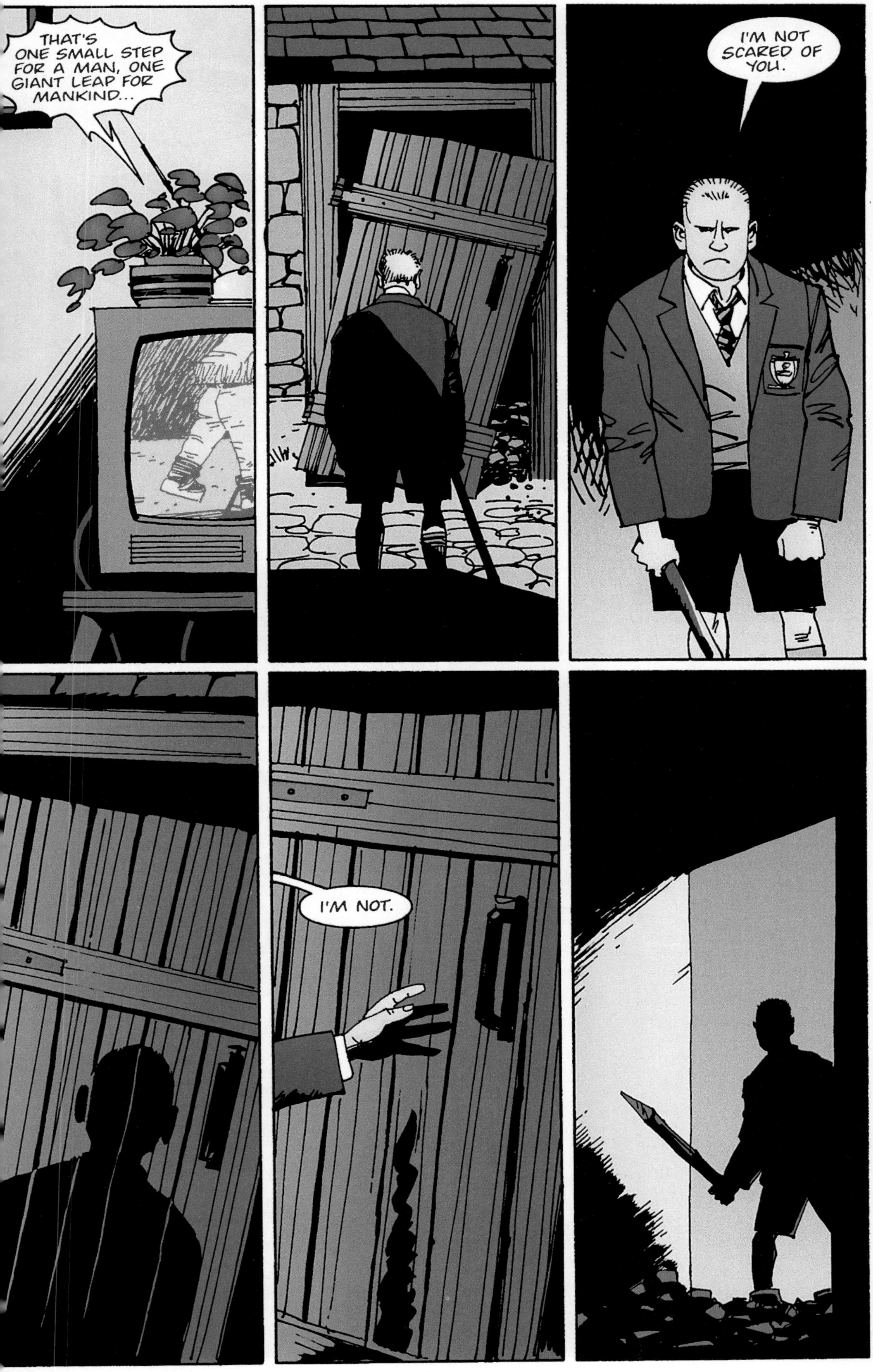
THAT'S ONE SMALL STEP FOR A MAN, ONE GIANT LEAP FOR MANKIND...
I'M NOT SCARED OF YOU.
I'M NOT.

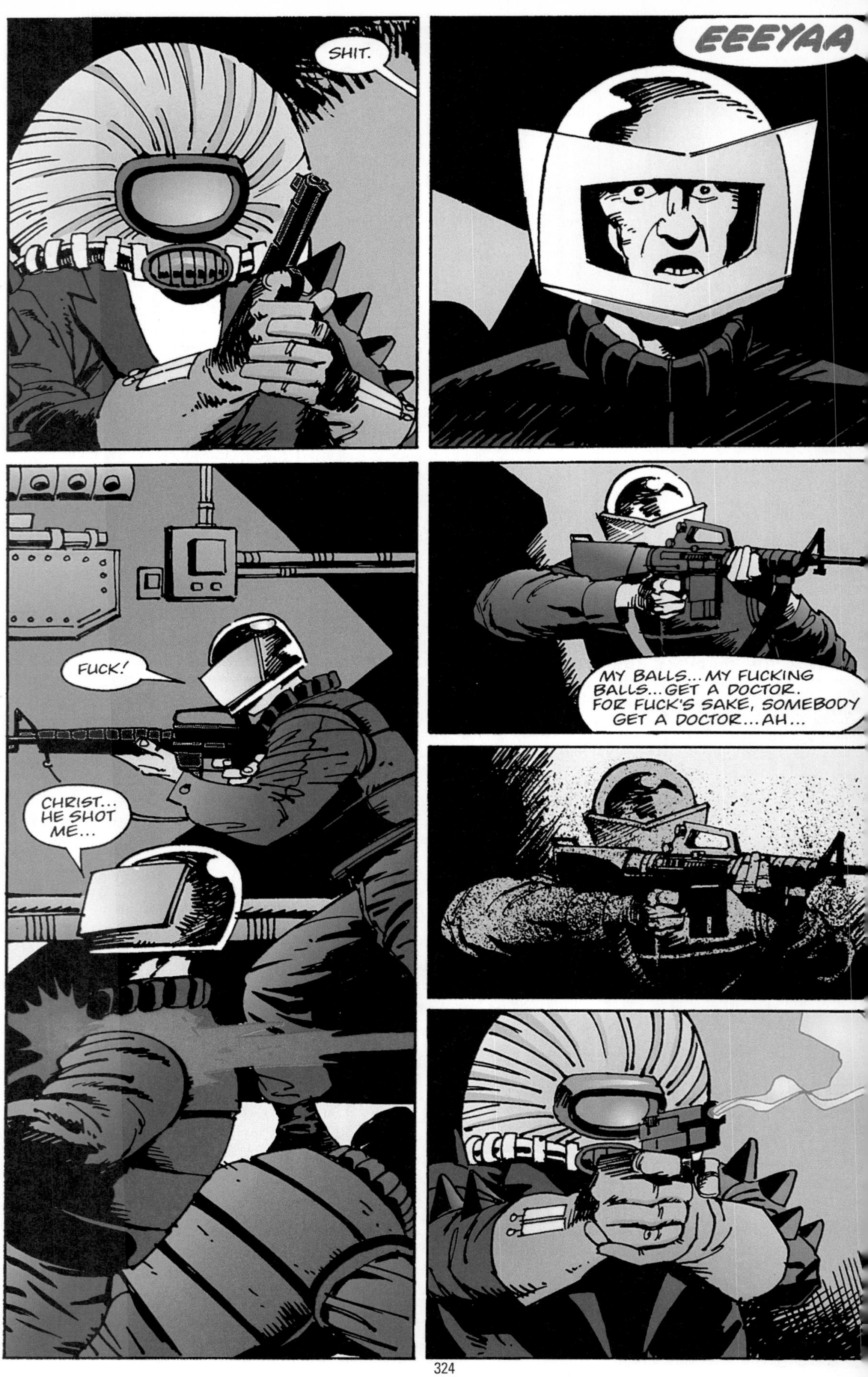
SHIT.
EEEYAA
FUCK!
CHRIST... HE SHOT ME...
MY BALLS... MY FUCKING BALLS... GET A DOCTOR. FOR FUCK'S SAKE, SOMEBODY GET A DOCTOR... AH...

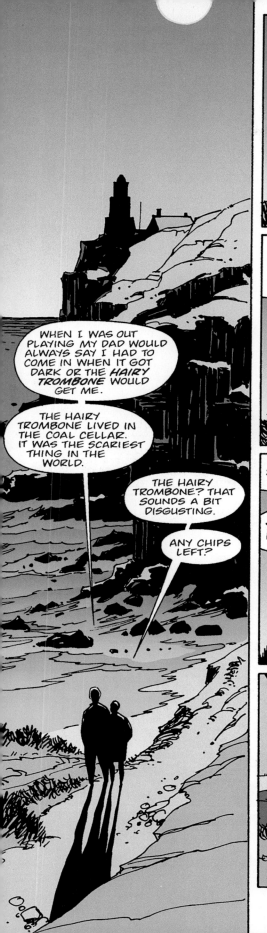

WHEN I WAS OUT PLAYING MY DAD WOULD ALWAYS SAY I HAD TO COME IN WHEN IT GOT DARK OR THE *HAIRY TROMBONE* WOULD GET ME.

THE HAIRY TROMBONE LIVED IN THE COAL CELLAR. IT WAS THE SCARIEST THING IN THE WORLD.

THE HAIRY TROMBONE? THAT SOUNDS A BIT DISGUSTING.

ANY CHIPS LEFT?

HERE. YOU CAN HAVE THE LAST ONE.

I USED TO BE REALLY SCARED OF THAT DOOR. IT WAS BLUE AND ALL THE PAINT WAS KIND OF PEELING OFF. I REMEMBER ONE NIGHT WHEN I WAS ABOUT NINE, I DECIDED TO GO OUT AND FIGHT IT. I KNEW I HAD TO.

SO WHAT HAPPENED THEN?

I DID IT. I OPENED THE DOOR AND I SAW THE SCARIEST THING IN THE WORLD AND IT WAS JUST A *GAS MASK.*

AN OLD GAS MASK, HANGING UP ON A NAIL ABOVE THE COAL.

IT'S STUPID WHAT SCARES YOU WHEN YOU'RE WEE.

WHAT'S *YOUR* MOST FRIGHTENING THING?

I DON'T KNOW. I'M SCARED OF DYING AND STUFF LIKE THAT, I SUPPOSE. JUST THE SAME AS EVERYBODY ELSE. GETTING OLD. BEING LONELY.

D'YOU EVER WONDER HOW YOU'LL DIE?

NO.

I'M GOING TO LIVE FOREVER.

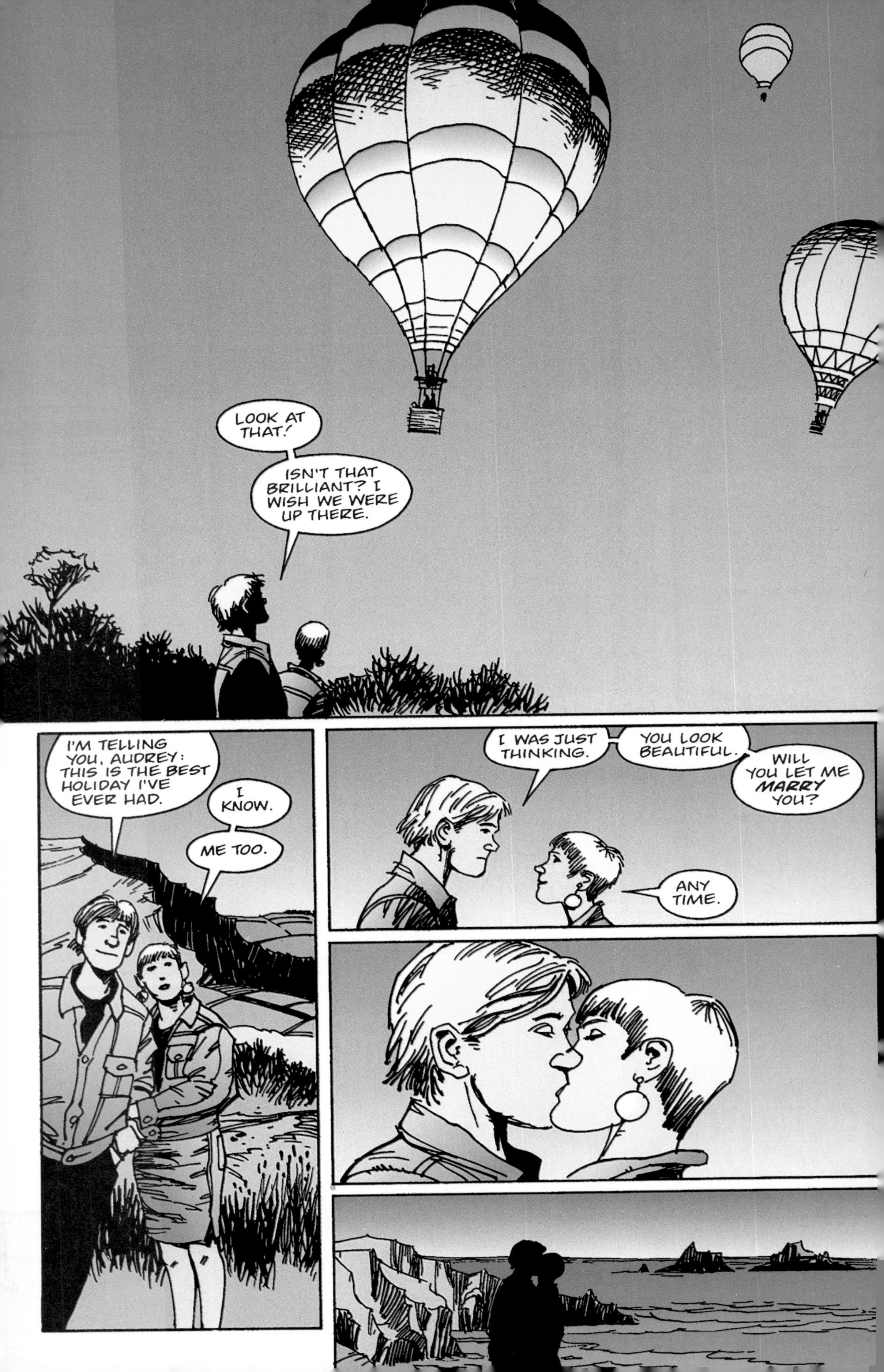
LOOK AT THAT!
ISN'T THAT BRILLIANT? I WISH WE WERE UP THERE.
I'M TELLING YOU, AUDREY: THIS IS THE BEST HOLIDAY I'VE EVER HAD.
I KNOW.
ME TOO.
I WAS JUST THINKING.
YOU LOOK BEAUTIFUL.
WILL YOU LET ME MARRY YOU?
ANY TIME.

...I can't see... nnn... I can't see... what's he done to my face... Is it bad?

nnf...fuck... This isn't happening...

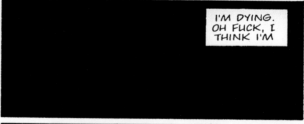

I'M DYING. OH FUCK, I THINK I'M

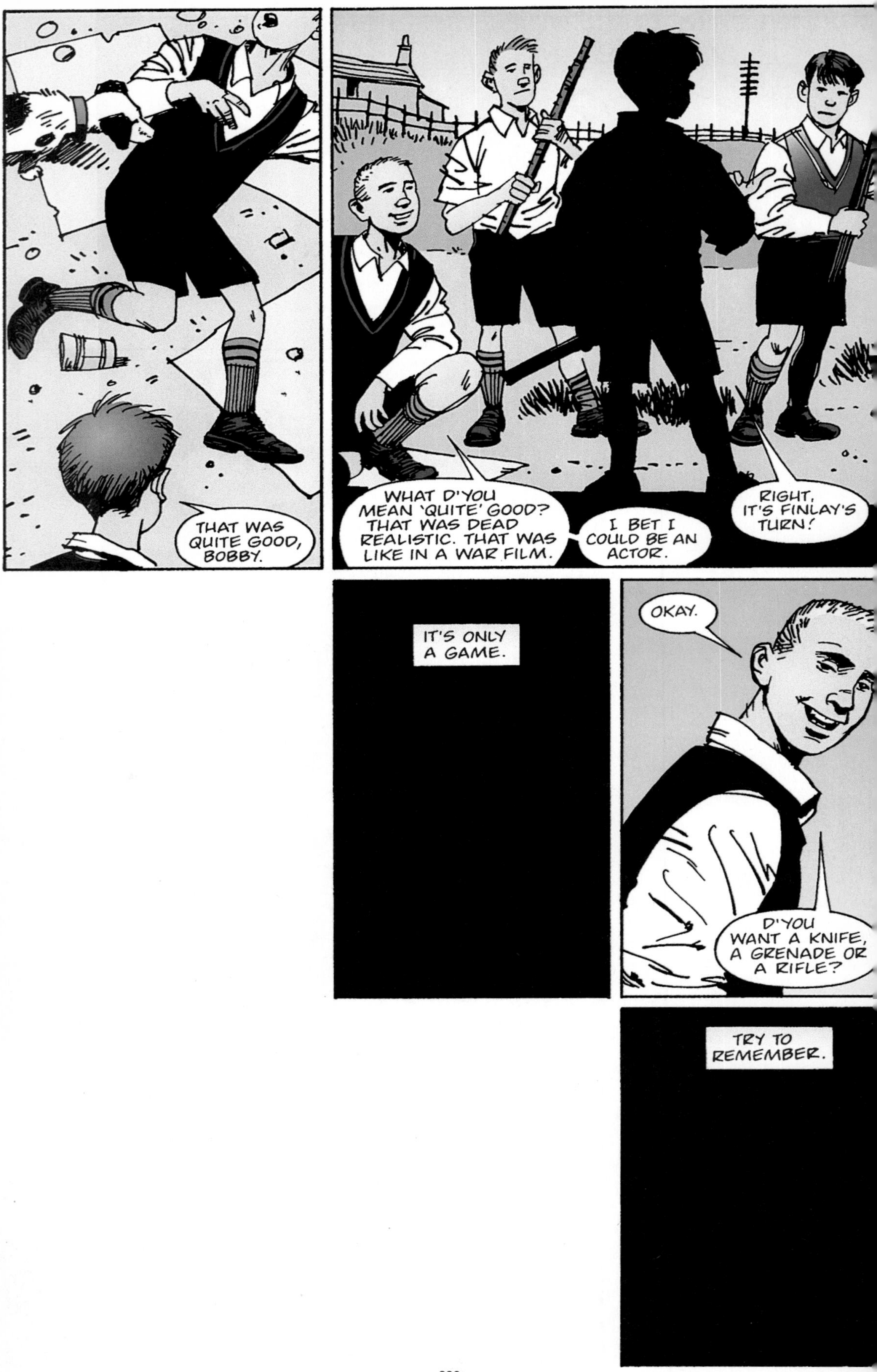
THAT WAS QUITE GOOD, BOBBY.
WHAT D'YOU MEAN 'QUITE' GOOD? THAT WAS DEAD REALISTIC. THAT WAS LIKE IN A WAR FILM.
I BET I COULD BE AN ACTOR.
RIGHT, IT'S FINLAY'S TURN!
IT'S ONLY A GAME.
OKAY.
D'YOU WANT A KNIFE, A GRENADE OR A RIFLE?
TRY TO REMEMBER.